MW00573553

Baseball's Last Dynasty

Charlie Finley's Oakland A's

Bruce Markusen

MASTERS PRESS

A Division of Howard W. Sams & Company

Published by Masters Press
A Division of Howard W. Sams & Company
2647 Waterfront Pkwy. E. Drive, Indianapolis, IN 46214

97 98 99 00 01   10 9 8 7 6 5 4 3 2 1

Library of Congress Cataloging-in-Publication Data Pending

Contents

Credits
_____

Cover design: Christy Pierce
All photos: Ron Riesterer, *Oakland Tribune*

Acknowledgments

As much as an author would like to believe that he has written a book by himself, such a massive undertaking requires the assistance of many people. I would like to thank those former Oakland A's who consented to interviews: Jack Aker, Sal Bando, Orlando Cepeda, Dave Duncan, Rollie Fingers, Mike Hegan, Reggie Jackson, Ted Kubiak, Tony LaRussa, Don Mincher and Rick Monday. I would also like to thank former Minnesota Twins' beat writer Bob Fowler and longtime sportswriter John Steadman of the *Baltimore Sun* for their insights on the A's. Other individuals have provided much-needed support and encouragement: Dan Bennett, Scot Mondore, Corey Seeman and Tim Wiles of the National Baseball Hall of Fame Library, and fellow author Joe Wallace. Also, thanks to Bill Burdick, Darci Harrington and Pat Kelly and Milo Stewart, Jr. of the Hall of Fame's Photo Department for their assistance in photo research. Finally, I would like to acknowledge the invaluable resources of the Hall of Fame Library's Research Department. The biographical files on each player, along with the availability of such periodicals as *The Sporting News* and *Sport* magazine have helped make *Baseball's Last Dynasty* more detailed and accurate than I could have otherwise hoped. I have found the Hall of Fame Library an essential element in writing an historical narrative about the A's of the early 1970s.

Thanks to Ken Samelson, the editor of this book, whose experience and professionalism have guided the project in the months leading up to publication. Thanks also to Holly Kondras, senior editor, and Heather Lowhorn, editor at Masters Press for their assistance in the process that transforms a manuscript into a book.

Finally, I would like to offer special thanks to Ron Bergman, currently a writer for the *San Jose Mercury News*. Bergman's reports on the A's, which appeared daily in the pages of the *Oakland Tribune* from 1968-76 and in each weekly issue of *The Sporting News*, proved critical in creating a foundation for *Baseball's Last Dynasty*.

Dedication:

Dedicated to the memory of my father, Stanley Markusen, 1917-1997, who taught me to become a baseball fan. For that, and many other reasons, I owe him a lot.

Introduction

I was seven years old when the Oakland A's won their first world championship in 1972. I had been a fan of the New York Yankees (and still am today), dating back to the final playing days of Mickey Mantle in 1968. Yet, the green and gold uniforms of Charlie Finley's A's caught my eye. At the time, most major league teams wore boring white uniforms at home and drab grays on the road, but I found the A's clothing refreshingly different. I even tried to dye my white undershirts green in tribute to Oakland's vividly unique baseball colors.

When the A's won the Series in the fall of '72, I became even more intrigued beyond the colorful uniforms. Given my youth, I couldn't fully appreciate how efficiently the A's won ballgames, but I had an inkling. Those teams, solid at every position, had no weaknesses. They made all the plays defensively, ran the bases with aggression and wisdom, hit well in the clutch and pitched with precision and power. In the 20-plus years that have passed since watching the A's of the early seventies, my appreciation of their ability has grown. I have followed many championship-caliber teams, but none have matched the level of play achieved by the A's from 1972 to '74.

Baseball observers have marveled at Oakland's ability to win in spite of constant in-fighting, persistent meddling by owner Charlie Finley and a never-ending stream of controversies. Experts tell us that championship teams require cohesion and harmony to win pennants, not arguments and controversies.

Maybe they have it all wrong. Perhaps teams filled with conflict and tension have such feelings because their players care more about achievement than players on losing teams, where mediocrity is too easily accepted. On losing teams, players tend to be far too forgiving of their teammates' mistakes. They create the perception of harmony, at the expense of complacency. Perhaps they simply don't care enough about winning to bruise other players' feelings. Everyone "gets along," but no one improves and the team comes no closer to reaching a championship level.

The A's of the seventies had a passion for the game and for winning. Players with passion tend to strive for perfection and become upset when they don't achieve it. When John "Blue Moon" Odom crumbled under the pressure of a fifth and decisive playoff game in 1972, Vida Blue took him to task for it. When Billy North didn't hustle in the eyes of Reggie Jackson, the A's slugger berated him about it. The ensuing confrontations created an uncomfortable tension in the Oakland clubhouse, which served as fodder for both the local and national media. Yet, it also served as a reminder that Oakland players considered winning far more important than hurt feelings.

Another intriguing aspect of these A's teams involved the maneuverings of Charlie Finley, who served as his own general manager. Finley never felt satisfied with the composition of his teams, regardless of the current won-loss record. He constantly traded for veteran "name" players, especially accomplished hitters he felt could help down the stretch. I was fascinated by Finley's ability to acquire a Matty Alou, an Orlando Cepeda, a Vic Davalillo, or a Rico Carty, to help his bench in the second half. Finley knew how to add pitching, too. When he needed a relief pitcher to assist a youthful Rollie Fingers, he acquired a capable veteran like Jim "Mudcat" Grant. When Blue held out in 1972, Finley swung a deal for Denny McLain. Some of the trades worked out and others didn't, but it was always fun to watch these newly-acquired notables put on the green and gold uniforms for the first time.

Gaudy uniforms, newsmaking controversies, a revolving door of baseball stars, and boatloads of winning. We find all of these storylines by exploring the Oakland A's of 1971-75, baseball's last dynasty.

Chapter One:
A Cross Between Branch Rickey and Vince Lombardi

During his controversial reign as owner of the Kansas City and Oakland A's, Charlie Finley had tinkered far too often with the managerial office. In 10 seasons as owner, Finley had plowed through 10 managers. Hank Bauer (twice), Eddie Lopat, Mel McGaha, Haywood Sullivan, Alvin Dark, Hall of Famer Luke Appling, Bob Kennedy and John McNamara had all experienced the feeling of being hired and fired by Finley. But on October 2, 1970, one day after the A's season had come to an end, Finley made perhaps the best move he had ever engineered as chieftain of the franchise. Finley named Montreal Expos' coach Dick Williams as manager, replacing McNamara. Yet, the reasoning behind the sacking of McNamara was neither logical nor fair.

Under McNamara, the A's had won 89 games, the most for the franchise in 38 years. The A's had finished a respectable second place, nine games behind a very good Minnesota Twins team. Most of the Oakland players liked playing for McNamara, including power-hitting first baseman Don Mincher. "John McNamara was probably the most striking gentleman I ever played for," recalls Mincher, who currently owns and operates the Huntsville Stars of the Double-A Southern League. "He was a guy that really insisted that you stay in shape and play hard, but he really didn't have the hard intensity you see of a lot of managers today and a few back in those days."

That lack of intensity may have played a part in Finley's decision to lay the ax on McNamara. Yet, Finley claimed he had other reasons for making the change. At a lengthy press conference announcing the firing, Finley spent the first half hour ranting and raving about one of the team's three catchers, Dave Duncan. Finley blamed Duncan for the firing of McNamara. Why would Finley fire McNamara because of the team's second-string catcher? The long-haired receiver had batted a respectable .259 with 10 home runs, but had seen a decline in playing time under McNamara the second half of the season. After the season's final game, Duncan fired away — not at McNamara, but at Finley. "There's only one man who manages this club — Charlie Finley," Duncan told reporters. "And we'll never win so long as he manages it."[1]

"We had the team to win it (the American League West)," Duncan continued. "But because of the atmosphere he (Finley) creates, there's no spirit, no feeling of harmony. We should be close like a family, but it's not here."[2] When Finley learned of Duncan's remarks, he decided to use the opportunity to fire McNamara. "He didn't lose his job," Finley claimed. "His players took it away from him."[3] Finley reasoned that a manager who could not prevent his players — Duncan and Reggie Jackson, in particular — from making critical remarks about their owner had lost control of his own clubhouse. Therefore, Finley felt justified in firing McNamara.

Duncan's comments most likely infuriated Finley on two fronts. Finley resented Duncan's portrayal of him as a meddler, as someone who tried to undermine his manager. That was bad enough. When Duncan took his criticism a step further, by portraying Finley as an incompetent meddler, one who prevented his team from winning, Finley felt motivated to take action.

Many players on the A's agreed with Duncan's remarks. Right fielder Reggie Jackson had publicly criticized Finley for interfering with the ballclub during the 1970 season. Jackson had also accused Finley of ordering McNamara to bench him on several occasions. Jackson's displeasure with Finley ran so deep, that on one occasion, he gestured obscenely toward the owner's box after clubbing a long home run. Such gestures and angry words typified the strange relationship that Jackson had with Finley. "Let's face it, Reggie would say outrageous things about Charlie at various times," says Rick Monday, Oakland's starting center fielder in 1970. "Then he'd run to the clubhouse and call Charlie."

While no other players had made their feelings known on the record, several had privately complained to the team's beat writers about Finley's constant meddling. In fact, some players had even used the unfortunate situation to their advantage by calling Finley directly and complaining about a lack of playing time in the hope that the owner would force McNamara into making lineup changes. On several occasions, a player contacting Finley found himself in the lineup within the next few days. Finley's interference had created an impossible situation for a well-liked baseball man like McNamara, whose integrity was now under interrogation. A more experienced, proven manager might have been able to ignore Finley's "advice," but McNamara had no choice but to follow along, or lose his job during the season.

In essence, Finley decided to use Duncan's scathing words as an excuse for firing the manager. Finley seized the opportunity to make a scapegoat of his backup catcher, while shielding himself from a critical media that was bound to roast him for firing yet another manager. After all, Finley wondered aloud, if McNamara's own players questioned his authority, then he must not be performing his role of leading the team.

Most of the Oakland media did not accept Finley's reasoning. Two beat writers following the A's had predicted — well before Duncan's remarks — that McNamara would be fired. Reports in the *Oakland Tribune* and the *San Jose Mercury News* had indicated that McNamara would not return for the 1971 season. Those published accounts had stated that either Finley would fire McNamara, or that McNamara would reject a new contract offer from the overbearing Finley.

Both McNamara and Duncan denied that the catcher's comments about Finley had rendered an impact on the manager's job security. "It's ridiculous to believe that the reason McNamara was fired was because of me," Duncan insisted. "It was obvious to everyone a long time ago that Finley was going to fire him." McNamara supported Duncan's contention. "I've been fired since last May when the club started out under .500,"[4] McNamara said. Furthermore, recently fired manager Billy Martin, late of the Minnesota Twins, claimed that Finley had offered him the Oakland job in mid-July, and then again in late-August, before he had decided to accept an offer from the Detroit Tigers.

After firing McNamara during a one-hour meeting, Finley immediately held a press conference announcing the change. Finley spent most of the press conference criticizing Duncan for several reasons, in particular his living situation. "One day I found out that Duncan was sleeping with (batting) coach Charlie Lau," Finley exclaimed, in an extremely poor selection of words. "By that I mean they were rooming together, sharing expenses. When I found out about this, I...asked them to break it up immediately, because as we all know, in the Army, troops don't fraternize with officers."[5]

Duncan and Lau, whose firing was also announced at the press conference, had refused to comply with Finley's order. Both men had recently separated from their wives, and had decided to cut costs by sharing an apartment. Now, Finley had tried to aggravate Duncan by intimating that he was "sleeping" with one of the team's coaches. It was as if Finley had intentionally used the phrase "sleeping with" as a way of falsely suggesting some romantic involvement between the player and coach. Later, after finishing his winter ball season in the Dominican Republic, Duncan would request a meeting with Finley and eventually reach a temporary truce with the owner.

With McNamara and most of his coaching staff out of the picture, the leadership of the A's now rested on the vast abilities of Dick Williams, who would officially sign a two-year contract at the World Series. The 41-year-old Williams represented the 10th managerial change Finley had made, covering a total of 10 different managers, since purchasing the franchise in 1960. Once a top prospect in the Brooklyn Dodgers' organization, Williams' hitting and throwing abilities had been undermined by a severe shoulder injury he had sustained while making a diving catch in left field. The three-way shoulder separation left Williams a pedestrian player, one who would encounter stops in Baltimore, Cleveland, Kansas City and Boston. Williams actually enjoyed two productive seasons for the Kansas City Athletics in 1959 and '60, but a trade to the Baltimore Orioles during the spring of '61 prevented him from playing for Charlie Finley, who had just bought the club in the aftermath of the death of A's owner Arnold Johnson.

As a minor league player, Williams had been strongly influenced by his manager in the Texas League, Bobby Bragan. Williams had noticed Bragan's strengths as a manager: the ability to teach and instill discipline. These attributes would become essential parts of the Williams dossier. Williams' manager in Baltimore, the successful and innovative Paul Richards, noticed the journeyman outfielder's knowledge of the game and encouraged him to pursue a managerial career. Williams decided to abandon a mediocre playing career for what he hoped would be a higher standard of achievement as a manager.

A fiery, militaristic kind of leader, Williams had patterned his "tough-guy" managerial style after that of men like Branch Rickey and Vince Lombardi. Williams stressed the importance of fundamentals and basic execution, demanded absolute hustle from his players at all times, and challenged them to play for more than themselves and the lure of a contract. "A player should have something other than the name of his city on the front of his uniform," Williams said. "He should have P-R-I-D-E written there."[6]

In his first managerial tenure in the major leagues, Williams had molded a soft group of ninth-place Boston Red Sox into a hardened, gritty American League pennant winner. The transition had taken just one season. Prior to his arrival in 1967, the Red Sox had been regarded as baseball's "country club," where team owner Tom Yawkey consistently spoiled his players. Two years later, the Red Sox had deemed Williams as too tough, overly militaristic and dangerously unyielding in the ways that he dealt with his players. Williams also clashed with Yawkey, who repeatedly undermined his manager by pampering Red Sox players after Williams had tried to discipline them. Williams believed that Yawkey regarded the Red Sox as a toy, a philosophy that conflicted with Williams' more businesslike approach. On one occasion, Yawkey belittled his manager in a Boston newspaper, giving him a rating of 2 on a scale of 1 to 4. The lack of confidence understandably angered Williams.

During the 1969 season, Yawkey fired Williams, who took a job as a coach under Gene Mauch in Montreal. Williams credited Mauch with equipping him to become a better manager the second time around. "The best manager in the business," Williams said of Mauch. "You watch him and you learn. If I ever had a seminar on managing, I'd want Gene to run it for me. He's a baseball genius — a marvelous organizer and the greatest handler of men I ever saw."[7] While with the Expos, Mauch also taught Williams to be more compromising and conciliatory when dealing with his team's owner. Williams would need to follow this advice with the A's. Although Finley was a different kind of owner than Yawkey, he found his own ways to circumvent the powers of his managers.

At least one Oakland player agreed with Finley's choice of Williams as the A's new manager. "If his reputation is what it's supposed to be, he will be an asset," predicted team captain Sal Bando. "We need a guy to kick us in the rear now and then. Mac (McNamara) said he just wasn't the type to jump all over guys, and we liked that. We knew that if we made a mistake, it wouldn't be too bad. But we didn't learn from our mistakes. We didn't take them seriously. I think that hurt us as the season wore on."[8] Bando added that he liked McNamara and would miss him as a friend, but maintained that the A's needed a tougher, more demanding manager to become a pennant contender.

"It was a different personality," says Sal Bando, now the general manager of the Milwaukee Brewers, in discussing the differences between Williams and his predecessor. "John McNamara, in most cases, we all grew up with John because we played for him in the minor leagues. So, in some ways, the familiarity was not an asset because we got too close to John. Whereas Dick had that distance between you and him, and you just zeroed in on baseball."

Williams owned a personality not only unique from McNamara's, but different from the parade of other managers that Finley had employed. "You've got to realize that also listed in there was Alvin Dark, Luke Appling, Bob Kennedy and Hank Bauer," says Rick Monday, who played for all of the above during his tenure with the A's. "So we really ran the gamut as far as the number of different managers that we had at that particular time." Williams'direct, no frills approach most similarly resembled one of his predecessors. "Hank Bauer, also no-nonsense," Monday says, "but a little bit differently." While Bauer had alienated some of the A's with his militaristic style, Williams' gruffness might have annoyed some of his players, but did not turn them off completely. "Dick Williams had a job to do," Monday says. "And he wanted to get through all the clutter to get down to the task at hand —

and that was to try and move his ballclub from day one in spring training...and get to the end of the season, where you have a chance to have a post-season."

As Monday puts it, Williams cared most about the end result of winning, to the extent that he occasionally bruised feelings. "He didn't care about the laundry list that it took to get from point A to point B," explains Monday, now a broadcaster with the Los Angeles Dodgers. "He didn't care if he ruffled your feathers or not. If you played well, you would be in the lineup. If you did not play well, well, he had other ideas and ways to approach it."

Don Mincher says that, in contrast to Williams, John McNamara's gentlemanly demeanor may have interfered with his managerial ability. "He was just such a nice person," Mincher says of McNamara, "that you wanted to go out and kill for him. He remains one of my best friends; I see him frequently even today. He was, maybe, to a fault, too nice. I mean, our ballclub at that time was just beginning to formulate and there were some pretty tough characters there, like Reggie and Sal, and some of those guys who were sometimes quite individual-like, but when they played together, their team was terrific. It was a time when we were just entering that stage of being a dominating team, and it was tough on John to handle that. Consequently, he didn't make it through."

When Mincher heard that Dick Williams would replace McNamara, he knew that the atmosphere on the ballclub would change drastically. "Well, I knew one thing right away," Mincher says. "There would be some confrontations; I knew that. I knew Dick Williams from playing against him, his reputation and what-have-you. And I knew there would be some confrontations that would take place, and I knew that Dick Williams would win 'em all!"

Mincher believed that turmoil would result from the heated inter-action between the feisty Williams and some of the egocentric players on the A's. "You could just feel it coming, and sure enough there was." More importantly, Mincher sensed that with the hiring of Williams, the A's were about to start winning a lot of games — and championships. "That was really the beginning of a great ballclub," Mincher says, "when Dick Williams was signed to that contract."

Although Finley had hired Dick Williams immediately after the conclusion of the 1970 season, his new manager did not meet the media until January 26, 1971. At his opening press conference, Williams spoke confidently of the A's potential to reach the post-season. "I don't see any reason why we can't win this division," Williams bellowed. "I don't see anyone running away from the rest of the division, unless it's us."[9] Williams viewed his A's as the most talented team in the American League West, and far better than the Boston Red Sox team he had led to the American League pennant only four years earlier. "This club is head and shoulders above the Boston club I had in '67,"[10] Williams said, surprising some of the reporters in attendance. Williams felt the A's had a stronger and deeper pitching staff, as well as more team speed than the "Impossible Dream" Red Sox.

Williams realized that he was joining the A's at just the right time. He recognized the work that Oakland scouts like Clyde Kluttz and Don Pries had done in assembling talent throughout the mid-to-late 1960's. The nucleus of young players, which featured Bert "Campy" Campaneris, Sal Bando, Joe Rudi, Rick Monday and Reggie Jackson among the position players and Jim "Catfish" Hunter and Vida Blue on the pitching staff, had just begun to flourish at the major league level.

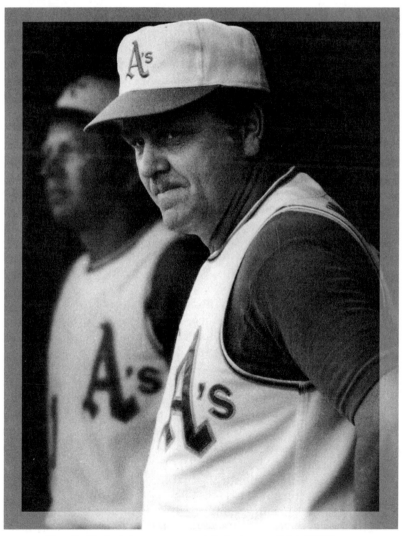

Charlie Finley's best managerial choice — Dick Williams.

Williams viewed the Minnesota Twins as Oakland's biggest obstacle in trying to win the American League West. The two-time defending divisional champs had dominated the A's during regular season play over the previous two seasons. In 1969 and '70, the Twins had forged identical records of 13-5 against Oakland. Williams realized that the Twins, though still very talented, were an aging team. Harmon Killebrew, the Twins' top slugger, was now 34 years old. Tony Oliva, though only 30 years old based on his birth certificate, hobbled around on the knees of a 40-year-old. Thirty-five-year old Jim Perry and 32-year-old Jim Kaat headlined Minnesota's pitching staff.

Although the A's had finished nine games back of the Twins each of the past two seasons, veteran baseball observers realized that a changing of the guard was about to occur. Minnesota Twins' beat writer Bob Fowler, who covered the team in the sixties and seventies, recognized two clubs proceeding in opposite directions. "Oh, I think you could see it," says Fowler. "We had a veteran team, with Harmon Killebrew, Tony Oliva, Bob Allison and Jim Perry, guys of that nature. Oakland had a young team, with Catfish Hunter, Sal Bando and Rick Monday. They were nine games out, (but) they had great talent. And then in 1971, the Minnesota team — we suddenly got old."

The astute Dick Williams soon recognized the identities of the A's three primary leaders: Sal Bando, Reggie Jackson, and Catfish Hunter. He moved quickly to bolster the confidence of the two position players in the group, both of whom figured to play regularly for Oakland. In one of Williams' first publicly announced decisions, he showed strong regard for the leadership abilities of Bando, his starting third baseman. Williams announced that he would retain Bando as team captain, even though he had seen fit to strip Carl Yastrzemski of his captaincy in Boston.

With one announcement, Williams had succeeded in gaining the confidence of one of the most respected players on the Oakland club. "They were very good," Bando says of his first impressions of Williams. "I had the opportunity to get together with Dick prior to spring training (at the A's winter caravan.) I got to talk to him a little bit there. I think the one thing Dick had going for him was his reputation, because he didn't have to live up to it, as being a tough disciplinarian. It was already in place."

After confirming Bando's captaincy, Williams made an even more significant announcement in discussing the important role that his new everyday right fielder would play in 1971. "I expect Reggie Jackson to play everyday. I have no thoughts of benching him against left-handers,"[11] Williams insisted. During the 1970 season, Jackson had held out for five weeks and had become embroiled in several verbal battles with Finley. The Oakland owner allegedly ordered John McNamara not to play the controversial young outfielder. At times, McNamara platooned

Reggie; at other times, he flat-out benched the potential superstar. Most people around the A's believed that McNamara did whatever Finley told him to do when it came to playing or sitting Jackson. At one point, Finley even threatened to demote Jackson to the minor leagues. As a result of the holdout and the benchings, Jackson finished the season with only 23 home runs.

Jackson, when first asked about Dick Williams, expressed skepticism about his new manager. "I've heard a lot of bad things about him from other players, unfavorable comments," Jackson admitted. "I heard that when things get tough, he wouldn't stick up for you."[12] Jackson would soon change his opinion of Williams, after meeting with the manager briefly during the off-season. Jackson initially asked Williams to trade him. Reporters circulated rumors that the A's might trade Jackson to the Pittsburgh Pirates for slugging outfielder Willie Stargell, or to the Baltimore Orioles for outfielder Paul Blair and pitcher Tom Phoebus. Jackson later retreated from his trade request. "I saw Reggie down in Puerto Rico," said Williams, who watched his slugger play for Santurce in the Winter League. "His attitude was so good it was scary."[13]

Williams clearly realized the potential of Jackson, who had been drafted by the Kansas City A's in 1966 after a terrific sophomore season at Arizona State University. After making Jackson the A's first pick in the draft, Finley personally recruited Jackson's signature on a contract. The owner offered the college star an $85,000 bonus and a new car, in the hopes that he would give up his football scholarship with the Sun Devils. "He came driving up in a big Cadillac," Jackson said of his first meeting with Finley. "He kept talking about what a big star I was going to be and how we were going to be champions. He really overwhelmed me."[14]

Finley wanted to start Jackson at Double-A, but Kansas City scouts Bob Zuk and Ray Swallow begged the owner to start him at a lower level. For once, Finley gave in. Jackson debuted professionally that summer, making two pitstops for Class A teams in Lewiston and Modesto. Reggie moved up to Double-A Birmingham in 1967 and so dominated Southern League pitching that he earned a promotion to the major leagues midway through the season. When Jackson batted only .178 in 35 games, the A's targeted him for additional work in the Instructional League. Kansas City coaches tutored Jackson on hitting inside pitches and cutting down on his frequent strikeouts.

In 1968, with the A's now entrenched in Oakland, Jackson spent his first full season in the majors and worked daily with batting coach Joe DiMaggio, the former New York Yankee great. For over an hour each day, DiMaggio schooled Jackson on the art of making better contact. "Reggie is still green as grass," DiMaggio admitted. "We've just got to bring his talents to the surface. They're all there, no question."[15]

Jackson terrorized American League pitchers during the first half of the 1969 season, setting a record with 37 home runs before the All-Star break. Jackson seemed destined to break Roger Maris' single-season record for home runs, but encountered a second half power drought brought upon by nerves and excessive media scrutiny. In addition to his obvious power, Jackson possessed all the other requisite skills to become a star: a burst of speed that reminded some of Willie Mays in his prime, and a thunderous throwing arm that reminded others of a young Al Kaline or even a vintage Roberto Clemente. When he was playing well, Jackson was merely the best player on the Oakland roster.

During the winter following the 1970 campaign, Jackson started to make some important changes in his approach to the game. While playing for Santurce in winter ball, Jackson tinkered with his batting stance by crouching at the plate. "I've torn down my batting style and I'm reconstructing it," Jackson told reporters. "I've forgotten about hitting the home run ball and I'm just hitting the ball somewhere."[16] The crouch helped Jackson improve his ability to make contact with the ball. "This way, as long as I stay down in the crouch and swing, I don't lose contact with my eyes and overswing and hit the ball all over."[17]

By accident, Jackson also discovered that he needed to wear eyeglasses. Jackson visited an eyewear store in search of some new sunglasses and met with an eye doctor. The doctor performed an examination of Jackson's eyes and discovered the slugger to be nearsighted. After donning his new eyeglasses, Reggie raised his batting average 70 points in Winter League play. "I've hit five home runs in the six games I played after I began wearing them," Reggie exclaimed. "It's amazing"[18]

Unfortunately, Williams could do little to help the third leader of his team — Catfish Hunter — as he battled Charlie Finley on the contract front. Hunter was upset by the offer of a $5,000 raise, which he considered inadequate in light of his career-high 18 wins in 1970. Finley preferred emphasizing Hunter's 14 losses and his ERA of 3.81, the highest of Catfish's career since 1966. Critics of Hunter also cited his extreme reliance on closer Jim "Mudcat" Grant, who had rescued eight of Catfish's wins with tightrope relief work in the late innings. One Bay Area sportswriter had come to call the duo the "Cat People," in reference to the similarities of their nicknames and the frequency with which they teamed up to post wins for the A's.

Hunter didn't appreciate the implication that he had depended heavily on Grant to enjoy a successful season. "Mudcat was a good relief pitcher last year," Catfish said diplomatically, "one of the best I've ever seen. But I didn't like it when some sportswriters suggested that he get half my salary this year. He did his job and I did mine"[19] One week before the start of spring training, Hunter and Finley would agree on a 1971 contract.

Hunter, Jackson and Bando formed the nucleus of the A's, with each player providing leadership in different manners. "Catfish was quiet," says Bando, "but he was ace of the staff. Catfish was a jokester, one of the guys, and very unassuming. He was liked by everybody. Reggie was outgoing, but Reggie did his leading by what he did on the field. And I was probably the guy in between. I was outgoing, but the not the Reggie Jackson-type of player. I was more outgoing than Catfish, but I was out there everyday at third base, so I kind of helped bridge that gap."

With Bando, Hunter and Jackson firmly in place, Oakland's prospects for a good season looked favorable. With the proper additions of veteran players to their young talent base, the A's seemed ready to contend — and win — the American League West. Finley and Williams set out to acquire, or in this case, re-acquire one of those veteran players, first baseman-outfielder Tommy Davis. In September, the A's had traded Davis to the Chicago Cubs. In another deal, Charlie Finley had sent his best relief pitcher, Mudcat Grant, to the Pittsburgh Pirates. Since the A's had fallen completely from the race, Finley had decided to trade Davis and Grant to two contending National League East teams. At the time, Oakland players had criticized Finley for the deals, but the owner had defended himself, saying that he needed those players to finish first, not second.

After the season, the Cubs released Davis, an aging, but still skilled right-handed hitter. Davis had long battled an unfair reputation as a clubhouse lawyer, a label that may have been created out of racism. Like other outspoken black players of the time, critics termed Davis a troublemaker. One prominent baseball publication mysteriously described Davis as a "problem"[20] player without further explanation, but Finley and Williams thought otherwise of the highly respected veteran, who had batted a solid .290 in 200 at-bats for Oakland. The A's high command viewed Davis as just the kind of steadying hand needed to supplement a team whose nucleus consisted mostly of younger players who had never experienced the rigors of a pennant race.

While the A's gained Davis, they had apparently lost the services of another important veteran, second baseman Dick Green. In 1970, Green had hit a career-worst .190, a performance that had prompted him to consider retirement. Green, saying he didn't like to travel, announced that he would probably devote himself to operating his family's moving business in Rapid City, South Dakota. Given the tone of Green's statements, the A's felt they would be without their starting second baseman by the time spring training began.

Aside from the hiring of Williams and the return of Davis, the A's made one other significant off-season change, though this move had nothing to do with the personnel on the field or in the dugout. Shortly after the firing of John McNamara, the A's had announced the departure of controversial broadcaster Harry Caray. The former St. Louis Cardinals' announcer had worked only one season in Oakland, where his work had drawn mixed reviews. Caray impressed some listeners with his candid, insightful pre-game interviews and his willingness to discuss controversial issues. Caray's frequent criticisms of Oakland players ruffled others, including the since-fired batting coach, Charlie Lau, who nearly exchanged punches with Caray on a team flight. Some writers speculated that Charlie Finley had pushed for Caray's removal, while others indicated that the veteran broadcaster merely wanted to retreat to the Midwest, where he had forged a popular following with the Redbirds. Caray would not return to the Cardinals, instead signing on to broadcast Chicago White Sox games.

Caray also clashed with the team's other broadcaster, veteran play-by-play man Monte Moore, a favorite of Finley's. When Caray first showed up in the Oakland booth, he allegedly told Moore to refrain from interjecting during any of his classic, humorous monologues. Caray made it clear that *he* wanted to be the lead broadcaster with the A's, not Moore. Whatever the reasons for his short tenure in the A's booth, the marriage of Caray and Finley, two headstrong personalities, had come to an abrupt ending.

The flurry of off-season maneuverings — the departure of Caray, the sacking of McNamara and the hiring of Williams — apparently did not please fans in the Bay Area, who had become disgusted with Charlie Finley's style of ownership. A group of fans manufactured and distributed bumper stickers, which had obviously not been endorsed by Finley. "FREE THE A's," read the stickers, summarizing the feelings of some fans toward the meddlesome owner.

Chapter Two:
Spring Training Follies

In February, the A's reported to Mesa, Arizona for their first spring training under the supervision of Dick Williams. The new manager immediately defended the way in which he ran his former team, the Boston Red Sox. "I had to be tough with the Red Sox," Williams insisted. "They'd finished ninth the year before. I had to change an I-don't-give-damn-attitude to a winning attitude."[1] Williams once again proclaimed his A's superior to the team he skippered in Boston. "This club here is a contending ballclub; they've finished second for the past two years. Basically, what I've got to do here is have the A's eliminate mistakes, mental errors, play good, sound fundamental baseball, and win head-to-head against the Twins."[2]

Williams immediately tried to create a new mindset among Oakland players. "What he set out to do first was establish a winning attitude," observed Charlie Finley. "I liked that tremendously. He didn't talk much about batting eyes or pitching arms. He talked attitude, attitude. He drummed it into their head at his very first clubhouse meeting."[3]

Williams raved about the talent available to him among his pitchers. "I've got a hell of a pitching staff here. They're 100 per cent better than the pitching staff I had in Boston."[4] Williams announced that he would deploy a five-man rotation, which would almost certainly include Catfish Hunter, Vida Blue, and, if healthy, Chuck Dobson. The other

13

two starters would come from a group that featured John "Blue Moon" Odom, and two relievers, Diego Segui and Rollie Fingers.

Williams did have some concerns about his pitching staff, however. In 1970, Odom had spent 44 days on the disabled list with elbow pain. Doctors had diagnosed the problem as floating bone chips, which needed to be removed from below his elbow in order to save his career. The surgery posed a risk; with the bone chips located so close to vital nerves and tissue, an operation could just as easily end Odom's career. With the prognosis of recovery listed at 50/50, Dr. William Bickel of the Mayo Clinic cut open Odom's elbow on December 14 and removed several bone chips, including a large one the size of a finger nail. Although Dr. Bickel declared the operation successful, he could not guarantee Odom's availability for the start of the new season.

Chuck Dobson, who had pitched five shutouts and won eight straight games before experiencing elbow problems, had finished the 1970 season with a sore arm. The question marks surrounding Odom and Dobson left Hunter and Blue as the only certainties in the starting rotation. Under a worst case scenario, Williams might have to pluck a pitcher from his bullpen, further depleting a relief staff that had been foolishly weakened by the late-season trade of fireman Mudcat Grant to the Pirates.

One of the contenders for a spot in the rotation caused a stir during spring training when he admitted to the use of "greenies," or legal pep pills. Chuck Dobson, who had gained a favorable reputation for being talkative, humorous and frank with the local media, told reporters that he had used greenies several times during his career. The use of greenies by major league players had first been disclosed in Jim Bouton's controversial book, *Ball Four*, which had been released after the 1969 season. Such pep pills enabled players to overcome fatigue and muster more energy to play in games. "I don't see anything wrong in it," said Dobson, who claimed that he had pitched a shutout in 1970 after taking a greenie. "A lot of guys use them, and I've used them."[5]

Commissioner Bowie Kuhn, who had tried to censor Bouton's book, did not agree with Dobson's opinion. Prior to spring training, Kuhn had already warned players to comply with federal and state drug laws. Although greenies were not considered illegal drugs in and of themselves, they were available through prescription only and often obtained through illegal means. "If the commissioner says we can't use them anymore, then the next time someone asks me whether I use them, I'll say no, go around the corner and pop,"[6] Dobson said. Dobson had just stepped over the line from honesty into stupidity.

In the April, 1971 issue of *Baseball Digest*, two team doctors expressed concern over the use of pep pills. Dr. Joseph Finegold of the Pittsburgh Pirates and Dr. Jacob Suker of the Chicago Cubs suggested the possibility of a player suffering a heart attack on the playing field after taking pep pills. The article indicated that pep pills posed a special danger to older, overweight players who did not play on a regular basis. "Amphetamines and speed — there is no place for them," Dr. Suker told Bill Jauss of *Baseball Digest*. "They won't make a Billy Williams out of a Billy Nobody. And they can be very dangerous and habit-forming."[7]

On March 9, Dobson revised his statements regarding the use of greenies. Dobson issued a press release that read as follows: "My recent statement in regard to taking a greenie was misunderstood and completely blown out of proportion. These are the facts: Yes, I did take a greenie last year prior to pitching a game after I'd had a bout with the flu. At that time, I was of the opinion it had been of help to me. Since it has been brought to my attention by medical authorities the harmful effects that greenies or any other drugs can have on an athlete, I want it known that I am strongly against anyone using drugs in any form."[8] After Dobson released his revisionist statement, Kuhn held a private conversation with the right-hander to discuss his use of greenies. Kuhn apparently accepted Dobson's new story, in which he claimed to have used greenies only one time during his major league career.

With that controversy averted, the A's suffered their first major setback of spring training when they learned that Blue Moon Odom would not be able to pitch until after the mid-July All-Star break. After making the All-Star team in 1968 and '69, the talented right-hander had encountered a series of elbow problems. As a result, Odom had won only 10 games since the 1969 All-Star break. Now healthy after off-season surgery, Odom had opened up spring training with a pain-free right elbow and had routinely pitched batting practice. Then, one day, without warning, Dick Williams approached Odom and told the right-hander that he would no longer be allowed to throw batting practice and would not pitch in an actual game until mid-season, at the earliest. Dr. William Bickel, the surgeon who had removed bone chips from Odom's elbow, had ordered the shutdown of Odom's arm, in order to allow scar tissue around the elbow to heal. With batting practice deemed off limits, Odom could do no more than field grounders on the mound and feign throws to second base.

In the past, the temperamental Odom might have reacted angrily to the doctor's orders. As one of the most fiercely competitive players in the major leagues, Odom hated the idea of going through the motions in spring training. Yet, Odom seemed to understand the long-term wisdom of Dr. Bickel's decision. "I'm not happy about this because I felt pretty good throwing in batting practice," Odom said diplomatically. "But one breaking pitch could ruin my whole career."[9]

The A's received some good news in spring training when Dick Green changed his mind about retirement. "I've had a chance of heart and I'm more anxious than ever to play in 1971," Green said in a press release. "My lousy season last year bothered me and I wasn't in the right frame of mind to play. I used to cringe just thinking about seeing my name in the lineup, but I feel entirely different now."[10] Prior to Green's turnabout, Charlie Finley had contemplated drastic measures in trying to goad his second baseman into returning. "I told him that I was going to put on some snowshoes and go up to see him in Rapid City, South Dakota, to try to get him to change his mind," said Finley. "Dick told me that I was getting too old for that, so I said I would hire a helicopter that would drop me into his front yard."[11] Considering that it was Finley making such a statement, it was hard to say whether he was kidding or not. Finley had been trying to make trades for veteran infielders Ted Kubiak of Milwaukee and Larry Brown of Cleveland. Neither of those players possessed the range or fielding skills of a healthy Dick Green.

The veteran second baseman's initial threat to retire had prompted the A's to invite a 26-year-old minor league second baseman named Tony LaRussa to camp and give him Green's locker. LaRussa had sipped cups of coffee with the A's in 1963, '68, '69 and '70 but had never been able to establish himself at the major league level because of a questionable bat. An incredible series of injuries had also curtailed LaRussa's progress. From 1964 to '67, LaRussa had suffered torn ligaments in his arm, a pulled muscle in his back and two shoulder dislocations.

The A's had apparently thought so little of LaRussa's potential that they had left him off their 40-man roster since 1968. Yet, the hardnosed LaRussa had played well enough at Triple-A stops Vancouver and Iowa to earn himself two brief promotions to Oakland in the interim. Now, with Green back in the fold, LaRussa would have to battle to make the A's roster as a utilityman instead of as the starting second baseman.

As the exhibition season began, Reggie Jackson began to offer proof that his winter league improvement might carry over to the regular season. In the first 10 exhibition games, Jackson ripped seven home runs, including homers in four straight games, and drove home 17 runs. Reggie credited the influence of his winter league manager Frank Robinson, who had skippered Jackson's Santurce team in Puerto Rico. Jackson roomed with Robinson, the Baltimore Orioles' right fielder, for seven weeks. "He's very inspiring," Jackson said of Robinson. "He has a great record so I have to respect his knowledge... And he battled back from bad years, so when he tells me I can do it, I feel he knows what he's talking about. He's been there."[12] Robinson emphasized to Jackson the importance of keeping his anger under control.

Jackson took full advantage of his day-to-day contact with Robinson. "Every time after I had a turn at-bat, I'd go to Frank and ask him how I did," Jackson explained. I was looking for his criticism and suggestions, and he helped."[13] Armed with a new philosophy and an improved attitude, Jackson seemed ready to embrace his new roles as the team's number three hitter and everyday right fielder. As Hall of

Famer Ted Williams had said about Jackson the first time he watched him play, "He's the most natural hitter I've ever seen."[14]

During the exhibition season, the A's experimented with one of Charlie Finley's many inventions: the three-ball walk. Finley had petitioned the other major league teams to adopt the rule as a way of speeding up the pace of games and introducing more offense into baseball. Finley also figured that since baseball could not bring violence to its game the way that football had, the three-ball walk would at least provide the game with more action. Yet, of all the teams the A's were scheduled to play in spring training, only the Milwaukee Brewers agreed to experiment with the rule, and only during spring training. On March 6, in the first of four scheduled Cactus League games between the two teams, the A's and Brewers played a nine-inning game using Finley's brainchild. Fans booed the pre-game public address announcement of the three-ball walk, and the in-game results proved predictable. The teams' pitching staffs combined to allow 19 walks and 6 home runs, as the A's won, 13-9.

Having seen the effects of the rule on their pitchers, the Brewers no longer liked the three-ball walk. Cleveland Indians' manager Alvin Dark expressed some interest, but most other teams looked upon Finley's new rule with disdain. When Commissioner Bowie Kuhn expressed his discontent with the rule, which created too many bases on balls and appeared to swing the balance of power too far to the side of the hitters, Finley's three-ball walk died quickly.

Rollie Fingers, like most of the A's pitchers, probably breathed a sigh of relief when he learned that Kuhn had ordered the three-ball walk to be discontinued. As an unproven 24-year-old right-hander, Fingers had already overcome one of his problems — that of an extended waistline. In 1970, an overweight Fingers had won just seven games and lost nine, while switching between the bullpen and the starting rotation. Critics had often suggested that Fingers' poor eating habits contributed directly to his mediocre pitching results.

Ironically, the six-foot, four-inch Fingers had been anything but heavy as a teenager growing up in Steubenville, Ohio. In 1964, the gangly beanpole had won the American Legion Player of the Year award and signed a professional contract with the Kansas City A's. After debating whether to make Fingers a pitcher or a position player, the organization assigned him to moundwork with Leesburg of the Florida State League. Fingers ascended the ladder slowly, making it to Class-AA Birmingham in 1967. On opening night, Fingers threw a change-up to a minor league hitter named Fred Kovner. A line drive soon returned in Fingers' direction. "I saw it," said Fingers, "about three feet from my face."[15] Fingers tried to block the ball with his glove, but reacted too late, the drive striking him in the jaw. Fingers fell to the dirt, face first. When manager John McNamara rolled him over, he fixated on a stream of blood flowing from Fingers' right eye. Doctors repaired the eye, which had caused blurred vision, and wired his jaw shut. Fingers spent three days in the hospital, losing several pounds along the way.

After the 1970 season, Fingers located the answer to his weight problems. Once again, the solution arrived in an undesirable way. Rollie experienced a severe bout with intestinal flu and lost 25 pounds in the process. The illness proved to be a blessing, as Fingers reported to spring training lighter, quicker, and more durable. In just over 36 spring training innings, Fingers compiled a record of 4-0, with an ERA of 2.23. On March 27, Fingers pitched the most masterful exhibition game of any Oakland starter to date. Despite struggling with his control, Fingers shut down the San Diego Padres, 9-2, with a complete game, five-hit effort. The performance marked the first complete game for an A's starter in spring training.

The A's had projected Fingers as their third best starter, after Catfish Hunter and Vida Blue. Finger's unforeseen spring training success convinced Williams to name him the A's No. 2 starter. Hunter, a notoriously poor spring training pitcher, fell to the No. 3 slot, despite leading the staff with 18 wins in 1970. Williams deemed Chuck Dobson healthy enough to merit the status of fourth starter, despite being slowed by a spring training back strain.

The improvement of Fingers strengthened the rotation, but weakened a thinning bullpen corps. Diego Segui, the American League's ERA champion in 1970, had reported to spring training late because of a contract dispute. Another right-hander, veteran Bob Locker, appeared nervous and fidgety during his spring training stints and experienced difficulty throwing his sinkerball for strikes. From the left side, Jim Roland allowed only three runs in 19 innings, but appeared best suited for the unglamorous role of long relief. The other southpaw, Paul Lindblad, pitched solidly in the spring, but like the other relievers, lacked the intimidating fastball preferred from a late-inning, game-saving reliever. With Mudcat Grant now in Pittsburgh, the A's lacked a dominating closer who could handle opposing batting orders in the seventh, eighth and ninth innings. The A's would have to find relief from a completely unexpected source later in the season.

Chapter Three:
Low Expectations

Opening Day Lineup, 1971
Campy Campaneris, ss
Felipe Alou, lf
Reggie Jackson, rf
Don Mincher, 1b
Sal Bando, 3b
Rick Monday, cf
Dave Duncan, c
Dick Green, 2b
Vida Blue, p

The play of career minor league veteran Tony LaRussa provided the A's with one of their most intriguing story lines of spring training. Once Dick Green had foregone retirement and reported to camp, LaRussa seemed destined to return to the minor leagues for a tenth consecutive season. The A's, however, did need a utilityman, someone who could back up Green, Campy Campaneris and Sal Bando.

In the past, LaRussa had played almost exclusively at second base but an offseason stint in the Dominican Republic had afforded him a chance to play the other infield positions. LaRussa successfully carried that experience over to spring training, where he impressed the A's with nearly flawless defensive play at second base, shortstop and third base.

The motivation of qualifying for a major league pension had also spurred LaRussa. "I'm 26 now. My oldest daughter is three," said

19

LaRussa, who had contemplated retirement in 1970. "I've still got a year and a third to get my pension and I'd like to get that if I can."[1]

Although LaRussa hadn't hit much during the pre-season, his fielding and versatility so impressed the A's that he made the team's 25-man roster over the more experienced John Donaldson and the more highly touted Dwain Anderson.

In spite of the good feelings provided by LaRussa's spring training climb from oblivion, the A's opened the 1971 season as only the third place choice in the American League West. Respected baseball writers like Joe Durso and Murray Chass of the *New York Times* made the upstart California Angels the fashionable choice in the American League West, leaving the A's and the Minnesota Twins to battle for second place. In general, most baseball writers seemed captivated by the Angels' off-season acquisition of Boston Red Sox slugger Tony Conigliaro, who had hit 36 home runs and driven in 116 runs in 1970.

The writers considered the Twins too much on the dark side of thirty, with key players like Harmon Killebrew, Leo Cardenas, Jim Kaat and Jim Perry creeping up in age. In contrast, the experts regarded the A's as too young, and too lacking in pitching depth to win the division outright. Oakland's 11-17 spring record left some doubt in the minds of the writers, who also noticed the unusual, poorly-balanced structure to the season-opening team. Oakland's 25-man roster included only nine healthy pitchers, and featured seven outfielders, an unusually high number. The A's had discussed the possibility of trading left fielder Felipe Alou to the Milwaukee Brewers, perhaps in exchange for utility infielder Ted Kubiak, but the veteran outfielder remained in Oakland. The failure to trade for Kubiak had also ensured that Tony LaRussa would remain with the team. With Alou stationed in left, Rick Monday positioned in center, and Reggie Jackson entrenched in right (and no designated hitter rule in effect at the time), quality players like Joe Rudi and Tommy Davis seemed destined for minimal playing time. The bevy of veteran outfielders left talented youngsters like Angel Mangual and Steve Hovley buried further on the depth chart, with little opportunity to develop their skills at the major league level.

The installation of Dave Duncan as the starting catcher indicated that Dick Williams might be more in charge of lineup decisions than his predecessor, John McNamara. After all, Charlie Finley had battled verbally with Duncan during the offseason. Williams seemed assured of production no matter whom he selected as his starting catcher. In 1970, Duncan, Gene Tenace, and Frank Fernandez had combined for 32 home runs and 93 RBI's.

Dick Williams surprised most of the Oakland media by naming Vida Blue as his Opening Day starter in Washington, where the A's would play the Senators in the traditional Presidential opener. At the start of the season, Williams had considered Blue as no better than his

No. 2 starter. The 21-year-old left-hander had made only a handful of major league starts prior to the season, while Catfish Hunter was coming off an impressive 18-win campaign. Blue, however, had been dominant in two late-season starts in September. In his fourth start of 1970, Blue hurled a no-hitter. Throwing 90 per cent fastballs, Blue shackled the Minnesota Twins, the eventual Western Division champions. Two starts earlier, Blue had nearly equaled that effort when he one-hit the Kansas City Royals, allowing only an eighth inning single to Pat Kelly.

The sleek left-hander had made a profound first impression, even on a Hall of Fame pitcher from an earlier generation, Whitey Ford. "The first time you see him — if you think like a pitcher — you have to say 'this one can throw the ball.'" remarked Ford. "He has a loose, easy windup. He coils himself up and that way he gets the most spring out of his body. He's smooth and he comes right over the top."[2]

Blue prepared to face the Senators, who had lost eight consecutive Opening Day games. Washington had also dropped its last 14 games of the 1970 season to finish a dismal last in the American League East, an unsightly 70-92. Yet, the Senators still had reason for optimism heading into the new season. Owner Bob Short had signed former All-Star outfielder Curt Flood, who was still in the midst of battling baseball's reserve clause, and had acquired former 31-game winner Denny McLain in a trade with the Detroit Tigers.

Blue started the game throwing hard but a bit wildly, surrendering three walks in the second inning. An error by Campaneris at shortstop allowed two unearned runs to score, putting the A's in an early hole. An unsettled Blue ended up surrendering four runs in a jittery start. "He didn't know where he was," observed third baseman Sal Bando. "Anything you said to him, he shook his head and said 'yes.' You could have said you're full of bull, and he would have said 'yes.'"[3] The Oakland bullpen did not help matters, either, allowing four runs to score over the final six and 1/3 innings. On offense, the A's managed only six hits and no runs against Dick Bosman, a competent, but hardly overpowering veteran starter. Lumbering left fielder Frank Howard, considered one of the worst defensive outfielders in the league, made two terrific catches on the run, preserving Bosman's six-hit, 8-0 shutout.

Two days later, the A's played their home opener at the Oakland Alameda County Coliseum. At the behest of Charlie Finley, the A's had scheduled an unusual home-opening doubleheader. A sparse crowd of just over 23,000 fans showed up to watch Catfish Hunter and Rollie Fingers pitch miserably in both ends of the doubleheader, as the A's lost 6-5 and 12-4 to the Chicago White Sox, who had somehow managed to lose more games — 106 — than any other team in 1970. Oakland pitching, which Dick Williams had raved about during spring training, appeared on the verge of an early-season collapse.

With his team's record sitting ugly at 0-3, Williams called his entire pitching staff into his office for a meeting. Having noticed his pitch-ers' unwillingness to challenge hitters, Williams encouraged them to stop nibbling at the corners. He urged them to concentrate on the most important task at hand: throwing strikes. The Oakland manager may have also recognized the organization's mistake in trying to open the season with only nine pitchers: Blue, Fingers, Hunter, Chuck Dobson, Diego Segui, Jim Panther, Bob Locker, Jim Roland, and Paul Lindblad. Dobson, the team's scheduled fourth starter, was clearly not healthy enough to pitch. He had performed poorly in his final exhibition start, and seemed to be favoring his arm during his delivery to the plate. "You know we can't get by with eight pitchers" Williams said after announc-ing that Dobson would be placed on the disabled list. "Heck, you know we couldn't even get by with nine."[4]

Armed with a surplus of outfielders, Charlie Finley decided to pull the trigger, or some might say the panic button, on an early-season trade. On April 9, just four days after the start of the season, the A's dealt Felipe Alou, the team's Opening Day left fielder. Instead of send-ing Alou to the Brewers for infield help, as had been rumored during the spring, Finley traded Alou to the New York Yankees for pitchers Rob Gardner and Ron Klimkowski. Yankee management was thrilled to have acquired a professional hitter and veteran leader like Alou, while some Oakland writers criticized Finley for not receiving equal value in return. Klimkowski had pitched well in 1970, with an ERA of 2.66, but had done so in the relatively low-pressure role of long and middle relief. Gardner, a 16-game winner for the Syracuse Chiefs of the International League, had failed to make the Yankees' pitching staff in the spring.

Oakland players knew they would miss Alou, one of the most well-liked and respected players in all of baseball. Captain Sal Bando had previously offered Alou the ultimate praise. "He's one of the greatest men I've ever met."[5] Dick Williams attempted to defend the deal, which he felt was mandated by the team's lack of pitching depth. "The name of the game is pitching," Williams declared, "and we haven't had it yet. In fact, we've been bombed."[6]

The timing of the trade — just a handful of days into the regular season — caught Alou by surprise. Although Alou maintained a perma-nent home in Atlanta, he had just moved his wife and children into an Oakland apartment, where they were scheduled to stay for the entire 1971 season. Those plans would have to be scrapped, but the Yankees graciously gave Alou the necessary time to move his family out of the Oakland apartment and make new accommodations in the New York metropolitan region. When Alou finally reported to the Yankees a few days later, he found a positive spin to the trade in the strangest of places — the simplicity of his new uniform. "At least I know this is the uniform I'm going to be wearing everyday," Felipe said of the traditional home Yankee pinstripes. "Out there (in Oakland), I didn't know which uniform to wear when. We had one uniform for the first game of a double-header and another for the second. Once I put on the wrong uniform."[7] The A's led both leagues in the number of uniform combinations, which featured Charlie Finley's favorite colors: Kelly green, Fort Knox gold, and wedding gown white. On some days, the A's wore green uniforms with gold undershirts, on other days they donned white jerseys and pants with green sleeves, and on still other days they wore gold uniforms with green undershirts. When the A's played home doubleheaders, they wore white jerseys in the first game and gold ones in the second game. The arrangement proved confusing to the players, but entertaining to Finley.

On Friday night, April 9, the same day that the trade had been announced, the A's finally displayed some of the championship potential that Williams had beamed about during the offseason and spring training. Oakland scored five runs against the Kansas City Royals in the second inning, thanks to four walks, an error, a two-run single by Joe Rudi and a sacrifice fly by Reggie Jackson. The offensive fireworks proved to be more than sufficient for Vida Blue, making his second start of the season. In stark contrast to his unsettled performance in the opener against Washington, Blue proved overpowering against the Kansas City Royals, striking out 13 batters in a 5-0 six-inning, rain-shortened win. For the first time in his brief managerial tenure with the team, Williams sat back and enjoyed a dominant pitching performance by one of the American League's most dazzling young pitchers.

The next day, Diego Segui made his first start of the new season. The fork-balling right-hander struggled, giving up four runs in five innings. As a result, the Aís trailed, 4-3, heading to the bottom of the ninth inning. With one out, No. 8 hitter Dick Green singled, and moved up to second on a walk to Steve Hovley. Royals' reliever Jim York then retired Campaneris for the inning's second out. Since Dick Williams had pulled a double-switch earlier in the game, the pitcher's spot, featuring relief pitcher Bob Locker, was scheduled to bat. Williams called upon his most experienced pinch-hitter, Tommy Davis. With two on and two outs, and the A's facing their fourth loss in five games to start the season, Davis belted a hard-hit ball into the left-center field gap. Green scored easily from second to tie the game, and Hovley raced all the way home from first base to give the A's a dramatic come-from-behind victory. Davis, who had been acquired from the baseball scrap heap known as the waiver wire, had paid his first major dividend as the leader of the A's bench brigade.

In the early 1960's, Tommy Davis was arguably the National League's best all-around hitter. In 1962, he had led the league with a robust .346 batting average and a Hack Wilson-esque 153 RBI's. In 1963, Davis' numbers fell, but he still led the league in hitting with a .326 mark. Two years later, Davis caught his spike on the second base bag while executing a take-out slide, shattering his right ankle. The fracture robbed Davis of much of his speed and power-hitting capacity. Davis learned to hit off his front foot, but the injury rendered him a journeyman player, as he floated from Los Angeles to New York (Mets) to Chicago (White Sox) to Seattle (Pilots) to Houston, to Oakland to Chicago (Cubs). Davis had been traded three times, sold twice, made available in the expansion draft, and even released — on Christmas eve, no less. Now, Davis had found a home in the Bay Area, as perhaps the best pinch-hitter in the American League. As Dick Williams would say of his skilled batsman in later years, "Tommy Davis can hit at midnight with the lights out."[8] By the time he ended his 18-year major league career in 1976, Tommy Davis would rank first on the all-time pinch-hitting list with a batting average of .320.

Chapter Four:
A New Sheriff in Town

In spite of the win over the Royals, the A's were not playing the kind of crisp baseball that Dick Williams had envisioned. After losing the next game to the Royals, 10-5, the A's fell to 2-4 on the season, further wearing the patience of their demanding skipper. While on the team bus at the Milwaukee airport, one of the Oakland players decided to play a practical joke by stealing a battery-operated megaphone from the team airplane. Williams was not amused. He angrily lectured his players about the incident, demanding the bullhorn be returned immediately.

"Gentlemen," Williams addressed his players, "some of you think you can be *bleeps*. Well, I can be the biggest *bleep* of them all. I've been mild up to now." Williams then delivered his first major pronouncement. "The serving of booze on planes is terminated for the rest of the season."[1] Williams continued his diatribe. "The plane can't leave without the megaphone, and we won't leave until the plane does."[2] As Williams continued his lecture, one of the players dropped the megaphone from the bus window onto the sidewalk. Williams saw the megaphone fall, but continued talking. "I suggest that you stay in your rooms the entire trip." And one more thing. "If any of you want to telephone Charlie Finley to complain," Williams said, "I have three phone numbers where he can be reached."[3] In other words, Williams was challenging his players to go over his head and complain to the owner. Oakland players had

25

never seen the mild-mannered John McNamara react in such a way. The reign of Dick Williams had officially begun.

Who stole the megaphone in the first place, setting off Williams on his first tirade as Oakland manager? In the years after the incident, several Oakland players have identified Catfish Hunter, perhaps the team's most cunning practical-joker, as the culprit. Sal Bando says that Hunter might have been assisted by an accomplice. "It was either he or (Paul) Lindblad," Bando says, "but they were both involved."

The A's responded to Williams' disciplinary measures by winning their next five games, including two-game sweeps of Milwaukee and Minnesota. After losing a single game to the White Sox, the A's strung together seven more victories, making it 12 wins in 13 tries. The A's moved into first place on April 16, slipped back to second briefly, and recaptured the top spot on April 20. The A's finished April with a record of 17-8, a ledger that became even more impressive in light of the club's three game losing streak at the start of the season.

The key man in Williams' plan, Reggie Jackson, contributed game-winning hits in three consecutive games, and powered two long home runs in a victory against the Twins. One of the home runs traveled an estimated 437 feet, while the other managed a distance of 422 feet. Jackson continued to credit his winter league manager — and American League rival — Frank Robinson. "Being around Robinson matured me as a person and as a player," explained Jackson, who had played for the Santurce Crabbers in Puerto Rico. "When I got down there, I was rock-bottom in morale and confidence...From then on, we talked almost continuously about baseball, and I did most of the listening. We talked about temper and then I learned things by watching him control his. We talked about being a black man in baseball, and he helped me put myself in perspective." Robinson's life lessons had seemingly taken hold on Jackson. "I feel I'm a different person because of Frank Robinson."[4]

Although Reggie was delivering timely power to the Oakland cause, he was struggling to make contact. In his first 51 at-bats, Jackson had struck out 20 times, or nearly 40 per cent of the time. Another Oakland slugger, third baseman Sal Bando, helped compensate for Jackson's early-season penchant for swinging and missing. Bando homered five times in his first 16 games, and enjoyed an incredible stretch of 12 plate appearances, which included four longballs, two singles, a double, and three walks. The Oakland captain also expressed extreme confidence in his team's ability to contend in the American League West. With less than a month of the regular season completed, Bando seemed to be looking ahead to a post-season matchup with the defending World Champion Baltimore Orioles. "Definitely, we're going to win our division," Bando boldly told reporters. "We haven't the depth Baltimore has, and of course, not the pitching, but in a short series, you never can tell."[5]

The play of second baseman Dick Green also bolstered the A's. Green had endured a miserable season in 1970, batting under .200 with four home runs and 29 RBI's. Green admitted that he had allowed his poor hitting to affect his usually reliable fielding. In general, he had grown disenchanted with the lifestyle of a baseball player, and had considered retirement. At the end of the season, Green returned his contract offer unsigned and later mailed back a check he had received for upcoming spring training expenses.

After considering trading for another second baseman, Boston's Mike Andrews or Cleveland's Larry Brown, Finley went to work. He telephoned Green, put on his best salesmen's pitch, and offered him some improved financial considerations. Green eventually agreed to return to the A's and once again teamed with his usual double play partner, shortstop Campy Campaneris.

In his first 24 games, Green batted only .205, but totaled four home runs and 15 RBI's. Those power numbers ranked behind only Sal Bando on the Oakland roster. More importantly, the slick-fielding Green had committed only one error, which had occurred on an errant throw and not because of his mishandling of the ball. Baltimore Orioles' second baseman Dave Johnson praised Green's defensive ability, especially his courage in turning the double play. "Greenie's the least scared of the opposing baserunners of all the second baseman in the league," Johnson said. "He shows the most guts. He sacrifices something, trying for that double play."[6]

On April 24, the A's finally managed to acquire Larry Brown from the Indians — at the cost of $100,000. Finley clearly overpaid for Brown, who had entered the 1971 season with a lifetime batting average of .239 and only 45 home runs in eight seasons. Now, with Green un-retired and playing well, the A's viewed Brown as a pricy backup, not as their starting second baseman.

The day before the acquisition of Brown — which, by the way, gave them three players named after colors of the spectrum, joining Dick Green and Vida Blue — the A's finished off a three-game sweep of the pre-season darlings, the California Angels. Blue picked up the victory, becoming the first four-game winner among American League pitchers.

Although Dick Williams had managed the club for only a month, he had already succeeded in gaining more authority than his predecessor. Williams had quickly and firmly dealt with the bullhorn incident, and had banned alcohol from team flights as punishment for the childish prank. Most importantly, Williams had accomplished his most important task as manager — helping his players to perform better. "He instills confidence in you," said Dave Duncan. "I think we are 75 per cent better than last year. It's a great feeling."[7]

Fortunately for Williams, Charlie Finley had not yet chosen to attend a game in Oakland, which removed an ominous shadow that might otherwise have lurked over the shoulders of Dick Williams. The Oakland media, however, had taken note of Finley's absence, and had decided to criticize the owner for his lack of interest. "The fans do not care whether Charles O. Finley comes out to the games,"[8] Finley said, attempting to defend himself from the latest criticism.

In early May, the A's record stood at 19-11, good enough for first place in the American League West. Still, Finley felt he could improve his team by tinkering with his roster. On May 8, the A's made a major trade, dealing veteran first baseman Don Mincher, backup catcher Frank Fernandez, reliever Paul Lindblad and cash to the Washington Senators for power-hitting first baseman Mike Epstein and lefty reliever Darold Knowles. Reports differed as to the amount of cash the A's included in the deal. Estimates ranged from $75,000 to $300,000, a massive amount of money to be included in such transactions at the time.

Prior to his tenure in Oakland, Mincher had played stints with the Minnesota Twins, California Angels and Seattle Pilots. Twins' beat writer Bob Fowler remembers Mincher well from his days in the Twin Cities. "Don Mincher was a very big guy, six-four, maybe 220 or so," says Fowler. "Excellent power hitter, pretty good fielder. A real quiet, gentlemanly type of guy, which frankly we had a lot of in Minnesota." The veteran first baseman's polite, easygoing demeanor made him popular with the other Oakland players, while offering a soothing balance to a team filled with more volatile personalities like Reggie Jackson and Vida Blue. Mincher's leadership, professionalism and hustle also made him a favorite of managers like John McNamara and Dick Williams.

On the surface, the deal seemed questionable for the A's. Mincher and Mike Epstein were similar players: left-handed power hitters with limited range at first base. Yet, Mincher had paced Oakland with his career-high 27 home runs in 1970, and had proven to be a clutch hitter, driving in the tying or go-ahead run 23 times. While Mincher had forged a reputation for being a solid clubhouse force, Epstein had created some friction in Washington through his brash, outspoken complaints about managers and playing time.

Paul Lindblad and Darold Knowles were both 29-year-old left-handed relievers, neither of whom offered the capability of pitching as a starter. The loss of "Broadway" Frank Fernandez — so dubbed because of his Staten Island heritage and his acquired dislike of New York and playing for the Yankees — seemed inconsequential. Fernandez, the third-string catcher, had come to bat only four times.

The A's, however, had their reasons for making the deal. Williams had lost confidence in Lindblad, whose ERA had risen to nearly 4.00, and who had struck out only four batters in 16 innings. Meanwhile, Knowles had displayed a more lively arm with the Senators, striking out 16 batters in 15 innings. In 1970, Knowles had earned 27 saves while pitching for a last-place team in Washington. Yet, Senators' owner Bob Short had criticized Knowles' most recent performance, suggesting that the left-hander had lost several miles off his fastball. Short hinted that Knowles' value was declining with each passing day. "I didn't realize I was so horsemeat," Knowles said sarcastically. "From the way he talked, I don't know how I've stayed in the big leagues for five years."[9]

The trade did not catch Mincher completely off guard. "I had heard rumors," Mincher says. "I knew that Darold Knowles...was what the club was really after. And Mike Epstein, who became a great player for them, really worked out well, too. I had heard rumors, and I could remember very vividly that I was called to Dick Williams' room that night along with Paul Lindblad. In the back of his mind, Mincher knew what he was leaving behind. "We also knew that Oakland was going to be a club that was really gonna be there," Mincher says. "I hated to leave Oakland because I could tell, and most people could tell, what was coming with that ballclub." Mincher did not know at the time that he would eventually be making a return to Oakland, thanks to the handiwork of Charlie Finley.

Although both Epstein and Mincher had endured poor starts to the 1971 season, the A's felt they enjoyed an advantage in trading for youth. After all, the 28-year-old Epstein was nearly five years younger than Mincher. Epstein, for his part, reacted with near ecstasy to a trade that brought him closer to family and friends who lived throughout California. When Senators' owner Bob Short informed Epstein that he had traded him to Oakland, the strapping first baseman responded sincerely, "Thanks for trading me to a first-class ballclub."[10]

A reporter quickly asked Epstein how he would react to platooning with the A's. In the past, Epstein had battled with Senators' manager Ted Williams, who liked Epstein but didn't feel he could hit left-handed pitching well enough. "Even in 1969, when I had my best year, I didn't face left-handers," Epstein gasped. "In 1970, the same story. I'd get hot and then they'd throw a left-hander against us, and I'd sit on the bench and cool off. I sat on the bench more and more. It was discouraging."[11] While Ted Williams had made up his mind to platoon him in Washington, Epstein held out hope Dick Williams might eventually change his status in Oakland. "Dick told me that Tommy Davis is playing against left-handers," Epstein acknowledged. "But I can get real hot with the bat and maybe not platoon."[12] Epstein was in for a rude awakening.

In spring training, the A's had envisioned Davis as a pinch-hitter deluxe, but the veteran batsman had a different plan in mind. When Mincher started the season in an 0-for-17 slump and went hitless in 12 at-bats against southpaws, Williams decided to increase Davis' playing time against left-handers.

On April 28, in a game against the Baltimore Orioles, Mincher had struggled badly in three hitless at-bats against left-hander Mike Cuellar. In the seventh inning, O's manager Earl Weaver brought in another southpaw, Grant Jackson, to face Mincher. Having seen enough of Mincher's futile swings against lefties, Williams summoned Davis to pinch-hit. Davis worked the count against Jackson, drawing a walk. Then, in the ninth inning, Davis faced tough right-handed reliever Dick Hall. With one out and the winning run in scoring position, Davis battled Hall, fouling off several two-strike deliveries, before lacing a game-winning single.

From that point on, Williams decided to employ Davis as his first baseman against all left-handed pitchers. "The next time a left-hander pitches against us," Williams told reporters after the game against Baltimore, "Tommy will be in there. I told him so... Tommy was upset tonight because he didn't start and I can't blame him. He wants to play. Now he's convinced me."[13]

Although the season was less than two months old, Davis had twice won games with ninth inning base-hits. He had also served as a batting mentor to several of Oakland's younger players, including superstar-in-waiting Reggie Jackson. The A's right fielder had struggled to make contact at the start of the season, striking out 11 times in his first 23 at-bats. During an early-season game against the Twins, Davis had noticed a flaw in Jackson's technique as he began his swing and strode toward the pitcher. Davis escorted Jackson to the clubhouse, showed him that he was making an improper movement with his back leg, and corrected the bad habit. Jackson returned to the dugout, and eventually blasted two home runs against Minnesota pitching. Without the benefit of film or videotape, Davis had helped Jackson make a critical in-game adjustment.

Chapter Five:
The Runaway

After losing the Presidential Opener to the Senators, Vida Blue had forged a run of seven straight complete game victories. The left-hander mastered American League hitters with a devastating fastball and an occasional curveball, also an overpowering pitch. Yet, Blue seemed surprised by his early run of success. "I was always confident I would win in the majors," Vida mused, "but 7-1?"[1]

Some sportswriters began calling Blue the "black Sandy Koufax," in reference to the former Brooklyn and Los Angeles Dodgers' left-hander, who was now broadcasting for NBC-TV. As the most dominant pitcher of the 1960s, Koufax had bagged three Cy Young Awards and authored four no-hitters. "Sandy Koufax came to me just before he was to interview Vida Blue," Dick Williams told *New York Times* columnist Arthur Daley. "Whom does he remind you of?"[2] Koufax asked Williams, a teammate of the future Hall of Famer during the 1956 season. "The guy I'm talking to,"[3] responded Williams. Koufax reportedly blushed when informed of his similarity to the A's pitching sensation. "I don't know if he's faster than I was," Koufax responded when asked for a comparison, "because I never saw me pitch...I always thought Jim Maloney threw harder than I did, anyway. I do know that I couldn't get the ball over the way he does at age 22. He's not only ahead of me, he's ahead of the world."[4]

Dick Williams agreed with Koufax's assessment of Blue. "This kid

31

has a five-year advantage over Sandy," Williams offered. "He has the control and the poise."[5] Koufax, a remarkable pitcher from 1962 to 1966, had struggled with command and control during his initial major league trials. The early part of his career — 1955 to 1960 — had included won-loss records like 2-4 and 8-13, and earned run averages as high as 4.91, 4.48 and 4.05. "I'd say (Vida's) already ahead of Sandy," said Tommy Davis, who had played with Koufax, covering a span from 1959 to 1966, and now shared an apartment with Blue. "There's no limit to (Blue's) future."[6]

When one New York reporter told Blue he looked like Koufax after one game, the African-American left-hander responded deftly: "You mean I look Jewish?"[7] In general, Blue reacted humbly to the continuing streams of Koufax comparisons, a man he knew little about. "I never saw Koufax pitch," Blue admitted. "Not in person or on TV. The only guy I used to try to imitate was Willie Mays — hitting."[8] American League teams couldn't hit Blue, who proceeded to win three more starts — including a three-hit shutout against the Brewers and a five-hitter against the Twins — to extend his winning streak to double figures. In 12 starts overall, Blue had amassed 10 wins, all before the calendar had turned from May to June. Except for his Opening Day loss and a no-decision on May 14 against the Royals, Blue had notched a complete game every time he had taken to the mound.

Blueís double-digit victory total included a pair of dominating performances against the defending champion Baltimore Orioles. In 18 innings against Baltimore's stacked lineup, Blue had allowed only one run, a mere eight hits, and had struck out 18 batters. "That's the best stuff Iíve seen in a long, long time,"[9] said future Hall of Famer Frank Robinson after the second loss to Blue. "It's not fair to compare talents but this kid takes a back seat to no one. He's as good right now as Denny McLain was three years ago," said Robinson, referring to McLain's outstanding 1968 season with the Detroit Tigers. "You know what he's going to throw and you still can't catch up to it."[10]

In another game, Blue had struck out 11 batters, while tossing a four-hit shutout against the powerful Detroit Tigers, whose lineup included another future Hall of Famer in Al Kaline, along with sluggers Bill Freehan, Norm Cash, and Willie Horton. Blue's performance impressed Kaline, who felt that Blue appeared more confident and relaxed than he did during his debut in 1970. "What impressed me was that when he got in a jam," said Kaline, "he could strike somebody out. That's important."[11]

A third future Hall of Famer marveled at Blue's ability to pinpoint his pitches on all four corners of the plate. "In the games I've faced him," said Minnesota Twins' slugger Harmon Killebrew, "I figure he's thrown about 30 pitches. Not one damned one has been down the chute. He's in, out, up, down — with something on every pitch."[12]

Dave Duncan, who caught most of Blue's 12 starts, had played an important role in the young left-hander's fast development. Duncan had beaten out the hard-hitting Gene Tenace for the A's starting catching job in the spring. Dick Williams had indicated early in spring training that he considered a catcher's defensive ability the most important facet of his game. "Catching is a defensive position," Williams had said. "To me, the biggest thing is handling the pitchers, calling the pitches, and defensive work."[13]

Duncan, an excellent receiver who provided a thinking man's approach to catching, played the position with surprising mobility for a large man. He also established a fluid game-day rapport with the team's pitchers, especially Blue. Duncan offered a variety of reasons for Blue's sudden success. "Vida has three things going for him," Duncan said. "First he's overpowering. Second, his ball moves. Third, he's sneaky. He has that nice, easy motion, so you think you can hit him. But you can't pick up the ball until it's too late."[14]

Although overshadowed by the powerful pitching of Blue, right-hander Catfish Hunter had quietly won eight consecutive starts after an 0-2 beginning. In the absence of an intimidating repertoire such as the one owned by Blue, Hunter relied on the less inspiring principles of control and movement. After one particular defeat of Milwaukee, Brewers' manager Dave Bristol admonished his hitters. "If you can't hit Catfish," said a scolding Bristol, "you can't hit anybody." [15] Hunter, unshaken by the critique, would win two more decisions against the Brewers in 1971, improving his season record to 3-0 against Bristol's team.

Hunter made up for his lack of arm strength with a discernible tenacity. As a result of his aggressiveness, Hunter often yielded home runs — usually solo home runs because of his ability to avoid bases on balls.

In their last 19 starts, Blue and Hunter had combined to win 18 games (17 complete games), while holding opponents to an average of 1.91 runs per nine innings. The devastating left-right combination provided by the Oakland aces made the A's the envy of the American League. Spearheaded by Blue and Hunter, the A's raced out to a record of 30-15. Oakland starters piled up complete games in 23 of the 45 games. The A's, who had been picked by most to finish third in the American League West, had emerged as the best team in the division, and perhaps the class of the American League.

Yet, Charlie Finley wanted more. The A's owner frothed at the possibility of adding another hammer to Oakland's intimidating staff of starting pitchers. Finley talked to the Chicago White Sox about the availability of left-hander Tommy John. But the A's owner desired a bigger name, one who would make headlines in the Oakland newspapers. Finley approached the Cleveland Indians about the status of their ace, hard-throwing left-hander Sam McDowell. Finley offered a package of players that included injury-plagued right-hander Chuck Dobson, who had been activated in May after starting the season on the disabled list. In spite of the rumors, the deal involving McDowell never did take place. In June, Finley claimed that he no longer possessed interest in acquiring "Sudden Sam." More likely, Finley found Cleveland's asking price for McDowell too high.

The A's might have regretted adding McDowell to their club, given his struggles with alcoholism and his recent feud with Oakland's Blue Moon Odom. In 1969, Odom had disparaged the Cleveland lineup, predicting he could shut out the Indians any time he faced them. The boast prompted some harsh words from Indians' slugger Hawk Harrelson, Odom's former teammate with the A's. Odom then ridiculed Harrelson who was hitting just .177 at the time. McDowell came to Harrelson's defense and challenged Odom. "You tell Blue Moon that I want a piece of his action when we get to Oakland," McDowell told a Cleveland reporter. "I want his game."[16] When a writer relayed the remarks to the Oakland clubhouse, Odom belittled McDowell's intelligence. "Sam's dumb," said Odom bluntly. "If I had his stuff, I'd win 25 games a year. He don't have no kind of brain. Why? He's just dumb. He don't know how to pitch."[17]

Such harsh words typified Odom, especially in the early stages of his career. "Blue Moon Odom came up as a very brash young fellow with a great arm," says Jack Aker, who pitched with the A's from 1964 to '68. "He's a fellow that went right to the major league mound, not a bit afraid, not a bit nervous. I can remember one incident especially, the first year that he was with us. We came into New York to play the Yankees, and it was a day game — a Saturday game — and we were gonna play a Sunday game, which he was gonna pitch. At the end of batting practice that day, I was walking off the field with Blue Moon. Whitey Ford was nearby on the other sideline. And Blue Moon stopped and asked me who it was. I said, 'That's Whitey Ford, he's gonna pitch against you tomorrow.' Blue Moon, at that point, turned around and yelled at Whitey, 'Hey tomorrow, Whitey, it's gonna be you and me dealin' in the sun.' Well, needless to say, Whitey just gave him a look like, 'Who is this guy?' The next day, Whitey was dealin' in the sun, but by the second inning, Blue Moon was in the clubhouse. He'd been knocked out of the game."

In May, the A's activated Odom from the disabled list — well ahead of his scheduled arrival in July. Odom pitched well in his first start, allowing two runs in six innings against the Royals. "I feel great," Odom said after the game. "I feel better now than I've felt in two years. I'm beginning a new life — pitching without that pain."[18] To make room for Odom and Chuck Dobson, Williams shifted Rollie Fingers to the bullpen in early May. Fingers, who had struggled as a starter, had been heavily sought after by the Washington Senators in trade talks. The Senators had wanted to include him in the recent deal involving Mike Epstein and Don Mincher, but the A's had refused to part with the talented young right-hander.

Williams had hoped that Fingers would prosper as a starter. In his first major league start in 1969, Fingers had pitched a complete game shutout against the Twins, whose lineup included Rod Carew, Tony Oliva and Harmon Killebrew. With his hard, sinking fastball that moved in two different directions and a knee-buckling slider, Fingers owned the physical requirements needed to become an excellent starting pitcher. Yet, Fingers' personality and make-up posed a problem, working against him as a starter. "When I was a starting pitcher," Fingers surmised, "I'd start thinking about it the day before the game. I'd be all shaky and everything."[19] An onslaught of nervous anxiety and anticipation plagued Fingers' mind and body. "I just couldn't handle a starting job," Fingers conceded in later years. "If Dick Williams hadn't moved me to the bullpen in 1971, I would have been out of baseball a long time ago."[20]

Fingers initially resisted the move to the bullpen, considered an unglamorous residential area in 1971. "Rollie thought it was banishment to begin with, to go to the bullpen," says Rick Monday. "Bill Posedel was the pitching coach and did a wonderful job, and constantly stayed on top of Rollie." At the time, the decision to move Fingers to the bullpen created few headlines. No one around the A's realized the significance of what was to become a critical career change. "Rollie Fingers was just becoming Rollie Fingers in 1971," recalls Don Mincher. "He had been a starter — a lousy starter before — and all of a sudden somebody realized the guy can get somebody out for two innings. So, he becomes a Hall of Famer." Fingers would establish himself as the game's most consistent reliever over the next 13 seasons, a span that included stints with the A's, San Diego Padres and Milwaukee Brewers. Fingers' 341 saves and 2.90 ERA would earn him election to the Hall of Fame — following Hoyt Wilhelm as only the second reliever to receive baseball's highest honor. If not for the foresight of Dick Williams, Fingers might have settled for a pedestrian career as a middling starting pitcher.

On May 22, the A's made a deal to further shore up their bullpen by acquiring right-hander Daryl Patterson from the Tigers for minor league second baseman John Donaldson. The addition of Patterson put the A's one player over the 25-man roster limit. As a result, the Oakland brass decided to outright spring training sensation Tony LaRussa to Triple-A Iowa. The timing of the move must have struck LaRussa as eerie, considering that he had been recalled by the A's exactly one year ago to the day.

LaRussa had played in only seven of Oakland's 43 games and had come to bat only twice. The durability of starters Dick Green, Campy Campaneris and Sal Bando, coupled with the in-season acquisition of utilityman Larry Brown had doomed LaRussa to afterthought status with the A's. Although LaRussa would earn another promotion to Oakland, his A's career had essentially come to a crossroads. On August 14, the A's would sell him to the Atlanta Braves. The intelligent, well-spoken LaRussa would not return to Oakland until July 7, 1986, when he debuted as the A's new manager. LaRussa would begin a terrific 10-year run as the leader of the A's, prompting some to call him the game's best manager of the late 1980s and early nineties. No one in Oakland in 1971 had any idea of the successes to come for LaRussa.

On May 26, the strange saga of left-handed pitcher Rob Gardner continued. The A's traded Gardner to the Yankees — the same team that had dealt the southpaw to the A's four days after the start of the season. Gardner had previously been optioned to Triple-A Iowa after seeing little action with the A's, primarily because of all the complete games being thrown by Catfish Hunter and Vida Blue.

In exchange for the human yo-yo and another minor league pitcher, the A's acquired the $40,000 contract of versatile backup Curt Blefary, who could catch, man first base or play the outfield. At first, Blefary considered the possibility of not reporting to Oakland, but quickly changed his mind when he realized the A's might make the playoffs. As a result, Blefary would shed baseball's most traditional uniform for the game's most radical doubleknits. "Hey, we play you guys next week, don't we?" Blefary said to his soon-to-be former Yankee roommate Bobby Murcer. "I wonder how I'll look in white shoes?" "Like a white whale,"[21] replied Murcer..

After a poor April, Reggie Jackson began to deliver on the promise that he had shown during his Winter League play in Puerto Rico. During the month of May, Jackson batted .337, crushed seven home runs, and collected 17 RBI's. Reggie attributed the resurgence to the shortening of his swing, coupled with his improved ability to hit with two strikes. "Why do people want me to hit 75 homers?" Jackson asked Ron Bergman of *The Sporting News*. "I'll hit my 30 with that .300 average and be satisfied."[22] With 10 home runs by the start of June, Jackson was on a pace to reach 30, but his batting average still lingered in the .270s.

Jackson had also improved his fielding in right field, which had been an inconsistent part of his game during his first three major league seasons. Jackson had begun to take advantage of his best defensive trait — a cannon-like throwing arm. Over the first two months of the season, Reggie had thrown out nine runners, including five at the plate.

While Jackson, Vida Blue and Catfish Hunter captured most of the media attention in April and May, another player had quietly assumed two important roles — as the starting left fielder and number 2 hitter in the lineup. Prior to the season, Joe Rudi figured to be a little-used backup, buried behind veteran Felipe Alou in left and Reggie Jackson in right. The trade of Alou to the Yankees during the first week of the season created regular duty for Rudi, except for those weekends when he had to fulfill his military requirements in the Marine Reserves. "I was driving to my Marine Reserve meeting when I heard Felipe was traded," Rudi said. "I was so high, I could have jumped off the roof."[23]

Rudi had overcome considerable odds just to make the major leagues. As a high school star in Modesto, California, Rudi impressed a horde of major league scouts until he suffered a badly broken hand on a pitched ball. Only one scout — the A's Don Pries — continued to show interest in him, even setting up medical treatment for Rudi's injured hand. Rudi rewarded Pries' loyalty by inking a contract with the Kansas City A's in 1964.

The A's signed the six-foot, two-inch Rudi as a shortstop but quickly realized that he was too tall for the position. A move to third base proved equally treacherous, as evidenced by his 37 errors, the most in the Midwest League in 1965. The A's finally settled on Rudi as an out-fielder, but after hitting .223 and .254 over his first two minor league seasons, the organization placed him on waivers. The Cleveland Indians claimed Rudi, only to return him to the A's in a subsequent minor deal. The A's assigned him to Modesto, his hometown, where he rejuvenated his hitting while playing for one of the greatest teams in minor league history. In 1966, Rudi batted .297 with 24 home runs and 95 RBI's for the California League champions. The Modesto club included 14 future major leaguers, including Rudi, Reggie Jackson and Dave Duncan.

Yet, Rudi struggled badly in major league trials in 1967 and '68, failing to hit as much as .200 each time. Rudi realized that his use of a sweeping, uppercut swing and his insistence on trying to hit home runs hurt his development at the major league level. In 1970, Rudi reported to spring training and encountered hitting coach Charlie Lau, who convinced him to change his approach at the plate. Rudi responded to the newfound tutelage by hitting .309 in 350 at-bats. Conversely, Rudi's defensive play in left field remained adventuresome.

Some writers questioned the decision to trade an established out-fielder like Felipe Alou for two unproven pitchers, while making room for an uncertain player like Rudi. Yet, captain Sal Bando defended Rudi's ability to step in and play left field. "I liked Felipe, but he can't do any more than what Joe can do," Bando insisted. "Joe can play everyday, hit the ball, and play good defense."[24] In early June, Rudi's batting average resided at a mediocre .260, but his productivity had impressed Dick Williams. In his first 52 games, Rudi totaled 27 RBI's and scored 31 runs. As the second hitter behind sparkplug Campy Campaneris, Rudi led the A's in sacrifice bunts and skillfully deployed his most effective offensive weapon — driving the ball to right field. Rudi's ability to execute the hit-and-run regularly created first-and-third situations for the A's.

Furthermore, Rudi had greatly improved his defensive play. "He was very below average, I'd say, with his fielding," reveals Jack Aker, who played with Rudi during his first two major league seasons. Rudi had shagged fly balls daily under the direction of then-manager Bob Kennedy, who supplied the young outfielder with an assortment of line drives and bloopers. After frequently butchering balls hit to him in 1970, Rudi evolved into an above-average flychaser. Rudi also lengthened an average throwing arm by embarking on a series of weight training exercises designed to strengthen his shoulder and arm.

In the meantime, Vida Blue had quickly become the American League's new sensation. In his first 16 starts of the season, Blue had pitched before crowds averaging over 21,000 per game. Although that number might not sound impressive in the context of baseball attendance in the 1990's, a team drawing 20,000 or more fans per game in the early seventies was considered a good drawing card. At times, Charlie Finley commanded Dick Williams to alter his rotation, in order to give Blue extra starts at home. On one occasion, Williams switched Blue

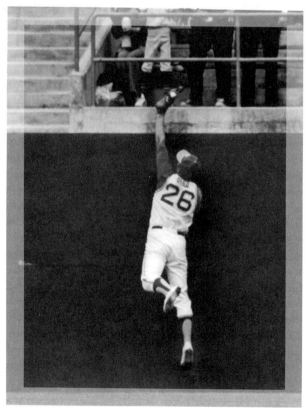

At first a poor defender, the hard-working Joe Rudi
displays the prowess that would eventually earn him a
Gold Glove in left field.

and Catfish Hunter, so that Blue would not pitch on Bat Day in Oakland.

Blue's Koufax-like pitching in the season's first half helped Oakland's opponents at the gate, as well. In a series in early June at Yankee Stadium, Blue drew a crowd of 30, 052. The Yankees sold approximately 20,000 tickets in their day-of-the-game gate sale, or about four times the usual rate. The Yankee fans watched Blue retire 17 batters in a row on the way to a 5-2 win over New York.

Blue displayed little nervousness in setting down the Yankees in front of the Bronx crowd, but expressed little desire for pitching in the big city. "I can't stand New York; it's too fast for me," [25] Blue complained to the *New York Times*. The more laid-back atmosphere of Oakland proved more attractive for Blue, who had thus far dealt well with the increasing media and fan attention. Blue kept his home phone number unlisted, but writers and potential girlfriends still called. "No, he's sleeping," said roommate Tommy Davis to an inquiring reporter. "He pitched last night. Certainly he'll talk to you. Vida's good about that. Can he call you back — say in about three hours? That should still give you plenty of time to talk, right?"[26]

Although Davis screened most of Blue's calls and supplied him with some advice, he admired his young teammate's ability to handle fame on his own. "What I do know from living with him is that everything that's happening to him is not getting to him," Davis said. "He knows how to relax. He knows what's going on. He's 22, but he acts like a man of 30."[27]

Blue reminded himself to remain level-headed as the media continued to shower him with attention. "I think I'm for real," Blue said of his pitching, "but I keep telling myself: 'Don't get cocky...Talk to the press...Be nice to the kids...Throw a baseball into the stands once in a while.'"[28] Blue wanted no part of becoming a prima donna, an affliction that had fallen on many players who had suddenly found stardom at the major league level.

Unlike Blue, Reggie Jackson did not handle himself well during a mid-season series at Yankee Stadium. As a reporter interviewed Blue in the Oakland clubhouse, Jackson watched from his neighboring locker. Reggie suddenly interrupted the conversation, which had been cordial in tone. "Don't talk to him, Vida," Jackson warned Blue sternly. "They're all the same. You don't need the press. Just wait until you ask for a raise next year. You'll see that they'll take the side of management. You'll see."[29] Jackson remembered his difficult contract negotiations after his breakthrough season of 1969 and the way that some of the media had sided with Charlie Finley in the dispute. The entire episode had convinced Jackson that the media at-large served as a mouthpiece for baseball ownership.

Left uncomfortable by Jackson's unprovoked diatribe, Blue politely wrapped up the interview with the reporter. Jackson remained ill-tempered. When a clubhouse attendant asked Jackson what kind of soft drink he wanted, the right fielder erupted again. "Get me the kind niggers drink," Jackson shouted. "I'm a nigger. You know I'm a nigger and we all drink the same thing."[30]

In contrast to Jackson, Blue had handled the barrage of media and fan requests diplomatically. "He has to put up with a lot," said Tommy Davis. "He's a bachelor, and mothers are always taking their daughters to meet him."[31] Blue, however, showed little interest in being set up on dates, or in involving himself with women that might be classified as baseball groupies. "They might be impressed with me, but I'm not impressed with them."[31] Blue preferred a quieter, simpler, stay-at-home lifestyle. "I don't usually go out more than three or four times during a two-week road trip," Blue said. "I do OK with women. But most of the time, I'd just rather get me a bottle of soda and a paper, watch some TV and go to bed."[32]

Blue seemed most at ease when relating to younger baseball fans. "He's great with kids," explained Davis. "We live in a middle-income to low-income project (in the Oakland area) and the kids are always knocking on the door. He has a lot of patience with them and he spends a lot of time talking to them."[33]

As well as Blue had pitched for the A's, he became involved with several controversies involving Charlie Finley. The owner had offered Blue a $2,000 bonus to officially adopt the middle name "True," giving him the rhythmical appellation of "Vida True Blue," already one of the many nicknames that had previously been administered by minor league sportswriters. Blue refused to accept what he considered such an undignified moniker. "I couldn't believe he was serious," Blue said of Finley's suggestion. "Vida was my father's name. I loved my father. He was a good, good man. Vida means life in Spanish...Now that my father is dead, I honor him every time the name 'Vida' appears in a headline. Why would I want to be called 'True Blue?'"[34] Blue also felt insulted by Finley's attempt at bribing him to change his name. Finley defended himself by claiming that he was only offering the money to Blue to defray the legal expenses of changing one's name in court. It was not until many years later that Blue comprehended Finleyís motivation. "That was his attempt at marketing," Blue says in a 1996 interview with Sports Collectors Digest, "and now I understand it."[35]

During one of Vida's starts, Finley ordered the scoreboard operator to flash the name "True Blue" on the message board at the Oakland Coliseum. Blue relayed a message to public relations director Michael Haggerty. "Tell Mr. Finley I don't like it and I wish he would have it stopped"[36] On several occasions, Finley told broadcasters Monte Moore, Bob Elson, and Red Rush to refer to his star pitcher as "True Blue." During a broadcast at Yankee Stadium, Elson repeatedly called Vida

"Charlie Finley's Blue Boy." Outraged by the racial implications of such a label, a San Francisco television announcer publicly criticized the Oakland announcing crew for using the word "boy" in association with an African-American player.

Another controversy occurred when Finley decided to reward Blue's standout pitching by giving him a new powder blue Cadillac, with the letters V-B-L-U-E adorning the license plate. Finley presented his prized left-hander with the $8,000 car during a game at the Oakland Coliseum. Although Finley claimed the Cadillac was a gift, an Oakland newspaper reported that Finley continued to hold the title to the car. Finley called a press conference to deny the accusation. Later, Blue resolved the controversy by saying that he himself held title to the car. Blue then said that he couldn't afford paying the insurance on the car, not to mention the gas and oil expenses created by a Cadillac. Finley initially balked at helping out, before agreeing to pay the expenditures.

In 1970, the A's had drawn only 778, 355 fans to the Oakland Coliseum, or about 200,000 fewer than their mark on the road. Spearheaded by the pitching of Blue, the A's had raised their level of play to a point higher than that of any of the previous Charlie Finley-owned teams, including the 1970 pennant contender. While Oakland's improved performance in 1971 had drawn the attention of their opponents and the national media, it had barely created a ripple with the Bay Area fans. Through their first 29 games, the A's had drawn a measly total of 310,640 fans — or an average of fewer than 11,000 per game. Even that figure was deceivingly high, considering that the A's had attracted two unusually large throngs for Cap Day and Helmet Day, which served to inflate the attendance totals at the Oakland Coliseum.

Most of the Oakland players had taken note of the paucity of fan support. The lack of rabid fan involvement represented one of the few negatives of a player's baseball existence in Oakland, where many of the A's liked the pace of life, the climate, and the people. "It's great here," said first baseman Mike Epstein, "even if you are playing before 2,000 people."[37]

In spite of the sagging attendance, Charlie Finley ventured into his wallet to procure a veteran player. On June 14, Finley made a quiet pickup, but one that would greatly strengthen the Oakland bench in the second half. The A's purchased first baseman Mike Hegan from the Milwaukee Brewers, the last-place team in the American League West. Although Hegan's batting average seemed unimpressive at .221, his penchant for drawing walks made his on-base percentage a respectable .358. Furthermore, Hegan's nifty glove work made him one of the best defensive first basemen in the American League, and a perfect backup to the iron-gloved starter, Mike Epstein.

Although the trade afforded Hegan the opportunity of leaving a bad team and playing for an improving one, he had some reservations about switching cities. "It was kind of a mixed emotion because my wife and I had just purchased a home in Milwaukee," recalls Hegan. "We had come to the Brewers as part of the Seattle Pilots, and at the time we had come to Milwaukee we were looking at planting some roots and living someplace year-round for a change, something we hadn't done. I think at first it was kind of a shock, although I knew the Brewers at that point really didn't have plans for me to be playing everyday. So, if I wasn't going to play everyday in Milwaukee with a team that was struggling, I think the best alternative at that time was to go to a winning team, and have a chance to go to the playoffs and World Series. After the deal set in and once I got to Oakland and I became comfortable with the surroundings, it turned out to be probably the best thing that happened in my career."

Like many other players who had joined the A's in mid-season acquisitions, Hegan appreciated the fact that Dick Williams sat down with him to explain specifically his new role with the ballclub. "I think Dick for a lot of reasons was probably the best man for that job at that time," Hegan says. "There are a lot of people who have negative impressions about Dick Williams; I'm not one of them. He sat me down, told me exactly what his plans were for me in certain roles. You know, that's all a player really wants is to know what kind of a role he's going to be used in, whether it be a starter, or a defensive player, or a pinch-hitter. Yeah, that was the first thing that Dick did, and very frankly, he stuck to it. That's the other thing. I've played for some managers who will tell you one thing, and another thing happens. That wasn't the case with Dick, and I appreciated the fact that he was very up front."

Hegan had never before played for Dick Williams, but he had encountered Charlie Finley during his days as an amateur player. "I've got lots of recollections of Mr. Finley," Hegan says. "Number one, back in 1960 or '61, after my freshman year at Holy Cross, I was playing summer league in Boston. Lenny Merullo and I were playing summer league and getting ready to head down to the Cape to play. And Len's dad was a scout with the Cubs. We had started to hear rumors that no longer was there going to be free agency, that a draft was gonna come in and it would restrict some of the ability for bonuses. In about early or mid-June of that year, we kind of passed the word around that instead of going back to Holy Cross for our sophomore years, that we were probably gonna sign (a pro contract).

"Mr. Finley came in himself to scout one ballgame and came back to my grandmother and grandfather's house. My father (ex-major league catcher Jim Hegan) was still coaching at the time and I was living with grandparents during the summer. He (Finley) came right to my grandparents' house, sat at the kitchen table, and wrote out a blank check and asked me to fill in the numbers that I wanted. I was stunned, you know. After our meeting, I talked to my father, who was coaching with the Yankees. And the only thing he said about Mr. Finley was that he was a maverick and an eccentric, and you make up your mind, but if you want to go with a 'quality' organization, give some thought to signing with the Yankees. That's what I eventually did."

When Hegan found out that he had been traded to the A's, he thought about meeting Finley for the second time. "You talked about that day I arrived in an Oakland uniform," Hegan says. "The first time I saw Mr. Finley, he shook hands and said, 'I finally got you.' So Charlie waited 11 years, but I finally joined his ballclub."

Perhaps inspired, or angered by the acquisition of another first baseman, Mike Epstein experienced a memorable two-game stretch on June 15 and 16. After struggling in April and May, Epstein's hitting had prospered in recent days. Playing against his former team, the Washington Senators, Epstein tied a major league record by homering in four consecutive at-bats. Epstein's overlapping power surge helped Chuck Dobson and Vida Blue coast to easy complete-game wins over Washington. In the meantime, former Athletic Don Mincher went 0-for-7 in the two games against his former mates.

Nine days after netting Mike Hegan, the A's continued to display their infatuation with husky backup catcher Frank Fernandez. In early May, the third-string receiver had been dispatched to Washington as part of the five-player deal that brought Mike Epstein and Darold Knowles to the Bay Area. Now, the A's had decided to re-acquire Fernandez, purchasing him from the Senators for cash, and assigning him to their Triple-A affiliate at Iowa. On the surface, the aquisition was hard to fathom since Oakland seemed well-stocked in major league catchers. Starting catcher Dave Duncan had successfully assumed command of the pitching staff, while Gene Tenace and the recently-acquired Curt Blefary provided excellent depth. But the A's knew that Duncan would be required to serve two weeks in the military reserves in August. Since Blefary lacked the defensive skills to catch on a regular basis, the A's desired a more reliable receiver like Fernandez, who had been Oakland's first-string catcher at the start of the 1970 season.

On June 25, Blue won his 16th game when he five-hit the Royals. The victory put Blue three games ahead of Denny McLain's pace in 1968, when the former Detroit Tigers' right-hander had won 31 games. Thus, the Oakland and national media began to regularly compare Blue's victory pace to that of McLain's. Aside from the pure numbers, the manner in which Blue won games left a stark impression on teammates and opponents. "I think overpowering," says Rick Monday, when asked to provide his own recollections of Blue during the summer of '71. "I mean to the point where you would see ballclubs come in and say, 'We're gonna get him tonight, we're gonna get him tonight.' And then they would leave town and say, 'Well, we'll get him next time.' He would just very, very quietly slice through a lineup."

Opposing hitters knew that Blue would throw his fastball the vast majority of the time, but still couldn't catch up to his particular brand of power pitching. Pitching coach Bill Posedel explained the key to the late explosion of Blue's fastball. "He has this extra flick of the wrist," Posedel pointed out. "You get the idea that his motion is all through, then he gets this extra snap on the pitch...Vida has that something else. It's the difference."[38]

Boston Red Sox star Carl Yastrzemski observed the last-second movement of Blue's fastball. "Maybe it's an optical illusion, maybe it isn't," offered Yaz. "Maybe we all get fascinated by that wrist flick, like a mongoose watching a snake."[39] Washington Senators' manager Ted Williams — the last man to hit .400 in a season — also focused his keen batting eyes on Blue. "This Blue throws a heavy fastball," explained the Hall of Fame outfielder. "It doesn't soar by you...It does most of its damage when it gets in close to you...When he comes into the plate, it either swoops away or sinks rapidly on you. When a batter makes contact, he's hitting something dead."[40]

Blue's pitching had created a nationwide stir; so did one of Charlie Finley's patented promotions. On June 27, the A's hosted the Kansas City Royals in a doubleheader at the Oakland Coliseum. Finley offered free admission to all women who wore hot pants to the game. Expecting about 1,000 not-so-shy women to accept the invitation and take part in the between games fashion show, the Coliseum staff found itself overwhelmed when 6,000 ladies showed up for the festivities. The lengthy parade of hot pants caused a one-hour delay in between games, compared to the usual 20 minute break. "Hot Pants Day" nonetheless represented a huge financial success for Finley, as the promotion resulted in an overall attendance of 45,302, with a paid crowd of 33,477. The next game, a Monday night tilt with the Minnesota Twins, drew only 4,654 fans to the Coliseum.

By the end of June, the A's had compiled the best record in all of baseball. On June 28, the A's became the first major league team to reach the 50-win plateau. At 50-26, the A's owned a double digit lead on the surprising Royals, who trailed by a full 11 games in the American League West. How did the A's manage to win 17 of 25 games in June, as they had done in April? Primarily because of a pitching staff that continued to dominate opposing lineups. Aside from Blue and Hunter, the A's received major contributions from a comebacking Chuck Dobson, who had won all six of his decisions while featuring an ERA of 3.14. After a shaky start, Blue Moon Odom had won three straight games. Odom sported an ERA lower than that of 11-game winner Catfish Hunter.

Prior to his three-game winning streak, several teammates had complained privately that Odom's presence was hurting the team's chances of winning. "Every time he pitches," one teammate had said snidely behind his back, "we know we've got to come from behind."[41]

Other players had maintained that Odom, at less than full strength, was taking up a space on the roster that belonged to a healthier, more deserving pitcher. Several fans had even written letters to Dick Williams, asking him to cease his use of Odom as one of the four regular starters. The criticism placed Odom in an awkward position. "I felt like a rookie," Odom said later. "Everyone was watching my every move and pitch, just to see if I would falter...Fans expected too much of me."[42]

In a related development, Charlie Finley had pushed for a new rule that would allow players who had undergone off-season operations to start the season in the minor leagues on a rehabilitation assignment. Under the existing rule, the A's could have tried sending Odom to one of their affiliates, but risked losing him on waivers to another team. Although the major leagues initially resisted adopting Finley's suggestion, they would eventually institute the rule during the 1980s. As the frequency of placing players on the disabled list increased dramatically, the ability to assign rehabilitating players to the minor leagues for extended stretches would prove extremely valuable to all major league clubs. Once again, Finley's thinking proved to be well ahead of his contemporaries.

In the bullpen, converted starter Rollie Fingers had surpassed veteran right-hander Bob Locker as the club's best reliever. In six relief stints during the month of June, Fingers did not allow a single run. The string extended his consecutive scoreless innings streak to 29 and two-thirds innings, covering 11 appearances. On July 9, Fingers pitched seven shutout innings during a 20 inning, 1-0 marathon win over the California Angels. Dick Williams had apparently found the bullpen successor to Mudcat Grant, who had been the club's best reliever in 1970 prior to the trade that sent him to the Pirates for outfield prospect Angel Mangual. "He's to us now in the bullpen what Vida Blue and Catfish Hunter are to us as starters," gushed Williams in a conversation with Ron Bergman of *The Sporting News*.

Although the Oakland brass loved the natural movement of his pitches, Williams and his coaches had become concerned over Fingers' tendency to daydream and become distracted. During a game early in his career, Fingers had tried to hold a potential base stealer close to first base. Fingers spun and pretended to throw to first base, a clear violation of the balk rule. While the rules permitted pitchers to fake pickoff throws to second or third base, Fingers had completely forgotten the most obvious aspect of the balk rule...no fake throws to first base.

On and off the field, Fingers' daydreaming had become legendary. "He has a rubber arm and a rubber head,"[43] one of the A's said good-naturedly. Several teammates recalled the time when Fingers was scheduled to take an at-bat during an exhibition game in Salt Lake City. Fingers left the dugout and grabbed his helmet, but forgot one important item — his bat — on his way to home plate. During another game in Oakland, Fingers and the other pitchers stood for the playing of the National Anthem. When the anthem ended, all of his teammates placed their caps back on their heads and sat back down, except for one. Fingers continued to stand, holding his cap over his heart. "I realized when I heard everybody clapping," Fingers said. "I asked myself, 'Why is everyone clapping?' Then I figured out that the National Anthem had ended. I was just thinking about the ballgame."[44]

On another occasion, Fingers' mind-wandering had actually avoided a tragic accident that might have claimed the life of one of the A's best players. Playing in the California League in 1966, Fingers drove one of his teammates, Steve Kokor, to the minor league stadium in Modesto. Fingers and Kokor became so riveted in conversation that Rollie forgot to pick up two other teammates, a pitcher named Stan Jones and an outfielder by the name of Reggie Jackson, on the way to the ballpark. As they neared the ballpark, Fingers drove his car through an intersection. Another vehicle ran through a red light and smashed into Fingers' car, damaging the left rear end. The impact crushed and rolled over the back seat, where Jackson and Jones would have been sitting if Fingers had not forgotten to pick them up. "Our roof came right down to the seats," Fingers explained. "If Reggie had been in the back seat, it probably would have been all over for him."[45] Fingers escaped with a bruised ribcage, while Jackson safely made his way to the ballpark in a taxicab.

The A's had also discovered that Fingers' tendency to drop down and throw sidearm harmed his most effective pitch — a sinking fastball. Catcher Dave Duncan and third baseman Sal Bando constantly harped on Fingers to throw over the top, in order to allow the natural "sink" in his fastball to take effect. "Sal is yelling on every pitch, 'Stay on top, stay on top!' Fingers disclosed. "I'm getting to the point where I can figure it out for myself. I'm not dumb."[46]

Among the offensive contributors was the newly-acquired Mike Epstein, who had overshadowed the other headline player that Oakland had acquired from Washington, Darold Knowles. While Knowles struggled out of Oakland's bullpen, Epstein batted over .300 with 10 home runs in his first 37 games with the A's. "Mike's always been a bear-down son of a gun," said Dick Williams, who praised Epstein for making better contact and expanding his one-dimensional power game. "He's hitting singles and doubles now to drive in runs and he's playing great defensive ball at first base, too."[47] Epstein had so impressed the A's that Williams temporarily abandoned the platoon arrangement with Tommy Davis. Then, Epstein went 0-for-13 against left-handers, prompting Williams to re-institute the platoon with Davis. The decision so upset Epstein that he requested a face-to-face meeting with Williams to discuss the situation.

Chapter Six:
He's Human After All

The A's continued to win games in July despite injuries to two starters, shortstop Campy Campaneris and right fielder Reggie Jackson. Campy missed several weeks with a severely sprained left ankle, while Jackson spent a few games on the sidelines with a pulled hamstring muscle. In their place, Dick Williams called upon his quality supply of reserves, including recently-acquired shortstop Larry Brown and young outfielders Angel Mangual and George Hendrick. Mangual, dubbed the "Little Clemente" because of his facial and physical resemblance to Pirates' right fielder Roberto Clemente, had especially impressed Williams. Through his first 152 at-bats, Mangual batted .322, while playing center and right. Mangual had played so well that he had taken away playing time from regular center fielder Rick Monday, who had been slumping.

Jackson, the team's regular right fielder, gained election to the American League All-Star team, as did Vida Blue, who had won 17 of 20 decisions, posted a 1.42 ERA and established himself as baseball's best pitcher over the first half of the season. On July 13, Blue started the midsummer classic at Detroit's Tiger Stadium against Dock Ellis of the Pittsburgh Pirates. The occasion marked the first All-Star game in history that pitted two black starting pitchers. Moments before the game, Blue admitted to an extreme case of nerves. "I'm scared stiff," Blue revealed. "I'm shaking."[1] Yet, Blue's first-inning performance showed

47

no effects of tension, as he retired the side on seven pitches.

The next two innings proved troublesome. Blue permitted a two-run homer to Johnny Bench in the second inning and a solo home run to Hank Aaron in the third. "When they say the guy throws harder than (Sandy) Koufax," said a skeptical Aaron, "then I gotta say they're a damn liar."[2] Aaron and National League teammate Joe Torre claimed that five pitchers in their league threw harder than Blue, including the Mets' Tom Seaver and Nolan Ryan, St. Louis' Steve Carlton, and Houston's Don Wilson. Astros' superscout John Mullen offered a defense of Blue. "You didn't see the real Vida Blue tonight," said Mullen. "His fastball was straight. I've seen him when his fastball moved three ways, in or out or up. He was nervous tonight."[3]

In the bottom of the third, American League manager Earl Weaver sent up Reggie Jackson, a last-minute substitute for the injured Tony Oliva, to pinch-hit for Blue. As Jackson left the clubhouse to prepare for his pinch-hitting appearance, Sal Bando jokingly advised him not to strike out. When Dock Ellis reached two strikes on Jackson, Reggie remembered Bando's words. On the next pitch, Jackson assaulted an Ellis fastball, driving it to the deepest lengths of right field. Still seemingly on the rise hundreds of feet from home plate, the ball carried over both decks and caromed off a Tiger Stadium light tower. If the ball had not struck the tower in right-center field, it would have easily cleared the outer dimensions of the ballpark. Some witnesses estimated the home run at 520 feet. "Hardest ball I ever saw hit,"[4] observed Detroit's Al Kaline, who had previously seen teammate Norm Cash hit several titanic shots into the right field deck at Tiger Stadium. A reporter asked Jackson for his opinion of the blast. "I didn't travel 2,000 miles to strike out,"[5] said Jackson, heeding the instructions of Sal Bando.

On the pitching side, Chuck Dobson won nine consecutive decisions before finally losing a game. On July 31, Dobson's record stood an incredible 10-1. Prior to the season, Dick Williams had looked up the veteran right-handerís career record. The losing ledger did not impress the demanding skipper, who called Dobson into his office before the season. "So I called him in and said, 'What the hell is this? You're 57 and 58 lifetime? With that arm? On this club?'" Williams continued his line of rhetorical interrogation. "'I'd be embarrassed if I were you. You're pitching on a pennant contender and you're 57 and 58. You know what that means? That means you haven't contributed. Your contributions have been nil.'"[6]

A sensitive player might have been crushed by Williams' biting commentary. Dobson, an intense competitor on the mound, took a different approach, taking Williams' remarks to heart. "Before this year, everybody told me how to pitch, but not how to win," Dobson explained. "I'd go out and lose, 3-2, on an eighth inning homer and everybody would shake my hand, tell me it was a nice game, tough luck. But it wasn't a nice game. It was a loss."[7]

Dobson was also involved in one of the most interesting social situations on the A's. In 1968, Dobson, a white man, had started rooming with Reggie Jackson, an African-American, on A's road trips. Earlier in the '68 season, Dobson had roomed with reserve outfielder Jim Gosger. When Dobson slept late and missed three Oakland bus trips, he complained that he needed a roommate who could wake him up. Jackson volunteered for the duty. "You know Reggie," Dobson said in 1969. "He kind of swaggered up to me and said, 'I'll get you up in the morning.'"[8]

In breaking one of baseball's long-standing traditions, Dobson and Jackson became the first regularly-paired interracial roommates in major league history. Jackson and Dobson tried to downplay the significance of the living situation, claiming they were not trying to make a civil rights statement. "I don't want to be known for rooming with a white guy and I don't think Chuck wants to be known for rooming with a Negro guy,"[9] Jackson said. Jackson added that he and Dobson simply enjoyed each other's company.

While such an interracial arrangement would become fairly commonplace in later years, (before teams generally adopted a policy of assigning one player to each hotel room) it was still highly unusual in 1971. Most major league teams continued to assign players of the same skin color to live with each other on the road. Furthermore, most white players preferred to room with each other and most black players did the same.

As well as the A's had played through the first four months of the new season, attendance continued to lag at the Oakland Alameda County Coliseum. For some reason, the Bay Area did not seem infatuated with a team that featured two dynamic young superstars (Vida Blue and Reggie Jackson) and an array of exciting support players (Campy Campaneris, Sal Bando, Joe Rudi, Catfish Hunter and Rollie Fingers). During the offseason, Charlie Finley had spent half a million dollars with an advertising firm that had suggested a makeover for the team. Finley had changed the official team name from "Athletics" to "A's," and had adopted the slogan, "The Swingin' A's," to lead the advertising campaign. Neither the formal name change nor the quantum leap in the quality of play had succeeded in attracting more fans to the ballpark.

Critics of the Oakland owner pointed to the lack of radio affiliates featuring the A's broadcasts, which minimized the team's exposure throughout Northern California. Others claimed that Finley did not spend enough money in staging promotions. The promotions that Finley did organize usually involved little cash outlay on his part: "Hot Pants Day," "Mustache Day," and the like. Prior to some games, players rode in on his pet mule, appropriately named "Charlie O" in tribute to the owner. "Many of the promotions he draws up are hick-town promotions that don't go over here," explained Bay Area columnist Glenn Dickey, a frequent critic of the owner. "The town is a lot more sophisticated than he is."[10]

Promotions aside, many fans in the Bay Area seemed turned off by Finley's brash, outlandish style of running the team. "People resent him," said Glenn Dickey, "because he overshadows the team and because he doesn't live here."[11] Finley lived in Chicago almost all-year round. He generally attended Opening Day at the Oakland Coliseum but rarely watched his A's play in person during the regular season.

The Oakland Coliseum represented another problem for Finley. Once dubbed the "Oakland Mausoleum," writers described the Coliseum as drab and cavernous, lacking the character and charm of some of the American League's more charming ballparks, like Fenway Park, Yankee Stadium and Tiger Stadium. Finley also faced direct competition across the bay. Critics questioned the wisdom of having two major league teams in the Bay Area, where the relatively small population base indicated a better chance of survival for a single franchise. In 1970, the A's and the San Francisco Giants had basically split a total attendance figure of about 1.5 million fans, with the A's drawing slightly more than half that figure. A team that drew 1.5 million fans in the early seventies was doing well; a team that was drawing half that number was probably losing money.

But not the A's of Charlie Finley. "He was a very shrewd businessman," says Dave Duncan. "He made a statement one time that he had never lost money on his baseball team, and there were a lot of years when there weren't very many fans coming to the ballpark." Only twice during Finley's reign in Oakland — 1973 and '75 — would the A's draw as many as one million fans in a season. Yet, by keeping player salaries and front office expenses to a minimum, Finley was able to keep his club profitable, at least until the latter stages of the decade.

On August 7, Vida Blue won his 20th game when he shut out the White Sox on five hits. Blue became the first pitcher in franchise history to reach 20 wins since 1952, when left-hander Bobby Shantz accomplished the feat for the Philadelphia Athletics. Blue managed to win the game, 1-0, despite a bout with nerves and an upset stomach. "I started shaking in the ninth inning because I wanted to win so bad," Blue explained afterward. "I took three Alka Seltzers during the game. That's how shaky I was."[12]

The milestone should have been a pleasant achievement for Blue, but the swarm of media pressure and fan expectation seemingly aggravated the young left-hander. Blue had failed to win his 20th in two previous starts, and had begun to show a dislike for the constant barrage of questions from newspaper reporters and television and radio broadcasters. According to Ron Bergman of *The Sporting News*, Blue had resorted to compiling a list of his ten most hated questions from reporters.

Earlier in the season, Blue had disclosed to reporters that he carried two dimes in his pocket, to signify his quest for 20 wins. When Blue won his 20th, a reporter asked him if he would carry a third dime as a symbol of his effort to win 30 games. Some athletes might have reacted to the question with humor, but Blue responded angrily. "There you go again," Blue snapped, while slamming his fist on a nearby table. "There's that damn pressure."[13]

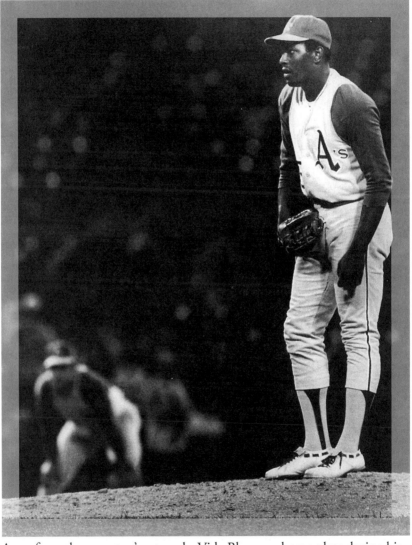

Away from the reporters' notepads, Vida Blue eyes home plate during his summer of domination.

After Blue won his 22nd game — a difficult 6-4 win over the Yankees which he called his "longest, hardest game" — Blue admitted to having difficulties with his emotional stability. "I feel the tension everyday," Blue told reporters. "Physically, I'm all right...but I sometimes feel like I'm going to crack up mentally."[14] In an interview with *Sport* magazine, Blue described how awkward he felt in the presence of so many media questions. "It's a weird scene," Blue explained. "You win a few baseball games and all of a sudden you're surrounded by reporters and TV men with cameras, asking you about Vietnam and race relations, and stuff about yourself. Man, I'm only a kid. I don't know exactly who I am. I don't have a whole philosophy of life set down."[15]

Although Blue was still pitching well, he had ceased being the dominant pitcher the A's had become accustomed to watching during the first half of the season. Blue's heavy reliance on the fastball may have contributed to his August falloff. "He threw 95 per cent fastballs in 1971," Dick Williams said two years later. "He just blew it by them. But he did tire some in the second half of the season."[16] American League hitters had started to familiarize themselves with Blue's simplistic pitching pattern.

Other factors caused Blue's performance to level off. Aside from the media pressure, Charlie Finley's insistence on using Blue on short rest, in order to maximize the number of starts he made at the Oakland Coliseum, had taken a toll on Vida's left arm. Extra starts on three days rest and a pileup of midsummer innings had removed some of the life from Blue's fastball. The unnecessary juggling of the rotation had also affected the timing and rhythm of Catfish Hunter, who was usually pushed back a day or two in order to accommodate the added starts for Blue.

In August, the A's had to face two weeks of play without the availability of starting catcher Dave Duncan, who had performed admirably in his role of quarterbacking the pitching staff. Duncan wasn't hurt; like many other major league players during the Vietnam War, he had to serve two weeks of duty in the Marine Reserves. The absence of Duncan forced Williams to use backup Gene Tenace in a starting role.

In 1965, the A's had drafted Tenace out of high school in Lucasville, Ohio, where he starred as an all-state shortstop and played on the same American Legion team as future major leaguers Al Oliver and Larry Hisle. The A's quickly switched Tenace to the outfield, where he appeared clumsy and unsure. In one minor league game for Peninsula of the Carolina League, the versatile Tenace played all nine positions, as a way of drawing more fans to the ballpark. In 1968, with the A's owning a bevy of young outfielders — including Joe Rudi, Rick Monday and Reggie Jackson — Tenace thought about quitting. The organization responded to the overload by converting Tenace to catcher. The A's felt confident that Tenace, an excellent hitter with power, could make the adjustment to a radically different position, which happened to be one of the thinnest throughout the Oakland system. Tenace worked with former major league catcher Gus Niarhos, the manager of the A's affiliate in Birmingham, Alabama.

Niahros compared Tenace to his former teammate with the New York Yankees, Yogi Berra, also a converted catcher. Tenace impressed Niahros with his strong throwing arm but struggled in other phases of defensive play. By 1970, Tenace reached the major leagues to stay, largely on the strength of his bat. He batted .305 in his rookie season and succeeded in wresting the number one catching job away from Frank Fernandez and Dave Duncan during the final month of the regular season.

When Dick Williams became the A's manager, he had announced his preference for a defensive-minded catcher who could handle pitchers. Prior to the 1971 season, Williams had declared an open competition on the catching position. Duncan, a far superior defensive receiver to either Tenace or Fernandez, had won the three-way battle during spring training.

Now Williams was entrusting his pitching staff to the defensively-challenged Tenace. On a thirteen-game road trip, Tenace batted a robust .500 with 11 RBI's, raising his season batting average to .322. That came as no surprise; the A's had always recognized Tenace's ample ability with the bat. On the same road trip, Tenace also displayed an improved knack for handling Oakland's pitching staff. None of the A's pitchers, privately or publicly, complained about Tenace's pitch-calling or general defensive skills behind the plate.

Tenace's surprising all-around performance on the long road trip helped the A's increase their lead in the American League West from 10 to 14 and a half games.

Oakland beat writers asked Tenace about the possibility of remaining in the starting lineup after Duncan's return. Tenace answered the question with a combination of diplomacy and chutzpah. "It's not up to me to decide who'll play. That's number 23's (Williams') decision," Tenace said politely. "But if I do my job and he takes me out, then I think he'll be making a mistake. But it's his decision."[17] Williams was clearly facing his first major controversy in regard to playing time for his catchers.

Despite Oakland's commanding lead in the West, Charlie Finley continued to tinker with his roster. During spring training, Pittsburgh Pirates' general manager Joe Brown had promised Finley that if and when he decided to unload veteran reliever Mudcat Grant, he would give the Oakland owner the first chance at trading for him. On August 10, Brown, living up to his promise, sold the soon-to-be 36-year-old Grant back to the A's for the waiver price of $25,000. After pitching brilliantly for the Pirates the first two months of the season, the aging Grant had gone into an extended pitching slump. The Pirate brass worried that Grant's days of effective pitching had come to an end.

In September of 1970, the A's had traded Grant to the Pirates for a player to be named later, which turned out to be young outfielder Angel Mangual. In an embarrassing mistake, the A's misspelled the outfielder's name, referring to him as Manguel five times in an introductory press release. Oakland writers and fans roasted Finley for making the deal. Oakland players privately questioned Finley's sanity. In 72 games with the A's, Grant had saved 24 games, forged an ERA of 1.83, and had emerged as one of the American League's most effective firemen. Without Grant, the A's lacked an established closer.

If not for Grant's presence in the bullpen, Rollie Fingers might not have developed into the game's most consistently effective reliever of the 1970s. "I learned how to become a reliever from Grant,"[18] Fingers said in later years. Rollie watched Mudcat attack opposing hitters by mixing his pitches, rather than trying to rely on one dominant pitch. Fingers also observed the different ways that Grant warmed up in the bullpen. "If a pitcher in the game gets out of a jam, I stop warming up and sit down," Fingers explained. "If he gets in another jam, I don't go at it hard in the bullpen. A lot of relievers burn themselves out in the bullpen."[19] Grant did not, and as a result, Fingers didn't, either

Grant had also supplied the A's with a positive clubhouse force, as he had done earlier in his career with the Indians and Twins. As an African-American, Grant became one of the few black stars to populate the Twin Cities area in the 1960s. "He was really the catalyst of that (Twins) team," says former Twins' beat writer Bob Fowler. "First of all, he was black. I think that was very significant to the Minnesota franchise. He wasn't Cuban. He was black. And the Minnesota area is basically Scandinavian. Sandy Stevens was a quarterback at the University of Minnesota in '61, when they went to the Rose Bowl. And Bill Muncie was a running back then. They had a couple of good (black) college basketball players...But we didn't have one (African-American star) in baseball."

Upon his arrival in Minnesota in 1964, Grant quickly made an impact on his Twins' teammates. "So anyway, Mudcat came in and he was a loosy-goosy guy," Fowler explains. "But the Minnesota team basically was a white team, outside of the Latins we had. It was basically a white team. And he came into that clubhouse, and he was the synergy of that ballclub. Harmon (Killebrew) was a quiet guy. Bob Allison was a quiet guy. We had a clubhouse of quiet guys. And Mudcat was sort of the spark, really."

Grant served as a role model for his black teammates, while helping to unite players from different racial backgrounds. "Oh, I think so," says Fowler. "Yes, I would definitely say that. He was a guy that players, whether they were black or white, looked up to. So, consequentially, if you were black, you may have looked up to him more so. Here was a guy who was admired by everybody. Liked by everybody. Didn't have an enemy." Well-liked by teammates and the Oakland media, the smiling Grant always seemed upbeat, supplying a counterbalance to the moodiness of stars like Reggie Jackson and Vida Blue.

By re-acquiring Grant, Charlie Finley also saw a chance to reverse his original trade, a deal that had brought him criticism from the players, media, and fans. Furthermore, Finley loved to bring back players he had previously traded or released. The list of re-acquisitions already featured Tommy Davis, Frank Fernandez and Diego Segui. Finley especially enjoyed bringing back such players in exchange for less compensation than he had surrendered in the first place. For example, Finley had originally traded Grant to the Pirates for Mangual, considered a top-flight prospect in the Pittsburgh organization. Now, Finley had re-acquired Grant for a small sum of cash, without having to yield any players in return.

Finley phoned Grant in Pittsburgh almost immediately. According to Grant, Finley told him, "We need you. Join the team in Boston as quick as you can."[20] Grant explained that he needed to take care of some business in Pittsburgh over the next couple of days. Finley would have none of it. "Charlie screamed into the phone, 'Oh no you don't,'" said Grant. "'You've got to be with the club tomorrow.'"[21]

Grant followed Finley's orders, reporting to the A's the following day, in time to pitch in the second game of the August 10 day-night doubleheader in Boston. In the nightcap, Williams summoned Grant to relieve Blue Moon Odom with two outs in the sixth inning. Sporting his trademark mutton chop sideburns, Grant proceeded to pitch three and a third innings of one-run baseball. Grant saved a 7-5 win for Odom and the A's, giving Oakland a sweep of its doubleheader against the Red Sox. A classic Finley trade had delivered an immediate reward for the A's.

Grant noticed a distinct change in the A's from the time he had spent with the club in 1970. "I've seen more guys give themselves up," Grant said, "like hit behind the runner, in one week than I did all of last year. You've got to give Williams credit. He's done a tremendous job to orchestrate things."[22] The re-acquisition of Grant also gave the A's of 1971 another distinct advantage over the team of 1970. Now, the A's had two quality closers in Grant and Fingers, as opposed to just one.

Much to the delight of Charlie Finley, Grant also added a dash of color — he had the A's clubhouse man stitch the letters "M-U-D-C-A-T" on the back of his uniform jersey, in lieu of the traditional use of the letters of his last name, "G-R-A-N-T." Finley liked the innovation so much that he encouraged other players to wear their first names or nicknames on the backs of their shirts. In 1973, Vida Blue would wear the name "V-I-D-A" on the back of his jersey and Billy Conigliaro would

feature the letters "B-I-L-L-Y C." Future Athletic Dick Allen would use
the letters "W-A-M-P-U-M" on the back of his jersey, signifying the name
of his hometown in Pennsylvania.

On August 15, the Yankees staged an unusual promotion. Instead
of giving away a traditional freebie or honoring one of the great players
from their rich and storied past, the Yankees paid tribute to the
opposition's starting pitcher. "Vida Blue Day" attracted over 45,000 fans
to Yankee Stadium. The Yankees granted free admission to all customers named Blue — 126 people showed up with identification proving
their monikers — and printed special game-day programs that featured
a blue tint. Blue, who battled fatigue but seemed undisturbed by the
Yankees' strange recognition of his celebrity, pitched the A's to a 6-4
victory. "I've been sharper, but I've never been more tired,"[23] Blue revealed to the New York reporters after the game.

On August 17, as the A's prepared to face the Washington Senators in the start of a two-game series, the Oakland players received an
audience with United States President Richard M. Nixon. President Nixon
chatted with manager Dick Williams, who then introduced each of his
players and coaches to the nation's highest-ranking official. President
Nixon, a die-hard baseball fan, exchanged several words with each player.
Vida Blue offered the President a modern "soul" handshake, saying,
"That's the way we do."[24] Later, President Nixon posed with the Oakland
players for a group photo, and then held up an A's cap, given to him by
Blue. "You must be the most underpaid player in the game," the President told the 22-game winner, who was making only $13,000. "Who is
the lawyer for this club? I would hate to negotiate your contract next
year."[25] Blue's best friend on the A's, Tommy Davis, commended the
President on his ability to talk baseball. "I was very impressed with his
knowledge of the game,"[26] Davis said.

The Oakland contingent at the White House included backup first
baseman Mike Hegan, who says the meeting with the President revealed
a side to Finley not often acknowledged or seen by the general public.
"Shortly after I joined the ballclub, of course Vida was having his big
year and was the talk of the country," Hegan says. "We were going into
DC and President Nixon wanted to meet Vida Blue. Charlie wouldn't
have anything to do with it; he said, 'Either he meets the whole ballclub
or he doesn't meet anybody.' So, they set up a reception for the entire
ballclub with the President in the Oval Office." With little publicity, Finley
had shown even the President that the concept of "team" mattered more
than individual celebrity.

Perhaps distracted by their visit to the White House, the A's would
lose two straight games in Washington. The defeats, however, did little
to dampen what had been a productive stretch for the team. Prior to the
visit to RFK Stadium, the A's had won seven straight games. They had
also captured 12 consecutive decisions on the road. The A's would go

on to win nine of their last 12 games in August to finish the month with 23 wins and a mere eight losses. As well as the A's had played from April to July, they had exhibited their best ball-playing ability during the month of August.

In spite of their high level of play, Oakland fans continued to show a lack of interest in the A's. In late August, the A's hosted the Yankees in a three-game set at the Oakland Coliseum. While the Yankees usually drew better on the road than any other team in the American League, the series with New York managed to lure a total of only 29,110 fans. Even that figure was deceptively high, considering that over 18,000 of those fans had shown up for the middle game of the series, a 1-0 game lost by drawing card Vida Blue.

On August 31, the frequent journeys of backup catcher Frank Fernandez continued. Now that Dave Duncan had returned from his stint in the Marine Reserves, the A's traded Fernandez — yet again! Oakland sent Fernandez and minor leaguer infielder Bill McNulty to the Chicago Cubs for minor league outfield prospect Adrian Garrett. Fernandez' 1971 itinerary read as follows:

— Oakland to Washington
— Washington to Iowa
— Iowa to Oakland
— Oakland to Iowa
— Iowa to Chicago

At the end of August, the A's record stood at 87-47, 40 games above the five hundred mark. With a 16-game lead on the Royals, the American League West had long since been decided. Only a few questions remained. Would Vida Blue reach the elusive 30-victory plateau? Would Catfish Hunter win 20 games for the first time in his career? Which Oakland player would win the American League MVP Award, Blue or third baseman Sal Bando?

Some baseball writers opposed the idea of selecting a starting pitcher for the Most Valuable Player Award. They reasoned that since a typical starter pitched only once every four or five days, he did not possess the same value as an everyday position player. Other writers felt that the MVP should be reserved solely for catchers, infielders, and outfielders. They surmised that pitchers had their own award — the Cy Young. A's manager Dick Williams shared that opinion. "That's why they made that special award, the Cy Young Award. That's why it was invented, in my opinion."[27]

Yet, recent history dictated otherwise. In 1968, Denny McLain had won 31 games for the pennant-winning Detroit Tigers. After the season, the Baseball Writers Association of American rewarded McLain with both the MVP and Cy Young Awards. If Blue could approach the 30-win level for the division-winning A's, precedent would dictate that Blue win both prestigious awards.

Williams, risking the wrath of Vida Blue, cast his unofficial, but public MVP vote for Sal Bando. After an early-season slump, Bando had cashed in on a tip from batting coach Irv Noren, who had suggested that Sal stop dropping his elbow during his swing. Through games of September 2, the A's captain was batting .278 with 19 homers and 84 RBI's, had played exceptional defense at third base, and had provided the team with its largest dose of day-to-day leadership. "You can see what Sal means to us when he's in there," Williams explained. "Whether he bats in a run or not. It's just his presence."[28] Williams credited several other players, including Reggie Jackson, Dave Duncan and the underrated second baseman, Dick Green. "But if I had to get down to one," Williams said, "it would be Sal."[29]

While some Bay Area writers expected a close vote between Bando and Blue, the Baseball Writers Association of America would issue a convincing mandate in favor of one of the two stars. The media coverage given Blue throughout the season helped his cause; he appeared on the covers of *Sports Illustrated* and *Sport* magazine, and even made the cover page of the respected non-sports weekly, *Time* magazine. Blue also made guest appearances on two nationwide television programs, the *Dick Cavett Show* and NBC's *Today* show. "He had such a dominant year," says Sal Bando, "that you couldn't help but write about him and talk about him. I've never seen anyone — maybe (Bob) Gibson's year in St. Louis (1968) would be comparable — but Vida just had a phenomenal year."

In the voting announced after the World Series, the writers named Blue on all 24 ballots, giving him 14 first-place votes. One week earlier, those same writers had made him the youngest winner in the history of the Cy Young Award. Blue thus became only the fifth pitcher to win both the Cy Young and the MVP in the same season, joining Denny McLain, Bob Gibson, Don Newcombe and Sandy Koufax — the man he had been compared to so often — on the list of double winners. Bando received four first-place votes and trailed Blue in the final MVP balloting, 268 points to 182.

Was Bando disappointed that he finished no better than second in the MVP balloting? "As it turns out," responds Bando, "I was the most valuable position player that year, being beaten out by a pitcher. Yeah, I was disappointed because that's something that comes once in a lifetime. I had a good year at an inopportune time and it didn't happen." Although Bando would enjoy a fine career with both the A's and Brewers, he would never win a Most Valuable Player Award. Bando would finish as high as third in 1974, when he finished behind MVP Jeff Burroughs of the Texas Rangers and Oakland teammate Joe Rudi.

On September 13, 19-game winner Catfish Hunter faced the Royals, the surprising second-place residents of the Western Division. Hunter edged the Royals, 2-1, to post his 20th win of the season. In the process, Catfish rapped out two hits to raise his season batting average to an incredible .357. Hunter may have been the second best pitcher on the A's staff behind Blue, but he ranked as the best hitting pitcher in all of baseball.

For the first time in his major league career, Hunter had reached the single-season, 20-win plateau. Charlie Finley promised to reward his ace right-hander with a Cadillac, much like he had done with Blue earlier in the season. Hunter told Finley that he wanted the car to be royal blue, with a white vinyl top, but later asked the owner to take the money he would have spent on the Cadillac and invest it in some stocks. Cadillacs and blue chips aside, the milestone represented the high point of Hunter's young career. "This 20th win," said Catfish, "is more to me than the perfect game in 1968."[30]

On May 8, 1968, Hunter had faced the minimum 27 batters. Using his trademark off-speed slider, Hunter struck out 11 in carving a 4-0 gem against the Twins. "Just two words," A's batting coach Joe DiMaggio had said after Hunter struck out pinch-hitter Rich Reese on a three-and-two count to end the game. "A masterpiece."[31] Much like he did in winning his 20th game, Hunter had ably supported his own cause at the plate, driving in all three runs in the perfect game against Minnesota. Hunter had also exhibited his typical modesty, refusing his teammates' attempt to lift him onto their shoulders. "I just wanted to get out of there as quickly as possible," Hunter explained. "I was too embarrassed."[32]

In 1970, Hunter had won 18 games, but had struggled through a typically torturous August, when he had failed to win a game. Hunter's August swoon had been caused, at least in part, by a loan given to him by Charlie Finley. Prior to the 1970 season, Finley had loaned Hunter $150,000, which Catfish planned to use to purchase some property. Hunter had agreed to pay back $20,000 at the end of each season in addition to six per cent interest. Finley, however, couldn't wait. He began pestering Hunter regularly to pay back the loan. "It seemed like he never called me about it except on days when I was going to pitch," Hunter revealed later. "I started eight games that August and didn't have a single win the whole month."[33] Hunter asked Finley why he insisted on calling on those days on which he was scheduled to start. "He said he didn't know who was going to pitch when," Hunter related. "That's bull. Charlie Finley knows more about the ballclub than the manager."[34] Exasperated by Finley's attempts to secure the loan money, Hunter decided to sell off several acres of the land he had purchased and pay the owner the money.

August of 1971 proved far more fruitful for Hunter, who went a career-best 5-1, putting him on track for a 20-victory campaign. Hunter had also displayed an ability to pitch deeper into games. He had already thrown 16 complete games, compared to only nine the previous season. Hunter credited much of his improvement to a change that his pitching coach Bill Posedel had made in his pitching motion. Instead of raising his hands above his head at the start of his windup, Hunter kept his hands closer to his waist. The adjustment allowed Hunter to hide the ball behind his left knee, thereby preventing opposing hitters from seeing the ball as quickly as they had in the past. Hunter credited his pitching coach.

Hunter's ability to pinpoint his pitches, his inclination to pitch quickly and his accommodating nature made him an attractive partner for his catchers, especially Dave Duncan. "Catfish adjusts easily," said Duncan. "If I call a curve ball and he's thinking fastball, he just reprograms himself for my pitch. He never shakes me off. He just reprograms his mind and then my pitch really becomes his pitch. This makes him an easy man to catch."[35]

Two days after Hunter claimed his 20th victory, the A's officially laid claim to their first-ever American League West title. Oakland won the first game of a doubleheader with the White Sox, and clinched the division when the second-place Royals fell to the Angels. Fittingly, Sal Bando hit a two-run home run in the top of the eighth inning to give the A's a come-from-behind, 3-2 win. The recently-acquired Mudcat Grant hurled three shutout innings of relief to pick up his first win for the A's since his trade from Pittsburgh.

The A's held a subdued celebration in the visitors' clubhouse at Comiskey Park. Oakland players decided not to revel too loudly for two reasons. First of all, the A's had lost the second game of the double-header, 7-3. Secondly, the clinching had come as a mere formality. The A's had held possession of first place since April 20. By the end of June, Oakland had constructed a 10-game lead. By the completion of August, the gap had bulged to a season-high 17 games. After building up such a sizable lead on the Royals, the team had known for weeks that it would win the division. The A's were now setting sights on beating the defending World Champion Baltimore Orioles, who would provide the opposition in the American League Championship Series.

After the clinching, Dick Williams elected to limit his starting pitchers to five innings per outing, unless their pitch counts were remarkably low. Williams wanted to ensure that his top three starters — Vida Blue, Catfish Hunter, and Chuck Dobson — would be fully rested for the playoff series against the favored Orioles. Blue and Hunter had already amassed a large total of innings, while Dobson required constant monitoring due to his troublesome elbow.

The A's played out the string over the final two weeks of the season, and finished September with 14 wins and 13 losses. Although the record represented the A's worst for any single month, they had still managed to post winning ledgers in April, May, June, July, August, September and October. Along the way to a record of 101 wins and 60 losses, the A's dominated their Western Division rivals. Oakland won 10 of 18 games against the Twins, who had dominated the A's the previous two seasons. The A's performed even better against the Royals and Angels, winning 13 and 11 games, respectively.

In team pitching, the A's finished second only to the Orioles. A fatigued Vida Blue tailed off in August and September, settling for 24 wins, second most in the American League to the Tigers' Mickey Lolich. Blue did capture the league's ERA title, allowing a mere 1.82 runs per nine innings. Catfish Hunter finished with 21 victories, 16 complete games, and an ERA of 2.96. Chuck Dobson and Blue Moon Odom, both huge question marks at the start of the season due to physical ailments, combined to win 25 games. Right-handers Rollie Fingers, Bob Locker, Diego Segui and mid-season pickup Mudcat Grant all pitched effectively in relief. Fingers saved a staff-high 17 games despite opening the season in the starting rotation. One of the few pitching disappointments was left-hander Darold Knowles, who saved seven games, but failed to re-capture the form that he had displayed with the Senators in 1970.

On the hitting side, Oakland scored 691 runs, putting them in a third place tie with the Red Sox in the American League rankings. Although Reggie Jackson did not experience the breakout season that many had anticipated, the slugging right fielder led all A's regulars with a .277 average, 32 home runs, and 19 game-winning hits. Jax hustled at all times, swiped 16 stolen bases, and greatly improved his defensive play. "My attitude is better," Reggie had explained during the season. "Last year I was thinking in my own little circle."[36] Team captain Sal Bando finished with 24 home runs and a team-leading 94 RBIís. Mike Epstein ripped 18 home runs and delivered 11 game-winning hits after joining the team from Washington. Epstein's platoon partner at first base, Tommy Davis, batted .324 with 42 RBI's in only 219 at-bats. Dave Duncan, Dick Green, Joe Rudi, and Rick Monday all contributed power hitting and defense.

Shortstop Campy Campaneris represented one of the few offensive disappointments for the A's. In 1970, Campaneris had slugged a career-high 22 home runs. "He hit some home runs leading off one year," Rollie Fingers says, recalling Campy's unusual power output in 1970. "Right out of the shoot, you were up 1-0, and that certainly helped."

In 1971, Campaneris struggled through an up-and-down season at the plate. Much to the chagrin of Dick Williams, Campaneris tried to hit home runs the way he had in 1970, rather than concentrate on putting the ball in play and getting on base. "We called him 'Baby Hondo,'" Fingers says with a chuckle, "because everybody thought he swung the bat like Frank Howard." The six-foot, seven-inch Howard weighed well over 250 pounds, while Campaneris measured five feet, ten inches tall and barely 155 pounds. Using a long, overextended swing, Campaneris hit only five home runs and saw his batting average, runs scored, and stolen base totals fall off from his career-best season of 1970. On the plus side, Campy rebounded from a poor start defensively — which had seen him make 10 errors in his first 24 games, including errors in four consecutive games — and began to emerge as a reliable, sure-handed shortstop who still had plus range to either side of the ball.

Chapter Seven:
Facing the Defending Champs

The A's had known since August that their play-off opposition would be provided by the Baltimore Orioles, the 1970 World Champions. The usually penurious Finley spared no expense in preparing to face major league baseball's elite team. Finley hired former Tiger manager Mayo Smith specifically for the purpose of tracking and scouting the Orioles in September. Thanks to the work of Smith and other Oakland advance scouts like Al Hollingsworth and Sherm Lollar, Finley presented Dick Williams with a thickly bound scouting report, replete with a green and gold cover. The document provided Williams and his coaches with infinite details on the strengths, weaknesses and tendencies of the defending AL champs.

While he was adding employees in the area of scouting, Finley was losing employees in other departments. As the A's were making Championship Series, and potentially World Series arrangements, public relations director Mike Haggerty announced his resignation. Haggerty's secretary, Mary Brubaker, also left the front office. The untimely departures left the A's without a public relations department, at a time of the season when they needed such a staff more than any other. Finley would not replace Haggerty until after the season, when he made play-by-play man Monte Moore the interim public relations director. In the spring of 1972, just before the start of the new season, Finley would finally get around to hiring a full-time person for the job when he transferred Art

Popham from the team's promotions department. In hiring Popham, Finley had saved himself from adding another salary to his skeleton front office payroll.

Prior to the playoffs, Dick Williams raised the possibility of benching his regular first baseman, Mike Epstein, and replacing him with Tommy Davis or mid-season pickup Mike Hegan. Although Epstein had initially hit well after joining the team from Washington, he had slumped in the second half. During one failed stretch, Epstein had gone 45 days without hitting a home run. "I'd stopped swinging," said Epstein. "I was just feeling for the ball."[1] Epstein's sullen nature had also annoyed Dick Williams. "He's too big to mope," the A's manager said of Epstein. "We've got to play the men who're doing the job. I don't know who'll start in the playoffs."[2]

Epstein presented a strange defense of his performance. "You can't expect superstar statistics from someone not making superstar money," Epstein reasoned. "I'm just an average ballplayer trying to do his job. Why do people expect me to hit 40, or even 30 home runs a year? I'll hit 20." In a lighter mood, Epstein joked about his abilities. "You can't polish a turd,"[3] said the wise-cracking first baseman. While most players tended to have overinflated opinions of their own value, Epstein seemed willing to belittle his own ability. Or, perhaps Epstein was making a ploy for a sizable pay increase after the season. If the A's pay me more money, Epstein seemed to be saying, then I will produce better offensive numbers.

Williams would ultimately retain Epstein's services against Baltimore's right-handers in the playoffs. Epstein would platoon with the righty-hitting Davis, who paid the Orioles the utmost compliment prior to the series. "The toughest (post-season) series will be with Baltimore, not the National League winner."[4] In other words, Davis and some of the other Oakland players regarded their series with the O's as the true World Series. Confident Baltimore fans had already dubbed their city "Flagtown USA."

On another front, the A's learned that Blue Moon Odom would be unavailable for the playoff series against the Orioles. Odom had experienced a dead arm, having accumulated a workload of 141 post-surgical innings. The A's deactivated Odom for the post-season, replacing him with journeyman Ron Klimkowski. The right-handed reliever, acquired in the Felipe Alou deal, had pitched effectively in between trips to the minor leagues.

The loss of Odom didn't figure to hurt the A's since Dick Williams figured to go with only three starters in the playoffs: Vida Blue, Catfish Hunter, and Chuck Dobson. But who would start in Game One, Hunter or Blue? Some players, including captain Sal Bando, suggested the possibility of using Hunter, who had been Oakland's best starter over the last six weeks. Williams chose Blue instead. On paper, the first game matchup of Vida Blue against any one of the Orioles' fine pitchers seemed to favor the A's; after all, Blue and Detroit's Mickey Lolich had outclassed all other American League starters in 1971. A closer look at Blue's season, however, revealed some reasons for worry. Blue had ceased being a dominant pitcher over the final two months of the regular season. He had won only four games since August 7, perhaps the result of pitching too heavy a workload. With his second-half struggles a concern, one reporter asked Orioles' slugger Frank Robinson if he expected to see a "different" Vida Blue in the playoffs. "Why?" Robinson responded sarcastically. "Is he pitching right-handed?"[5]

An even greater concern for the A's involved the mindset of Blue, who continued to display a high level of irritation with the media. Blue arrived late as the A's worked out prior to the first game against the Orioles. Blue did not dress with the other players and brushed off several attempts at interviews. "I can't talk to you," Blue said to one reporter. When the writer asked why, Blue responded, "Because I don't want to."[6] Any reporter looking for cogent analysis would have to look elsewhere.

Blue walked off to the sanctuary of the trainer's room — declared off limits to reporters — putting a quick end to the media's attempts at interrogation. Blue's shortness with the media was apparently prompted by a recent gossip column item. The article, written by a non-baseball writer, speculated as to the skin color of Blue's girl friend. The invasion of privacy did not sit well with Blue. "I don't know whether that's what has him put out," said roommate and friend Tommy Davis, "but if that's what it is, I don't blame him one bit."[7] The gossip column's invasion of Blue's privacy, coupled with its racial implications, clearly angered Davis. "What business is it of anyone?" Davis asked rhetorically. "He goes out with a number of girls. Maybe his girl friend is chartreuse, who knows? Who keeps track?"[8]

Although Blue had justification to be upset with the gossip column, his outward personality had undergone reconstruction since the first half of the season. "I think he's changed," said Sal Bando. "The fame has changed him some. He's been more of a loner. He doesn't talk to many people...He's not as carefree as when he first started."[9]

The oddsmakers installed the Orioles as favorites to win the playoff series, perhaps out of consideration for the recent spate of lackluster pitching by Blue, perhaps out of respect for Baltimore's previous post-season experience. The negative prognostications aside, Dick Williams expressed confidence over his team's ability to challenge the defending American League titlists. "I don't think they'll beat us three straight," proclaimed Williams, "but I think we can beat them three straight."[10]

The best-of-five playoff series opened at Baltimore's Memorial Stadium. Playing the first two games on the road didn't figure to faze the

A's, who had won an American League record 55 games away from home. The A's also expressed relief that Earl Weaver had chosen Dave McNally to start Game One. "I'm surprised they are going to go with McNally in the first game," said backup catcher Curt Blefary, a former Oriole. "I think they should go with Jim Palmer. Palmer's fastball, maybe the best in the league, explodes...Once he gets his rhythm, it's all over. He'll take you every time."[11]

Although Oakland hitters had examined Mayo Smith's scouting reports on the Orioles, they also relied heavily on Blefary's input in developing strategies against the Oriole pitchers. "I've caught everyone of their pitchers," Blefary said, "and I've also batted against them, so I think I know what I'm talking about."[12] Dick Williams certainly seemed to think so. "I'm depending on Blefary to help out with the more personal touches about the individual players," said the A's manager, "things such as habits, what a player can be expected to do in a certain situation."[13]

The series opened a day later than scheduled because of a day of rain in Baltimore. The rainout marked the first in the short history of the Championship Series. Although the rains ceased the next day, they had been replaced by small swarms of bees which infiltrated the humid air above the playing field. Amidst the stings, the A's touched McNally for two runs in the second inning to take the lead. With Dave Duncan on second base and still no one out, Williams ordered number eight hitter Dick Green to lay down a sacrifice bunt. With Blue the next scheduled batter, Williams predictably called for the squeeze play. The Orioles anticipated the strategy, pitched out, and nailed Duncan in a rundown between third and home.

The A's scored a run in the top half of the fourth to extend the lead to 3-0, but the Orioles answered with a run of their own in the bottom half of the inning. Blue held the Orioles scoreless in the fifth and sixth innings, before running into trouble in the seventh. Frank Robinson drew a leadoff walk, followed by a Boog Powell strikeout. Brooks Robinson singled, before Andy Etchebarren's fly ball pushed Frank Robinson to third. With runners on first and third and two outs, Blue prepared to face the light-hitting Mark Belanger. On paper, Belanger seemed like an easy target for Blue, but the reed-thin shortstop responded with a line single to center, scoring Frank Robinson.

By now, Blue had thrown 120 pitches. Belanger's ability to turn on Blue's fading fastball should have sent a red flag to Dick Williams, but he chose to ignore the signs of fatigue. Another non-threatening batter, the .189-hitting Curt Motton, pinch-hit for McNally and pounded a double into the left field corner, scoring Brooks Robinson with the tying run. Leadoff man Paul Blair, who had hit only .196 vs. Oakland during the regular season, followed with another ringing double to left, scoring Belanger with the go-ahead run and Motton with an insurance tally. Blue finally retired Dave Johnson to end the rally, but not before a two-run lead had turned into a two-run deficit.

Baltimore's top reliever, Eddie Watt, blanked the A's over the final two innings to preserve a 5-3 victory. Afterwards, reporters questioned Vida Blue about his schizophrenic game; he was great for six innings, then awful in the seventh. Why? Blue answered the questions in whispers, sighing often during his pauses in speech. "I blew my lead; that's the big thing."[14]

During the seventh inning, home plate umpire Hank Soar had called a few borderline pitches balls, when they might have been strikes. "The umpiring was tough," Blue said diplomatically, refusing to blame Soar directly. "There were a lot of close calls, but I guess they were just calling them the way they saw them."[15]

For one of the few times all season, reporters and fans roasted Williams for what they considered major strategic gaffes. Several writers criticized Williams for several of his choices in Game One, principally his questionable decision to bunt with his eighth place hitter in the second inning. Sal Bando had started the inning with a double, Angel Mangual had followed with a triple and Dave Duncan had completed the extra-base hit parade with a double. With Duncan on second and still no one out, Williams asked Dick Green to lay down a bunt, rather than play for a large rally against a struggling McNally.

The second-guessers also wondered about Williams' failure to lift a tiring Blue during the Orioles' seventh-inning rally. According to Orioles' manager Earl Weaver, Blue's mounting pitch count through the first six innings may have sapped his fastball of necessary life by the seventh inning. "He was throwing a lot of pitches," noted Weaver, "and we felt that had to have an effect on him. We figured maybe he'd slow down a bit or his fastball would straighten out."[16] Both effects had taken place, making Blue an easier mark for mediocre hitters like Curt Motton and Mark Belanger.

Down one game to none, Williams called upon his other 20-game winner, Catfish Hunter, to pitch Game Two. Hunter faced left-handed craftsman Mike Cuellar, who like McNally, had won over 20 games during the regular season. Even though the A's would return home for Game Three, and possibly a fourth and fifth game, they needed to win Game Two to have a realistic chance of winning the series.

The Orioles led 2-1 in the top of the sixth inning, when Reggie Jackson led off with a double. That brought up first baseman Tommy Davis, the cleanup hitter against left-handed pitching. To everyone's surprise, including Dick Williams, Davis bunted, pushing Jackson to third. Cuellar then retired Sal Bando and rookie Angel Mangual, stranding Reggie at third.

The A's had lost out on their last remaining scoring opportunity. Oakland would fail to score a run over the final three innings, while

Baltimore would tack on a single run in the seventh. In the eighth, the Orioles put the game away despite a lapse in fundamental play. Boog Powell, playing with a painfully sore wrist, tried twice to sacrifice a runner over to second base, failing each time. Powell then pulled a Hunter delivery into the right field bleachers for his second home run of the game. The Orioles won, 5-1, on Cuellar's six-hitter.

Much like they had done after Game One, reporters questioned Williams about the decision to have Davis bunt in the sixth inning. "I did not have the bunt sign on," Williams revealed. "I would have preferred it if he took the shot."[17] Although Williams explained that he had not ordered the bunt, he deflected some of the blame from Davis by admitting that he, as manager, had put too much recent emphasis on advancing runners from second to third with no one out.

Hunter blamed himself for the loss, especially for the two home runs to the injured Powell, whose wrist injury should have sapped much of his power-hitting ability. Powell had originally injured his hand two and a half weeks earlier when Tigers' relief pitcher Tom Timmerman hit him with a pitch. Powell re-aggravated the injury earlier in Game Two, when he slid awkwardly into second base on a double play takeout. "Even though his hand hurt, he still looks like 900 pounds up there," Hunter said. "With a hurt hand, a broken leg, or anything, he's tough."[18]

An ultra-conservative offensive approach, coupled with the failures of Blue and Hunter, had put the A's in a two-game hole, facing elimination. The A's would host Game Three at the Oakland Coliseum, where they figured to play with a more relaxed sense of security, even though only 33,176 fans bothered to show up, leaving over 17,000 empty seats. Charlie Finley hoped to change Oakland fortunes by resorting to several superstitions. The Oakland owner wore his patented Blue blazer, or as he called it, his "Vida Blue" blazer. Finley brought out his pet mule, aptly named "Charlie O," for a pre-game stroll at the Coliseum. Lastly, Finley made arrangements for one of his own players, the multi-talented Mudcat Grant, to sing the National Anthem. In 1970, Grant had become the first major league player to sing the anthem on Opening Day.

Good-luck charms and superstitions aside, the more pertinent issue centered around the game's pitching matchup, which did not favor the A's. As if the playoffs hadn't gone badly enough, Dick Williams learned that Chuck Dobson would not be available to start Game Three. The fragile 15-game winner informed Williams that he could not pitch because of a sore elbow. With Blue Moon Odom already sidelined, Williams turned to veteran Diego Segui, who had pitched primarily as a reliever during the regular season. Segui would have to match the performance of Baltimore's Jim Palmer, the Orioles' best right-handed pitcher.

Williams made several lineup changes in an effort to counteract

Palmer. The manager benched catcher Dave Duncan, first baseman Tommy Davis and left fielder Joe Rudi, all right-handed hitters. In their place, Williams inserted Gene Tenace behind the plate, the lefty-hitting Mike Epstein at first base and rookie Angel Mangual in left field. The strategy would not work, however, as the trio would manage a combined 1-for-11 against the future Hall of Famer.

At his best, Diego Segui baffled hitters with his sharp-breaking forkball — or spitter, as some claimed. At his worst, Segui's inability to hold runners close and his deliberate pitching style undermined the Oakland defense. Over the first four innings, Segui allowed only one run. Then, in the top of the fifth inning, with the score tied at 1-1, the Orioles put runners on second and third with two outs. Dick Williams ordered Segui to walk the lefty-swinging Elrod Hendricks in favor of Brooks Robinson. Segui had mastered Robinson in head-to-head matchups, holding Brooks to a mere .154 average over the last three seasons. Segui fired his first pitch, which Robinson promptly lined up the middle. The two-out safety scored two runs, giving Baltimore a 3-1 lead. Williams summoned Rollie Fingers to finish out the inning.

Williams' strategy in the fifth inning seemed dubious. Hendricks had managed only two hits in 16 regular season at-bats against Oakland pitching. Robinson, in contrast, had collected nine RBI's in 11 games vs. the A's in 1971. Robinson was a future Hall of Famer; Hendricks was a platoon player. "Walking Hendricks was a percentage move," Williams would explain after the game. "Hendricks hurt us more, and by putting him on, we have a force play at any base."[19] Robinson had foiled the strategy by lining a hard-hit ball over second base, out of the reach of Dick Green and Campy Campaneris.

In the bottom of the sixth inning, Sal Bando slammed a solo home run to draw the A's within one. Unfortunately for Oakland, Fingers and Darold Knowles could not keep the A's close. In the seventh, a Frank Robinson double and a Knowles wild pitch enabled the Orioles to stretch the lead to three runs. Jim Palmer gave up a harmless run to the A's in the eighth inning, but returned to the mound in the ninth. Palmer ended the game and the series by striking out former Oriole Curt Blefary, who had made several outspoken comments about the Orioles before the playoffs. One reporter had quoted Blefary as predicting an easy victory for the A's. "Curt gave Oakland 24 positions over us,"[20] crowed Curt Motton, one of Baltimore's stars in Game One. For his part, Blefary claimed he had been misquoted.

As the Orioles celebrated their return to the World Series, photographers captured telling shots of a heartbroken Reggie Jackson, who was slumped on the steps of the dugout, his shoulders hunched over, his eyes moistened by tears. Unlike many professional athletes who had been taught to hide, or at least lessen their outward displays of emotion, Reggie was crying — openly.

Another star player, Vida Blue, reacted differently to the Game Three defeat. Blue expressed a desire to put the long, pressurized season behind him and begin a stage of off-season relaxation. "I'm going home, if they want me (there)," Blue said in the clubhouse. "I'm going to get a job standing on the corner — just resting."[21]

Oakland problems did not end with the Game Three loss. "In fact," says Rick Monday, "when we came back from Baltimore to Oakland, we went to the plane we chartered to go back, and there were fire trucks all around the airplane — because there had been threats coming in. And people had to offload their luggage."

For the A's, a 101-win regular season had translated into a three-game sweep in the playoffs at the hands of the defending World Champions. The playoff losses left the A's stunned. Granted, the Orioles had won more games than any major league team, but were they *this* much better than the A's? How could a team that had played so efficiently during the regular season lose three straight games in the playoffs? How could a club featuring two Cy Young candidates in Vida Blue and Catfish Hunter fall so quickly in the post-season? "I think we were surprised, certainly," says Rick Monday, who played in only one of the three games. "Surprised from the standpoint that we felt we had a pretty good ballclub. I don't remember the exact number, but I think that year, too, we had a remarkable road record...Going into that series, we thought that we had a very good chance to at least prolong that series, and all of a sudden, we turn around and we're not only having trouble in the series, that series is over and we're sending it home."

Mike Hegan says the lack of post-season experience damaged Oakland's chances of advancing to the World Series. "I think there was probably more pressure in the playoffs back then than maybe there is now," explains Hegan. "Baltimore was a very experienced ballclub, and although we won the 100 games, I think when we went into the playoffs, the Orioles' experience paid off for them."

Sal Bando agrees with Hegan in regards to the differences in the teams' post-season experience. "I think there were two things that stood out in my mind," Bando says, trying to explain the three-game sweep. "One, their experience was greater than ours, and that was a big, deciding factor. And we also at that point did not have a solid (or deep) rotation. We had Vida and Catfish. And after that it was Diego Segui, Chuck Dobson." While Segui and Dobson were respected veteran starters, they were no match for the likes of Jim Palmer, Mike Cuellar, Dave McNally and Pat Dobson, all of whom won 20 or more games that season.

The rainout in Game One of the playoffs had succeeded in further shortening the paper-thin Oakland rotation, by eliminating the scheduled off day between the second and third games of the playoff series. "You're right," Bando says. "That rain (out) would not allow you to come back with Vida right away. We ended up having to have four starters, and in reality, we only had two."

The realization that the season had come to an end especially frustrated the veterans on the club who had played together since the mid-1960s. "Disappointing, I think certainly," says Rick Monday, "because this is a ballclub that had really battled at the minor league level. Almost everybody that had signed had been under the magnifying glass of all the experts: what were they going to do, how could you draft that guy first, why was he a No. 2 pick? All of a sudden, boom, here we are collectively and we turn around and it was the same guys that had been on that bus and the same guys that had been on that field for a number of years. It was a good ballclub. Of course, we happened to be matched against a terrific ballclub and some outstanding pitching of their own."

As frustrated as the Oakland players felt, they were able to learn from the losing experience in the playoffs, as part of the process of bettering themselves in 1972. "Absolutely," says Mike Hegan. "When I arrived in Oakland and you've got the Bandos and Campanerises and Reggie Jackson and Vida Blue and Joe Rudi and Catfish Hunter, the interesting part about that is that this is a club that kind of started together back in '67, '68; some of those guys played in Kansas City. But it was a growing experience for them, watching those young players, and they were at that time still very young, kind of mature and then win 100 ballgames. There is a stepping stone, if you will, and you win a hundred games, but then it comes down to pressure time of the playoffs, and at that juncture, nobody made big money, so to get to the World Series and get a World Series share that was a big accomplishment. Back at that time, some guys could make twice as much money from World Series shares as they were making in salary."

Rick Monday says the A's eventually succeeded in turning an emotional low into a motivating force. "Devastated?" Monday asks himself. "I don't know if we were devastated. I think, if anything else, that (playoff loss) may have driven a ballclub that had a taste of post-season play, and the initial stages of it, to come back and play even better."

Several writers criticized Dick Williams for being too conservative throughout the series, perhaps overemphasizing the bunt and various one-run strategies. Mike Hegan says that the second-guessers failed to understand the true nature of the Oakland offense, which was not capable of producing many big innings. "That ballclub was a club which won on pitching, defense and execution. Dick Williams did not play like Earl Weaver did for the three-run inning, the home run, the big hit. We always tried to execute to manufacture runs. Maybe in a short series and against a club like Baltimore where you know that you're not gonna score many runs because of their pitching, there are certain things that you have to do more of. If that was a criticism from the press, it certainly wasn't a criticism from the players."

Some players, like Sal Bando, don't remember such critical attacks being directed at Williams. "No, I don't," says Bando. "In fact, I don't remember reading about him being second-guessed because we were just outplayed by a superior team; there wasn't anything he could have done."

Nonetheless, Williams heard rumors that he would fired. Finley had questioned him throughout the playoffs, especially his decision to start Diego Segui in Game Three. But who else could have started? Vida Blue had pitched only two days earlier and Chuck Dobson was hurt. That Finley would even consider a firing seemed ridiculous, given the widespread feelings of respect toward Williams. Termed a "giant in this clubhouse"[22] by pitching coach Bill Posedel, Williams had taken a perennial also-ran to a 100-win season and its first playoff berth. He had been responsible for placing Rollie Fingers in the bullpen and had integrated mid-season pickups like Mike Epstein and Mudcat Grant into the Oakland equation. Williams had also succeeded in establishing his managerial rules. "I only ask two things," Williams had said. "I want a player to give 100 per cent on the day he plays, and I don't want him to make mental mistakes...We have the same sign in our clubhouse that the old Yankees used to have. It says, 'Don't mess with my money.'"[23] Playoff money, that is.

Unlike rumors about previous Oakland managers, the rumblings about a Williams firing proved to be false. Williams would return to the A's in 1972, a just reward for the Associated Press Manager of the Year. "He was very demanding," says Rick Monday, "from the standpoint that once the season was over, there were no shortcomings that you did not allow yourself the opportunity to go ahead and take care of as a club, individually or collectively." Williams would soon address those shortcomings. Unfortunately for Monday, the solutions to those shortcomings would result in his own departure from baseball's developing dynasty.

Chapter Eight:
Off-Season Shuffle

Charlie Finley and Dick Williams realized that changes needed to be made to improve the A's. With both Chuck Dobson and Blue Moon Odom ailing, Oakland needed to acquire another starting pitcher. Perhaps the A's could use their surplus of quality outfielders and first basemen as part of a package for a third starter behind staff aces Blue and Hunter.

In late November, major league executives and general managers convened at the annual winter meetings in Phoenix, Arizona. The meetings had traditionally become a mid-winter trade fest, where major league general managers discussed and engineered blockbuster deals. On November 29, the first day of the meetings, the San Francisco Giants and Houston Astros traded away future Hall of Famers Gaylord Perry and Joe Morgan, respectively, in separate deals they would come to regret. On the same day, the A's announced a deal of their own, one they would not regret. The A's sent starting center fielder Rick Monday to the Chicago Cubs for left-handed pitcher Ken Holtzman.

The A's parted with Monday reluctantly. In 1965, the A's had selected Monday with the first pick of the first-ever free agent draft of amateur talent. Finley had given Monday a $100,000 signing bonus and a new car, in the anticipation that the former University of Arizona outfielder would blossom into major league stardom. Monday had exhibited flashes of potential with his considerable power, speed, throwing arm and defensive skills. He had also impressed the A's with his constant hustle and strong character. A series of frustrating injuries had hindered Monday's progress: a broken wrist in 1967, torn tendons in his leg in '68, another broken wrist in '69, and a fractured rib and bruised kidney in 1970. Monday had also shown little improvement in mastering his biggest weakness: left-handed pitchers. Monday struck out too often, failed to make consistent contact and tried to pull almost every pitch.

As much as the A's liked Monday's potential and personality, they deemed him expendable because of the emergence of Angel Mangual, who had patterned his style of play after his favorite player, Roberto Clemente. The 26-year-old Monday, an everyday player in the past, had not felt comfortable in a platoon role. "I figured that something was going to happen," Monday says. "You never know that you're going to be traded, but I figured that certainly from a platoon situation, that's what Dick Williams had decided to do. He was going to go with Angel Mangual against left-handed pitching and go with me against right-handers. I would also go in and play defense in later stages of the ballgame. That's a situation for a young player that you're not particularly pleased with, because that's the first time it had ever taken place."

The A's reasoned that they had a greater need for a starting pitcher than for a platoon center fielder. Yet, critics of the deal wondered why the A's settled for Holtzman. The veteran southpaw had suffered through a miserable season in 1971, winning only nine of 24 decisions while posting a bloated ERA of 4.48. "I just had a bad year," the left-hander explained. "There were no physical problems. I just couldn't get started. I couldn't get straightened out."[1] On several occasions, Holtzman had found his season interrupted by stints in the Marine Reserves. Holtzman had also experienced difficulties in his relationship with Cubs' manager Leo Durocher.

Holtzman and Durocher had hardly spoken during the second half of the season. Durocher had previously criticized Holtzman for not using his fastball often enough and relying too much on a "lollipop" curve. Durocher had also questioned Holtzman's effort. "I wasn't happy when Leo Durocher was quoted in the paper saying I wasn't trying,"[2] Holtzman said later. After Durocher publicly criticized Holtzman, the left-hander asked Cubs' general manager John Holland to trade him. Holtzman claimed that Durocher's handling of the team, rather than his own relationship with the manager, had prompted his trade request. "I didn't have any real trouble with Leo," Holtzman explained. "I got along all right with him. But I didn't like the way he'd criticize players sometimes in the papers, instead of confronting a player directly."[3] Other Cubs' players had struggled to get along with "The Lip," whose interpersonal skills had always been lacking. In recent years, the aging Durocher had cultivated increasingly strained relationships with the new wave of "mod" players. "Baseball has changed a lot since Leo was a player," Holtzman reasoned. "You're not getting a lot of players from small towns in the south anymore. The players are very intelligent now. You've got players in the game with college degrees, sometimes even masters degrees. I don't think Leo understood that."[4]

Given his problems in 1971, Charlie Finley welcomed Holtzman by cutting his salary by 10 per cent. Still, the A's liked Holtzman for many reasons. Despite his off performance in 1971, Holtzman was still only 26 years old — and healthy. "I've never had arm trouble in my life," Holtzman told Oakland reporters. "I've worked between 275 and 280 innings a season for the last five years and that's a lot of pitching."[5] Once likened to his pitching hero — another Jewish left-hander by the name of Sandy Koufax — Holtzman had enjoyed back-to-back seasons of 17 wins in 1969 and '70, and had forged a lifetime record of 65-54. Holtzman had twice pitched no-hitters, a sign of his powerful repertoire of pitches. His most recent no-hitter had occurred during the 1971 season, when he shut down a Cincinnati Reds lineup that featured dangerous right-handed hitters like Hal McRae, Lee May, Johnny Bench, Tony Perez, and George Foster. Furthermore, Holtzman managed to no-hit the Reds despite his inability to spot his most effective pitch — the curve ball — for strikes. Over the last five innings of his June 7th no-hitter against Cincinnati, Holtzman threw only two curve balls. Using his fastball almost exclusively — much to the delight of Leo Durocher — Holtzman dominated one of the National League's most feared line-ups.

Holtzman's new manager, Dick Williams, hoped that the stylish left-hander would dominate American League batters and balance the starting rotation. Oakland already had three excellent right-handed starting pitchers in Catfish Hunter, and when healthy, Blue Moon Odom and Chuck Dobson. Yet, the A's had only one capable left-hander in Vida Blue. Williams figured that Holtzman would prove effective against some of the American League's best left-handed hitters, like the Twins' Tony Oliva and Rod Carew, the Orioles' Boog Powell, Boston's Carl Yastrzemski, Detroit's Norm Cash, and the Yankees' Bobby Murcer.

The trade of Monday represented the initial breakup of a nucleus of players that had come up together with the Kansas City Athletics in the mid-sixties. Dick Green, who had been with the A's longer than any other player, remembered the Kansas City teams of 1963 and '64. "Those A's were the worst," Green said. "I don't know how bad the Mets were then but I don't see how they could have been any worse than we were."[6]

Although those early Finley teams had struggled, Monday remembers the Kansas City days as important in laying the groundwork for future success in Oakland. "They selectively rushed some guys because quite frankly, we didn't have a real strong ballclub at Kansas City," Monday says. "We were really a very close group because we had to band together as a young club that went out and basically continued to get beat upon by other clubs. We were trying to gain that experience, trying to learn fundamentals."

By 1971, the seeds of struggle had given way to a cash crop — a team filled with leaders, not dependent on any one player. "It finally came together," Monday says. "And then finally, collectively, we got together. When you (try to) single out any one person, I don't think you can single out one person. Everybody played an integral role depending upon what they were gonna be called upon to do.

"If you look around major league baseball (today), those guys are still sprinkled around, in and around the game in one way or another." A scan of post-playing career resumes bears out Monday's contention. Since finishing a productive major league career with the A's, Cubs and Dodgers, Monday himself has worked as a broadcaster for the Dodgers and Padres, while Mike Hegan has performed similar duties for the Brewers and Indians. Felipe Alou, who played briefly for the A's at the start of the '71 season, has become one of the game's finest managers with the Montreal Expos. Sal Bando has worked in the front office for the Brewers, eventually becoming the team's general manager. Reggie Jackson has served George Steinbrenner as an executive with the Yankees. Dave Duncan has become one of the most successful pitching coaches in the major leagues, working under Tony LaRussa in Chicago, Oakland and St. Louis. Gene Tenace has worked as a coach for the Houston Astros and Toronto Blue Jays. George Hendrick, a backup on the '71 A's, became the hitting instructor for the Cardinals. Joe Rudi, Tommy Davis and Darold Knowles coached briefly for the A's, Mariners and Cardinals, respectively.

In perhaps the most intriguing story of success after a playing career, former A's slugger Don Mincher has become one of the few ex-major leaguers to own and operate a minor league franchise. As the Minnesota Twins' beat writer throughout the sixties, Bob Fowler covered Mincher during his playing days in Minnesota. Fowler isn't surprised that Mincher has become successful in baseball management. "He's doing a great job today," Fowler says of Mincher's involvement with the Huntsville Stars of the Double-A Southern League. "He's the Huntsville general manager, has done a terrific job with that. I think that's another aspect of that era that you see nowadays. Here's Don Mincher, I mean, here's a guy that could so something other than play first base. He could do something other than play professional baseball; he had other talents. And now they're coming out. Quality guy."

The day after making the Monday-for-Holtzman trade, Charlie Finley made a puzzling move when he announced the unconditional release of 36-year-old right-hander Mudcat Grant. The A's cited concerns over Grant's age, but the veteran reliever had pitched brilliantly for Oakland since being re-acquired from the Pirates in August. Grant had picked up a win and four saves, at the tune of a 2.00 ERA. "It looks awful strange when Finley could buy me back from Pittsburgh just to release me," said a bewildered Grant, who expressed skepticism over Oakland's emphasis on age as the reason for his release. "They keep telling me I'm an old man and that I'm through," Grant told reporters, "but I look around and see guys as old as me not doing as well."[7] In reality, Finley had been motivated by financial concerns. In 1971, Grant earned $60,000, a figure that Finley considered too lofty for a relief pitcher.

Rather than attempt to re-sign with the A's at a reduced salary, Grant would receive a spring training invitation from the Cleveland Indians, one of his former teams. Mudcat would fail to make the big league roster, instead signing a contract with the A's Class-AAA affiliate at Iowa. Incredibly, Grant would never again pitch in the American or National Leagues. Given the constant need for pitching, the exclusion of Grant from the major league scene ranked as near criminal.

With Chuck Dobson set to undergo surgery to remove a piece of bone from his right elbow, Finley set out to acquire another starting pitcher. The A's offered first baseman Mike Epstein to the New York Yankees for one of their starting pitchers, believed to be right-hander Mel Stottlemyre. Epstein, a left-handed pull hitter with tremendous power potential, would have provided a natural fit for Yankee Stadium. The Yankees, however, did not want to part with Stottlemyre, and turned down the deal.

Epstein himself contemplated retirement during the off-season. As Epstein and his family celebrated the Thanksgiving holiday, the emotional first baseman considered quitting the game. His second half slump and Dick Williams' decision to platoon him in the playoff series against Baltimore had preyed on his mind. "I'd let a lot of people down," Epstein explained later. "Things had snowballed."[8] Having decided that mental fatigue had caused his late-season problems, the 235-pound first baseman embarked on a stern weight-reducing program. After losing 30 pounds during the winter, Epstein would report to spring training weighing 205 pounds, the lightest weight of his professional career.

With Dobson's health a major question mark, the A's nearly lost another one of their pitchers — for good. On January 6, 1972, Blue Moon Odom, attempting to prevent a burglary near his mother's home in Macon, Georgia, was shot twice when he attempted to question three youths who had broken into a nearby house. Odom's wife, Perrie, had noticed three young men trying to enter the home of a neighbor. She phoned the police and her husband, who was working at a liquor store only four blocks away. Odom grabbed a gun that he kept in his car and made his way to the neighbor's home. Odom actually passed the youths on the street when his wife signaled to him that they were, in fact, the perpetrators.

"Hey, I want to talk to you," Odom said to the young men as he followed them. One of the robbers turned around to face Odom, asking him, "What for?"[9] Almost simultaneously, the youth pulled out a .38 caliber pistol and fired three shots. Two bullets struck Odom, one in the neck, and another in the side of the chest. Odom returned fire with his own gun, but missed both men. For a moment, Odom first thought his baseball career, and then his life, had come to an end. "I was thinking I never would pitch again after that first shot," Odom said afterwards. "After the second shot, I thought it was all over."[10]

Medics rushed Odom to the Medical Center of Georgia Hospital, where he received treatment for three days. "I didn't bleed enough to cover a small wash rag,"[11] Odom joked, trying to minimize the severity of his injuries. Fortunately, each gunshot had passed through Odom's body while causing only minimal, non life-threatening. damage. Odom's doctor predicted the gunshot wounds would not affect his pitching career, and believed that the veteran right-hander would be able to resume throwing in about a month. Considering that he had almost lost his life just a few days earlier, the doctor's words had to sound very good to the man known as Blue Moon.

Chapter Nine:
1972 — Holdouts, Mustaches, and McLain

With spring training only two weeks away, half of the A's 40-man roster remained unsigned. In one case, the A's braced for what seemed to have all the makings of an ugly contract showdown, one that reminded team observers of the 1970 salary battles between Reggie Jackson and Charlie Finley. Vida Blue had earned under $15,000 in 1971, despite winning 24 games, the Cy Young Award and the Most Valuable Player Trophy. Blue's agent, Bob Gerst, wanted a contract that would make Blue one of the ten highest-paid pitchers in all of baseball, somewhere in the range of $100,000. Finley had offered a raise to about $50,000.

On January 8, Gerst met with Finley for five hours to discuss a new contract. The meeting left Finley outraged. Gerst had informed Finley of his initial asking price — $115,000. After a few moments of heated self-deliberation by the owner, he asked Gerst if he knew what floor of the building they were standing on. When Gerst told him that they were on the 27th floor, Finley shot back: "Mr. Gerst, you have as much chance of getting $115,000 as I have of going out that window and landing on my feet."[1]

After making an initial demand of six figures, Gerst and Blue lowered their sights to an asking price of about $92,000. Finley continued to balk at Blue's demands, refusing to move from his $50,000 figure and insisting he would not raise ticket prices to meet the salary request. Contract negotiations became bitter. Gerst accused Finley of blackmail, lying, and attempting to end Blue's career. "I won't trade him and I won't sell him," Finley told the agent. "Either he accepts what we have offered or he is through in baseball."[2]

In explaining his negotiating stance, Gerst attempted to justify the figure of $92,500. "He is at a minimum one of the 10 best pitchers in baseball and should be paid accordingly."[3] Gerst pointed out the salaries of star pitchers like Bob Gibson ($150,000), Ferguson Jenkins ($125,000), Tom Seaver ($120,000), and Gaylord and Jim Perry ($90,000 each). "In addition," continued Gerst, "he's proven his importance to the financial well-being of his club and to the league."[4] Nearly one million fans had watched Blue pitch in 41 games, including the All-Star game and the American League Championship Series.

Yet, Finley felt lack of service time weighed heavily against Blue's case. "I don't mind paying a player that has proved himself, but a player can't prove himself in just one year,"[5] countered Finley. The owner explained that if he conceded to Gerst and gave Blue a contract for $92,000, and the pitcher responded with a poor season, he could cut his salary by only 20 per cent in 1973. "Nope, I have to be firm on paying him $50,000 for 1972," insisted Finley. "Based on the fact that Vida has had only one full year in the majors...I think it is a fair offer."[6]

The A's opened up spring training in Mesa, without the presence of Blue. As negotiations continued, Gerst explored the avenue of making Blue a free agent. Gerst raised the possibility that Blue had signed an illegal contract with the A's in the first place. "When he signed the contract (back in 1967)," Gerst explained, "he was a minor. When a minor signs a contract with a movie studio, it has to be approved by the courts. We're checking to see if this applies in this case."[7] It didn't. On another front, Gerst hinted that Finley may not have made a payment of $2,500 due to Blue on his original contract. "There is a clause in the contract," Gerst said, "that says the contract will be rescinded if the club does not live up to any part of the agreement."[8] Gerst was clearly grasping at loopholes, but to no avail.

Two weeks into spring training, with Blue still unsigned, and with the status of Chuck Dobson and Blue Moon Odom uncertain, the A's took major action. No, Finley did not reach a contract agreement with his star left-hander. Instead, Finley announced the acquisition of another former Cy Young Award winner — 27-year-old Denny McLain.

Oakland picked up McLain from the Texas Rangers (formerly the Washington Senators) for two pitching prospects, Jim Panther and Don Stanhouse, a 21-year-old reliever who had drawn rave reviews. At first, the A's had offered either Blue Moon Odom or Chuck Dobson, but Rangers' owner Bob Short had rejected the oft-injured veterans. Short called Stanhouse and Panther the two best pitching prospects in Oakland's organization. At 27-years-old, Panther was virtually the same age as

McLain but had yet to win a single major league game.

In 1968 and '69, McLain had won a combined total of 55 games, captured an MVP award and earned two Cy Young awards as the American League's most dominant pitcher. Only a few years removed from his peak, and still three years short of his 30th birthday, the A's now had the services of the talented McLain. Unfortunately, McLain had experienced one of the most precipitous declines in major league history. In 1970, Commissioner Bowie Kuhn suspended McLain for half of the season because of his involvement with illegal bookmakers and unsavory ties with the gambling world. McLain also received suspensions for carrying a gun and for maliciously treating the Detroit press. After the season, the Tigers traded McLain to the Senators, where he feuded with manager Ted Williams and struggled with increasing weight and a decreasing fastball. In 1971, McLain won only 10 games while losing a league-leading 22.

Plain and simple, McLain had pitched badly for a bad team in Washington. Yet, the controversial right-hander blamed his struggles on the way that Ted Williams used him in the starting rotation. "I threw the ball up until July as well as I ever have for both velocity and strikes," McLain insisted. "Then Ted Williams said after he had seen me for two months that it would be better for me to pitch every fifth or sixth day. I thought I was better every fourth day. He had two months of statistics. I had six years of statistics."[9]

Dick Williams explained that the trade for McLain had occurred as a direct result of the failed negotiations with Vida Blue. "We started talking on and off with other clubs when it looked like we would have trouble signing Vida," Williams said. "When you don't have your big starter in camp, and it's been open for two weeks, you've got to take action."[10] Although McLain had struggled over the past two seasons, he had generally been impressive in games against the A's. Over his career, McLain had posted a lifetime record of 15-5 against Oakland. Considering his relatively youthful age and overall history of success, the A's considered the acquisition of McLain a reasonable gamble. Furthermore, the Rangers had agreed to swallow $25,000 of McLain's $75,000 salary. In other words, the A's would pay him $50,000 — the same amount as their offer to Blue.

McLain reported to the A's, joining the club in Arizona. McLain arrived in Phoenix, where the team's spring training hotel was located. As McLain relaxed by the hotel pool on his first day with the team, a reporter from ABC television approached him in an effort to record his reaction to the trade. The volatile right-hander, who had once dumped a bucket of water on two sportswriters, yelled at the reporter and made indirect threats against ABC sportscaster Howard Cosell, who had previously criticized McLain. While McLain had changed teams, he had unfortunately retained the same nasty streak he had displayed in both

Detroit and Washington.

McLain's disposition matched his dreadful spring training performance. In his first exhibition start for the A's, a shell-shocked McLain
allowed 10 runs on 10 hits and six walks. McLain defended himself by
explaining that he had thrown only curve balls and change-ups and
had refrained from unleashing his best fastball early in the spring. Yet,
his second start produced another series of ghastly numbers: seven
runs on a cache of 14 hits. Although McLain had not pitched well for
Washington the previous summer, he hadn't pitched this badly, either.

Meanwhile, the A's enjoyed no progress on the Vida Blue front.
The acquisition of McLain annoyed Gerst, who couldn't understand
Finley's willingness to assume a $50,000 salary for a pitcher who lost
22 games. "Finley is not acting the part of a man who wants to be fair,"
Gerst assessed, "but that of a man who wants to be in command."[11]
Nonetheless, Finley refused to budge on what he called his first, last
and only offer to Blue — $50,000. On March 2, Finley invoked baseball's
rarely used reserve clause, which allowed an owner to automatically
renew an unsigned player's contract. If Finley had invoked the clause
earlier, he could have given Blue a 20 per cent pay cut from his 1971
salary of $14,500. Since Finley had already offered Blue $50,000, he
had to agree to pay his star left-hander that much money in 1972. "I
think Vida is entitled to a 300 per cent pay increase because he accomplished quite a bit," Finley acknowledged before launching an attack on
Bob Gerst. "Vida has been brainwashed and browbeaten by his attorney. I do not like the image his attorney is creating for him."[12]

Blue refused to sign the renewal or report to spring training. Surprisingly, most of Blue's teammates expressed their agreement with the
stance taken by Finley. Curt Blefary and Mike Epstein, in particular,
voiced remarks critical of Blue and Gerst. "He's foolish for giving up
$50,000," Blefary said. "He could have made it $100,000 with endorsements."[13] Epstein placed most of the blame on Gerst. "I'm sorry for
Vida," Epstein claimed. "He obviously hooked up with the wrong guy."[14]
Another player, team captain Sal Bando, sided with Finley. "I'm for a
guy getting all he can, but Charlie has offered Vida a fair contract,"
Bando reasoned. "We can win without Vida Blue. It would be harder,
but we can."[15] Only one Oakland teammate publicly showed support for
Blue. Tommy Davis, also a Gerst client, offered Blue some sympathy.
"I'd like to see him in uniform," Davis told Ron Bergman of The Sporting
News, "but I respect his decision."

Blue and Gerst offered Finley several proposals. They would agree
to Finley's offer of $50,000 if Blue could become a free agent after the
1972 season. Finley called the request absurd. Gerst then asked to
submit the contract negotiation to Commissioner Bowie Kuhn, who
would arbitrate a settlement. Finley, a bitter enemy of the commissioner,
turned thumbs down on Kuhn's involvement. Gerst then suggested that

he might take his client to the Japanese League. By international agreement between the major leagues and the Japanese teams, no player
could jump from one continent to the other without receiving his owner's
permission. Once again, Finley laughed off such a possibility.

The player and his agent decided to explore their options. Even
though he had no professional acting experience, Blue reportedly signed
a deal with MGM to star in the second of a series of planned sequels to
the movie studio's successful venture, *Shaft*. Blue appeared at a press
conference with actor Richard Roundtree, the star of *Shaft*, but would
never appear in such a film. Blue and his agent called another press
conference in Oakland. Blue, reading from a prepared statement, Blue
told the gathered reporters that he had accepted a position as vice-
president of public relations for Dura Steel Products, a company that
specialized in making bathroom and toilet fixtures. "It is with deep regret and sadness I announce my leaving baseball," Blue said, making
his retirement official. "I had hoped my career could have been longer.
While it was short, it was packed with excitement."[16] Gerst did not allow
Blue to answer any questions at the press conference.

None of the reporters took Blue seriously, especially when he smiled
and giggled repeatedly while reading from the press release. Finley reacted to Blue's announcement with sarcasm. "I'm happy to hear that he
is entering the steel industry and starting as a vice-president," Finley
chortled. "I too was associated with the steel industry, as a worker with
U.S. Steel, Corporation in Gary, Indiana. I worked there for five years,
the first four of which I served my machine shop apprenticeship."[17] The
following night, Finley and Blue met at the Edgewater Heat Motel in
Oakland. Blue was still clearly interested in playing baseball, but Finley
refused to budge from his initial offer.

According to some players, Finley could be at his worst during
long contract negotiations, often forcing his players into bad moods. "I
remember once Charlie called me up during the offseason," recalls Rick
Monday. "We were talking contract. And he basically just — he really
irritated me. And then there was namecalling."

Monday says he tried to use an agent during one off-season negotiating session, but the strategy did not please Finley. "I did (have an
agent) one year, and Charlie and I did not leave on the best of terms. He
made some promises that he came considerably short of, and some of
those were in writing. There was a lawsuit that was going to be instituted, and finally, at the last second, he made amends for it. There was
a financial arrangement that was taken care of. He called my attorney
once; he said, 'Get that bird off my back, or I'll squash him.' Charlie was
different."

After repeatedly failing in efforts to lure Blue to signing a new
contract, Finley adopted a bizarre strategy, while revealing a strange
chain of command in the Oakland organization. On the advice of equip-

ment manager Frank Ciensczyk, the self-proclaimed "sock and jock man," Finley ordered several of his players to fly up to Oakland to talk to Blue. At first, Finley dispatched catcher Gene Tenace, with orders to bring Blue to Arizona, where the A's trained. Tenace returned without the ace left-hander. Finley then assigned utilityman Curt Blefary the duty of baseball bounty hunter. The third-string catcher dined with Blue one night, then met with him for two hours the next day. Blefary returned to Arizona empty-handed, except for $60.00 in taxicab receipts. Finley referred to Blefary as the "last of the goodwill ambassadors."

As the start of the season neared, Dick Williams resigned himself to the fact that Blue would not be with the team come Opening Day. Several other pitchers, however, impressed Williams in the spring. The newly-acquired Ken Holtzman pitched brilliantly in exhibition games, making the Rick Monday trade look like a potential coup for the A's. Blue Moon Odom, now recovered from his offseason gunshot wounds, threw the ball harder than he had in the last two seasons. Perhaps the veteran right-hander had fully overcome his chronic elbow troubles. Catfish Hunter pitched well in his last two spring starts. Out of the bullpen, both Rollie Fingers and Bob Locker looked impressive. To some observers' surprise, Fingers expressed a preference for working as a starting pitcher. "Starting is where the money is,"[18] Fingers said succinctly.

The holdout of Blue and the trade for McLain overshadowed another building Oakland controversy. One of the A's had reported to spring training wearing a mustache. Keeping in mind that no major league player had donned such facial hair during the regular season since Wally Schang in 1914, Reggie Jackson's decision to sport a mustache made major news in 1972. Jackson bragged to teammates that he would wear a mustache, and possibly a beard, come Opening Day. The new mustachioed look quickly cornered the attention of Charlie Finley and Dick Williams. "The story as I remember it," says Mike Hegan, "was that Reggie came into spring training in '72 with a mustache, and Charlie didn't like it. So he told Dick to tell Reggie to shave it off. And Dick told Reggie to shave it off, and Reggie told Dick what to do. This got to be a real sticking point, and so I guess Charlie and Dick had a meeting, and they said well, 'Reggie's an individual so maybe we can try some reverse psychology here.' Charlie told a couple of other guys, I don't know whether it was (Dave) Duncan, or Sal (Bando), or a few other guys to start growing a mustache. Then, (if) a couple of other guys did it, Reggie would shave his off, and you know, everything would be OK."

According to Sal Bando, Finley wanted to avoid having a direct confrontation with Jackson over the mustache. "Finley, to my knowledge, did not want to go tell Reggie to shave it," says Bando. "So he thought it would be better to have all of us grow mustaches. That way,

Reggie wouldn't be an individual."

Rollie Fingers, Darold Knowles, Catfish Hunter and Bob Locker followed Reggie's lead, each sprouting his own mustache. Instead of making Jackson fell less individualistic, thus prompting him to adopt his previously clean-shaven look, the strategy had a reverse and unexpected effect on Charlie Finley.

"Well, as it turned out, guys started growing 'em, and Charlie began to like it," Mike Hegan recalls. Finley offered a cash incentive to any player who had successfully grown a mustache by Father's Day. "So then we all had to grow mustaches," says Hegan, "and that's how all that started. By the time we got to the (regular) season, almost everybody had mustaches." Even the manager, Dick Williams, known for his military brush-cut and clean-shaven look in Boston, would join the facial brigade by growing a patchy, scraggly mustache.

The mustache-growing represented only part of the grooming and fashion changes that had begun to take root among the Oakland players. Sal Bando, previously the owner of a short, close-cropped haircut and one of the most conservative dressers on the team, showed up at spring training looking like one of the feature characters on the television show, *The Mod Squad*. "My hair is growing over my collar," Bando had warned Ron Bergman of *The Sporting News* prior to spring training. "It's going to cover my ears."[19] Bando also parted ways with the traditional line of clothing that he has worn throughout the 1960s. His wardrobe now included bell-bottom trousers, large lapel shirts, sportscoats with vents and wrap-up around belts in the back, and new-style ties. "I like wide ties," Bando said enthusiastically. "I really like those wide ties."[20]

As late as 1969, most major league players still wore their hair short and preferred conservative-looking clothes. Any player daring to wear high-heeled shoes, plaid bell-bottoms, gaudy multi-colored shirts and wide-lapeled suits with vests would have become the immediate target of public ridicule. Over the next few years, such fashions started to become accepted among professional athletes. Some managers, like Dick Williams, loosened the requirements of the team's dress code on road trips. For example, starting in 1971, Williams allowed his players to travel on buses and plains without ties. Such a practice had previously been considered taboo by the major league establishment. Fashions and dress codes were changing around baseball, and the A's were at the center of the revolution.

The A's also created a stir in 1972 when they unveiled a major change in their on-the-field appearance. Oakland players sported baseball's newest uniforms, which Charlie Finley hoped would stimulate marketing and fan interest. Finley retained his favored color scheme of green and gold, but eliminated the two-tone effect of a sleeveless jersey over a contrasting colored undershirt. The new double-knit uniforms now featured bright, pullover V-neck tops, elastic waist lines instead of the traditional buckle belts, and shimmering white pants with green and gold racing stripes. Finley announced that the A's would alternate jerseys, wearing a bright "kelly green" one day, followed by a gaudy "California gold" the next. The shirts featured "A's" in white lettering on the left side of the chest, the player's uniform number in smaller white lettering to the right, and three bright stripes — either green or gold — on the edge of the sleeves. On Sundays, the A's would wear all white — "wedding gown white" as Finley called it.

The A's had first adopted the green and gold pattern in 1963, while still in Kansas City. In breaking with the tradition of wearing white, gray, and one-color trim — a color scheme that Finley abhorred, referring to it as "eggshell white and prison gray" — the A's became the first major league team to employ multicolored uniforms, along with white shoes. "We were embarrassed the first time we went on the field," says Jack Aker of the radical new uniforms. "We saw the uniforms, we wore them on the field, we were embarrassed. I think almost everybody on the ballclub. We did feel clownish. This was not baseball as we knew it. The white shoes especially grated on a lot of players. We'd never had white shoes; everybody wore black in those days."

Former sportswriter Bob Fowler has distinct memories of observing a Hall of Famer who looked hopelessly out of place in the A's unusual uniforms. "I'll never forget," Fowler says, "Joe DiMaggio was the hitting coach. People were teasing DiMaggio about being in this green and gold and 'wedding gown' white, whatever the colors were. Gold, green, and they had gray on them. White was used at home. Anyway, they were teasing DiMaggio, saying, 'Gee, you know, we're used to see you in Yankee pinstripes and now you got on this clown outfit.' It was going on around the batting cage before the game; it was quite humorous. That was the institution of color into baseball, you know."

The revolutionary new uniforms of the A's brought howls of amusement from some observers in the baseball community, especially those who considered green and gold inappropriate colors. Fans in the stands taunted the A's players. "They would call us clowns," recalls Jack Aker. "They would start the music that goes with Ringling Brothers, Barnum and Bailey, they'd start singing this." A's players eventually became more comfortable with their new outfits and other teams started to follow suit. In 1972, the San Diego Padres began using brown and gold as their signature colors. The Chicago White Sox, Milwaukee Brewers, Montreal Expos, Philadelphia Phillies and St. Louis Cardinals started to wear powder blue road uniforms as a substitute for the traditional gray appearance. By 1975, the Houston Astros instituted rainbow striped shirts, the Baltimore Orioles adopted an alternate uniform consisting of bright orange shirts, and the Cleveland Indians a blood-red uniform featuring matching jerseys and pants.

Whether they cared to admit it or not, several owners had followed Finley's lead in creating colorful new uniforms for their own teams. This was not the first time that Finley's influence had fueled change, nor would it be the last. During the 1960s, Finley had called for the playing of World Series games at night. By 1971, the first night game in Series history had taken place. Finley had also pushed for the adoption of a designated hitter rule, a radical concept that American League owners would ratify in 1973. "He was a great innovator," says Reggie Jackson."Night All-Star games, night World Series games for the working man to be able to enjoy. He wanted to do things that added color to the game and created excitement for the game that the fan could enjoy."

"He was very creative," says Dave Duncan. "He was always trying to attract more interest in the game of baseball from the fan's standpoint. He was always trying to entertain. You have to give him credit for that." Yet, few owners wanted to give Finley credit for anything, given his abrasive style, pushiness, and stubborn demeanor. They refused to heed his warnings about the systems of free agency and arbitration and grudgingly listened to his reasons for supporting the DH, night World Series games and interleague play. "Charlie was different," says Rick Monday, "but at the same time he certainly left his footprint on baseball. A lot of things that he said about baseball way back in the seventies, if they had listened to him a little bit closer, maybe things would not have gotten out of hand like they have."

Aside from the changes in fashions and uniforms, the spring of '72 produced several baseball-related surprises for the A's. Angel Mangual, expected to be the starting center fielder, reported to spring training with a torn leg muscle. The A's optioned him to Triple-A, instead of having him start the season on the disabled list. Mangual's injury opened up center field for an obscure seven-year minor league veteran named Bobby Brooks, who had started the spring as a non-roster player. Nicknamed the "Hammer," the hard-hitting Brooks batted .344 with three home runs and 11 RBI's in 61 pre-season at-bats. As the end of spring training neared, Dick Williams announced to the media that Brooks would be his Opening Day center fielder.

In an even more shocking development, the A's waived veteran first baseman-outfielder Tommy Davis. "I knew I was in trouble when I got my contract," Davis said of the pact that Charlie Finley had mailed him during the winter. "I hit .324 for him and he offered me (only) a $3,000 raise."[21] The 33-year-old Davis had performed exceedingly well as the A's best bench player in 1971. He had led all American League pinch-hitters in batting average and had responded brilliantly to clutch situations, collecting 13 RBI's with his 12 pinch-hits. Davis had also continued to hit well in the spring exhibition games, assaulting pitchers at a .563 clip prior his release. So why did the A's throw away such a valuable bench player while receiving nothing in return? The A's claimed that the condition of Davis' oft-injured legs prevented him from playing a position in the field. "He could no longer do the job defensively,"[22] explained Dick Williams.

In reality, Davis' defensive limitations had little to do with his sudden unemployment. The real reason could be found in the name of Davis' agent — Bob Gerst — the same man representing holdout Vida Blue. Davis had first introduced Blue to Gerst, an act which Finley now considered unconscionable. "If that's the reason they cut me," Davis reasoned, "there's nothing I can do about it. If it is, it's very childish"[23]

Davis later explained that he had brought Blue and Gerst together during the first half of the 1971 season, when Vida's assault of American League batters had attracted commercial suitors. "I didn't introduce Gerst to help Blue with his contract," Davis explained. "I introduced him to help him with endorsements and personal appearances — and that was early in the season."[24] Regardless of Davis' intentions, Finley sought retribution for the current crumbled state of salary negotiations with his star pitcher. "He wanted a scapegoat," Davis said. "He didn't want to get rid of Blue, but he wanted to show how strong he could be."[25]

With teams looking to reduce their rosters late in spring training, the timing of the release did not help Davis. "I figure I had a job, hitting for Oakland and maybe playing sparingly...the next thing I'm out of baseball."[26] Davis would eventually find work with the Chicago Cubs and later make Finley regret his foolish decision to release him.

After a players' strike, which delayed the start of the season, the A's announced their Opening Day 25-man roster. The list of newcomers included the following: pitchers Denny McLain and recently signed reliever Joel Horlen, whom the Chicago White Sox had surprisingly released; third string catcher Larry Haney; and a trio of outfielders, youngsters Bobby Brooks and George Hendrick, and veteran Brant Alyea. The A's placed Chuck Dobson, still recovering from off-season elbow surgery, on the disabled list. That left the A's with a decision to make on Vida Blue. Since Blue was not injured, he could not be put on the disabled list. Charlie Finley thus placed Blue on the rarely-used restricted list, which allowed Dick Williams to replace him with another pitcher. In spite of the absence of Blue and the delicate status of both Dobson and Blue Moon Odom, Williams expressed satisfaction with his Opening Day roster.

On the eve of the opener, Curt Blefary issued a play-me-or-trade-me order. The veteran utilityman had become famous for making such proclamations during his journeyman career with the Orioles, Astros, Yankees, and A's. Blefary had begun spring training as the team's second-string catcher behind Dave Duncan. After hitting .360 during the spring, Blefary had managed to fall to fourth-string catcher behind

Duncan, Gene Tenace and Larry Haney, and third-string first baseman behind Mike Epstein and Mike Hegan. Blefary's clumsy play behind the plate made him too much of a liability to play except on an emergency basis. "Sometimes my mouth went into gear before my brain was engaged," Blefary said of his frequent criticisms of managers who did not play him regularly. "I had to play everyday or I was mad."[27] The next day, Blefary apologized to Williams for making such a public outburst and putting his manager on the spot right before Opening Day.

Sporting their new Finley-mandated uniforms, the A's opened the regular season on Saturday, April 15, against the Minnesota Twins. The fans didn't seem too curious about the new look in pullover polyester, considering that only 9,912 showed up for at the Oakland Coliseum. With Vida Blue still unsigned, Dick Williams handed the Opening Day ball to former Chicago Cub Ken Holtzman, who had worked out, by his own estimation, for only five minutes during the 13-day strike. The rest of the Oakland lineup looked much the same as it had in 1971:

Campy Campaneris, ss
Joe Rudi, lf
Reggie Jackson, rf
Sal Bando, 3b
Mike Epstein, 1b
Bobby Brooks, cf
Dave Duncan, c
Dick Green, 2b
Ken Holtzman, p

Aside from the installation of the unknown Bobby Brooks in center field, the biggest surprise involved the catching position. At the start of spring training, Williams had declared an open competition between Dave Duncan and Gene Tenace. In spring training play, Duncan batted only .138, while Tenace sizzled at .316. Tenace believed that his superior spring hitting had earned him the first-string position, but on Opening Day, Duncan found himself behind the plate. Duncan's shotgun throwing arm and agility behind the plate gave him a stronger defensive presence than the offensive-minded Tenace. Williams diplomatically told Tenace that he wanted Duncan to catch Holtzman in the opener since the two had worked together more frequently during the spring. In actuality, Tenace had caught Holtzman more often. Once again, Williams had decided to reward his better defensive catcher with the honor of starting the first game of the season.

Williams respected Duncan's ability to read other teams' hitters and help his own pitchers make in-game adjustments. After his playing career, Duncan would become one of the game's most respected pitching coaches. As part of his coaching duties, Duncan would maintain records on every opposing batter. Duncan's files would indicate the type of pitch each batter hit, the location of the pitch, and a description of where the batter hit the ball. Every game, every batter.

Holtzman pitched well in his Oakland debut, giving up just two runs in eight innings. The A's won the game in the 11th inning, when Joe Rudi raced home from third on a one-out grounder to third base. Eric Soderholm's throw easily beat Rudi to the plate, but catcher George Mitterwald dropped the ball when the Oakland left fielder crashed into him. The miscue gave the A's a dramatic 4-3 win.

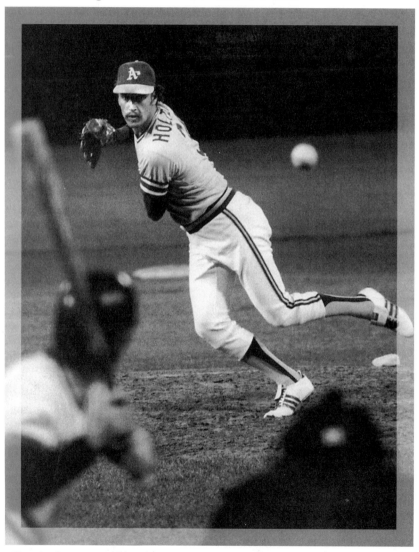

Ken Holtzman, Oakland's key off-season acquisition and Opening Day starter, wearing one of the three new uniforms debuted by the A's in 1972.

After losing to the Twins on Sunday afternoon, Denny McLain made a memorable debut for the A's on Tuesday night against the Kansas City Royals. McLain scattered eight hits over seven plus innings, giving up a pair of unearned runs. With relief help from Darold Knowles and Rollie Fingers, and the longball support of Dave Duncan and Mike Epstein, McLain earned a 3-2 win.

Although McLain had dressed in the green and gold of the A's uniforms for less than two months, he had already determined Oakland to be baseball nirvana. "It's great to be back in the big leagues," exclaimed McLain, while taking a shot at his former team, the Washington Senators-turned Texas Rangers. "Fundamentally, (Oakland) is the best team ballclub I've been on in my life...The execution here is almost flawless. They hit the cut-off man, they make the double play, they do just about everything they're supposed to do."[28] Keep in mind, McLain had previously played for the Detroit Tigers, the 1968 world champions.

The next day, Ken Holtzman topped his Opening Day performance by blanking the Royals, 4-0, on five hits. Through his first two games, Holtzman had pitched 17 quality innings, and had yet to surrender a single walk. Although the season was less than a week old, Holtzman had made a dynamic first impression on his new team and had lessened the A's worries about the continuing absence of their other left-handed starter.

On May 2, 12 days after the start of the strike-delayed season, the Vida Blue saga would finally end. Charlie Finley, having agreed to raise the ante on his initial offer of $50,000, reached agreement on a one-year deal with his unhappy pitcher. Finley consented to give Blue a contract for $63,000, which would be prorated dating back to April 27, but only after Commissioner Bowie Kuhn had interceded in the talks. In the days leading up to the agreement, even President Richard Nixon had put pressure on Finley by raving about the talent of Blue. "Maybe Finley ought to pay," mused the President. "It would be a great tragedy if a young player with all that talent stayed out too long."[29]

Since all of spring training and the start of the regular season had already elapsed, Blue expressed little optimism over his ability to pitch well. "I'll be lucky if I win 10 games,"[30] said Blue, who would need three to four weeks of conditioning before returning to game action. Blue's words could not please Finley, who had agreed to prorate his contract. In other words, Finley had agreed to give Blue back pay even though he would not be able to pitch for another month. Now Blue was hinting that he might not be able to regain his dominant form once he actually returned to the mound.

Blue had actually come to terms with the A's in Chicago on April 27, when Finley agreed to pay him a base salary of $50,000, give him a $5,000 bonus for his 1971 performance and set aside another $8,000 that would be put toward the pitcher's continuing college education. The package, totaling $63,000, satisfied Blue, but he refused to sign the deal when Finley insisted that all terms of the contract be publicly revealed. At the time, most major league teams did not announce the specific stipulations of contracts signed by their players.

After the disagreement over "public revelation" led to a collapse in the talks between the two sides, Kuhn had stepped in to the negotiations, much to the chagrin of Finley. At first, Kuhn told reporters that Finley had made a fair offer, and felt Blue should agree to the $63,000 contract. Kuhn then ordered Finley to keep the offer on the table until May 2. Finley resented the notion of the commissioner ordering him to do anything when it came to offering contracts. An angry Finley tried to remove the offer, but Kuhn insisted otherwise. "I am ruling that the offer has been made and will remain in effect,"[31] stipulated Kuhn.

"The commissioner has no business being in this," Finley fumed. "I don't believe he had the authority to do so. I didn't like it one damn bit."[32] The commissioner later fined and reprimanded Finley for criticizing him through the media. Finley and Kuhn didn't see eye-to-eye on most matters; the handling of the Blue case just added to the list of angry disagreements between the two men.

The holdout of Blue had not only created hard feelings between Finley and the commissioner, but also between the owner and his star pitcher. Blue had not appreciated Finley's condescending tone throughout their protracted contract negotiations. As he prepared himself to resume playing baseball, Blue rapped the owner for his handling of the contract stalemate, "Charlie Finley has soured my stomach for baseball." Blue also introduced racial overtones to the recently concluded dispute. "Finley treated me like a damned colored boy,"[33] claimed the angry pitcher. Blue's claim represented the first time — but certainly not the last time — that he would charge Finley with racism.

As he looks back on his holdout in 1972, Blue regrets some of the negotiating tactics that he and his representatives employed. "I was doing what I thought was in the best interests of Vida Blue," the former major league pitcher said in a 1996 interview with *Sports Collectors Digest*. "The unfortunate part of it, at that time, was I still thought of baseball as a game, but the people I had assisting me in contract negotiations knew it was a business and approached it that way. If I had to do it all over again, I would probably change many of those things."[34] Yet, Blue maintains that he deserved to be paid commensurate with his 1971 performance and not based on his lack of major league longevity at the time. "You're getting paid for what you did last year in this business," Blue explains, "especially back then. Thus, that gives you a legitimate negotiating right to say your value is this amount in dollars and cents."[35]

Now that the A's had signed Blue, they had to face another controversy, one that involved the all-important catching position. Although Dick Williams had given Dave Duncan the honor of starting on Opening Day, he had subsequently decided to employ Gene Tenace in a time-sharing program behind the plate. Williams alternated the two back-stops, playing each man every other day. The plan didn't sit particularly well with Duncan, the team's number one catcher in 1971. Despite his unhappiness, Duncan enjoyed one of the hottest hitting streaks of his career, blasting four home runs in his first seven games. Duncan hadn't shown such power-hitting capacity since his minor league season of 1966, when he had clubbed 46 home runs for Modesto of the California League. Williams would now have to consider playing Duncan on an everyday basis.

During the strike-shortened month of April, the A's won seven and lost four, before reeling off four consecutive wins. After 16 games, Oakland's record stood at 12-4. Even reserve players like Mike Hegan had contributed to the quick start. On April 25, Dick Williams had installed Hegan as a pinch-hitter in the top of the 12th inning of a 3-3 tie. With a runner on second base, the lefty-swinging veteran faced right-hander reliever Lindy McDaniel, one of the Yankees' best relief pitchers. Hegan laced a McDaniel fastball into right-center field, just a few feet in front of his father, Jim, the Yankee bullpen coach. As the elder Hegan watched from the Yankee bullpen beyond the right field fence, Mike chugged into second base, the owner of a game-winning base hit.

Hegan's clutch pinch-hit may have won the game, but he was still thinking about his father, who would have preferred to see him draw an intentional walk. "I kind of took a look toward the bullpen when I got to second," said the younger Hegan, "but I didn't see him."[36] Mike remembered that he scheduled a post-game dinner date with his father. While the dinner with Jim was still on, Mike knew his base hit would cost him a few dollars. "I bought lunch," Jim pointed out, "so he better buy dinner."[37]

The A's had managed their fine start with no contribution from Vida Blue, who hadn't signed until May 2, and wouldn't pitch his first game until three weeks later. Without Blue, Dick Williams had smartly used a three-man starting rotation — Ken Holtzman, Catfish Hunter and Denny McLain — which had been facilitated by several open dates and rainouts. The bullpen had also picked up the slack for the absence of the reigning Cy Young award winner. Through the first 17 games of the season, Oakland relievers had allowed only one run in 33 and a third innings. The bullpen corps of Rollie Fingers, Bob Locker, Diego Segui, Joel Horlen, and Darold Knowles had played a direct hand in winning or saving nine of the A's first 12 victories.

"Without a doubt, the best bullpen in baseball," Dick Williams assessed of his five relievers. "They throw hard and have good control. My three stoppers, Fingers and Locker from the right side and Knowles from the left, can get either right-handers or left-handers out... My two long and middle men, Segui and Horlen, are just outstanding."[38]

During the 1960s, the side-arming Locker had used his hard, moving sinker to become the relief ace of the Chicago White Sox and one of the best firemen in the American League. As a 27-year-old rookie in 1965, the off-beat Locker had drawn snickers from his veteran teammates by wearing a 10-pound weighted canvas vest that looked like a bullet-proof jacket usually reserved for members of a SWAT team. When Chicago reporters asked him about wearing the vest during spring training drills, Locker offered some unconventional logic. "You see," said Locker, "most of the players come to camp about 10 pounds overweight, while I never gain an ounce. The fellows with the extra weight are strengthening their legs just carrying it around during these workouts before they finally take it off. Since I never am overweight, I saddle myself with those extra pounds to put me even with them."[39] At least Locker didn't wear the vest while pitching.

Locker loved to hunt and fish, to the extent that he often woke up at 2:30 in the morning to embark on various expeditions. An expert fisherman, Locker once caught 100 fish in a lake — in one day. Locker avidly followed the philosophies professed in the book, *Jonathan Livingston Seagull*, which he encouraged his A's teammates to read as a way of life.

The success of the bullpen enabled the A's to overcome a series of adversities. A bad back sidelined starting second baseman Dick Green. Joe Rudi missed several games with the flu. Chuck Dobson, still recovering from elbow surgery, started his season pitching in Double-A. Denny McLain, after pitching well in his Oakland debut, struggled in his next three starts.

In his second start, McLain lasted only four innings against the Yankees, giving up five hits and three runs. In his next outing, McLain pitched creditably against the Brewers, but took the loss after pitching six and one-third innings of three-run baseball. On May 7, McLain failed to reach the fourth inning, giving up eight hits and five runs to the Yankees. Five days later, McLain lasted only two innings after the Red Sox pounded him for four runs. The latest start left McLain with an earned run average of 6.05.

Most alarmingly, in all five of his starts, McLain had exhibited extremely poor velocity. One rival player was asked to compare the difference between McLain's fastball in 1972 as opposed to the heater he threw in 1968, when he won 31 games for the Tigers. "About 20 miles an hour," said Boston Red Sox catcher Duane Josephson. "McLain's ball comes up to the plate as straight as a string."[40]

Dick Williams exiled McLain to the bullpen. Rumors circulated that Charlie Finley would offer McLain a $25,000 settlement if he would retire and forego the balance of the $50,000 the A's owed him. Another report said that Finley would release McLain. The right-hander reacted philosophically to such speculation. "If the game ends tonight," McLain told reporters after his last appearance as a starter, "I've had thrills other people never dreamed of having...They'll have to rip the uniform off me."[41] A few days later, the A's did the next best thing. Instead of releasing him and paying off his guaranteed contract in full, the A's demoted McLain to their Double-A affiliate at Birmingham in the Southern League.

As a veteran player, McLain had the choice of refusing the demotion, but that option would have meant sacrificing the balance of his salary. McLain delayed reporting to the minor leagues for three days, causing some writers to speculate that McLain was pondering retirement. Others claimed McLain was intentionally stalling, so as to continue drawing his $75,000 annual salary for an extra few days. That theory didn't make sense, however, since the A's would have to pay McLain his major league salary regardless of whether he pitched for them or in the minor leagues. Finally, McLain agreed to report to Birmingham — as a matter of survival. "There were a lot of reasons for my decision (to report to the minor leagues)," McLain explained. "But when you come right down to it, it's a matter of eating."[42]

Eating may have been the root of McLain's problems in the first place. In Washington, McLain had gained too much weight, which had affected his pitching. Prior to the trade to Oakland, he had begun taking diuretic pills, a medication that results in weight loss. The pills helped McLain lose weight, but also resulted in loss of fluids and a reduction in potassium, which had caused a general weakening of the muscles. Although observers in Washington insisted McLain had already lost his good fastball in 1970, the loss of strength may have been responsible for robbing him of further velocity. "He can't throw that high, hard one any more,"[43] said Dick Williams, whom McLain had called his best major league manager only a few weeks earlier. A reporter asked Williams if McLain could still pitch at the major league level. "From the way he's throwing, and the statistics show it," said Williams, "I don't think he could help anybody right now."[44]

Based upon McLain's poor performance, Williams had sufficient reason to demote him to the minor leagues. But there was more. Although Williams said McLain was a "good fellow and didn't cause us any problems,"[45] he knew of the pitcher's past, which included a burdensome gambling habit and associations with illegal bookmakers. The A's manager, a strict believer in self-responsibility and discipline, felt McLain's habits presented a potential threat to the winning atmosphere that he had successfully established in the Oakland clubhouse.

Other factors may have contributed to McLain's decline. He had been stricken with the flu almost immediately after joining the A's in the spring. The players' strike had limited his ability to work out and improve his conditioning. Furthermore, his wife, Sharon, had undergone a difficult pregnancy that had forced her into an unexpected stay in the hospital.

McLain made his first start for Birmingham on May 20. Even though he was facing batters two classes below the caliber of major league hitters, McLain continued to struggle — embarrassingly. In five innings against Montgomery, McLain gave up nine hits, including three home runs, and suffered a 9-3 loss. Somehow, McLain had managed to pitch worse in Double-A ball than he had in the major leagues.

Chapter Ten:
Revolving Doors

The A's played well throughout most of April and May, but Charlie Finley continued to tinker with his roster. On April 28, the A's made a strange move, selling quietly effective reliever Jim Roland to the Yankees, which left them with Darold Knowles as the sole left-hander in the bullpen.

Ten days later, the A's replaced Roland with a pitcher of lesser potential in Mike Kilkenny. The curveballing left-hander came over from the Tigers for minor league outfielder Reggie Sanders, whom the A's regarded as nothing more than a very good Triple-A player. On May 15, Finley sent backup infielder Dwain Anderson to the Cardinals for lefty reliever Don Shaw. Two days later, the A's made their most puzzling move of the month, trading valuable backup Curt Blefary, a player to be named later, and the recently acquired Kilkenny to the San Diego Padres for veteran outfielder "Downtown" Ollie Brown, whom Charlie Finley had sought since 1969. The trade left the A's with only one reliable left-hander in the bullpen (Darold Knowles), deprived them of Blefary, one of their best left-handed bats off the bench, and gave them yet another right-handed hitting outfielder in Brown, who was hitting just .171 at the time with no home runs and three RBI's. The next day, Finley dealt backup outfielder Brant Alyea to the Cardinals for utility infielder Marty Martinez. Oakland then sold Opening Day center fielder Bobby Brooks to the Detroit Tigers' organization. In the span of three weeks, Finley had made six transactions involving 12 players.

The trade of Blefary appeared mystifying on the surface. Although Blefary had requested a trades moments before the start of the season, he had served the A's well in a backup role, rapping out five hits in 11 at-bats. "I got off to a good start there," Blefary said later, "but I've stopped trying to figure things out. I do what I'm told now and keep my mouth shut. (Dick) Williams told me it wasn't his idea to trade me."[1]

So why did the A's trade him for Ollie Brown, who figured to be a third-string right fielder? Blefary's constant complaints over playing time may have sealed his fate with Charlie Finley, but former teammate Mike Hegan offers another theory. "When you did look at the other people that were there, I think that Dick (Williams) felt and maybe Charlie (Finley) felt that we had enough left-handed hitting coming off the bench, and that we needed some right-handed hitting coming off the bench. Very frankly, Curt — and I love him, Curt and I are great friends — but very frankly, he was kind of a one-dimensional player, if you will, and that was offense." Blefary had long since earned the nickname "Clank," which represented the imaginary sound the ball made when it caromed off any of his less-than-reliable gloves. Blefary carried around eight different gloves, in the eventuality that he might catch, play first, second or third base, or patrol the outfield. Although Blefary brought enthusiasm and versatility to the utility role, he represented a defensive liability everywhere.

After the announcement of the trade, Blefary threatened to retire and become a policeman if the Padres did not renegotiate his contract, but soon changed his mind. "Clank" played sparingly with the Padres, who released him after the season. The move ended Blefary's career at the age of 29, only one season before the American League adopted the designated hitter rule.

Hegan says that Ollie Brown, despite playing the same position as Reggie Jackson, brought some strengths to Oakland. "I think that we needed some right-handed power and some defensive help," Hegan says, "and Ollie Brown provided both." Cincinnati Reds' superscout Ray Shore once called Brown's throwing arm the best he'd ever seen from an outfielder. Other scouts rated Brown's arm on a par with Roberto Clemente of the Pittsburgh Pirates. In 1970, Brown had enjoyed his most productive season, reaching career highs with 23 home runs and 89 RBI's. Yet, that season would represent the pinnacle of Brown's journeyman major league career.

The series of player moves reflected general concerns about the Oakland ballclub. After winning five straight to open up the month of May, the A's lost three games in a row. For the first time all season, the bullpen played the part of culprits. In a 7-6 loss to Boston, the Red Sox tagged both Bob Locker and Rollie Fingers for late-inning runs, including a game-winning home run in the 12th inning. The next day, Joel Horlen allowed a three-run homer in relief of Ken Holtzman, who suffered the loss. A week later, starting second baseman Dick Green underwent surgery to remove a herniated disc in his back. Green had suffered the injury on April 25 after bending over to lay down a sacrifice bunt. At first, the A's worried that Green would miss the entire season, but doctors encouraged him by telling him that he could return by the first of September. On May 19, the A's suffered their most one-sided loss since Charlie Finley moved the franchise from Kansas City to Oakland in 1968. Oakland pitchers gave up 20 hits in a 16-1 loss to the Royals. Blue Moon Odom lasted only three and a third innings. Rollie Fingers allowed three runs without retiring a batter. Newly-acquired Don Shaw, exhibiting why the Cardinals had given up on him, surrendered nine runs in a torturous three-inning stint.

"It was a circus," Sal Bando said of the embarrassing loss to the Royals. "It should have been played in a tent."[2] The performance did not amuse Dick Williams, who watched his pitchers toil miserably, witnessed physical errors by Reggie Jackson and Bob Locker, and observed numerous mental lapses by his fielders and baserunners. Williams called a team meeting after the game to let the players know of his displeasure. The A's responded by winning their next four games. After a loss to the Angels on May 24, the A's won five more games in a row, and six of their next seven. The stretch gave the A's 18 wins in 26 games during the month of May, and an overall record of 25-12 heading into June.

The A's had started to solve some of their nagging personnel problems. Vida Blue had returned to the starting rotation, and Blue Moon Odom had returned to health, giving Dick Williams two more viable starters after Catfish Hunter and Ken Holtzman. Utility infielder Larry Brown, though hitting only .168, had successfully replaced Dick Green's fielding ability at second base, giving the A's a reliable double play partner for Campy Campaneris. Top prospect George Hendrick had been summoned from the minor leagues to fill the center field gap created by the off-season trade of Rick Monday to the Cubs. Hendrick responded by hitting game-winning home runs in two consecutive games against the White Sox.

The A's offense ranked as the best in the American League, thanks largely to the play of Joe Rudi. The anonymous left fielder, who hadn't even been listed on the American League's All-Star ballot, had emerged as an early MVP candidate. On June 1, Rudi's .324 batting average ranked him second in the league. Rudi rated in the top five in runs scored, hits, doubles, and triples, all while batting out of the demanding No. 2 slot in the batting order. Rudi would later put together a 17-game hitting streak, the longest in the short history of the Oakland franchise. "If I had been scouting him, I'd have been completely wrong," says Jack Aker, a teammate of Rudi during his first two major league seasons. "I really didn't feel he was gonna be a major league everyday player; I thought possibly a fourth outfielder and extra man, but he just kept improving, made himself into a star, really."

Rudi claimed that previous stints in the U.S. Marine Reserves, which caused him to miss 35 to 40 games a year, had affected his timing and rhythm at the plate. As an example, Rudi had fallen off to a mediocre .267 in 1971. Now that Rudi's military obligations had ended, he was free to pursue the art of hitting to the fullest. A pull-hitting power hitter in the minor leagues, he had transformed himself into a successful gap-hitting, opposite field hitter. "Joe has the ideal temperament for a professional athlete," said an admiring Dick Williams. "He's always working to improve."[3] Under former Oakland batting coach Charlie Lau's tutelage in 1970, Rudi had worked hard to radically change his batting approach. Rudi began choking up on the bat while adopting a severely closed stance with a deep crouch. Using an unusual diagonal stance, Rudi placed his left foot close to the front corner of the plate, while nearly planting his right foot outside of the batter's box. In the meantime, Rudi rested his bat flat on his right shoulder. Although Rudi hardly seemed ready to handle an incoming pitch, the new stance actually made his swing quicker and more compact. "Charlie Lau changed my whole theory on hitting and what I was trying to do with the ball," Rudi said. "He taught me about hitting behind the runner, thinking about what I wanted to do with the ball... All of a sudden, it was there. It was like being in the boonies all your life and walking into a big city and finding a metropolitan library. I just milked that guy every second I could about hitting."[4]

Charlie Finley had obviously not consulted Rudi when he had fired Lau for "sleeping with" catcher Dave Duncan. "It was the turning point of my career," Rudi said of the first time he met Lau. "Charlie got me to shorten up on my swing and to forget about hitting home runs. He also taught me how to hit to right field."[5] Rudi pointed out that the departed Lau had also helped Dave Duncan, who had tended to overswing and chase too many bad pitches, making his hitting a chronic struggle. Aided by a shortened swing, Lau's former housemate had hit 10 home runs, which left him tied with Reggie Jackson for the team lead.

While Rudi garnered a few headlines with his surprising hitting, Jackson enjoyed a quietly productive season at the plate, providing the team with a measure of longball and a decent batting average. In June, Jackson described his philosophy of power at the plate, and his love of "taters," a nickname that Boston Red Sox slugger George Scott had originated to describe his own home runs. "The home run is very important to me," Reggie Jackson explained to *Sports Illustrated*. "Sure, I like to keep a respectable average, like .280 or .290, but average is like the wind; it can disappear overnight. Those taters, them they can't ever take away from you."[6]

Jackson and Rudi enjoyed a special relationship, even though their personalities differed as much as the color of their skin. In 1966, Jackson and Rudi had played for Modesto, the Class-A affiliate of the A's. The next season, both players moved up to Double-A Birmingham, where segregation in the South prevented Jackson from enjoying the same experiences as his white teammates. Jackson found Rudi the most accepting among his fellow players. "Joe was the first player ever to have me over to his house for dinner," Reggie said of his days in Birmingham. "There were a lot of places in Birmingham I couldn't eat. I couldn't even live where the Rudis were staying."[7] Rudi found the racial attitudes of some of his neighbors distasteful. "Our landlady kept coming around asking why that black guy was coming over all the time," Rudi told *The Sporting News*. "For the (rent) money we were paying her, we figured we could have anyone over we wanted."[8]

In May, Charlie Finley called a press conference to announce that the A's would hold a special promotion on Father's Day. Major league baseball's first-ever "Mustache Day" would take place at the Oakland Coliseum. In a continuation of a story that had begun with Reggie Jackson's sprouting of a mustache in spring training, Finley promised to pay $300 bonuses to each player who featured a mustache on Father's Day. In addition, all mustache-bearing fans would receive free admission to the ballpark.

Finley had gone full circle — from an initial dislike of Reggie Jackson's mustache to a desire to have every player on his 25-man roster wearing one. "Guys that didn't have mustaches, and I was one of them, were required to grow a mustache so that Charlie could put on a 'Mustache Day' at the Coliseum," Mike Hegan recalls. Some players, like Rollie Fingers, willingly fulfilled Finley's request for mustaches. "For $300," Fingers admitted, "I'd grow one on my rear end."[9]

A small group of players felt differently. "There were three guys that didn't want to do it," says Sal Bando. "Larry Brown, Mike Hegan and myself. (Finley) had to call us in and convince us — not twist our arm or anything — but just reiterate he wanted us to do it." After initial misgivings, Hegan eventually caved in to the owner's wishes. "I finally grew a mustache, did it for about six weeks until 'Mustache Day' and then shaved it off." In ridding himself of the mustache, Hegan gave in to a higher authority than Finley. "My wife didn't like it."

All 25 players on the active roster, Bando and Brown included, sported mustaches by Father's Day. In return, Finley fulfilled his promise of cash considerations. "Yeah, at the end of the game, there was a couple of hundred bucks in everybody's valuable box," confirms Hegan. "(There was also) a little thank-you note for growing the mustaches." At the cost of $7500, Finley had put together a successful promotion.

By July most of the other A's would shave their mustaches, only to bring them back later in the season. Why did so many of the Oakland players revert back to the hairy-lipped look? "Well, we had success as a team," explains Sal Bando, "so everybody stayed with it." As a team, the A's long-haired, mustachioed and eventually bearded look would stamp them with an identity starkly different from the rest of major league baseball.

Rollie Fingers profited most from the facial hair episode, growing a stylish handlebar mustache that became his trademark and helped him become the "best-looking guy in all baseball," according to Joe Falls of *The Sporting News*. Fingers even made sure to negotiate Finley's $300 bonus into his 1973 contract with the A's. In a comically-written press release, Finley discussed his contract talks with Fingers. "Rollie not only got a substantial increase in salary," Finley expounded, "but his 1973 contract also includes a year's supply of the very best mustache wax available. In fact, this is what held up the final signing. I wanted to give Rollie $75.00 for the mustache wax and he wanted $125.00 for it."[10] The two parties settled at $100.00, allowing Fingers to wax the tips of his mustache two times a day.

More than any other player, catcher Dave Duncan embodied the image of the A's as hippies. Not only did Duncan grow a mustache; he sported a scraggly, unkempt beard that made him suitable to appear at a Grateful Dead concert. Duncan also allowed his blonde hair to flow past his shoulders, far longer than any of his teammates. Duncan's appearance proved disconcerting and intimidating for some observers, especially those who didn't know him. "With that long hair, he kind of looked goofy as a player," said Detroit Tigers' shortstop Eddie Brinkman, who would serve with Duncan as a coach with the Chicago White Sox in later years. "But once you get to know him, you realize he's one of the kindest, smartest men you'll ever meet."[11]

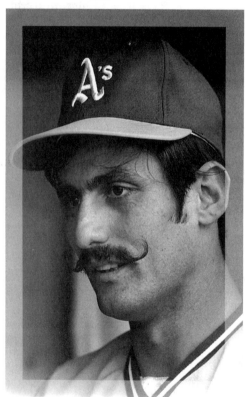

Hall of Fame relief pitcher Rollie Fingers, sporting the most famous of the Oakland mustaches.

In the meantime, Denny McLain continued his stay of execution in Class-AA Birmingham The former Cy Young winner aggravated some of his minor league teammates by continuing to live a major league lifestyle. McLain lived in an expensive suite at the Savannah Inn and Country Club, where he roomed with another former Athletic,

Chuck Dobson. McLain spent most of his days playing golf and sun-tanning before riding to games in a luxurious El Dorado Cadillac driven by another former Athletic, Ken "Hawk" Harrelson, a resident of Savannah. "How you like my 'team bus' boys,?"[12] McLain said to his teammates, many of whom made minimum minor league salaries.

McLain also failed to make any friends with his on-field performance. After bombing in his first start, McLain fared no better in his next, giving up three more home runs. In his first 11 innings at Double-A, McLain had given up six home runs, 19 hits and 16 runs. In his third start, McLain appeared on the verge of extinction, giving up two walks and a single in the first inning. The sore-armed right-hander told manager Phil Cavarretta that his shoulder was "killing him," but insisted that he be left in to pitch. Somehow, McLain recovered to throw seven innings of one-run baseball, while striking out eight. The positive performance soon gave way to harsh reality, as McLain gave up four homers and 12 runs in his next start. "My report will be exactly what I saw," Cavarretta said candidly. "A man pitching with no real velocity, no real control, and a man who must be hurting inside."[13] Out of shape, overweight, and his shoulder causing him pain, McLain appeared light years away from the major leagues.

After losing the first game of June, the A's racked up a season-high eight-game winning streak, which also represented the best stretch in the history of the Oakland franchise. Ken Holtzman, Catfish Hunter, and rookie Dave Hamilton pitched three consecutive shutouts against the Orioles. Hunter's game was a 91-pitch, two-hit masterpiece. Catfish faced only 28 batters, one above the minimum, and retired the last 20 batters he faced. In the next series, Blue Moon Odom threw only 76 pitches in beating the Indians, 3-2, in 10 innings. Despite the win, Dick Williams laced into his players for a series of baserunning mistakes. The tongue-lashing, even in the wake of a victory, impressed some players. "I liked that," Gene Tenace said of Williams' reaction. "It showed he cares. Some managers will let you get away with a mistake. Not Dick."[14] Not satisfied with playing badly in a win, Williams demanded near perfection from his players. The A's responded well to the Williams tirade, pounding out 20 runs in back-to-back wins over the Indians and Tigers. The A's put together two more winning streaks in June, one of five games and another of four games. The streaks gave Oakland another winning month — 18 wins against 11 defeats.

Even high profile players like Reggie Jackson respected the demanding nature of Williams. "If you don't win," said Reggie, "he's ready to fight. I'm loyal to him. He's the best baseball man I've ever known. He keeps you scared enough so you've gotta do your job."[15] Jackson's assessment of his manager had evolved considerably since his initial negative description of Williams in 1971.

Despite their winning ways on the field, Charlie Finley continued to maneuver his players in the transactions column. On June 7, he sold former ERA champion Diego Segui to the Cardinals. The fine pitching of Dave Hamilton and Joel Horlen had made Segui expendable. The sale of the utility pitcher marked the third time he had been traded or let go by the A's. Some players wondered how the move might affect Campy Campaneris, who felt closer to Segui than any of the other A's. The two Cubans had spent so much time together that fans regularly mistook one for the other, and Campaneris and Segui had simultaneously enjoyed career seasons in 1970.

Mike Epstein remained an Athletic, despite his rollercoaster status with Dick Williams. In early June, Epstein had embarked on a home run tear, cementing his favor with the manager. Then, on June 17, Epstein hit a weak pop fly in a game against the Indians. Frustrated by his poor swing at the ball, Epstein failed to run out the pop-up. Williams, furious over Epstein's lack of hustle, pulled him from the game immediately. The next day, Williams returned Epstein to the lineup and watched the left-handed slugger collect two hits in four at-bats and drive in four runs.

The day after Epstein returned to Williams' good graces, Vida Blue finally won his first game. During his spring holdout, Blue had spent much of his time making public appearances for Dura Steel Products and Jantzen Sportswear and had neglected to work out on a regular basis. The lack of conditioning seemed to cost Blue, who had lost three consecutive starts before pitching a 9-0 shutout vs. the Indians. In contrast, Blue had already won eight games by the same date in 1971. Blue would struggle throughout much of the season, paying the price for the spell of inactivity created by his contract dispute with Charlie Finley. Did Blue hold the upper moral ground during his lengthy holdout, or did Finley? "At this point," counters Sal Bando, "I'm not sure it matters who was right or wrong, but the bottom line was Vida Blue was never the same dominant pitcher he was in '71. He still had a good career, but coming off that '71 season he was unhittable. I think he became hittable after that. He just never had the same fastball, the consistency with it. So, if anybody suffered, I think Vida did for missing that time."

Blue also began his drug use during the 1972 season. His involvement with illegal drugs, including cocaine, would lead to his arrest in 1984. Blue would spend 81 days in a federal institution in Fort Worth, Texas, for attempting to purchase cocaine. After his release from prison, Blue began serving another drug-related punishment — a year-long suspension from major league baseball. Commissioner Bowie Kuhn banned Blue — now with the Kansas City Royals — and three of his teammates, Willie Mays Aikens, Jerry Martin and Willie Wilson.

The end of June would bring another flurry of trades for the A's. On June 28, the A's acquired first-baseman outfielder Art Shamsky from the Cubs in a cash deal. Shamsky, a member of the 1969 "Miracle Mets," figured to replace Curt Blefary in the role of left-handed pinch-hitter. Finley announced two more deals the next day. The A's dispatched outfielder

Ollie Brown, the former third-string right fielder who had most recently moved into the starting lineup after Dick Williams had decided to move Reggie Jackson to center field. Not satisfied with Brown's hitting, the A's sent him to Milwaukee for what was announced as cash considerations. Finley secretly acquired the rights to negotiate with recently retired outfielder Billy Conigliaro. On the same day, Finley finally resolved the Denny McLain dilemma.

McLain had pitched much better after his first two disastrous starts with Double-A Birmingham. With his minor league record now a respectable 3-3, McLain telephoned Dick Williams, asking him to be placed on the A's 25-man roster. "I've done everything they've asked," McLain told reporters. "My instructions were to get myself in shape and get my arm in shape. I've done that."[16] Even though the A's possessed only nine healthy pitchers at the time, Williams told McLain that he had no need for a starting pitcher. "We're not recalling him," said Williams, who had noted that McLain had give up 10 home runs in his five major league starts. "We have five starting pitchers and they are all going a good job. What we need is a left-handed reliever and the last time I looked, McLain didn't fit that bill." [17]

Since McLain had no plans to become a left-handed pitcher, it appeared that his future rested with another major league organization. McLain said that two major league teams — the Atlanta Braves and Montreal Expos — had expressed interest in him. The right-hander asked Charlie Finley to work out a deal. Finley said he would do his best to trade to him, which would alleviate the A's responsibility of having to pay McLain's $75,000 salary. Finley certainly didn't want to release McLain outright. Under baseball's new collective bargaining agreement, McLain's salary was 100 per cent guaranteed. If the A's released McLain, they would still have to pay his contract in full.

Faced with having an unwanted player at an exorbitant salary, Finley made an unusual transaction on June 29. The Oakland owner sold his Double-A albatross to the Braves, who had earlier turned down a deal with the A's. "I'm as happy as hell,"[18] responded McLain, who hated pitching in the minor leagues. Finley simultaneously purchased 1967 National League MVP Orlando Cepeda from the Braves. Although the A's and Braves announced the transactions as separate sales, the two teams had essentially traded one former league MVP for another, the first time in history that such a deal had taken place. Knee troubles had limited Cepeda to only 84 at-bats, but he had still managed four home runs and a .298 batting average.

If this trade had been made five years earlier, it might have been hailed as the deal of the century. At his peak in 1967, Cepeda had batted .325 with 25 home runs and 111 RBI's for the world champion St. Louis Cardinals. In 1968, McLain had forged an eye-popping record of 31-6 with an ERA of 1.96. By 1972, both players had fallen on hard times,

McLain victimized by his weight and gambling problems and the 34-year-old Cepeda undermined by his chronically bad legs. Since each player had to clear waivers before the trade could be officially consummated, any of the other 22 major league teams could have claimed McLain or Cepeda for $25,000. *New York Times* columnist Arthur Daley aptly summarized the trade of former MVP's. "It is a trade that is a lot more historic than it is momentous."[19]

Like McLain, Cepeda was pleased to hear the trade news. "I am always happy," said Cepeda. "Only when I do not play am I unhappy."[20] With the Braves, Cepeda had lost his starting job when manager Luman Harris decided to move Hank Aaron from the outfield to first base. Cepeda balked at his demotion by walking out on the team and the Braves suspended him — albeit for only two days. Harris questioned whether Cepeda could play everyday because of his wavering physical condition. Cepeda recalls the Braves' thinking behind the deal. "The reason they trade me was because of my knees," says Cepeda, who had originally injured the knee in 1963 and had waited two years before undergoing surgery.

Now that he had arrived in Oakland, how would the A's use Cepeda? Perhaps Dick Williams envisioned a platoon of Cepeda and Mike Epstein at first base, with Orlando playing against left-handed pitchers. Although Epstein had managed a respectable .250 average against portsiders, he had hit only one home run against lefties. Cepeda says Williams made a point of explaining his role with a new team. "Yes, he told me," Cepeda says, "because see they didn't know I had a bad knee. They didn't know that. But he told me that Mike was the first baseman, but when they have a tough left-handed pitcher, to be ready because you're gonna be playing many games with this ballclub."

Predictably, the arrival of Cepeda angered Epstein, who had been enjoying his status as an everyday first baseman. Epstein wondered aloud why Williams didn't approach him to explain how his role might be affected. "What hurt me is that Dick Williams hasn't called me into the office and told me what they're going to do with Cepeda," said a frustrated Epstein. "I busted my tail for this team and then I read in the paper where we got another player to platoon with me,"[21] Williams countered by saying it wasn't the responsibility of the manager to explain his every lineup decision. "All a player has to do is check the lineup card every day and see if his name is on it," Williams said angrily. "If it is, he goes out and busts his rear."[22] When a reporter pointed out Epstein's reputation as a moody player, Williams shot back, "Well, I'm a moody manager."[23]

Epstein had become associated with moodiness dating back to his days in Washington. Although his critics considered his moody nature a detrimental flaw in his personality, Epstein disagreed. "Moodiness is an outgrowth of pride in a person," Epstein explained. "My so-called moodiness stems only from desire. Now, at 29, I feel I've matured enough to handle problems."[24] When Cepeda learned of Epstein's concerns over his arrival in Oakland, he sought out the big, left-handed hitting first baseman. "Yes, I told him, 'I didn't come here to take your position away. I just came here to try to help win some games and see what happens." Cepeda's chat evidently eased Epstein's mind. The incumbent first baseman proceeded to pick up 13 hits in his next 20 at-bats, including seven safeties against left-handed pitchers. As it would turn out, Epstein and Williams would have little to worry about with regards to a first base controversy.

The trade of the unhappy McLain ended one of the shortest chapters in his baseball life. In the spring, Finley and Williams had quietly hoped that McLain would recapture his former pitching dominance, or at least some percentage of it. By mid-season, those hopes had been transformed into the realities of a lost fastball and an expanding waistline. Although McLain lasted less than half a season in Oakland, he succeeded in leaving an impression on his teammates. "Yes, I got to know Dennis," says Sal Bando. "He was still kind of recovering from being on the downward cycle of his career. Even at that point, he was a gambler; he liked to go play golf for money, bowl for money, whatever it was. He was a character."

According to Bando, McLain posed no problems for his teammates, despite his reputation as an annoying egotist who had antagonized teammates in Detroit and Washington. "In the clubhouse he was fine," Bando insists. "He was a kibitzer. He was a guy who'd like to have a good time and yet he worked. He did his baseball work."

McLain's quick departure from the A's was sad for several reasons. Still only 28 years old, McLain seemed to be wasting his talents, which earlier in his career had him pointed in the direction of Cooperstown. Furthermore, his flamboyant, somewhat abrasive personality would have been a natural for the A's, given their colorfully controversial tendencies throughout the early 1970s. "He would have fit in very well," agrees Bando. "Now that we can look back, you can see obviously that there were some problems in his life." McLain's problems continued after his retirement from the game. After allowing his weight to balloon to 300 pounds, McLain, looking unrecognizable to those who remembered him as a player, suffered a heart attack. He later served 29 months in prison on racketeering, drug, and gambling convictions. McLain's daughter, Kristen, died in a 1992 car accident. In 1997, McLain returned to federal prison after a jury convicted him of stealing millions of dollars from a union pension plan.

Players like Denny McLain and Ollie Brown were now gone from the fast-changing Oakland scene. Art Shamsky and Orlando Cepeda had entered the revolving door. The latest influx of players left the minds of players and writers spinning. With more than half the season to go, Charlie Finley had already orchestrated 34 personnel moves to date. "He was probably one of the only guys who told you that he treated the game as a business," Vida Blue says of Finley's attitude toward player transactions. "He was real cut and dried with trading or cutting or releasing or swapping a player. He was quoted as saying he would trade his mother if he could get the right player he felt he needed."[25]

One writer, Ron Bergman, noted that the addition of Art Shamsky gave the A's three Jewish players — along with Mike Epstein and Ken Holtzman — on their 25-man roster. Bergman pointed out the oddity to Holtzman, who responded, "I hear we're going to have Golda Meir as a shortstop."[26]

While Holtzman was willing to joke about the religious makeup of the team and Epstein reveled in calling himself "Super Jew," both players took pride in their heritage. Later in the year, when terrorists murdered several Israeli athletes during the Olympic Games, Holtzman, Epstein and Reggie Jackson wore black armbands in tribute to those who had been slain. "It hit us like a ton of bricks," Epstein said when the players heard of the tragedy. "Of course, Ken and I are Jewish, but we'd feel the same way if it was any other team. The Olympics are supposed to foster international brotherhood."[27]

The constant changes in personnel might have affected a less talented, or weaker-willed team, but seemed to do little harm to Oakland. The A's continued to pile up wins, while separating themselves further from the second place White Sox and the third-place Twins, who had paced the West the first month of the season. While Finley had tried desperately to upgrade his bench and his bullpen, he had wisely not tinkered with the core of his team: Holtzman, Hunter, and Blue in the starting rotation, Fingers and Knowles in the bullpen, Duncan behind the plate, Campaneris and Bando on the left side of the infield, and Rudi and Jackson in the outfield. These ten players represented the most important segment of the A's; if Finley had traded any of them, he might have done irreparable harm to the team's chances of making the World Series.

No Oakland player had been more indispensable than Holtzman, who had filled the void created by the long holdout of Vida Blue. Though not a power pitcher in the mold of Blue, Holtzman had won 11 of his first 17 starts, compiled 11 complete games, and given up slightly over two runs per nine innings. Holtzman credited his catching partner with his improvement. "Dave Duncan and I think a lot alike," Holtzman said. "I'd say Duncan and I try to challenge the hitters 99 per cent of the time."[28] By attacking opposing hitters with fastballs early in the count, Holtzman had cut down on his walk total, while also reducing his pitch count. In 135 innings, Holtzman had walked only 19 batters, or just over one per start.

Such numbers represented major improvement over his final season in Chicago, where he had pitched in a ballpark (Wrigley Field) that was much friendlier to hitters than the Oakland Coliseum. Holtzman had also struggled under the managerial style of Leo Durocher, whose antiquated style of dealing with players had affected the thoughtful left-hander's performance. Holtzman liked his relationship with his new manager, Dick Williams. "Williams is just super," Holtzman gushed. "He's a great fundamentalist. I think he's as fair as a manager can be in the major leagues."[29]

Holtzman's businesslike professionalism on the mound impressed his teammates and the media, but some observers had begun to take note of his aloof personality. Holtzman refrained from socializing with most of his teammates, showing little interest in visiting bars or restaurants after games. "I'm not really outgoing," Holtzman explained. "When we go on the road, I like to buy four or five paperbacks in the terminal so I'll have something to read in my hotel room."[30]

On the field, Holtzman had pitched far better than expected. So had comebacking right-hander Blue Moon Odom, who had regained his arm strength after persistent elbow problems the past two seasons. Although Odom hadn't made his first start until early May, he had quickly emerged as one of the American League's most effective right-handed pitchers. Odom had regained the good, moving fastball that he had featured prior to his elbow problems.

"He's one of the few guys I've ever seen in baseball that could not throw a ball straight, which was great," says Jack Aker. "He would have had a little trouble at another position." In a 1968 game against the Washington Senators, Odom had tried to pickoff speedster Ed Stroud three times. With the three throws, Odom hit Stroud, first baseman Danny Cater and umpire Larry Napp in succession.

Odom had actually benefited from his elbow surgery in 1970. In 1971, when he could not throw his fastball with its same level of pre-surgical pop, he had worked diligently at developing a change-up and improving his breaking pitches. Now adept at the art of pitching and equipped with a more deceptive motion, Odom had won six straight games.

Odom also made strides in curbing his temper, which he had often vented at teammates when they made fielding errors behind him. "I know they're not perfect," said Odom, "and there's no reason to get mad. I just tell them to get them next time or try to make it up with the bat. I guess I'm more grown up this year. I used to have a quick temper. I know how to control it now."[31]

The pitching of Odom helped carry the A's while Blue scuffled to regain his 1971 form. The lack of spring training had left Blue physically ill-prepared for the new season; the ugly contract negotiations with Charlie Finley had left him emotionally tainted. "Yes, I'm bitter," Blue said in July. "It all seemed unnecessary to me, all that trouble."[32] Blue claimed he no longer wanted to play for Finley and asked for a trade to one of three teams: the Cardinals, Mets, or Yankees.

A series of injuries threatened to undermine the A's. Second baseman Larry Brown encountered back pains, which forced him into traction for 10 days. With starting infielder Dick Green already on the shelf after back surgery, the A's were now down to their third-string second baseman — former Washington Senator Tim Cullen, who had been picked up on waivers prior to the start of the season. Smaller injuries nagged the A's, as well. Blue missed a turn because of a severe bruise on his leg. Joe Rudi,

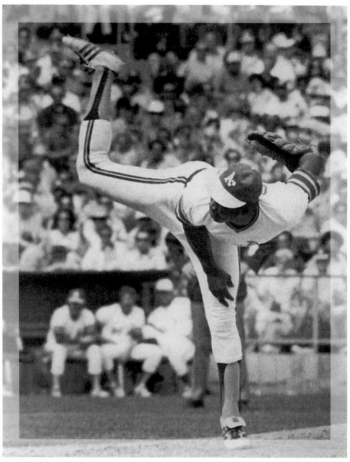

John "Blue Moon" Odom finishing off his unorthodox
delivery, his weight shifted onto the left leg while the other
kicks high.

vying for the American League batting lead, found his swing hampered by
a sore left hand, which had been hit by a pitch.

As the A's prepared to face the White Sox in Chicago for a weekend
three-game set, Dick Williams learned about another setback to his personnel. One of his recent acquisitions was in no condition to play. Orlando Cepeda, who had recently undergone surgery on his knee, could
not run well enough to play the field or move along the basepaths. In a
way, Cepeda's injury delayed a difficult decision for Williams. "Even if
Orlando could play," said the manager, "I don't know where I'd put him.
The guy we have at first base now (Mike Epstein) is doing the job. He's got
the hot bat."[33]

On June 30, Shamsky made his Oakland debut. With the Cubs,

Shamsky had come to bat only 16 times, mostly as a pinch-hitter, and had collected only two hits. Worn down by rust, the veteran outfielder pinch-hit unsuccessfully for second baseman Tim Cullen. The next day, Dick Williams asked Shamsky to do the near impossible: pinch-hit against Angels' ace Nolan Ryan, the most intimidating right-hander in the American League. "He was really throwing the ball," Shamsky said of Ryan, who regularly approached the 100 mile per hour barrier on the radar gun. "I figured I'd go up swinging, and I did — I fouled out."[34] At least Shamsky made contact with the ball, something that most of the A's failed to do that night at Anaheim Stadium. Ryan struck out 16 Oakland batters in earning a 5-3 win for the Angels.

On July 3, Orlando Cepeda finally made his Oakland debut when he pinch-hit for Cullen in a game against the Angels. Three days later, Williams called upon Cepeda to pinch-hit for Joel Horlen against the Yankees. The next day, Cepeda appeared as a pinch hitter for Bob Locker during a 9-4 loss to the Brewers. Cepeda failed to register a hit in any of the three at-bats. More alarmingly, Cepeda looked bad in each of his plate appearances. The "Baby Bull" could hardly run. His knees ached severely. Cepeda and the A's came to a logical conclusion; he would need another surgery to be performed on his knees.

Doctors performed the operation on Cepeda's knees. The A's hoped that Cepeda might become useful to them by early September, but the big first baseman didn't seem confident that he would be able to return before the end of the season. Either way, Finley was furious. While he had traded away Denny McLain and his $75,000 salary, he had picked up an even larger tab — the balance on Cepeda's $90,000 contract. Finley had gone from a pitcher who had no fastball to a first baseman who couldn't even walk. Neither was of much use to a baseball team.

Although the sorry condition of Cepeda's knees prevented him from enjoying a longer stay in Oakland, the "Baby Bull" traveled with the team on a few occasions and relished the opportunity to witness a great team first-hand. "Yes, I made a couple of trips with the team," Cepeda recalls. "In Oakland, I had the opportunity to play with Reggie and Bando and Vida and some of the great ballplayers...They had a great ballclub. I mean, what a baseball team."

Even though Cepeda's season ended quickly, it didn't take long for him to notice the swirl of conflict surrounding the A's, and how it emanated from the team's controversial epicenter. "You know Reggie," says Cepeda. "You know how Reggie is."

Reporters, whether they be local or national, print or electronic, swarmed around Jackson. If a writer needed a quote to spice up a bland story, he ran to Reggie. Some reporters interviewed Jackson reluctantly, turned off by his ego and mood swings. Others, like Twins' beat writer Bob Fowler, found Jackson an engaging personality. "Well, the best guy, the best guy on the A's, the guy I really enjoyed the most — and I don't mean that we became buddy-buddy — but...I liked Reggie Jackson," Fowler says. "I mean, Reggie Jackson was a real businessman. Reggie Jackson knew what you wanted. I don't know that he had ever been schooled at Arizona State in media relations, but he could sense what was a good story, what was a good quote. And he was willing to give it. Other writers said, 'Oh, he's an egotist.' I don't feel that way at all. He knew his role, he knew your role. He was happy to give you his part of the mutual relationship, the working agreement that you had. And then that was it. He would go his way and you'd go your way."

Some writers felt intimidated around Jackson, but not Fowler. "Oh no," Fowler says, "not at all. Not a twit." In general, Fowler found the A's of the early seventies to be an agreeable group of players. "Vida was very good, Sal was very good. They were all good. I can't really think of — I'm desperately trying to think of someone that I didn't like in the Oakland clubhouse and I can't think of anybody." Fowler says that the A's, a team filled with talented and confident players, made his job as an inquisitor that much simpler. "Players who are good players," Fowler says, "are the easiest to interview. Players who are marginal players are the most difficult to interview because those marginal players are always fearful that you will write something that will cost them a trip to Triple-A. Whereas you couldn't beat a Brooks Robinson. You couldn't beat a Reggie Jackson."

When Jackson first joined the Kansas City A's in 1967, he irritated most of his veteran teammates. "Personally, Reggie was very hard to like," says Jack Aker. "Reggie was so brash; he actually was a braggart. It started right from his first day in a major league clubhouse. He came in and told us how good he was, what he expected to do, that he expected to be a regular player. That he was gonna lead our team. Of course, all the players who had been around for awhile sat back and said, 'Well, let's see what you can do.'"

Jackson gained acceptance by backing up his words. "The thing about Reggie," says Aker, "is he could do everything he said he could do. He turned out to be a magnificent player. As soon as we saw him in spring training throw the ball from right field — a rifle arm. He could run like a deer. When he made contact, he hit balls farther than anybody on the club. Really, looking at him as a young player, I was thinking to myself, 'This is as close to Mickey Mantle as I'm gonna see; this guy can actually do everything he said.' As I saw him play, both in spring training and then a little later when he joined our club, he also impressed me with his hustle. I've never seen Reggie not hustle in a ballgame."

Did Jackson back off on his bragging, as he began to establish himself in the late sixties? "No, he continued," Aker says with a laugh. "Reggie, as I say, is hard to like off the field. For me, he throws in a lot of 'I's' and 'ME's' in his conversation, but I have to admire him as a ballplayer. I really do."

In spite of Jackson's brashness, few players on the A's developed an outright dislike of Jackson. Reliever Darold Knowles resented Jackson's arrogance more than most. In one of baseball's most famous quotations, Knowles characterized Jackson during the 1974 season. "There isn't enough mustard in the whole world to cover that hot dog," Knowles said, describing his most famous teammate.

Another relief pitcher enjoyed Jackson's presence in the clubhouse. "Reggie and I have always gotten along," says fellow Hall of Famer Rollie Fingers. "We kind of came up together through the minor leagues. I played with him in Birmingham, Alabama, played with him in Modesto, California. We had a lot of fun in the minor leagues together. Reggie came up the year before I did. Reggie and I always got along. I never had any problems with Reggie. You know, I'd get on him a lot; of course, I got on everybody. But he knew it was in jest. We always had a good time."

Tony LaRussa, who played with the A's over parts of four seasons (1968-'71), respected Jackson as a teammate committed to winning. "I

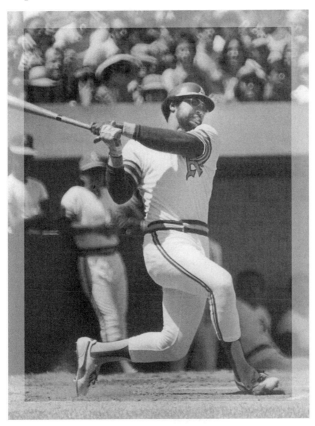

Reggie Jackson unleashing one of the era's most ferocious swings.

had a chance to watch Reggie from the beginning and watch him develop," LaRussa says. "Just a very competitive player with great talent. He really knew the value of winning and was a really good teammate. It was just a thrill to say that you were in the same lockerroom as people like that."

In early July, Jackson and another Oakland star found themselves in the midst of a mid-season slump. On July 6, Jackson took a seat on the bench, the result of a 4-for-46 slump and a drought of 14 games without a home run. With the A's facing Yankee left-hander Mike Kekich, Dick Williams made an unusual move, placing catcher-first baseman Gene Tenace in the unfamiliar environment of right field. Tenace played the new position without incident and went 1-for-4 with a run scored against Kekich and Sparky Lyle, but couldn't stave off a 6-2 loss to the Yankees.

The next day, Vida Blue endured his worst start as a major league pitcher and a small fallout with some of the Oakland fans. Blue allowed eight runs in six innings against the light-hitting Brewers, who saddled Vida with an embarrassing 9-4 loss. In the fifth inning, Blue ran slowly to first base on a routine grounder to shortstop, prompting a few boos from the fans at the Oakland Coliseum. Those fans, believing that Blue was failing to hustle, didn't realize that the left-hander had twisted his knee one inning earlier. "I hope better days are coming," Blue told *The Sporting News* after the debacle, which dropped his season record to an unsightly 2-5. At the same time a year ago, Blue's record stood at 17-3.

Blue's inconsistency proved especially frustrating to the A's. In his previous start, he had shackled the Angels, striking out eight batters in an impressive 3-1, complete game victory. Incredibly, the win represented only his second of the season. "It would be nice to see the season start over," moaned Blue, "so I could have some spring training."[35] Of course, Blue had no one to blame but himself for missing all of spring training and failing to keep himself in proper pitching condition.

Much like the quick disappearance of Orlando Cepeda, the A's didn't have much success, or patience, with another one of their June 29 acquisitions. On July 19, Finley released Art Shamsky, after the former New York Mets hero went hitless in seven pinch-hit appearances. The Oakland owner replaced Shamsky the next day, when he announced his 40th transaction of the season. Finley re-acquired former A's first baseman Don Mincher and utility infielder Ted Kubiak from the Texas Rangers for infielders Marty Martinez and Vic Harris, who had been recalled from the minor leagues only a few days before but had not appeared in a single game for the A's. On the surface, the deal seemed to heavily favor the A's, but Oakland sources indicated that the A's would also surrender a promising young pitcher to the Rangers once waivers could be obtained. Six days later, the A's sent Triple-A prospect Steve Lawson to Texas to complete the deal for Mincher.

Like many of Finley's acquisitions, the trade caused some contro-

versy. Since the deal occurred after the traditional June 15 trading deadline, each player had to wait to clear waivers. As a result, Kubiak, Mincher
and Martinez actually knew about the trade two days before it was announced. In his last game with the A's, Martinez started and collected
three hits against Milwaukee. The Brewers, who had gotten wind of the
deal with Texas, protested the game, claiming that the A's had announced
the trade of Martinez before the game. They reasoned that a player who
already been traded should not be allowed to play for his old team. As
with most protests, the American League turned down the appeal.

"I do remember some odd things (about the trade)," Mincher recalls
25 years later. "I knew of the trade early because we had some friends
from Huntsville staying with us; they had just come by on vacation. And
I remember having to stay quiet for a couple of days, even while they were
there... And I even played, I think I dressed out (with Texas), and was still
in (a Ranger) uniform, knowing that I was traded already." Such was the
cloak-and-dagger life of a baseball player who had been involved in a
Charlie Finley trade.

The acquisition of Mincher gave Dick Williams a quantity he desperately wanted — a left-handed power hitter to bring off the bench. The A's
had tried, and given up, on both Art Shamsky and Curt Blefary in that
role. Although Mincher had struggled to a .236 average in 61 games, he
had been hitting the ball well of late. Mincher had lifted his batting average 70 points in the last three weeks, and continued to lead the Rangers
in RBI's, despite his status as a platoon player. With six home runs, Mincher
figured to provide the A's with a decent long-ball threat in the late innings.

Mincher would have to make the difficult adjustment from playing
regularly to being used in spots. At first, Mincher objected to the trade.
"I'm just not ready to sit on the bench," explained Mincher, who had
played fairly regularly for the Rangers. "Although I don't want to get into a
lot of name-calling, and I won't, but I'm really disappointed...This trade
knocked me off my feet."[36]

Charlie Finley did not approach Mincher to explain his new role with
the A's, but Dick Williams quickly stepped in to soothe the disappointed
slugger. "Finley, of course, didn't," Mincher replies. "Charlie and I never
really talked about baseball; we talked about a lot of other things. We
were good friends. But Mr. Williams sure did and I appreciated it so much.
It's what made him a great manager. He told me right away that I was
going to play occasionally, that I was gonna be the No. 1 pinch-hitter.
When I got there, Dick sat me down and we had a long talk, and he told
me exactly what was gonna go on and I appreciated that."

Williams also realized that the announcement of a trade for a first
baseman might have a damaging effect on the psyche of incumbent Mike
Epstein. Williams quickly sought out Epstein, telling him that the A's had
acquired Mincher to improve the bench, not to play first base everyday.
"You're my first baseman as long as you can do the job,"[37] Williams as-

sured Epstein.

The trade provided renewed life for Mincher and Kubiak, who went from rebuilding mode in Texas to World Series hope in Oakland. In contrast, the deal cost Martinez his best chance at playing post-season ball for the first time in his career. After his three-hit game, Martinez boarded the Oakland bus, soon to be joined by reliever Bob Locker. The well-traveled Locker, who had pitched for the White Sox, Seattle Pilots, Brewers and A's, tried desperately to supply some philosophical psychology from his own experiences. "I don't know what I can say to make it easier for you," Locker admitted. "These things happen."[38]

The A's arrived at the All-Star break with a comfortable six and a half game lead in the Western Division. The margin, however, seemed less substantial when compared to Oakland's 11-game lead prior to the break in 1971. Nonetheless, a fine first half translated into ample All-Star rewards. American League fans chose Reggie Jackson to start the '72 classic; in fact, Jackson led all AL outfielders in votes. Orioles' manager Earl Weaver selected five other Oakland players for the All-Star Game: infielders Campy Campaneris and Sal Bando, outfielder Joe Rudi, and pitchers Catfish Hunter and Ken Holtzman.

Several other Oakland players felt they should have been selected, as well. Weaver overlooked catcher Dave Duncan, whose 14 home runs and 48 RBI's highlighted his power-hitting and whose defensive play placed him among the elite of the league's receiving corps. Weaver's snub upset Duncan, who had yet to play in an All-Star Game during his career. "I'm the best defensive catcher in the league," argued Duncan, "and I'm doing the best with the bat."[39] Weaver instead chose Boston Red Sox' catcher Carlton Fisk and Milwaukee Brewer mediocrity Ellie Rodriguez as backups to the Tigers' Bill Freehan. Weaver ignored A's first baseman Mike Epstein, who ranked in the league's top five in both home runs and RBI's. "I guess statistics don't mean anything,"[40] Epstein said with resignation. Weaver also bypassed the surprising Blue Moon Odom, who felt the Oriole manager had played favorites by choosing his own pitcher, Pat Dobson. Odom said Weaver should have picked either himself or Angels' left-hander Clyde Wright.

On the same day that he learned of his All-Star Game rejection, Duncan relieved his frustrations in a game against the Brewers. After being struck three times by the backswings of Brewer batters, Duncan felt the impact of a breaking ball thrown by Milwaukee right-hander Jim Colborn. Duncan charged the mound, only to be intercepted by several of the bench-clearing Brewers. Players and coaches from both dugouts piled onto the field, followed by residents of the bullpens. Even 50-year-old bullpen coach Vern Hoscheit tried to catapult himself over the bullpen wall, only to break his arm while tumbling to the ground.

Of the four Oakland players selected for the All-Star Game, three received a chance to play against the National League. American League manager Earl Weaver chose not to play Campy Campaneris, upsetting the veteran shortstop. Campy vowed to himself that he would exact revenge on Weaver, by playing as well as he possibly could in head-to-head matchups against Earl's Orioles.

Orlando Cepeda, who played with Campaneris briefly in 1972, raves about the subtle, understated importance of the scrappy shortstop to the Oakland teams of the seventies — offensively, defensively and in the clubhouse. "Campy Campaneris, it's too bad he don't get the recognition he deserved," laments Cepeda. "Boy, he was the guy. I remember that Dick Williams told me that year, 'This is my MVP. If we don't have this guy on this ballclub, no way we're gonna win no pennant.' Campy was a guy who play every day, he's a great teammate, a great human being. I'd like for him to be there in the Hall of Fame someday."

Campaneris first became eligible for Hall of Fame consideration in 1989, but received only 14 votes from the Baseball Writers Association of America — well below the five percent minimum needed to stay on the ballot. As a result, Campaneris is currently not eligible for election to the Hall of Fame. Rollie Fingers, who gained election to the Hall of Fame in 1992, won't go as far as Cepeda to say that Campaneris deserves enshrinement, but does believe the shortstop merits closer examination. "I think he should certainly be given a close look," Fingers says. "I don't know exactly what his lifetime batting average is, but he certainly was our starter for our ballclub."

Although Campaneris batted only .259 for his career, he nonetheless ignited the A's offense with speed and aggressive baserunning for 12 full seasons. "He was the guy who got everything started for us," Fingers says. "He played for years, stole a whole lot of bases, was a good leadoff hitter." Campaneris also cemented a middle infield that found itself in a state of flux due to a constant jumble of second basemen.

Great pitching kept the A's in front in the Western Division. On July 31, Vida Blue shut out the Rangers, 2-0, on a pair of hits. The next day, Ken Holtzman spun a three-hit shutout against the Royals. Catfish Hunter then made it three consecutive blankings with a five-hitter against Kansas City. Oakland managed to win despite scoring only 11 runs combined in the three games.

The series against the Royals proved costly to Oakland's manpower. In the August 2nd game won by Catfish Hunter, Royals' pitcher Dick Drago fired a fastball that clipped Sal Bando in the ankle. Bando stepped toward the mound, only to be intercepted by Kansas City's burly catcher, Ed Kirkpatrick. Bando and Kirkpatrick tangled, leading to an eruption of players from the bench onto the playing field. Dave Duncan tackled Kirkpatrick, preventing him from doing any further bodily harm to Bando. But Reggie Jackson pulled a muscle in his ribcage during the melee, aggravating an injury that already existed.

Just as Mike Epstein had returned to the lineup from an eye injury, the brawl with the Royals forced Jackson to miss a series of games with what doctors diagnosed as bruised ribcage cartilage. Later, the doctors discovered that the cartilage had actually torn away from the ribcage, forcing Jackson onto the 15-day disabled list. Jackson would miss three weeks of playing time.

When healthy and in the lineup, Epstein and Jackson provided the A's with the necessary lethal combination of left-handed hitting power. Ironically, the two sluggers had experienced difficulties relating to each other off the field. Jackson had started referring to himself as "Mr. B and B," an abbreviation for "bread and butter," as if to say that he drove in all of the important runs for the A's. Epstein didn't appreciate the arrogance of the self-appointed nickname and let Jackson know about it. Prior to another game, Epstein approached Jackson, the team's player representative, about obtaining some complimentary tickets for an upcoming A's game. Jackson asked Epstein whom he intended to give the tickets to, reminding the first baseman that he could only provide passes for relatives, not friends. "It is none of your business,"[41] Epstein snapped at Jackson, prompting a conversation filled with curses and shouts. Angry words soon gave way to the throwing of fists by the two strongest men on the A's roster.

Jackson, a taut, muscle-bound man, proved no match for Epstein. According to witnesses in the Oakland clubhouse, Epstein floored Jackson with his first punch. Although not as well-known as Reggie for power hitting on the field, Epstein's show of strength in the lockerroom should not have surprised any of his Oakland teammates. After growing up in the Bronx, where he had experienced frequent neighborhood fights, Epstein had starred in football at the University of California at Berkeley. A ramming fullback during the season, Epstein built himself up during the summers by engaging in the most physical of jobs: lugging carcasses around a meatpacking factory, toting bags of sand for an oil rig and running a jackhammer on a construction crew.

After the back-to-back shutouts against the Royals, the A's headed to Minnesota and Kansas City for a seven-game road trip. The A's, who had enjoyed 17 consecutive winning or break-even road trips, lost six of seven on their journey to the Midwest. After struggling to a record of 16-15 during July, the A's had followed up by losing six of their first nine games in August. In the midst of their worst stretch of the season, Oakland prepared for a critical four-game home series against the Chicago White Sox, who had managed to climb within a half-game of first place.

A Chicago radio station circulated reports that Charlie Finley was ready to fire Dick Williams, whose contract was scheduled to run out at the end of the season. Former A's announcer Harry Caray talked about Williams' imminent firing during a White Sox game broadcast. Reports out of Chicago and California indicated that the Cubs and Angels would pursue Williams — either immediately, if Finley were to fire him, or after the season, when Williams' contract would expire.

Prior to the first game against the White Sox, Finley telephoned Williams. The two men verbally agreed to a two-year contract extension that would keep Williams in the green and gold of the A's through the 1974 season. Williams summoned Sal Bando to his office, putting the captain on the phone with Finley. Bando, upon hearing of Williams' contract extension, told the other Oakland players the news. Almost to a man, the A's greeted Finley's decision with approval. "It's good," said Campy Campaneris. "Some people (the players) had pressure (on them). They thought maybe he wasn't coming back. Everybody started to say he wasn't coming back. Everybody started to say he might be fired. But now he can be more loose. He's a good manager. I think we can get to the World Series with him."[42] Joe Rudi offered his full support of Williams. "We all had been worried about him," Rudi said in reaction to Williams' extension. "We knew he had other offers. It eased my mind a lot. I love that man."[43]

While many baseball historians have classified Williams as abrasive and dictatorial in his managerial style, players like Sal Bando say such descriptions are inaccurate. "I think a lot of things are mislabeled on Dick," Bando says. "I mean, he was a strong disciplinarian, in terms of fundamental baseball and what he expected. As far as being a disciplinarian in terms of your curfew, your dress, your hair, no, Dick was very flexible there."

"He's very fair," utility infielder Ted Kubiak said of Williams during the 1972 season. "Once he chewed me out when I missed a hit-and-run sign in Kansas City," said Kubiak, "but when Jerry Adair, the first base coach, told Dick he had missed the sign, too, Dick apologized."[44] Bando says Williams' orderly, militaristic style of managing in Boston had created a false notion about his personality. "He was really a very friendly and outgoing guy," Bando says, "but everyone knew his reputation, so everyone kind of stayed in line." Bando says many sportswriters and broadcasters have helped created the myth of Dick Williams as a mean-spirited, inflexible tyrant. "I think a lot of it has to do with the media buildup," Bando says, "because he wasn't the ogre that everybody thought him to be."

Many sportswriters considered Williams an ogre, at least on the surface. On one occasion, *Sport* magazine writer Al Hirshberg approached Williams and asked him what he had done to improve Mike Epstein as a hitter. "Nothing," Williams fired back angrily while giving Hirshberg a glaring stare. Former sportswriter Bob Fowler contends that Williams' gruff exterior often proved misleading. Fowler enjoyed interviewing Williams, in spite of his outward appearances. "Oh, Dick Williams was outstanding," Fowler says without hesitation. "He was, how can I say? You had to accept the gruffness. And I don't mean to sound like an old-timer. But you had to accept if you asked (Williams) a dumb question, and Dick Williams said, 'Gee, that's a dumb question.' You wouldn't retreat with your tail between your legs. You would say, 'Well, OK, give me a dumb answer.' And then you would go on."

With Williams in tow, Catfish Hunter bested Stan Bahnsen, 5-3, in the opener of the series against Chicago. In the second game, the White Sox edged the A's, 1-0, on the shutout pitching of left-hander Dave Lemonds. Chicago then took the third game, 3-1, in 11 innings, as knuckleballing Wilbur Wood baffled the A's lineup. At their peak, the A's had built up an eight-game lead in the American League West. Now, with the calendar reading August 12, the A's had lost eight of their last ten and found themselves a half-game and .001 percentage points behind the resurgent White Sox. For the first time in 46 days, the A's were no longer in first place.

After the Saturday loss to the White Sox, Finley officially made his new contract offer to Williams. The two-year deal would pay the manager $60,000 a year. Williams accepted the deal, which would keep him on the Oakland payroll through the 1974 season. With Williams' new contract in hand, the A's prepared for the final game of the series against Chicago. Another loss and Oakland would fall a game and a half back of the Sox, who would enjoy the momentum of a three-game winning streak. Vida Blue took the ball against Stan Bahnsen, who was pitching on only two days after pitching in relief in the series opener. The A's pounded out 11 hits, including home runs by Campaneris and Duncan, and knocked out Bahnsen after six innings. Blue, pitching on three days rest, shut down the White Sox on four hits. The 3-0 win put the A's back in first place by one-half game. "We won that one for Dick Williams," said injured second baseman Dick Green. "Everyone played a lot looser. It (the contract extension) helped a lot."[45]

Spurred by the win over Chicago and the knowledge that Williams would remain in place for the foreseeable future, the A's proceeded to win their next three games. The White Sox, however, won their next four games to remain even with Oakland in the standings. The A's then lost five of their next seven to fall out of first place. During the stretch, even Williams made a mistake when he sent up left-swinging outfielder Bill Voss as a pinch-hitter against an Oriole southpaw. Williams fined himself $100 for the embarrassing oversight.

By August 27, the A's faced a crisis. Although Reggie Jackson had just returned from the disabled list, the team was still not hitting. Angel Mangual remained mired in a season-long slump. Voss, acquired from Milwaukee in the Ollie Brown deal, did not appear to be the answer to the center field problem. The A's had virtually no depth in the outfield. But Charlie Finley had one more trading card to play.

In June, Finley had practically given pitcher Diego Segui to the Cardinals, who fancied themselves contenders in the National League East. Segui had pitched brilliantly as the Cardinals' number one reliever, but by late August St. Louis had faded from the pennant race. Cardinals' general manager Bing Devine, looking to shed salary and rebuild with younger players, realized that now was the right time to repay Finley for the favor of giving him Segui earlier in the season. Devine agreed to send veteran outfielder Matty Alou and his $110,000 salary to the A's for Voss and minor league pitcher Steve Easton.

Although the Cardinals felt that the 33-year-old Alou was no longer capable of playing the outfield on an everyday basis, he was still a competent major league hitter. At the time of the trade, Alou paced the Cardinals with a .314 batting average, a better mark than that of hard-hitting teammates like Joe Torre, Lou Brock and Ted Simmons. Alou's hitting placed him fifth in the National League, behind only Cesar Cedeno, Billy Williams, Ralph Garr and Dusty Baker. The 33-year-old Alou had also retained enough footspeed to steal 11 bases.

Dick Williams immediately installed Alou as his everyday right fielder. In his first game in an Oakland uniform, Alou batted in the No. 3 slot against Indians' right-hander Steve "Stunning" Dunning.

The hard-throwing right-hander shackled the Oakland lineup over the first six innings. With the A's trailing 2-0 in the bottom of the seventh inning, Matty Alou began to figure out Dunning. Alou led off with a single, igniting a five-run rally against Dunning. The sudden offensive outburst helped the A's to a come-from-behind, 5-4 victory.

After helping the A's to victory in his Oakland debut, Alou struggled in his next few games, as the A's team-wide batting slump continued. Sal Bando had collected only six hits in 66 at-bats during one stretch. Joe Rudi, bothered by the flu, went only 4-for-24. Dave Duncan managed only two hits in 26 at-bats and went to the bench in favor of Gene Tenace. Thanks to the bullpen, however, the A's won five consecutive games to recapture first place from the White Sox. Dick Williams called upon his relievers in each of the five games. Middle reliever Bob Locker extended his scoreless games streak to 11. Short man Darold Knowles had now gone nine games without allowing a safety. Rollie Fingers had pitched scoreless relief in nine of his last ten outings.

The timely winning streak did not prevent Finley from engaging in controversy. In September, Finley issued an edict barring beat writer Ron Bergman from traveling with the team. Bergman had upset Finley with an item he had included in the September 16 edition of *The Sporting News*. "Listening to the A's play-by-play announcers," Bergman wrote about broadcasters Monte Moore, Jimmy Piersall and Jim Woods, "you get the impression they're in some sort of contest to see which one can make the most complimentary remarks about owner Charlie Finley."[46] Finley said that Bergman made "my announcers look like prostitutes."[47] Finley told A's traveling secretary Tom Corwin to physically remove Bergman from any charter flights he tried to board. Finley also ordered Corwin not to speak to Bergman, and not to make any of the writer's hotel reservations, as had been a customary practice by the ballclub.

Finley's treatment of Bergman typified his stormy relationship with the Oakland media. When local reporters wrote negatively of the A's and Finley, the owner responded vindictively. If a reporter described Finley in a positive light, he became an instant friend. "Such an irascible individual, almost difficult to describe in a pattern of words," says John Steadman, the longtime *Baltimore Sun* sportswriter who dealt with Finley as far back as his days in Kansas City. "I remember once when he was going to build his porch in right field to emulate what they had at Yankee Stadium. I wrote that he had every right in the world to do that. Charlie reacted in a very positive manner, and I guess he thought I was kind of a bright sportswriter. So he called me to thank me. And he talked and talked and talked. Someone in the office put the clock on it, and it was two hours and 45 minutes with one conversation." How much did Steadman get to speak during the marathon talk? "I was able to do a lot of listening," says Steadman, "I can tell you that."

Steadman recalls an incident during Finley's stay in Kansas City, when a local sportswriter named Ernie Mehl implied that A's manager Joe Gordon was acting as the owner's puppet. Mehl wrote that Gordon had once filled out a lineup card, with the words "Approved by C.O.F." scrawled across the bottom. The letters "C.O.F." represented the initials of Charles Oscar Finley. Although Mehl's sentiments did not reflect any unusual or uncommon view, Finley felt a need for retribution. "He ridiculed Ernie Mehl, the sports editor of the *Kansas City Star*," Steadman says. "Ernie Mehl was one of the most delightful men that the newspaper business has produced." Finley decided to exact some revenge on Mehl, in a very public way. "He had a 'Poison Pen Day' (at Municipal Stadium) to denigrate a lovely man like Ernie Mehl. I'd say in the newspaper business, you could go to the end of the world and not find a nicer, more compassionate or equitable man than Ernie Mehl. But that was Charlie."

Steadman felt special sympathy for the local writers in Kansas City and Oakland who had come under Finley's fire. "I know that Charlie had to be a tough man to live with if you were a sportswriter and you were working and covering his games. It had to be a test — a terrible test — to your patience."

Another of the out-of-town sportswriters found Finley an engaging and charismatic interview subject. "Oh yeah, great guy," says former Minnesota sportswriter Bob Fowler. "Great, great, great guy. Charles Finley was... he was a character, obviously. I have to personally qualify this. I like different type of people. People that are of the same ilk from a media point of view weren't interesting to me. I liked the different kind of guys. Certainly Charlie was that way. But the thing I like about Charlie — he was articulate. He was always willing to give you a quote. Now, all the people said, 'Well, he's an egotistical whatever' I always felt he was cooperative with me. He would answer your questions. He wouldn't duck them."

While the Bergman controversy did not involve any of the A's themselves, the 1972 season represented the beginning of an era marked by ill feelings between certain Oakland players. "It was beginning in those days," remarks Don Mincher, one of the few players who never seemed to be involved in conflict. "I can remember a lot of animosity in that clubhouse between individual guys, and it became a little bit cliquish to some degree at that time. Not very much, but I remember it forming. It was amazing the guys that had trouble with each other just forgot about it when they went out on the field, and then picked it up after the game. It was amazing to do that."

Mincher says the manager deserved most of the credit for keeping the players unified in their goal of playing winning baseball. "I still attribute a lot of that to Dick Williams, who really controlled that clubhouse," Mincher says. "He had good rapport with everybody, and everybody really respected him. A guy like that who was real intense, but once you know he knows what he's talking about, then you follow him. He managed to keep that (team) together for awhile until he couldn't keep his own job, reluctantly and sadly."

Mincher would be long retired by the time controversy had fully taken over the team in 1973 and '74, and by the time Williams had stepped aside after the '73 World Series. Yet, Mincher had seen the seeds of controversy grow. "Yeah, I can remember it beginning in '72. Of course, I wasn't there when it really got hectic, but I can imagine what happened, and I can imagine who was in the middle of it. It wasn't any fistfights or brawls or anything like that (in '72), but I remember the bickering, sure."

Second Basemen Used by A's in 1972
Tim Cullen — 65 games
Ted Kubiak — 49 games
Larry Brown — 46 games
Dick Green — 26 games
Dal Maxvill — 24 games
Marty Martinez — 17 games
Ron Clark — 11 games
Gene Tenace — 2 games
Dwain Anderson — 1 game
Sal Bando — 1 game
Curt Blefary — 1 game
Larry Haney — 1 game

According to Mincher, the media coverage of one player, in particular, served as a stimulator to controversy. "Reggie (Jackson)," Mincher says, "who is probably the most intelligent individual I ever played with, was always the center of the media attention, either good or bad. And he seemed to always be there. I can remember some bickering with other players and him. You know, Dave Duncan, who was Reggie's good friend, they had some problems. But David was a very stern individual himself, just like he is now, really demanding a lot of the pitching staff and himself. When an outfielder causes a pitcher to get in trouble with an overthrow or an error or something like that, there could be some things said and some words exchanged in those situations. And I can remember some of those. Of course, my old roomy, Sal (Bando), he wasn't very shy about stepping up to the plate either as far as telling people exactly what he thought. And there would be some words back and forth."

Mincher says the uncomfortable feelings created by such verbal outbursts never seemed to interfere with the team's on-field playing ability. "Like I say, these guys were great, great players, and they learned from most things, and while I was there we never had any fistfights or anything like that. And all of the confrontations led to good things, and they just played better, it seemed like, as they went along."

On August 30, just before the deadline for freezing a team's potential post-season roster, Charlie Finley made one last move to improve his team for the stretch run. Finley once again turned toward the rebuilding Cardinals, who surrendered longtime shortstop Dal Maxvill for minor leaguer Joe Lindsey and a player to be named later. Although the A's already possessed a fine shortstop in Campy Campaneris, they viewed Maxvill as another option at the troublesome second base position. Dick Green and Larry Brown had been sidelined by serious back problems, and Marty Martinez had been sent away in the Mincher deal. Although Maxvill had never been a threatening hitter, he still possessed fairly reliable defensive skills as a middle infielder and brought championship experience from his days with the Cardinals in 1967 and '68.

Shortly after the acquisitions of Maxvill and Alou from St. Louis, rumors sprang up that the A's would release both players after the season due to their salaries. Alou, at $110,00 per season, ranked as one of the highest paid players in the game. Maxvill made only $40,000, but even that figure was considered high for a 33-year-old infielder considered past his prime. Another rumor indicated that the A's owed the Cardinals another player as part of the Alou transaction. One newspaper report claimed the player would be starting pitcher Ken Holtzman, Oakland's best pitcher during the first half of the season. Dick Williams emphatically denied the preposterous rumor. After the season, the A's would send minor league catcher Gene Dusan to St. Louis to complete the trade.

Dick Williams, at the behest of Charlie Finley, had devised an intriguing, but strange plan to use Maxvill and the other second basemen on the team. "It was always a circus atmosphere with that ballclub," explains Don Mincher. "Charlie had decided that the second baseman on our ballclub should never hit. Therefore, we had four pinch-hitters ready. Every time the second base position come up, we'd pinch-hit." Williams installed Maxvill as his starting second baseman, but pinch-hit for him during his first or second at-bat of each game. Williams then installed Ted Kubiak at second base, before pinch-hitting for him. Williams followed with Tim Cullen, before replacing him with another pinch-batter. Once Maxvill, Kubiak, and Cullen had been exhausted, Williams employed catcher Gene Tenace at second base, despite the fact that he had never played the position before during his professional career.

With Green and Brown on the disabled list, Finley felt it best that

Williams give his second baseman as few at-bats as possible in order to mask their offensive deficiencies. In his first 14 games with the A's, Maxvill came to bat only 23 times, and totaled only five singles. Tim Cullen was batting .250 with no power or speed. Ted Kubiak was faring even worse, with an average of .196. "Well, I don't think any of us really liked it," says Kubiak, now the manager of the minor league Watertown Indians. "The way I looked at it after awhile — since I was a utilityman — I just said, 'Well, this is my job. I have to do it.' It was nerve-wracking...I mean you were under pressure to perform there."

While Maxvill's lack of hitting came as no surprise, given his .219 lifetime batting average heading into the season, the struggles of Matty Alou did concern the A's. Alou batted a mediocre .266 in his first 17 games with Oakland. Given his lack of power and unwillingness to draw many walks, the A's needed a higher average from Alou, their No. 3 hitter against most pitchers. Some writers reasoned that Alou, a line-drive, ground ball hitter, missed the artificial turf of St. Louis' Busch Memorial Stadium. Alou disagreed with such an assessment. "When you've got more than 1500 hits in your career, you've got to have all sorts of hits," explained Alou, "line-drive hits, high-bouncing hits, bunts. There are 300 players over there in the National League, and they don't have that many guys hitting .300, do they?"[48] Furthermore, Alou had once won a batting title by playing the majority of his games on natural grass. More likely, Alou had suffered in his transition to the American League due to his lack of knowledge of opposition pitchers.

Alou's defensive play in the outfield had come as a pleasant surprise. Prior to the trade, the Cardinals had already decided to move Alou to first base. National League scouts and beat writers had criticized Matty's range and poor throwing arm in center field. The A's had wisely moved Alou to right field, where he had handled all of his fielding chances without incident and had made a fine running catch to save a game against the Tigers. "I'm a good defensive outfielder," Alou insisted. "Reading that I'm not doesn't bother me because I know a lot more about baseball than they (sportswriters) do. I read these things and I laugh."[49]

By September 11, the A's had opened up a three and a half game lead on the White Sox, who had lost a key doubleheader to the Twins and had begun to fade. The A's then lost a doubleheader of their own to the Twins, allowing the White Sox to move to within two games of first. On September 12, Matty Alou enjoyed his best game to date, driving in four runs with two singles and a sacrifice fly. Alou's timely hitting sent Oakland to an important 7-4 victory over Minnesota. Alou collected two more hits the following day to help the A's to an 8-0 win, while expanding the lead over the White Sox to three games. In the A's next game, Alou drove in four more runs with a sac fly and a bases loaded double, spearheading a 12-3 win over the Rangers. Meanwhile, the White Sox lost a 1-0 heartbreaker in 11 innings to fall four games back of the A's. In three straight games, when the A's needed his timely hitting the most, Alou had rapped out five hits in 10 at-bats, collected nine RBI's, and scored three runs.

After his initial struggles with the A's, Alou had vindicated his supporters. The unorthodox batting approach of the five-foot, nine-inch Alou — his swinging at pitches out of the strike zone and hitting off of his front foot while using a remarkably heavy bat — had drawn criticism for several years. Alou strode with his right foot first, kept his bat back as long as possible, and then flicked his wrists. The result? Alou often blooped balls into short left field for base hits. Steve Carlton had once called Alou "the worst .300 hitter I've seen" and Ted Williams had remarked, "He violates every hitting principle I ever taught."[50] Yet, by bunting, hitting down on the ball, and spraying line drives to all fields, Alou won the National League batting title with a .342 average in 1966, and bettered the .330 mark each of the next three seasons. At the time of his trade to Oakland, Alou ranked fifth in career batting average among established major league regulars, behind only Hall of Famers Hank Aaron and Roberto Clemente and stars Rico Carty and Tony Oliva.

On Sunday, September 17, the A's expanded their lead to five games when Catfish Hunter registered his 20th win, a 4-1 knockdown of the Rangers. Hunter became the first pitcher in franchise history since Hall of Famer Lefty Grove to win 20 games in consecutive seasons. Considering his pedestrian repertoire of pitches and his struggles with mediocrity in the late 1960s, Hunter's emergence as a two-time 20-game winner ranked as an unexpected development.

In 1964, the year before baseball established an amateur draft, a horde of scouts had launched an all-out assault on Hertford, North Carolina, and its population of 2,012 residents. That's where Jim Hunter, one of the best high school pitchers in the country, resided. Charlie Finley shooed away other major league scouts when he arranged for a police escort and a black limousine to bring him to the modest Hunter home. "Mr. Finley started passing out green warm-up jackets and green bats and orange baseballs, and it sort of scared off all the other scouts. They figured Mr. Finley had me all sewed up."[51] Finley and the Kansas City A's didn't, at least not yet. The owner refused to give Hunter the new Thunderbird he wanted, but relented on a $75,000 bonus and a major league contract. For the hard-working farming community of Perquimans County, a $75,000 check represented an unheard-of windfall.

Shortly after his signing in June, Finley discovered that Hunter's right foot contained 30 shotgun pellets. During a high school rabbit-hunting expedition, Hunter's brother had tripped and accidentally shot him in the foot, resulting in the loss of his small toe. "My folks worried I would get hurt playing football," said Hunter, an all-round athlete during his high school years. "So, instead, my brother shot my toe off accidentally."[52] His brother fainted, forcing Hunter to slap him in the face in an effort to bring him back to consciousness. The two boys then walked off together to a local hospital.

Taking a passive approach, a local doctor had decided to leave the buckshot pellets in Hunter's foot. Finley wanted to tear up his major league contract with the injured teenager and replace it with a minor league deal, for far less money. The commissioner's office ruled that the original contract remain valid. Having failed to destroy the contract, Finley wanted to repair Hunter's foot. Finley instructed the scout who had signed Hunter, Clyde Kluttz, to take the teenager to the famed Mayo Clinic in Rochester, Minnesota. Doctors removed half of the pellets and some bone fragments from Hunter's four remaining toes, but the surgery knocked him onto the disabled list for all of the 1964 season. Baseball's bonus role and the possibility of losing Hunter to the first-year draft forced the A's to keep the 19-year-old on the big league roster in 1965, even though he had displayed only an average repertoire in spring training. The following spring, the A's planned to send Hunter to the minor leagues, but his surprising maturity and injuries to a few veteran pitchers enabled him to stay with Kansas City.

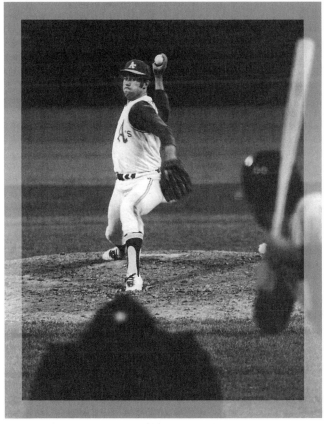

Jim "Catfish" Hunter pushes off his right foot, the one he injured in a boyhood hunting accident.

"It just so happened that he was my roommate," says Jack Aker, a reliever who had first joined the A's in 1964, one year before Hunter's arrival. "They decided he could stay with me, that I was safe and wouldn't lead him astray. Catfish was so impressive, not because of what he did pitching, but here's a kid right out of high school who goes on the major league mound and pitches as if he were a veteran. Catfish never showed a bit of fear or nervousness, anything that most rookies would show in that situation. He just picked up on major league baseball like it was another day back at his high school in Hertford, North Carolina." Hunter remained with the A's on a full-time basis, never spending a single day in the minors.

Hunter quickly impressed the veteran A's players with his demeanor, both on the pitching mound and in the clubhouse. "Very calm, cool customer on the field," Aker says. "Very personable off the field. Very shy when he was young. But a guy that, even though it took awhile to get to know him, everybody liked."

Although Hunter insisted that he continued to push off the mound with his foot as hard as ever, the high school hunting misadventure appeared to have robbed Hunter's fastball of some its velocity. Still, baseball scouts liked Hunter's control, movement and pitching instincts so much that they predicted he would become a right-handed Whitey Ford. The A's liked Hunter enough to reject an enticing trade proposal from the Orioles, who had offered former American League Rookie of the Year Mike Epstein and two pitchers for Hunter. From 1966 to 1970, Hunter pitched creditably, earning selection to a pair of American League All-Star teams. Yet, Hunter fell short of the level of stardom predicted by Charlie Finley, who had hoped Hunter would become a 20-game winner in 1968. That didn't happen until 1971, when Hunter finally became a bonafide star, aided by the development of a slider, continued improvement of his control and the addition of deception to his pitching motion.

On the same day that Hunter won his 20th, Wilbur Wood lost his bid for his 25th win when the Angels turned back the White Sox. Two days later, the A's and White Sox opened up a brief, but critical two game series at the Oakland Coliseum. The Sox needed to sweep in order to have a realistic chance of catching the A's with less than two weeks remaining in the regular season.

Blue Moon Odom and Tom Bradley started the opener of the series. Four hours and fifty one minutes later, the White Sox remained hopeful of catching the A's when they emerged with an 8-7 victory thanks to Jorge Orta's 15th inning home run. The two teams combined to use 51 players, establishing a new major league record. The White Sox used 21 players to snare the win, while the A's set a record by employing 30 players on the night. Dick Williams used so many players that he was forced to utilize veteran minor leaguer Allan Lewis, who almost never played a defensive position, in right field. Dal Maxvill, Ted Kubiak, Dick Green, Tim Cullen, and catchers Gene Tenace and Larry Haney all made appearances at second base, setting a record for most second sackers used in one game. Only Tenace and Haney came to bat, as the others saw themselves lifted for pinch-hitters under Charlie Finley's revolving door plan at second base.

The A's now needed a victory in the second game of the series to keep the White Sox five games back. Reggie Jackson and Sal Bando, who had struggled all season, hit second inning home runs against 24-game winner Wilbur Wood, giving Ken Holtzman a 3-0 lead. The White Sox scored twice in the fourth inning, but the A's rallied for two more runs in the fifth and one in the sixth. Rollie Fingers pitched three and two-thirds innings of brilliant relief to maintain a 6-3 win and a five game lead in the West. With only 12 games remaining, the A's had effectively closed out the White Sox' pennant hopes.

With a week to go in the season, the A's lost one of their most valuable pitchers to a freak injury. Darold Knowles, Oakland's best lefty reliever, broke his pitching thumb after flying out to left field. Knowles hadn't suffered the break on the swing; he had tripped while running out the ball, and had fallen awkwardly on his left thumb. The injury ended Knowles' season, forcing the A's to find another southpaw reliever. Charlie Finley summoned Don Shaw, who had pitched miserably with the A's during a brief early-season stint. Finley reached Shaw at the Palace Car Club in St. Louis, where the veteran pitcher was working as a bartender.

On September 27, a White Sox loss to the Royals, coupled with Oakland's doubleheader sweep of the Twins, reduced the A's magic number for clinching the division to one game. The next day, the A's hosted the Twins, who raced out to a 7-0 lead against Blue Moon Odom and Bob Locker. The A's pecked away, scoring single runs in the fifth and sixth, three runs in the seventh and two more in the eighth, to tie the game. Twins' reliever Dave LaRoche hit Sal Bando with a pitch to lead off the bottom of the ninth. Dal Maxvill, the fourth second baseman of the game, came to bat in the cleanup spot of Dick Williams' jumbled batting order. Williams instructed Maxvill to bunt, but LaRoche threw three straight balls before finally finding the strike zone. With the count three-and-one, Williams flashed the hit sign to Maxvill, who ripped a double. The extra-base hit scored Bando with the winning run, clinching the A's second consecutive American League West title.

Bando possesses a strong recollection of the moment prior to scoring the division-clinching run "I'll tell you what I remember most," Bando says. "I was having a good day offensively — I felt very good. I was leading off the inning, and in the on-deck circle, and I said to Maxie, 'I'm gonna get hit with a pitch,' and he said, 'Just get a base hit.' Sure enough, I got hit with a pitch, and Maxie couldn't believe it."

Maxvill had made two exceptional defensive plays in the recent critical win over the White Sox. Now, with Dick Williams having run out of pinch-hitters, Maxie had turned one of his rare at-bats into a pennant-clinching double. Much like Matty Alou earlier in the month, one of Charlie

Finley's late-season pickups had played an important role in the A's defense of the West against the White Sox.

Twins' beat writer Bob Fowler, who covered the pennant-clinching game at the Coliseum, says that the hitting heroics of a role player like Maxvill typified the A's newfound success. "I think that the Oakland team — yes, they had superstars like Reggie Jackson and and Sal Bando — but you look down the line, their bench was good, too. They had role players. They knew their roles. They were veteran guys, like a Dal Maxvill, who could come in and do things."

Fowler says that by adding such veteran role players as Maxvill and Alou to the mix, the A's had completed the transition from being a contender to winning a title. "When they added to their ballclub through trades, they were really destined for great things. They were a complete 25-man unit versus some of these other teams you see even today, where they've got 10 or 15 top-of-the-line players and they've got 10 guys sitting on the bench who don't know their roles or who aren't content sitting there; they're too young, they want to be playing, they're itchy. So you need that type of player, a Dal Maxvill. That's a good example of the Oakland team. They didn't clinch it by Reggie hitting a home run. They didn't clinch it by Vida Blue pitching a shutout. They won it with a Dal Maxvill hit."

After the game, the A's celebrated their Western Division championship with a variety of beverages. Backup first baseman Don Mincher, who had missed out on the 1971 division title because of a mid-season trade with Washington, dumped water on the head and shoulders of manager Dick Williams. In another corner of the clubhouse, veteran reliever Joel Horlen poured a bottle of wine on star pitcher Catfish Hunter.

Oakland would finish the season with a record of 93-62, far inferior to their 101-win season of 1971. Yet, the 1972 A's had overcome much more adversity: the spring training strike which delayed the start of regular season play, the holdout and mediocre pitching of Vida Blue, the season-long slump of Sal Bando, mid-season injuries to Reggie Jackson and Mike Epstein, and a constant upheaval of personnel which dramatically altered the composition of the starting outfield and the bench. Left fielder Joe Rudi enjoyed a breakthrough season, batting a team-high .305 with 19 home runs and 75 RBI's. Epstein and Jackson combined for 51 home runs, though neither broke the 80-RBI mark. Catcher Dave Duncan banged a career-high 19 home runs before slumping in September. On the pitching staff, Catfish Hunter won over 20 games for the second straight year. Ken Holtzman added 19 wins as the rotation's top left-hander, making up for Vida Blue's interrupted season. Blue Moon Odom earned votes for Comeback Player of the Year honors by winning 15, losing 6, and spinning an ERA of 2.50. Rollie Fingers, Bob Locker, Darold Knowles and Joel Horlen comprised the best bullpen in the American League.

Chapter Eleven:
A Catcher Plays Second, and a Shortstop Blows His Stack

T he A's prepared to play the American League Championship Series against the Detroit Tigers, who had unseated the Baltimore Orioles as Eastern Division champions despite sporting a roster that averaged 32 years of age per man. The Tigers, an aging team considered too old to contend prior to the season, had reacted well to the fiery personality of new manager Billy Martin. Tiger pitching carried an offense that was harmed by injuries to Al Kaline and Willie Horton. Mickey Lolich won 22 games, while Joe Coleman missed the 20-win plateau by just one decision. Woodie Fryman won 10 games in 14 starts, while Tom Timmerman and the comebacking John Hiller (back from a 1971 heart attack) fortified the bullpen. Veteran players like Bill Freehan, Norm Cash, Dick McAuliffe and Mickey Stanley brought post-season experience to the Championship Series.

The matchup of the A's and Tigers brought another intriguing storyline to the playoffs. These two teams simply did not like each other. They had already engaged in one full-scale brawl during the course of the regular season. Furthermore, Billy Martin and Charlie Finley had carried a grudge against each other ever since Martin had rejected Finley's managerial overtures in 1970. Prior to the playoffs, Martin called Finley a "chicken-*bleep* owner." Finley responded by labeling Martin with three insults, terming him "a liar, a phony and a 24-karat kook."[1]

Finley faced a more significant concern heading to the post-season, one that ranked slightly higher on the priority list than Martin's mental condition. Who would replace Darold Knowles on the 25-man roster? The A's had already moved rookie starter Dave Hamilton to the bullpen, giving them one competent left-handed reliever. If Williams desired another left-handed reliever, he could choose Don Shaw, whose ERA of 18.00 testified to his ineffectiveness.

Even though Williams loved the idea of having two left-handers available in the bullpen, the Oakland brass did not have enough confidence in Shaw to include him on the 25-man roster. Instead, the A's decided to carry a little-known first baseman named Gonzalo Marquez. The 26-year-old Venezuelan had been summoned in August from Triple-A Iowa, where he had batted .309. Due to his lack of power, the A's did not consider him a long-term prospect. Yet, the singles-hitting Marquez responded with seven hits in 16 pinch-hit at-bats for Oakland, including a game-winning RBI the final week of the season. Marquez's ability to handle the bat so impressed team broadcaster Monte Moore that he dubbed the Venezuelan "Mandrake the Magician." With Finley still insisting that Williams pinch-hit for his second baseman whenever possible, the A's recognized the value in keeping an extra left-handed hitter like Marquez on the post-season roster.

Williams selected Catfish Hunter, the A's best second half starter, to pitch the first game of the series at the Oakland Coliseum. Tiger manager Billy Martin countered with his ace, left-hander Mickey Lolich. Hunter and Lolich each surrendered an early run, before pitching shutout baseball over their remaining innings. Hunter lasted eight innings, before giving way to Vida Blue and Rollie Fingers. Lolich kept the A's off the scoreboard through ten innings. The Tigers' future Hall of Famer, Al Kaline, managed to break the tie in the top of the 11th, connecting for a solo home run against Fingers.

Martin elected to stay with Lolich in the bottom half of the inning. Lolich allowed the first two batters, Mike Epstein and Gene Tenace, to reach base safely. Martin called upon right-hander Chuck Seelbach to relieve his best starting pitcher. Seelbach faced Gonzalo Marquez, Oakland's 11th hour addition to the post-season roster. Marquez roped a single which dropped in front of Kaline in right field. Pinch runner Mike Hegan scored easily to tie the game, as Tenace raced from first to third base. Possessing a strong right fielder's arm, Kaline attempted to gun down Tenace for the inning's second out. Kaline's throw bounced in front of awaiting third baseman Aurelio Rodriguez, who could not block the ball from caroming past him into foul territory. Tenace scurried home with the game-winning run, giving the favored A's a dramatic win at home to start the series.

The A's carried the emotion of the extra-inning victory into the second game, as they pounded out seven hits in the first five innings, scoring a single run in the first inning, and four more in the fifth against

Woodie Fryman. The offensive outburst sent Fryman to the showers, forcing Billy Martin to dip into his weak bullpen. Meanwhile, Blue Moon Odom dominated the Tiger batting order, holding Detroit to three singles, in a 5-0 shutout. The second game, however, would be remembered most for an ugly incident that took place in the bottom of the seventh inning.

A's leadoff man Campy Campaneris faced Tiger reliever Lerrin LaGrow, who had entered the game in the sixth inning. Campaneris had done considerable damage in his first three at-bats, with three hits, two runs scored, and a pair of stolen bases. Throughout the game, Tiger pitchers had thrown fastballs in the general direction of Campy's legs, in an attempt to either injure the Oakland catalyst, or at least brush him back off the plate. Predictably, LaGrow threw his first pitch — a fastball — down and in on Campaneris, hitting the Oakland short-stop in the ankle.

Most of the Oakland players knew that one of the A's batters, given the Tiger struggles in the early part of the series, would eventually be-come the victim of a deliberate brushback pitch. "I was in the on-deck

Gene Tenace trots home with the winning run in Game One of the 1972 playoffs against the Tigers. As Reggie Jackson (No. 9) emerges from the left side of the Oakland dugout, Mike Hegan (No. 20) and Dick Williams (No. 23) compete in the high jump. Note the vertical leap of the 42-year-old Williams.

circle," said Joe Rudi, "and I feel the Detroit pitcher threw at him. Campy had run the Tigers ragged in the first two games, and when (Billy) Martin gets his ears pinned down, he's going to do something about it."[2]

Mike Hegan observed the pitch from the Oakland dugout. "There's no question in anybody's mind, and I think if the truth be known," Hegan says, "I think we saw something was gonna happen, but didn't know exactly what it was gonna be. Those orders to Lerrin LaGrow came right from Billy Martin — to start something, to do something. We had won the first game, and I think Billy Martin wanted to light a fire under his ballclub, and Campy was the guy that they were going after because he was the guy that set the table for us. There's no question that Billy Martin instructed Lerrin LaGrow to throw at Campaneris."

There was recent history of ill feeling between the Tigers and A's. Earlier in the season, Tiger relief pitcher Bill Slayback had thrown at Campaneris and Angel Mangual back-to-back, prompting Mangual to charge the mound. During the ensuing melee, Mangual had punched Slayback, Billy Martin had run after Mangual, Willie Horton had decked Mike Epstein, and Duke Sims and Oakland coach Jerry Adair had brawled. Another Oakland coach, Irv Noren, had been injured by Tiger relief pitcher Tom Timmerman. The 15-minute incident, which included fights and pileups, had left simmering feelings of hatred between the two teams.

When LaGrow's fastball struck the bone of Campaneris' ankle, the Oakland shortstop staggered for a moment, glared at the Tiger pitcher, and then, in an unusually violent reaction, flung the bat toward LaGrow. Spiraling about six feet off the ground, the bat helicoptered toward the pitching mound. LaGrow ducked down, barely avoiding contact with the bat, which ended up a few feet behind the mound.

Billy Martin led the charge of Tiger players and coaches from the dugout. Martin ran directly toward home plate, but three of the umpires managed to hold back the Tiger manager, preventing him from completing his assault on Campaneris. Nestor Chylak, the home plate umpire and crew chief, ejected both Campaneris and LaGrow, while attempting to calm an infuriated Martin. "You bet I was after him," said Martin, who tried to fight Campaneris in a sixty-foot area located between the two team clubhouses. "There's no place for that kind of gutless stuff in baseball," seethed Martin. "That's the worst thing I've ever seen in all my years of baseball...I would respect him if he went out to throw a punch, but what he did was the most gutless of any man to put on a uniform. It was a disgrace to baseball."[3]

Why did Campaneris resort to throwing the bat, rather than the standard charging of the mound? "I don't know why I threw the bat," Campaneris said later. "My ankle hurt so bad. I knew he was going to throw at me, but people now tell me it's better to go and fight. I don't know. I just lost my temper."[4] Campaneris' reaction left him confused and apologetic. "I'm sure he was regretful about it," Mike Hegan says. "You know, sometimes in the heat of a battle like that you do things that you don't think about, contemplate the consequences. Unfortunately, Campy did it, and had to live with it for the rest of the playoffs and the Series." The incident left Campaneris stigmatized for the balance of his career.

After the game, American League President Joe Cronin suspended Campaneris for the balance of the playoff series against the Tigers, and added a $500 fine. On the matter of Campy's availability for the World Series, Cronin chose to defer to Commissioner Bowie Kuhn. To the disappointment of Charlie Finley, Cronin elected not to suspend either Billy Martin or Lerrin LaGrow. "Nestor Chylak said he didn't think LaGrow was throwing at Campy," Cronin said, defying credibility, "so he isn't being punished," said Cronin. "Martin didn't hit anybody because the umpires subdued him quickly and so there will be no action against him."[5] The A's had lost on all counts.

Several days later, Commissioner Bowie Kuhn announced that Campaneris would have to sit out the first seven games of the 1973 season, but would be deemed eligible for any potential World Series games involving the A's. The A's were now 1-for-4. Mike Hegan says that Cronin and Kuhn handed down appropriate and fair punishments. "I think that was the right thing to do," claims Hegan. "The incident happened within our league, and against the Tigers, so he got the suspension for the rest of that series, which took him out of those games, and that was punishment enough for him for that period of time. Then you're going to a World Series, kind of a neutral set of ballgames, if you will, and then you go back to league play (in 1973), where you punish him and the ballclub the following year. I just think that was the right thing to do."

According to Dick Young of the *New York Daily News*, Bowie Kuhn had initially planned on a much longer suspension — one lasting 30 days. Negotiations with Charlie Finley and the Players' Association resulted in a more lenient punishment, a suspension of 10 days, which Kuhn later whittled down to one week. Young estimated that the suspension would cost Campaneris about $3,000 but speculated that Finley would make it up to his favorite shortstop by paying him a larger salary in 1973.

Although Odom held the Tigers scoreless over the final three innings to maintain a 5-0 win, Campaneris' bat-throwing escapade served as motivating anger for the Tigers. Campy's indiscretion also removed one of the hottest bats from the Oakland lineup, while depriving Dick Williams the services of his best leadoff man. Trailing two games to none in the series, Detroit rallied to win Game Three, 3-0, as the series shifted to Tiger Stadium. Joe Coleman pitched a seven-hit shutout, striking out a then-playoff record 14 Oakland batters along the way.

The series' low scoring theme continued in the next game, as the A's and Tigers played even through nine innings. With the score tied at 1-1, hard-luck Mickey Lolich left for a pinch-hitter in the ninth inning. The Tigers failed to score, forcing extra innings for the second time in the series. The A's scored two runs against Chuck Seelbach in the top of the tenth, closing in on what appeared certain to be the franchise's first American League pennant since the Philadelphia A's of 1931.

Unfortunately for the A's, Dick Williams had already burned his best reliever, Rollie Fingers, who had bailed out Catfish Hunter in the bottom of the eighth. Williams had followed with Vida Blue, who pitched a scoreless ninth but left the game for pinch-hitter Gonzalo Marquez. Those moves had left Williams with a choice of three middle relievers to work the tenth: right-handers Bob Locker and Joel Horlen, or left-hander Dave Hamilton. Although left-handed hitter Dick McAuliffe was scheduled to bat first in the inning, Williams opted for the more experienced Locker over the rookie, Hamilton.

McAuliffe and Kaline started the inning with singles, sending Locker to the dugout in favor of Horlen. Horlen uncorked a wild pitch, moving the tying and winning runs into scoring position. Facing the lefty-swinging Gates Brown with no one out, Horlen walked the veteran pinch hitter, loading the bases. With the A's playing the infield back, Bill Freehan followed with a grounder to Sal Bando at third base. Conceding the Tigers' second run of the game, the A's opted for what seemed like a sure third-to-second-to-first double play. The A's, however, were playing with a second-string infield. With Campaneris suspended, Dal Maxvill had started the game at shortstop, before giving way to a pinch hitter and utility infielder Tim Cullen. Starting second baseman Dick Green had been lifted for a pinch-hitter, but with Maxvill, Cullen and Ted Kubiak committed to playing shortstop, Dick Williams used his starting catcher, Gene Tenace, at second base in the late innings.

Tenace ran to cover second base, readying himself to receive the throw that would give the A's a forceout, and perhaps the start of a twin-killing. The novice infielder bobbled the toss from Bando, allowing Gates Brown to reach second base safely. "I think he heard my footsteps," offered the 230-pound Brown, "because he got out of there before he had the ball."[6] McAuliffe scored from third, to make it a 3-2 game, while the bases remained loaded. Instead of recording at least one, and possible two outs, the makeshift Oakland infield had come up empty. Reliever Dave Hamilton prepared to face two left-handed hitters, Norm Cash and Jim Northrup. Hamilton, perhaps rattled by Tenace's error, walked Cash to tie the game. Hamilton then watched helplessly as Northrup lashed a game-ending single to right field, in front of Matty Alou.

For one of the few times all season, the A's strange second base shuffle had cost the team a game, and a critical one at that. Williams had never really liked the constant lifting of second baseman for pinch-hitters, but for the first and only time during his Oakland tenure, he had agreed to follow one of Charlie Finley's in-game orders. Finley had often made pre-game lineup suggestions, which the manager felt compelled to follow, but once the game started, Williams usually did what he wanted, not what Finley demanded. Now, Williams' decision to go along with Finley's rotation of second basemen had led directly to an important playoff loss. Williams vowed to himself never to use the second base shuffle again.

The Tigers had managed to tie the series at two wins apiece, and now enjoyed the benefits of momentum and home field advantage heading into Game Five. The A's, meanwhile, seemed preoccupied with finding a way to restore the suspended Campy Campaneris to the lineup. Or at least Charlie Finley was obsessed with the Campaneris matter. At midnight, Finley held a press conference in his hotel room, pleading desperately for Campy's reinstatement. With Campaneris in attendance, Finley claimed his starting shortstop was legitimately sorry for the act he had perpetrated against Lerrin LaGrow. Standing off to the side of Finley, Campaneris nodded in agreement — perfectly on cue. Campaneris said only two words during the press conference: "I'm sorry." Dick Williams looked on, wondering why he couldn't be getting some much-needed sleep in his own hotel room.

After presenting his defense of Campaneris, Finley proceeded to attack the character of Billy Martin, whom he blamed for starting the bat-throwing incident. "I say with all sincerity that Mr. Martin instructed — no, demanded — that his pitcher throw at this young great star,"[7] said Finley in his best prosecuting-attorney voice. Finley claimed that he had tried to hire Martin in 1970, only to be talked out of the move by one of Martin's former employers. "Cal Griffith, owner of the Twins, told me I would be taking a chance with Martin's past record,"[8] Finley explained, before detailing Martin's rap sheet. A fight with Twins' pitcher Dave Boswell. A scuffle with Twins' vice-president Howard Fox. A knockdown of Chicago Cubs' pitcher Jim Brewer, breaking the left-hander's jaw. "That's Billy Martin," said Finley. "He suckered Brewer, he beat up a club executive, and he took advantage of one of his own players who was intoxicated."[9]

"He's a liar about the managing job," Martin retaliated. "We shook on the job and I was all set to go with them. Then the A's started winning and he couldn't very well fire Johnny McNamara with the team moving towards first place."[10] According to Martin, Finley agreed to send him scouting reports and films on the Oakland players, but never followed through. Martin then wrote the owner a letter, telling him he was no longer interested in managing the A's.

Without Campaneris and with Martin fully inflamed, the decisive matchup pitted a nervous Blue Moon Odom against Woodie Fryman.

The two starters had met in the series' second game. Odom hardly slept before the final game, perhaps two hours, if that much. The game started ominously for the A's, when the Tigers reached Odom for a run in the first inning and Oakland lost its most dynamic position player in the second inning. With Mike Epstein at first and Reggie Jackson at third base, Dick Williams called for a delayed double steal. Jackson crashed feet-first into Tiger catcher Bill Freehan, scoring the tying run. On the play, Jackson injured his hamstring muscle severely, forcing him to leave the game. The A's faced the undesirable situation of having to play the final seven and a half innings without Jackson and the suspended Campaneris.

At six feet, 200 pounds, Jackson possessed the build of an Adonis. His muscular arms, strong wrists and whipping bat speed made him one of the game's feared power hitters, but his 27-inch thighs and 17-inch biceps made him susceptible to frequent muscle pulls and strains, such as the one he incurred running home on the double steal. Dick Williams and several Oakland players helped a teary-eyed Jackson leave the field for treatment in the trainer's room. Mike Hegan and Darold Knowles then moved Reggie to a spot in the clubhouse where he could watch the remainder of the game on television. Jackson watched his center field replacement, George Hendrick, reach base in the fourth inning against Fryman. With Hendrick on second base and two men out, the slumping Gene Tenace stepped to the plate. Tenace, 0-for-15 in the series and one of the principal goats in the fourth game, delivered a sharp single. Hendrick rounded third, fast approaching home plate. The fleet-footed, lanky center fielder slid feet first, away from Bill Freehan's sweeping glove. As Freehan tried to apply the tag, he bobbled the ball, allowing Hendrick to score the go-ahead run.

Blue Moon Odom continued to shackle the Tigers, holding them to just one unearned run through the first five innings. Although Odom appeared fine on the mound, he complained to Dick Williams that he was having difficulty breathing. Odom asked to be taken out of the game. Williams complied, turning the ball over to Vida Blue to start the bottom of the sixth inning. The hard-throwing Blue responded with one of his best efforts of the season: four innings, three hits, no walks, and three strikeouts. As Detroit fans repeatedly hurled debris onto the field, Blue continued to keep the Tigers off the scoreboard. With two outs in the ninth inning, Tony Taylor lined a Blue fastball to center field. Perfectly positioned, George Hendrick made the catch with ease. A 2-1 victory gave the A's a three-games-to-two win in the American League Championship Series. For the first time in 41 years, the A's franchise had won an American League pennant.

Reggie Jackson watched the final out from the clubhouse. After shouting "We're champions!" to himself, Jackson limped over to his locker to wait for his teammates and cover his belongings from the upcoming onslaught of champagne. Jackson's teammates soon arrived. Vida Blue and Blue Moon Odom quickly embraced. Gonzalo Marquez immediately walked over to Jackson's locker, where Reggie stood by with the help of crutches. Jackson let the crutches fall to the ground, hugged Marquez, and cried. Later, utility infielder Dal Maxvill shook Jackson's hand and assured him of his importance to the team. "You're the biggest reason this club is here,"[11] Maxvill told Jackson, whose immediate future had fallen into doubt due to an injured hamstring.

The tears of camaraderie in the clubhouse soon gave way to feelings of bitterness. Blue chided Odom, his best friend on the A's, for leaving the game early. "Hey man," Blue snapped at Odom, "Why didn't you go nine?"[12] Odom explained that the tension of the situation had caused him to gag, almost to the point of throwing up. "Oh man, I know why you didn't go nine," Blue said, answering his own question. Blue held his hand up to his neck. "I know why."[13] The charge of "choking" infuriated Odom, who retreated to his locker momentarily before making a move toward Blue's nearby locker. Joe Rudi intercepted Odom, preventing him from completing his charge on Blue. Moments later, Blue apologized to his ally, explaining that he was only kidding.

Like many other fights in the Oakland clubhouse, what had begun as good-natured ribbing had turned into near fisticuffs. "I think a lot of that had to do with the intensity of the ballclub and the fact that the players were there to win games," says infielder Ted Kubiak. "Guys would be a little edgy, maybe because they weren't performing that well. Some of the guys would be getting on them in a fun kind of way, and it wasn't taken that way at that point. So things got out of hand. But they were able to stop and turn around and do what they had to do."

The presence of Charlie Finley as team owner may have indirectly led to more fights in the Oakland clubhouse. "I think Charlie Finley had something to do with that because he was so outspoken," Kubiak explains. "I don't know whether it was his design or whether it was just his method or just his personality, but he allowed the players to speak out also. There were guys that would be pissed off at him and they'd get angry and they'd say things in the papers."

Vida Blue fired a blast in the direction of Finley, whom he had battled since their vicious spring training contract negotiations. Blue charged Finley with "trying to destroy my career."[14] When Blue asked an attendant to give him a bottle of champagne he held in his hands, the clubhouse man refused, telling him that the bottle was reserved for Finley's wife, Shirley. "What did she do?"[15] Blue responded, wondering what the owner's wife had contributed to the playoff victory over the Tigers. Blue also turned his wrath toward Dick Williams, who had elected not to use him as a starter during the playoffs. Rather than tell Blue directly that he had planned to use him as a reliever, Williams had instructed pitching coach Bill Posedel to relay the message. "Why didn't he tell me himself I wouldn't start a playoff game?"[16] Blue lamented.

Jealousies and resentment aside, the Game Five win had lifted the Oakland A's to a status never before achieved. Reggie Jackson assembled his words appropriately in discussing the meaning of winning the pennant. "It gets us over the hump," Jackson explained. "It makes a lot of us pros. It makes guys on this club leaders. Now we don't have to talk about doing it, we don't have to get ready to do it. Now we've done it. We're the best, man, we're the best."[17]

Chapter Twelve:
The 1972 World Series — Liberals vs. Conservatives

Reggie Jackson hoped that he had suffered nothing more than a severe charley horse or a slight hamstring pull and might be able to play in his first World Series. As he sat next to his friend Dave Duncan on the team flight, Reggie suspected otherwise. Duncan cried, as did Jackson.

The A's flight would take them to Cincinnati. The National League champion Cincinnati Reds had defeated the Pittsburgh Pirates in a riveting five-game playoff. The matchup of the A's and Reds offered a series of clashing physical images: the green and gold uniforms of Oakland against the staid red, white and gray colors of Cincinnati; the clean-cut, conservative Reds against the brash, rebellious, hippie-like A's. As an organizational rule, the Reds prohibited all of their players from donning facial hair, either mustaches or beards. A few Reds — Johnny Bench, Pete Rose and Bobby Tolan — wore their sideburns fairly long, but nowhere near the dimensions of some of the A's. In contrast, 19 of the 25 players on the Oakland roster sported mustaches and/or beards, and some featured sideburns so long and thick that they touched the points of their mustaches in mutton chop fashion.

"There's nothing wrong with mustaches or beards,"[1] acknowledged Reds' superstar Pete Rose, who had worn one of baseball's shortest buzz-cuts during the 1960s before allowing his hair to grow longer in a mop-top style. "I wear them in the off-season, in fact."[2] Once Reds play-

141

ers reported to spring training, they had to part with all forms of facial hair. "The boss says no," Rose said, referring to Reds' executive vice-president and general manager Bob Howsam. "If he says no mustaches, no mustaches."[3] The more rebellious A's likely would have posed a different reaction had Charlie Finley tried to implement a similar ban on facial hair.

One of the A's few clean-cut players returned to the lineup for the World Series. Oakland regained the services of Campy Campaneris, who had been ordered to sit out the first five games of the 1973 season as part of his bat-throwing punishment, but would be considered eligible for all World Series games.

On the down side, Dick Williams learned that Reggie Jackson would indeed miss the entire Series. In the last playoff game against the Tigers, Jackson had initially pulled his hamstring about 30 feet from home plate. If he had stopped running at that moment, he might have been able to play against the Reds. Instead, Jackson kept running, scored a critical run, and did massive damage to the leg. "I could feel everything tear loose when I went into Tiger catcher Bill Freehan at the plate," Jackson wrote in an article that appeared in *Baseball Digest*. "I ruptured my hamstring, pulled it away from the bone, stretched the ligaments in my knee."[4] As gory as Jackson's description sounded, the pain felt worse. "Imagine," Reggie suggested, "someone reaching inside your leg and just pulling everything apart."[5]

Jackson's leg hurt him so badly that he could not sleep that night. Over the next several days, he could not dress himself, instead needing assistance to put on his shoes and socks. Reggie's outfield mate, Joe Rudi, offered tangible support to the injured right fielder. "He's the best friend I have," Jackson said of Rudi. "The man came over. He fed me. He helped me put my underwear on, my pants on."[6] Rudi's assistance typified the caring nature of a man whom Oakland pitching coach Bill Posedel, a veteran of 43 baseball seasons, once dubbed, "the nicest guy I've ever met since I've been in baseball."[7]

The absence of Jackson forced Williams to move the unproven George Hendrick into the center field slot on an everyday basis. Without Reggie, the A's found themselves stripped down to just one left-handed power bat. The inconsistent Mike Epstein moved into the cleanup spot against both right-handed and left-handed pitchers.

The injury to Jackson added to the general feeling of Reds' superiority. The oddsmakers made Cincinnati the favorite to win the Series. As the Reds' most outspoken player, Pete Rose, showed little regard for the talent of the A's. "The real World Series was between the Reds and Pirates," Rose claimed, referring to the hard-fought National League Championship Series. "Those are the two best teams in baseball."[8] The A's quietly took note of Rose's pre-Series comments.

As part of baseball ritual, the Riverfront Stadium public address announcer introduced the starting lineups for both teams prior to Game One. As the announcer read off the names of the A's, each Oakland starter ran from the dugout to the third base line. Reds' fans booed Campy Campaneris loudly as he took his place next to manager Dick Williams. After the starters sprinted onto the field, the announcer made a special introduction of Oakland's injured star, Reggie Jackson. Dressed in a long suede coat and assisted by a pair of crutches, Jackson made his way slowly onto the field. The fans at Riverfront Stadium rewarded Reggie with a louder set of cheers than any other A's player.

The outlook for the A's appeared even more dire since Williams could not use Catfish Hunter in the first game of the World Series. Since Catfish had pitched in Game Four of the playoffs, he was unavailable to start the opening game of the Series. Dick Williams chose Ken Holtzman as his replacement, a decision that likely did not please the Reds' offense. In his last start at Riverfront Stadium, Holtzman had pitched his second career no-hitter while still a member of the Chicago Cubs. Reds' manager Sparky Anderson selected ailing right-hander Gary Nolan to represent the Reds in Game One. Nolan, a 15-game winner and the ace of the Reds' staff, had battled shoulder soreness over the last two months.

According to the Reds' scouting reports, the ability to retire leadoff man Campy Campaneris and handle middle of the order threats like Joe Rudi, Matty Alou, Mike Epstein and Sal Bando ranked as the highest priorities for Cincinnati pitchers. Little attention was given to Oakland's No. 7 hitter, Gene Tenace. The Oakland catcher had hit only five home runs and batted .225 during the regular season before continuing to struggle in the playoffs, with just one hit in 17 at-bats. Yet, versus the Tigers, Tenace had swung the bat like a man on a hitting streak. "I was smoking the ball real well, hitting a lot of hard shots straight at somebody,"[9] Tenace told the *New York Post* in 1990. Furthermore, Tenace's lone single had produced the pennant-winning run in the final game against Detroit.

In each of his first two at-bats, Tenace lofted a Nolan offering deep into the left-field bleachers at Riverfront, thus becoming the first player to homer in his first two Series at-bats. The two-run blast and solo shot gave the A's a 3-2 lead. "I never hit two home runs in one game before," Tenace revealed. "The first one was on a fastball out over the plate. The second was on a hanging curve."[10] Tenace had taken advantage of a pair of mistake pitches — both thrown in poor locations by Nolan. "No scout in the world could help you on those (pitches),"[11] said Sparky Anderson, defending the Reds' scouting report and pitch selection against Tenace. Prior to the Series, Anderson had told his pitchers to throw Tenace strikes and not walk him under any circumstances.

In the meantime, the Reds hit Holtzman well, collecting four hits in the first five innings, while scoring single runs in the second and fourth frames. Holtzman struggled in each inning, but avoided further damage by stranding eight Cincinnati baserunners. Dick Williams allowed a teetering Holtzman to face the leadoff batter in the sixth inning. When Johnny Bench doubled of the right field fence, Williams called upon his best reliever, Rollie Fingers.

Fingers fanned Tony Perez and Denis Menke and retired Cesar Geronimo on a line drive to Joe Rudi. In the seventh inning, Dave Concepcion grounded a leadoff single to left field. With pinch-hitter Ted Uhlaender at the plate, Concepcion took off for second base. Gene Tenace threw high to Campy Campaneris, who arrived late in covering the bag. Campy applied a sweeping tag that appeared to miss Concepcion. Second base umpire Mel Steiner saw the play differently, calling Concepcion out.

Concepcion briefly protested what seemed like a questionable call. Steiner pointed to Concepcion's head, indicating where Campaneris had placed the tag. But television replays, utilizing a ground-level camera angle, showed that Campaneris had missed Concepcion completely. Since Campy had arrived at the bag late, and had been forced to reach for the high throw, he had been left with only one choice: the sweep tag. Campaneris had come up empty, missing both Concepcion's shoulder and head. A proper call would have allowed Concepcion, the potential tying run, to remain at second base with no one out.

After striking out Uhlaender, Fingers walked Pete Rose on four pitches and gave way to Oakland's newfound relief ace, Vida Blue. The unhappy left-hander, previously offended by Williams' refusal to use him as a starter, hurled shutout baseball the rest of the way to preserve the 3-2 win and give the A's the early edge in the Series. "He was told the other day that he'd pitch relief," Williams told reporters. "He volunteered for it today."[12] Perhaps reluctantly, Blue had offered his services to Williams as a Game One reliever. "Pitching is my job," Blue said tersely. "And when I throw the ball, I'm contributing more than anybody else."[13] Williams planned to rest Blue for the next two games and use him as a starter in Game Four.

Prior to Game One, few baseball fans outside of the Bay Area knew much about Fury Gene Tenace (pronounced "tennis"), who had grown up in Lucasville, Ohio, a small Midwestern town. His grandparents had immigrated from Italy and had decided to Americanize the pronunciation of their last name, changing it from its original "Tenacchi." Tenace's maternal grandfather branded the youngster with the nickname "Steamboat," in tribute to the unusually clumsy way that he walked — like a steamboat carrying heavy cargo.

Despite his awkward gait, Tenace began playing baseball at a young age, encouraged by his father, a former semipro player. Tenace's father drove him so hard to excel at baseball that he developed an ulcer at the age of 13. As a youngster, Tenace idolized the New York Yankees, until an unpleasant encounter with one of their scouts. Having just led his team to the Ohio state baseball finals, Tenace approached a Yankee scout who had attended the game. "He told me there was no way I could play in the big leagues," said Tenace. "That's when I quit liking the Yankees."[14] Tenace also experienced rejection from a Reds' scout, Gene Bennett, who informed Tenace that he had no future as a professional baseball player. Tenace eventually signed a bonus contract with the Kansas City A's organization. With the Yankees in the midst of a long post-season drought that would continue until 1976, Tenace was enjoying life as a World Series hero with the A's — against the Reds, no less.

Tenace had served as the A's second-string catcher, backup first baseman and pinch-hitter over the first half of the season. At mid-season, when starting catcher Dave Duncan found himself in a lengthy batting slump, Dick Williams had encountered one of his first lineup dilemmas. Since Duncan represented the strong defensive catcher that Williams liked, the manager preferred that he remain in the lineup, but knew that he needed better offensive proficiency, as well. Finally, Williams approached Tenace, asking the utilityman if he could catch. At any other time, Tenace would have leapt at the opportunity. Riding a temperature of 104 degrees, Tenace had lost 10 pounds from a case of the summer flu, and as a result, was in no condition to catch. Tenace begged out of the backstopping assignment, but did feel well enough to play first base. Williams gave him a start there, and Tenace responded with a triple. The next day, Tenace felt well enough to wear the catcher's equipment and squat behind home plate for nine innings. Dick Williams had suddenly found himself another number one catcher.

Given the lack of attention to him prior to Game One, Tenace was able to spend most of his pre-game routine taking batting practice. "There must have been 500 reporters, photographers, and guys with tape recorders cluttering up the field and wanting to talk to Sal Bando and Rudi and Bert Campaneris during batting practice," Tenace said in 1990. "No one wanted to interview me, so I stayed in the batting cage, taking my cuts, swinging at one ball after another and looking for Bando, Campy or some of the other guys coming into the cage to take their licks. But they were all tied up talking to somebody with a pad and pencil or a mike, so I just stayed in there, taking more cuts. That didn't hurt."[15]

Tenace received more media attention prior to Game Two, which attracted the largest baseball audience in the history of Cincinnati. A crowd of 53,224 fans, standing room only, watched Hall of Famer Jackie Robinson throw out the ceremonial first pitch only nine days before his death from a heart attack. In his final public appearance, the 53-year-old Robinson spoke eloquently of his desire to "see a black face managing in baseball." After Commissioner Bowie Kuhn assisted a nearly sightless Robinson to his seat along the first base line, inexperienced left-hander Ross Grimsley took to the mound at Riverfront Stadium.

Grimsley encountered trouble early against an Oakland lineup heavily loaded with capable right-handed bats. In the second inning, Sal Bando, Dick Green, opposing pitcher Catfish Hunter and leadoff man Campy Campaneris massaged four singles around a pair of outs, to give the A's their first run. One inning later, Joe Rudi reached the seats for the first time in his post-season career, connecting on a solo home run on a "thigh-high" fastball that Grimsley left over the inside third of the plate. "I was surprised how he had developed into a real good hitter," Reds' advance scout Ray Shore said of Rudi during the Series. "Two years ago I didn't think Joe Rudi would be a good player."[16] Rudi's defensive play in the ninth inning would provide an even more lasting image, one by which the '72 Series would be most remembered.

Hunter held the Reds scoreless through the first eight innings. In the ninth, Hunter surrendered a leadoff single to Cincinnati's powerful first baseman, Tony Perez. Third baseman Denis Menke followed with a line drive toward left field. The ball carried well, appearing to have a chance to clear the wall for a game-tying home run. Rudi raced back, neared the wall, and peeked over his head toward the flight of the ball. Within a few feet of the unpadded wall, Rudi turned to his right, made a forceful leap, bracing himself against the wall with his right hand. With his back to the infield, Rudi climbed the wall in spider-like fashion. With his left arm fully outstretched and his right hand braced against the wall, Rudi leapt for Menke's drive. His legs hovering several feet above the ground, the six-foot, two-inch Rudi attempted a backhanded snare of the ball. When Rudi's feet returned to the warning track turf, he held the ball up to the umpires, proving that he had robbed Menke of an extra-base hit. "It was as great a catch as you'll ever see,"[17] gushed Dick Williams, not usually prone to hyperbolic praise. If Rudi had not caught the ball, Perez likely would have scored from first and Menke would have coasted into second base with a stand-up double. Instead, the disappointed players in the Reds' dugout had to watch Perez, who had already rounded the second base bag, scurry back to first with one man out.

Rudi credited Hall of Famer Joe DiMaggio with preparing him to make such a play. In the late sixties, DiMaggio — an A's coach and executive — had instructed Rudi on how to turn his back on a fly ball, run for the wall and then turn his body back toward the flight of the ball. Did Rudi feel confident in his ability to make the catch as soon as Menke made contact with the pitch? "I didn't think I had a chance," Rudi said, while revealing that he had been unable to flip his sunglasses down prior to making the catch. "I thought it was gone." Rudi says he made a key snap decision after initially cradling the ball in his glove. "I jumped for the wall and hit it the same time I caught the ball.

I pulled my glove away fast because if it had hit the wall, the ball probably would have popped out."[18]

Mike Hegan, playing first base in the ninth inning, saw the play unfold in front of him. "I was pulling for Joe all the way," Hegan says. "I mean when it was hit, you couldn't tell, it was difficult to tell (if the ball would clear the fence). You're in a ballpark that you're not familiar with. If that ball is hit in Oakland, you probably know that it had a chance to go, or it wasn't gonna go. But there, you're just not sure. Joe Rudi was an excellent hitter, but Joe Rudi, for those of us who saw him play left field everyday, may have been one of the best left fielders that I've ever seen. He wasn't very quick, because he was a big country boy, and had heavy legs, but he got a great jump on the ball. Everything that he could get to he caught. Fortunately, he caught that one."

Onlookers at Riverfront Stadium immediately compared Rudi's leaping catch to heroic defensive plays in earlier World Series. "I'd put it ahead of two other World Series catches that have been written about a lot," Dick Williams said definitively. "The one by Al Gionfriddo of the Dodgers against Joe DiMaggio in 1947 and the one Willie Mays made off Vic Wertz in 1954."[19] Several writers mentioned Sandy Amoros' running catch in 1955 and Ron Swoboda's sliding grab in the 1969 Series. While Mike Hegan says there may have been better catches than Rudi's play, few carried more weight within the context of a critical Series game. "I don't know if it rates with the Willie Mays catch," Hegan says, "but in terms of what it meant in a big game at that point in the ballgame, it was as important a catch as any I've seen, or been personally involved. It saved the game and therefore won it for us, and gave us an edge in the World Series."

The next batter, Cesar Geronimo laced a screeching line drive to the right of Hegan, who had been inserted for defensive measures three innings earlier. Hegan dove, smothered the ball, retrieved it, and scrambled on his hands and legs to record the inning's second out at first base. "At that point in time," remarks Hegan, "what we didn't want to have happen was any doubles down the line, so that that run could score all the way from first, or you'd have runners at second and third. So, I was just trying to not get too far off the baseline." Hegan says the late afternoon start time of Game Two made the play even more problematic. "It was very difficult to see because you're in the shadows, and fortunately, when the ball was hit, I just reached out and stabbed; I didn't catch it cleanly, and had to kind of scramble back to the bag. That was another, I guess, game-saving play."

Although Joe Rudi's play against Menke would receive more attention, some in attendance at Riverfront Stadium claimed that Hegan had actually executed a more impressive play. Dick Williams praised Hegan fully, calling him "the best left-handed fielding first baseman in all of baseball, and that includes Mr. (Wes) Parker."[20] Williams' assessment tweaked the senses of some National League observers, since many considered Parker, the veteran Los Angeles Dodger infielder, the slickest first baseman in either league.

Williams certainly had ample reason to believe in Hegan's credentials. During the regular season, Hegan had set an all-time major league record for first baseman by playing in his 164th consecutive game without making an error. In addition to sure, reliable hands, Hegan possessed cat-like range to either side. Unlike slower first baseman, Hegan felt equally comfortable playing on either grass or artificial turf, where batted balls tended to travel faster and skid more often.

Although the Oakland defense had brought the A's within one out, Catfish Hunter had allowed several hard-hit balls in the ninth. Sal Bando walked to the mound from his position at third base, urging Hunter to finish the game off. "You're not even trying," Bando yelled, according to Catfish. "He's on me all the time in tough spots, trying to get me mad at myself so I'll pitch out of it,"[21] said Hunter, explaining Bando's psychological ploys. Sparky Anderson called back his No. 8 hitter, Darrel Chaney, replacing him with pinch-hitter Hal McRae. The backup outfielder grounded a single to left, scoring Perez to make it a 2-1 game.

Recognizing that the last three batters had hit the ball solidly, Dick Williams walked to the mound to remove a tiring Hunter from the game. "I wanted to finish," said Hunter. "I begged to finish."[22] Williams refused to listen and called upon a refreshed Rollie Fingers. The Oakland relief ace faced pinch-hitter Julian Javier, the former St. Louis Cardinals' second baseman who had played for the Redbirds' championship teams in 1964, 1967 and '68. In his final official major league at-bat, the right-handed hitting Javier weakly popped up a Fingers slider into foul territory along the first base line. Hegan ran into foul territory, planted himself squarely in the first base coaching box, and nestled the ball into his glove for the game's final out.

The pair of excellent defensive plays in the ninth inning typified the way that the A's won games, more so with their gloves than with their bats. "Really, when you look back at it," Hegan says, "we were not a great offensive ballclub. We were a very good offensive ballclub and had some explosive people. But Dick Williams, from day one that I remember being in Oakland, talked about pitching, defense and execution. Those are the things that we tried to do, and what he tried to do was plug the right people in the right spots. Fortunately, Joe made the play, then I made the play, and we win the ballgame."

The acrobatics of Rudi and Hegan overshadowed the clutch pitching brilliance of Catfish Hunter, who had sidestepped several potential Red rallies. In the second inning, the Reds had put runners on second and third with no one out, only to watch Hunter strike out three straight batters. Hunter told a group of reporters that some of the Reds' hitters may have underestimated the speed of his fastball, which featured late movement within the strike zone. When Pete Rose heard about Hunter's public comments, he erupted. "I don't want to make any excuses, but it's just that we put so much into that series with Pittsburgh," said Rose, referring to the playoffs against the Pirates. "Now he (Hunter) goes and says we were underestimating his fastball."[23] A reporter, sensing Rose's anger at Hunter, asked the Reds' left fielder if he would characterize the Catfish as a "super" pitcher. "No, I wouldn't," Rose responded tersely. "He's a good pitcher, but hell, I'm not gonna make him out to be a super pitcher because he's not."[24] Rose offered an uninspiring comparison of Hunter to two lesser known National League pitchers. "He reminds me of Rick Wise," said Rose, referring to the veteran right-handed pitcher with the Cardinals. "That's about how hard he throws, or maybe like Jim McAndrew (of the New York Mets), but he certainly is no Tom Seaver or Bob Gibson."[25] Rose then extended his criticism to the entire Oakland pitching staff. "Don't tell me their pitching is that much better than Pittsburgh's,"[26] Rose said, referring to a Pirates' staff regarded by several scouts as only slightly better than average. In the space of a few paragraphs, Rose had supplied the A's with sufficient bulletin board material to last an entire Series.

Although Rose's remarks upset the A's, they remained consistent with the advance reports compiled by the Reds' scouts. In an interview with Phil Pepe of the *New York Daily News*, Reds' scout Ray Shore echoed Rose's sentiments. "I wouldn't say they have the best pitching in baseball but they're good," assessed Shore. "Catfish Hunter is a lot like Rick Wise. Ken Holtzman is like Dave Roberts of Houston…If Vida Blue throws like he threw in Detroit the other day, he's in a category with Steve Carlton."[27]

Sparky Anderson added to the Oakland bulletin board by making a bold prediction. "I'm not a betting man," said the Reds' manager, "but even if the Las Vegas people make us 20-1 underdogs now, I still bet we'll win the Series in seven games."[28] Anderson did concede some concern, however. "I'm not going to panic just yet," Anderson told Red Smith of the *New York Times*, "but I'm close to that."[29]

Although Anderson felt confident in his ability to defeat Dick Williams' team, he held a special regard for the Oakland manager. The two men had played together in the Brooklyn Dodgers' farm system. In 1955 and '56, Williams and Anderson played as teammates at Ft. Worth and Montreal, two of the Dodgers' top affiliates. As a result, the two future managers had become good friends. In a World Series marked by hostile statements between opposing players, Anderson and Williams felt no motivation to make any inflammatory comments about one another.

Yet, some members of the national media questioned Williams' on-field strategy. Some writers wondered aloud why Williams had seen fit to make so many trips to the mound. Those same scribes criticized him for making too many pitching changes and substitutions during the first two games of the Series. "I've overmanaged two in a row now," Williams said sarcastically to his critics in the media, "and I'm tickled pink!"[30]

Yet, Williams did second-guess himself over his handling of his pitchers in Game Two. "I left (Catfish) Hunter in two hitters too long," Williams said of his decision to allow Hunter to face Denis Menke and Cesar Geronimo in the ninth inning. "Rudi and Hegan took me off the hook. But they shouldn't have to. I made a mistake."[31] Williams' self-effacing statement indicated his growth as a manager. By his own ad-mission, Williams never would have conceded error during his first managerial reign in Boston. Now a more mature and secure manager, Williams felt comfortable in pointing out his own strategical mistakes.

The Game Two victory left Williams and 24 of the 25 A's happy. The lone holdout was first baseman Mike Epstein, who was furious with Williams for having removed him from the game for pinch-runner Allan Lewis in the sixth inning. Epstein, known as a below-average defensive player, claimed that he could have pulled off the same kind of play that Mike Hegan had made against Cesar Geronimo.

On the flight to Oakland, Epstein rose from his seat and walked to the front of the plane, where Williams usually sat. Epstein seated him-self next to Williams, politely admonishing his manager for taking him out of a World Series game. Williams listened patiently to his frustrated first baseman, who did his best to calmly explain his feelings. "He did not want to come out (of the game)," recalls Mike Hegan. "Apparently, Epstein told Dick (Williams), and if I don't know if it was tongue-in-cheek or not, that if he was in the ballgame at the time, that would have been a double play," Hegan says, laughing. Anyone who had watched the defensively-challenged Epstein play first base on a regular basis would have held a radically different opinion.

Perhaps Epstein's touch with reality had been skewed by his con-sumption of alcohol aboard the light. Epstein and Williams would ad-mit later that they had both been drinking. According to Williams, Epstein issued him a kind of warning, instructing the manager to never take him out of a game again. "I just feel you don't appreciate the way I've been busting my tail," Epstein said to his manager. "I don't want this to happen again."[32] Williams, who moments ago might have been feeling some sympathy for Epstein, was now ready to strangle his first baseman. Williams exhibited unusual courage in shouting at Epstein, an oversized man once described by rugged backup catcher Curt Blefary as being so strong that, "He could pinch my head off."[33]

Epstein and Williams exchanged angry words for the next few moments. Yet, Hegan says he doesn't recall Williams and Epstein com-ing to blows during the argument. "I had heard that something had gone on up front (in the plane) where the coaches and managers were sitting," says Hegan, who was seated in the back. "As far as I know, it was nothing more than verbal." Nonetheless, the exchange left Williams convinced that Epstein was a selfish player, one who was more concerned about the personal issue of playing time than the team's goal of winning the World Series.

While Epstein's complaints had placed him squarely in the manager's doghouse, three other players had earned the monetary affections of an appreciative owner. "I don't know how well-known it is," Hegan says, "but on that plane ride back to Oakland from Cincinnati, he gave Joe Rudi, Gene Tenace and myself each checks for $5,000 for what we did in games one and two." Commissioner Bowie Kuhn later ruled that the payments were actually illegal bonuses, while Finley insisted they were merely "retroactive" pay raises. "Tenace was getting a minimal salary," Finley pointed out to reporters in an effort to justify his discussion of pay raises. "He was getting only $20,000."[34] Finley hoped to increase Tenace's salary to $25,000.

"The commissioner found out about it and tried to void it," Hegan recalls. "Charlie fought it and we ended up able to keep the money. At that point in time, it was interpreted as a bonus, which in contracts, you're not supposed to be able to do. Charlie did it anyway." In an article in *Sport* magazine, A's captain Sal Bando sided with Finley in voicing his complaint over Kuhn's action. "The ban on cash bonuses for outstanding play is one of the silliest of all concessions to tradition," Bando wrote in the first-person article. "Finley tried to change all that at the World Series. He failed because Commissioner Bowie Kuhn wouldn't let him do it. It transformed something very decent on Charlie's part to something looking underhanded and sordid."[35] Even a generous, kind-hearted act on the part of Finley had prompted a negative reaction from baseball's highest power.

Finley also announced that he had rewarded Dick Williams with a new contract, which included a pay raise. Media reports speculated that under terms of the new deal, Williams would make between $65,000 and $75,000. If so, Williams would become the highest paid manager in all of baseball. Kuhn could do nothing about that.

After a travel date, the ninth consecutive day of rain in the Bay Area forced postponement of Game Three. Amidst reports that the Series might be shifted to San Francisco's Candlestick Park, which featured artificial turf, Commissioner Bowie Kuhn ordered the use of two helicopters to dry the natural grass playing field of the Oakland Coliseum. The strategy enabled the Series to resume the next day — in Oakland. All three games at the Coliseum would start at 5:15 PM local time, forcing the A's and Reds to experience the alternating light and shadows created by the Oakland twilight. The unusual start times had been mandated by NBC-TV, which preferred airing the games at 8:15 PM on the east coast.

With the field softened by the continuous rain and puddles dotting the vast expanse of foul territory at the Oakland Coliseum, the Reds sought their first victory before a hostile crowd. Perhaps angered by Pete Rose's disparaging remarks about Catfish Hunter, a group of fans seated down the left field line pelted the Reds' left fielder with an array of foods and other disposable household goods. "One guy out there must have been a grocer," Rose said. "They threw everything, including oranges and eggs at me."[36]

Rather than use Gary Nolan on three days rest, Sparky Anderson opted for Jack Billingham, while Dick Williams countered with Blue Moon Odom. Both hurlers pitched brilliantly over the first six innings, maintaining a scoreless tie. Dick Green made two spectacular plays at second base, robbing Joe Morgan and Pete Rose of certain singles. In the seventh, Tony Perez led off with a single and moved to second base on Denis Menke's sacrifice bunt. Cesar Geronimo, better known for his fine defensive skills, swatted a line single toward center field. Perez stumbled rounding third, falling to the wet ground face-first, but still managed to score easily when George Hendrick tossed the ball toward Campy Campaneris, the cut-off man who was stationed in between the pitcher's mound and second base. Geronimo's single held up, as Clay Carroll saved the 1-0 game for Billingham with a scoreless ninth.

When a reporter questioned Hendrick's decision to throw to second base and Campy Campaneris' failure to throw home, Williams sprang to their defense. "Don't make a goat out of Hendrick," Williams said, scolding the media. "He was worrying about Geronimo trying for two bases... As for Campaneris, he couldn't hear our third baseman yelling about Perez because of the crowd noise."[37]

The sinkerballing Billingham, a .500 pitcher during the regular season, struck out seven batters and allowed a mere three hits over an eight-inning stint. "I don't usually strike out that many batters," said Billingham, not known for power pitching ability. "The twilight no doubt helped me."[38] The tenuous mix of shadows and glare also helped Blue Moon Odom, who struck out 11 Reds in seven innings. During the regular season, Odom had managed a high-water mark of nine K's.

Although the Reds won the game, a piece of unique Dick Williams strategy left a lasting impression on the fans watching the game at the Coliseum and on national television. With Joe Morgan on third and Bobby Tolan on second in the eighth inning, Rollie Fingers faced the Reds' cleanup batter, Johnny Bench. Fingers ran the count to three-and-two, prompting a visit from Williams. The manager pointed to Bench and the on-deck circle, and then aimed his finger in the direction of first base, as if to indicate to Fingers and Gene Tenace that he wanted to intentionally walk Bench. As he went through the motions of calling for the ball-four pitchout, pointing at just about everyone in sight, Williams told Fingers to throw a slider over the middle of the plate. After the conference on the mound broke up, Tenace stood straight up behind the plate, signaling for the intentional walk with his right hand. As Fingers began his delivery, Tenace stepped out briefly, then retreated toward his usual position, squatting to receive the pitch. Bench, anticipating the automatic ball four pitchout, watched as Fingers threw a sharp slider that crossed the outside corner of the plate. Bench started to throw his bat away and run to first, before realizing that he had just witnessed "strike three."

Williams had tried the unusual trick play during his minor league managerial career. "It never worked for me the few times I tried it in the minors," Williams admitted. "I never tried it in the majors until tonight. I think the only guy in the ballpark who saw it coming was (Joe) Morgan. At the last minute, he yelled to Bench, 'Be alive!' but it was too late."[39] Home plate umpire Mel Steiner watched Fingers' slider nick the outside corner and signaled strike three, sending an embarrassed Bench back to the Reds' dugout. After an intentional walk to Tony Perez, Fingers retired Denis Menke on a pop-up to keep the Reds from scoring another run.

The 1-0 win for the Reds underscored the domination of pitching in the Series. Through the first three games, the Reds and A's had combined for nine runs, for an average score of 2-1. NBC television opened up its broadcast of Game Four by discussing the extreme low-scoring nature of the Series, which had left some critics pining for more offensive action. Given the absence of Reggie Jackson from the lineup, the A's lack of offense was somewhat understandable; the Reds' batting order, however, featured Pete Rose, Joe Morgan, Johnny Bench and Tony Perez in its top five.

In the fourth game pitching matchup, Sparky Anderson chose hard-throwing left-hander Don Gullett to face Ken Holtzman. With the game again scheduled to be played during the twilight hours, Anderson hoped that A's hitters would have difficulty seeing Gullett's quick, rising fastball and hard slider. "The twilight here is hell for hitters,"[40] said Dick Williams, describing one of the most distressing hitting features of the Oakland Coliseum. The twilight had already played a part in determining the nature of Game Three.

Holtzman kept the Reds off balance with an excellent curveball, while Gullett overpowered Oakland batters with his 90 mile-per-hour fastball. The game remained scoreless until the bottom of the fifth, when Gene Tenace measured a Gullett fastball, pounding it over the left field wall. The solo home run by the newly-discovered World Series hero gave the A's a 1-0 lead heading into the late innings.

In the eighth inning, Reds' shortstop Dave Concepcion bounded a leadoff grounder between short and third. Campy Campaneris made a fine, backhanded pickup, but had no chance to throw out his fleet-footed counterpart. Instead of allowing Gullett to attempt a bunt, Sparky Anderson inserted Julian Javier as a pinch-hitter. An experienced handler of the bat, Javier softly bunted toward third baseman Sal Bando, who threw to Mike Hegan at first base, as Concepcion moved up to second. Pete Rose followed by smashing a pitch up the middle. The ball deflected off Holtzman's glove toward second baseman Dick Green, who retired Rose at first base. The 1-4-3 putout allowed Concepcion to advance to third.

With two left-handed hitters scheduled to bat and Holtzman still pitching well, Dick Williams walked to the mound. The manager surprised several observers on press row by asking for the ball from Holtzman and summoning Vida Blue from the bullpen. Why bring in another left-hander when you already have one in the game? The manager explained later that he had asked catcher Gene Tenace how well Holtzman was throwing. "He said he thought Ken had lost a little off his pitches," Williams related. "I had a fresh arm in the bullpen in Vida Blue."[41]

Blue walked Joe Morgan, the most patient of the Reds' hitters, and one of the National League's fastest and smartest baserunners. Bobby Tolan followed by stroking a clean double down the right field line. By the time Matty Alou retrieved the ball in the corner and returned it to the infield, both Concepcion and Morgan scored. Williams' unorthodox decision to use Blue over Holtzman had backfired. "The decision was mine," Williams emphasized. "I'll live and die with it, and believe me, for awhile, I was dying."[42] The Reds now led, 2-1, and would continue to hold the advantage as they entered the bottom of the ninth.

Reliever Pedro Borbon faced backup first baseman Mike Hegan, who had once again replaced Mike Epstein for defensive purposes in the seventh inning. Hegan grounded weekly to Denis Menke at third base for the first out. Dick Williams pinch-hit for George Hendrick, calling upon late-season sensation Gonzalo Marquez. The Reds' scouting report, compiled by Ray Shore, indicated that Marquez usually hit ground balls up the middle. Strangely, shortstop Dave Concepcion, who had played with Marquez in the Venezuelan Winter League, positioned himself several strides to the left of second base. Using a compact swing, Marquez chopped the ball — up the middle. The high-hopper was not hit hard, but managed to elude both Concepcion and Joe Morgan for a one-out single.

Pinch-runner Allan Lewis, the "Panamanian Express," entered the game for Marquez. Sparky Anderson told Borbon to check Lewis at first base, but not to throw over. Borbon ignored the order, tried to pick Lewis off of first base, and then ran the count to two-and-one on Gene Tenace. Annoyed by Borbon's lack of concentration, Anderson decided to bring in his best reliever — "The Hawk" — Clay Carroll. Tenace responded with a ground single to left, pushing Lewis to second. With Dick Green representing the next scheduled batter for the A's, Dick Williams instructed his most seasoned pinch-hitter to make his way to the plate.

Don Mincher had struggled after his mid-season acquisition from Texas, batting a mere .148 in an Oakland uniform. When Mike Epstein went to the sidelines, Mincher filled in at first base and failed to drive in a single run. "The Mule" ultimately returned to the bench, where he failed to hit a single home run and managed only five RBI's. Mincher finished the season with a career-low .216 batting average, but Williams trusted him in the pressurized situations of World Series play. "A lot of times when you're in slumps, like the 2-for-21 (earlier in the season)," Mincher recalls, "I knew in my head — Dick Williams knew in his head — it was nothing pressure-wise that was causing that; it was all physical. My mind-set was right." Williams realized that Mincher was one of only four Oakland players with previous World Series experience. Late season pickups Matty Alou, Mike Hegan and Dal Maxvill had played in the World Series for the San Francisco Giants, New York Yankees and St. Louis Cardinals, respectively.

Playing for the Minnesota Twins, Mincher had hit poorly in the '65 Series against an intimidating Los Angeles Dodgers' pitching staff, collecting only three hits in 23 at-bats. But Mincher had hit an important home run during that Series, connecting against Don Drysdale in Game One. Mincher says Williams realized his ability to block out the pressure created by a World Series game. "I was aware of the (pressure) situation," Mincher says, "but when I stepped in the box, it's just the pitcher and me. That's the only two people on the face of the Earth. And I think Dick knew that my thinking was still that way, even though my bat was sometimes kind of slow. And Clay Carroll was a sinkerball pitcher — he didn't throw hard — and those were the guys that all my career I could hit very well. The fans and the pressure and the TV, all those things did not enter into my mind because I had been there before."

By using Mincher, Williams was taking at least one major gamble. Mincher's ability to hit the ball hard, coupled with his plodding running speed, made him susceptible to grounding into a game-ending double play. Mincher says he never allowed himself to think about that possibility during the at-bat. "I can't think that way," Mincher insists. "I really can't. I know one thing. After my first two or three years in major league baseball, and through my minor league career, with a guy on first base and a ball hit well to second base or shortstop, it's a double play. I'm not gonna outrun a double play. I knew that. So, I learned not to even be concerned about it."

Later in the World Series when Mincher came up as a pinch-hitter, Sparky Anderson would counter with one of his left-handed relievers. "All the other appearances that I had had in the World Series, and ended up having," Mincher says, "they always switched to a left-handed pitcher and I was hit for. This was the only official at-bat I had in the World Series. I remember Sparky Anderson saying afterward that he had wished that he had done it again." Anderson resisted the urge to play the percentages and call upon hard-throwing left-hander Tom Hall, who was already warming up in the bullpen. Anderson decided to stay with Clay Carroll, who had handled left-handed hitters throughout the regular season.

Mincher had not swung a bat in a game since the final game of the regular season. Although he had been used as a pinch-hitter in the playoffs against Detroit, Mincher had taken three pitches — all called strikes. Dick Williams reminded Mincher to be more aggressive in his at-bat against Carroll. "I told him to go up there swinging," Williams said after the game. "I told him he hadn't swung the bat the last time he was a pinch-hitter."[43]

The advice not withstanding, Mincher took the first pitch for a ball. With the count 1-and-0, Carroll threw a fastball over the middle of the plate. "I was lucky enough to be able to get a good pitch I could drive, down in the strike zone," Mincher says, in recalling "The Hawk's" second pitch. "I tried to get a ball that you can drive up the middle or pull in the hole to first base. Those were the things I really thought about, and I thought about on that day. The ball went directly over the second baseman's head. If it had been on the ground, it'd been a double play." Mincher's upper-cut swing enabled him to lift the ball over the infield. "I remember it just like it was yesterday," says Mincher. "I got it in the right-center field gap, which probably should have been for a double, but I was cold and couldn't run." Mincher's golf shot into the alley scored Lewis with the tying run and sent Tenace, representing the potential game-winning run, to third base.

"It's the last hit I ever got," Mincher says, "and certainly it's the most vivid in my memory." Mincher left the game for a pinch runner, while Williams called on his third pinch-hitter of the inning, Angel Mangual, as a replacement for Rollie Fingers at the plate. The young outfielder represented an interesting choice for Williams, given the manager's displeasure with Mangual's frequent failures to advance runners during the regular season. With the infield drawn in, Mangual hacked at the first pitch, sending a routine grounder toward the right side of the infield. With second baseman Joe Morgan playing shallow, Mangual's dribbler squeezed through the infield, giving the A's their most dramatic win of the Series.

"Dick Williams keeps making mistakes, and he lucks out every game,"[44] said one National League manager, observing from the World Series press room. What game was he watching? What mistakes by Williams was he referring to? In the ninth inning, Williams had used three pinch-hitters, all of whom delivered, and two pinch-runners, one of whom scored. If Williams had managed less aggressively, the A's might not have won.

Game Four proved a testament to the depth of the A's bench, which Charlie Finley had tinkered with so often during the regular season. Marquez and Mincher, two players not with the team at the beginning of the season, had delivered key pinch-hit singles. Mangual, who had fallen out of a starting role after an impressive debut in 1971, had won the game with the most important hit of his career. Although many of Finley's critics had snickered over the incredible number of roster moves he had made during the season, the end results of Finley's maneuvering had left the A's with the best bench in all of baseball.

Ted Kubiak, one of the many mid-season pickups, says Charlie Finley had a knack for acquiring key role players at just the right time. "I guess that's his credit," Kubiak says, "finding guys that he needed to fill in. How about Marquez, the pinch-hitter that we had? I mean every time he'd come up, he'd get a base hit."

Another late-season acquisition had also helped the A's to their third win of the World Series. In the fifth inning, right fielder Matty Alou had robbed the Reds of a certain double when he one-handed a Pete Rose drive and crashed into the outfield wall. One inning later, Alou made another fine one-handed catch when he raced in and snared Johnny Bench's sinking line drive. The defensive play of Alou had helped

Captain Sal Bando (No. 6) leads the charge of A's after Angel Mangual's pinch-hit single ended Game Four of the 1972 World Series. Others pictured, from left to right: Gene Tenace (No. 38), Joe Rudi, Mike Hegan (No. 20), and Ted Kubiak (No. 11).

draw the A's within one victory of Oakland's first world championship.

Oakland pitching had played an even larger role throughout the first four games, shutting down the front three of the Reds' intimidating lineup. The first three Reds' hitters — Pete Rose, Joe Morgan and Bobby Tolan — had combined to produce four hits in 34 World Series at-bats. As a result of Oakland's concerted pitching efforts against Rose, Morgan and Tolan, the Reds' fourth and fifth place hitters had enjoyed few run-scoring opportunities. Johnny Bench and Tony Perez had teamed up for 12 base hits, but had not collected a single RBI between them.

The Series resumed on Friday afternoon at the sold-out Oakland Coliseum, where the A's — regardless of the outcome of the Series — would play their final home game of 1972. Catfish Hunter faced Reds' starter Jim McGlothlin in what appeared to be another major pitching mismatch in favor of the A's. The Reds' offense quickly did its best to remove the advantage. Pete Rose led off the game against Hunter and cracked his first pitch over the 375-foot marker in right-center field.

The A's eclipsed the 1-0 deficit in the bottom of the second inning, scoring three runs on Gene Tenace's record-tying fourth home run of the Series. Tenace, who had hit only five home runs during the regular season as the backup to Dave Duncan, had matched the all-time mark for most home runs in one World Series. The scoreboard at the Oakland Coliseum flashed the message that Tenace had equaled a record shared by Hall of Famers Babe Ruth, Lou Gehrig and Duke Snider and former Yankee slugger Hank Bauer. "I remember looking up at the scoreboard when they made that announcement and thinking, 'I don't belong with those guys,'"[45] Tenace said 18 years later. The Reds probably thought the same.

The Reds and A's traded runs in the fourth, before Cincinnati closed to within one run in the fifth. Yet, Hunter failed to last the minimum five innings needed to claim the win for himself. With Rollie Fingers on the mound in the eighth and the A's just six outs away from the title, Joe Morgan walked, stole second, and scored the tying run on Bobby Tolan's single to right. Tolan eventually made it to third base with two outs, but was left stranded when Fingers fanned Denis Menke.

Fingers stayed in to pitch the ninth, surrendering a leadoff single to Cesar Geronimo. Sparky Anderson decided not to pinch-hit for Ross Grimsley, instead allowing the relief pitcher to attempt a sacrifice bunt on his own. Grimsley popped the ball in the air, a few feet in front of the mound. Instead of catching the ball for a sure out and attempting to double Geronimo off first, Fingers listened to the advice of third baseman Sal Bando and allowed the ball to drop. Fingers hesitated for a moment, then fumbled the ball, realizing he had no chance to retire Geronimo, who had already started running toward second. Fingers recovered and threw to first, but his toss sailed wide of Ted Kubiak. The throw pulled Kubiak into foul territory, but the acrobatic second baseman managed to tag Grimsley out. At worst, the A's should have recorded one out and held Geronimo at first. At best, they might have turned a critical double play. Another mistake soon followed. Dave Concepcion hit a ground ball to third, but Sal Bando bobbled the ball for an error, with Geronimo holding at second base. Pete Rose then laced a single to center field, scoring Geronimo with the go-ahead run.

For the first time on the afternoon, the A's found themselves trailing. Sparky Anderson left Grimsley in to start the ninth, but the erratic left-hander walked leadoff man Gene Tenace. Playing for the tie, Williams elected not to hit for Kubiak. The second baseman squared to bunt but popped up to Tony Perez at first for an easy out. Williams decided to insert pitcher Blue Moon Odom as a pinch-runner for Tenace, and sent up to Dave Duncan to pinch-hit for Dave Hamilton. Anderson countered by bringing in right-hander Jack Billingham, usually a starter, to relieve Grimsley. Duncan, the forgotten man of the post-season but an accomplished low-fastball hitter, lined a single down the left field line. By the time Pete Rose retrieved the ball, Odom reached third base. Billingham prepared to face the righty-swinging Campy Campaneris, who had gone hitless in four at-bats.

Campy lofted a soft fly ball down the right field line, just a few yards past the first base bag. Joe Morgan drifted into the spacious foul territory of the Oakland Coliseum. Morgan called off first baseman Tony Perez, and with his back to home plate, made the catch for the inning's second out. Surprisingly, Odom sprung from third base and began an all-out dash for home plate. Morgan stumbled momentarily on the wet grass, fell to one knee, whirled, and threw a strike to catcher Johnny Bench, who blocked the plate and applied his glove to Odom as he crossed the plate.

Later, when questioned by the media, Dick Williams explained his decision to use one of his pitchers as a pinch-runner, a strategy not favored by many managers. "I hated to do it and usually don't, but we had already used Allan Lewis," Williams reasoned. "You have to take the chance. Odom loves to run the bases and knows how. He took a calculated risk and nearly got away with it."[46] Nearly. Home plate umpire Bob Engel, down on one knee, his mask off and his eyes pointed directly toward home plate, fired his right arm into the air. "Out," Engel bellowed, ending the game. Odom immediately yelled at Engel, enraged by the call. Odom sprung himself from the dirt and bumped into Engel, who had stationed himself in a low crouch near home plate. "I wonder what the commissioner will do about that?"[47] pondered Reds' general manager Bob Howsam. In a controversial decision that would upset the Reds, Bowie Kuhn elected not to suspend Odom for the final two games of the Series, but issued only a $500 fine against the volatile pitcher.

As he sat at his locker, bandaging his bleeding right knee, Odom refused to answer questions from the media. After showering, the angry pitcher finally agreed to talk. "I was safe," insisted Odom. "I know I was."[48] Television replays showed otherwise. Johnny Bench, who had blocked Odom from the plate and tagged him before he touched home, questioned the pitcher's decision to run in the first place. "He was dead," Bench said flatly. "It wouldn't even have been close if the guy (Morgan) hadn't slipped."[49] Dick Williams, who agreed that the umpire had made the right call, contradicted Bench's criticism of Odom. "Anytime you get a ball like that down the foul line," Williams said, "even though short, you've got a chance. We had both men tagging up and when Morgan slipped, Odom kept going."[50] Odom, however, hadn't noticed Morgan's brief fall. "I didn't actually see him slip," Blue Moon admitted. "I was going all the way because he had difficult position catching the ball and because he doesn't have the strongest arm."[51] Yet, Morgan had delivered a perfect throw to Bench. A lesser throw would have allowed the A's to tie the game.

Even though the Reds had won the game to draw closer in the Series, they had clearly been upset by the quality of umpiring in Game Five. Both Pete Rose and Clay Carroll flashed first base umpire Bill Haller the choke sign. Haller ejected Carroll in the ninth inning, one inning after he had already left the game. Haller allowed Rose to remain in the game, thereby averting a near riot from the Reds. Bowie Kuhn later fined Carroll for using abusive language.

In addition to arguments with the umpires, the A's and Reds had shown hostilities toward each other throughout the Series. In the second inning of Game Four, Hal McRae had toppled Dick Green in an effort to break up a double play at second base. McRae, one of the toughest players in the game, hadn't even slid on the play, instead lowering his hip and shoulder into Green, rolling the second baseman about ten feet behind the bag. McRae felt he had executed a clean play; some of the A's thought differently. Two innings later, Johnny Bench viciously knocked Green to the ground. "I don't mind it," Green said of the takeout slides. "I want to be in there playing, that's all. Actually I like it."[52] Some of Green's teammates, however, considered McRae's rolling block unnecessary and dangerous.

Several A's had also grown to dislike Pete Rose, the Reds' brash left fielder, who had belittled Catfish Hunter earlier in the Series. Neither Hunter nor Gene Tenace, in particular, cared for Rose's abrasive and blunt personality. Rose had tried to ride Tenace verbally throughout the Series, repeatedly insulting the Oakland catcher in exchanges at home plate. In Game Five, with Tenace behind the plate, Rose came to bat. Rose took several close pitches, which home plate umpire Bob Engel called balls. When Tenace questioned Engel's judgment, Rose responded by telling Tenace to cease complaining. Rose's interruption infuriated Tenace, who told the Reds' leadoff man to stop taking pitches and start swinging the bat.

The loss in Game Five prevented the A's from clinching on their home field, necessitating a long and uncomfortable plane trip back to Cincinnati. In order to accommodate numerous guests of Charlie Finley, the plane carried a full capacity of 163 passengers. "That was the worst plane ride I ever had," complained Dick Green, after the plane had arrived in Cincinnati at 1:30 in the morning. "It was crowded and there was little service... The bathrooms were filled with luggage and you couldn't even use them. It was a four-hour flight and I didn't get served dinner until 25 minutes before we landed."[53] Another Oakland player placed the blame squarely on Finley for the unusual airplane conditions. "Finley had his whole damn entourage on the plane,"[54] said the player, who preferred to remain anonymous.

Finley, meanwhile, had experienced his own difficulties on the plane. According to a report in the *New York Daily News*, Finley had invited an unnamed reporter from Chicago to fly the Oakland charter. When the writer boarded the plane, Finley allegedly threw a punch at him, although reports varied as to whether Finley's hand actually connected. Finley had decided to exact revenge for what he considered a negative story the reporter had written the previous week. The reporter, for his part, considered the story as a favorable one about the Oakland owner.

More tension awaited the A's in Cincinnati. Prior to Game Six, a woman waited to purchase standing-room tickets at the Riverfront Stadium ticket booth. She overheard a man utter the following words: "If Gene Tenace hits a home run today, he won't walk out of this ballpark."[55] The woman reported the threat to ballpark authorities, who quickly informed the A's of the news.

Dick Williams and Charlie Finley asked Major League Baseball to provide extra security, but elected not to tell Tenace about the menacing phone call until after the game. The police also supplied Finley and his wife, Shirley, with extra security. Three officers stood by the owner as he and his wife sat in a front row box near the Oakland dugout.

Finley's mood grew more worried as he watched the A's play miserably in Game Six. Vida Blue lasted only five and two-third innings in his first post-season start. Dave Hamilton allowed four runs in less than an inning. Bobby Tolan and Dave Concepcion teamed up to steal three bases against the ragged tosses of A's catcher Gene Tenace, whose awkward release and throwing motion appeared strained and painful. In the meantime, Oakland managed only seven hits against a quartet of Reds' pitchers. Angel Mangual typified the A's ineptitude when he beat out a ground ball to Denis Menke for an apparent infield single, but was called out for overstepping the first base bag. The gory details added up to an 8-1 rout for the Reds.

The A's did not take the Game Six drubbing lightly. As Campy Campaneris walked to the plate in the eigtth inning of the blowout loss, he sounded a message to Reds' catcher Johnny Bench. "We never lose three in a row," Campy told the future Hall of Famer. Bench replied quickly. "You've never faced the 'Big Red Machine,'"[56]

The "Machine" had handled one of Oakland's best starting pitchers with ease. Prior to the game, Vida Blue had annoyed some of the Reds with what they interpreted as degrading comments. "Vida's a fine pitcher, I'm sure," said Joe Morgan, who had collected two hits in the seven-run rout. "But we faced Steve Carlton all through the year, and he's the best left-handed pitcher in baseball."[57] In other words, Morgan felt Blue, who hadn't pitched as well as Carlton in 1972, might be well-advised to keep his mouth shut the next time.

While Blue's statements to the media had upset the Reds, the A's had come away from Game Six burning with resentment toward Cincinnati's players. In the seventh inning, with the Reds already leading by five runs, Bobby Tolan had decided to steal second base. The Reds had stolen at will throughout the Series, party because of Gene Tenace's subpar throwing arm and partly due to the inability of Oakland pitchers to hold Cincinnati baserunners close to first base. Yet, several A's considered Tolan's stolen base unnecessary and un-sportsmanlike, given the one-sided score. Later in the inning, Tolan reached third base. Gene Tenace tried to pick him off by firing quickly to Sal Bando, who drove his leg and arms into Tolan. Bando claimed that he tripped and fell onto Tolan, but the Reds didn't believe him. "We're out to win a world championship" said Joe Morgan, defending Tolan's late-game stolen base. "You never have enough runs."[58]

The only good news the A's received during the game involved the apprehension of the man who had placed a threat on the life of Gene Tenace. Police arrested a 32-year-old Louisville, Kentucky man who possessed a loaded gun and a bottle of whiskey. "It's terrible something like that has to happen," said a stunned Tenace. "It's terrible people can't go to a ballgame and enjoy the game without that kind of thing. It scares me, but I'll play tomorrow," Tenace vowed. "I'm a little scared, but what can I do, tell the manager not to play me?"[59]

Even in the face of death threats and arrests, the A's attempted to deflect the situation with morbid humor. As Tenace fielded questions from writers in the clubhouse, Reggie Jackson offered him some twisted encouragement. "If you got to go, Gene," Jackson said, "at least it will be on national television."[60]

Tenace didn't hear anything more about the incident until 10 years later, when he was playing in another World Series — as a member of the St. Louis Cardinals. "I was opening my mail," Tenace said, "and there was a letter from this guy saying he was sorry for what he did and that he was glad they caught him."[61] Instead of comforting him, the letter disturbed Tenace, who felt the man may have been following him. Tenace quickly contacted the police and gave them the letter. Fortunately, Tenace never heard from the man again.

Chapter Thirteen:
The Machine vs. The Mustaches

Now that the issue of the death threat had been settled, the A's needed to regroup for Game Seven. "We were overmatched today, but we'll show up tomorrow," proclaimed a hopeful Dick Williams, who had managed only about three hours worth of sleep the previous night. "They got to my secondary pitching today for most of their runs, but we're still confident that we can win."[1]

Williams' confidence aside, the A's had blown a two-game lead, and had forced themselves into having to win a decisive game on the road. The Reds now had momentum, home field advantage and one of their hottest starters, Jack Billingham, in their favor heading into Game Seven. Williams would have to rely on his third-best starter, Blue Moon Odom, whom many writers felt should have suspended for his bumping of umpire Bob Engel in Game Five. Oddsmakers liked the Reds' chances of winning a third consecutive game, making Cincinnati 3-to-2 favorites to win the seventh game. With a win, the Reds would become the first team in major league history to capture a World Series after losing the first two games at home.

Williams, who had placed his stamp on the Series with his incessant visits to the pitching mound, prepared several lineup changes for Game Seven. Ever the strategist, Williams wanted to leave nothing to chance in his quest for his first world championship. Concerned about the Reds' success in stealing six bases over the last two games of the

163

Series, and 11 in 13 attempts over the length of the Series, Williams inserted Dave Duncan as his catcher and moved the weak-throwing Gene Tenace to first base. The dual moves resulted in the benching of regular first baseman Mike Epstein, who was hitless in the series. Consistent with his managing philosophy, Williams believed in benching slumping, unproductive players and replacing them with others who might be more helpful.

The news did not please Epstein, who felt he had swung the bat well throughout the Series, despite going 0-for-16. "I've been hitting the ball hard," Epstein insisted. "I've hit seven good shots on the nose, but they've been caught."[2] The absence of Reggie Jackson had placed extra pressure on Epstein to produce left-handed power. With Jackson unavailable, the Reds had pitched carefully to Epstein, throwing him off-speed pitches just off the outside corner. For his part, Williams didn't care why Epstein hadn't been hitting; he preferred looking at bottom-line results.

After cloudy skies and light rain threatened Game Seven, the weather cleared moments before gametime. A paid crowd of 56,040 fans — including 5,000 standing room customers — streamed into Riverfront Stadium, eclipsing the Reds' franchise mark set earlier in the Series. The record gathering witnessed two small doses of good fortune for the A's in the first inning. With one out, Angel Mangual hit a medium depth line drive into right-center field. Center fielder Bobby Tolan misjudged the liner, first running in, then trying to retrace his steps backward. Tolan leapt, the ball caromed off of his glove for a critical three-base error. The A's must have felt special satisfaction in watching Tolan falter on the play, considering his late-inning stolen base in the Game Six blowout. After the Series, Tolan admitted that many of the hard feelings between players on both teams had been initiated by the Reds. "We tried to get them upset after we lost the first two," Tolan would reveal to Dick Young of the *New York Daily News*. "You're down 2-and-0, you gotta try something."[3]

After the Tolan error, Joe Rudi flied to shallow left field, with Mangual holding at third. Gene Tenace then chopped a grounder to third baseman Denis Menke. The veteran infielder readied himself to field the routine grounder on a large carom, then watched the ball bounce high after hitting a seam in the artificial turf. The ball nicked the top of Menke's glove before rolling into short left field. The bad-hop single gave the A's an early 1-0 lead.

In the fourth inning, Dick Williams' seventh game defensive changes paid a critical dividend. Joe Morgan drew a one-out walk. Having been burned by Reds' base stealers throughout the Series, Blue Moon Odom threw over to first base seven times. Undeterred by the extra attention, Morgan broke for second two pitches later. Catcher Dave Duncan snapped quickly out of his crouch and hurled a strong, high throw toward second base. For the first time in the Series, the A's had thrown Morgan out on an attempted steal.

Odom held the Reds scoreless until the fifth. Tony Perez doubled down the left field line and moved up to second on a one-out walk. Odom then ran the count to two-and-one on Dave Concepcion. Playing it like the seventh game of the World Series that it was, Williams pulled Odom and replaced him with his best starting pitcher, Catfish Hunter. Catfish completed the walk by throwing two more balls to Concepcion. With the bases loaded, Hunter allowed two long fly balls to Angel Mangual in right-center field, the first one scoring the tying run.

Sparky Anderson paid a price for tying the game in the fifth, however, since he used Hal McRae as a pinch hitter for the effective Jack Billingham. Pedro Borbon entered the game and allowed a leadoff single to Campy Campaneris. After a sacrifice bunt by Mangual, Joe Rudi grounded to second for the second out, as Campy advanced to third. With two out and two bases open, Borbon faced Cincinnati nemesis Gene Tenace.

For some reason, Anderson decided not to intentionally walk Tenace, who had already driven in eight runs and collected four homers in the Series. Tenace promptly lined a Borbon delivery into the left field corner to score Campaneris with the go-ahead run. Williams inserted Allan Lewis as a pinch-runner for Tenace, a move that upset the Oakland World Series hero. Lewis had successfully stolen six bases in six late-season tries, but Tenace considered himself the fifth fastest runner on the team, trailing only Lewis, Campaneris, Reggie Jackson and Matty Alou. "Look I'm not a slow runner," complained Tenace. "I scored plenty of times from second base during the regular season and I could have done it again."[4]

Sal Bando followed with a soaring fly ball toward deep center field. When Bobby Tolan reached the warning track, his left leg collapsed underneath him, the result of pulling a hamstring. The ball landed on the track, bounced off the wall, and into the glove of the injured Tolan. Oakland now led 3-1. The A's eventually threatened to put the game away when they loaded the bases with two outs, but reliever Clay Carroll fanned Dick Green to end the threat.

In the sixth inning, the Reds put runners on second and third with two outs before Hunter retired Denis Menke on a fly ball to short right field. In the seventh inning, Hunter retired the Reds in order. Dick Williams left Hunter in to pitch the eighth, with the top of the Reds' order scheduled to bat: Pete Rose, Joe Morgan, and George Foster, who had replaced the hobbled Bobby Tolan.

Rose bounced a grounder up the middle past Hunter into center field. With the left-handed Morgan set to bat, Williams replaced Hunter with Ken Holtzman, who had started Game Four. The strategy did not work. Morgan doubled to right field, advancing Rose to third base. When Morgan's liner bounced off the corner wall away from Matty Alou, Reds' third base coach Alex Grammas momentarily waved Rose home, then changed his mind. Several Reds players believed that Rose would have scored easily if Grammas had not told him to retreat.

Sparky Anderson sent up the veteran Julian Javier to pinch-hit for George Foster, who had not yet established himself as a feared major league power hitter. Williams countered with ace reliever Rollie Fingers, who had already appeared in five of the six Series games. With his trademark toothpick hanging from his mouth, Fingers casually strode in from the visiting bullpen. Three days earlier, Fingers wouldn't have believed that he could pitch in Game Seven. "After the fifth game, my arm was completely dead," Fingers would say later. "I couldn't comb my hair, wipe my... whatever you want to write."[5] With an off-day for travel and no need to pitch in the Game Six rout, Fingers now felt rejuvenated for the Series' decisive matchup.

Sparky Anderson called Javier back to the dugout and sent up the lefty-hitting Joe Hague. The backup first baseman popped up harmlessly to Campy Campaneris in short left. Williams instructed Fingers to intentionally pass Johnny Bench, in order to set up a double play opportunity. The strategy seemed dubious, since it brought a hotter hitter to the plate in Tony Perez and put the potential go-ahead run on first base. Perez, hitting over .400 in the Series, lofted a fly ball to right to score Rose with the Reds' second run. After Bench stole second, Fingers induced Denis Menke into hitting a routine fly ball to Joe Rudi in left.

The A's had stopped the Reds' rally just in time, preserving an uncomfortable one-run lead. Williams allowed Fingers to bat in the ninth, not wanting to remove his best reliever. In the bottom half of the inning, Fingers retired Cesar Geronimo on a pop-up and Dave Concepcion on a grounder. Sparky Anderson, having already used up his best pinch-hitting options, sent up the weak-hitting Darrel Chaney to bat for pitcher Tom Hall.

Much to the displeasure of Dick Williams, Fingers hit Chaney with a pitch. That enabled the Reds to bring Pete Rose to the plate. "Charley Hustle" had batted only .220 in the Series, but had powered a home run while batting left-handed to lead off Game Five. Dick Williams walked to the mound, considering the possibility of bringing in Vida Blue to make Rose hit right-handed — his weaker side. Dave Duncan, huddling with Williams, convinced his manager to keep Fingers in the game.

Batting out of his severe left-handed crouch, Rose intensely eyed Fingers and drove a letter-high fastball to left-center field. The ball was hit well and appeared to have a momentary chance of splitting the gap, though well short of home run distance. The most reliable of the A's defensively, Joe Rudi calmly took several short strides toward left-center, stopped in front of the warning track and made a sure, two-handed catch, finalizing the Bay Area's first world championship.

Rollie Fingers hugged his catcher, Dave Duncan, while Sal Bando jumped on Fingers from behind. Dick Williams ran across the third base line and headed toward first baseman Mike Hegan, who readied himself for an embrace with his manager. Hegan had played very briefly for the New York Yankees during their championship year of 1964, but had come to bat only five times during the season and only once during that Series. With the A's, Hegan had played a meaningful role on a world championship team for the first time in his life. "After having gone through the loss the year before in the playoffs to the Orioles — and really, despite all of the headlines of how much adversity and animosity and hard feelings there were among the (Oakland) players, and very frankly, a lot of that is overrated — I think it was the culmination," Hegan says. "I came in on it a year before, and Dick (Williams) was there, and of course, Sal and Dick Green, Dave Duncan, Rudi, and Catfish, John Odom and all those guys had been together from the Kansas City days — for them especially it was something that meant a great deal. For all of us to be a part of accomplishing something, because in that Series, the Reds were favored, and they were "The Machine" and they had all the veteran players. Even though we had won

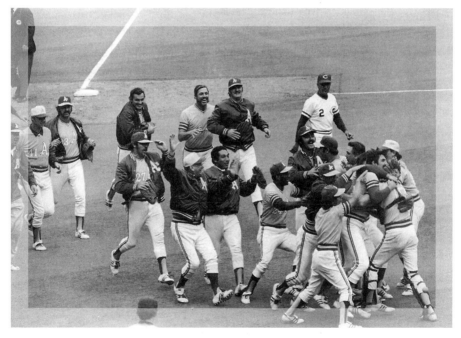

As Reds' third base coach Alex Grammas looks on, the A's celebrate their first world championship since the franchise's move to Oakland.

the division the year before, we weren't expected to beat them in the Series, and we did.

"The thing about that Series that a lot of people don't remember is that there were six one-run ballgames in that Series. The only game that wasn't a one-run game was when they blew us out in Cincinnati in the sixth game. But every other game was a one-run ballgame. So it was a gut-wrenching Series, to cap a tough playoff with the Tigers. It was a very emotional time."

After Hegan, Williams, Duncan, Bando, Fingers and the rest of the A's completed their on-field jumping and back-slapping, the A's moved their celebration to the clubhouse. In the clubhouse showers, Campy Campaneris, Dick Green, Joe Horlen, and Don Mincher sang a strange rendition of the national anthem under the guidance of conductor Vida Blue. Another group of A's — Mike Epstein, Dave Duncan, Joe Rudi and Sal Bando — poured champagne over their own heads in front of a movie camera. That part of the celebration would later appear on commercial television as part of an advertisement for hair spray. Outside of the clubhouse, several of the Oakland wives chanted, "We're number one! We're number one."

While most of the A's sang, laughed and poured champagne, one player experienced feelings of emptiness and despair. Reggie Jackson, unable to play because of a ruptured hamstring, felt out of place in the clubhouse. "The worst feeling I've ever had, as an athlete and a human being, was the day we won the World Series," Jackson would say the following summer. "I was so disassociated from it. I couldn't even get out onto the field to shake a hand."[6]

Fortunately for the A's, Gene Tenace had made up for the omission of Jackson's bat from the Oakland lineup. Tenace received word that he had been named the Series Most Valuable Player by *Sport* magazine, which would reward him with a new car. The previously obscure utilityman represented the lone Oakland hitting star of the Series. "How the hell can you win a car, Gino?" shouted Darold Knowles, needling Tenace over being removed for a pinch-runner in the sixth inning of Game Seven. "You can't even go nine innings."[7]

What Tenace had done was impressive. In a Series criticized for the lack of hitting by both teams, Tenace had tied a Fall Classic record by powering four home runs, and had driven in nine of Oakland's 16 runs. The little-known catcher-first baseman had also established a new Series record with a .913 slugging percentage, bettering the marks of Hall of Famers like Babe Ruth and Lou Gehrig. Tenace modestly discussed his role in beating the Reds. "I don't feel like a hero," Tenace told reporters, while overlooking the fact that he had mauled Cincinnati pitching at a .348 pace. "There was no one hero on this club," Tenace insisted. "There were 25 heroes."[8] The statistics told another story. Other than Tenace, no other Oakland player had driven in more than one run in the Series.

Near the lockers, a west coast baseball writer poured champagne over the head of Charlie Finley. "This is the greatest day in my life," Finley cried out. "None of you can appreciate what this means to me." A reporter asked Finley about the second greatest occurrence in his life. "That was when my wife accepted my (marriage) proposal," Finley gushed. "But wait a minute. You better make this my second biggest thrill. My wife might not like it the other way."[9] Two of Finley's children, 17-year-old Martin and 15-year-old Luke, joined their father as he held court with the media. When one of his sons tried to answer a reporter's question, the elder Finley instructed him otherwise. "You nod, I'll answer the questions,"[10] the owner said in typically Finleyesque manner.

In another section of the clubhouse, Dick Williams talked to members of the national media, some of whom had questioned his moves during the Series. Why, in Game Seven, did Williams pinch-run for Gene Tenace? After all, the A's had led only 2-1 at that point, and Tenace had been their best hitter against the Reds. Why did Williams order Rollie Fingers to intentionally walk Johnny Bench in the eighth inning? The strategy violated the basic baseball rule: never intentionally put the potential game-winning run on base.

Other writers felt Williams was more concerned with making appearances on television than actually devising pertinent strategy. At one point in the Series, Williams had decided to coach first base. The writers had also taken note of Williams' frequent visits to the mound. Williams had walked to the mound 38 times during the seven-game series, including 12 trips in the final game. The repeated delays would result in a change in baseball legislation. Commissioner Bowie Kuhn wrote Williams a letter informing him of the new rule. Beginning in 1973, the regular season rules that limited the number of mound appearances by managers and pitching coaches would also apply to the post-season. "I won't need a clean uniform for the playoffs," Williams would say in 1973. "The fans won't be seeing me as much this year."[11]

One writer asked Williams to compare the '72 A's to the Boston Red Sox team he had guided to the pennant in 1967. "This is a much better club than we had in 1967,"[12] Williams responded without hesitation. Williams cited the depth of the A's as far superior to that of the Red Sox. Williams then compared the A's to the Brooklyn Dodger teams he had played for two decades earlier. "This club is even better than the Dodgers of the fifties,"[13] Williams proclaimed. Those Dodger teams had featured Hall of Famers Roy Campanella, Jackie Robinson, Pee Wee Reese, and Duke Snider, and secondary stars like Gil Hodges, Billy Cox, Carl Furillo, and Don Newcombe.

Although the national media had pegged them as slight underdogs at the start of the Series, the A's had managed to defeat a Reds' team laden with Hall of Fame offensive talents. The meticulous scouting work of Sherm Lollar and Al Hollingsworth had played an important role in the Series victory. Lollar and Hollingsworth had assembled a scouting report so detailed that it advised the A's of even the most obscure tendencies of the Reds. By reading the report, Dick Williams had learned that the Reds liked to bunt in situations with runners on third and two out. In Game One, the Reds had placed the tying run on third in the ninth inning. With two outs and Pete Rose at the plate, Williams had motioned Sal Bando to move in at third and instructed Vida Blue to throw high fastballs in anticipation of the bunt. Rose fouled off a bunt attempt before grounding out to Ted Kubiak to end the game.

"We had a meeting the first time we played Cincinnati," Kubiak recalls, "and the scouting report that we got on them was just excellent. We went out to play them and I swear to God it was like we had played them all year. I made the last out of the first game when Pete Rose bounced the ball over the mound — kind of towards second base — but to the right of second base. I made the play, and the next day Rose says in the paper, 'How the hell could he be in that spot?' Well, I played with Pete in the minor leagues, so I now how he hits. I mean, we knew what he would do in certain situations, but that's what that intelligence does. It helps you out."

Long-haired and bare-chested, Dave Duncan joins three of his teammates in pouring champagne for the benefit of a camera crew after the 1972 World Series. The photo, featuring Mike Epstein, Duncan, Joe Rudi and Sal Bando from left to right, would become part of an advertising campaign for a hair spray company.

Some media observers had regarded the World Series between the A's and Reds as representative of a political battle between contrasting ideologies. Several baseball and political writers contrasted the conservative, old style, straight-laced Reds, whose players were forbidden to wear their hair long or don facial hair, against the liberal A's, a rowdy, unkempt group of players known for rebelliousness. "They said this Series was between the long hairs and the short hairs, the liberals against the conservatives," observed scruffy-bearded catcher Dave Duncan, "I think we proved that it's not how a person looks like outside that counts, but what he's got inside. We had it inside, heart and guts."[14]

In the *New York Daily News*, baseball writer Joe Trimble referred to the A's as the "bad guys, the ones with the mustaches and beards," and the Reds as the "good guys, the clean-shaven Cincys."[15] Another writer termed the World Series as "The Bikers against the Boy Scouts."

"Obviously, that was a focal point of the media," recalls Sal Bando, "simply because you had more of a radical personality in a Charlie Finley, and we had the longer hair and the mustaches. And then you take this very conservative, very inflexible Sparky Anderson and the Cincinnati Reds and their short hair and their high socks and their nice pants. It was a contrast between two different styles."

"Yeah, I guess it was a big deal," says Mike Hegan, laughing loudly. "Of course, the Reds had their rules that they couldn't wear the high stirrups. They couldn't have facial hair, and they had to have their hair cut so that it didn't reach the back of the uniform." Under the lead of Dick Williams, the A's had few rules when it came to fashion and grooming. "We're a free-lance club," explained Ray Fosse, who joined the A's in 1973. "We don't dress like other clubs. We didn't have to wear a coat or tie on airplanes or in hotel lobbies. We have the mustaches, and playing in California is kind of casual. As long as the hair is neat, everything's fine."[16]

Did players on the A's feel that the majority of the population was rooting for the Reds, since they seemed to convey the "boy-next-door" image, while the A's represented the anti-establishment? "I think you probably had the youth of the day rooting for A's," Bando explains, "and the elderly, or the older population rooting for the Reds. We never even thought anything of it. It was no big deal to us."

Yet, the A's liberal, hippie image did not necessarily reflect the political beliefs of the Oakland players. "We might have worn our hair longer and had mustaches," Bando admits, "but probably in today's political climate most of us were conservative anyhow." Liberal or conservative, conforming or rebellious, the A's had managed to change simultaneously with the American culture. More importantly, they had emerged as baseball's best team in 1972.

The Oakland players engaged in a rowdy, but enjoyable plane ride back to the Bay Area. "I remember the plane trip back," Don Mincher says. "It was such a great time. And Finley made sure that we had a good time, don't kid yourself. He had two airplanes chartered. He done all the things that let us enjoy ourselves. I don't remember a whole lot of sleep for the next two or three days, but we did celebrate, and it was a great time for me. It's just a cherished memory now. I have that World Series replica trophy displayed for all my friends to see right out in the open. And the ring and what-have-you. I was very, very proud."

Once the two planes arrived, the A's received a welcome from about 25,000 fans at Oakland's International Airport. Amidst rumors that the A's might eventually move the franchise to New Orleans, Charlie Finley sang the chorus of his favorite song, "Sugar in the Morning," shouted messages of encouragement and held up the World Series trophy. Gene Tenace, the World Series MVP, yelled "We're No. 1"[17] repeatedly to the collection of fans an friends. Some of the onlookers chanted "We want Vida!" but Blue was nowhere to be found. Blue had decided to skip the reception at the airport. "I just can't stand being in crowds like that," explained Blue, who had also missed the airport reception after the A's had won the pennant against the Tigers. Blue would later skip the team's private victory party and the public victory parade in downtown Oakland. Blue's string of absences would anger Charlie Finley.

On October 23, the A's officially celebrated the Bay Area's first championship with a 15-block parade through downtown Oakland. A convoy of antique cars escorted Oakland players along the parade rout, as an estimated crowd of 150,000 spectators looked on. Finley accepted the keys to the city — of Oakland that is, not the rumored destination of New Orleans. A number of fans held up signs that read "Tenace the Menace," the new nickname given to their sudden World Series hero.

Having grown up in a small town, Gene Tenace felt uncomfortable in the spotlight afforded to a player who had performed so well in front of an entire country. When he accepted a sports car from *Sport* magazine as the World Series MVP, Tenace showed little interest or enjoyment in the glamour associated with stardom. "See all this," said Tenace, pointing to the cameras and television lights surrounding him. "I couldn't care less about it all. I'm the same old me."[18] A quiet reserved man with a dry sense of humor, Tenace preferred spending time with his wife and two young daughters as opposed to traveling the banquet circuit. "Tony Perez called and wanted me to do an act with him, Johnny Bench, Vida Blue and others at Las Vegas," Tenace said. "But me? I just want to get back to my family."[19]

The unexpected power hitting of Tenace, the clutch pitching of Fingers, Hunter, Holtzman, and Odom, the strange but productive strategy of Williams, and yes, the endless maneuverings by Charlie Finley, had translated into a World Series victory. Even though the Reds had outscored the A's in the Series, 21-16, and had featured a lower team earned run average, Oakland had managed to overcome a series of obstacles to win. The injuries to Darold Knowles and Reggie Jackson, the playoff suspension of Campy Campaneris, the clubhouse argument between Blue Moon Odom and Vida Blue, the strange rotation of second basemen, and the lack of a proven center fielder had not been enough to prevent the A's from completing their evolution from American League also-ran to major league champion.

The feeling of winning a World Series represented a special satisfaction for a player like Mincher, who had already decided to retire after the season. "Yeah, it was," Mincher says. "I knew and I had announced that I was gonna retire. To go out as a winner, and as a World Champion. I had come close to it before, and I had done most of the things that I really wanted to do. My career was somewhat above-average; it wasn't the great-type career. But I had done some good things. I played in the All-Star game. But I still missed that big ring. When we won that thing, my roommate Sal Bando and the guys that I really got close to, one of them being (Mike) Epstein, we had such a great feeling of, I guess, kid-like joy. Like you were 17 years old and you just beat your high school rival."

Shortly after the Series, the A's players voted on how to divide their World Series shares amongst themselves. Such votes have historically proven both difficult and controversial, given the necessity of dividing 25 shares amongst a group of players that usually numbers in the thirties or forties. For the '72 A's, the task proved even more daunting, considering the revolving door theme to the season. Charlie Finley had engineered 65 transactions involving 41 different players. As a result, Finley had employed a total of 47 players throughout the season. The A's elected to hand out 27 full shares, with each player receiving a World Series record payment of $20,705. Strangely, the A's voted infielder Larry Brown a full share and Tim Cullen a one-third share, even though Brown had spent far less time on the active roster. In another notable decision, the A's elected to shut out Denny McLain completely from any World Series money, while giving other short-timers at least a small amount of post-season loot.

Finley spared no expense in rewarding his A's for a job well done. Finley placed an order with a jewelry company for a set of beautiful, half-carat diamond rings, which would be distributed to each of the Oakland players. Finley announced that the World Series rings, probably the most expensive to date in major league history, carried an estimated value of $1500 apiece. Several players, including captain Sal Bando, had the rings appraised for insurance purposes. The appraiser put the value even higher — at $3500 apiece.

As satisfying as the World Series victory had been, the A's status as World Champs did not prevent the loss of key players from the ranks. Although media reports indicated that backup first baseman Don Mincher was only contemplating retirement, and only if the A's did not meet his contract demands, "The Mule" says he had already made up his mind. "I had announced, as a matter of fact, my retirement," Mincher says. "I was done, quit, I was through. I didn't want to play anymore. My kids were graduating from high school age, you know tenth, eleventh grade. And I had never ever had a normal Fourth of July, or anything like that. I was 35, and I wanted to quit.

"It had been a tough season. I knew my bat was slowing down some. And I didn't really enjoy the fact that I was riding the bench so much, even though I understood the situation. So I had announced my retirement, and I was done. I'm telling you, I was absolutely done."

One Oakland writer, Ron Bergman, speculated that Mincher might have been more likely to return had he not achieved a significant milestone during the 1972 season. In July, Mincher had clubbed his 200th career home run, while still playing for the Rangers. Would Mincher have returned had he finished the season one or two home runs short of the milestone? "No," Mincher responds definitively. "No, no, remembering my feelings back in those days, is that I really, in my mind, had had enough. I do remember getting my 200th off of Joe Coleman in Detroit. And it was a big milestone for me. But I don't think that would have kept me from retiring. I think once I had my mind made up, I was done."

For awhile, Mincher considered the possibility of maintaining a baseball career, only in a different capacity. "I had thought about maybe managing in the minor leagues a little bit, but then I soured on that, too. I had some offers to do that. But I went home." Mincher would eventually return to baseball, but not as a manager or coach. "The Mule" would become the general manager and owner of his own minor league franchise, ironically one that had an affiliation with his former team — the Oakland A's.

Although Mincher says that he had announced his retirement near the end of the season, the A's did not officially publicize the news regarding their popular slugger until December 20. On that day, the A's issued a sloppily-written press release informing the fans and media of Mincher's decision to step aside. The media release contained several embarrassing factual errors, including a statement that Mincher had finished his career with over 200 home runs when he had hit exactly 200. The release also maintained that Mincher had played in one All-Star Game, when he had actually played in two. The release mentioned that he had played for the Twins, Angels, Pilots, Rangers and A's during his career, but omitted his stints with the Washington Senators. Charlie Finley should have been ashamed. A well-respected professional like Mincher deserved a better farewell.

Mincher knew about the erroneous contents of the press release. "I was aware of it," Mincher reveals. "I remember being somewhat upset, but it was one of those things back in those days that was a fleeting moment of being upset, and then I forgot about the whole thing. I never carried it around with me. As a matter of fact, I gotta be honest, I had forgotten all about it, until you just now brought it up. But I do remember now about that."

The sloppiness of the press release may have been attributable to Finley's insistence on employing a skeleton crew of employees in his front office, coupled with the frequent departure of beleaguered public relations staff members. "You call three people a skeletal staff?" Mincher says good-naturedly while laughing loudly. "Naw, I'm sure he had a couple more than that." Whatever the number of employees, Mincher agrees that the poor press release may have been the result of too few people trying to do too much work. "It could have been," Mincher says, "because I remember so many things during those days that we didn't have. You know, we didn't have a media relations-type guy. We had to do it ourselves; Dick Williams did it. And Charlie. But I'm sure that probably had something to do with it."

With Mincher gone, writers speculated as to whether the A's would keep expensive veterans like Matty Alou and Dal Maxvill, who were still useful players but were making too much money for Finley's liking. Finley might have been willing to pay them their salaries if they were still in their primes, but Alou could no longer play center field, and Maxvill lacked the hitting ability to play on an everyday basis. With Finley looking to cut payroll, the two former Cardinals wondered whether they, like Mincher, might soon become former A's.

Chapter Fourteen:
World Series Fallout

On October 30, Charlie Finley made his first move to bolster the team that he wanted to defend its world championship. The A's re-acquired left-handed reliever Paul Lindblad from the Rangers for minor league third baseman Bill McNulty, outfielder Brant Alyea (whom Finley had re-acquired from St. Louis in July) and $150,000 in cash. Lindblad had led the major leagues with 66 appearances, and had pitched exceptionally for a bad team. A 2.61 ERA and nine saves convinced Finley and Dick Williams to bring Lindy back to the Bay Area, perhaps as protection against Darold Knowles' comeback from a broken thumb. The addition of Lindblad gave the A's potentially three left-handed relievers, provided that Dick Williams did not return Dave Hamilton to the starting rotation. With the return of Lindblad, Finley had succeeded in re-acquiring all three players — Don Mincher and Frank Fernandez being the others — he had originally traded to Washington in the Mike Epstein deal.

Mincher, who played with Lindblad in Washington, Oakland, and Texas, remembers the left-handed reliever as a man of boundless energy, one who always needed to keep busy. "He could not sit still," says Mincher, who recalls Lindblad's trademark habit of searching for money with a metal detector "He'd go to the ballparks and look for pennies and nickels all day long." By Lindblad's own estimation, he collected an average of $11 per city on Oakland's road trips and gave the money to his coin-collecting children. When the metal detector beeped, Lindblad used a small screwdriver to dig into the outfield turf and warning track. Yet, Lindblad had to be careful not to dig too deep, for fear of striking a water hose or electrical line. Trips to Cleveland's Municipal Stadium posed a special problem, since groundskeepers Harold and Marshall Bossard took special pride in maintaining the grass field. "If I dig too deep into the Indians' field," Lindblad said, "those two guys would tan my hide."[1]

Although Charlie Finley was happy to have an effective relief pitcher like Lindblad in tow, he would make a far more important transaction on November 21, when he decided to deal one of his other veteran relievers. Finley sent 34-year-old right-hander Bob Locker to the Chicago Cubs for minor league outfielder Bill North, who would be given a chance to battle Angel Mangual for the starting center field position. The switch-hitting speedster had hit only .181 in 66 games for the Cubs before being demoted to Wichita of the American Association. Reports out of Chicago indicated that North had an attitude problem, dating back to his days at Central Washington State College. North had also reacted badly to a lack of playing time with the Cubs. One unsubstantiated report claimed North had threatened to leave the Cubs during the season to become a school teacher.

Casual Oakland fans questioned the trade, wondering why the A's would deal an effective reliever like Locker for a virtual unknown with a questionable attitude. Locker had gone 6-1, with a 2.65 ERA and 10 saves during the regular season. Finley, however, paid more attention to Locker's dismal post-season performance. An inconsistent Locker had pitched so poorly in two playoff games against the Tigers that Dick Williams had lost all confidence in the sinkerballing reliever. As a result, Locker made only one brief appearance during the World Series.

The A's saw much more in North than his .181 batting average would attest. During spring training, the Cubs had played the A's several times in Cactus League play. North had impressed the A's with his all-around play during those spring matchups. After his demotion from Chicago, North had batted .351 with 10 stolen bases in 28 games. Oakland scouts had noted North's ability to make contact, aggressively run the bases, and skillfully patrol the outfield. The scouting reports would prove accurate. North would become an effective leadoff hitter for the A's over the next three seasons and enable Dick Williams to drop Campy Campaneris to the more suitable No. 2 slot in the batting order.

With North in contention for the troublesome center field position and Reggie Jackson slated to move back to right field, the A's decided to part ways with Matty Alou, "the man I feel got us into the playoffs,"[2] according to Gene Tenace. Three days after the North acquisition, Finley sent Alou and his $110,000 contract to the Yankees for infielder Rich McKinney and (oh no, not him again!) pitcher Rob Gardner. This was

Players Acquired and Re-Acquired
by Charlie Finley: (1970-80)
      Brant Alyea
      Pat Bourque
      Rico Carty
      Tommy Davis
      John Donaldson
      Frank Fernandez
      Rob Gardner
      Mudcat Grant
      Dave Hamilton
      Larry Haney
      Ted Kubiak
      Paul Lindblad
      Bob Locker
      Dal Maxvill
      Don Mincher
      Diego Segui

the same Gardner that the A's had acquired from the Yankees in 1971 for Felipe Alou, before trading him back to New York later that summer. Thus, Finley's bizarre infatuation with the journeyman left-hander continued.

The A's continuing interest in Gardner remained a mystery. Although Gardner had pitched well at the Triple-A level, he possessed neither an overpowering fastball nor a particularly deceptive breaking ball. Most scouts termed Gardner's repertoire as pedestrian. Several weeks after the trade, Gardner had still not heard directly from Finley, either by telephone or through the mail. Gardner himself questioned why the A's had re-acquired him, when they already had two capable lefty relievers in Darold Knowles and Paul Lindblad, a promising swingman in Dave Hamilton, and two fine southpaw starters in Ken Holtzman and Vida Blue. "I've sat down and thought about it many times," Gardner said from his home in Binghamton, New York, "and wondered exactly why Oakland made the deal. I'm not too sure why they did. I'm not even sure they know they did because I haven't heard anything from them. Maybe they don't realize yet they made the trade."[3] Dick Williams indicated that he would use Gardner as a long reliever and spot starter, but some writers speculated that the journeyman lefty would be traded again before he donned the green and gold of Oakland.

Gardner had now been traded six times during his ten-year professional career. Three of the trades had involved the A's. In two of the transactions, Gardner had been traded for an Alou brother, first Felipe and now Matty. If the pattern continued, Finley would soon trade Gardner to the Astros for Felipe and Matty's younger brother, Jesus. "Where's he, Houston?" Gardner asked a reporter. "Oh well. Two out of three isn't bad."[4]

The 40-man roster took on a strange look. After the addition of North and the subtraction of Alou, the A's now owned only five outfielders, which represented the same bloated number of first baseman available to Dick Williams. Mike Epstein, Mike Hegan and Gene Tenace had all seen playing time at first base during the World Series. Don Mincher remained on the roster even though he had apparently decided to retire. Orlando Cepeda, he of the three regular season at-bats, remained on Finley's payroll, collecting his exorbitant $90,000 salary. Clearly, one or more of the first sackers would have to go. The A's also possessed a glut of second basemen, retaining Dick Green, Dal Maxvill, Ted Kubiak, Larry Brown and Tim Cullen. Dick Williams didn't need that many middle infield types, or did he? Perhaps Charlie Finley would try to resurrect his plan of revolving second baseman in 1973. In 1972, the A's had used 12 different players at second base including unlikely candidates like Tenace, Sal Bando, Curt Blefary, and Larry Haney, in addition to Marty Martinez and Dwain Anderson.

Finley continued to talk trade with other teams. A blockbuster deal remained a possibility, albeit remote. Finley asked the Philadelphia Phillies about the availability of ace left-hander Steve Carlton, who had won an incredible 27 games for a last place team. In turn, the New York Yankees and San Francisco Giants inquired about the availability of Vida Blue, who had annoyed Finley by refusing to partake of any of the post-season celebrations.

On November 30, Finley relieved the logjam at first base. Instead of ridding himself of backups Orlando Cepeda or Mike Hegan, Finley surprised Bay Area writers by dispatching his second-best left-handed power hitter, Mike Epstein. Finley traded Epstein to the Rangers for right-handed reliever Horacio Piña, who had gone only 2-7, but had pitched well during the second half and had saved 15 games for Texas. Piña would replace the departed Bob Locker as a set-up reliever.

One of the few people to welcome the deal was Rollie Fingers, who had been overworked during the regular season and had pitched in a record six World Series games. Fingers hoped the acquisition of Piña would lighten his pitching load from 65 games to about 55 appearances. In contrast, most of the Oakland media criticized the trade, wondering why the A's would deal the productive Epstein for a little-known reliever from a last place ballclub.

Why did the A's trade Epstein, who had enjoyed such a productive season in Oakland? Was it his temperamental nature? His battles with Dick Williams over playing time? Perhaps his 0-for-16 in the World Series had sealed his fate. None of the above, Finley answered. Instead, he had been forced to trade Epstein in order to make room for Gene Tenace at first base. Finley said that Tenace had recently suffered a shoulder injury which prevented him from catching on a regular basis. Due to the injury, Tenace could not make the throws to second and third base required by the catching position.

The shoulder injury came as a complete surprise to the Oakland beat writers who followed the A's on a regular basis. Although Tenace had struggled to throw out Cincinnati Reds' runners, no one had remembered Tenace hurting his shoulder during the World Series. They hadn't heard of Tenace injuring himself during the off-season, either. One writer asked Finley and Williams to describe the injury. Both men said they lacked the "medical knowledge" to give the injury a specific name. One reporter, Glenn Schwarz of the *San Francisco Examiner*, followed up by interviewing A's team orthopedist Dr. Harry Walker. According to Schwarz, Dr. Walker said he knew nothing about an injury to Tenace.

Oakland beat writers arrived at a logical conclusion: Finley had made up the injury to justify trading a malcontent player who had criticized both him and Dick Williams. A's observers wondered why the team hadn't acquired more than Piña for a left-handed power hitter coming off a 26-home run season. "We didn't get as much for Mike Epstein as we wanted," admitted Finley, "but we got as much as we could."[5]

Finley expounded on the alleged injury to Tenace. "Tenace came to me at the World Series and told me he had tendinitis," Finley revealed. "We had to keep him in the lineup, so I made room for him at first base. He can play there but he can't catch with his present arm problem."[6] In actuality, Tenace's problems had been caused by a bout with bursitis, which had affected his elbow, not his shoulder. Yet, the problem wasn't severe enough to jeopardize his future as a catcher.

Whatever the condition of Tenace's arm, Epstein had clearly worn the patience of both Finley and Williams. "Mike wanted to play everyday," explains Mike Hegan, who had served as Epstein's backup in 1972. "There was some growing problems between he and Dick simply because he didn't like being taken out in the sixth or seventh inning if we had a lead...With some of the other problems that they had had with Mike and some of his complaining, they felt that was the move to make."

Was Tenace really injured at the time of the trade? "I don't know if there was any shoulder ailment," Hegan says in retrospect. "The fact is, Dave Duncan was the better defensive catcher and he worked very well with the pitching staff. Geno (Tenace) was on the verge of — especially after winning the MVP in the World Series — you gotta think about playing him every day some place. The natural place was first base...I think Charlie and Dick were looking for a way to get them both in the lineup the following year."

Tenace credited Hegan with unselfishly tutoring him on the art of fielding bunts and how to take throws without getting his feet tangled. The better that Tenace became, the fewer the opportunities for Hegan to play. "All the time Mike was doing this," Tenace pointed out, "he was pushing himself further and further away from the job. He knew it and I knew it, but he still kept helping me."[7]

The status of another first baseman remained questionable. Orlando Cepeda had undergone knee surgery during the summer and had expressed a desire to play winter ball in Puerto Rico. Finley said that Cepeda should not play at all before being examined by Dr. Walker. Even if Walker proclaimed Cepeda healthy, where would he play in

Oakland? The A's seemed committed to the idea of playing Tenace at first base. Platooning was not an option, since Tenace and Cepeda both batted right-handed. Given the balky condition of his knees, Cepeda was not capable of playing another position.

In late December, Finley telephoned Cepeda to update him on his status with the ballclub. Orlando remembers his final conversation with the irascible owner. "After the 1972 season, I didn't care about playing baseball because I was in such pain. My knees. And he called me in Puerto Rico and said, 'If you don't call me tomorrow, I gonna release you.' I said, 'Go ahead and do it, because I don't want to call you.' I didn't call him; he released me."

Cepeda's disinterest in playing baseball stemmed only partly from the condition of his knees. Orlando no longer wanted any part of Oakland or the A's. "I didn't like the people," Cepeda said in a 1973 interview. "They were sour on me. I was surprised the A's got me. My knees hurt so much; my mind wasn't on baseball."[8] Mostly, Cepeda didn't want to return to Oakland because of his feelings for Finley. Although Cepeda lasted only a brief time with the A's, he still managed to fully experience the strangeness of the owner. "Yeah, Charlie Finley," Cepeda says, pondering the name for a moment. "He's a weird guy."

Finley's bizarre personality motivated Cepeda not to call him back from Puerto Rico, thus expediting his departure from the Bay Area. "I don't want to play for him," Cepeda says. "He was very difficult." In contract negotiations? "On everything."

Finley said good-bye to a total of three veterans the week before Christmas, including Cepeda. The A's also placed Larry Brown and Joel Horlen on waivers, in the hopes that some team would place a claim, take on their salaries and pay the A's the waiver price. When none of the other 23 major league teams put in a bid, the A's gave the trio their unconditional releases. To his credit, Finley notified the players personally. Finley offered Horlen and Brown minor league contracts with Tucson of the Pacific Coast League, but both players refused.

Cepeda, for his part, shed no tears over leaving the A's. "My mother was crying, my friends in Puerto Rico were all excited," Cepeda said several months later. "But I tell them don't worry because this is best for Orlando. I didn't like playing in that ballpark in Oakland. The weather was going to be lousy for me."[9]

Twenty-five years later, Cepeda has softened his stance on the Oakland Coliseum. "Let me tell you this," Cepeda says with emphasis, "compared to San Francisco, it's a much better ballpark. Better weather, better hitting ballpark. It's a nice ballpark." Many hitters have criticized the Coliseum for its expansive amount of foul territory, which makes many more foul balls playable, thus having a downward effect on batting averages. Cepeda, however, says that criticism is overblown. "I never thought about it," Cepeda insists. "People don't think about it."

Aside from Finley, Cepeda's largest concern in Oakland had to do with a lack of playing time. In Atlanta, Cepeda had bristled at a pinch-hitting role forced on him by manager Luman Harris. "In Oakland, all Williams and Finley wanted me for was to pinch-hit."[10] Cepeda believed that once he rehabilitated his knees, he would be able to resume a regular playing role — somewhere.

Finley felt otherwise, informing the press that he had been told that Cepeda no longer had cartilage in one of his knees. Finley believed the 35-year-old first baseman would never play again. The A's also doubted whether the 32-year-old Brown would play after electing not to undergo an operation on a herniated disc in his back. The veteran infielder had opted for a non-surgical treatment recommended by Chicago White Sox third baseman Bill Melton. Brown hinted that he would either sign a contact with the Detroit Tigers, or manage a golf course in Florida. In contrast, the release of Horlen was a bit bewildering. Although Horlen did have a bad knee which made his status for 1973 questionable, he had pitched well for the A's in long relief after being released by the White Sox in spring training.

The timing of Cepeda's release could not have been worse, as Finley would soon learn. Earlier in the month, American League owners had voted unanimously to adopt the controversial new designated hitter (DH) rule for at least the next three years, beginning with the 1973 season. If passed by the Playing Rules Committee of major league baseball, American League managers would be allowed to designate a hitter to bat in place of the pitcher throughout the game.

The National League owners bristled at the idea of a designated hitter, voting against such a concept. The National League also expressed its displeasure with two other American League attempts at innovation: the designated runner and inter-league play. The Playing Rules Committee (which consisted of three N.L. members, three AL representatives, and three minor league executives) agreed with the National League owners, rejecting the American League's bid for a DH rule and the other innovations. American League President Joe Cronin, who strongly favored the DH, requested a joint hearing with the National League and asked Commissioner Bowie Kuhn to attend the session. Cronin wanted Kuhn to cast the deciding vote on the issues of the DH, the designated runner, and inter-league play.

The National League eventually consented to forming a joint major league committee to study the DH further. On January 11, National League owners once again declined the DH for their own teams but voted to allow the American League to use the DH on an experimental basis, beginning in 1973. The Playing Rules Committee also followed with its approval. "We like the rules the way they are," maintained NL president Chub Feeney, "but we'll be watching the American League, and who knows, someday we may go along."[11] Charlie Finley, long a champion of the DH, actually voted against the rule in the final American League ballot because his fellow owners refused to adopt another one of his favored rules, the designated runner. Finley wanted both rules, not just one.

Finley might have had another reason for voting against the DH. Finley had already released Cepeda, a productive power hitter who seemed like a natural for the designated hitter slot. Although Cepeda could no longer move well enough to play a position in the field, he likely possessed enough leg strength to sprint four or five times a game, the maximum amount of running that would be required from the designated hitter.

Finley had picked up Cepeda's $90,000 contract in late June, paid off the majority of it, and received a grand total of three at-bats in return. Now, just before Cepeda might become productive again under a new rule, Finley had released the slugger and received no compensation in return. Finley thought he had ridded himself of a sizable headache when he had essentially traded Denny McLain to Atlanta for Cepeda; the "Baby Bull's" short tenure in Oakland had turned into a knottier problem.

One week after the designated hitter became reality, the Boston Red Sox announced the signing of Cepeda to a one-year contract. The Red Sox became the first American League team to sign a player specifically for the role of DH. Meanwhile, with Cepeda gone, Don Mincher retired, and Mike Epstein and Matty Alou traded, the A's were left without a logical choice for the DH slot. Ironically, the team whose owner had pushed harder for the designated hitter than any other executive was now left holding an empty bag of DH candidates.

The A's owner tried to save face by insisting that he would not have kept Cepeda even if he had been certain that the DH rule would be adopted. "Cepeda's salary didn't bother me," Finley claimed. "What bothered me was that our team physician...said that all the cartilage in his knee was gone — that it was almost bone on top of bone. Dr. Walker advised me that it was very, very questionable whether he could hold up. And even if he does hold up, if he gets on base, you have to put in a pinch-runner for him because he can't run. That's two players used right there."[12] The Red Sox obviously thought differently.

In December, Finley had tried to talk one of his former players into making a return specifically to fill the role of designated hitter. Finley had targeted the recently-retired Don Mincher. "The real tempting stage came after I had established a business and was working, my wife and I together," recollects Mincher, "and I got a call in December from Charlie Finley." Mincher replays the conversation, mimicking the deep-throated, slow-paced speaking style of Finley.

"I... want ... you... to come back... and...play for me," Finley told Mincher.

"Charlie, I don't want to," Mincher responded politely. "You don't want me, either."

"Yeah, I do," Finley insisted without hesitation. "We just passed the rule... called the designated hitter rule...and that's all I want you to do."

"What are you talking about?" replied Mincher, who hadn't even heard of the designated hitter.

"The pitcher hits no more," Finley explained. "And I need a guy to hit in that spot."

"You gotta be kidding me," said a disbelieving Mincher. "Baseball's not like that."

"Well, it is now," Finley snapped back.

After his initial skepticism, Mincher decided to give the DH some consideration. "So I had to take a couple, three days to think about it," Mincher reveals, "and I was very tempted to go back because that sounded so great. I knew that club was gonna win again and again. But in the end, my wife and I had established a business here (in Huntsville), and the kids were here. I was really enjoying being here, so I said, 'No,' and that took care of it."

Dick Williams and Charlie Finley also thought differently on how the DH would affect the composition of the Oakland roster. At a winter banquet, Williams predicted that the A's would reduce the number of pitchers on their roster from ten to eight, and would also carry more offensive position players. Three days later, Finley painted a different picture. "Dick and I talked for three hours in Oakland," Finley said. "I told him that it would be very difficult to carry only eight pitchers because very few of our pitchers have options left (to be demoted to the minor leagues)."[13] Finley also disagreed with the notion of using the singles-hitting Gonzalo Marquez as a DH. Finley said he preferred a DH with more power and speed than Marquez, and listed several other candidates for the DH role, including newly acquired players like Billy North and Rich McKinney, and holdovers Angel Mangual and Billy Conigliaro. Finley failed to mention that none of the above players possessed consistent or proven major league power. Only North had outstanding foot speed. In other words, the A's were in major trouble when it came to finding a qualified DH.

Oakland pitchers weren't necessarily pleased with the news that they would not be allowed to hit during the regular season. Catfish Hunter, Blue Moon Odom and Ken Holtzman each bemoaned the new rule. Although Odom had batted well under .200 the previous season, he prided himself on his ability to swing the bat, not to mention his two home runs in 1972. "I may have hit only .121 last year, but I was a threat every time up. I'm a better hitter than most pinch-hitters." Hunter echoed the thoughts of Odom. "I don't like the rule," Hunter said flatly. "I like to hit myself because it makes me feel like I'm more in the game,

Charlie Finley puts his arm around Gonzalo Marquez during the 1972 World Series. By the spring of 1973, Marquez had fallen into some disfavor with the owner who considered him ill suited for the newly created DH rule.

especially if I come up there to bunt."[14] Hunter had even more reason not to like the DH, given his .350 batting average during the 1971 season.

As they neared spring training, the A's seemed to be receiving very little attention, either through commercial endorsements or from the national media. The defending champions — filled with colorful, well-known stars like Reggie Jackson, Catfish Hunter and Vida Blue and a newly discovered World Series hero like Gene Tenace — seemed like perfect fodder for commercial spots and television appearances. Yet, few opportunities arose. "I was not asked to endorse anything," revealed Tenace, the World Series MVP. "I made no commercials. None of the talk shows invited me to be a guest, including Johnny Carson, who's just down the road in Los Angeles. I made no appearances in the Bay Area and only a few elsewhere."[15]

Although Tenace himself preferred exclusion from the spotlight, the lack of attention given to the A's on the whole disappointed him. "It's a strange thing that none of the Oakland Athletics made money by capitalizing on being world champions,"[16] Tenace said. Perhaps Oakland's status as a small market team had discouraged sponsors and corporations from contacting Oakland players. Or, perhaps the A's had felt the backlash of a general public that was unwilling to embrace a team of rebellious, long-haired, non-traditional baseball players. The general indifference of fans in the Bay Area reinforced the absence of recognition. "It's hard to believe that our ballclub couldn't draw a million in attendance despite winning the championship,"[17] moaned Tenace. "Here we are the world champs and no one pays attention. I don't know, maybe the people in Oakland don't deserve a champion. I know I expected more."[18]

On the field, the A's chief concern involved the lack of a proven center fielder. The A's had ended the 1972 regular season with Reggie Jackson in center field and Matty Alou in right field. Given Jackson's running ability, and Alou's sound defensive instincts, that seemed like a workable arrangement. Jackson, however, asked Williams to return him to right, while Charlie Finley had deemed Alou's contract too extreme at $110,000 per season. Williams had agreed to move Reggie back to right but now needed to pick a center fielder from among a platoon of candidates.

How about Angel Mangual? The Roberto Clemente look-alike had qualified for the Topps All-Rookie team in 1971 before flopping both offensively and defensively in 1972. Mangual misjudged several fly balls and batted only .246 with little power. Scouts wondered whether Mangual possessed enough speed to play center field.

Another prospect, George Hendrick, had played well for a brief stretch before showing that he was not ready to handle major league pitching. While Hendrick's supporters lauded his style of play as smooth and effortless, his detractors considered him too nonchalant, perhaps even lazy. Opposing coaches criticized Hendrick. "He's a real dog," Yankee coach Elston Howard would say in 1973. "You could see that the way he played against us. Half-trying. What a shame."[19] Hendrick's reputation as a loner and his unwillingness to speak to the media also concerned some members of the A's organization. According to one rumor, Oakland had considered a winter trade that would have sent Hendrick to the Rangers for right-handed starter Dick Bosman, but the deal never took place.

The most intriguing "name" among the center field candidates was that of Billy Conigliaro, the younger brother of former Boston Red Sox star Tony Conigliaro, who had retired in 1971 due to severe problems with his vision. Billy himself had briefly retired during the season, prompting the Brewers to trade his rights to the A's as part of the Ollie Brown swap.

At the time of the trade, neither the A's nor the Brewers had mentioned the name of Conigliaro. Since the outfielder had been placed on Milwaukee's disqualified list and the trade had taken place after the June 15 deadline, neither team could announce Conigliaro's inclusion. The Brewers stated that they had acquired Brown for the waiver price of

$20,000.

Conigliaro detested playing in Milwaukee, and was unhappy over his sporadic playing time. In June, Billy left the team to work with his brother Tony at a Boston golf course and night club. Tony had retired from the California Angels earlier in the season. In December, Finley finally contacted Conigliaro, offering him a contract for the 1973 season. At first, Billy wondered whether he should report to the A's. He remembered that Tony had experienced problems with Dick Williams in Boston. Ultimately, Billy found Finley's offer too good to refuse. Billy accepted, knowing that he would have a chance to play for a world championship team, one that needed a center fielder. Conigliaro reported to spring training in Mesa with an improved attitude. In his first five exhibition games with the A's, Conigliaro would hit two home runs while using a new, shortened swing.

Aside from Conigliaro, Mangual, and Hendrick, the A's seemed intrigued by their fourth center field option. Switch-hitting Bill North, who had been acquired from the Cubs for Bob Locker, featured better speed and defensive instincts than any of the other outfield possibilities. The Cubs had seemingly mishandled North's development. After an impressive spring training, manager Leo Durocher had played North in right field, instead of his accustomed center field position. When North struggled initially, Durocher damaged his confidence by playing him sporadically and then demoting him to Triple-A.

Dick Williams worried about other positions, although not as much as the center field dilemma. Would former catcher Gene Tenace be able to handle the defensive responsibilities of first base? Tenace had played almost exclusively as a catcher in the major leagues, after coming up in the Oakland system as an outfielder. Tenace expressed his preference for wearing the tools of ignorance. "I worked so hard to become a catcher," Tenace explained, "and I never had the chance to prove myself there."[20] Would 31-year-old Dick Green return from major back surgery and stabilize the troublesome second base position? Otherwise, with Tim Cullen already announcing his retirement, the light-hitting duo of Dal Maxvill and Ted Kubiak would be asked to share time at the pivot. Would Gonzalo Marquez and off-season pickup Rich McKinney effectively man the designated hitter platoon? Charlie Finley had already questioned the qualifications of Marquez, who lacked both speed and power.

As the A's searched high and low for DH contenders, the Bay Area media couldn't help but notice the success of another team's designated hitter. Oakland ex-patriot Orlando Cepeda was batting .346 for the Red Sox in Grapefruit League play, having banged out nine hits in 26 at-bats. While the "Baby Bull" could not be retrieved, the A's seemed to be overlooking an obvious solution to their designated hitter dilemma. Why not make Gene Tenace, an untested defender, the regular DH and play Mike Hegan at first base? In 1972, Hegan had batted a career-high

.329 in a reserve role. Furthermore, his everyday presence at first base would have strengthened Oakland's interior defense while lessening the burden on the comebacking Dick Green.

Hegan says the A's wanted more power from the first base position than he could provide. "Other than Reggie, and Sal, who hit some home runs, we were not what you would call an awesome offensive ballclub," Hegan says, dismissing the misconception of the A's as a power-packed team. "I think in '72 we only had one .300 hitter (Joe Rudi) and we only had one guy that hit more than 30 home runs (Mike Epstein led the team with 26). And I don't know if anybody drove in a hundred... It was a club that (had) to take advantage of that DH spot and put somebody in there who would drive in some runs and hit some home runs."

One player who might have to perform designated hitting duties out of necessity was Reggie Jackson. Reggie had injured his knee in the final game of the American League Championship Series, forcing him to miss the entire World Series. During the offseason, Jackson favored the knee in workouts, and ended up damaging his other knee. The lingering pain in both knees caused Reggie to struggle at the start of spring training. Jackson gradually worked his knees into better condition, which helped him lead the A's in spring training home runs while pushing his average close to .400. "I still can't go 100 per cent on the knees for an entire game," Jackson said by the end of spring training, "but I can still steal a base, run hard down to first, cover ground in the outfield, and throw."[21] Well, maybe he wouldn't have to DH after all.

Jackson seemed determined to have his best season ever in his quest for a $100,000 contract. Jackson felt that if he could avoid injuries and play up to his ability, he would be able to ask Finley for a six-figure deal in 1974. "To get that kind of salary, you have to put a lot of good years together," explained Reggie, "not just one streak. I'm not taking anything away from Gene Tenace, but he just had one good week and it happened to be in the World Series. It means a lot more when you do it day in and day out, year after year."[22] Jackson felt the key to reaching his salary milestone could be found in his ability to hit for average. "I still need to learn the strike zone," Jackson admitted. "I know I've got to be more patient. I'm trying to hit .300 because that's something I've never done. I know I can hit 40 home runs, I know I can knock in 100 runs, because I've done those things. I haven't hit .300."[23]

The A's made news on several fronts early in spring training. George Hendrick requested a trade. Finley had already told the second-year outfielder that he wouldn't be considered for the starting center field job. As a result, the A's planned to have Hendrick start the season at Triple-A Tucson. Hendrick, who had experienced the thrill of starting games in the World Series, wanted no part of extended duty in the minor leagues.

Vida Blue refused to sign his contract, which Charlie Finley had the right to renew automatically at $51,000. Blue's action led some observers to forecast another long holdout by the left-hander. The predictions proved exaggerated, as Blue reported to Mesa in early March, but again kept his signature off Finley's contract renewal. Blue said he would approach the head of the Players' Association, Marvin Miller, to inquire about the possibility of becoming a free agent after the season. "I could be a test case,"[24] Blue told United Press International.

Catcher Dave Duncan also decided to hold out at the start of training camp before reporting late. On March 10, Finley automatically renewed the contract of Duncan, who had received an offer of $40,000 in the mail. Three days later, Finley publicly informed both of his dissatisfied players that they were replaceable. "We're going to make every effort to repeat as world champions," Finley vowed. "A Vida Blue or a Dave Duncan aren't going to stand in my way. We certainly hope they play, but if they don't, I assure you we'll get along without them very well."[25]

In recalling the contractual tactics of Finley, Duncan has bitter memories. "That's the one area where I might have a little bit of resentment," says Duncan, "because negotiating those contracts was always very difficult. The game, the way it was at that particular time, you had no alternative but to sign the contracts that they were offering. (Finley) certainly wasn't going to do you any favors when it came to contracts. He was pretty difficult that way."

In the meantime, Finley executed a major change in contract policy with another player. Finley gave Campy Campaneris a two-year deal — the first multi-year contract he had ever agreed to since buying the A's in 1960. The contract would earn Campaneris an estimated $65,000 over each of the two seasons.

Perhaps the most interesting news item involved the revelation that Gene Tenace might be able to catch after all. The A's had tried to justify the Mike Epstein trade by citing the poor condition of Tenace's shoulder. Most Oakland writers hadn't bought the injury story initially; they became even more justified in their skepticism when Finley said that Tenace's shoulder injury had healed sufficiently over the winter. If that was truly the case, why hadn't the A's waited until spring training to see how Tenace's shoulder had responded before making a hasty trade with the Rangers? More likely, the A's had traded Epstein because of his public arguments with both Finley and Williams during the post-season.

Tenace's role came more into focus on March 24, when the A's made a four-player trade involving one player who had asked to be dealt and another who was playing without a signed contract. Finley sent Dave Duncan, who had refused to sign his renewed pact, and the unhappy George Hendrick to the Cleveland Indians for former All-Star catcher Ray Fosse and utility infielder Jack Heidemann. On the surface, the deal allowed the A's to rid themselves of two malcontent ballplayers and return Tenace to first base.

Duncan had initially held out of spring training. When he finally reported to Mesa, without the long blonde beard that he had sprouted in 1972, he agreed to work out with the team but declined to sign his renewed contract. The longtime catcher wanted a raise from $30,000 to $50,000. Finley wouldn't budge from $40,000. Duncan hinted that he might not play for the A's come Opening Day. Dick Williams reacted to Duncan's indecision by moving Tenace back to the catching position, and placing Gold Glove left fielder Joe Rudi at first base. "Even after the great Series I had," Tenace said in reaction, "they still don't know what they want to do with me."[26] Why would the A's remove the best defensive left fielder in the American League and relocate him to a less demanding position, one that he had played only briefly during his major league career? The moves smacked of Finley.

Finley claimed that Duncan's subtle threat of not playing during the regular season had not influenced the trade. "We believe we got the best catcher in baseball,"[27] Finley said of Fosse. The revelation probably came as news to the Reds' Johnny Bench, the Pirates' Manny Sanguillen, and the Yankees' Thurman Munson. Finley said that Fosse possessed a better arm than Duncan, most likely an accurate claim.

Duncan felt as if he had been released from a prison operated by a vindictive warden. "I was very happy to be traded," Duncan told reporters shortly thereafter. "It eliminated a lot of the mental hassles I had."[28] Duncan accused Finley of trying to strip away his dignity and orchestrating his benching during the second half of the 1972 season. The veteran catcher didn't completely absolve Dick Williams of blame, either. "He had been close to the players," Duncan said of his former manager. "Then all of a sudden that changed and he wasn't as close anymore. It's funny it happened around the time he got a new contract and a raise."[29]

The trade involving Duncan and the Indians also provided a fresh start for George Hendrick, previously regarded as one of Oakland's top prospects. Not only had Hendrick asked to be traded, he had asked to be traded to the Indians. Finley obviously had a warm spot for his young center fielder.

The trade appeased both departing players, but it did not soothe Reggie Jackson, who considered Duncan one of his best friends in baseball. "I don't have many friends, but the ones I have are close ones," Jackson had said during the 1972 World Series. "On this club, my closest friends are Duncan and Joe Rudi and Vida Blue. When I'm looking for somebody to talk to, I go to Dave and Joe. We'll go to dinner together. I usually don't make any plans until I check with them."[30]

While the trade figured to affect the chemistry of the ballclub, the acquisition of Fosse also seemed risky. In 1970, he had played at an

All-Star level for the Indians, earning a spot in the midsummer classic. Fosse's baseball life changed when Cincinnati Reds' All-Star Pete Rose lowered his shoulder and slammed into him while scoring the game-winning run in the twelfth inning. Rose collided so brutally with Fosse that he left the muscular catcher with a separated and broken left shoulder.

At first, X-rays showed that Fosse had suffered only a bruised collarbone. Eight months later a follow-up X-ray revealed the full extent of the injuries, which would continue to cause him pain even after his playing days. The hardened Fosse — nicknamed "The Mule" for his toughness and determination — continued to play after the All-Star break and never went on the disabled list that season, even though he could not lift his left arm above his head. Since the injury was to Fosse's left shoulder, it didn't bother his throwing but affected his swing, sapping him of much of his power. Then, in September, Fosse broke his right index finger on a foul tip by Mike Epstein, then with the Senators. The latest injury ended Fosse's season, but didn't prevent him from being selected to *The Sporting News* All-Star team.

Yet, Fosse was no longer the budding star catcher. Although his defensive skills remained well above average, his offensive game fell off severely the next two seasons. Fosse endured his worst full major league season in 1972, batting only .241 with 10 home runs and 41 RBI's. Those numbers represented nine fewer homers and 18 fewer RBI's than Duncan, who had shared time with Gene Tenace behind the plate. Still, Finley's belief in Fosse's superior defensive ability was supported by several Indian players, who criticized Cleveland management for making the trade. Ace pitcher Gaylord Perry was particularly incredulous over the deal. "You've got to be kidding?" Perry said in reacting to the news. "How can they trade our quarterback?"[31] Perry had previously credited Fosse with helping him win the American League's Cy Young Award in 1972.

Finley had included the talented Hendrick in the deal as a mere throw-in, perhaps because he regarded the young center fielder as too lackadaisical to achieve his considerable potential. Finley may have regretted his decision to unload Hendrick after an exhibition game against Cleveland. The Indians had agreed to play the game using orange-colored baseballs that Finley had been pushing heavily on major league baseball. Finley believed the orange baseball would prove more visible for fans and hitters. As commissioner Bowie Kuhn watched from the stands, Hendrick deposited three of those brightly colored baseballs into the bleachers against his old team. Ironically, several hitters complained that they couldn't see the orange baseballs as well as the traditional white ones. Other players criticized the baseballs because of the similarity in coloring between the red stitching and the dyed-orange horsehide. Much to Finley's chagrin, major league baseball would never adopt the orange baseballs in regular season play. To make matters worse, George Hendrick would go on to hit 21 home runs with 61 RBI's in 1973, on his way to a fine major league career.

Would the unsigned Vida Blue soon join Hendrick and Duncan on the list of former A's? One rumor made the rounds at Mesa, indicating that Finley would send his former Cy Young and MVP to the lowly Rangers for right-hander Pete Broberg, whom the A's had once drafted with their first round pick, and former Athletic Mike Epstein. In fact, Finley had been trying to reacquire Epstein practically from the day that he had dealt him to Texas in the first place.

Yet, the prospective trade made little sense for the A's. Broberg, although considered a live-armed prospect, had pitched poorly in 1972, with a record of 5-12 and an ERA of 4.30. Broberg's career record stood at 10-21. As for Epstein, the A's had only recently traded him away, in part because of his strained relationships with Dick Williams and Reggie Jackson. Why would Finley give up a franchise left-hander, one of baseball's rarest commodities, for an underachieving right-hander like Broberg and a player that his manager and star player didn't like?

On March 18, the *Oakland Tribune* reported that the A's had traded Blue to the Rangers for Broberg, "possibly catcher-outfielder Dick Billings, and one other player plus cash."[32] The story said the trade would be announced "as soon as a check drawn on a Pompano Beach, Florida, bank by Rangers' owner Bob Short clears."[33] Curiously, the *Tribune* article also quoted Finley as denying the reported trade. "I can tell you it's not true," said the A's owner. "If he has been traded, then my manager did so without my authority."[34] For his part, Dick Williams said he knew nothing of the trade.

Finley had no intention of making the trade. In fact, he hadn't even talked to the Rangers about a Broberg-for-Blue swap. Finley had floated the false rumor himself, as a way of scaring Blue into thinking that if he didn't sign the owner's contract offer soon, he would end up in the baseball hell known as Texas. The strategy worked. Ten days later, after a three-hour negotiating session, Blue finally signed his contract. Vida received $53,000 dollars, $2,000 more than what Finley had offered but $10,000 less than what he wanted. "Now that we've signed Vida," Finley announced, "we have the best team in baseball. I predict another world championship for the Oakland A's."[35]

On April 2, just before the start of the regular season, the orange baseball championed by Finley made its final appearance. Oakland's opponent, the California Angels, committed five errors in a losing the exhibition game by the final of 8-3. California players complained about the difficulty in seeing and gripping the orange-tinted ball. Unlike the designated hitter, one of Finley's pet inventions had died a quiet spring training death.

The final cuts of spring training brought few surprises, with the exception of pitcher Dave Hamilton. The rookie left-hander, who had pitched so well in 1972, had come to spring training 16 pounds lighter and seemed determined to avoid a sophomore slump. Faced with a surplus of left-handed pitchers, the A's optioned Hamilton to Triple-A Tucson so that they could hold on to Rob Gardner, who was out of options. Gardner, who would serve as the ninth man on the a nine-man staff, didn't figure to see much action since the advent of the DH meant the A's wouldn't have to pinch-hit for their pitchers.

Chapter Fifteen:
The Encore

The A's looked nothing like their 1972 world championship team when they opened up the season against the Minnesota Twins. Billy North became the first designated hitter in the history of the A's and batted leadoff. Dal Maxvill batted second and played shortstop in place of Campy Campaneris, who had been suspended for the first five games of the season after his ugly bat tossing incident during the League Championship Series. Gene Tenace played first base, not catcher. The recently-acquired Ray Fosse made his debut behind the plate. Billy Conigliaro emerged as the Opening Day center fielder, ahead of incumbent Angel Mangual. Several members of the '72 A's remained in the organization, only not at the major league level. Dave Hamilton and infielder Allan Lewis, both playing at Triple-A Tucson, were flown in to attend Opening Day ceremonies and receive their World Series rings.

The A's also played nothing like world champs in their first game. Catfish Hunter allowed nine hits in a disappointing three-inning stint. Fosse, Dick Green and Sal Bando committed costly fielding errors. The Oakland offense managed only a three-spot of runs in the fourth inning against complete game winner Bert Blyleven. The A's played better in their second game, thanks to a complete game start by Blue Moon Odom and a home run by Gene Tenace. The Twins won the game, however, when they scored four of their five runs against Odom in the fifth inning.

The Twins completed the three-game sweep on Sunday, winning an afternoon game, 4-2. Minnesota reached Ken Holtzman for two runs in the first, a run in the third and another run in the fifth. Errors by Sal Bando and Ted Kubiak made two of the runs unearned. Although the season was only three games old, the A's had managed to look like a complacent team that was already resting on its championship laurels. The suspension of Campaneris for the first five games of the season wasn't helping matters either. "I feel miserable," Campaneris said of his exclusion from early season games. "I sit around and can't help. It drive me crazy."[1]

Not so coincidentally, the A's had lost all three games without the services of perhaps their most unappreciated star. When Campaneris played, the A's didn't usually lose three games in a row to any club, much less a rebuilding team like the Twins.

A native of Cuba, Campaneris had arrived in the major leagues in 1964 with the Kansas City A's, as a replacement for injured shortstop Wayne Causey. After an all-night, sleep-depriving plane ride, Campaneris arrived at the ballpark. The A's equipment manager thought the 155-pound Campaneris too frail to be a ballplayer and initially refused to give him a uniform. Campaneris surprised the equipment manager by homering in his first at-bat against Minnesota's Jim Kaat — on the very first pitch. Campaneris followed up by hitting a second home run against Kaat in the seventh inning. The dual home runs tied a modern day record for most home runs in a major league debut. The 22-year-old speedster added a single, a stolen base and a running catch on a short pop-up into left field.

Separated from his mother, father and seven brothers and sisters, who still lived in Cuba, the shy, reserved Campaneris had few American friends, no girlfriend or wife, and lived by himself in a small apartment near Kansas City's Municipal Stadium. "He was such a loner," says Jack Aker. "I played with him there for three or four years and never really got to know him." Several of the A's attempted to incorporate Campaneris into the social atmosphere of the clubhouse. "We tried to get him at least psychologically to be a part of the team," Aker explains, "which we never were able to achieve while I was with the team."

Campaneris' tendency to stay to himself may have been caused by his problems with a new language. At first, Campaneris spoke such little English that teammate Diego Segui, who eventually became his best friend on the team, served as his interpreter for interviews with the media. Although A's coaches had difficulty communicating with him, they quickly came away impressed with his speed and daring base-running style. "He's got guts," said Kansas City coach and Hall of Famer Gabby Hartnett in 1964. "He's got the best pair of wheels I've ever seen. I saw a lot of great base stealers, including Max Carey, but I wouldn't rate any of them ahead of this kid."[2] A's third base coach Luke Appling, also a Hall of Famer, raved about Campy's baseball instincts, calling them "exceptional."

The language barrier forced a determined Campaneris to study pitchers on his own and develop base-stealing techniques by himself. In 1965, Campaneris led all American League base stealers with 51 thefts. Campy topped the 50-stolen base mark three straight seasons, before swiping 62 bases in 1968. At the plate, Campaneris hit consistently in the .260 to .270 range. "We felt he was more of an offensive weapon than a defensive weapon at that time," recalls Jack Aker. Only elements of his defensive play remained a concern. "An outstanding defensive player as far as his range at the time," Aker says. "He wasn't as steady as Dick Green was at second. But he made the spectacular plays." Campaneris' quick, scam-

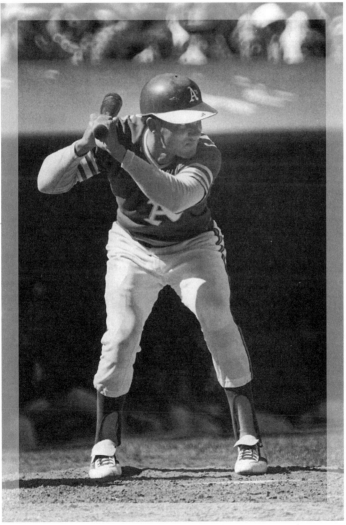

Bert "Campy" Campaneris, the catalyst to Oakland's lineup, coils into his unusually deep batting crouch.

pering feet allowed him to reach grounders that other shortstops couldn't touch, but he tended to bobble grounders because of his unsure hands. Campy made over 30 errors in three of his first four full seasons before settling down defensively in 1969. As with his base-stealing, Campy improved his field work through his self-imposed work ethic.

Campaneris wasn't satisfied with improvements on the field. He hoped to learn English to the point where he no longer would need bilingual teammates like Orlando Peña and Diego Segui to help him conduct interviews. He spent one winter with his second cousin, Angels' outfielder Jose Cardenal, whose wife gave him lessons in the new language. Thanks in part to his improved skills in speaking English, Campaneris eventually met and married an American woman.

The temporary loss of Campaneris had affected the A's in the season-opening set against the Twins. Writers and scouts had also begun to question off-season deals that had permanently sent away Mike Epstein, Matty Alou, and Dave Duncan. In exchange for three productive regulars, the A's had acquired a middle reliever, a platoon DH, and a catcher in decline. Critics claimed that the A's had too many pitchers and needed a better designated hitter with more power.

After the 0-3 start, the A's boarded a plane to Chicago's O'Hare Airport. On the bus ride to the hotel, Dick Williams noticed loud noises coming from the back of the bus, where Billy North was needling Blue Moon Odom. "Are you guys 3-0, or 0-3?" Williams snapped sarcastically.

Odom provided an answer. "We're 0-3."

"Well, you better start busting your rears,"[3] Williams shot back, not at Odom in particular, but at the whole team.

Williams' outburst was eerily reminiscent of the stern lecture he had given the A's on the team bus two years earlier. In 1971, the A's had responded to Williams' words by winning five straight games and 12 of 13. How would they respond this time?

Oakland routed Chicago, 12-2, knocking White Sox ace Wilbur Wood from the game. Joe Rudi snapped out of an 0-for-13 slump to hit a home run. Although several players tried to downplay the connection between the win and Williams' anger at them, it seemed the manager's temper had once again motivated the team, albeit for the short term. The A's dropped their next game, to fall to 1-4. Fortunately, Campy Campaneris would return to the lineup, his five-game suspension having come to an end.

The new designated hitter rule was forcing Wlliams and Finley to make changes with their team. Since Williams no longer had to pinch-hit for his pitchers, he tended to leave his starters in for longer periods. As a result, the A's bullpen became under-worked. Even ace reliever Rollie Fingers found himself spending too much idle time in the bullpen. "It's a terrible thing for relief pitchers," Fingers said, pointing his finger at the DH rule. "It seems like I'm throwing more on the sidelines this year instead of in games."[4] Fingers felt the new rule would hurt his chances of earning a pay raise. "We've got four good relievers," Fingers explained. Some clubs, like the Yankees, have one guy they use all the time. Sparky Lyle will still probably get about 30 saves this year. I'll have something like 13. That will be great when I go in to talk contract with Charlie Finley."[5]

With four quality relievers and the designated hitter in place, Dick Williams realized he didn't need a nine-man staff; four starters and four relievers would be sufficient. The A's dispatched the thoroughly well-traveled Rob Gardner to Tucson. In his place, Charlie Finley substituted Triple-A outfielder Jay Johnstone, one of the biggest flakes in 20th century baseball history.

In 1971, Johnstone had hit 16 HR's for the White Sox, but his struggles the following year prompted his release in the spring of '73. Envisioning problems in center field, the A's signed Johnstone to a minor league contract and assigned him to Tucson. Upon his promotion to the major leagues, Johnstone reported to Kansas City, where the A's were scheduled to play a night game against the Royals. At 7:45 PM, Johnstone received a telephone call in the dugout from Finley. The Oakland owner wanted to wish his newest player luck, and asked Johnstone if he needed anything prior to his first game. Over the phone, Finley heard a loud roar from the fans at Royals' Stadium. Thinking that the fans were reacting to an impressive batting practice display, Finley asked Johnstone specifically what had prompted the cheers from the crowd. Johnstone replied matter-of-factly that the fans were reacting to a play in the game going on between the A's and Royals. Finley felt a lump in his throat. He had thought that games in Kansas City started at 8:00, not at 7:30. The embarassed owner hurriedly said good-bye to Johnstone and promptly hung up the phone. Johnstone now realized the strangeness of the new baseball world he had entered.

Johnstone became one of the A's newest candidates to fill the designated hitter role. The A's needed a productive one. The absence of a power hitter to fill that role, coupled with the lack of a proven center fielder, left the A's with two major holes in their starting lineup. Plus, with Dick Green struggling in his return from back surgery, second base had once again become a problem. The pitching staff, although strong on paper, did not fare well the first two weeks of the season. Other than starter Ken Holtzman and reliever Horacio Piña, none of the pitchers were performing up to their past resumes.

While Blue Moon Odom was in the midst of an 0-5 start, Horacio Piña represented the other end of the success-failure spectrum. The 28-year-old Mexican had already faced pressure from the Oakland fans and media, who criticized his acquisition from Texas in the Mike Epstein trade. (Fortunately, Piña didn't hear many of the criticisms, because he understood and spoke virtually no English.) When A's fans took their first look at Piña, with his long, bushy hair and gangly frame, they must have wondered whether he was even an athlete. At six-feet, two-inches, and 160 pounds, the reed-thin right-hander had earned the nickname "Ichabod Crane" during his early major league days with the Cleveland Indians. An impressive physical specimen he was not.

Piña had also failed to impress pitching coach Wes Stock, who noted his inability to handle left-handed batters. Piña, an effective side-arming pitcher against right-handed hitters, seemed unwilling to use that style against lefties. "He was coming over the top to left-handers and his ball always was up," Stock explained. "His natural motion is side-arm, and his ball sinks when he throws it that way."[6]

Stock convinced Piña to chuck the overhand delivery and show courage in using his side-winding motion at all times. Piña had been given such advice in the past, but the recommendations never stuck — until now. With his long fingers and large hands, Piña already threw his best pitch — a sinking palmball — more effectively than most pitchers. Piña's palmball now became lethal to left-handed hitters, as well. Piña piled up three wins and a save, which represented the best pitching of anyone on the Oakland staff over the first month of the season.

On May 2, the A's finally addressed their troublesome problem at DH. Charlie Finley acquired 34-year-old right-handed slugger Deron Johnson from the Philadelphia Phillies for minor league infielder Jack Bastable and cash. Since the Phillies were retooling with youth, they had decided to trade the aging, slow-footed first baseman. "Deron Johnson is the DH we've been looking for," announced Dick Williams, who said that Johnson would serve as the designated hitter against both left-handed and right-handed pitching. "We changed our thinking on the DH," Williams admitted. "At first we thought we needed someone with speed who made contact."[7] In Johnson, the A's had decided to go with power and run production.

"Deron Johnson was a prototypical DH," explains Mike Hegan. "Well, he could play first base, too. But I mean he was a professional hitter. That was a pretty good acquisition. He would provide a little more power for the ballclub, as well." Prior to Johnson's arrival, the Oakland lineup featured only three home run hitters: Gene Tenace and Sal Bando from the right side and Reggie Jackson from the left. Although Williams might have preferred another left-handed power hitter to balance the middle of the order, he now had the services of four players capable of hitting at least 20 home runs.

Johnson delivered immediately as Williams' newfound DH. In his first at-bat with the A's, Johnson plated two runs with a soft line-drive single. Shortly after his arrival in Oakland, the A's reached .500 for the first time in 1973. In surrendering a minor leaguer utility infielder, who would never make the major leagues, for a respected, productive power hitter like Johnson, Charlie Finley had made one of his best trades as Oakland's combination owner-general manager.

On the same day that Johnson debuted as the Oakland DH, Dick

Williams unveiled the team's latest second base innovation. Unlike the rotation of second baseman that had been initiated by Charlie Finley in 1972, the latest brainstorm seemed to come from the mind of the manager. Williams filled out a lineup card that featured Gonzalo Marquez, a left-handed thrower, at second base. Only Willliams had no intention of playing Marquez at the position. With the A's playing on the road, Williams batted Marquez in the No. 2 slot in the order, after leadoff man Campy Campaneris. Marquez took his at-bat in the top half of the first inning, and when the A's took the field in the bottom half, gave way to Dick Green at second base. Williams then planned to pinch-hit for Green, and all subsequent second basemen, according to game situations.

"Of course," Williams said, in explaining the strategy, "you can only do this on the road."[8] In a home game, Marquez would have had to take the field in the top of the first inning, leaving the A's with a major defensive liability in the middle infield. Williams had first learned of such strategy by observing his minor league manager, Bobby Bragan, in the Texas League during the late 1940's. Williams himself had first used the strategy as a minor league manager in 1966.

While the A's had filled their designated hitter vacancy by acquiring a player like Deron Johnson from another organization, they thought they had solved another one of their problems — the center field situation — through internal means. Billy Conigliaro started the season hitting .295 while fielding reasonably well in the outfield. Then, on April 21, Conigliaro damaged interior cartilage in his right knee while sliding into second base. Conigliaro tried playing with the injury for two weeks before agreeing to have the surgery. Doctors predicted that Billy C. would miss anywhere from one to two months. Dick Williams hoped he would have the veteran center fielder available as a pinch-hitter by mid-July, and perhaps in the regular lineup by August. The injury would prove to be a blessing for the A's, who would soon discover their new center fielder.

Billy North had started Opening Day as Oakland's designated hitter before settling into his role as a third-string center fielder. Despite his status as an occasional starter, North was leading the American League in stolen bases. When Conigliaro went down with a bad knee and Angel Mangual pulled a chest muscle, Williams turned to North. The former Cub collected four hits and three RBI's in the first game of a doubleheader. In the second game, North sat on the bench because Williams had already promised to give Mangual a start. When Mangual committed a two-base error and went 0-for-8 over a two-game span, Williams had seen enough. "Bill North is my center fielder," Williams declared. "He stays in there unless he falls flat on his face."[9]

North would not. The 25-year-old switch-hitter raised his batting average with regular playing time, continued to lead the league in stolen bases, and played spectacular defense in center field. "He covers more ground in center than anyone we've ever had,"[10] stated Reggie Jackson, who had played with center field partners like Rick Monday, Angel Mangual, George Hendrick, and Billy Conigliaro since debuting with Kansas City in 1967.

On May 18, North enjoyed a particularly productive game against the Royals, stealing a base, driving home the tying run and scoring the winning run. In the eighth inning, North faced reliever Doug Bird. North swung and missed, letting the bat fly out of his hands toward shortstop. As North walked out to the infield to retrieve the bat, he mouthed a few words to Bird and then charged the pitcher's mound.

None of the players on either team, except for Bird, understood why North had reacted so violently. After the game, North explained that he had sought retaliation for a minor league incident in 1970, when the two players had faced each other in the Midwest League. Bird, pitching for Quincy, had given up two consecutive home runs to Waterloo batters when North stepped to the plate. In what seemed like an obvious purpose pitch, Bird beaned North. In their first head-to-head meeting since the beaning, North had fulfilled his quest for revenge.

American League president Joe Cronin handed North a three-game suspension for his actions, prompting an angry reaction from the A's brass. Dick Williams and Charlie Finley pointed to an incident 10 days earlier, when two Kansas City reporters quoted Royals' outfielder Lou Piniella as saying that he had intentionally thrown his bat at Detroit pitcher Jim Perry. Yet, Cronin had elected not to suspend Piniella. The A's felt that Cronin had victimized them by enforcing a double standard against North.

Williams did not excuse North, however. "If you've got a grudge against a guy," Williams lectured his young outfielder, "don't take it out on my ballgame. The team should come first."[11] North had learned an important lesson from his new manager.

The day before North's attack on Bird, the A's had received an unexpected boost in the American League West pennant race. Dick Green belted a three-run homer against Rudy May at Anaheim Stadium, helping Catfish Hunter to a 4-0 win over the California Angels. On the play, Angels' center fielder Bobby Valentine made a leaping attempt at Green's drive. Valentine's spikes caught in the center field wall, and with his momentum pushing his body toward the fence, two bones in his right leg snapped. The multiple fractures ended the season for Valentine, who was hitting .302 at the time. The Angels considered Valentine one of the American League's up-and-coming stars, and a key to their chances of claiming their first Western Division title.

Five weeks later, the A's would once again benefit from the misfortune of one of their rivals. Chicago White Sox first baseman Dick Allen, the American League's MVP in 1972, collided with former Oakland first baseman Mike Epstein, since traded from the Rangers to the Angels. The crash of muscle-bound sluggers resulted in a fracture of Allen's leg. The White Sox' best hitter, who was hitting .316 with 16 home runs and 41

RBI's at the time of the injury, would bat only five more times in 1973. With Allen out of the lineup for virtually the rest of the season, the White Sox would lack the power hitting needed to sustain a serious threat in the Western Division.

Dick Williams had his own reasons to be concerned, however. Both Gene Tenace and Sal Bando were struggling to drive in runs. After a solid April, Williams had promoted Tenace from No. 7 to No. 3 in the lineup, but the 26-year-old first baseman proceeded to go hitless in 18 at-bats. Williams then moved Tenace back to the seventh spot. Bando was also having problems getting runners home, and was dropped as low as No. 8 in the batting order.

After dropping his first five decisions, Blue Moon Odom finally won a game, beating the Rangers, 4-2, on May 12. The victory exacted a price, however. Odom developed a blister on his right index finger, forcing him to leave the game after five innings. Odom proceeded to lose his next three decisions, making his record a dismal 1-8. After losing to the Tigers on May 28, Dick Williams removed him from the starting rotation and placed him in the role of long relief.

Odom's ineffectiveness, coupled with the enigmatic struggles of Vida Blue, left Williams with two holes in his rotation. Williams began to contemplate the recall of two promising pitchers from Triple-A Tucson: left-hander Dave Hamilton and right-handed prospect Glenn Abbott. While both pitchers appeared to have solid futures, neither offered the talent to match the performance of Blue, especially the way that he had pitched in 1971.

Even though Blue had signed his 1973 contract fairly quickly, thus avoiding another prolonged salary battle with Charlie Finley, he was clearly groping to find his old form. His early-season difficulties prompted Williams to make a change in his catching rotation. In five straight games in which Blue started, Williams benched regular catcher Ray Fosse, moved Deron Johnson to first base, and installed Tenace as Vida's personal receiver. Tenace had caught Blue frequently since the 1969 season, when both were in Oakland's farm system. The two had been paired during Blue's two most significant milestone games: his no-hitter in 1970, and his 20th win in 1971. "A lot of things are still in his head," said Tenace, trying to explain Blue's subpar pitching. "I've known him a long time, so I can make a statement like that. I can tell when something is bothering him. Mentally, he's still not ready to pitch."[12] Tenace believed that Blue was still upset by his contract negotiations with Finley, and by a demanding fan base that expected him to duplicate his 1971 pitching standards.

"A year like that will never happen again," Blue warned his fans. "I was new to the league. They didnt know me. I had 150 strikeouts before they realized I wasn't throwing anything but fastballs."[13] Yet, Blue was not throwing his fastball as hard as he had in the past. Some observers of the A's pointed to Blue's workload in 1971, when he had pitched a burdensome total of 312 innings. Prior to that season, Blue had never pitched as many as 150 innings in a season, including his years in the minor leagues.

While some observers have speculated that Blue might have hurt his arm trying to come back too quickly after his 1972 holdout, some players, like Sal Bando, disagree. "I don't think he hurt his arm; for some reason I don't think he had the total recovery that you need and the buildup of the arm strength. He just, for some reason, was never the same pitcher. Occasionally, he would have a game where it looked like the '71 Vida Blue was there, but again, I can't help but think that the holdout hurt him more than anyone else."

On May 25, Campy Campaneris returned to Detroit for the first time since throwing his bat at Lerrin LaGrow in the 1972 playoffs. LaGrow claimed that he held no grudge against Campaneris. "Heck, I've forgotten all about it," said a forgiving LaGrow. "That's all over."[14]

Surprisingly, Tiger manager Billy Martin agreed with the sentiments of LaGrow. "It's all over. It's history," said Martin, before admitting that his mindset had been a bit different during the playoff game. "If I would have gotten to him at the time, I would have kicked the *bleep* out of him."[15] Martin said recent media reports of him continuing to seek revenge on Campaneris were greatly exaggerated. "I was quoted as saying that if there was another fight, Campaneris would be the first guy I would go after. That was a little misquote there."[16]

As much as Martin despised Campaneris at the moment he twirled his bat at LaGrow, the Tiger skipper respected him as a fiery, combative sparkplug who always hustled. In 1983, Campaneris would conclude his major league career with the Yankees, who were being managed at the time by none other than Billy Martin. After a one-year layoff from major league ball, Campy arrived at the Yankees' spring camp in Ft. Lauderdale, Florida — uninvited. Knowing that the Yankees needed a middle infielder, Campaneris asked Martin for a playing job and the Yankee manager challenged him to make the team. Campaneris proceeded to earn the final spot on Martin's 25-man roster, and hit .322 as a backup second baseman and third baseman to Willie Randolph and Graig Nettles, respectively.

Tiger fans were not as kind as Martin and LaGrow in their reaction to Campaneris' visit to Detroit. Fans at Tiger Stadium lustily booed Campy each time he stepped to the plate. "After I do it," Campaneris said of throwing the bat, "I am sorry. In Detroit, they boo me, but others don't. When people bring it up, I no say anything. I want to forget."[17] Some of the Tigers wouldn't let him forget. In the field, Campaneris took a fall when Tiger catcher Bill Freehan knocked him down with a fierce takeout slide at second base. The collision with the rugged Freehan resulted in a pulled right shoulder muscle, which forced Campy to the sidelines for six games. The A's proceeded to lose the first five of those games before salvaging a win, dropping their season record to 2-9 in games in which Campy did not play.

Vida Blue incurred a no-decision in the team's fifth consecutive loss, as the A's dropped a 4-3 decision to the Yankees. Blue didn't pitch badly, giving up only two earned runs in six innings. Yet, the left-hander remained dissatisfied with his performance. "I'm not really worried, but I am concerned," Blue said, contradicting himself in the same sentence. "I feel tired. I don't know why. The ball goes but not the way it should."[18]

The five-game losing streak represented the worst for the franchise since Dick Williams had been named manager after the 1970 season. The frequent losses resulted in roster changes. With Rob Gardner already on the disabled list, Oakland recalled Dave Hamilton from Tucson. Williams called upon Hamilton to replace the disappointing Blue Moon Odom in the starting rotation.

Upon his promotion, a reporter asked Hamilton about one of his Tucson teammates, an outfielder named Charlie Chant. The reporter asked Hamilton whether Chant, whose name sounded like film detective Charlie Chan, was actually of Chinese descent. "No," Hamilton answered. "He's a right fielder."[19] Perhaps Hamilton didn't understand the question.

The five-game losing skid during Campaneris' absence left the A's with a mediocre record of 23-24, an embarrassing mark for a defending world champion. Finley decided the time was right to send Rob Gardner packing. While revealing that the disabled Gardner wasn't hurt very seriously to begin with, the A's sold the oft-traveled southpaw to the Brewers. Oakland fans, however, hadn't seen the last of Finley' favorite pitching yo-yo.

The A's managed to win three of their next four, salvaging the nine-game eastern road swing with a record of 3-6. In one of the wins, Ken Holtzman retired the first 20 Yankee batters he faced before allowing a seventh inning single to former Athletic Matty Alou. In the eighth inning, Yankee designated hitter Jim Ray Hart hit a line drive that caromed off Holtzman's leg so hard that it landed in the mitt of first baseman Deron Johnson — on the fly. Calling it the "hardest ball ever hit at me,"[20] Holtzman limped off the field with a large red welt on the back of his left leg. The A's sent him to the hospital for precautionary X-rays, which showed no break. Holtzman had been victimized by Hart earlier in his career. "Jim Ray Hart hit the first pitch I ever threw in the major leagues for a home run,[21] Holtzman said, recalling his debut in 1965.

In another victory, a 12-1 rout of the Red Sox, Mike Hegan's error-less games streak finally ended. Hegan handled a ground ball cleanly, but misfired his toss to Vida Blue, who was covering the first base bag. The harmless throwing error halted Hegan's streak, which had lasted 178 games and overlapped four seasons.

The green and gold returned home for a 12-game homestand, only to drop two straight to the lowly Brewers. The defeats included a frustrating 5-4 loss to the recently traded Rob Gardner. The previous day the A's had played perhaps their worst game of the season. Although the final score of 2-0 didn't appear unsightly, a review of the game's circumstances proved otherwise. With runners on first and third, Dick Williams signaled for a double steal. Normally an excellent base runner, Campy Campaneris broke from third, then stopped, and was caught off the bag as he tried to return to third base. Later in the game, Campy foolishly cut off a throw from the outfield, preventing Ray Fosse from making a catch and tag at the plate on what seemed like a certain out. In the outfield, Billy North and Reggie Jackson nearly collided on a fly ball that should have been caught routinely in right field. Jackson caught the ball, but not without a few histrionics. After Reggie scolded North for venturing too far from his post in center field, Jackson started to run for the dugout, thinking that he had notched the third out. Unfortunately, only two were out. Later in the game, Ray Fosse failed to make contact on a squeeze bunt attempt, leaving the slow-footed Deron Johnson an easy victim at home plate.

"It's been like this all year," said an exasperated Sal Bando after the game. "We just haven't been executing."[22] Bando pointed out the following conventional baseball wisdom: teams are generally destined to win one-third of their games and lose one-third of their games, leaving another third up for grabs. According to Bando, the A's failure to complete fundamental plays was preventing them from winning their share of those critical games.

On June 9, in an historic Finleyesque moment, the A's debuted their all-green uniforms. In 1972, the A's had worn solid green tops, but with traditional white pants. The new green pants, another Finley innovation, gave the A's a surreal, softball-like appearance. Sal Bando claimed the matching green tops and bottoms provided a helpful, camouflaging effect against Oakland opponents. "The batters can't see us," Bando explained tongue-in-cheek, "because we blend in with the grass and they hit it right at us."[23]

Ably assisted by their new look, the A's won their next two games against the Tigers. In the June 10 game, Joe Rudi made a catch strikingly similar to his spider-like snatch against the Reds' Denis Menke in the 1972 World Series. Rudi deprived Willie Horton of extra bases with a sprawling grab, helping preserve Catfish Hunter's 5-0 shutout win.

The A's finished a mediocre 7-5 on the homestand, despite a boom period at bat for Reggie Jackson. Reggie powered six homers and totaled 17 RBI's during the home stretch, putting himself on pace for a 100-RBI season. In one of the games against the Brewers, Jackson drove in five runs but still heard boos when he misplayed three catchable flyballs in right field. "I had that one bad game (defensively)," Reggie conceded. "But that's like striking out four times in one game. Those things happen."[24]

Ever since his record-breaking home run streak during the first half of the 1969 season, some of the media had been tempted to call Jackson a superstar. Few players in either league matched his combination of brute strength, raw speed, and powerful throwing arm. "His strength is just unbelievable," said former Athletic Dave Duncan in an interview with *Sport* magazine. "He should be able to hit 30 home runs a year just by accident."[25] Yet, Jackson had reached the single-season milestone only twice in his first five full major league seasons. Reggie's lack of patience at the plate, coupled with his tendency to overswing had limited his home run totals while creating too many strikeouts and too few walks. "It's no secret what they get him out on," said Duncan, the Indians' everyday catcher. "He strikes out on pitches over his head or in the dirt. When the pitch is in the strike zone, he hits it."[26]

Some observers also felt that Jackson had suffered from an identity crisis. In spring training, some of the A's players and media had whispered about Jackson's tendency to model himself after controversial White Sox slugger Dick Allen, whom he had known from his days growing up in the Philadelphia area. Allen had become a kind of guru to a number of black ballplayers throughout the majors. Although as talented as any power hitter in the game, Allen's strained relationships with managers and fans had undermined his reputation, calling into question his desire to win. "I like Allen as a person and admire him as a ballplayer, but I'm not trying to be like him,"[27] Jackson insisted. Still, others in the Oakland clubhouse saw a resemblance. "There's a little of Dick Allen in him," said Sal Bando. "A little of Frank Robinson. He has to learn to be Reggie Jackson."[28]

His strikeouts and insecurities aside, Jackson had played well enough and shown enough improvement in his game to merit election to the American League All-Star team. The same could not be said of Reggie's outfield partner, Joe Rudi, who remained mired in a season-long slump. When Rudi's average fell to a season-low .217, Dick Williams placed him on the bench for five straight games. Dubbed "Gentleman Joe" by the Bay Area media, Rudi normally handled such adversity with a calm, even demeanor. On this occasion, however, the benching angered him.

Jackson wasn't happy either. Williams had decided to sit his right fielder for a couple of days, saying that Reggie needed to be "rested." Jackson refuted Williams' reasoning. "Why should I need a rest? I just had a birthday, but I'm 27, not 37. I'm not tired. What's he thinking of? What did I do wrong? I'm hitting .285 and driving in runs."[29]

On the A's, complaints weren't restricted to stars like Jackson and Rudi. Even reserves joined in the discord. Angel Mangual had moved into Rudi's spot in left field, in what amounted to his last chance to resurrect his career in Oakland. In the late innings of one game, Williams sent up Jackson to pinch-hit for Mangual. Angel reacted by throwing his helmet. Williams reacted by fining Mangual $200. While that amount may not have sounded like much, it represented the largest fine that Williams had doled out during his tenure as Oakland manager.

In a matter of days, Williams had heard and seen signs of disharmony from three of his outfielders. The recurring question of playing time, paired with the team's stumbling play on the field, irritated the manager. "I can't be concerned whether a guy is unhappy or not," said an unsympathetic Williams. "I just want them to go out and play."[30]

Mangual said Williams misunderstood his gesture. "I wasn't tossing my helmet because Reggie pinch-hit for me," Mangual insisted. "I did it just to relax." Mangual then let his frustration toward the manager show. "If Williams no like me, why doesn't he trade me?"[31] Williams and Charlie Finley faced a basic problem: who would want Mangual, given his poor 1972 season and continuing struggles at the plate and in the field?

During the offseason, Charlie Finley had pushed his fellow owners to adopt a rule allowing a "designated runner," a player who could be substituted at any time for the slowest batter in the lineup. Although American League owners had ratified the rule change, the National League had refused to go along. Even though the rules wouldn't allow a "designated" runner, Finley still believed in the importance of carrying a player whose only value was his ability to pinch-run. Finley called up Allan Lewis from Double-A Birmingham, and demoted Gonzalo Marquez to Triple-A Tucson.

Allan Lewis, a favorite of Finley nicknamed the "Panamanian Express," had been with the A's sporadically since 1967. In 1966, Lewis had set a Florida State League record by stealing 116 bases for Leesburg. Incredibly, opposing catchers had thrown out Lewis only 10 times that season. In spite of his eye-popping speed, few players had poorer baseball instincts and understanding for the game than Lewis.

Lewis had already attempted to defend his playing abilities. "When I play regularly, I hit .280,"[32] Lewis had said during the 1972 World Series. During his minor league career, Lewis had compiled respectable batting averages of .280 and .288 over full seasons, and averages as high as .319 and .322 during partial seasons. Yet, he had totaled only 13 home runs over 12 minor league seasons and had shown no ability to hit in part-time duty as a major league player. "He's a .300 hitter," Dick Williams had once said tongue-in-cheek. "One-fifty left-handed and .150 right-handed."[33] Lewis had also demonstrated himself to be a major liability in several other areas. He ran fast, but often negated that ability with his failure to get good jumps, and played no position particularly well, even though the A's listed him as an outfielder on their roster. The decision to promote Lewis to the major leagues angered several of the players, foremost captain Sal Bando, who criticized the 31-year-old pinch runner's baseball skills. Quite simply, the majority of Lewis' teammates felt he had no business wearing a major league uniform.

Bando became even more incensed when Lewis made his 1973 debut on June 18, pinch-running for Bando himself in the seventh inning of a 9-5 win over the Royals. The fact that Lewis scored a run did little to soothe Bando, who resented being replaced by an inferior ballplayer during a close game. Bando probably became more infuriated when he watched his replacement at third base, Rich McKinney, commit a late-inning error in the same game.

Other Oakland players publicly expressed their opposition to Lewis' presence on the roster. The resentment grew after a game on June 20, when the A's played the Royals in Kansas City. Dick Williams used Lewis as a pinch-runner for designated hitter Deron Johnson. One inning later, with a chance to break a 4-4 tie in extra innings, the A's loaded the bases with one out. It was now Johnson's turn to bat. Only Johnson had already been removed for the pinch-running Lewis, and was now out of the game. Williams sent McKinney up to pinch-hit for Lewis. McKinney failed to deliver the game-tying run, and the A's went on to lose the game in the bottom of the 12th.

The strategy left Oakland players incredulous. Williams had used Lewis as a pinch-runner in two earlier games, but the A's had managed to win both times. On this occasion, the use of Lewis had cost the A's their best chance to win in extra innings, at least according to most of the players in the clubhouse. Why did Finley insist on carrying Lewis on the 25-man roster, the players thought out loud, and why did Williams insist on playing him?

"At that time, it was kind of new to us to carry a player who would not have made the team based on his baseball skills," Bando explains. "I don't think it was anything personal against Allan as much as it was we were carrying somebody who really, all he could do was pinch-run. It's like putting somebody on the club, that when other guys are competing who have more skills to hit or field, couldn't make the club."

One year later, Finley took his experiment a step further when he signed a sprinter named Herb Washington, who had never played professional baseball at any level. "Actually, Allan Lewis was a better fit than Herb Washington," Bando points out, "because Allan Lewis could play a position here or there if you needed somebody."

Several days later, another controversy infiltrated the A's, though this one involved one of the team's announcers. Television play-by-play man Monte Moore had long been considered a Finley house man, one who constantly sang the praises of the Oakland owner on the air, and who allegedly served as a snitch for Finley around the ballpark and clubhouse. Some players and writers believed that if someone made negative comments about Finley in the presence of Moore, those remarks would eventually find their way to the all-knowing owner.

Most players suspected Moore of acting as a conduit to Charlie Finley. Moore knew about the allegations, and realized that some of the accusations came from baseball writers. Moore would soon enjoy some payback. In late June, the A's played the White Sox in a weekend series in Chicago. During one of the games, Billy North reached first base on what official scorer Edgar Munzel deemed an infield error. Moore, broadcasting the game back to Oakland, disagreed with Munzel's decision. Moore felt Munzel should have credited North with a base hit. Moore took his criticism a step further when he accused newspaper reporters, in general, of not paying attention to the action on the field. Several writers resented the accusation. "You newspaper men are so sensitive," Moore told a reporter after the broadcast. "A lot of newspaper men have criticized me, and if they've got a right to criticize me, then I've got a right to criticize them."[34]

Although most writers probably didn't want to admit it, Moore was right. Although one might have questioned his motives, he did have every right to criticize writers, provided that he could back up his accusations. Moore was also right on the Munzel scoring decision, and played a part in having the ruling changed. To his credit, Munzel asked all of the players involved on the play whether it should be scored a hit or an error. Munzel collected all of the testimony, and two days after making his original decision, he changed the scoring of the play. Munzel gave North a hit, drawing the praise of Dick Williams in the process. "Edgar Munzel showed me a lot of class,"[35] Williams said afterward.

Controversies, slumps, and personnel changes characterized the first half of the 1973 season. On June 28, the A's moved into sole possession of first place in the AL West for the first time. Vida Blue pitched seven and two-thirds strong innings before giving way to Rollie Fingers, who preserved a 3-2 win. It had taken 75 games, but the A's had finally taken the lead from the Angels, White Sox, Twins, and Royals, who all remained within two games of first place.

After allowing only three hits to Kansas City in his strongest outing of the season, Blue sounded off to those members of the media who had previously reported the death of his left arm. "All you guys from UPI and AP and SI (*Sports Illustrated*) and all the other initials — and anyone else who thinks my arm is dead — come out to the park and get a bat," Blue challenged the assembled reporters. "I'll throw you guys 100 pitches and give any man $500 for each ball he fouls off."[36]

The return to health of Dick Green gave the A's an excess of second basemen. Even though Green and Kubiak were slumping badly at the plate, Charlie Finley decided to part ways with classy veteran Dal Maxvill, who had helped Oakland clinch the 1972 divisional crown. Four clubs expressed interest in Maxvill, before Finley settled on making a cash deal with the Pittsburgh Pirates.

The A's arrival at the top spot of the Western Division didn't mean they had abandoned controversy. Far from it. In early July, Reggie Jackson committed two errors during a four-game stretch, dropping easy flyballs each time. After a game against the Angels, a reporter asked Jackson how he felt physically. Jackson said he felt fine, then quickly changed the subject to Oakland's coaching and managerial staff. "We make a mistake," a frustrated Jackson said to a gathering of writers, "and they act as if you did it on purpose. The coaches don't contribute anything. We make their money for them."[37] Jackson added a dose of sarcasm to his diatribe. "The way these guys criticize you, you'd think they were all Babe Ruth when they played."[38]

First base coach Jerry Adair fired back at Reggie. "I'm getting sick and tired of seeing him play half the time,"[39] said an angry Adair. Jackson tried to clarify his remarks, indicating that he hadn't intended to include Adair in his critique. Jackson said that he had actually directed his statements at manager Dick Williams and third base coach Irv Noren, who had criticized Dick Green and Ray Fosse for recent on-the-field mistakes.

The remarks represented the first publicly negative statements Jackson had made about his manager since his hiring in 1970, when Reggie had cited Williams' reputation as a man who would not stick up for his players. Williams didn't appreciate Jackson's most recent sentiments, especially about his underpaid coaching staff. "Everything we do is constructive criticism," Williams said before borrowing an old cliche. "If you can't stand the heat, get out of the kitchen."[40]

On the team's flight from California to Baltimore, Jackson approached Williams. A Baltimore newspaper would later report that Jackson challenged his manager to a fight on the plane. Jackson denied the story. "I never told him to get up and fight," said Reggie. "I told him never to talk to me again, just to write my name in the lineup."[41] What was Williams' reaction to Jackson's orders? "He didn't say anything," Jackson replied, "but I could tell he was ticked off." To his credit, Jackson later apologized for the way he had spoken to his manager. "The next day I knew I was wrong and I went up to him and said I wanted it to be forgotten."[42] Williams agreed to do so, hoping to reestablish his solid relationship with his All-Star right fielder.

Oakland beat writers wondered what effect Jackson's recent public comments might have on the future of Williams and his coaches. There had already been speculation that Williams might voluntarily leave the organization at season's end and try to find another managerial job. How would Charlie Finley react to his star player's dissatisfaction with the manager? Some writers speculated that Finley might use the opportunity to make public his own criticisms of Williams. Perhaps Finley would reprimand Williams for being overly critical of his players. Three days after the Jackson firestorm broke out, Finley made an announcement. Instead of firing any of his coaches, or Williams himself, Finley surprised most everyone concerned by announcing that he had renewed the contracts of Williams, Noren, Adair, pitching coach Wes Stock, and bullpen coach Vern Hoscheit for another season.

Finley denied that he had been motivated by Jackson's complaints about the "overcritical" managerial and coaching staff. Finley insisted that the timing of his decision to reward Williams and his coaches with extensions was merely a coincidence and had nothing to do with Reggie. According to Finley, he was simply rewarding his workers for a job well done.

More likely, Finley had decided to send Jackson the following message: *Don't knock your managers and coaches. You work for them, and they work for me. Keep your mouth shut and play.* Finley was making it quite clear that he was in charge of the team, not Jackson. In a way, Finley seemed to be punishing Jackson by rewarding Williams and the coaches.

The Jackson controversy overshadowed several positive developments in July. Home attendance, which had been awful during the first month of the season, had prompted Dick Williams to make the following remarks: "We're world champions. We've proved ourselves. The area hasn't."[43] In 1972, the A's had drawn a total of 921,323 fans — the worst total for a world championship team since World War II.

In his continuing frustration over the lack of fan support, Williams had warned fans about the possibility of the A's moving to another city. The A's wouldn't need to relocate the franchise, though, since attendance had improved considerably during the month of July. The rise in fan interest led some writers to speculate that the A's might break the one million fan mark for the first time in Oakland franchise history. Better play and warmer weather had given A's fans stronger incentive to visit the Coliseum.

Reliever Darold Knowles started to throw hard again, much like he had during his early major league days in Philadelphia and Washington. Knowles said overwork during his last two seasons with the Senators had robbed life from his fastball. Earlier in the season, Williams had admonished Knowles for his seeming unwillingness to challenge hitters. Knowles claimed that he never intentionally meant to nibble at the plate; he simply had been unable to throw the ball where he wanted. "I'd hate to have to tell him this," Knowles said of Williams' complaints, "but I'm trying to throw the ball right down the middle of the plate."[44] With Knowles throwing his good fastball and throwing it for strikes, the A's now had someone to relieve some of the late-inning pressure from closer Rollie Fingers.

Ray Fosse started to drive in runs, something he had failed to do over the first half of the season. Fosse hit three home runs during a four-game series against the Brewers, and collected 13 RBI's in Oakland's final 12 games before the All-Star break. Prior to that stretch, Fosse had driven in only 19 runs over the entire first half, having failed miserably with runners in scoring position. The hitting surge gave the A's excellent all-around play from their new catcher. Fosse had played remarkable defense throughout the season. In his first 98 games, opposing teams attempted only 48 stolen bases against the rocket-armed receiver. Fosse threw out 24 of those runners, for an even 50 per cent. In contrast, former Oakland catcher Dave Duncan had struggled in his efforts to nail base stealers in Cleveland. While Indian pitchers did not hold runners as well as Oakland hurlers, Duncan simply did not possess the kind of arm strength boasted by Fosse.

For the first time all season, Vida Blue notched back-to-back complete games. Blue followed up a four-hit effort against Baltimore with an impressive three-hitter against the Indians. Vida's new-found success didn't dissuade him from taking a subtle shot at Dick Williams. After the win over the Orioles, Blue hinted that Williams had been too quick in taking his starting pitchers out of games. Blue's observation conflicted with the general media consensus that Williams had been anything but quick in removing his starters; after all, the new designated hitter rule had eliminated the need for pinch-hitting for the pitcher and had resulted in an underutilized bullpen.

While the A's had started to play better baseball, Dick Williams' health had taken a turn for the worse. On July 19, Williams suffered an attack of appendicitis, which required an emergency appendectomy that day. The appendectomy would force Williams to miss several regular season games, but he would return in time to lead the American League in the All-Star game. Some writers speculated that Finley had ordered his manager to work the All-Star classic, even though he didn't feel anywhere close to perfect health. Williams later denied that Finley had made such a demand.

Catfish Hunter entered the All-Star break at 15-3, having won 10 consecutive decisions. Hunter's pitching earned him a spot on the American League All-Star team, which in this case, turned out to be bad news for the A's. Hunter's selection also provided Charlie Finley with an opportunity to unveil his inherent cheapness. The producers of a special All-Star Game portrait asked the A's publicity office (translation, Finley) to provide them with a photograph of Hunter. The photograph would serve as the model for the painter of the portrait. Instead of providing an updated photo of Hunter, with his longer hair and mustache, Finley sent a five-year old picture of "The Cat" to be used in creating the portrait. Hunter's appearance had changed considerably in the last half decade, perhaps more so than any Oakland player. No longer short-haired and clean shaven, Hunter looked unrecognizable to most fans in the outdated photograph and portrait. One of Finley's cost-cutting measures had ended up embarrassing his star pitcher, and even more so, the organization itself.

Hunter's appearance in the All-Star game became a regrettable one. In the second inning of the game, Hunter faced Chicago Cubs' outfielder Billy Williams, who smacked a line drive toward the mound. Instinctively, Hunter tried to field the ball bare-handed — an unfortunate decision, as it turned out — and incurred a hairline fracture to his right thumb. Dick Williams' stomach turned over as he observed helplessly from the American League dugout.

Doctors placed Hunter's thumb in a splint for several days before removing it. A hardy Catfish began throwing six days after sustaining the injury, which led doctors to predict a quick recovery period of only two weeks. If so, the break would force Hunter to miss about four or five starts; he had last missed a starting assignment seven years earlier in 1966 due to an appendectomy. An optimistic Hunter mused that the injury might provide a long term benefit. "Heck, it might help me," Hunter reasoned. "I need the rest. I'll be strong for August and September."[45]

Thumb injuries continued to affect the A's when, two days after the All-Star break, Joe Rudi jammed his thumb badly after slipping on a wet patch of outfield grass in Minnesota. Rudi then developed a bad case of strep throat, which forced him into a short hospital stay. Doctors treated Rudi for sores in his mouth and swollen tonsils before releasing him from the hospital.

The injury to Catfish Hunter left the A's wondering whether to disable their star right-hander. At first, Charlie Finley decided to place Hunter on the injured list and called up nine-year minor league catcher Jose Morales from Tucson. Finley then changed his mind, and told Morales to report back to Tucson after just one day with the major league club. One day later, Finley decided to disable Hunter, and left instructions with Morales to return to Oakland from Tucson. Incredibly, Finley changed his mind a third time and decided to keep Hunter on the active list, but instead of demoting Morales, sent pitcher Dave Hamilton back to Triple-A. Dick Williams finally rewarded Morales with a start as designated hitter in a game at Boston's Fenway Park. The 28-year-old rookie responded with a double in four at-bats against Luis Tiant in his major league debut. After nine years of pounding the minor league pavement, and then a series of indecisive moves by the Oakland brass, Morales had finally collected his first big league hit.

The A's initially hoped to place Hunter on the disabled list retroactive to the All-Star game, but Commissioner Bowie Kuhn refused to allow the move. A New York City doctor informed Hunter that he wouldn't be able to pitch for two weeks, but the A's physician, Dr. Harry Walker, refuted that prediction, saying that Catfish could return in less than seven days. Dr. Walker's prognosis initially upset Hunter, who claimed the thumb was still very sore. Hunter subsequently tried to throw batting practice but revealed that his thumb hurt appreciably, preventing him from cutting loose with his fastball or his needed out pitch — the slider. A few days later, Catfish reported improvement in the hand's condition, lending credence to the soothsaying skills of the Oakland doctor.

Billy Conigliaro returned to the lineup on July 27, just in time to face the Twins' Bert Blyleven. The young right-hander possessed one of the biggest-breaking and most deceptive curve balls in the major leagues, in addition to an above-average fastball. Not so surprisingly, Conigliaro went 0-for-4 in his start against Blyleven, who struck out nine Oakland batters. One reporter asked Conigliaro why he hadn't delayed his return so as to avoid facing the sweeping curve ball of Blyleven. "You can't wait to come back against some guy you like (to face),"[46] responded Billy C., who explained that there weren't many pitchers he found easy to hit.

Although the A's improved their level of play considerably in July, their record still lagged behind their won-loss pace of 1972. Charlie Finley believed one of the reasons for the fallback could be found in the poor play of the once sturdy bench. Oakland's pinch-hitting statistics revealed plenty about the inability of reserve players to deliver timely hits. Jay Johnstone went 0-for-12 as a pinch-hitter since his recall from Tucson. Angel Mangual also went hitless in a dozen pinch-hitting appearances. Rich McKinney, expected to be one of the designated hitters at the start of the season, was just 2-for-17 off the bench. Even Mike Hegan, an exceptional pinch-hitter in 1971 and '72, had failed in pinch-hit situations, with just one hit in 17 at-bats. Last year's late season sensation, Gonzalo Marquez, had since been demoted to Tucson.

On July 30, the Oakland bats fell completely silent against Texas Rangers' starter Jim Bibby. The giant-sized right-hander, who had been acquired in a June trade with the Cardinals, struck out 13 batters in compiling a no-hitter. Ranger outfielder Jeff Burroughs blasted a grand slam to support Bibby's 6-0 win.

The following day, Charlie Finley reacted to the embarrassment of being no-hit by the last-place Rangers, and the club's continuing pinch-hitting inadequacies, by announcing three transactions. Finley signed infielder Mike Andrews as a free agent and purchases two veteran pinch-hitters: the Pirates' Vic Davalillo and the Astros' Jesus Alou. In order to make room for the new players, the A's demoted Johnstone and McKinney to Triple-A, and also optioned rookie pitcher Glenn Abbott, who had thrown the ball poorly in his major league debut.

Much like he had in 1972, when he picked up Matty Alou and Dal Maxvill for the stretch run, Finley swiftly and directly addressed the team's greatest need. In 1972, the A's had needed help at second base and in the outfield; suddenly, Maxvill and Alou appeared out of thin air through trades. Now, with the A's requiring capable clutch hitting in the late innings, Finley had hand-delivered Matty's brother, Jesus, along with Andrews and Davalillo.

Andrews had asked for his release from the White Sox earlier in the summer. He had clashed with Chicago's unpopular general manager Stu Holcomb, who had publicly criticized Andrews' playing ability, saying he couldn't hit, field or throw. Dick Williams, who had managed Andrews during his first managerial tenure in Boston, had different memories of the veteran infielder. In 1967, Andrews had contributed to the Red Sox' pennant cause by hitting a respectable .263, playing a solid second base and teaming well with shortstop Rico Petrocelli. More importantly, Andrews had impressed Williams with his professionalism and hard-working attitude.

Davalillo employed one of the strangest batting styles in either league. A left-handed slap hitter, Davalillo bailed out severely on pitches, step-

ping toward the first base dugout with his front foot. Although this approach contradicted most fundamentals of good hitting, Davalillo had set
a single-season major league record in 1970 by collecting 24 pinch-hits
for the St. Louis Cardinals. The following year Davalillo joined the Pirates
in a trade, hitting .285 in a reserve role. Davalillo filled in ably at first base
and at all three outfield positions, contributing to the Pirates' world championship. After another fine season in 1972, Davalillo had seen his playing time and hitting effectiveness diminish in 1973 under Pirate manager
Bill Virdon. Davalillo's dwindling role upset the 36-year-old Venezuelan.
"I was doing nothing at Pittsburgh except pinch-hitting once every four or
five days," Davalillo told Ron Bergman of *The Sporting News*. "I don't mind
pinch-hitting. It's just hard to do when you do it only once a week. I don't
mind it three or four times a week."[47]

Jesus Alou, whose high leg kick and twitching neck characterized
his physical hitting style, became the third member of the Alou clan to
play for the A's. The three brothers had appeared in Oakland uniforms in
a neat, orderly succession: Felipe had played for Oakland in 1970 and
'71; Matty had joined the team late in 1972; and now Jesus was joining
the green and gold in '73. Although Felipe, Matty, and Jesus had once
played for the rival San Francisco Giants in the same outfield in 1963,
they never played with each other as teammates in Oakland.

Reggie Jackson offered a classic reaction to Finley's latest round of
trades and signings. "I want to be a member of the Oakland A's forever,"
Jackson declared tongue-in-cheek. "That way I get to meet all the famous
ballplayers coming and going."[48] During Reggie's tenure in the Bay Area,
Finley had acquired the following list of notable players in mid-season
transactions:

      1973 — Jesus Alou, Mike Andrews, Vic Davalillo, and Deron
             Johnson (soon to be followed by Rico Carty)
      1972 — Matty Alou, Ollie BrownOrlando Cepeda, Dal Maxvill, Don
             Mincher, and Art Shamsky
      1971 — Curt Blefary, Mike Epstein, Mudcat Grant, Mike Hegan,
             and Darold Knowles
      1970 — Tommy Davis and Bob Locker
      1969 — Bob Johnson, Juan Pizarro, and Fred Talbot
      1967 — Ken "Hawk" Harrelson

Finley's penchant for mid and late-season trades had allowed Jackson to play with members of one of baseball's most famous families (the
Alous), one of the game's greatest stars of the early sixties (Tommy Davis),
one of the top stars from the late sixties (Orlando Cepeda), two important
contributors to the Twins' 1965 American League championship team
(Don Mincher and Mudcat Grant), a key member of the lovable Mets championship team of 1969 (Art Shamsky), and one of baseball's most colorful
characters, a true symbol of the "mod" generation (Hawk Harrelson). In
many ways, Finley had assembled a "who's who" of baseball from 1967 to

1973.

Smart man that he was, Reggie Jackson expected more well-known names from the recent past to be playing for the A's before the end of the season. "Charlie will probably go over to the National League in September and get someone with 300 to 400 career home runs," Jackson predicted with a grin. "I wouldn't be surprised to see Willie McCovey over here."[49] Although Reggie was being facetious in his comments, he wasn't too far off base, just a bit ahead of schedule. The 35-year old McCovey, who was in the midst of a productive 29-home run, 75-RBI season in San Francisco, wouldn't be arriving in Oakland in 1973; his arrival would have to wait three more years, when he would join the A's for 24 late-season at-bats. When it came to star players who were winding down their careers but still had some productivity left in their bats, no one loved them more than Charlie Finley.

Mike Hegan had been one of Finley's mid-season pickups during the 101-win season of 1971. Although Hegan had never been a star player along the lines of an Orlando Cepeda or Tommy Davis, he had gained notoriety for two reasons. First, he was the son of former major league catcher Jim Hegan, a fine defensive receiver with the Cleveland Indians and later a long-time coach with the Yankees. Second, Hegan had played for the 1969 expansion Seattle Pilots, an awful team forever immortalized by Jim Bouton in his famed book, *Ball Four*. Hegan was now making news for another reason. In late July, he announced that he would retire after the current season. Although Hegan was just 31 years old, he had tired of performing as a bench player since his departure from Milwaukee, and longed for an opportunity to play elsewhere as an everyday first baseman or outfielder. With a still youthful Gene Tenace entrenched at first base, and with Joe Rudi, Billy North, and Reggie Jackson established in the outfield, Hegan saw little opportunity to break into Oakland's starting nine.

Hegan realized he had the ability to pursue other careers, having worked as a television sportscaster for WTMJ-TV in Milwaukee during the winter. The A's recognized his speaking ability; they had actually asked him to fill in for one of their regular announcers, Jim Woods, earlier in the season. Moments before the July 18th game against the Orioles, Dick Williams told Hegan to put on dress slacks and a collared shirt and report to the broadcast booth as a replacement for Woods, who had taken ill. Incredibly, Hegan announced the first three innings of the game against Baltimore, then rode the elevator back to the clubhouse. The backup first baseman-turned-broadcaster hurried into his A's uniform and returned to the dugout. As it turned out, Hegan didn't need to hurry, since Dick Williams chose to use Jay Johnstone — and not Hegan — as a pinch-hitter for Dick Green in the late innings. Hegan, by the way, received union scale wages for his three-inning effort in the booth.

Although Hegan enjoyed his part-time broadcasting gigs, a full-time announcing job would have to wait. Hegan wanted to continue his on-field career, assuming he could find another team, one that would provide him with a regular playing role. "It did get a little frustrating," Hegan says. "I had been getting less and less playing time. At that point, it got frustrating. I knew there were other clubs looking for left-handed hitting." Just a few days after announcing his retirement plans, Finley rescued Hegan, sending the backup first baseman to the Yankees for $20,000.

At the time of the trade, Hegan left one first-place team for another. Within a few days, the Orioles stormed past the Yankees on their way to winning the American League East. Does Hegan, in retrospect, feel any regret over leaving a winning team, one that had just begun to tap its championship ability? "The winning is fine," says Hegan, "but from a personal standpoint, the one reason we all play the game is to play the game, if possible. I wanted one more opportunity to play every day again."

Yet, Hegan fully realized he was departing a special team, one that would emerge as a dynasty in the early part of the decade. "I knew that I was leaving probably what would have been and should have been the dominating team of the entire seventies. If it hadn't been for free agency, they certainly would have been."

Chapter Sixteen:
Second Half Soap Opera

The A's soon discovered that their new infield acquisition, Mike Andrews, was damaged goods and could not make a routine throw from his position at second base. Andrews claimed that his arm was fine, but the physical evidence dictated otherwise. After watching him make two bad throws, Dick Williams announced that he would not use Andrews in the field anymore. Williams would restrict his new acquisition to pinch-hitting and designated hitting appearances.

Illness had become one of the unfortunate themes of the Oakland summer. In July, Dick Williams had been stricken by appendicitis. Charlie Finley had not been feeling well for much of the season, either. On August 7, Finley suffered a heart attack — the probable result of too many long hours spent questioning his manager's decisions and trying to make trades. Unfortunately for Dick Williams and the A's, Finley's heart attack would affect his behavior for the duration of the season.

On August 12, the A's played perhaps their wildest game of the season against the Yankees. Oakland trailed the Yankees 11-5 after six innings, before scoring six runs in the seventh and two more in the eighth. The incredible late-game rally gave the A's a 13-12 comeback win on the road. Yet, the A's had played so poorly early in the game that Dick Williams had almost pulled his regular players in favor of a wave of reserves. "It was so bad," Williams said, "that if we didn't score a few runs in the seventh, or at least get within striking distance, I was going to put in all of our other guys. I had six guys on the bench ready to go in the sixth inning."[1] The victory, inspiring enough in and of itself, proved even more meaningful since it allowed the A's to move within one game of first place in the West.

In August, Williams made two important strategic decisions. Leadoff man Campy Campaneris had been having difficulty getting on base and had failed to steal a base over a three-week period of time until finally picking up a theft against the Red Sox on August 16. The next day, Williams flip-flopped Campaneris and Billy North, putting North in the leadoff spot and pushing Campaneris to the No. 2 slot in the batting order. Williams recognized that the younger North was hitting for a higher average, drawing more walks, and stealing bases more efficiently than the more experienced Campaneris.

While baseball statisticians might have argued that Williams' decision was an obvious one, it still required a large degree of courage. Campaneris was one of the A's veterans, one of their most popular players in the clubhouse. Campy and his teammates might have considered Williams' lineup adjustment to be an outright demotion; after all, the leadoff spot carried with it a notion of glamour and excitement, while the No. 2 spot was considered a position for lesser hitters and baserunners. Yet, Williams understood that while the speedy, slap-hitting Campaneris looked like a leadoff hitter, he really wasn't a leadoff hitter. Campy didn't hit for a high enough batting average or exhibit nearly enough patience at the plate to reach base the requisite 38 to 40 per cent of the time, figures considered acceptable for a table-setting hitter. Williams had used Campaneris as a leadoff man in past years, but only because the A's had not possessed any other players even remotely capable of handling the job. With North batting leadoff, and Campaneris able to utilize his bunting and hit-and-run skills in the second spot, the A's shaped up as a much better offensive team.

Williams made an even more daring decision with his pitching staff, which counted only Vida Blue and Ken Holtzman as certified starters. Faced with a sudden shortage of starting pitchers, a void that was created by the loss of Catfish Hunter and the continuing slide of Blue Moon Odom, Williams turned to his ample bullpen corps for his best left-handed relief pitcher, Darold Knowles. The nine-year veteran hadn't started a game since 1967, when he had made one start for the Washington Senators. On August 14, Knowles made his fourth start of the season for the A's. Knowles faced the powerful Red Sox at Fenway Park, a noted graveyard for left-handed pitchers. Pitching carefully to a lineup that included dangerous hitters like Tommy Harper, Luis Aparicio, Carl Yastrzemski, Orlando Cepeda and Carlton Fisk, Knowles walked five batters on the night and struck out only one. But Knowles scattered only six hits and kept the Red Sox off the scoreboard for nine innings. Knowles pitched under pressure all night, given that the A's managed only one run against Boston's Bill Lee on a sixth inning squeeze bunt by Dick Green. Knowles' complete game shutout at Fenway Park represented one of the most amazing, and unlikely pitching performances of the 1973 season.

Five days after Knowles' masterpiece against the Red Sox, Catfish Hunter returned to the mound. Hunter pitched five innings of three-run baseball, earning himself a no-decision in Oakland's 6-4 win over the Brewers. In that same game, Jesus Alou collected two hits as he continued to fill in ably for the sidelined Joe Rudi. In his last four starts, Alou had managed three two-hit games. Charlie Finley could pat himself on the back for another deal well done.

The return of Hunter, however, was the big story. "The Cat" had initially been expected to miss only a couple of weeks; he ended up missing nearly a month. During his absence, the A's had seen their two and a half game lead in the West transform into a two-game deficit, before a late surge enabled the A's to reclaim a two-game lead by the time Hunter returned. For nearly a month, Dick Williams had scrambled around trying to find starting pitching, plucking Knowles and others for emergency duties.

When healthy, Hunter didn't dazzle onlookers with gasping fastballs or high strikeout games. Even though he lacked the velocity of Vida Blue, he nonetheless challenged hitters. Hunter also pitched to the scoreboard, giving up few enough runs to win games by the slimmest of margins. "He isn't afraid of giving up a lot of hits," remarked Reggie Jackson. "If he's got a big lead in the eighth, he'll just lay it in there and make them hit it. He doesn't care if he beats you 11-10, as long as he beats you."[2]

Without Hunter, the A's lacked their most important pitcher, the man most inclined toward winning. "There's the most valuable player on our club," shouted Jackson, while pointing directly at Hunter. "He's fouled up a whole pitching staff by himself."[3] A humble Hunter wouldn't accept Reggie's humorous praise. "I don't think I am the club's most valuable player," Hunter told reporters. "I would have to say Jackson is with the year he's been having."[4]

In a sense, Hunter was right. During Catfish's layoff, when the A's needed their offense to pick up the requisite slack for a faltering pitching staff more than ever, none of the Oakland hitters raised their level of hitting as much as the maturing Jackson. On August 18, Jackson simultaneously reached the two seasonal milestones considered most important to accomplished power hitters: 30 home runs and 100 RBI's. Jackson's benchmark game included a three-run, first inning home run against Milwaukee's Jim Slaton, highlighting a 6-3 win over the Brewers. On August 24, Jackson decided to shave his beard but retained his hot stroke with two singles and a pair of RBI's, helping Hunter to his first win since his return from the injured list. "He still looks the same to me,"[5] Dick Williams said of his beardless slugger.

Ray Fosse did notice some differences in Hunter, making only his second start since his return from the disabled list. After the game, Fosse told reporters that Hunter was "not popping, just pushing the ball, maybe afraid to cut loose after his layoff."[6] Since most baseball people considered Fosse an astute observer of pitching, Hunter's right arm would bear watching over his next several starts.

During an east coast trip that included stopovers in Detroit, New York, and Boston, the A's finally began playing the kind of high-caliber baseball that they had achieved throughout much of the '71 and '72 seasons but had eluded them for most of the summer of '73. The A's won two straight games against the Yankees, three consecutive vs. the Red Sox, continued the assault at home with three straight wins against the Brewers, and finished the stretch with a single victory over the Tigers. The string of games against Eastern Division clubs added up to a season-high nine-game winning streak. The A's lost their next game to Detroit, ending the succession of wins, but the defeat proved to be a minute blip in the day-to-day evolution of the standings. Oakland won the final game of its series with the Tigers, and then swept the Yankees in a three-game set. The new four-game win streak gave the A's 13 victories in their last 14 outings.

In the finale against the Yankees, Ken Holtzman and Vic Davalillo teamed up on a 1-0 win. Unlike another July 31st acquisition, Jesus Alou, Davalillo had struggled badly since trading in his Pittsburgh whites for the green and gold of Oakland. His first hit in 13 days drove home the only run of the game in support of Holtzman, who actually used an injury to improve his pitching. Holtzman sprained his ankle slightly while tripping over a loose bat, but the twist in his foot helped prevent him from over-throwing his fastball while fine-tuning his control. Partially aided by the unfortunate circumstance-turned-benefit, Holtzman set down the final 18 Yankees he faced en route to a complete game shutout.

While the development of Billy North settled Oakland's long-standing search for a center fielder, it made another outfielder extraneous in the playing time plan. Billy Conigliaro, the No. 1 center fielder at the end of spring training, had fallen into a state of disuse. "They're going to retire my uniform," said Conigliaro, "with me still in it."[7] At least Billy had retained his sense of humor, something he had failed to do during his miserable experience in Milwaukee the previous summer.

According to the latest press box rumors, Oakland seemed prime to become the hub of a Conigliaro family reunion. Newspaper reporters discussed the possibility of the A's signing Tony Conigliaro, who had retired from the Angels due to eye problems in 1971. Ironically, Tony C. had played his final game against the A's. In a 20-inning marathon loss that night, Conigliaro suffered through a strikeout-filled 0-for-8, twice engaging in shouting matches with home plate umpire Merle Anthony over balls and strikes. Tony C's five strikeouts convinced him he could no longer see well enough to hit a major league baseball.

If the A's signed Conigliaro, where would they play him? With Reggie Jackson marching toward an MVP, right field with the A's was out of the question. The designated hitter void had long since been filled by National League castoff Deron Johnson. Perhaps the A's were considering Conigliaro for left field, where Joe Rudi's play had been undermined by prolonged hitting slumps, repeated viral infections and subsequent losses of weight.

As quickly as the Conigliaro rumor arose in the press box, Dick Williams fired it down. He denied that the A's possessed any interest in the former Red Sox and Angel slugger. Williams' denial seemed plausible, given the strains between him and Conigliaro in Boston a few years back. After Tony C. had been struck in the head by a Jack Hamilton fastball in 1967, he laid near death in a hospital bed for several days. Conigliaro remained a captive of the hospital for a few more weeks, and bitterly complained when Williams did not visit him even once. Williams reacted to the criticism by insisting that he felt sympathy for Conigliaro, but regarded his obligation to a pennant-contending Red Sox team as his most important job priority. Since it seemed questionable whether Conigliaro wanted to attempt a comeback with any team two years after his retirement, even observers of the A's (who had come to expect surprises) had to wonder why he would consider a return to a manager whom he felt had abandoned him six years earlier.

The A's did make a roster move, albeit one of less headline-making ability than any signing of Conigliaro. Charlie Finley gave up his World Series pinch-hitting hero, sending Gonzalo Marquez the way of another 1972 bench stalwart Mike Hegan, who had departed in a trade earlier in the summer. Marquez had fallen victim to an unexpected by-product of the newfangled DH rule. Since pinch-hitting for the pitcher's spot had become a moot point, the general importance of a pinch-hitter deluxe like Marquez had been largely reduced. On the few occasions that Dick Williams had seen fit to use him, Marquez found his batting stroke wanting due to extended stretches of inactivity.

Finley dealt Marquez to one of his favorite trading partners, the Chicago Cubs, perhaps hoping that he would strike gold for a third time after reeling in Ken Holtzman and Billy North from the Windy City. In exchange for the one-dimensional Marquez, the A's acquired another left-handed first baseman named Pat Bourque. Although the Cubs considered Bourque an unremarkable prospect, he did possess two traits foreign to Marquez' game: a competent glove and slightly above-average power. The A's hoped that Bourque would fill the gap created by the dual partings of Marquez and Hegan.

Although Ken Holtzman had pitched well during a major league career that began in 1966, the veteran left-hander had never reached the 20-win plateau in a single season. In 1972, Holtzman had settled for 19 wins, falling short of the milestone due to a run of bad luck and poor run support. On September 4, Holtzman faced the Angels, trying to push his win total from an unglamorous 19 to the magic circle. Holtzman faced hard-throwing right-hander Bill Singer at Anaheim Stadium. Holtzman thinly out-dueled his veteran counterpart, winning a 4-3 decision. In his eighth major league season, Holtzman had finally achieved the notoriety of a 20-win season.

The next day reporters asked Holtzman how he felt in the aftermath of win No. 20. "Super," replied the normally reserved Holtzman, who was now speaking candidly. "A little hung over, but super."[8] Holtzman seemed relaxed on his off-day, in sharp contrast to the way he usually behaved on days in which he was scheduled to pitch. "Ken is always nervous before a game," observed Dick Williams. "He bites his fingernails and the skin around them. Have you ever seen his nails? Also, he's pretty silent on the days he pitches."[9]

Holtzman's catcher and pitching coach agreed on the reason behind the left-hander's newfound success in the American League. "His control is what makes him so effective," offered Ray Fosse. "He has good stuff...but the main thing is, he can get the ball where he wants it."[10] Pitching guru Wes Stock marveled at Holtzman's ability to throw strikes at such a high velocity. "I've never seen a pitcher who throws as fast as he does who has his control," Stock said. "He gets the ball exactly where he wants it time after time. You keep waiting for him to miss, but he almost never does."[11]

While Stock praised Holtzman's fastball, Dick Williams had actually wanted the left-hander to rely more heavily on his array of breaking pitches. On this issue, Holtzman politely disagreed with his manager. "My fastball is my best pitch," Holtzman insisted. "I have much better control with it than with the curve. If I get in a tight spot, 99 per cent of the time I'm going to throw my fastball."[12] In one game alone, Holtzman had thrown a total of 97 pitches, 91 of which had been fastballs. Williams could hardly argue with the results.

On September 8, Reggie Jackson sustained a pull hamstring, an injury that he frequently encountered due to the muscle-bound nature of his sculptured legs. Jackson, leading the league with 112 RBI's, strained his hamstring running hard from first to third on an extra-base hit. A similar, but more serious injury had prevented Jackson from participating in his first World Series in 1972; fortunately, the A's believed the latest occurrence would sideline Reggie for a moderate length of seven to 10 days, allowing him to return for any post-season games.

Jesus Alou, hitting .322 since his arrival from Houston, stepped into the right field vacancy. Alou had previously filled in well for an ailing Joe Rudi in left field. "It's funny," remarked Alou, discussing his new role as Oakland's fourth outfielder. "I was on a team like Houston, in fourth place, and I didn't play. Then I came over here to a team that is running for a pennant and I play."[13]

Alou attributed his latest spree of hitting success to a curious habit at the plate. "I have always swung at bad pitches," admitted Alou, whose aggressive style at the plate reminded observers of the free swinging nature of contemporaries like Roberto Clemente or Manny Sanguillen, or older generation stars like Yogi Berra. "But now I am swinging and missing. I used to swing at bad pitches and hit them. That was hurting me because every time I hit a bad pitch, it was so bad I couldn't get good wood on it. Now I swing and miss the bad ball and that gives me a chance to come back and hit a better pitch."[14] In a strange way, Alou's bizarre analysis made sense, but left one question unanswered. Why was he swinging and missing more often than before? Even Alou could not provide an answer to that mystery.

Although the least talented of the Alou brothers, Jesus possessed the most distinctive style at the plate. Jesus typified the term "nervous hitter," with his constant body twitchings, Clemente-like neck rotations, and stylish bat twirling. Alou exhibited so many extraneous movements before, during, and after each one of his many swings that Dick Williams could not bear to watch him during his at-bats. Instead, Williams waited to hear the sound of Alou's bat meeting the ball before daring to look up from his position in the dugout.

When Oakland's top farm club, the Tucson Toros, saw their Pacific Coast League playoff run come to an end, Charlie Finley decided to summon reinforcements for the final weeks of the regular season. The A's recalled infielder Rich McKinney and pitcher Dave Hamilton, both of whom had spent some time in Oakland earlier in the season. When neither player reported immediately to the A's, Dick Williams castigated both of them for their tardiness. Hamilton tried to explain that their late arrival had resulted from a simple misunderstanding, but Williams had little tolerance for such excuses during a pennant race.

Another late-season recall paid his first dividend on September 11. Heralded prospect Glenn Abbott won his first major league game, an impressive five-hit complete game effort against the Royals. Earlier in the day, the A's announced the surprising purchase of outfielder Rico Carty from the Cubs. The onetime National League batting champion had endured a fractured season in 1973, beginning with a failed stint as the first designated hitter in the history of the Texas Rangers. Claiming he couldn't adjust to the new DH role, Carty had hit only .232 for Texas. The Cubs then acquired Carty for the waiver price, hoping that the friendly dimensions of Wrigley Field would remedy Rico's once-thundering bat. Carty hit even worse for the Cubs than he did for the Rangers, batting only .214 in 22 games.

A supremely talented offensive player and arguably the best two-

strike hitter of his era, Carty had enjoyed his best major league season
only three seasons earlier. In 1970, as a member of the Atlanta Braves,
Carty had led the National League with a .366 batting average and a
.456 on-base percentage. He had also hit for power, accumulating career highs with 25 HR's and 101 RBI's. Then, trouble struck. A winter
league collision with Matty Alou crushed his kneecap, preventing him
from playing at all in 1971. A pulled leg muscle plagued him the following summer.

The self-proclaimed "Beeg Boy" had also clashed with teammates
throughout his career. In Atlanta, Carty had brawled with Hank Aaron
and pitcher Ron Reed. Carty's continuing problems with Aaron had
influenced his trade to Texas. After his trade to the Windy City, Carty
sparred with another legend — Ron Santo — one of the Cubs' leaders
and most popular players. Upon his arrival in Oakland, Carty pointed
the finger at Santo, terming him a selfish player. Carty predicted the
Cubs would never win a division title or league pennant until they rid-
ded themselves of their longtime third baseman. Although Carty's criticism likely had little to do with it, the Cubs would trade Santo to the
cross-town White Sox after the season.

Like many of Charlie Finley's acquisitions, the pickup of Carty
seemed puzzling on the surface. Since the A's had picked him up after
September 1, he would be ineligible for any post-season games. Furthermore, where would he play during the stretch run? Given his poor
throwing arm, Carty posed no threat to play right field, which was already occupied by MVP candidate Reggie Jackson. How about left field,
where Joe Rudi had been slumping much of the summer? Rudi's bat,
however, had shown signs of a recent revival. On September 16, Rudi
clubbed his first career grand slam and added a two-run double in a 9-
4 win over the Rangers. Under any circumstances, Rudi's six-RBI performance ranked as eye-popping; it became even more noteworthy since
Rudi was still fighting in his recovery from a persistent, recurring virus.

Though listed as an outfielder, Carty's chronically fragile knees
made him best suited to serve as a designated hitter, a role that he
didn't like, as evidenced by his flop in Texas. Deron Johnson had been
a productive DH over the first half of the season, but had struggled in
recent weeks. Johnson's deepening ineffectiveness at the plate had
started to concern Dick Williams. In an August 12th game against the
Yankees, Johnson had torn a tendon in his right hand and badly jammed
his thumb while sliding into third base. While Johnson tried not to use
his bad hand as an excuse, the injury had robbed him of much of his
bat speed, while making him vulnerable to inside fastballs and sliders.
American League pitchers, quickly taking note of Johnson's injury, had
wisely exploited the designated hitter's vulnerability.

The A's played well against the Rangers, as they should have,
sweeping the three-game series. On September 14, in the first game of

the set, Gene Tenace experienced what he called "my biggest day in the majors." The hard-hitting catcher went 4-for-4 and drove in five runs in support of Catfish Hunter's 19th win, a 10-inning decision. "I looked at the scoreboard and saw that (second place) Kansas City had lost," Tenace explained, "and then I thought if we could win this game, we'd give Reggie Jackson another week's rest."[15] Jackson, who had been sitting out action with a hamstring pull, actually did make an appearance in the game when he pinch-hit for Dick Green.

Earlier in the month, the A's had played some of their worst baseball in another set against Texas. The ways in which the A's had lost to an inferior team particularly vexed Dick Williams, who expressed his anger at a team meeting. Williams hadn't liked the players' carefree behavior during and after games with the sad-sack Rangers. After Williams' team-wide lecture, the A's had captured two of three from the Royals to move six and a half games in front in the American League West.

Unlike other managers who avoided confrontations with their players, Williams believed in addressing mistakes quickly and directly. "When you make a mental error," Joe Rudi explained, "Dick chews you out right on the spot. You miss that cutoff man, or something like that, and when you come in from the field, you hear about it, right now. And you better not make the same mistake again."[16] While some managers frowned on such directness out of fear of embarrassing their players, Williams' approach worked because of its consistency. "He's fair, though," said Rudi. "He'll rip into Reggie Jackson the same way he'll chew a rookie. He treats everybody the same."[17]

Two of the most pleasant individual developments of the season involved the pitching of middle reliever Horacio Piña and the growth of center fielder Billy North, both much-maligned off-season pickups. As a long reliever, Piña fooled hitters with his sidearm delivery and deceptive palmball. During one stretch in September, Piña belied his frail, stringbean appearance by working in eight of ten games. The play of North proved even more vital. "We haven't had anybody who can go get a ball like that since Rick Monday,"[18] assessed Dick Williams. By May, North had wrested the center field position away from Angel Mangual and Billy Conigliaro. By August 17, North had moved into the leadoff spot, bumping Campy Campaneris to the second position. On September 15, North stole his 50th base of the season. Given the aforementioned milestones, the news of September 20 came as a crushing strike to Oakland fortunes. With a runner on third and one out, North bounced a routine grounder to Twins' second baseman Rod Carew. When Carew threw home to retire the lead runner, North turned his head back momentarily toward home plate as he landed awkwardly on the first base bag. The misstep resulted in a sprained ankle. The prognosis arrived as quick and cutting to the A's; North would miss the balance of the regular season, and most likely, any playoff and World Series games.

North's impact on the A's had been considerable. He had also left an imprint on American League rivals, who had come to detest his combative, feisty, and some would say, dirty style of play. On May 18, North had tangled with Kansas City's Doug Bird. North had also become involved in two subsequent incidents. On August 31, the Royals' Kurt Bevacqua pushed North twice while he stood a third base, in apparent retaliation for the assault on Bird. A's captain Sal Bando, standing at home plate, ran toward third base, tackling Bevacqua. North responded well to the attack, going 6-for-14 in the three-game series with Kansas City. North said he felt special motivation for two reasons: series-long booing from the fans at Royals Stadium, and racial catcalls he heard from a few select Royals partisans.

In early September, the A's played the rival Angels in a series marked by cursing and trash talking between opposing players. In the September 6th game, California's Dick Lange threw a fastball directly over North's head. North had done nothing to provoke the "message" pitch; he had merely had the misfortune of coming to bat after Lange surrendered a home run. Rather than accepting the time-honored knockdown practice, North dragged a bunt between the mound and the first base line, hoping that Lange would field the ball. Angels' first baseman Mike Epstein ruined the plan by reaching the bunt before Lange. The former Oaklander planted an unnecessarily firm tag on North's neck in an obvious effort to injure the pesky A's catalyst. Epstein proceeded to drop the ball allowing North to reach first base on an error. Moments later, as Epstein prepared to hold North on the bag, the Oakland outfielder referred to the muscular first baseman as a "big goon." The remark prompted an abrupt reaction from Epstein, who was held back by an intervening Reggie Jackson. After the game, North expressed no remorse for his derogatory characterization of Epstein. "There's no one in this game who can intimidate me," North said proudly. "There will be a time for him."[19]

North's brash speaking manner, teamed with his on-field combat-

---

Charlie Finley's Best Trades:

- Ken Holtzman from the Cubs for Rick Monday
- Billy North from the Cubs for Bob Locker
- Mike Epstein and Darold Knowles from the Senators for Frank Fernandez, Paul Lindblad and Don Mincher
- Horacio Piña from the Rangers for Mike Epstein
- Deron Johnson from the Phillies for Jack Bastable
- Matty Alou from the Cardinals for Steve Easton and Bill Voss

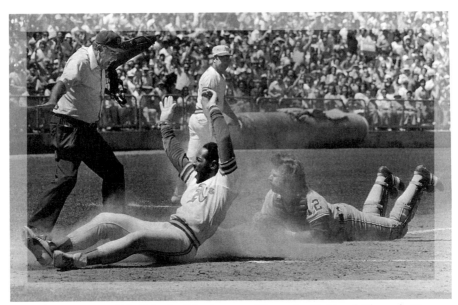

A catalyst in 1973, Billy North slides home safely at the Oakland Alameda County Coliseum, avoiding the tag of Chicago White Sox' catcher Ed Herrmann.

iveness, had made him an unpopular player around the American League. Those same qualities rated him highly in Dick Williams' mental scouting report. "North's an aggressive player," said Williams, refuting charges that his center fielder played dirty, over-the-line baseball. "He's a heck of a ballplayer. Some people say he's a hot dog, but he can play for me anytime."[20]

North's contributions not withstanding, the A's had played uninspired, even listless baseball for much of the season. Yet, their pitching and bullpen depth, buttressed by the hitting of Reggie Jackson and the relative weakness of the division, catapulted the A's to favored status in the West. On September 23, the A's officially laid rest to their Western Division opponents by beating the White Sox, 10-5. An Oakland clinching had become such a yearly routine that the A's celebrated mildly after the win, quietly drinking champagne in the clubhouse.

Vida Blue won the clincher, which coincidentally represented his 20th win of the season. After a slow start, Blue's fastball had improved considerably, as had his control. Supplemented by a newly-developed harder breaking pitch, Blue had succeeded in putting his dismal 1972 season behind him "We've got him throwing a change-up and a hard breaking ball," explained pitching coach Wes Stock. "Vida's made up his mind he wants to be a good pitcher. Eighty per cent of pitching is determination and he has all the determination in the world."[21]

Blue's teammates had noticed the changes in the left-hander's pitching philosophies. "In the first part of 1971, Vida was overpowering everybody," recalled Sal Bando. "Now he is overmatching them. He found out that you can't throw the fastball for 300 innings."[22]

In addition to recapturing some of his success from 1971, Blue had also dropped the surly demeanor that had marked much of his behavior during the latter stages of '71 and much of the '72 season. "Vida tried very hard to be an SOB," pointed out an anonymous member of the Oakland organization, "but he's really too nice a kid to bring it off."[23]

Yet, Blue's personality had not completely reverted back to 1971 form. "Vida's changed. The fame changed him some," acknowledged Sal Bando, one of the most observant of the Oakland players. "He isn't so carefree. He's become more of a loner."[24] Blue served as a classic example that success did not translate into a higher degree of happiness.

With his win against the White Sox, Blue joined Ken Holtzman and Catfish Hunter in the 20-win circle; for only the 14th time in American League history, three teammates had simultaneously won 20 games. The collaboration had occurred only once before in the history of the A's franchise. In 1931, Hall of Famer Lefty Grove, George Earnshaw and Rube Walberg had each reached the 20-win plateau for Connie Mack's legendary Philadelphia Athletics.

Hunter, Blue and Holtzman attacked opposing hitters with distinctively contrasting styles. Hunter relied on one key out-pitch — the slider — featured by neither Blue or Holtzman. Against left-handed hitters, Hunter augmented his repertoire with a deceiving change-up. Yet, more than anything else, Hunter succeeded because he possessed precise control of his pitches. "Know what I hate to do?," Hunter once said, thinking out loud. "I hate to walk a man. It bugs me somethin' fierce, because every time you put a man on base for free it seems like he scores. I'd rather give up a hit than a walk — that's how strongly I feel about it."[25]

Hunter's control, as great as it was, barely exceeded that of Holtzman, whose pitches featured more snap than those of Catfish. Holtzman threw with the most fluid of deliveries, which made his deceptive fastball approach hitters with late explosion and movement. "What I try to do," said Holtzman, "is set up the hitter for a pitch that I think will bother his timing."[26] When batters began to anticipate his sneaky fastball, Holtzman countered with a large, looping overhand curveball that doubled as a change of speed.

Whereas Hunter and Holtzman relied on control, economy of pitches and effective breaking balls, Blue employed a style that centered on pure power, requiring more pitches and more labor. Blue's hard-driving though seemingly effortless mechanics, which included a high kick of his powerful right leg, helped his fastball reach a pace of 94 to 95 MPH, replete with late, rising movement. Blue's recent addition of a harder breaking pitch, which featured a smaller but sharper break than his standard curve ball, made him more similar in effectiveness to the scintillating pitcher of 1971 than the discounted 1972 model.

The presence of three 20-game winners on the Oakland staff vindicated the work of first-year pitching coach Wes Stock, who had replaced the amiable and popular Bill Posedel. "Bill Posedel knows more about pitching than any man I know,"[27] Catfish Hunter once said of the venerable pitching coach. Several Oakland pitchers had anonymously criticized Stock's relatively abrasive approach, which contrasted with the friendly, down-home style of predecessor Posedel. Yet, the comeback of Blue, the continuing improvement of Holtzman, and the sustained brilliance of Hunter had served as testimony to Stock's effectiveness.

The combined domination of Blue, Holtzman and Hunter made the Oakland rotation the envy of baseball. In some scouts' minds, the A's had even managed to surpass the excellence of the Orioles' starting rotation, which just two years earlier had featured four 20-game winners. Yes, the Orioles still had Jim Palmer, Dave McNally, and Mike Cuellar, but they had parted with Pat Dobson, who had been traded to the Braves. One could at least make the argument that, based on 1973 results, the A's now boasted the best group of starters in all of major league baseball.

Three 20-game winners. A third straight American League West title. A return to health of Joe Rudi and Reggie Jackson. Except for the injury to Billy North, all appeared well and calm in the Oakland kingdom. Well, not quite. In late September, the A's fired part-time scout Bill Rigney. Only Charlie Finley refused to call Rigney's departure a "firing."

Finley had hired Rigney as an administrative assistant prior to the season. Rigney's job description included a variety of duties, including broadcasting and scouting. Rigney served as a color announcer on radio and television for most of the season. In early September, Finley had removed Rigney from the booth, assigning him the more important duty of scouting the leaders in the American League East, the Baltimore Orioles. Rigney joined full-time scout Billy Herman in following the A's likely opponent in the upcoming American League playoffs.

When the Orioles clinched the AL East, Rigney left his road assignment, figuring he didn't need to observe Baltimore's second-string lineup of backups and Rochester recalls. Rigney also felt it more important to be with his wife, who had been injured in a recent fall.

Not surprisingly, Finley wanted Rigney to remain on the road stalking the Orioles. With four games to go in the regular season, Finley instructed Rigney to meet with manager Dick Williams and farm coordinator John Claiborne. Under Finley's orders, Rigney would reveal the contents of his scouting report to Williams and Claiborne, and then head home for the winter. Rigney understood Finley's directive to mean that he was fired; Finley insisted he had not actually fired Rigney. "This was not a job on a permanent basis," Finley explained during the post-season. "Because of financial conditions we eliminated the job at the end of the season."[28] Finley acknowledged that with two weeks remaining in the regular season he had instructed Rigney to scout the Orioles. "He returned at the end of one week and it was so close to the end of the season and since Bill had done such a fine job during the year, I told him the job was over."[29] In Finley's mind, he had actually given Rigney a one week's paid vacation as a reward for a job well done.

Rigney felt otherwise. His departure left a vacancy in the broadcast booth. To replace the man that Finley called the "greatest color man that I've heard in baseball,"[30] the owner hired 30-year-old Bob Waller, who had broadcast Chicago White Sox games during the 1973 season, to work the post-season games with Monte Moore. In yet another Oakland oddity, a man who had broadcast regular season games for one team would now announce playoff games for another club. Waller would broadcast Oakland's games in the postseason and then return to Chicago, where he teamed with former A's broadcaster Harry Caray. Only in Finley's Oakland.

Rigney could take solace in knowing that many other A's employees had lost their jobs during the season. Some had been fired; others had left on their own. The A's playoff program depicted seven front office officials and secretaries no longer with the team. The outdated program also contained photographs of four former Oakland players — Larry Haney, Mike Hegan, Gonzalo Marquez and Dal Maxvill.

The departure of Rigney angered many of the players, who became more upset when they learned they could not take their wives on the team flight to Baltimore. All of the players had expected to be able to travel with their wives, but some of the spouses were placed on standby when Finley brought extra passengers on the flight. When the players found out that their loved ones had lost out to some of Finley's cronies, they were ready to put a stranglehold on the owner.

A more minor incidence of controversy occurred during the best-of-five playoff series against the Orioles. Former A's pitching coach Bill Posedel was supposed to travel with the team on its trip to Baltimore and suit up in an Oakland uniform in the dugout. When Posedel didn't make the flight, several players wondered whether Finley had interfered with the attempt at the reunion.

Controversies aside, the A's outfield had been undermined by injuries and sickness. Billy North's sprained ankle would sideline him for the entire playoff series, while Reggie Jackson's strength and weight had been affected by a viral infection and a sore throat. The A's expected Jackson to play in Game One, but the injury to North left them without their center fielder and most capable leadoff batter. Dick Williams moved Campy Campaneris back to the leadoff spot, moved Joe Rudi up to the No. 2 position, and made Sal Bando his third-place hitter. Williams also announced that Angel Mangual would assume North's position in center field.

The Oakland coaching staff might have expected that Mangual would react to the news with several leaps for joy. Earlier in the season, Mangual had stated his unhappiness as a backup and his preference for a trade. When he did play, he had botched fly balls in the outfield, missed signs from the coaches, and failed to execute basic plays like the hit-and-run. Despite his frequent mental and physical mistakes, Mangual would now be the starting center fielder in the playoffs, with a chance to play a prominent role in the World Series. So how did Mangual react to being named Billy North's replacement? He did what any Oakland player would have done; he asked to be traded. At least Mangual had the decency to say that his trade request could wait until after the season.

The collection of injuries and controversies, coupled with a general lack of respect for the Oakland ballclub, led the oddsmakers to install the Orioles as 6-to-5 favorites to eliminate the A's. "I don't believe people think of us as legitimate world champions," Sal Bando complained rightfully. "We are out to prove that we are."[31] The prevailing sentiment of Baltimore superiority left Dick Williams laughing. "I heard Jimmy the Greek made the Orioles 11-to-10 favorites," said Williams. "That tickles me to death. Why? Because he's been wrong the last five years. And he picked Bobby Riggs, too."[32] Riggs had predicted he would defeat Billie Jean King in the greatly hyped "Battle of the Sexes" tennis match a month earlier, only to lose decidedly to the world's best female player.

With his makeshift starting lineup now in place, Dick Williams selected Vida Blue to start the first game of the American League Championship Series against the Orioles. Williams opted for his hardest-throwing left-hander, rather than staff ace Catfish Hunter, in an effort to keep Baltimore's two hot-hitting rookies, Al Bumbry and Rich Coggins, on the bench. Both left-handed hitters with intimidating speed, Bumbry and Coggins had hit .337 and .319 respectively, and had combined to steal 40 bases during the regular season. "Our job is to keep their speedsters off the bases," explained Williams. "That's one reason why I'm starting Blue."[33] Even without Bumbry and Coggins in the starting lineup, the Orioles hoped to take advantage of Blue's poor pickoff move to first base. "He's got a terrible move,"[34] said one of the Orioles, choosing to remain anonymous.

Williams hoped that the lack of experience of rookies like Bumbry and Coggins would hurt them later in the series, when they would encounter their first taste of the post-season. "They haven't played in a Championship Series before," Williams told reporters. "Anybody who doesn't get butterflies is crazy."[35] The throwing of Ray Fosse also posed a hindrance to base stealers like Bumbry and Coggins. Oakland catchers had thrown out nine of 16 Oriole base stealers during the course of the regular season.

Williams selected Blue to start Game One for reasons other than the fact he threw with his left arm. Blue had pitched exceptionally down the stretch, making him the choice over another southpaw, Ken Holtzman. "It wouldn't surprise me if Blue was even better now than when he was having that great year in '71," observed Baltimore's Jim Palmer. "He is not as tired now. He looked it (fatigued) in the '71 playoff. He had pitched an awful lot of innings."[36]

Although Blue had pitched much better in 1973 than the previous year, his relationship with the media had hardly improved. *Sport* magazine writer Don Kowet reminded Blue of the interview that he had scheduled for the aftermath of Game Two. "Well, you better get to me fast," Blue warned, "because when that game is over, I'm on leave. I take off that uniform. I put on my civvies. I go underground. I disappear."[37] Dealing with the press ranked low on Vida's list of priorities.

Williams' reasoning in choosing Blue made perfect sense on several levels, but Earl Weaver's right-handed platoon lineup torched the left-hander, who failed to last the first inning. Leadoff man Merv Rettenmund, replacing Coggins in right field, singled and scored on a double by former Athletic Tommy Davis. Don Baylor, subbing for Bumbry in left field, drew a walk and scored another run, helping give the Orioles an early 3-0 advantage. Baylor went on to go 2-for-3 with two runs scored and an RBI. The early offensive showing proved more than enough for Jim Palmer, who struck out 12 A's en route to an easy 6-0 win.

Much like their playoff series in1971, the A's seemed to have met a superior opponent in the Orioles. Baltimore possessed advantages in the areas of pitching experience and overall depth. Over the span of two different post-seasons, the A's had met the Orioles four times, and had lost each time. Much like the Championship Series of two years ago, Dick Williams heard the cries of second guesses from the media after the game. In the top of the first, the A's had put their first two batters on base, but left the runners stranded when the middle of the order came up empty. One reporter asked Williams why he hadn't asked his No. 3 hitter, Sal Bando, to bunt the runners over. "I'm not gonna bunt Sal Bando in the first inning for all the tea in China," responded an incredulous Williams. "Look, you people can second-guess, but I get paid to manage. Bando and (Reggie) Jackson are my two biggest RBI guys. Why would I bunt them in the first inning? If Bando bunts, then they walk Jackson."[38]

Although very few managers would have played for the bunt in the first inning, even Baltimore players took subtle shots at Williams for his supposed strategical mistake. "I read where Dick Williams said they were going to play for runs, move the runners along," chimed in Jim Palmer. "I guess he forgot he said it."[39]

Al Bumbry and Rich Coggins returned to the lineup for Game Two, as Dick Williams countered with Catfish Hunter. For a change, the A's played longball, hitting four home runs against Dave McNally, while the homer-prone Hunter surrendered none. Sal Bando connected twice against McNally to lead the A's to a 6-3 win — their first ever playoff win against the Birds.

Bando narrowly missed a three-homer day when Orioles' left fielder Al Bumbry leapt and stretched his glove hand over the fence, bringing back a long drive. "Unbelievable,"[40] Bando said of the catch. Bando seemed just as surprised by his own performance, considering the nerves that he had felt earlier in the day. "I woke up at 7:30," recalled Bando, "and I had to get out of the hotel room. It was just nerves. I knew we had to win this game to stay alive."[41]

Prior to the series, Jim Palmer had pointed to Campy Campaneris as Oakland's most critical offensive player. With Billy North out of the lineup, Campy had returned to the leadoff spot. "I think the key to beating Oakland," Palmer had remarked, "is keeping Campaneris off base."[42] In Game Two, Campaneris reached base three times in five plate appearances, swiped a pair of bases and scored two runs. In contrast, Baltimore tablesetters Al Bumbry and Rich Coggins went a combined 2-for-9 against Catfish Hunter and Rollie Fingers. Not so coincidentally, the A's won the game handily.

Since the A's had managed a split of the two games in Baltimore, they now held the home field edge, with the third and fourth games, and if necessary, Game Five, set for the Oakland Coliseum. Heavy rains on Sunday and Monday in the Bay Area posed a threat to Game Three, which was scheduled for Monday afternoon. Twenty minutes before game-time, American League President Joe Cronin called for a postponement, based on wet grounds and a continuing forecast of rain. Cronin's quick and early decision prompted an angry display from Charlie Finley, who argued loudly with the AL chief in the runway leading from the Oakland clubhouse to the playing field. As several media types and an embarrassed Dick Williams watched on, Finley screamed at Cronin for calling the game so early in the day. Cronin's decision infuriated Finley on two counts: the A's had lost an almost certain sellout at the Coliseum, which was a rare event for the attendance-starved franchise, and the rainout would prove beneficial to the Orioles, who could now use Jim Palmer in Game Four on three days rest.

"I don't think we should discuss it here in public," Cronin informed Finley. "I don't give a damn what you think,"[43] Finley fired back. Finley continued his mouthy diatribe, but Cronin's ruling stood. The continuing rain in Oakland justified Cronin's initial decision; no game could have been played, either in the afternoon or evening.

A day later, Ken Holtzman outpitched Mike Cuellar in a game that featured a combined seven hits, three runs, and 18 strikeouts. "I never pitched a more important game or one that meant more,"[44] Holtzman would say later. With the game tied at 1-1 in the bottom of the 11th inning, Campy Campaneris led off against Cuellar. Campy, who had reached the seats only four times during a regular season of spray hitting, worked the count to one-and-one before pulling a low-and-in pitch into the left field bleachers. "I look for a slider and when I see it, I hit," Campy said, simplifying the thinking behind his at-bat. "When I go up, I want to pull the ball because the third baseman is playing close to the line and there is a hole. But when I see the slider I hit it."[45]

The A's raced out to a 4-0 lead in Game Four, but Vida Blue and Rollie Fingers failed to protect the sizable margin in what had all the earmarks of a clinching game for Oakland. Fingers allowed a game-deciding solo home run to Bobby Grich in the top of the eighth, while left-hander Grant Jackson held the A's scoreless over the final two and two-thirds innings.

Rather than accept a difficult defeat gracefully and look forward to a decisive fifth game, Oakland players stewed over what might have been. "We had them by the nostrils and we let them get away from us,"[46] a disgusted Fingers said out loud in the clubhouse. Although Fingers was speaking to no one in particular, his next-door locker mate, Blue Moon Odom, felt Rollie was directing his comments to Vida Blue as a way of placing blame for the defeat. "You shouldn't be talking," Odom snapped at Fingers. "If you don't give up that home run (to Grich), we don't lose the game."[47]

Fingers yelled back at Odom, escalating the latest shouting match in the Oakland clubhouse. While the outburst might have concerned some players, others viewed the skirmish as a good sign. After all, the A's played their best when clawing at each other's throats. "We'll probably score 25 runs tomorrow," observed a wise and confident Reggie Jackson. "You know us."[48]

Aside from the A's ability to play well under a veil of adversity, Jackson might have realized that Orioles' manager Earl Weaver had made the curious decision to use his least experienced starter, the soft-tossing Doyle Alexander, in Game Five. Weaver's decision raised several eyebrows, but the manager had lost all confidence in veteran left-hander Dave McNally, who had allowed two Sal Bando home runs in a Game Two loss. Still, several writers wondered about the wisdom of switching from an experienced pitcher like McNally to a neophyte like Alexander. "To be honest," said Weaver sarcastically, "it never occurred to me until about the time Bando's last shot was going over the wall."[49]

Meanwhile, Dick Williams was concerned about the sustained ineffectiveness of his designated hitter, Deron Johnson. A productive stretch from may through July had helped Johnson become the first player in major league history to hit at least 20 home runs in a season split between the National and American Leagues. (Johnson had hit one home run for the Phillies before hitting 19 for the A's.) Unfortunately for the A's, DJ had become an offensive nonentity in August and September. His struggles had spilled over into the postseason, where he had collected only one hit in 10 at-bats against Baltimore pitching. The extended slump stemmed from a game in August, in which he had torn tendons in his right hand, causing severe pain in his thumb. Johnson talked little about the injury, until after the season. "The tendon was lying on the bone," Johnson would explain, "and that's why it was giving me so much."[50] Johnson had tried taking pain-killing shots and wrapping the thumb in sponges but neither strategy lessened the pain.

Dick Williams had shown patience with Johnson, but with the pennant on the line, he decided he could wait no longer. Williams made two adjustments in facing the junk-balling Alexander, inserting Jesus Alou as his DH replacement for Johnson, while giving Vic Davalillo the start in center field. Since Alexander tried to ruin batters' timing with off-speed pitches, Williams leaned on Alou and Davalillo, two of his best and most experienced breaking-ball hitters. Once again, Williams had made the appropriate moves at the opportune time.

In the third inning, Ray Fosse reached on a rare error by Brooks Robinson, moved up to second on a sacrifice by Dick Green, and scored on a two-out single by Joe Rudi. The A's created a comfort zone in the fourth inning, when Gene Tenace singled, Davalillo laced a triple and Jesus Alou capped the rally with another single. Thanks to the July 31st acquisitions (Alou and Davalillo), the A's had vaulted themselves to a 3-0 lead, which Catfish Hunter maintained over the final five innings.

Hunter pitched brilliantly in perhaps his best performance under pressure to date. "You know what I like to do, really like to do," Hunter asked a reporter rhetorically. "I like to pitch. I'd rather be out there on the mound than anywhere. That's my business and my pleasure and man, I work at it."[51] While other pitchers cowered under pressure circumstances, Hunter embraced them. Orioles' manager Earl Weaver spoke reverently about Hunter, a man that he would have preferred pitching for his team in a critical fifth game situation. "He's got his doctorate in pitching," Weaver said of the leader of the Oakland pitching staff. "He's had his B.A., he went on and got his masters, and now he's got his doctorate."[52] Few would argue with the Weaver allegory. While the A's had exposed Doyle Alexander's youth, the Orioles had failed to break the calm of an efficient, workmanlike Hunter. "When you have a fifth game, he's the one you want pitching for you," said Reggie Jackson. "He's good and has the composure."[53]

Timely, pressurized performances like the one he authored in Game

Five would earn Hunter membership in the Hall of Fame in 1987. Rollie Fingers joined Catfish in Cooperstown five years later. "Catfish, he's probably the greatest right-handed pitcher I played with," Fingers says. "When Catfish was on, I didn't even go down to the bullpen — he was that great of a pitcher. He had great control. If you had a game to win, that's who you wanted on the mound when we were playing."

In spite of a poor playoff for Vida Blue, the absence of the catalytic Billy North, and the continued helpless swinging of an injured Deron Johnson, the A's had won their second consecutive American League pennant. Of their regulars, only Campy Campaneris had produced well-rounded offensive numbers vs. the Orioles. As the A's celebrated in the clubhouse, Campaneris tried to drink simultaneously from four different champagne bottles, encouraged in Spanish by a group of Latino teammates that included Vic Davalillo and Jesus Alou. The two bench players had contributed some of the timeliest hits of the series. Davalillo, a member of the Pirates' post-season teams in 1971 and '72, had filled in at first base and in center field, collecting five hits in eight at-bats. Alou had added two hits in six at-bats in the first post-season series of his career.

Even in victory, the A's failed to sidestep controversy. After the clinching victory, Reggie Jackson found himself stuck behind a pair of motorcycle police officers, who were driving under 10 miles per hour. Jackson sounded his car horn, which prompted the officers to pull him over. An angry exchange followed and a police computer check found two outstanding warrants against the Oakland star: one for a parking violation, the other for speeding. The two tickets carried a combined fine of $82.00. According to the police sergeant, Reggie refused to pay the fines. "I'm Reggie Jackson and I don't have to pay," the sergeant said, doing his best imitation of Jackson. Reggie spent two and a half hours in city jail before the posting of bail.

Chapter Seventeen:
Same Series, Different Team

Even with nearly half of the players having departed from their 1972 world championship team — Mike Epstein, Don Mincher, Mike Hegan, Gonzalo Marquez, George Hendrick, Bob Locker, Matty Alou, Dave Duncan, Tim Cullen, Dal Maxvill and Joel Horlen — the A's had scratched their way back to the World Series. Although oddsmakers placed the A's in the roles of slight favorites over the upstart New York Mets, Oakland faced several manpower challenges. The designated hitter would not be allowed in any World Series games, negating any dividends that a slugger like Deron Johnson might pay. Center fielder Billy North remained hobbled by a bad ankle, even though Oakland continued to list him as "questionable" for the Series. Williams announced tentative plans to use Reggie Jackson in center field, while employing Jesus Alou in right field against left-handed pitching. Although Alou had hit well in the playoffs against Baltimore, the new outfield alignment represented a significant drop-off in terms of speed and defensive abilities.

In reality, North would not be able to play at all in the Series, forcing Williams to make do with his "plan B" outfield. Although his ankle remained in a cast, North hoped to travel with the team to New York for the middle three games of the Series. After Game Two, North would make his way to the Oakland Airport, only to be told that the A's had made no arrangements for him to be included on the team charter. The snub offended North, but the story would receive little attention due to another budding controversy, whose seeds were just being sown.

The issue of post-season eligibility superseded all others prior to the World Series. In the American League Championship Series, the Orioles had allowed the A's to replace two of the players on their 25-man roster. Since Charlie Finley had sold backup catcher Jose Morales to the Montreal Expos on September 18 (after the September 1 deadline for freezing post-season rosters), the A's needed to petition the Orioles to employ a replacement. Baltimore gave Oakland permission to use pinch-running specialist Allan Lewis. The Orioles also agreed to allow the A's to replace injured center fielder Billy North with minor league infielder Manny Trillo. Thanks to the Orioles' generosity, the A's played the Championship Series with a full complement of 25 players.

While the Orioles had been gracious in making roster allowances, the A's would have to repeat the petition process with the New York Mets prior to the World Series. The Mets agreed to permit the use of the one-dimensional Lewis, but refused to allow Trillo to play in the Series. When Finley learned of the Mets' rejection of Trillo, he tried to re-acquire Jose Morales from Montreal. Morales would first have to clear National League waivers. He did not, leading to speculation that the Mets themselves had claimed Morales in order to prevent the A's from using him. Whatever the case, Morales would not be allowed to rejoin the A's for the World Series. The failed maneuvering, which had started with Finley's unwise sale of Morales after the September 1 roster-freezing deadline, left the A's with only 24 players available for their most important series of the season.

The Mets' action, though perfectly within their rights, infuriated Finley. Charlie O. ordered his public address announcer to make an awkward declaration prior to Game One, emphasizing that the Mets had refused to allow the A's to use Trillo in the 1973 World Series. If Finley's motivation were to simply provide Oakland fans with information, the announcement might have been defensible. But Finley had clearly tried to embarrass the Mets, who in Finley's mind, had shown audacity in refusing to play along with his roster games.

Commissioner Bowie Kuhn interpreted Finley's announcement as one inspired by sheer spite. Kuhn publicly reprimanded his favorite sparring partner among major league owners, and promised further disciplinary action after the World Series.

The eligibility issue would die down considerably after Game One, and appeared destined to become a afterthought to the Series. The late innings of Game Two would soon change the course of history, and the way that Finley would be seen by players, the fans, and the media.

Prior to Game One, the lavish pre-game ceremonies included appearances by three celebrities. Actor Jim Nabors, a veteran of the popular *Andy Griffith Show*, performed the National Anthem. Atlanta Braves' playing great Hank Aaron threw out the ceremonial first ball, marking one of the few times in history that an active major leaguer had performed such an honor. And Oakland's owner, Charles O. Finley, stepped out onto the field, reveling in his team's second consecutive appearance in the World Series.

Bay Area fans seemed less enthusiastic about the A's return to the World Series. Only 46,021 fans bought tickets to Game One, far less than the capacity of the Oakland Coliseum. The atmosphere surrounding the ballpark reflected that of a spring training Cactus League game. "When I was a kid there was excitement at the Series," bemoaned Catfish Hunter. "There was electricity everywhere. But there wasn't any bunting on the walls at the Coliseum. The place wasn't sold out. The crowd was acting dead. It was like an exhibition game."[1] Hunter then delivered a message to the fans of the Bay Area. "These people don't deserve us."[2]

Gene Tenace continued the criticism of the fans after the game. "That crowd was a joke," crowed the Oakland catcher-first baseman. "The people here just don't appreciate us and I'm tired of hearing excuses for them. They should have been standing in the aisles. If the game was played in any other city in the country, the park would be packed."[3]

Oakland players also found fault with Charlie Finley, who had decided to allow the sale of seats in the center field bleachers, a section normally left empty to provide the batters with a better hitting background. "The man is ridiculous," one anonymous player said about the owner's ticket policy. "Here they have all these empty seats in the upper deck and they let all those people sit in center field... There's simply no background (for hitting) this way."[4]

The first game pitted two left-handers, neither of whom was the ace of his respective staff. Ken Holtzman faced Jon Matlack, who owned the highest earned run average of any of the Met starters and a sub-.500 record of 14-16. Matlack would pitch well, except for one inning. In the bottom of the third, Matlack retired Ray Fosse. Dick Green walked, but was thrown out stealing. Matlack hoped to polish off the inning by disposing of Holtzman, Oakland's ninth-place hitter. The right-handed hitting Holtzman surprised all observers by smacking a double down the left field line, and then scoring when second baseman Felix Millan allowed Campy Campaneris' simple grounder slip through his legs. Millan, normally a sound defensive player, had committed only nine errors during the regular season. Campy, taking advantage of Millan's fielding abnormality, stole second and came home on Joe Rudi's clutch single. The two-out, two-run rally gave the A's a one-run lead heading to the ninth.

Rollie Fingers faced Ed Kranepool, pinch-hitting for Don Hahn. Kranepool lined to Campaneris for the inning's first out. Fingers then walked Ron Hodges, the pinch-batter for Bud Harrelson. When Yogi Berra called upon his third consecutive pinch-hitter, the lefty-swinging Rusty Staub, Dick Williams countered with Darold Knowles. Fingers' lack of control had clearly upset Williams, who had visited the mound several times in an effort to coax his best reliever into throwing strikes. "He wasn't concentrating," Williams said of Fingers. "Some guys you have to pat on the back, others you have to kick in the butt. Fingers is a kickee"[5]

Knowles came on to retire Jim Beauchamp, hitting for Staub, and then disposed of Wayne Garrett on a fly ball to short right field for the game's final outs. Thanks primarily to the surprising hitting of Ken Holtzman, the A's had taken the upper hand in the Series.

Holtzman, who had never come to bat during the regular season, took batting practice during Oakland homestands, but didn't usually fare well. "The coaches get me out easy,"[6] Holtzman said with a laugh. Unfortunately for the Mets, Matlack hadn't experienced similar results. "I'm not a natural hitter," Holtzman said after Game One. "I'm not even a good one."[7] Even though Matlack had been burned by his counterpart, the Mets' left-hander didn't seem impressed. "He's a fair hitter,"[8] Matlack said, grudgingly.

If Millan had handled Campaneris' grounder, Matlack might have pitched a shutout. The two unearned runs put the Mets in an early hole, forced New York manager Yogi Berra to pinch-hit Ken Boswell for Matlack in the seventh inning, and led to an early Series appearance for Tug McGraw. The screwballing Mets' closer pitched two impressive shutout innings of relief. Even in a losing effort, the talents of Matlack and McGraw caught the attention of the A's hitters. "I've seen good pitching for a week and haven't got a piece of the ball," lamented Dick Green, one of five Oakland regulars to come up hitless in Game One. "The screwball of that last pitcher — what's his name? That's a great screwball."[9] Rollie Fingers, who came to bat against McGraw in the eighth inning, agreed with Green's assessment of McGraw's deceptive screwball, a pitch that moved away from right-handed hitters. "I couldn't have hit it with a tennis racket,"[10] Rollie admitted.

The A's had expected that the Mets would pose a threat because of their strong pitching. The Oakland scouting staff — comprised of Al Hollingsworth, Sherm Lollar, and Billy Goodman — had performed well in preparing the A's for the Mets. "You can't tell an awful lot from one game," said captain Sal Bando, "but I got the impression they were just like the reports said."[11]

In contrast to the crisp play of the first game, the Mets and A's played sloppily in Game Two. A bright October sun interspersed with dark shadows created a hazy background for fielders on both teams, leading to six errors, including five by the homestanding A's. "The conditions here are very tough this time of year," explained Dick Williams. "Luckily, we'll only have to play two more games here."[12] Oakland players offered far less diplomatic opinions of playing at the Coliseum in mid-October. "The seeing out there is just terrible — in the field, at bat, all over," complained Joe Rudi, usually one of the quieter A's. "It's just a shame that World Series games have to be played under such conditions,"[13] said Sal Bando, always an outspoken critic of the Coliseum.

Fielding errors by the A's contributed to two unearned runs, which gave the Mets a 6-4 lead heading to the bottom of the ninth inning. With two outs and runners on first and second, Reggie Jackson and Gene Tenace cracked crucial RBI singles. The pair of timely hits tied the game, forcing extra innings.

The Mets threatened to take the lead back in the top half of the tenth, when Bud Harrelson led off with a single and moved to second on Tug McGraw's bunt. Wayne Garrett followed with a hard grounder to first, which Gene Tenace fielded nicely before throwing wildly to Rollie Fingers at first base. The error put runners on first and third with one out. Felix Millan lofted a short fly ball to left field, where Joe Rudi made the catch. Harrelson, with above average speed as a runner, tagged and ran home, deciding to challenge the average throwing arm of Rudi. The Series' first major controversy ensued.

Home plate umpire Augie Donatelli called Harrelson out at the plate on a very close play. Willie Mays, the Mets' on-deck batter, fell to his knees, pleading with the veteran umpire to change his call. Donatelli ruled that Ray Fosse had tagged Harrelson on the hip just before he touched the plate. Fosse, however, claimed that he had touched him on the arm, while Harrelson insisted that he hadn't been tagged at all. Television replays, while somewhat inconclusive at first, seemed to support Harrelson's claim that he had avoided the tag entirely.

Game Two remained deadlocked until the top of the 12th. With Buddy Harrelson on third and Tug McGraw at first, Willie Mays bounced a two-out, run-scoring single over Rollie Fingers' outstretched arms. "I knew Fingers was going to throw me fastballs," Mays explained afterward. "That seems to be the only pitches any (Dick) Williams team throws me."[14] When Cleon Jones lined a single to load the bases, Dick Williams replaced Fingers with lefty Paul Lindblad, who would face John Milner. Milner bounded a routine grounder to second base, where Mike Andrews was now playing. Andrews had pinch-hit for Ted Kubiak in the eighth inning and remained in the game to play defense.

Milner's ground ball had all the earmarks of the inning's final out, which would leave the A's one run down with a chance to come back in the bottom half of the inning. An uncertain Andrews stabbed clumsily at the ball, allowing it to dribble through his legs. McGraw and Mays both scored, with Milner and Jones taking second and third, respectively. The A's now trailed by three runs. Jerry Grote then grounded a ball to the right side of the second base bag. Although a more difficult play than its predecessor, the grounder remained eminently playable. Andrews handled the bouncer without difficulty, but threw wide of first baseman Gene Tenace, pulling him off the bag. Andrews' second error enabled Jones to score the Mets' fourth run of the inning. The next batter, Don Hahn, mercifully pulled a grounder to the left side of the infield, away from Andrews. Sal Bando fielded the ball without problem and threw to Tenace for the third out of the prolonged inning.

The three additional gift runs took on added significance in the bottom of the 12th, as the A's attempted to rally. Reggie Jackson tripled, Gene Tenace walked and Jesus Alou singled to start the inning. One run in, runners on first and second and still no one out.

If not for the three extra runs created by the Andrews errors, Dick Williams might have been able to utilize the mediocre-hitting Ray Fosse to sacrifice the runners over to second and third. Now, still trailing by three runs, the bunt had ceased being an option for the A's. Fosse hit a slow ground ball to shortstop Buddy Harrelson, who tossed to Felix Millan at second base for the first out. Andrews, of all people, stepped to the plate. Desperately hoping to atone for his infield butchering, Andrews worked a walk to load the bases, putting the tying run at first base. With a chance to continue a dramatic comeback, Vic Davalillo popped up to Millan and Campy Campaneris grounded to Harrelson, ending the rally — and the game.

Prior to his key hit in the 12th inning, much of the media had watched with anguish as Willie Mays struggled to play his position in the outfield. Several writers questioned Yogi Berra's decision to use Mays as a pinch-runner for Rusty Staub, which resulted in Don Hahn moving from center to right field and Mays entering the game as the new center fielder. Mays failed to make two plays — when he allowed fly balls by Deron Johnson and Reggie Jackson to drop in — that he would have corralled easily during his prime seasons with the Giants. "I didn't play that bad," Mays said, disagreeing with the media's consensus that he had embarrassed himself in the field. "I'll catch the next one tomorrow."[16]

The post-game topic of conversation soon shifted from an aging Willie Mays to an embattled Mike Andrews. After the disastrous top half of the 12th inning, Sal Bando had noticed Charlie Finley placing a call from the owner's box, located near the A's dugout. On the other end of the line, as Bando later discovered, Oakland team physician Dr. Charles Hudson listened patiently to his employer.

Andrews accepted blame for the loss and willingly described both crucial misplays. "I have no excuses," Andrews said bravely before detailing the first error. "I put my glove down for the ball and thought I had it." The second error, according to some of the A's, may have resulted from Andrews' bad back. "As I started to throw, my back started to slip and go out from underneath me."[17] Yet, Andrews did not cite any injury in explaining why he had committed the error.

After the game, a reporter asked Dick Williams if the absence of Manny Trillo had cost the A's the game. Williams refused to use the omission of Trillo from the World Series roster as an excuse. "Let's face it," said Williams bluntly, "when you get down to the 25th man, you're in trouble."[18] Trouble was just beginning, thanks to Charlie Finley.

Chapter Eighteen:
Finley vs. Andrews

Moments after the disheartening defeat, Mike Andrews received instructions to report to Dr. Harry Walker. For a period of about five to 10 minutes, Dr. Walker examined Andrews' right shoulder. Andrews then met with Charlie Finley and Dick Williams in a private office. In a sermon that lasted approximately 40 minutes, Finley tried to persuade Andrews to sign a statement, dated October 14, 1973, that made the following claim:

Mike Andrews is unable to play his position because of a bicep groove tencosynotitis of the right shoulder. It is my opinion that he is disabled for the rest of the year.[1]

Dr. Walker had signed his name to the statement. Under the words, "I agree to the above," Mike Andrews finally agreed to place his signature.

In essence, Finley had "fired" one of his players. The player "firing," a first in World Series history, was not unprecedented for Finley. In 1967, the Kansas City A's had been struggling, a source of irritation to Finley. "Things were building to a head on one particular road trip," says Jack Aker, who was the A's player representative that season. "One of our broadcasters was riding on the plane with us — a fellow by the name of Monte Moore. Lew Krausse, who was a prankster right from the time he first came up, started ragging on Monte Moore a little bit and some other fellows came in on it. Before we know it, we had an

245

argument on the plane. It was rowdyism, even though it was nothing that any of the stewardesses on the plane complained about. When the flight was over, they didn't complain to anyone about it, until Mr. Finley actually asked them. So, it wasn't a big deal, we didn't think.

"Then the next day, of course, we have another meeting, where Mr. Finley comes in and starts chewing everybody out. He ended up suspending Lew Krausse. At that time, Hawk Harrelson, who was outspoken, made a comment. And Mr. Finley said, 'You're gonna be gone.'" Harrelson allegedly called Finley a "menace to baseball," a statement that Harrelson denied ever making. "So we thought, well, he probably will do it, he'll probably trade him for somebody. The next day we find out he released him." Harrelson, one of the best players on the team, had been "fired," with the A's receiving nothing in return. The move surprised the baseball world, which regarded Harrelson as a quality ballplayer. Many writers wondered why Finley hadn't simply put "The Hawk" on waivers. If claimed, Finley would have received $50,000. Others felt Finley should have waited until after the season, when the trade deadline would lift, allowing him to deal Harrelson to another team. Harrelson ended up signing with the Boston Red Sox, more than doubling his salary with the eventual American League pennant winners.

Finley was now angry with Mike Andrews, not for anything that he had allegedly said, but for what he done on the field. Finley contended that Andrews' shoulder injury, supposedly sustained prior to the Series, made him unavailable to play during the balance of the World Series. Finley now hoped to make the case that he be allowed to reinstate Manny Trillo to Oakland's post-season roster. In one fell swoop, Finley had attempted to break the rules of eligibility, force his team physician into lying about a player's health, and publicly embarrass a respected veteran like Mike Andrews.

"The game was over and we sat for a long period of time in the bus waiting to go to the airport," says Sal Bando, recalling the scene at the Oakland Coliseum. "We did not know what was holding us up. Now we were getting cranky and complaining. It was getting ridiculous. Finally, after I'd swear it must have been an hour or so, we left. It was all during that time where Finley was meeting with the team doctor and Mike Andrews and trying to disable him and activate Manny Trillo."

The A's reacted with disbelief when they saw that Andrews had not boarded the flight. "We found out on our way to New York," Bando says. "We were really upset because of the fact that Mike Andrews was no different in that World Series than he had been the second half of the season. He just happened to make a couple of errors." Oakland players had become accustomed to Finley's bizarre habits: his obsession with minutia, his rampant pettiness, his interference with coaches and managers. Yet, none of those nasty habits had prepared the players for the sinister act that he had committed in trying to rid himself of

Andrews in mid-Series. Oakland players simmered on the flight from Oakland to New York. Finley angered them further when he ordered the stewardess to stop the showing of the flight's in-house movie, *1776*. Finley apparently didn't like the movie, which he had already seen.

On the off-day scheduled between games two and three, a furious band of A's reported to Shea Stadium for a required workout. "I suggested at the workout that we wear Mike Andrews' number on our shirts," Bando reveals. In response to the captain, several players taped makeshift patches containing Andrews' No. 17 on their uniform sleeves. "Manny Trillo even wore the number of Mike Andrews," says Bando. "It wasn't anything against Manny, it was just the way it was handled with Mike (by Finley)."

Some of the A's considered taking their displeasure a step further. Reggie Jackson, who had become the A's player representative after the trade of Mike Hegan, threatened a player boycott of the World Series. "There is a possibility of refusing to play," said Jackson, acting as a team spokesman. "There are a bunch of guys who are close to that point."[2] Jackson also expected a grievance to be filed on Andrews' behalf with the Players' Association. If the Oakland players themselves could do little to make Finley change his mind, perhaps Marvin Miller could. Miller himself pondered the question of whether Finley had done emotional harm to Andrews, thereby justifying a grievance. "Public humiliation of a player, humiliating him in the eyes of other players, aspersing his ability so as to damage his standing as a professional in the field where he earns a living — does this do him injury?,"[3] Miller asked aloud. In asking the question, Miller seemed to be providing his own answer, in the affirmative.

The unified front presented by the Oakland players in the face of the treatment of Andrews provided the country with a different image of the A's. The publicized fights involving Vida Blue, Blue Moon Odom and Rollie Fingers had led fans to believe that A's players didn't like each other. "People think we hate each other and that we're always fighting," Sal Bando said at the time. "That's not true. The Andrews thing proves it. We all stood behind Mike when this happened." [4] Now the A's were fighting Finley.

A report by United Press International painted Finley as the villain, at least according to the testimony of Andrews himself. Andrews told UPI that Finley had threatened to "destroy me in baseball,"[5] if he did not sign the statement that declared him injured and unfit to play. Andrews said he really didn't want to sign the agreement, but did so out of fear that Finley might follow up on his verbal threats.

Finley called a press conference that evening to respond to the verbal salvos he had been receiving. Finley reiterated his claim that Andrews' shoulder was sufficiently injured, making him unfit for World Series play. Finley added one other nugget of information; Finley said

Andrews had expressed his willingness to sign Dr. Walker's statement in exchange for a guaranteed 1974 contract. "In the presence of my secretary and my farm director, John Claiborne, Mike said he would sign that letter if I would guarantee him a contract for next year."[6] Finley said he refused the offer. Later, Andrews denied that he had ever suggested making such a "trade" — a playing contract for the following season in exchange for his agreement to sit out the remaining games of the Series.

After Game Five, Finley would make another stunning "revelation," when he indicated that Dick Williams had played a role in the attempt to disable Andrews. "Dick thought it would be a good idea if that we should have him examined by a doctor," Finley told the Associated Press on October 20. "Dick thought we had about a 10 percent chance of getting the commissioner to O.K. it."[7]

One day after the Finley press conference, Bowie Kuhn met with Andrews. Then, just a few hours prior to Game Three, the commissioner rendered his ruling on the latest Finley-initiated controversy. Kuhn explained that an injured player can be replaced during the World Series, but only if he suffers a new injury, one that is serious enough to create an immediate emergency requiring a new player be added to the roster. Kuhn said that he found no proof that Andrews' pre-existing shoulder condition had "changed or worsened since the Series began, or that he had been injured in the Series."[8] As a result, Kuhn ordered the Oakland owner to reinstate Andrews, while denying Finley's request to use Manny Trillo as a substitute player on the 25-man roster.

Kuhn wasn't done. In addition to reinstating Andrews, he admonished Finley for trying to circumvent the rules while humiliating one of his players. "I might add," said Kuhn, "that the handling of this matter by the Oakland club has had the unfortunate effect of unfairly embarrassing a player who has given many years of able service to professional baseball."[9] Although Kuhn failed to mention Finley by name, it was quite clear who he meant in citing the "Oakland club."

Finley offered a predictable response to Kuhn's admonishment. "It is my ballclub, my money and I don't appreciate anyone telling me how to spend my money to run my business," Finley bellowed defiantly. "I don't think the commissioner treated us fairly in turning down this request. He's talking about embarrassing Andrews. We're not out to embarrass Andrews. But I sure as hell was embarrassed by what he (the commissioner) did."[10] Finley charged Kuhn with issuing his denial letter to the media before he, as owner of the team, had received a copy of it.

Andrews attended a separate press conference in an effort to explain what had transpired between him and Finley after the second game. Andrews described an atmosphere in which a persistent, persuasive Finley had played with his emotions, making him feel guilty about the way he was hurting the team by playing with a supposedly injured shoulder. "I'm sorry I signed it," said Andrews, "but if I were in the same state (of mind), I'd probably do it again."[11] Finley had tried to coerce him into signing a statement that represented, in Andrews' view, a complete fabrication. "I read a report which in my opinion was a total lie," Andrews said. "Maybe (Manny) Trillo could help the team (I thought). I said, 'Give me the damn thing, I'll sign it.'"[12] Andrews apologized for endorsing a dishonest statement that he knew misrepresented the facts surrounding his health. "I was embarrassed. I was beaten. For the first time in my life, I just quit,"[13] Andrews said with shame in his voice.

Throughout the episode, Dick Williams had observed the machiavellian efforts of his owner with quiet disdain. On October 16, prior to Game Three, Williams met with his players in the clubhouse, finally ending his silence. "I'm going to deny this if it leaks out from this room," Williams said in prefacing his bombshell declaration, "but I'm resigning at the end of this World Series, win, lose or draw."[14] According to some players, Williams explained that Finley's disgraceful handling of Andrews had pushed him to this decision, one he had been contemplating for several weeks.

Up until now, Williams had said little publicly or privately about his opinion of the Andrews mess. Williams still wasn't speaking candidly with the media about the issue, perhaps out of fear that Finley might fire him on the spot. But Williams had already begun to make plans for the future. After first using a third party to let another team know of his interest in becoming their manager, he secretly telephoned officials of the New York Yankees.

One Oakland player claimed that Williams had previously told him of his desire to quit, well before the Andrews case had become an issue. Reggie Jackson said that Williams, talking to him on September 22, had informed him that he would step aside after the season. Williams supposedly wanted to use Jackson as a DH while the slugger recovered from a minor hamstring pull. According to Jackson, Finley told Williams not to use Reggie at all, apparently in an attempt to deflate his statistics and thereby reduce his negotiating power for the 1974 season. Although Finley had often tried to dictate lineup changes to his manager in the past, Williams felt he had stepped over the line of integrity with his latest demand.

Williams' announcement prior to Game Three did not come as a major revelation to a veteran player like Sal Bando. "It had been floating around," Sal says, "and I think he decided he better let everyone know right then and there. It wasn't that big of a surprise. But we understood. Working for Charlie was not a normal, everyday occurrence. I mean, there were things that would happen, or he'd call Dick at the last minute. It was not baseball, and it was tough."

Andrews, who had not made the team flight from Oakland to New

York, did not play in Game Three, perhaps the most dramatic and well-played game of the Series. The A's won, 3-2, on Campy Campaneris' RBI single in the 11th inning. Campy's night included three hits, a stolen base, and some rare credit being sent his way. Reporters surrounded his locker after the game, putting the humble Campaneris in the spotlight usually reserved for Reggie Jackson or Catfish Hunter. Unlike his early days in the major leagues, when he hardly spoke a phrase of English, Campaneris could now answer questions posed to him by the media. "I'm no banjo hitter," said Campy, "but I'm no hero, either. Many times I wish I could be a big hitter like Hank Aaron or Willie Mays, but I must be satisfied with what I've got."[15] As Mets' manager Yogi Berra put it, Campy rarely beat the opposition with a home run, "but he'll hurt you in a dozen other ways."[16]

In the eighth inning, Campaneris stole a base against rifle-armed catcher Jerry Grote and scored the game-tying run on Joe Rudi's single. Although Grote threw very well, Campaneris felt confident that he could time his jump against Tom Seaver. "I watch Seaver on television in the playoffs," Campaneris explained. "I watch him very close. Seaver is slow in his move to home plate. So I get the jump and I go."[17] By studying pitchers on his own, as he had done since joining the Kansas City A's, Campy had once again helped his team win.

Unfortunately, Campaneris' moments with the media were interrupted by the continuing coverage of another Oakland middle infielder. After the 11-inning victory, Catfish Hunter claimed that the treatment of Mike Andrews had inspired the A's to play with greater intensity. "I think we busted our ass a little harder tonight," said Hunter, who had started Game Three. "If Finley fired everybody but nine players, we'd still go out and do our best to win."[18] Sal Bando also sounded off on the Andrews theme. "That stuff about Mike Andrews was actually good for us in the end," Bando told reporters. "For two whole days it made us completely forget the fact we had to face Seaver."[19]

The win didn't completely appease Bando, however. The third baseman expressed his wishes to be traded after the Series, provided that Charlie Finley did not improve the condition of the Oakland Coliseum or the state of the team's travel arrangements. "Traveling conditions are not good and everything about the set-up at the Coliseum is not favorable," Bando complained. "For one thing, it takes too much time to get things done at the ballpark. Why do you need a written order for them to cut the grass?"[20] Bando would later rescind his trade request.

Unlike Bando and Hunter, Reggie Jackson said that Finley's handling of Andrews had played no part in the Game Three victory. "We win in spite of him," Jackson declared. "He's a financial empire and that's all. That's all I respect about him. It's too bad he doesn't use his money to help humanity."[21] When a reporter asked Jackson whether Finley had ever treated him poorly for racial reasons, Jackson offered only a backhanded endorsement of his owner. "To him, all people are the same color — green."[22]

Andrews telephoned Jackson from his home in Massachusetts. Andrews wanted to know how his teammates felt about the episode and how they would react if he decided to return to the team. When Jackson told Andrews that the players supported him "100 per cent," the embattled infielder decided to book a flight to New York.

In the fourth game, a 6-1 Mets' triumph, Williams inserted Andrews as a pinch-hitter. Andrews came to bat for Horacio Piña in the eighth inning of the one-sided game. As Andrews strode toward home plate, the crowd of 54,817 fans at Shea Stadium treated him as one of their own, bathing him in a prolonged, standing applause. Andrews then topped an easy grounder to third baseman Wayne Garrett, who threw to first base for a routine out. As he jogged toward Oakland dugout, the Mets' fans once again rose in support of the embattled infielder. Two standing ovations for an enemy player during the World Series. Andrews expressed appreciation for the gesture from the New York fans, not exactly known for their sensitive or sympathetic ways. "The ovation gave me chills, it surprised me," said an appreciative Andrews. "I don't think I've ever had a standing ovation in my life. To me that meant everything."[23]

Surrounded by Met fans, Charlie Finley remained motionless in his owner's box. As Andrews ran back to the dugout, an uncomfortable Finley offered some polite applause and awkwardly waved an A's banner. Thanks to Dick Williams' decision to use Andrews as a pinch-hitter in a lost cause of a game, the owner had received his own unsavory taste of humiliation.

Dick Green, the A's regular second baseman, decided to have some fun with Andrews after the Game Four loss. Usually an impeccable fielder, Green had committed a fourth inning error on a Felix Millan grounder, leading to an unearned run for the Mets. "Damn Andrews," Green said out loud to a reporter in the Oakland clubhouse. "He fouled up that position so much I can't play it."[24] Hopefully, enough time had passed since the pratfalls of Game Two for Andrews to appreciate the gallows humor.

The consensus of media opinion placed Andrews in a sympathetic spotlight, while targeting Finley as the proprietor of a plantation-like atmosphere in Oakland. In the November 3, 1973 issue of *The Sporting News*, Bay Area columnist Art Spander charged Finley with the following crimes:

- ruining Vida Blue mentally during their protracted salary hassle in 1971
- vindictively trading Mike Epstein to a last-place team as punishment for his critical assessments of the Oakland owner

- firing scout Bill Rigney without just cause during the September stretch run

- committing acts of pettiness, such as refusing to place decorative post-season bunting on the walls of the Oakland Coliseum for Games One and Two of the World Series.

In summary, Spander accused Finley of fostering an "atmosphere of hate" in the A's clubhouse, with most of the anger directed toward the dictator-like owner. Spander indicated that no matter the Series' outcome, Finley had succeeded in tainting the best-case scenario of an Oakland championship.

Finley had managed to alienate most of his players, along with the rest of the baseball world. While Finley had previously involved himself in bizarre statements and schemes, his behavior had taken a turn for the worse since suffering a heart attack in August. The irrational badgering of Dick Williams not to play Reggie Jackson, the inexplicable decision to sell Jose Morales before the playoffs, the unjust firing of Bill Rigney, the faking of attendance figures on the final day of the regular season, the cursing at Joe Cronin during the playoffs, and now, the inhumane treatment of Mike Andrews had all occurred within weeks of the heart attack.

Sal Bando agrees with the theory that Finley's heart attack led to a major transformation in his personality. "No question," says Bando. "There was a big change in the man because I would tell you that most players — prior to the 1973 season anyhow — would consider Mr. Finley a father figure, a good friend, because he was very helpful. It seemed that with the success of the team, and with his heart attack, things started to change; he became more vindictive and more difficult to get along with."

A scene at the following year's World Series would offer further evidence of Finley's growing nastiness in the aftermath of the heart attack. "They had the incident where his wife got the beating during the World Series," Bando says. "His wife and him got into an argument and she had to wear sunglasses because she had a black eye. She ended up divorcing him. I'm not sure when, but it wasn't too long after the incident... It just wasn't a healthy Charlie Finley."

By 1974, Finley had made enemies of almost every player on the A's roster. "I would say that 22 of the 25 guys on our team hate him," Bando would say in July of 1974. "That holds us together."[25] A's players often argued with each other, often fought with each other. Yet, they could find common ground in their dislike of Charlie Finley.

The stirrings of the Mike Andrews affair overshadowed another item of consternation to Charlie Finley — poor crowds throughout the post-season at the Oakland Coliseum. The defending champions drew little interest from their own fans, who seemed to take the A's success for granted. "The people here just don't appreciate us,"[26] said an exasperated Gene Tenace. The fans didn't appreciate Finley either. When the A's returned home for Game Six, a group of fans displayed a large banner that read: "HOW COULD FINLEY HAVE A HEART ATTACK?" The banner answered its own question. "HE DOESN'T EVEN HAVE A HEART."

Another group showed little appreciation for Reggie Jackson, but in a much more sinister way. Although the story would not be revealed publicly until after the World Series, Jackson was playing the post-season under the protection of the FBI and a personal bodyguard named Tony Del Rio. The reason? A group calling itself "The Weathermen" had sent the ominous letter to A's broadcaster Monte Moore, who passed the note along to Dick Williams and Charlie Finley. Perhaps distracted by the death threat, Jackson had struggled during the Championship Series against the Orioles, ending up with a paltry three hits in 21 at-bats, and an uncharacteristic total of no extra base hits or RBI's. In the World Series, Jackson had started out 0-for-5 before collecting four hits in the Game Two loss in extra innings.

As he sat in his hotel room during the Series, Jackson thought about the assassinations of Martin Luther King, and John and Robert Kennedy. Even though he knew that the six-foot, five-inch, 290-pound Del Rio and a full complement of FBI agents were on the premises, Jackson wondered about his safety. "What could they do for a man standing all alone out there on the diamond?" Jackson wrote in an article that appeared in *Guideposts* magazine. "I began to visualize a fanatic on a roof overlooking the park. He's holding a high-powered rifle; I'm in the batter's box waiting for the pitch. He lines up the cross-hairs of the telescopic sight and slowly squeezes the trigger..."[27]

Jackson quickly realized that he could not play baseball with such thoughts running through his mind. Playing in a World Series provided sufficient pressure in and of itself, without also having to wonder about one's own livelihood. Jackson sought inspiration and comfort from a letter he had recently received from his father. Jackson had already read the letter once; he would read it again.

On October 18, two days after Dick Williams had privately told his players of his imminent departure from the clutches of Charlie Finley, media reports circulated that Williams would leave the A's and might be headed to New York to manage the Yankees. Even though Williams had made it clear to interested third parties that he was extremely interested in working for the Yankees, he publicly denied the newspaper stories.

As the Mets and A's prepared for Game Five, one of New York's coaches engaged in some playful banter with one of Oakland's pitchers. "If Williams is going to manage the Yankees," Mets' bullpen coach Joe Pignatano said to Darold Knowles, "does Finley manage the A's?"[28] The colorful Knowles suddenly jumped up from his seat in the A's dugout, giving Pignatano an exaggerated look of mock surprise and shock. Even in the face of the Mike Andrews story, with the team fighting for a championship, with the loss of their manager imminent, the A's had retained their sense of humor.

Chapter Nineteen:
Oh, By the Way, the A's Win Another World Series

In Game Five, New York's Jerry Koosman and Tug McGraw held the A's to just three hits in the Mets' 2-0 victory. The Mets led the Series three games to two, but now had to go back to Oakland for Game Six, and possibly a decisive seventh game. On Friday, the A's landed at the Oakland Airport to a smallish reception of fewer than 200 fans. Most of the players walked off the plane with frowned, serious expressions on their faces, while failing to wave to the few onlookers who had bothered to attend their arrival. The results of the first five games of the Series, the distasteful handling of Mike Andrews and the fatigue caused by a cross country flight had left many of the Oakland players in foul moods.

Gene Tenace found two other causes of heartache — his own lack of hitting and the brilliant play of Mets' shortstop Bud Harrelson. "I've hit some good shots they took away from me," Tenace complained. "I think they've got two shortstops out there."[1] Harrelson's defensive play had dominated the on-field theme of the Series.

Mets' manager Yogi Berra faced an important decision with regard to his starting rotation. He could pitch Tom Seaver on three days rest in Game Six, and use Jon Matlack, if necessary, in Game Seven. Under that scenario, Matlack would also start on three days rest. Or Berra could pitch 12-game winner George Stone in the sixth game, saving a well-rested Seaver for the eventuality of a seventh game. Berra opted for a more aggressive approach, starting Seaver on short rest in what he hoped would be a climactic Game Six. "He's Mr. Baseball," Reggie Jackson said of Seaver. "They've heard about him in China. Blind people come to the park to hear him pitch."[2]

The prospects of facing Seaver represented only part of the problems the A's faced in trying to square the Series at three games apiece. The sideshow created by Charlie Finley's handling of Mike Andrews had proven to be a minor distraction to at least some of the players. "I'm a man split in two," admitted Reggie Jackson. "Half of me is trying to think about Mike Andrews, the other half is trying to think about Tom Seaver."[3] In 21 Series at-bats, Jackson had managed only five hits and two RBI's and had left eight runners in scoring position. As a result of the Andrews incident and his own struggles at the plate, Jackson seemed to be talking like a man who felt his team was on the verge of losing the World Series. "Our attitude is bad," Jackson revealed. "It just doesn't seem like a World Series."[4]

While veteran second baseman Dick Green disagreed with Jackson's contention, an unnamed player reflected the feeling of discontent surrounding the A's. "I can hardly wait for Monday," stated the anonymous player, "when all this is over."[5] The player was not referring to Rick Monday, either.

Dick Williams had other thoughts on his mind — thoughts of Tom Seaver. Williams felt pressure to maximize the offensive output of his lineup against New York's best starting pitcher. Williams benched his defensive-minded catcher, Ray Fosse, moved Gene Tenace behind the plate and inserted Deron Johnson at first base. Johnson had not started the first five games of the Series, in a decision that may have been sparked by Finley. "It's no secret," said one Oakland player, who predicted that Johnson would not return to the A's in 1974. "Deron is gone. Finley doesn't like him."[6]

One New York newspaper gave the A's little hope of coming back in the Series. The headline in the October 20th edition of the *New York Daily News* read as follows:

FOR THE A'S...THERE'S NO TOMORROW
Seaver Figures to Wrap It Up Today

In the accompanying article, Jon Matlack predicted that he would not have to pitch a Game Seven. He believed that Seaver would end the Series in six. Dick Williams felt more optimistic about Oakland's chances — at least publicly. "You know the '52 Dodgers had a 3-2 lead over the Yankees," Williams said, referring to the Brooklyn club he had played for during his major league career. "We went back to Ebbets Field to wrap it up. Only it didn't turn out that way. We lost both games and blew the Series."[7]

Williams could take some consolation in the knowledge that the A's would be facing a right-handed pitcher, albeit a great one in Seaver, rather than the left-handed starters who had proved so troublesome against Oakland. Even though the A's lineup tilted heavily to the right side, Oakland had managed only 35 hits and 13 runs through the first five games. "Their lefties have been throwing the ball exactly where they wanted it," Williams said, referring to starters Jerry Koosman and Jon Matlack and relievers Tug McGraw, George Stone and Ray Sadecki. "You can't give enough credit to (New York scout) Dee Fondy for the scouting report he gave the Mets on our hitters."[8]

Williams' optimism proved prophetic. In the first inning, Joe Rudi singled against Seaver and scored on Reggie Jackson's double. In the third inning, Sal Bando and Jackson teamed up, contributing a single and a run-scoring double, respectively. The A's added an insurance run in the eighth, when pinch-hitter Jesus Alou scored Reggie with a sacrifice fly. Catfish Hunter, Darold Knowles and Rollie Fingers made the runs hold up in a 3-1 victory.

Rudi, Jackson and Sal Bando all noticed a difference between Seaver's performance in Game Six as compared to his earlier showing in the Series. "I think it's dead or something," Bando said bluntly of Seaver's arm. "His arm must be bothering him because he threw much harder in the game at Shea."[9] "He needs an extra day's rest,"[10] offered Jackson, indirectly second-guessing Berra's decision to use Seaver on three days rest. Seaver, for his part, claimed that his right shoulder felt fine.

The A's had regained the momentum but the Mets still held the advantage on the mound. Jon Matlack, the Game Seven starter, had not allowed an earned run in 23 innings of post-season work. Both Holtzman and Matlack kept the opposition lineups hitless through the first two innings. The game remained scoreless until the bottom of the third.

With one out, Holtzman came to bat and rocked a double down the left field line. Campy Campaneris followed with an uncharacteristic show of strength, lifting a hanging curveball over the fence in right field. Campy's first Series home run gave the A's a 2-0 lead. Joe Rudi followed with a sharp single to center, and after Sal Bando popped out, Reggie Jackson lofted a drive deep into the right field stands. After rounding third base, Jackson trotted slowly, stopped himself one stride short of home plate, leapt in the air and stomped both of his feet on the plate. A tight, scoreless seventh game had suddenly become an Oakland runaway.

With his signature Game Seven home run and memorable landing on home plate, Jackson began to shape the World Series reputation that would earn him the nickname "Mr. October" in later years. "If you needed a home run in the ninth inning, he usually gave it to you," says Rollie Fingers. "He was that type of player. He played great under pressure, a great pressure ballplayer in situations where the game was on the line."

The A's added another run against Matlack in the fifth, before the Mets posted their first run on consecutive doubles by Felix Millan and

Rusty Staub in the sixth. Rollie Fingers relieved Holtzman and closed out the rally by retiring Cleon Jones and John Milner. Fingers remained in the game until the ninth, when a walk, a single and an error by Gene Tenace at first base gave the Mets one last hope. With two outs and a left-handed hitter scheduled to bat, Dick Williams summoned Darold Knowles. The veteran sinkerballer had now appeared in each of the seven games against the Mets, establishing a new World Series record.

With one out to go in the ninth inning, several fans had hurled themselves over the railing at the Coliseum onto the playing field. A small group headed in the direction of Reggie Jackson, stationed in right field. Jackson, who had played the post-season under a death threat, decided to take no chances and ran away from the fans, who thought the game was already over as Tenace bobbled pinch-hitter Ed Kranepool's apparent Series-ending ground out.

Darold Knowles and the A's still required one more out. Don Hahn led off third base and pinch-runner Teddy Martinez inched off first base. The Mets, having closed to within 5-2, had managed to bring the potential game-tying run to the plate. With the left-handed hitting Wayne Garrett

Gene Tenace lies at the bottom of the pile as the A's celebrate their world championship win over the Mets.

scheduled to face the southpaw Knowles, the situation cried for Mets' manager Yogi Berra to insert Willie Mays as a pinch-hitter. Mays, a right-handed hitter with power, stood a better chance of hitting a game-tying home run against Knowles than Garrett. Mays also seemed like the appropriate sentimental choice, given that he had already announced he would retire at the end of the Series. Berra chose neither the percentages nor sentiment. He allowed Garrett to face Knowles. Garrett popped a Knowles fastball weakly to the left side of the infield.

As Campy Campaneris nestled the ball into his glove, a storm of Oakland players unleashed itself onto the field, toppling Knowles and Gene Tenace to the ground. For the second straight year, the Oakland A's celebrated their status as baseball's best team. For the first time in 12 years, a major league franchise had claimed back-to-back titles. The Yankees of 1961 and '62 had been the last team to repeat as world champions.

Players, reporters and various officials jammed their way into the A's smallish clubhouse. Sal Bando admitted that the A's had taken the Mets lightly at the start of the Series. "We beat Baltimore and figured the Series was going to be easy," Bando acknowledged. "But once the Mets had us one game from elimination, we woke up."[11]

The bullpen had contributed heavily to the awakening. Rollie Fingers and Darold Knowles had combined to pitch five scoreless innings over the final two games. Except for the second and fourth games, the Oakland bullpen had prospered throughout the post-season. "Our bullpen was the difference," said Dick Williams. "Our bullpen was deeper than the Orioles and Mets...I think our staff was better than theirs because of the bullpen."[12]

As Charlie Finley's band played his favorite song, "Sugar in the Morning, Sugar in the Evening," Reggie Jackson answered questions from a large gathering of writers and broadcasters. Jackson pleaded with the media not to misrepresent the owner's involvement in the Series victory. "Please don't give Finley credit," sounded Jackson. "That takes away from what the guys in this dressing room have done."[13] After struggling in the early games of the Series, Jackson had collected four hits in eight at-bats over the final two games. He had driven in four runs, including two on his Series-cementing home run in the seventh game. Jackson's hitting appeared aided by the playing of the final two games during the daylight hours. In night games during the Series, Jackson had managed only one hit in 12 at-bats. In contrast, his day-game performances numbered eight hits in 17 at-bats.

Once again, controversy attached itself to the winning atmosphere in the clubhouse. Although Jackson had hit well late in the Series, his lack of hitting in games one through five had held back the A's. *Sport* magazine nonetheless named Jackson the Series MVP, ignoring the player whom many writers felt deserved the award: Campy Campaneris. Veteran baseball writer Dick Young chided *Sport* magazine for making what he considered a political selection.

"In this phony, commercial world of ours," Young wrote in the *New York Daily News*, "Reggie Jackson, who had two good games, wins the MVP car instead of Bert Campaneris, who had seven good games. Do you know why?... Because Reggie Jackson is great copy, Reggie Jackson can make a fine forceful speech in New York when he gets the car."[14] Young proceeded to describe Campy's exploits throughout the Series, including his impressive fielding and critical Game Seven home run against Jon Matlack. "He does it all, except one," Young wrote of Campaneris. "He can't speak English. This, if you're giving a car for a magazine promotion, is a terrible weakness."[15]

"Bert Campaneris has been so great for us," raved Dick Williams, "that this has to be the best World Series shortstopping since Phil Rizzuto and Pee Wee Reese were dazzling everyone in my younger days."[16] Williams went as far as to compare Campaneris to another Hall of Fame middle infielder. "I've never seen anyone since Jackie Robinson who gets such a jump and who makes the opposition to nervous,"[17] Williams gushed. Even Jackson acknowledged that Campaneris, among other Oakland teammates, had built a stronger case for claiming the Series MVP award. "I thought Bert, or Joe Rudi or Catfish should win it,"[18] Jackson said amongst a gathering of players and reporters in the clubhouse.

Campaneris, usually one of the most modest of the A's, agreed that he deserved the award. In the dugout near the end of Game Seven, teammates Jesus Alou, Sal Bando and Gene Tenace had told him to expect to win the car from *Sport*. "I never in my life been so disappointed," Campaneris told the *New York Times'* Dave Anderson, who disagreed with Dick Young's contention that *Sport* had chosen Jackson based on his articulation. "I think I do better job than Reggie do. I think I have seven good games."[19]

The post-game celebration contained two other bittersweet moments. Longtime second baseman Dick Green, the glue to Oakland's right side of the infield, indicated that he would retire. "I think it's time to quit," Green told reporters. "I'm happy to be going out on top."[20] Green's announcement soon became overshadowed by another revelation. A's manager Dick Williams, speaking on national television, publicly announced his resignation, effective immediately. The news that A's players had been aware of since Game Three and had been rumored throughout the working press had now become official.

Reggie Jackson put his arm around his former manager and delivered an emotional message. "You taught me how to win," said Jackson, as he kissed Williams on the cheek. "I'm sorry you're leaving."[21] Jackson had analyzed Williams for the media over the last few days, as rumors of his move to the Yankees circulated. "He's got two rules," Jackson had said. "You hustle all the time and you don't make the same mental mistake twice."[22] Jackson had also credited Williams for treating all players similarly. "He doesn't play favorites. But he likes you better if you are hard-nosed. If you are a candy ass, you may have trouble making his team."[23]

Only four months earlier, Jackson had resented Williams and his coaches for being too critical. "He's the kind of guy you might like for a month and hate for a month," Jackson said now. "But he doesn't care. He just wants to win...That's what Dick has taught us."[24]

Williams maintained that his decision to leave the A's had not been motivated by any problems with Finley. "I am leaving for personal reasons," Williams insisted, "not out of any dissatisfaction over my relations with Finley."[25] Williams explained that working on the west coast while maintaining a home near Ft. Lauderdale, Florida, had created problems in maintaining a relationship with his family. Few onlookers believed Williams' graceful public sentiments. During the playoffs, Williams had confided to a friend. "I've had it up to here. I'm quitting after the season. I've had only five peaceful days all year, the five days (Finley) was in the hospital."[26] Many players, including Catfish Hunter sympathized with Williams. "He couldn't run the team the way he wanted," assessed Hunter. "He had to check everything out first with Mr. Finley."[27] Williams had finally decided to check out of Finley's neighborhood.

Hunter and Vida Blue decided not to attend the team's rain-soaked victory parade, which drew nearly 200,000 fewer fans than the 1972 celebration. Those players who did show up for the motorcade looked sullen and disinterested. Given the resignation of Williams and the mistreatment of Mike Andrews, the A's were in no mood to celebrate their second world championship.

Chapter Twenty:
No More Dick Williams to Push Around

Dick Williams said he would consider any of-
fers from major league teams, but he clearly had one club in mind.
"Sure I'd love to be with the Yankees," said Williams. "Anyone who says
he wouldn't is crazy."[1] As Williams discussed his resignation during the
A's victory celebration, Charlie Finley told his manager that he wished
he would return. Speaking on national television, Finley added that he
would not stand in Williams' way should he not change his mind.

Two days later Finley changed his mind regarding Williams' future. Oakland farm director John Claiborne had suggested to Finley
that he exact some form of compensation in exchange for Williams'
services. Any major league team wishing to hire Williams as manager
would have to compensate the A's — with players and/or cash, but
preferably players. When Yankee owner George Steinbrenner asked
Finley for permission to contact Williams, he received a blunt response.
"Absolutely not," Finley said. "They seemed stunned and wanted to know
why."[2] Finley explained that he had recently given Williams a two-year
contract extension. If the Yankees did not properly compensate the A's,
"there will be court action,"[3] Finley vowed.

Finley referred to several precedents which supported his claims
for compensation. In 1934, the Washington Nationals exacted $225,000
from the Boston Red Sox in exchange for the rights to manager Joe
Cronin. In 1967, the New York Mets sent pitcher Bill Denehy and

$100,000 to the Senators for the right to hire Gil Hodges as manager. The compensation the Mets turned over to Washington was well worth it — in 1969, the Mets would win the first world championship in franchise history while under the direction of Hodges.

Precedents aside, Williams felt that the most pertinent issue was Finley's failure to live up to his initial vow. In less than a week, Finley's words had changed from "won't stand in the way" to "over my dead body." Williams expressed surprise at Finley's turnabout. "It's not like Mr. Finley to go back on his word. But this is an about-face."[4] In subsequent interviews, Williams went further, practically calling his former boss a liar. "Charlie says one thing and does another. He's giving out a lot of false information."[5]

Finley responded to Williams' claims by trying to clarify his initial remarks during the A's post-game celebration. When he said he would not "stand in the way," he was referring to Williams' options in the business world, not in the baseball community. Finley said he never intended to allow Williams to walk off to another managerial job, without some sort of compensation coming his way.

Although Finley also claimed that he preferred Williams return as his manager in Oakland, reports out of Baltimore indicated otherwise. In a story written by Doug Brown that appeared in the December 8, 1973 edition of *The Sporting News*, Finley had supposedly contacted the Orioles about the availability of their manager, Earl Weaver, during the World Series. Finley had placed the call prior to the conclusion of the World Series, while Williams was still Oakland's manager, several days before his publicly-expressed intention to leave the A's. According to Brown's story, Baltimore's vice-president and general manager, Frank Cashen, had refused to give Finley permission to talk to Weaver.

Baseball legalities prevented the New York Yankees, or any other team from negotiating with Williams. Yet, the Yankees made it clear they wanted Williams, who expressed mutual affection for wearing pinstripes. Prior to the winter meetings, the Yankees agreed to compensate Finley, offering starting second baseman Horace Clarke. Finley said no to the mediocre Clarke, but counter-offered by asking for one of three players: catcher Thurman Munson, outfielder Bobby Murcer, or pitcher Mel Stottlemyre. In other words, Finley wanted one of the three best players on the New York roster, while the Yankees were offering about their 15th best player.

In stage two of negotiations, Finley met with Yankee general manager Gabe Paul at the winter meetings in Houston. Finley backed off on his request for Munson, Murcer or Stottlemyre. Instead, he asked for two minor league prospects: first baseman-outfielder Otto Velez and left-handed pitcher Scott McGregor. "Both?" exclaimed an incredulous Gabe Paul. "You can't have either."[6]

Finley talked further with Paul, asking for either Velez or McGregor, plus a sum of cash. No sale. Finley agreed to eliminate the cash part of his request, but wanted the Yankees to include one of the following prospects — Steve Coulson, Kerry Dineen, John Shupe or Terry Whitfield — along with either McGregor or Velez. Paul's response was the same as before — no deal. The two sides had reached a stalemate, ending their meeting in Houston.

Finley's stubborn posture on ample compensation left Williams furious and frustrated. The former A's manager told reporters that he was considering filing a lawsuit against Finley on the grounds that his former employer was running interference on his legitimate efforts to find new work. Williams also mentioned his disappointment with the American League's failure to intervene in the matter. Why didn't AL president Joe Cronin step in and determine which players the Yankees should surrender to the A's in a trade for Williams?

"The problem is between New York and Oakland,"[7] claimed a neutral Cronin. Perhaps Cronin wanted to steer away from any involvement in the case as he prepared for his own retirement from the American League office. Williams would later criticize Cronin for refusing to involve himself in the dispute. "Not letting me go to the Yankees was one of the last of many years of non-decisions by...Joe Cronin,"[8] Williams told Sport magazine.

Williams wanted the Yankees, the Yankees wanted him, Cronin wanted no part of the dispute, and Finley insisted he wanted Williams to continue managing the A's. Since Williams still had a signed contract with the A's for the 1974 season, Finley reasoned, he still considered Williams his manager. In fact, he continued mailing Williams paychecks on the first and 15th day of each month through the end of the calendar year. "There is no way I'll go back to Oakland,"[9] Williams said adamantly. Williams later revealed that he had received the checks on a timely basis from Finley, but had neglected to cash any of them after his resignation. Williams did not want to feel beholden to Finley, at least not in any financial way.

On December 13, the Yankees, exasperated in their negotiations with Finley and by Cronin's foot-dragging, decided to force the issue. George Steinbrenner announced that he reached a contractual agreement with Williams to manage the Yankees. Gabe Paul introduced Williams to the media at a press conference. Williams donned a Yankee cap and uniform jersey and smiled widely for reporters. Photographs of Williams wearing Yankee paraphernalia would become collector's items; Williams would find an immediate roadblock in his efforts to wear a Yankee uniform during a regular season game.

Charlie Finley filed an immediate protest with Joe Cronin. The owner expressed his rage over his manager's refusal to honor an existing contract. Finley also informed the media of his contempt for the Yankees, who had tried to steal one of his contracted employees. "What if I tried to sign Bobby Murcer," supposed Finley. "Wouldn't the Yankees be furious with me for trying to sign one of their best players, one who was already under contract to New York?"[10]

In contrast to his disagreement with Finley over the cancellation of Game Three of the American League Championship Series, Cronin sided with the Oakland owner on the issue of control over Williams' contract. On December 20, just one week after the Yankees had signed Williams, Cronin ruled that Finley still held rights to Williams. Without Finley's approval, the Yankees would not be allowed to employ Williams as their manager in 1974.

"Dick Williams was my manager yesterday, he's my manager today and he'll be my manager tomorrow,"[11] declared Finley, who now refused to even negotiate the compensation issue with the hated Yankees. After several last-ditch legal efforts to secure Williams, the Yankees finally surrendered in their pursuit of the world championship manager. On January 3, 1974, the Yankees introduced former Pittsburgh Pirate skipper Bill Virdon as their new manager. Although the Yankees publicly decided to leave their managerial door slightly ajar (just in case they could work out a compromise with Finley and obtain Williams), the organization had basically conceded defeat on the legal front. While Finley had been both technically and morally wrong in his handling of the Mike Andrews affair, he was now acting within his legal rights in maintaining possession of Williams.

Dick Williams (right) in happier times with catcher-first baseman Gene Tenance. By the end of the 1973 World Series, Williams had experienced enough of Charlie Finley's world to call it quits.

Chapter Twenty-one:
Great Players, No Manager

The Mike Andrews incident had represented the final insult for Dick Williams, convincing him to expedite his departure from the organization. Andrews soon followed Williams out the door, though not of his own volition. Finley placed the veteran infielder on waivers, the first step in giving him his release. Finley refused to let Andrews' exit go at that; he insulted Andrews by quoting baseball's waiver rules. "Any team that wants him can have him for $1."[1]

Andrews insisted that his arm and shoulder felt fine. A Boston doctor confirmed Andrews' positive feelings about the shoulder, saying that he found nothing physically wrong with the arm. Andrews did admit that he had developed a mental block that affected his throws to first base. In spite of the problem, Andrews believed he could play a capable first base while still hitting major league pitching. Andrews contacted 22 of the 24 major league teams, but none of the clubs offered him as much as a tryout.

In the aftermath of his release, and Finley's embarrassing $1 crack, Andrews received an invitation to appear on the *Dick Cavett Show*, but still no interest from any of the ballclubs. The major league career of the former Red Sox and White Sox second baseman had come to an end at the age of 30. After sitting out the 1974 season completely, Andrews would play one unproductive season in Japan before retiring for good.

Unfortunately, much in the tradition of Bill Buckner, most fans remembered Andrews for the one World Series incident, rather than his career accomplishments from 1966 to 1973. In 1967, Andrews contributed to the Red Sox' "Impossible Dream" team, which, ironically enough, was managed by Dick Williams. From 1969 to 1971, Andrews reached double figures in home runs, while playing a consistently solid second base, where he efficiently turned double plays with shortstop partner Rico Petrocelli. Although Andrews was no star he deserved better than the shabby treatment he received from Finley, and the stigma of disgrace attached to his post-season firing.

While the Williams and Andrews sagas had dominated conversation since the World Series, the Oakland players had created further controversy when they met to distribute World Series shares. The players, already resentful of Allan Lewis' inclusion on the 25-man roster, cast votes on how much Series loot to give to the veteran pinch-runner. Lewis had appeared in a career-high 35 games, or well over 20 per cent of Oakland's regular season contests. Yet, the A's saw fit to give Lewis, who had failed to come to bat a single time during the regular season, a mere one-tenth of a share. At least Lewis was well-liked in the minor leagues. Fans of the Southern League's Birmingham Barons, where Lewis had played for most of the season, voted him the most popular player on the team.

Lewis did fare better than one of his teammates in earning some of the World Series loot. Oakland players decided to shut out late-season acquisition Rico Carty, who had already been denied his first opportunity at World Series play. Carty's Oakland experience worsened when Charlie Finley decided not to give him a World Series ring. On December 14, Carty received another slap in the face. "I was really hurt when Finley sent me a telegram in December telling me I was released," Carty said three years later. "Here I was released and I had been a .300 hitter all my life."[2] Carty was also leading the Dominican League in home runs, RBI's and batting average at the time. As with his releases of Tommy Davis and Orlando Cepeda, Finley would come to regret his severance of Carty. The "Beeg Mon" would make a successful comeback in 1975, emerging as one of the American League's best designated hitters. By 1978, Carty would impress Finley so much that the Oakland owner would re-acquire him in a trade with the Toronto Blue Jays.

While turmoil had begun to infiltrate the A's during the 1972 championship run, it had reached its peak in 1973. One controversy after another had arisen: Reggie Jackson's complaints about the coaching staff, the resentment toward Allan Lewis, the Bill Posedel affair, the Mike Andrews escapade, ad nauseam. Somehow, the A's had sidestepped each roadblock on their way to a second straight title. Catcher Ray Fosse felt the Oakland players, in combination with the out-of town media, had exaggerated the extent of the tension. "The Oakland writers are used to it, so they just laugh when something like that gets started.

But strange writers think it's dissension and fighting, so they make it into a big story.

"Sure, we had turmoil all year," Fosse acknowledged, "but it's not really dissension. We kind of blow it up."[3] Fosse felt the A's actually played better in the face of trouble. "We try to stir things up," said Fosse, "because we think we're a better team when everybody's yelling at one another."[4]

Most of the post-season news surrounding the A's carried an unsavory stench, with one exception. The Baseball Writers Association of America rewarded one of the A's — Reggie Jackson — by making him the overwhelming selection as American League Most Valuable Player. Jackson garnered all 24 first-place votes, becoming only the sixth American Leaguer to earn a unanimous vote. Jackson joined Hall of Fame first baseman Hank Greenberg, future Hall of Famers Mickey Mantle and Frank Robinson, and standouts Al Rosen and Denny McLain in sweeping the vote.

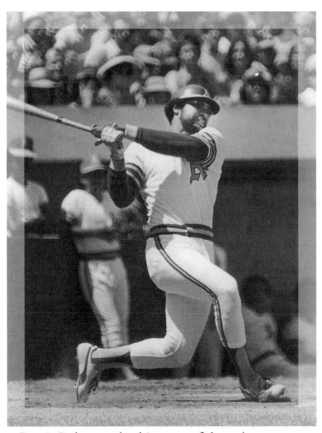

Reggie Jackson unleashing one of the era's most ferocious swings.

Although bogged down by the Dick Williams-to-the-Yankees tug-of-war, Charlie Finley did manage to make a trade during the December winter meetings in Houston In a bizarre move, Finley sent 28-year-old reliever Horacio Piña to the Cubs for former Athletic reliever Bob Locker, who was now 35 years old.

Locker had pitched well in his one season with the Cubs, with his 18 saves, 63 appearances and 2.55 ERA all leading the Chicago staff. So why did the Cubs trade their best reliever? When the Cubs had acquired Locker the previous winter, the sinkerballing right-hander had informed general manager John Holland that he would agree to pitch one season in the Windy City, then expect to be traded. Otherwise, Locker planned to retire after the 1973 season.

Threatened with the loss of an effective relief pitcher, the Cubs found Locker a new team, while gaining seven years in the process. Locker and Piña were pitchers of similar abilities, but the difference in their ages was substantial. Why did Finley make his trade, taking on the much older of the two pitchers? Piña had encountered some shoulder soreness during the season, but had still pitched effectively, managing a 2.76 ERA as a long reliever. Piña had responded favorably to the coaching of pitching mentor Wes Stock, who had recommended that the Mexican right-hander throw sidearm to both right-handed and left-handed hitters.

The Oakland media theorized that Finley had traded Piña merely to spite Dick Williams. In 1972, Williams had suggested the A's acquire Piña in exchange for Mike Epstein, a player that Williams had lost all respect for during the 1972 World Series. Finley had quickly soured on that deal, trying to reacquire Epstein almost immediately from Texas before the Rangers later dealt him to the Angels in mid-season.

As for the other player involved in this latest deal with the Cubs, Locker had fallen into Williams' doghouse during the 1972 post-season run. By reacquiring Locker, Finley seemed to be sending a subtle message to Williams that his opinions no longer mattered in the Oakland scheme.

"How could Charlie make that trade?" asked an incredulous Williams. "He says he wants me back as manager and then he goes and trades Piña for Locker. Piña is seven years younger and he trades him for Locker!"[5] Williams was right; the trade broke all the rules of logic and common sense.

Upon hearing of the deal, the flaky Locker promised not only to contribute to the Oakland bullpen but also offered to replace Williams, as well. "I talked to Charlie about that," Locker told reporters. "I told him I would be a player-manager. He thought I was kidding, but I was half-serious."[6]

Finley had other candidates in mind for the managerial vacancy. Third base coach Irv Noren and Tucson manager Sherm Lollar topped the list of in-house candidates. One Bay Area writer even mentioned the name of second baseman Dick Green, one of the most intelligent players on the team. Candidates from outside the organization included former Cincinnati manager Dave Bristol, who had led the Reds to three consecutive solid finishes in the late sixties before giving way to Sparky Anderson. Bristol then managed the Brewers with little success over two-plus seasons, losing his job 30 games into the 1972 campaign. Like Dick Williams in 1970, Bristol had experienced a demotion from major league manager to third base coach of the Montreal Expos, whom he had served in 1973.

While Bristol seemed like a solid manager-in-waiting, he possessed very little star appeal, lacking the glamour that Finley preferred in his managers and coaches. Finley appeared to be considering more intriguing candidates, including former Texas Rangers' skippers Ted Williams and Whitey Herzog. The other names all belonged to former or current major league stars who happened to be black: Satchel Paige, Frank Robinson and Maury Wills.

The inclusion of Paige in the Oakland rumor mill seemed like the unlikeliest of all the possibilities. Although the Hall of Fame pitcher had worked one game for Finley's Kansas City A's in 1965 — which at least gave him some connection to the organization — he had rarely been mentioned as a possible major league manager. Paige did not fit the managerial profile; as a player, he was a flamboyant showman who often jumped from team to team and abhorred basic conditioning regimens that included such unpleasant exercises like running. While Paige was a great competitor and a determined, resilient athlete who pitched well into his fifties, he seemed to lack the disciplinary skills required of managing professional athletes.

Maury Wills provided the A's with a more realistic managerial package. A star player throughout the 1960's, Wills had retired from the Los Angeles Dodgers after the 1972 season. In a stunning example of perseverance, Wills had arrived on the full-time major league scene at the late age of 27. Within three seasons, he had established himself as one of the National League's best all-around shortstops and its most prolific base stealer — setting a single-season major league record with 104 stolen bases.

In 1973, Frank Robinson had slugged 30 home runs and driven in 97 runs for a bad California Angels' team. But Robinson was now 38, and didn't figure to be around by the time the rebuilding Angels fielded a quality on-field product. The Angels were willing to trade him for a prospect or two, perhaps with some cash thrown into the deal. In turn, the A's could employ Robinson as their full-time manager, and as a part-time designated hitter, first baseman and outfielder.

The presence of Robinson on the A's figured to appease American League MVP Reggie Jackson, who was upset by the departure of Dick

Williams. Jackson had raved about Robinson's positive influence on him during the 1970-71 Winter League season, when F. Robby skippered Reggie's team in Santurce, Puerto Rico. Jackson had subsequently played his best extended stretch of baseball from 1971 to 1973, perhaps as a result of Robinson's calming, professional hand.

As speculation concerning Dick Williams' future had run rampant during the World Series, Reggie had publicly recommended that Robinson stay away from the turmoil of managing the A's. "Robby has too much class to manage for Charlie Finley,"[7] Jackson told reporters. Reggie seemed to be sending his friend a less-than-subtle warning about life as an Oakland skipper. As major league baseball's first African-American field boss, Robinson would be facing ample pressure already; the looming presence of a meddling, often irrational owner like Finley might make Robinson's task nearly unbearable.

Two weeks after his World Series warning, Jackson changed his public stance on the Robinson-to-the-A's scenario. Jackson compared Robinson to Dick Williams, who had managed to survive three seasons under the oppression of Finley. "Both Frank and Dick are similar in personality and in handling people," Jackson explained. "Now I think all the class he (Robinson) has might be what he needs to manage our club. What Finley is interested in is production. He's only concerned about winning."[8] Assuming that the A's could adequately compensate the Angels, the addition of Robinson made perfect sense for Oakland. The former Cincinnati and Baltimore star had often been mentioned as a managerial candidate; his combination of intelligence, work ethic and on-field fire made for a superior managerial resume. Robinson possessed a streak of nastiness, too, which ensured that he wouldn't he tempted to retain too congenial a relationship with his players, many of whom were still his contemporaries. As a bonus, Robinson could still hit with power. As well as Deron Johnson had produced as the Oakland designated hitter for much of the season, his home runs, RBI's and batting average all lagged Robinson's basic numbers.

On another front, the hiring of Robinson as baseball's first black manager would represent a public relations coup for Finley. Stung by the fallout of the Mike Andrews and Dick Williams episodes, Finley might now regain some favor with the Oakland and national media by playing the 1970s role of Branch Rickey. "Knowing Charlie Finley, it's possible that Frank Robinson could be hired," Jackson said optimistically. "Finley wants to be first in everything and the fact that he likes the publicity wouldn't hurt either."[9] It was inevitable that some team would hire Robinson sometime soon; why not Finley, the game's most daring, innovative, and controversial owner? The plan fell through when Finley and the Angels could not agree on compensation for the future Hall of Famer.

Finley had already maliciously and willingly rid himself of one of his second baseman when he dumped Mike Andrews after the World Series. Now Finley was losing another second baseman, one that he wanted back in 1974. Dick Green, who had mentioned retirement after Game Seven of the World Series, made it official with an announcement from his home in Rapid City, South Dakota. The 32-year-old Green, who had made retirement statements an almost annual ritual since the 1970 season, said that he fully intended to step aside this time. Charlie Finely, remaining unconvinced of Green's sincerity, elected not to accept his retirement gracefully. "I am going to Rapid City to try to talk him into changing his mind," Finley vowed. "He is too young to give up the game."[10]

Green had successfully returned from back surgery, managing to hit a respectable .262 with three home runs and 42 RBI's. He had lost some range defensively, but remained a deft fielder with an aptitude for positioning himself properly against hitters' tendencies. Yet, Green insisted he had made up his mind and expressed resentment toward Finley for not believing his retirement statement to be serious. Green, however, did concede that Finley might be able to persuade him to return — if he did something crazy like double his salary. "Well, I'd have to think about it," Green conceded. "I won't say yes or no. I'm not a dummy, you know."[11]

Some of Green's teammates put little stock in his retirement claim. When a reporter asked Catfish Hunter to comment on the loss of Green and its impact on the pitching staff, the ace right-hander replied confidently, "He'll be back." Finley himself delayed sending Green's official retirement letter to the American League office. Finley knew that if he mailed the letter, making the retirement official, and Green were to decide to return, he would have to wait until 60 days had passed since Opening Day before becoming eligible to play again. By holding on to the letter, Finley was protecting Green and the team's interests.

In mid-January, media speculation centered on Dave Bristol as the man Charlie Finley would tab to replace Dick Williams. One newspaper reported that Finley had actually hired Bristol as a "head coach," who would manage the team only as a contingency against Williams returning. In other words, by giving Bristol the nebulous title of "head coach," Finley could still claim Williams to be his manager, thus preventing him from signing with another team. Finley tried to put the Bristol rumors to a quick rest. He denied that he had hired Bristol to manage, "head coach," or do anything else for the organization.

Williams put forth his own candidate for the job. "For a time I thought Dave Bristol was going to be the head coach of the A's this summer," said Williams, "but now I'm leaning toward Sal Bando. He's the only guy not having salary problems with Finley. He could do the job."[12] Several other major league managers considered Bando the smartest on-the-field player in the American League. Bando quickly turned down the offer that hadn't even been made. "I was flattered that Dick thought enough of me to say what he did," Bando said, "but I'm really not interested in managing now."[13]

As an amateur player, Bando had starred at Arizona State University, where he played with his future Oakland teammate, Rick Monday. His collegiate coach — future A's coach and manager Bobby Winkles — worked with him on the principle of hitting to all fields, rather than trying to pull every pitch. Winkles hoped to make the slow-footed Bando a catcher in his senior season, but the young third baseman foiled the plan by making himself eligible for the professional draft. After hitting .480 in the 1965 College World Series, the Kansas City A's made him their sixth-round choice in that year's amateur draft.

Bando showed improvement in each of his three minor league seasons, hitting for a higher average while advancing one level each summer. Kansas City scouts loved Bando's game, especially the powerful throwing arm that had made him an all-city quarterback in Warrensville Heights, Ohio. Scouts from other teams labeled Bando the best third base prospect they'd seen in years.

In 1967, the A's traded journeyman Ed Charles to make room for Bando, whom manager Alvin Dark considered the second coming of Brooks Robinson. At the urging of Dark, Bando altered his batting stance, adopting a deeper crouch. Bando should have retained his old approach; he hit only .192, injured himself and received a return ticket to Triple-A Vancouver.

Bando returned to the major leagues the following season — sans the crouching stance preferred by Dark. Batting out of a straighter, more comfortable position, Bando continued to struggle. A subsequent tip from Hall of Fame batting instructor Joe DiMaggio reversed his failures at the plate. "I was getting jammed on everything," Bando explained. "Then Joe D. told me to close up my stance."[14]

By 1969, Bando became the A's cleanup hitter and team captain. Even though Bando was only 25 years old, manager Hank Bauer recognized the leadership qualities and intelligence of his rugged, respected third baseman. "We didn't have a lot of veteran players when I was with Oakland," Reggie Jackson says of his first few years with the A's. "My intensity on the field was helped by playing with our captain, Sal Bando. We lived near each other in our very early years and he was very influential in my career."

Jack Aker, a former teammate, considered Bando a natural selection as team captain. "In the late sixties, all these fellows, like Bando, Campaneris — who was already there — Catfish came along, Reggie Jackson, Rick Monday, all of these fellows came up at almost the same time. I think everyone knew right away, as far as the veteran players, that they were gonna have some kind of team here. We didn't have a veteran who was in the right age group that could have carried on as

Sal Bando eludes the tag of Twins' catcher George Mitterwald during a game at the Oakland Coliseum. Note Bando's white helmet, which the A's had abandoned by 1971.

captain when these young fellows came in. So I think partly the reason that Sal Bando was named the captain and fit in so well: number one, he had the aptitude for it; he was a hard-nosed type of player who gave all he had everyday and expected everybody else to do. And he also was a very bright player; he made very few mistakes on the field...I think they definitely picked the right fellow."

Yet, Bando did not want to manage the A's in 1974, at least not until his playing days had ended. Bando's lack of current interest in the job seemed moot, given Charlie Finley's denial of the Bando-as-manager rumors. While Bando as player-manager was not going to occur, it was now becoming unclear whether Finley would be back as the A's owner. In January, Finley raised the possibility of selling the team, assuming he could exact the right price in return.

Finley had already spent much of the winter aggravating his relationship with the Oakland fans. For some bizarre reason, Finley had decided to reduce the number of "Family Night" promotions from 12 to four. In 1973, the A's had drawn over 330,000 fans for the dozen "Family Nights." That figure represented more than one-third of the A's total attendance for the season. Although the A's charged only half-price admission on "Family Nights," they generally made up for the reduction with improved concession sales and higher parking revenues.

Finley had also decided to eliminate a 25 per cent discount for purchasers of season tickets. The hefty discount had encouraged patrons to buy season tickets prior to the start of the season. By discontinuing the discount, Finley had removed all incentive to buy season tickets ahead of schedule. Fans who wanted to go to games at the Oakland Coliseum would be wiser to purchase tickets on the day of the game. In a final slap at the fans, Finley declared that he would no longer employ his popular ballgirls at home games and would discontinue the practice of ballpark fireworks.

Finley seemed so oblivious to the Oakland fans that some wondered if he had an ulterior motive for his cost-cutting. The owner confirmed suspicions when he announced his willingness to sell the team — for a sum of $15 million. Doctors had suggested selling the A's, as a way of reducing the stress that had led to his recent heart attack. As usual, Finley was noncommittal on the issue of whether he would definitely sell the club before the start of the season. "Maybe I will and maybe I won't,"[15] offered the typically cryptic Finley.

A Bay Area advertising executive expressed immediate interest in buying the franchise. John Hays (whose name had been misspelled "Hayes" in several newspaper reports) headed up a group that claimed to have the $15 million needed to complete the purchase. Hays announced that he already had a manager in mind to replace Dick Williams — recently fired scout and broadcaster Bill Rigney.

Hays may have made a tactical error by expressing his interest in Rigney, a man who had been fired by Finley only six months earlier. Finley may have interpreted Hays' interest in Rigney as a slap in the face. How dare he hire Rigney, a man I just got rid of, Finley might have wondered aloud.

In early February, Finley made a predictable announcement. "In my opinion, the A's will not be sold,"[16] Finley wrote in a form letter to season-ticket holder. When asked to expound on this pronouncement, Finley questioned Hays' ability to formulate a group with the necessary financial backing to purchase the team. Finley also seemed annoyed that Hays had publicly declared his interest in buying the club. "If he keeps on talking the way he has," Finley warned, "I may not sell him the club for twice the amount."[17] The words smacked of vindictiveness and pettiness, while lacking any sound business sense.

In the meantime, Finley continues to alienate many of his best players by offering them very small salary increases. Unlike his salary battles with Reggie Jackson in 1970 and Vida Blue in 1972, Finley didn't run the risk of any extended spring holdouts. The players and owners had agreed to a new system of settling contract disputes — arbitration. Under arbitration, a player would submit a salary figure, the team would counter with another figure, and an independent judge would select one of the two figures. The judge, or arbitrator, would not be permitted to select any figures in between those submitted by the player and the team. As a result, both player and team would feel motivated to submit a fairly representative figure, and not one that was substantially too high or too low.

In spite of the looming threat of arbitration, Finley had offered skimpy $5,000 raises to his four best pitchers: Catfish Hunter, Vida Blue and Ken Holtzman and closer Rollie Fingers. Hunter, Blue and Holtzman had each won at least 20 games, while Fingers had established himself as arguably the American League's second-best relief pitcher after the Yankees' Sparky Lyle. Hunter expressed bewilderment over Finley's hard-line stance on new contracts. "From what I understand, the whole Oakland team may be going to an arbitrator. I don't know what Finley is thinking," said a puzzled Hunter, who then provided an answer to his own question. "I think he's got the hots out for all of us ballplayers because we stood up for Mike Andrews."[18]

Unlike the other stars on the Oakland pitching staff, Chuck Dobson possessed virtually no leverage in seeking a new contract. After two straight years of mediocre pitching at Triple-A Tucson, the comebacking right-hander was pleased just to receive an invitation to Oakland's spring training camp. The elbow surgery that Dobson had undergone after the 1971 season had rendered him the status of a non-roster player, with no guarantee that he would have a job with the A's, or with their top minor league affiliate. If Dobson pitched poorly in the spring, he might be witnessing the end of his career as a professional pitcher.

In 1973, Dobson had managed a record of just 9-13 for the Tucson Toros, and had been lucky to receive a brief in-season promotion to Oakland. "Last year, I was working on my high slider and hanging curve,"[19] Dobson deadpanned. Yet, Dobson had fared much better in winter ball, impressing Oakland scouts with improved control of his slider and curve ball. Dobson had also shown the ability to pitch as both a starter and reliever, an unusual trait for a pitcher with such a fragile arm. Dobson's versatility would increase his nearly minuscule chances of making the A's Opening Day roster.

If nothing else, Dobson had caught Finley's attention with his intense desire to make a full-time return to the major league lifestyle after a nearly two-year hiatus. "When I came back (to Oakland) last year," Dobson explained, "I noticed how great everything was — the planes, the schedule, the big league towns... And clubhouse guys that do something except just sit around and gripe after giving you a spread that consists of nothing except two pieces of bread and one slice of bologna."[20] In Finley's mind, so many of the A's were unappreciative of major league perks; Dobson, in contrast, had developed a special regard for the luxurious life of a world championship major league team.

With spring training just a few days away, the A's had a surplus of pitching and good position players, but a dearth of other employees. No manager, no full-time public relations director, and no sidekick for No. 1 announcer Monte Moore. In mid-February, Charlie Finley filled the latter vacancy by hiring 24-year-old Jon Miller, who hailed from Walnut Creek, California, a suburb of Oakland. Miller was a broadcasting no-name, a recent college graduate who had little on-the-job experience. By the 1990s, Jon Miller would become one of baseball's most well-known announcers as the lead commentator for ESPN's *Sunday Night Game of the Week*.

With Miller and Moore now in place as the broadcasters, all the A's needed was an outlet to air the games. Finley had failed to sign a deal with either a television or radio station. Although most teams in the early seventies made very few of their games available over free TV, every team made sure to broadcast all, or at least most, of their games on the radio. Radio coverage served as an excellent — and inexpensive — way to promote a ballclub. Only Finley, who had put together very poor radio networks in past years, didn't seem to regard a radio contract as a very high priority. Finley reached a new low in broadcasting history one season when he arranged for a college radio station to air the A's games.

Chapter Twenty-two:
The Return of the Dark Ages

The absence of a radio contract paled in comparison to the team's largest vacancy — the managerial office. With spring training only days away, Charlie Finley had struck out in efforts to bring Frank Robinson or Dave Bristol aboard as manager. By now, Finley realized that Dick Williams had no interest in returning and would rather sit out the entire 1974 season. So, in late February, Finley placed a call to one of his many former managers — Alvin Dark. Finley asked Dark if he were willing to manage the team, but refrained from actually offering him the job. "It's a tough spot to put a man in," said Dark, who had been fired by Finley during the 1967 season. "No matter what he does he'll probably be wrong. The first time he loses a close game the second-guessers will have a field day."[1] Dark realized that the new manager would be subjected to endless comparisons with predecessor Dick Williams and would be expected to win a third consecutive World Series. Dark knew that any lesser accomplishments would be considered disappointing. "So to answer your question," Dark said slyly, "I'd love to."[2]

On February 18, Finley told Dark to visit him in Oakland immediately. As soon as Dark arrived at Finley's home, the owner made him a monumental offer of a one-year contract, with bonuses for winning the division, the pennant and the World Series. The deal lacked security, to say the least. Yet, Dark agreed to the contract, calling it "better than I've ever had in baseball."[3]

Dark must have had some horrendous contracts during his career. Although it was not publicly known at the time, Dark's contract provided him with an even smaller degree of security. According to reports that would circulate after the 1974 season, the contract between Finley and Dark was essentially an non-guaranteed, day-to-day agreement. In other words, Finley could fire Dark at any time without having to pay off his manager for the rest of the season.

On February 20, three days before the start of spring training, Finley staged a press conference to officially introduce Dark as the 12th manager in his reign as A's owner. An impatient Finley did his best to anticipate reporters' questions, answering their queries before they had even had a chance to ask them. "Yes, he was hired by me in 1966...Yes, he was fired in 1967...Yes, I hired him again... Yes, he expects to be fired again someday."[4]

A reporter asked Finley how much input he himself would have in managing the team. "If I have any suggestions, such as putting (Ray) Fosse at shortstop and he (Dark) doesn't like it, then he'll explain to me why he doesn't," Finley responded ominously. "And if I say Fosse is at shortstop, then Fosse will be at shortstop." Finley then contradicted himself later in the press conference. "Alvin had free reins then (in 1966) and he'll have free reins now."[5] Now that Finley had made that clear, Dark had to sideswipe an even more difficult obstacle — trying to repair a racist image that he had developed during the 1960s.

Oakland beat writers wondered how Latinos like Campy Campaneris and Jesus Alou and African-American players like Reggie Jackson, Billy North and Blue Moon Odom would respond to a manager who supposedly held them in less regard than white players of similar talents. In particular, how would Odom relate to his new manager? In 1967, Dark had demoted Odom to the minor leagues, prompting a charge of racism from the young pitcher. Dark maintained that such criticism was unfair. "I'm a born-again Christian," explained Dark. "Being a born-again Christian, there is no color involved or race involved as far as love is concerned. Everyone will be given the fairest chance. If a player makes a mistake, I don't care as far as color is concerned. He made a mistake, that's all."[6]

Critics of Dark had their doubts, especially those who remembered his stormy managerial tenure with the San Francisco Giants in the early 1960s. Dark had gained an especially bad reputation with the blacks and Latins on the Giants, who felt that he too often pointed the finger at them after losses. The minorities on the Giants became even more infuriated when they read a series of disparaging quotes attributed to Dark in an article in *Newsday*, a newspaper in Long Island, New York.

"We have trouble because we have so many Spanish-speaking and Negro players on the team," *Newsday* reporter Stan Isaacs quoted Dark as saying. "They are just not able to perform up to the white ballplayer when it comes to mental alertness."[7] In the article, Dark went on question to the pride and intelligence of black and Latin players. Dark later claimed that Isaacs had badly misquoted him throughout the story.

In a 1974 *Sports Illustrated* article that contained excerpts of his book written with John Underwood, Dark tried to clarify his remarks to Isaacs. Dark explained that several Giants, including Jesus Alou and Orlando Cepeda, had been guilty of "dumb base running" in recent games. Since Alou and Cepeda happened to be dark-skinned Latinos, Dark felt that Isaacs had inferred his comments to be racist. Dark accused Isaacs of taking some of his remarks out of their proper context and placing undue emphasis on certain negative statements that he had made.

During his days with the Giants, Dark had encountered a number of run-ins with Cepeda. Dark cited several examples of what he considered Cepeda's lack of hustle on the basepaths, which had led to verbal reprimands after games. Dark described one game against the Milwaukee Braves where Cepeda was "pinch-hitting, the last out of a game on national television, and he hit a ground ball, ran about 30 feet, stopped and walked back to the dugout." When Cepeda reached the dugout, Dark shouted at him loudly, continuing the barrage as the two men walked to the clubhouse. Although Dark admitted that he had gone too far in "showing him up in front of the other ballplayers,"[8] he made it clear that Cepeda's failure to run hard on a ground ball had prompted the reaction.

"I recall when I played for Alvin Dark," Cepeda says. "Alvin Dark segregated the team. He put (divided) the whites, the blacks and Latins. We had to strike against that, you know, being black and being Latin." In addition to separating the players by race and color in the clubhouse, Cepeda says Dark banned the speaking of Spanish in the Giants' clubhouse, a decision that upset the Latin players, many of whom struggled with the English language. Cepeda adds that Dark habitually blamed tough Giant losses on the team's black and Latino stars, including himself, Willie Mays and Willie McCovey. Given Cepeda's and Dark's feelings for one another, Charlie Finley could be thankful that Orlando no longer played for the A's. Otherwise, Oakland players might have had to break up fights between Cepeda and Dark on a daily basis. Of course, they had already become accustomed to breaking up conflicts between two teammates, as evidenced by previous skirmishes involving Vida Blue, Blue Moon Odom and Rollie Fingers.

Unlike the Giants of the early 1960s, the A's encountered few racial conflicts or incidents. When players did fight, they generally did so for non-racial reasons. Yet, some of the players remained dissatisfied with the lack of interaction between different ethnic groups on the club. Vida Blue had previously described the A's as a team that broke down into strict racial divisions. Pointing to the starting outfield one day, Blue illustrated his contention. Joe Rudi (a white) played left, Angel Mangual (a Latino) patrolled center, and Reggie Jackson (a black) played right. "There are three cliques on this team," Blue said, pointing to the outfielders, "and you can see them all out there."[9]

The cover story in the June 3, 1974 edition of *Time* magazine supported Blue's assertion. The article, which centered on Reggie Jackson's stardom, claimed that the A's were generally "free from tangible racial tension," but surmised that "an undercurrent of division persists. Black players tend to stick together socially, as do the Latin Americans and whites. This atmosphere of tolerance minus affection is now commonplace in baseball."[10]

Other players did not share the opinion of Blue or the *Time* feature. "We never felt that we were black or white or Latin or American," Sal Bando says, insisting that he witnessed no racial divisions during his days in Oakland. Bando says the common enemy found in the owner's box may have contributed to general racial harmony. "We were just one baseball team that cared for each other. I think the reason might have been the friction that Charlie caused that had us all stick together and rely on each other. It's a negative way of getting a team concept, but in a roundabout way I think it worked."

Questions of racism aside, Alvin Dark promised to be more tactful and sensitive in relating to his players. Dark also emphasized that his strong religious faith, which had come under criticism due to a well-known incident of marital infidelity. Since re-married, Dark quoted the Bible frequently and vowed that he had become a changed man — for the better. "I've reassessed my commitment to the Christian life and where I had failed in it, and my faith in Jesus Christ,"[11] Dark vowed.

One day after Finley officially hired Dark to replace Dick Williams, Reggie Jackson awaited the results of his arbitration hearing, which would determine his 1974 salary. After failing to reach a contract agreement on their own, Jackson had taken Finley to arbitration. A total of nine A's had decided to resolve their contract disputes through arbitration, more than any other major league team. While Jackson had asked for $135,000, Finley had countered with an offer of $100,000. The independent arbitrator sided with Reggie, making him the highest paid player in the history of the A's franchise.

Another star player, third baseman Sal Bando, had already won his arbitration case. Bando would receive $100,000, rather than the $75,000 offered by Finley. Bando and Jackson now joined Catfish Hunter as the three A's making $100,000 or more in 1974. Other Oakland players did not fare as well as Bando and Jackson at the arbitration table. Left fielder Joe Rudi and utilitymen Ted Kubiak and Jack Heidemann all lost their cases, as did first baseman Gene Tenace. The arbitrator ruled that Tenace would have to settle for $45,000, as opposed to the $52,500 that he had sought. Tenace reacted bitterly to the decision, declaring that he would only play first base, and would no longer serve as an emergency catcher behind Ray Fosse. "If they're not going to pay me to play two positions," Tenace fumed, "then I'll play only one."[12]

Faced with an angry Gene Tenace, an overbearing owner and questions about his racial beliefs, Dark embarked on his second term as A's manager. During his previous tenure with the Kansas City Athletics, Dark had managed several of the organization's current stars: Dick Green, Campy Campaneris, Sal Bando, Catfish Hunter and Blue Moon Odom. Those players, representing one-fifth of the A's 1974 roster, had come to know Dark as a hot-tempered, impatient man who often feuded with A's management — i.e. Charlie Finley.

Those players hardly recognized the new Alvin Dark that descended on Mesa, Arizona in spring training of 1974. Refusing to lose his temper, Dark no longer cursed or yelled at his players. When his players made mistakes, Dark talked about religion and love. Those reporters who had heard Dark profess to being a born-again Christian at his opening press conference realized that he had meant what he said. Dark had undergone a deep, religious conversion and intended to transfer his new lifestyle to the playing field.

Dark also received some good news with regard to player personnel. Dick Green, to no one's surprise, announced that he had changed his mind about retirement and reported to spring training in prime physical condition. Green's arrival in camp gave the A's a veteran fallback at second base in the event that young Manny Trillo struggled to hit American League pitching. Dark also learned that Tenace had reversed his decision about catching and would be willing to go behind the plate if needed. "I'm not crazy about catching," Tenace admitted, "but maybe in the long run it can help me career-wise and financially."[13] Dark announced plans to use Tenace as a backup catcher, and as a bullpen catcher on those days when he was not playing first base.

Tenace's change of mind came as especially good news to the A's, whose 40-man roster contained exactly one catcher, Ray Fosse. The A's had invited three other receivers, all of the non-roster variety, to spring training. The group included once-and-future Athletic Frank Fernandez and minor leaguers Tim Hosley and Buzz Nitschke, none of whom inspired much confidence in the event that Fosse experienced a season-ending injury.

Meanwhile, Vida Blue indicated that he might give up baseball after the season, in favor of a career in the fledgling World Football League, a rival to the established National Football League. The combination of unpleasant salary negotiations with Charlie Finley and the sense that he had accomplished his baseball goals left Blue pining for a new a challenge. Blue had starred at quarterback at Mansfield High School in Louisiana, throwing 35 touchdowns in his senior season. Blue's quarterbacking impressed recruiters so much that he received offers from 25 college football powers, including a southern school like the University of Houston. The Cougars hoped to make Blue the first black quarterback in the history of the Southwest Conference.

Blue had signed a letter of intent to play at the university, but family tragedy interfered with the plan. In 1968, during his senior year at DeSoto High School, Blue's father died suddenly from a heart attack. Vida Blue, Sr. had supported his wife and six children with his income as a factory worker. As the oldest child, Vida felt compelled to assume the leadership of the household. The high school senior opted for an immediate profes-

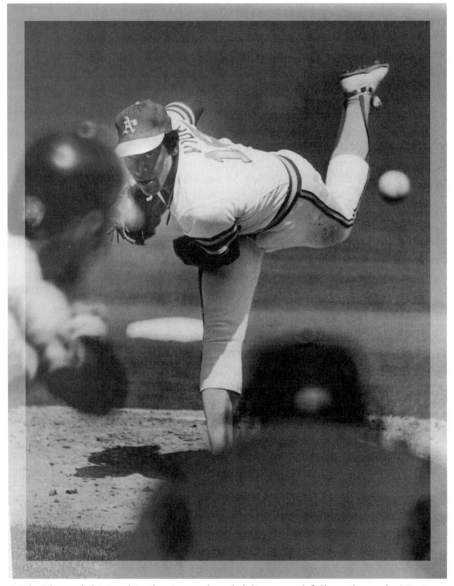

Vida Blue exhibiting his classic overhand delivery and follow-through. Notice the use of his first name of the back of the jersey.

sional baseball contract, rather than a four-year college scholarship, as a means of supporting his family.

The A's selected Blue with their first pick in the 1967 amateur draft. As he did with most of his highly recruited talents, Charlie Finley paid Blue a personal visit in an effort to secure a signed contract. Finley and Blue agreed on a salary of just over $10,000, a bonus of $40,000 and an important stipulation. At the behest of Blue's high school baseball coach, Clyde Washington, the A's agreed to pay for Blue's tuition to a four-year college. In the short-term, Blue wanted to care for his mother and siblings, but Washington hoped that Vida would return to his schooling in the future.

Blue went only 8-11 in his minor league debut season, but struck out 231 batters in 152 innings. His arm strength and athleticism so impressed officials in the A's organization that he earned a promotion to the major leagues only two years later, at the age of 19. Although Blue spent relatively little time in the minors, he gained a valuable social experience. Having grown up in the predominantly black neighborhood of Mansfield, a town of fewer than 10,000 residents, Blue had never before played with or against players from other racial and ethnic groups.

After Blue first arrived in the major leagues in 1969, principally on the strength of his fastball, he received help from a 32-year-old Latino pitcher named Juan Pizarro. The Puerto Rican left-hander showed Blue how to improve the control and break of his curve ball while providing other fatherly advice on the art of major league pitching. "I got to be a high-class batting practice pitcher," Blue said of his struggles before meeting Pizarro. "Juan showed me how to grip the ball for a curve. I really didn't have any idea."[14]

While Gene Tenace had made peace with the A's, the team faced controversies and distractions on several other fronts. Reggie Jackson annoyed Charlie Finley when he signed a deal with Puma, agreeing to wear the company's baseball shoes in exchange for a payment of $30,000 over the next three years. Finley pointed to a pre-existing contract with Puma's chief rival, Adidas. The terms of Finley's arrangement with Adidas required all of the Oakland players to wear Adidas shoes during the regular season. Jackson refused to wear Adidas, saying that he would fulfill his contract with Puma. Finley threatened to suspend Jackson $1,000 a day. Reggie said he'd think about it.

Finley butted heads with Jackson, and the rest of the players, on another issue. Early in spring training, Finley instructed the team's traveling secretary, Jim Bank, to distribute the team's new World Series rings. The rings, supposedly a reward for the team's second consecutive World Championship, contained no diamonds, only cheap-looking synthetic emeralds. "These are trash rings," assessed Jackson. "It's not fair, it's not right."[15] Even quiet, reserved players like Catfish Hunter, who usually resisted controversy, sounded off on the rings. "The new rings are horsemeat," said Catfish. "This ring isn't even as good as a high school ring."[16]

Sal Bando says the World Series rings provide another example of the personality differences exhibited by Finley after his 1973 heart attack. "To show how he changed," Bando explains, "the first World Series we won he gave us a ring with a full carat; he gave our wives a pendant that they wore around their necks with a half a carat. He gave each player a replica of the World Series trophy that ownership receives, in appreciation for what we did. Then he comes back the next two years and we got the cheapest rings you'll ever see a World Series team have. No stones, no nothing. It was just the way he was. He went from being very generous on the one hand to being very cheap on the other."

In the spring of 1973, when Finley had rewarded his players with lavish rings in appreciation for winning the first world championship in Oakland franchise history, he had vowed to furnish his players with even better rings the next time around. The players had fulfilled their part of the arrangement, defeating the New York Mets for their second consecutive World Series triumph. Finley, apparently hurt that his players had not bothered to show him any gratitude for the luxurious rings of the previous year, reneged on the promise. "Screw 'em," Finley told *New York Daily News* sportswriter Dick Young, who came out in support of the owner in the ring controversy. "The next time we win I won't give them a thing."[17] Finley's disdain for players he considered unappreciative and ungrateful had reached a vengeful level. He also hadn't forgotten that these were the same players who had dared to criticize him for his handling of Mike Andrews during the 1973 World Series.

With two weeks to go in spring training, Finley angered his players by announcing an unprecedented signing in baseball history. Finley added 22-year-old Herb Washington to the roster, despite the fact that he had never played baseball above the high school level. In fact, Washington hadn't played baseball since his junior year in high school, several years earlier. Washington, a world class sprinter, had set records in the 50-yard dash, running it in five seconds flat, and the 60-yard dash, with a time of 5.8. With Allan Lewis drawing his release over the winter, Finley viewed Washington as a pinch-runner extraordinaire, someone who could win a game with his speed in the late innings.

The A's distributed a press release — written by Finley — that heralded the arrival of Washington. "Finley and Dark feel that Washington will be directly responsible for winning 10 games this year," the release declared. Dark actually had said nothing of the kind, but Finley believed it, and that was seemingly all that mattered. Dark, however, did predict that he would use Washington as early as the sixth inning, depending on the game situations.

The A's also announced the hiring of former major league shortstop Maury Wills as a spring training base running instructor. Under a special six-day program, Wills would tutor Washington on basic base running skills, everything from taking a proper lead to the correct way of rounding the bases. In other words, Wills would serve as Washington's personal coach. The A's had many standout players on their roster, including Reggie Jackson, Catfish Hunter and Vida Blue, but none of them had their own individual instructor.

Wills' instruction did benefit Washington, a novice at running the bases. The former Dodger shortstop refined Washington's sliding skills, which were coarse at best and had left him susceptible to injuring himself. Wills taught Washington the method of sliding headfirst, as a way of reducing the wear and tear to his sprinter's legs.

The signing of Washington, a football and track star at Michigan State with no college or professional baseball experience, upset most of the A's veterans. "That's a joke," exclaimed Gene Tenace. "This is going to cost somebody who should be in the major leagues a job."[18] Other Oakland players tried to joke with Washington, perhaps in an effort to make him feel more comfortable in hostile surroundings. After one player compared Washington to a race horse, second baseman Dick Green approached the ridiculed pinch-runner. "If you break a leg," Green said to Washington, "we'll have to shoot you."[19] When a reporter asked Washington to assess how long he needed to warm up before entering a game as a pinch-runner, Catfish Hunter interjected, addressing Washington by his new nickname. "'Hurricane,' by the time you're warmed up," Hunter chided, "the game will be over."[20]

Tenace was also angered by some of Charlie Finley's many cost-cutting features of spring training. The veteran first baseman-catcher complained loudly about a spring training bus ride from Yuma to Palm Springs, wondering why Finley hadn't sprung for the cost of a flight. "We shouldn't have to travel like this," Tenace said, sniping at the owner. "We go out and bust our rears for the owner. He should do the same for us."[21] Several other players griped that Finley had supplied only one case of soda and soft drinks for the long bus ride, prompting Reggie Jackson to buy two more cases of refreshments with his own money. Oakland veterans later discovered that Finley had invited two minor leaguers to the major league camp in Mesa, yet had elected not to pay them major league meal money.

Finley's repeated penny-pinching maneuvers undermined Alvin Dark's efforts to create a more serene, unified, and familial atmosphere than the A's had become used to in recent years. Dark extended an olive branch to Blue Moon Odom, the same man who had accused him of racism in 1967. Dark promised the veteran right-hander the fourth spot in the starting rotation, despite his horrid pitching numbers of 1973: a 5-12 record and an ERA of 4.49. Dark's attempts at establishing a positive backdrop to preseason camp did not go unnoticed by one of the team's stars. "I feel for him," said a sympathetic Reggie Jackson, one of the few A's willing to keep an open mind about his new manager. "He's bent over backwards to create harmony, to preserve dignity. I want him to do good."[22]

Yet, many players found the born-again Dark overbearing in his religious kindness. Others wondered if he truly lived the words he preached. Some players laughed at his biblical quotations, his meekness, his avoidance of confrontation. They mocked his mannerisms and style of speech. They ridiculed his refusal to use obscenities. They noticed how he refused to discipline players who had made mistakes. They wondered aloud how a major league manager could be so lacking in fire and fury, so unwilling to use anger as a motivating force.

"Alvin, I know he was very religious," says Ted Kubiak, now a minor league manager himself. "and I think that interfered with it a little bit at times. And I think that was resented. And maybe some hypocritical stuff going on, too. I know there were a lot of questions." Oakland players had remembered Dark's alleged racism toward black and Latino players and had heard stories of his infidelity to his first wife in the 1960s.

Dark's two and a half year absence from managing had clearly damaged his knowledge of the American League. When Dark discussed other teams that the A's needed to beat during the regular season, he often referred to players since departed from those clubs. In some cases, he mentioned players who were no longer active major leaguers. The A's players cringed at a manager who lacked so much credibility and seemed out of touch with baseball in 1974.

"You know, I'd always heard what a good manager Alvin Dark was," says Kubiak, who had first played for Dark in 1967. "To be honest with you, I didn't really see it...His style was so different from Dick Williams, you know, I might not have had a fair advantage of making a comparison in that one quick year. I don't think he had as much command of things as Dick did. That's the one thing that stood out."

Dark made it clear that his own managerial wishes would run second to those of his owner. For example, Dark wanted to retain pitcher Chuck Dobson in the organization, keeping him at Triple-A Tucson at the start of the season, with the possibility of being promoted to the major leagues later in the summer. Although Dobson had struggled early in spring training, Dark had seen improvement and predicted that the veteran right-hander would help the A's later in the season.

One day later, Charlie Finley released Dobson, apparently not wanting to pay him $28,500 to pitch in the minor leagues. Dark offered little objection. Finley telephoned Dobson at a nearby golf course, giving him the unpleasant news as he played the 17th hole. "He told me he hated to do it but he was having problems, like his divorce," said Dobson. "I'm getting released and he's crying on my shoulder! Incredible!"[23]

Dobson returned to the team's workout facilities in Mesa to gather his belongings. "What can I tell you," said backup catcher Frank Fernandez, somewhat unsympathetically. "Good luck on your life?"[24] A few days later, "Broadway" Frank would receive his release. Dobson would remain in

Mesa for a few days, eventually signing a contract with the Mexico City Leones of the Mexican League before returning to the majors with the California Angels. Fernandez would never again play in the major leagues.

Fernandez lost out on his bid to make the team when the A's reacquired veteran catcher Larry Haney from the Cardinals. The A's had sold Haney to the Cardinals the previous September, but now felt the need for another catcher in the event that Dark chose to pinch-run Herb Washington for either Ray Fosse or Gene Tenace. In turn, the inclusion of Washington on the roster robbed Billy Conigliaro of his best chance of making the team. The A's, concerned by Conigliaro's surgically-repaired knee, released the veteran outfielder. "We kept Angel Mangual instead of Billy C.," explained Dark, "because Angel can run better, hit better and throw better."[25] Some of the Oakland veterans, however, pointed to Conigliaro's superior defensive abilities as the reason why he, and not Mangual, belonged on the Opening Day roster.

The A's still needed to make three more cuts to make the 25-man limit. Finley and Dark decided to send down veteran infielder Rich McKinney, once hailed as the A's designated hitter of the future, and right-handed pitcher Glenn Abbott, who remained a highly regarded prospect. After Bob Locker surrendered a grand slam home run to Milwaukee's George Scott, the A's placed the veteran reliever on the 21-day disabled list. Locker had complained of recent elbow pain, similar to the discomfort that had bothered him the previous spring before disappearing prior to the start of the regular season. "It only hurts when I throw hard,"[26] cautioned Locker. Oh, is that all?

Team doctors told Locker not to pick up a ball until May, in the hope that he would be able to start pitching sometime during the first half of the season. The doctors' timetable proved to be overly optimistic. The right-handed reliever would spend the entire season on the disabled list, the by-product of surgery to remove bone chips from his elbow. The questionable trade that had sent the healthier and younger Horacio Pina to the Chicago Cubs for Locker looked even worse now.

The A's left Mesa with a dreadful spring record of 8-16, their worst since 1970, when John McNamara managed the team. McNamara would be fired after that season. Was a similar fate awaiting Alvin Dark, who had endured a spring full of off-the-record sniping, owner-induced controversy, and annoying distractions? Dark realized that the A's needed a prosperous start to eliminate the inevitable comparisons to the successful regime of Dick Williams.

Chapter Twenty-three:
Gunning For The Three-Peat

The A's played the Rangers in Arlington on Opening Day. Much to their dislike, the A's faced huge right-hander Jim Bibby, the same man who had no-hit them the previous summer. Bibby proved far more hittable on this occasion, giving up eight hits and six runs in four and one-third innings. Reggie Jackson collected a home run, two doubles and a single to lead Oakland to an impressive 7-2 win over Texas.

The mood in the A's clubhouse after the game reflected anything but a well-played Opening Day rout. In the seventh inning, with the A's leading 7-0, Alvin Dark had made a bizarre move, removing starting left fielder Joe Rudi for pinch-runner Herb Washington. The decision angered Rudi, normally the most placid and agreeable of all the A's. "I want to play nine innings of all 162 games," Rudi told reporters in the clubhouse. "When they take you out for a pinch-runner, it makes you look like half a ballplayer."[1]

In the second game against the Rangers, Dark removed Ken Holtzman after only four and a third innings. Holtzman had surrendered eight hits, but only two runs. The next day, Dark hooked Vida Blue after he faced two batters in the fifth inning. As he walked to the dugout, Blue shouted loudly enough for Dark to hear him. "All right, Alvin Dark, it's all right the first time," Blue warned his manager. "But the next time you do this to me, I'm going to lay every word in the book on you."[2]

291

Although Blue had directed his anger at Dark, he knew that the manager was merely following orders from a higher authority. "I knew Alvin Dark was a religious man," Blue said somewhat tongue-in-cheek, "but he's worshipping the wrong god — C.O.F."[3] Those initials belonged to one Charles Oscar Finley.

The A's scored three runs in the fifth and three more in the ninth, capping off an 8-4 win over the Rangers and removing any possibility that Blue might lose the game. Strangely, Alvin Dark used Rollie Fingers for five innings of relief, his longest stint ever in a nine-inning game. Reggie Jackson supported Fingers and Blue with one of his best games as a major leaguer, driving in seven runs with two home runs and a single. Ranger fans in the right field bleachers rewarded Jackson with a standing ovation. "I tipped my hat to them three times because it was the least I could do," explained Reggie. "I appreciated them recognizing my performance."[4] After the game, several Oakland players rewarded Jackson with an enormous balloon shaped like a hot dog. Reggie smiled as he carried the balloon through the Dallas Airport onto the team's flight to Kansas City.

The A's won two of three from Texas in the season-opening series, but most of the conversation centered on Alvin Dark's strange managerial moves. In addition to removing his starters earlier than usual, Dark had raised eyebrows by employing Herb Washington as a pinch-runner in each of the games. Several writers speculated that Charlie Finley had ordered Dark to use his glorified pinch-runner as often as possible in the early stages of the season.

The extent of Finley's stranglehold on Dark became even more evident during the A's next series. Prior to the April 10th game against the Royals, Dark explained to the media why he had decided to bench his regular designated hitter, Deron Johnson. The move seemed to make sense for two significant reasons. Johnson had struggled badly during the first series against Texas and didn't figure to break out of his slump against a tough right-hander like Kansas City's Steve Busby. As a result, Dark had announced that he would use the left-handed hitting Vic Davalillo as the DH.

Moments before the game, Charlie Finley telephoned Dark in the Oakland dugout. "He asked who the DH was going to be," Dark revealed. "I said Davalillo. He said he'd rather have Johnson."[5] Dark made the appropriate changes on the lineup card, handed it to captain Sal Bando and instructed him to give it to the umpires.

Dark should have stayed with his original lineup. Johnson went 0-for-4 against Busby, and then went on the 15-day disabled list. A doctor's examination had determined that Johnson had suffered a pulled muscle in his right hand, the same hand that had been surgically repaired during the off-season.

On Saturday, April 13, the A's returned to the Oakland Coliseum for the first time since Game Seven of the 1973 World Series. Vida Blue pitched miserably in front of the crowd of 22,743, giving up seven runs in only one and a third innings — his worst start as a major league pitcher. Campy Campaneris and Sal Bando added errors and Oakland batters struck out 10 times against complete game winner Jim Bibby.

The A's on-field play represented only a fraction of the home opener embarrassment. Much like he had done during the 1973 World Series, Charlie Finley decided not to pay for any decorative red, white and blue bunting, leaving the stadium walls barren. The Oakland grounds crew had let most of the grass grow too long, while improperly cutting the grass around the bases. "If this grass was a little higher," surmised Reggie Jackson, "we could have an Easter-egg hunt."[6] Stadium workers had also neglected to store the canvas backdrop in center field, letting it sit out all winter long. The winter cold and rain had badly faded the green-colored canvas, which now appeared the same shade of color as the bleachers. "Another year and they still haven't cleaned the tarps," pointed out Sal Bando. "Or bought new ones. They're filthy. Why couldn't someone scrub them down?"[7] As a result of all the cost-cutting neglect, the Coliseum took on an even more drab, depressing appearance than usual.

The A's played better after their home opener fiasco, winning five of seven games. Reggie Jackson's bat carried the offense, as the reigning American League MVP totaled four home runs, 11 RBI's and a .429 batting average during the stretch.

One of the A's victories occurred in particularly dramatic style, a 4-3 win over the White Sox in extra innings. With two outs and a runner on second in the 13th inning, Gene Tenace faced White Sox relief ace Terry Forster, who had pitched five shutout innings. Tenace cracked a solid single to left, scoring journeyman John Donaldson from second base with the winning run.

Alvin Dark's — or rather Charlie Finley's — handling of the pitching staff continued to mystify the Oakland players. Dark repeatedly lifted his starters early, but for some reason, showed little confidence in any of his relievers, except for Rollie Fingers. As a result, Fingers became ineffective due to overwork while the rest of the bullpen struggled to remain sharp due to a lack of game action. Outspoken reliever Darold Knowles tried — and failed — to be diplomatic in his criticism of Dark. "I don't agree with the way — and how can I put this delicately — Alvin Dark is handling the pitchers as a whole," Knowles assessed. "He's got to realize that there are other pitchers in the bullpen besides Rollie. I'm not ripping Alvin, but he's got a quick jerk sometimes and not quick enough other times."[8]

Dark apparently thought Knowles was ripping him and called for a face-to-face meeting with the veteran left-hander. The two men exchanged angry words for about 45 minutes before finally breaking up the heated conversation. Most neutral observers agreed with Knowles' take on the situation, and pointed to games like that of April 21, when the A's hosted the Angels. With the A's leading 4-3 in the eighth inning, Dark pulled Vida Blue from the game. Blue said nothing to Dark, but proceeded to grab a bat and smash it against a bat rack in the Oakland dugout. Rollie Fingers, whom Dark called upon to relieve Blue, allowed three runs while retiring only one batter. A six-run Angel explosion in the eighth gave California a 9-5 victory, while saddling Fingers with his first loss of the season.

In that same game, Angels' reliever Skip Lockwood threw a fastball up and in on Reggie Jackson, knocking the A's cleanup hitter to the ground. Jackson, believing that Angels' manager Bobby Winkles had ordered the knockdown, shouted toward the California dugout. "I'm not going to forget that," Jackson warned Winkles. Ironically, Winkles had coached Jackson during his college career at Arizona State. "We'll still be friendly," Jackson told a reporter after the game, "but I'm going to bear down harder when I come to the dish against them."[9]

Aside from the bizarre deployment of the pitching staff, the most prominent theme of the early season centered on the presence of Herb Washington on the 25-man roster. Through the team's first 16 games, Washington had stolen only one base in four attempts, missed several steal and hit-and-run signs, and showed a complete lack of baseball instincts in running the bases. In one game, with runners on first and second base, Alvin Dark sent Washington in to pinch-run at first base. Washington, perhaps not realizing that second base was already occupied, asked Dark if he wanted him to steal on the first pitch. Dark patiently told him no, while Oakland players looked on in disbelief.

Reports of Washington's salary created resentment in the clubhouse. One newspaper story claimed that Washington's salary paid him over $42,000, in addition to a bonus of $35,000. Charlie Finley denied that he was paying Washington that much, but another reporter said Washington's salary approached the $30,000 level and featured a bonus of $25,000. Either way, Herb Washington qualified as major league baseball's most overpaid player. "It's still ridiculous,"[10] one of the Oakland players said anonymously.

On May 3, the A's decided to release one of their players, but it wasn't Washington. Veteran outfielder Vic Davalillo, hitting only .174 through the team's first 21 games, was given his walking papers. Granted, Davalillo hadn't played well as a part-time DH and outfielder, but his off-the-field reputation for excessive drinking may have expedited his release over Washington's.

One day after the release of Davalillo, Vida Blue continued his season-long struggles, losing an 8-2 blowout to the Indians. The latest loss dropped Blue's record to 0-4, lifted his ERA to 5.18, and left Alvin Dark wondering whether he should pull his star left-hander from the

starting rotation completely. Although Blue had visibly showed his anger toward Dark for early removals from games, his pitching had done
nothing to support his disagreements with the manager. Blue had likely
annoyed his manager further with an action that smacked of sarcasm.
After Dark had fined Blue $250 for one of his acts of insubordination,
the pitcher dumped an enormous load of pocket change on the manager's
desk. Blue had decided to pay the fine in pennies, nickels, dimes and
quarters.

Blue pitched much better his next time out, defeating the Orioles,
7-3. The victory gave Blue his first win of the season, while providing a
much-needed psychological uplifting. "that was important for my head,"
Blue said in the clubhouse. "After four losses, you wonder whether you're
still alive."[11]

In early May, Charlie Finley continued his reign of thriftiness by
announcing that the team would no longer pay the postage for players
responding to fan mail. Finley informed the players that they, regardless of their status on the team, would have to spring for the requisite
number of stamps. The Finley mandate represented a policy different
from the operating procedures of most other major league teams, whose
ownerships generally paid for return letters of fan mail.

The surly atmosphere of the Oakland clubhouse, teamed with the
continuing mediocrity on the field, left the A's in a state of near rebel-
lion. One player even suggested that Charlie Finley should fire Alvin
Dark immediately and name captain Sal Bando as player-manager.
Sensing that such sentiments had placed the A's in a no-win situation
under Dark, Bando called a players-only meeting. At the meeting, several players assailed Dark for allowing fundamental mistakes to go un-
checked. The players, however, reached an important resolution. They
agreed to cease their public criticism of the manager, perhaps realizing
that such second-guessing served no useful purpose. "We just weren't
playing the way we should," Gene Tenace said after the meeting. "I don't
think Alvin Dark was losing those games. We were."[12]

Bando, one of the manager's staunchest critics early in the 1974
season, says he harbored no ill feelings toward Dark as a person. Bando
acknowledges that circumstances made it more difficult for Dark to
succeed in his return as a major league manager. "To Alvin's credit,"
Bando says, "he really didn't know the team that well simply because
he had been out of baseball. He was going by things he had read or
remembered, and it took him awhile to see the makeup of the club. At
the beginning, it was an adjustment period for him and for us. We had
some disagreements but they were strictly baseball strategy in using
the strengths of our club."

Dark, to his credit, accepted much of the blame for the A's middling record. The veteran manager admitted that his lack of knowledge
of the team's personnel had cost the team several wins in April and

May. "I'll be honest with you," Dark told a reporter. "I'm not doing a good job, yet. We've lost about three games we should have won...I haven't learned my pitching staff yet. I've made a few mistakes with the rest of the players, too, but no one can tell you about your pitching staff. You can talk to your players and pitching coach, but you've got to learn about the staff yourself."[13]

In fairness to Dark, the A's had suffered a number of injuries, which had left the manager shorthanded around the infield and off the bench. Second base continued to be a nagging problem, as the A's used five different players at the troubled position through the first 30 games of the season. In the fourth game of the year, Dick Green had strained his arch while turning a nifty double play. The injury resulted in his placement on the disabled list. Ten days later, Manny Trillo joined Green on the shelf when he pulled a thigh muscle running the bases. Ted Kubiak stepped into play second base but a calf injury to Sal Bando forced Dark to move the veteran utilityman to third base shortly thereafter. Bando's bad leg prompted the recall of journeyman John Donaldson from Triple-A Tucson. Donaldson played second base for two games, then collided with center fielder Billy North on a short pop-up to the outfield. The A's then signed one of their former players, veteran middle infielder Dal Maxvill, who had drawn his release from Pittsburgh two weeks earlier. In his second game at second base, Maxie received a spike wound from the Twins' Tony Oliva. Twenty-three stitches later, Maxvill found himself on the disabled list next to Green and Trillo.

The injury to Maxvill left Alvin Dark desperate for a second baseman. The A's considered highly-touted prospect Phil Garner, but the scrappy infielder had reported to spring training late and had since been moved to third base, where he suffered a back injury. Garner's status left the A's with no other choice but to promote an obscure infielder, the oddly-named Gaylen Pitts, from Tucson. Pitts would become the seventh player to man the second base position for the A's in 1974, a season that had not yet entered the month of June. The 27-year-old Pitts had started his professional career in 1964, but had never graduated to the major league level.

Ten years after first signing a major league contract, Pitts finally made his major league debut on May 12 when the A's played the rival Twins. Alvin Dark inserted Pitts as his second baseman and number nine hitter. Moments before the game, several veteran A's warned Pitts about playing second base, a position that had become a black hole for Oakland. Six players had tried their hand at second base prior to Pitts and all had come up injured. "A few of the fellows told me not to go out and play second base," Pitts said later. "They said it was jinxed."[14] Pitts made a fielding error in his debut but made up for it with a 1-for-4 performance at the plate and a run scored, helping the A's to a 9-2 win.

Later in the day, the A's found out that Pitts really wasn't a second baseman after all. He had played virtually all of his minor league career at shortstop, but hadn't wanted to admit to Dark his lack of experience at second base. Who could blame Pitts, considering how long he had waited for a chance to play in the major leagues? Besides, Pitts knew that he had no future with the A's at shortstop, not with Campy Campaneris around.

Two nights later, Dark flip-flopped his infield, returning Ted Kubiak to second base and sliding Pitts over to third base. In the second game of a doubleheader against the Royals, Pitts enjoyed a dreamlike performance, collecting three hits in four at-bats and driving in the game-winning run in the bottom of the tenth. Pitts accounted for the A's only two runs of the game, both coming on run-scoring doubles, as Oakland prevailed 2-1 at the Coliseum.

On May 17, Charlie Finley finally reached an agreement with a television station to carry 20 games. While all other major league teams had signed television deals during the off-season, Finley had waited until over five weeks of the regular season had passed to finalize his arrangement. With about 130 games to go in the season, the A's would appear on local television an average of only once for every six to seven games.

Finley, ever the penny-pincher, added that he wanted to use members of the Oakland pitching staff to serve as color announcers on the game broadcasts. So, for example, on a night when Catfish Hunter was not scheduled to start, he would take his place in the broadcasting booth next to play-by-play man Monte Moore. Vida Blue, Ken Holtzman and Blue Moon Odom would do the same. Under the bizarre plan, Finley would save himself the cost of hiring a full-time color commentator. Of course, Finley had no intention of paying his starting pitchers any extra money to pull double duty.

The next day, the A's lost one of their most wrenching games of the season, a 3-2 decision to the White Sox. The A's left 11 runners on base, negating a 10-strikeout performance by Vida Blue. Any loss upset Charlie Finley, but especially a loss to the White Sox, who played in his hometown of Chicago. After the game, Finley berated Dark in the manager's office for nearly 20 minutes. Although the lecture occurred behind a locked door, Finley shouted loud enough for several of the A's to hear him. "I'm playing to win," Finley screamed at Dark. "If you don't start playing aggressive baseball, I'll kick your *bleeping* ass out of here. We won two years without you and we can win again without you."[15] If Oakland players felt no sympathy for Dark prior to the outburst, they probably did now.

The A's, coincidentally or not, rallied behind Dark after hearing Finley's demeaning dress-down. Oakland strung together four consecutive wins, capped off by a 7-4 victory over the Twins. Reggie Jackson continued his strong offensive showing, while exhibiting few effects of a badly pulled hamstring. Jackson powered a home run and a three run double early in the game, while Joe Rudi capped off the scoring with a tie-breaking two-run double in the ninth inning. After the game, Rudi paid Jackson a compliment, one that might have been hard to dispute. "'Super' is unbelievable," Rudi said, referring to Jackson by his nickname. "He's the best player in the league."[16] Reggie returned the favor when he termed Rudi "underrated and underpaid," a statement that likely rankled Charlie Finley, the man responsible for paying Rudi. "He's the nicest guy in baseball," Reggie continued, "and the best left fielder in the league."[17]

Rudi had also made himself into the most fundamentally sound player on the A's. "There are six things I look for in a ballplayer," said Alvin Dark, "and Rudi checks out perfectly in all six."[18] The six categories? Hitting, hitting behind the runner, bunting, running, fielding and throwing. Although some Oakland players hit with more power and many possessed faster running speed, no one hit the cutoff man, executed the hit-and-run, or ran the bases more wisely than Rudi.

Angels' right-hander Dick Lange ended the Oakland mini-streak on May 24, besting Catfish Hunter in a 4-3 decision. The tight game, the latest in a series of hard-fought matches between the A's and Angels, exemplified the growing rivalry. Earlier in the season, the Angels had angered the A's when Skip Lockwood floored Reggie Jackson with an inside fastball. "They started it last year," said the five-foot, nine-inch Lange, the shortest pitcher in baseball, "when they referred to us as a bunch of Triple-A players."[19] Triple-A or not, California had managed to split its first four matchups with the A's on the season.

On May 31, Dick Green returned to the active roster, having missed 43 consecutive games with an injured arch. The return of the veteran second baseman figured to restore some normalcy to the Oakland infield, where minor league refugees Gaylen Pitts and John Donaldson had been seeing too much playing time. For the first time since the opening series of the season, Dark would be able to start his regular infield: Gene Tenace at first, Green at second, Campy Campaneris at short, and captain Sal Bando at third. To their credit, the A's had played well without Bando in the lineup, winning seven and losing three during their captain's stint on the shelf.

Chapter Twenty-four:
The Fight

T he A's had also fared well without Reggie Jackson, who had missed a handful of games with a bad hamstring. With Jackson in the lineup, however, the A's offense operated at a higher level, as one of the best in the American League. In late May, Jackson's hitting streak finally ended after 15 games. Yet, Reggie's season-long average stood at .404. The A's had long since become accustomed to Jackson's mammoth home runs and pace-setting run production, but hadn't ever seen the slugger hit so consistently during his major league career.

On June 5, the A's players dressed in the clubhouse at Tiger Stadium, preparing for their game that evening against Detroit. Billy North, already fully suited in his Oakland uniform, suddenly shouted a few words at Reggie Jackson, who was completely undressed. Jackson returned North's verbal volley and the two men proceeded to brawl on the clubhouse floor. Vida Blue jumped in first, attempting to break up the combatants. In the meantime, a trio of A's who were playing cards — Dick Green, Ken Holtzman and Darold Knowles — ignored Blue's request for help in stopping the fight. Knowles, who in particular didn't like Jackson, saw that North was winning the fight and elected not to step in.

Another player, Ray Fosse, decided to play the role of peacemaker. Assisted by Blue and other players, Fosse helped separate North and

299

Jackson, albeit only momentarily. A few minutes later, North and Jackson tangled again, only to be broken up by Sal Bando and Gene Tenace. Unlike previous clubhouse fights involving the A's, the North-Jackson brawls contained a tinge of hatred. "I'll tell you one thing," said one of the A's anonymously. "It wasn't the regular clubhouse fight. There was no backing off. They went at it hot and heavy — twice."[1]

The skirmish between Jackson and North came as a surprise to some observers of the team, considering that the two men had become friends during the 1973 season. In fact, North believed that he was Jackson's only friend on the team. Their friendship had seemingly strengthened during the off-season, since both lived in Arizona. During spring training, they often ate breakfast together at Jackson's home and rode to the ballpark in the same car. So why the flurry of fists in the clubhouse?

Some players claimed that the fight might have resulted from an incident one month earlier. North had hit a routine ground ball to the second baseman and did not appear to run hard to first. As North jogged back to the dugout, in full view of his Oakland teammates, Jackson yelled at North, chiding him for his failure to hustle. During the encounter, North defended himself by explaining that he had been bothered by a nagging groin pull, which prevented him from running at his usual speed or effort. North then shouted at Jackson, "You're not No. 5," referring to manager Alvin Dark's uniform number. "I only take orders from No. 5."[2] When Jackson stepped to the plate later in the game, several A's players complained about his obscenity-filled attempt to embarrass North.

Alvin Dark and Charlie Finley denied that the aforementioned incident had played a significant part in causing the clubhouse fight, but Dick Young of the *New York Daily News* maintained otherwise. In the June 8, 1974 edition of the *Daily News*, Young reported that North had taken such offense to Jackson's charge of loafing that he had decided to stop talking to Reggie the next day, thus halting the friendship.

North not only gave Jackson the silent treatment but refused to shake his hand after he hit his next 10 home runs. North also tried to rile Reggie in retaliation for his recent criticism. In his column, Young wrote that North repeatedly uttered derogatory comments about Jackson within earshot of the slugger. One of those remarks had triggered the fight in Detroit. "I guess Reggie couldn't take it any more," an unnamed Athletic told Young. "He (North) let go with one of his nasty cracks. Reggie, who was sitting there undressed, yelled, 'I've had enough of it,' and he charged at him."[3]

Captain Sal Bando claimed that the problems between the two outfielders had started much earlier than the loafing incident. "It goes back deeper than that," Bando said. "It is a problem that doesn't exist between the baselines, but between two very strong-headed individuals."[4]

Race relations may have played a part in creating the tensions between North and Jackson. In April, North had informed Jackson that he was spending too much time with whites and not enough time with other blacks. North told Jackson that he too often criticized black players for mistakes, while excusing his white teammates from similar errors. Jackson took offense to North's accusations. "I've made a special effort to help my own kind," said Jackson, who regularly donated thousands of dollars to African-American community groups, "but it has backfired. I'm having trouble communicating with them, and that upsets me. I know they mistrust me because I spend so much time with white people. But I'll tell you something. On the field I don't respect anyone just because he's black or white. I respect him if he performs."[5]

Having grown up in the racially mixed community of Wyncote, Pennsylvania — a suburb of Philadelphia — Jackson had always made a strong effort to integrate himself with other ethnic groups. Jackson had previously roomed with Chuck Dobson, a white pitcher, dated several Caucasian women, and frequently spoke Spanish with Latino players. Jackson wanted to be liked by everyone, regardless of race. "Now ain't that some bleep?" Jackson asked rhetorically. "Is that supposed to be bad?"[6]

The state of his relationship with North disturbed Jackson. "This whole thing is bad," Reggie said. "Two black guys, two teammates, It shouldn't be like this."[7] Jackson explained that he had tried to repair his relationship with North on at least six occasions. "He was my friend," Jackson said sadly. "He's a stubborn kid, but he's also a very intelligent kid. He's really a good person and a great ballplayer and we had a lot of good times together. I miss his friendship."[8]

For his part, North said little, except to deny innuendo that he had initiated the fight with his former friend. "I was not the aggressor," North told Clint Roswell of the *New York Daily News*. "I am not the heavy in this situation. I was trying to defend myself."[9] North would say little more publicly about the incident.

Unlike previous fights involving Oakland players, Charlie Finley reacted aggressively to the latest controversy. Finley booked a flight to Milwaukee, in order to meet the A's on the next stop of their road trip. He met with Alvin Dark, Billy North and Reggie Jackson in the trainer's room, and ordered his two outfielders to shake hands. The angry owner then addressed the team for about 20 minutes in the clubhouse. "You're world champions," Finley screamed aloud. "Stop acting like a bunch of kids!"[10]

As Finley scolded his players, images of a father screaming at his children came to mind. "He'd come in and have tirades," says Ted Kubiak. "He was the father of the family. He was the guy who led everything. Guys would talk back to him in meetings like kids would talk back to their parents. I always marveled at the fact that he listened. You know, he was open. He was an open guy. I just learned a lot from him, I think."

In this case, Finley had good reason to be upset, considering that the dual fights between Jackson and North had proved costly to the A's health. During the second go-round, Jackson fell and suffered a bruised shoulder, which prevented him from taking his usual ferocious swing. More importantly, the first fight caused a serious injury to one of the peacemakers. Ray Fosse separated his cervical disk and pinched a nerve in his neck, necessitating that he be placed in traction in an Oakland hospital. As a result, the A's lost their starting catcher for what they feared would be a significant amount of time.

Fosse replayed the fight between North and Jackson, and his subsequent attempt at peacemaking, for the Oakland media. "I was just sitting there in my underwear. Billy walked in and made a few remarks to Reggie and all of a sudden they started fighting. Instinctively I jumped in and tried to break it up. Vida was also one of the guys who tried to break it up. I was concerned about Vida because he was pitching that night."[11] Fosse saved Blue from injury, but not himself. During the melee, Fosse ended up on the floor with North and Jackson. When Fosse returned to his feet, he found himself being pushed up against a locker. Later that night, Fosse felt pain in his right shoulder as he tried to make a throw to second base.

Although Finley made no public statements in assessing blame, he told Jackson that he held him most responsible for the altercation with North. Finley's finger-pointing bothered Jackson, who felt betrayed by the owner. The criticism would affect Jackson's play in both the field and at the plate. North noticed Jackson's failing spirit and eventually initiated a meeting with his former friend. The meeting eventually led to a reconciliation. "It was hurting the team," North said about Jackson's fragile insecurity. "Hell, the man wasn't hustling or really swinging the bat."[12]

With Ray Fosse sidelined as a result of the North-Jackson fight, Alvin Dark slid Gene Tenace from first base to catcher, moved Deron Johnson from designated hitter to first base, and installed Angel Mangual as his DH. The new lineup weakened the A's defensively and in the standings, as they lost seven of their next 10 games. Oakland's four-game lead in the West slipped to just one.

Shortly after Fosse's injury, Tenace pinched a nerve in his neck while swinging the bat awkwardly. The latest setback shelved Tenace, forcing Alvin Dark to turn to his third-string catcher, Larry Haney.

On June 19, the A's lost their second straight game to the Red Sox, an excruciating 2-1 loss in extra innings. In the top of the 11th inning, backup catcher Bob Montgomery delivered a bases-loaded sacrifice fly against reliever Paul Lindblad. Former Athletic Diego Segui handled the A's in the bottom of the 11th, retiring Sal Bando for the

game's final out. The loss, and the managerial gaffes committed by Alvin
Dark earlier in the game, left Bando in the foulest of moods.

"We had battled back, tied the game," Bando recalls, "and we led
off (the tenth inning) with the eighth hitter getting on. Instead of putting up someone to bunt him over with the top of the order coming up,
he (Dark) sent up Reggie, who was not playing that day, and Reggie
ended up hitting into a double play." In actuality, Jackson pinch-hit for
the sixth-place hitter, first baseman Deron Johnson, and ended up flying to center field, but Bando disagreed with Dark's strategy nonetheless.

"And then we ended up losing in extra innings," Bando says, continuing the story. "To make matters worse, I made the last out of the
game. So as I came up the runway and into the clubhouse just frustrated and disgusted with losing, and making the last out, the fact that
I thought we could have bunted him over in the top of the inning, I
kicked a trash can and said, 'You can't manage a meat market.'"

Bando did not intend for the remark to be heard by his manager.
"Alvin Dark never came into the clubhouse after the game," Bando explains. "But for some reason he was in there that day. As I looked up,
he was standing right in front of me. To make matters even worse,
Glenn Dickey, the writer for the (San Francisco) *Chronicle* happens to
be in there, which was unusual. And he heard it. So the next day,
headlines in the paper say, "BANDO SAYS DARK CAN'T MANAGE A
MEAT MARKET."

To his credit, Dark refrained from responding angrily to Bando.
"Alvin and I had a conversation right after that happened," Bando says.
"I went into his office. I told him where I disagreed with him. He said
there was some merit to it, but I apologized for saying that. I mean, that
was more temper than any substance, and he accepted my apology.

"But what was really funny about the whole thing is the next day
I got a telegram from the meat packers union. They said, 'If you think
managing a meat market is easy, you don't know what you're talking
about.' To me, that was hilarious."

After the controversial post-game scene, the A's won three straight
games and six of their next seven, leading the manager to place a positive spin on the outburst by his team captain. "It kind of relaxed the
team," Dark said of Bando's meat market remark and his subsequent
meeting with his third baseman. "I'll tell you, I felt better after the game
than before it. I thought we'd been in a state of lethargy for about a
week."[13]

On June 24, the A's decided to part company with one of the players instrumental to their success in 1973. Designated hitter-first
baseman Deron Johnson, hitting just .195 with seven home runs, was
sold on waivers to the Brewers. Although less than a year removed from
one of his most productive seasons, Johnson had been unable to find

his stroke after initially injuring his thumb in August of 1973. In February, Johnson had expressed his wish to remain a member of the A's for the balance of his career. "For six years, before I came to Oakland, I was with losing clubs," Johnson said, referring to stints with the Phillies, Braves, Reds, and the Kansas City Athletics. "I want to stay here (in Oakland) until I quit baseball."[14] In selling Johnson's contract to the Brewers, the A's had ended that dream while removing one of the most popular players from their clubhouse. The A's had also decided to entrust the inconsistent Angel Mangual with the daily responsibilities of the designated hitter role.

The injury to Ray Fosse and the ineffectiveness of Deron Johnson had left the A's short at three positions: catcher, first base and DH. The A's had initially hoped that Fosse could return to the lineup quickly, but now realized that his cervical disk injury was serious enough to mandate his placement on the disabled list. Oakland scouts recommended the acquisition of veteran catcher-outfielder Ed Kirkpatrick, hitting .278 in a reserve role for the Pittsburgh Pirates. The 29-year-old Kirkpatrick, a strong left-handed hitter with some power, had played for the rival Kansas City Royals from 1969 to 1973. Although a liability defensively, some in the Oakland organization viewed Kirkpatrick as a perfect fit for the A's; the Curt Blefary play-alike could DH against right-handed pitching while providing Gene Tenace with a capable backup behind the plate.

Charlie Finley tried to pry Kirkpatrick loose from Pittsburgh but could not satisfy the Pirates' trade demands. Finley had also telephoned Mike Epstein, recently released by the California Angels. Epstein was also considering a contract with the Cubs. When the Angels had cut loose Epstein in May, they had made him available to any other major league team for the waiver price of $1. Any team claiming Epstein on waivers would have had to pay the balance of his $60,000 salary. Now that Epstein had cleared waivers and become a free agent, the A's or Cubs could sign him for the major league minimum, leaving the Angels with the balance.

Epstein may have burned any bridges leading toward Oakland with a series of scathing remarks about Finley that appeared in print during the 1973 season. Epstein had explained the reasoning behind Finley's vindictive decision to exile him to the Texas Rangers. "You either kiss Finley, or you don't play for him,"[15] Epstein said not-so-subtly. "Charlie Finley got rid of three of us — me, Dave Duncan and George Hendrick — because we wouldn't kiss his fanny," Epstein contended. "What's more, he buried us. He sent the other two to Cleveland and me to Texas."[16] Epstein believed that Finley had passed up the opportunity to trade him to another team, one that would have surrendered more value than Horacio Piña in return. "The Cubs wanted me," Epstein revealed. "They offered (Joe) Pepitone and a pitcher, but instead he called up Bob Short and said take Epstein and give me anything. So they gave him Piña."[17]

Epstein said that, despite his problems with the owner, he had enjoyed playing for the A's. "I got along good with everybody but Finley. The night he traded me, six guys in the Oakland area, guys on the team, came over to my house and threw me a party to cheer me up. I felt awful."[18] After his release by the Angels, Epstein did not return to Oakland, despite the fact that he appeared to suit the A's, a team in need of a left-handed power threat. Epstein's major league career came to an end while perennial prospect Rich McKinney earned a promotion from Triple-A. Unlike Kirkpatrick, McKinney couldn't catch, and unlike Epstein, had little power, but had hit .311 against Pacific Coast League pitching.

On July 9, Ray Fosse underwent surgery to repair a ruptured disc in his neck. Fosse, who had already missed over a month of action, learned that he would be sidelined for another six to eight weeks. The prognosis meant that the A's would be without their best defensive catcher. Gene Tenace would continue to serve as the regular catcher, with Pat Bourque taking over for Tenace at first base. Fosse's absence would weaken the A's at not one, but two positions.

The night of July 9 brought big changes to the Oakland organization. Instead of making a trade, Finley gave manager Alvin Dark permission to make an unusual in-season move — axing two of the team's coaches. Third base coach Irv Noren and bullpen coach Vern Hoscheit, both holdovers from the Dick Williams regime, found themselves unemployed. In their place, Dark hired Bobby Hofman, one of his former coaches with Kansas City, and Bobby Winkles, the recently fired Angels' manager, who had angered Reggie Jackson earlier in the season by supposedly ordering a knockdown of the Oakland slugger. Winkles would take Noren's place in the third base coaching box, while Hofman would assume Hoscheit's duties in the bullpen.

The dual firings surprised some of the Oakland players, but not Catfish Hunter, who hurled an impressive three-hitter shutout against the Indians earlier in the evening. "If they told me that half the team had been traded — Reggie Jackson, Joe Rudi, Sal Bando, Billy North — to Mexico, I'd believe them. Nothing on this club surprises me anymore."[19]

Noren's firing represented a strengthening of Alvin Dark's power base. Noren didn't like or respect Dark and felt more loyalty to his predecessor, Dick Williams. In turn, Dark didn't trust Noren, whom he had accused of intentionally making bad decisions as third base coach. Oakland players, such as pinch-runner Herb Washington, didn't agree with Darks' assessment of Noren. Washington told Noren, "You're the best third base coach I ever had."[20] Of course, Washington hadn't had a third base coach since high school, the last time that he had played baseball. Dark, for his part, had wanted to fire Noren back in May, only to be restrained by Finley, who didn't want to eat the coach's contract.

While the firing of Noren seemed inevitable, the departure of Hoscheit fell into a more surprising category. According to one media report, Hoscheit and Dark had experienced a fallout over a relatively trivial item — the availability of baseballs for extra batting practice. When Hoscheit threatened to quit, Dark saved him the effort, firing him instead.

Hoscheit reacted bitterly to the treatment he had received from his former employer, Charlie Finley. "I'm going home and retire," Hoscheit announced. "When you meet people like this in baseball, it's time to quit. Charlie Finley is no good. He promised the coaches last year that if we did good, we'd get a raise. We won the World Series and we never got the raise. He doesn't keep his word."[21] Hoscheit, who had been the A's senior coach, offered no praise of Dark, either. "The manager is no good, too. He's just a horsemeat manager."[22] Hoscheit, like Noren, would receive his full salary for the balance of the year.

The previous week, Finley had experienced a reunion of sorts with Hoscheit and Noren's former boss, Dick Williams. On July 1, the ex-Oakland manager returned to the major leagues as the manager of the California Angels. Finley had given California permission to sign Williams out of friendship for Angels' owner Gene Autry. That same night, Williams and the Angels hosted the A's in the beginning of a four-game series at Anaheim Stadium. The A's swept all four games, ruining Williams' debut in southern California.

In the second game of the series with the Angels, Joe Rudi, perhaps longing for Dick Williams, revealed his own lack of respect for Alvin Dark. When Dark pulled Rudi from the game in favor of pinch-runner Herb Washington, Rudi provided the media with a sarcastic post-game nugget. "John McGraw must be turning over in his grave,"[23] said Rudi. And Dick Williams must have been chuckling in the Angels' dugout.

On July 14, Alvin Dark reached his boiling point. Upset by two instances when his starting pitchers flipped him baseballs instead of handing them off upon their removal, Dark yelled at his players in a private meeting. "When I come out to the mound," one player quoted Dark as saying, "I don't want to play catch out there. Just hand me the ball."[24] Dark also delivered a message to all players who had criticized him with wisecrack remarks throughout the season. "I'm the manager of this ballclub. If you want to be the manager, phone Charlie (Finley) and ask for the job. But don't be second-guessing me."[25]

Dark's speech, eerily reminiscent of Dick Williams' angry lecture to his players after the 1971 megaphone incident, drew a surprisingly favorable response from the majority of Oakland players. Several Oakland veterans had considered Dark too tolerant of fundamental mistakes and too unwilling to ride players who had failed to play smart baseball. "I thought it was good," Reggie Jackson said of Dark's meeting with the club. "I was glad to see Alvin do it."[26]

For the first time in 1974, Dark had made it clear that he would no longer accept public criticism and ridicule of his managerial style or strategies. Much like Dick Williams' fire and brimstone talk in 1971, the A's seemed to carry Dark's message to the playing field, where they responded by winning four straight games.

A change in player personnel also aided the Oakland cause. In early July, the A's had sent infielder Gaylen Pitts back to Tacoma, and had replaced him on the 25-man roster with a 19-year-old outfielder from Double-A Birmingham. Claudell Washington, a line-drive-hitting outfielder with speed, played a decisive role in a game against the Indians on July 8th.

Cleveland ace Gaylord Perry had won 15 consecutive decisions, dating back to the 1973 season. With one more win, Perry would tie the all-time American League record for most consecutive victories. Perry allowed only three runs through nine innings, but was matched by Vida Blue. In the bottom of the tenth, with the score still tied at 3-3, Perry walked pinch-hitter Pat Bourque to start the inning. Blue Moon Odom, running for Bourque since Herb Washington had already been used, moved up to second on a sacrifice bunt by rookie catcher Tim Hosley. Perry retired Campy Campaneris for the second out. With Odom still at second, Perry faced Claudell Washington, who had tripled earlier in the game for his first major league hit. In a pressurized situation against a future Hall of Famer, Washington lined a pitch into right field for a clean single, scoring Odom with the game-winning run and halting Perry's run at the record books.

Dissatisfied with the performance of Angel Mangual, Charlie Finley had demanded Washington's recall from Double-A and ordered Alvin Dark to insert Washington into the DH role. The ascent of Washington through the organization had impressed Finley, the team's scouts and the coaching staff. In the early seventies, Washington had elected not to play baseball at Berkeley High School, an expression of his dislike for extracurricular activities. Washington's self-imposed exile from scholastic baseball had prevented most major league scouts from learning his identity. Jim Guinn, a part-time Oakland scout who happened to live in Berkeley, visited the school's athletic department and asked for a list of students who possessed the most athletic ability but had not tried out for the baseball team. Informed of the 17-year-old Washington, Guinn contacted him immediately. "He's a loner," Guinn said of Washington. "Someone had to encourage him."[27] Guinn took on the role and farm director John Claiborne eventually signed Claudell to a $3,000 bonus.

On the afternoon of July 14, Washington delivered two RBI's, including a tie-snapping sacrifice fly, which helped the A's to a 7-3 win over the Yankees. Three days letter, the left-handed hitting Washington stroked two hits against southpaw Mike Cuellar, as the A's blanked the Orioles, 2-0. Washington then went 3-for-4 against Gaylord Perry, the same pitcher he had defeated earlier in the month, helping the A's to a 3-2 win over the Indians.

Washington's smooth transition from Double-A to the major leagues amazed his teammates, many of whom had taken note of the size of Claudell's bat. Although he weighed only 190 pounds, Washington swung a 42-ounce bat, a size matched by Chicago White Sox slugger Dick Allen. After a few days, Washington switched to a 32-ounce model in an effort to quicken his bat speed during the hottest months of the season.

On July 19, Oakland's inconsistent offense fell victim to Indians' right-hander Dick Bosman. The journeyman pitcher, who had pitched so brilliantly in stifling the A's on Opening Day of the 1971 season, threw a no-hitter, missing a perfect game on his own fourth inning error. The 30-year-old Bosman, who appeared on the verge of a trade near the June 15th deadline, became the second pitcher to no-hit the A's over the last two seasons.

Two days later, Alvin Dark shuffled his lineup in a desperate attempt to inject more offensive firepower. Dark inserted Angel Mangual in left field, moved his best defensive outfielder, Joe Rudi, to first base, and benched the struggling Pat Bourque. The moves made little sense. Mangual, hitting in the .250 range with negligible power, represented only a very small improvement over Bourque. More importantly, the changes damaged the quality of Oakland's defense at two positions. Rudi, the best defensive left fielder in the American League, found himself playing an uncomfortable position at first base. Mangual, a poor defensive outfielder, often misjudged fly balls, which dropped in for singles and doubles. In essence, the A's had greatly reduced their fielding ability while doing little to improve the offense. Bizarre.

At the end of July, the A's lost the services of perhaps their most important defensive player, shortstop Campy Campaneris. The starting shortstop sustained a severely sprained left ankle, which forced him into a stint on the 15-day disabled list. The A's promoted infielder Phil Garner from Tucson, where "Scrap Iron" had been playing mostly third base. The injury to Campaneris meant that utility infielder Ted Kubiak would receive most of the playing time at shortstop.

On August 7, the A's ended their mystifying use of Angel Mangual in left field and Joe Rudi at first base — at least temporarily. In the two weeks since he had become their regular left fielder, Mangual had seen his batting average plummet 20 points. No, Alvin Dark and Charlie Finley didn't come to their senses; an in-game injury forced their hand. During an 8-4 win over the Rangers, Mangual pulled a hamstring muscle. Rudi returned to left field, Tenace reverted back to first base, and backup catcher Larry Haney moved in behind the plate. The injury to Mangual made the A's stronger at three defensive positions, but not for long.

Mangual returned to the lineup the next day and contributed with a hit and two runs scored. Rudi, however, proved to be the game's biggest star, as he homered, doubled, singled twice, and drove in half of the A's runs in a 10-2 rout of the Rangers. The outburst lifted Rudi's season average to .310, second best to Reggie Jackson among Oakland regulars, while improving his home run and RBI totals to 13 and 72, respectively. Rudi's excellence, in the face of ill-advised position switches, impressed observers of the game, who continued to call him one of baseball's most underrated stars. The "underrated" label began to wear on Rudi. "I get more ink about not getting ink than about the things I do,"[28] complained the A's most gentlemanly player. Underrated or not, Rudi had made himself into a legitimate candidate for the American League's MVP Award.

In early August, the A's wrapped up a nine-game road trip with the three-game swing in Texas. While in Arlington, Vida Blue experienced severe chest pains and paid a visit to a doctor's office. The physician suggested Blue consult a heart specialist, who decided to check Vida into Dallas' Baylor Hospital for a series of examinations, including a test for sickle cell anemia, a disease afflicting black males. Hospital technicians then tested Blue's heart with an electrocardiogram, which revealed an irregularity.

Although the test showed abnormalities, a cardiac specialist explained that electrocardiograms performed on young black males occasionally showed irregularities even though their heart functions were actually normal. When the doctor compared Blue's most recent EKG with one that had been conducted earlier as part of a life insurance exam, he found that the test results matched. In other words, nothing was wrong with Blue's heart; his chest pains may have been the result of simple indigestion.

With Blue in the hospital and unable to make his scheduled start on August 7, Alvin Dark handed the gameday ball to Darold Knowles. Knowles, who had questioned Dark's use of the bullpen earlier in the season, had lost his status as Oakland's top left-handed reliever to Paul Lindblad. The underused sinkerballer responded with five effective innings against the Rangers, besting Oakland-killer Jim Bibby in the process.

The missed start not only proved a benefit to Knowles, but to Blue himself. On August 10, a well-rested Blue surrendered only one run, scattered eight hits and earned an impressive 5-3 win over the Boston Red Sox. The victory, which improved his record to 14-9, left Blue's catcher awestruck. "His fastball was exploding, really moving around," remarked Gene Tenace, continuing to serve as the A's top receiver in the absence of Ray Fosse. "He's throwing like he did in 1971."[29] The A's had waited two and a half years to hear such words.

The A's lost their next game to the Red Sox, 2-1, as an aging Juan Marichal barely outpitched rookie right-hander Glenn Abbott. The lackluster defeat, which dropped the A's record in August to a mediocre 6-6, upset Alvin Dark to the point that he made a stunning announcement the next night prior to a game against the Yankees. Dark would no longer permit the drinking of hard liquor on any team flights for the duration of the season. Players would be allowed to drink wine and beer, but the use of anything stiffer would be strictly prohibited. "I just feel that the rest of the year we all have to suffer a little, sacrifice a little to keep things going," explained Dark, a teetotaler who abstained from all kinds of alcohol. 'The hard stuff isn't too good for a ballplayer. It isn't too good for anyone."[30]

Dark's sudden prohibition pleased crusaders against the evils of drink, but resulted in a sarcastic reaction from several of his players. "I think the flask is coming back in style,"[31] said one anonymous player. When Dark urged his players to abandon hard liquor and give "100 per cent of 100 per cent," another player wrote those words on a piece of tape, mockingly sticking the message to the back of his uniform. Other players offered more constructive criticism of the Dark directive. "I think it's kind of bad," said Catfish Hunter. "I haven't seen anyone drunk on a plane or even high."[32]

Perhaps Dark had imposed the restriction as a delayed reaction to an incident that had cost him his job as the manager of the Kansas City A's. On a 1967 commercial flight from Boston to Kansas City, an eyewitness had claimed to have seen rowdy behavior by several drunken Athletic players, principally pitcher Lew Krausse. Charlie Finley had suspended Krausse and ordered a ban on the serving of alcohol on all team flights. When several players came to Krausse's defense, Dark supported his players and stood up to Finley. The owner fired Dark shortly thereafter.

On the same day that Dark announced the latest ban on liquor, Campy Campaneris came off the disabled list. Campaneris told Dark that he didn't feel well enough to leave the disabled list, but when Finley stepped in and asked Campy to play, the manager penciled his veteran shortstop into the designated hitter's role. Campy went 0-for-3 as the DH but the A's managed a 3-2 victory over the Yankees, as Catfish Hunter ran his record to 17-9.

Four days later, Campy played his first game at shortstop since spraining his left ankle. Campaneris went one-for-three at the plate and played all nine innings in the field. The next game, however, Campy showed ill effects of trying to come back too quickly from the injury. In the eighth inning, Campy banged out his second hit of the game, only to come up hobbling as he reached first base. Trainer Joe Romo started to run from the dugout to first base, but Campaneris quickly waved him off. The Oakland players knew that their star shortstop was hurting badly, but Campy refused to leave a close, one-run game that the Tigers eventually won, 4-3.

After the game, Charlie Finley berated Romo, as if he were to blame for the fragile condition of Campaneris' ankle. Romo hadn't insisted that Campaneris return to the lineup a week earlier; Finley had. Perhaps Finley was upset that Romo hadn't run out onto the field to tend to Campy right away.

Campy started the next night, going 1-for-2 in a 13-3 demolition of the Tigers. After Campaneris reached on a single in the late innings, Alvin Dark had the good sense to pull him from the game, replacing him with pinch-runner Herb Washington. The question remained, however. Why did Dark start Campaneris in the first place? If Oakland's lead were only one or two games in the American League West, the decision to use an ailing Campaneris might be more understandable. With a fairly comfortable lead of five and a half games over the second-place Royals, why were the A's risking the long term health of their most important middle infielder and second-best base stealer? Like many of Dark's strategies, the decision seemed to make little sense.

Speaking of Dark's strategies, the 13-3 win over the Tigers produced another mild controversy. In the sixth inning, with the A's up 4-1 and two men out, center fielder Angel Mangual dropped a routine fly ball, allowing two unearned runs to score. Dark hooked Holtzman, replacing him with another left-hander, Darold Knowles. Why? Holtzman had pitched well and couldn't be faulted for Mangual's latest misadventure in the outfield. Furthermore, to take Holtzman out and replace him with another left-hander pitcher, instead of waiting for a right-handed batter to come to the plate, made even less sense.

Dark contended that he was concerned about the condition of Holtzman's left thigh, which had been struck by a batted ball one inning earlier. The left-hander, for his part, said the leg didn't bother him and had no effect on the quality of his pitching. "I just didn't deserve to be taken out," said Holtzman. "I felt fine and I still had good stuff."[33]

In the meantime, the play of the Oakland bench had become a concern to Finley and Dark. Phil Garner, called up to replace Campaneris during his stint on the disabled list, had come to bat 20 times as a major leaguer before recording his first base hit. Garner, a talented prospect, seemed overmatched at the plate. Another backup, first baseman, Pat Bourque had gone 12 consecutive pinch-hit at-bats without a hit. Finally, in the Sunday rout of the Tigers, Bourque had delivered an important two-run pinch single as a substitute for light-hitting shortstop Dal Maxvill.

Bourque's late-inning heroics against Detroit failed to save his roster spot in Oakland. The next day, in a classic example of trading "my flat tire for your flat tire," Finley dealt him to the Twins for another left-handed pinch-hitter, Jim Holt. A veteran outfielder, Holt was hitting a mediocre .254, had not delivered a single pinch-hit and had not managed a single home run in nearly 200 at-bats. Perhaps Finley just wanted to bring back one of his former farmhands. Holt had played in the organization seven years ago, when the franchise was still in Kansas City.

On August 24, the A's received a double dose of positive developments when Catfish Hunter earned his 19th win, allowing the Red Sox no earned runs in a route-going effort. That same day, Ray Fosse returned to active duty for the first time since undergoing surgery on his damaged cervical disk. Although Fosse did not start the game, he came in for defensive purposes after Alvin Dark used Claudell Washington to pinch-hit for Larry Haney.

Hunter won his 20th game his next time out, shackling the Brewers over eight innings. The 3-1 victory gave Catfish four consecutive seasons with 20 or more wins. Reggie Jackson supported the A's pitching stalwart with two monstrous County Stadium home runs. While Jackson's tape-measure shots drew much of the attention away from Hunter, Catfish didn't seem to mind. After the game, Hunter calmly fielded questions about reaching the 20-win circle. "The thing about winning 20 is that it makes you hungry to win 20 again,"[34] remarked a philosophical Hunter. Only four years ago, the A's had questioned whether the soft-spoken right-hander would ever amount to anything more than a 15 or 16-game winner.

Claudell Washington also contributed to Hunter's 20th, rapping out two hits while filling in for an injured Billy North in center field. The young, left-handed hitting outfielder continued to show remarkable aptitude for handling major league pitching. On the day before his 20th birthday, the rookie played center field, went five-for-five and drove in three runs in a 10-5 thumping of the Tigers. The August 30th display so impressed Charlie Finley that he graciously rewarded Washington with a $2,000 bonus. Considering Commissioner Bowie Kuhn's dislike of bonuses, Finley decided to call the money a retroactive pay raise. Yes, Mr. Finley still had a generous side to his complex personality.

In 1973, Washington had torn up the Class-A Midwest League, hitting .322 with 38 stolen bases and 81 RBI's. The fine season earned him a promotion to Double-A Birmingham, where he terrorized Southern League pitching over the first half of the 1974 season. In search of a left-handed hitting DH, the A's decided to promote Washington to the big leagues, bypassing the usual stop at Triple-A Tucson. The 19-year-old sensation showed no fear of playing in the major leagues, earning him praise from Reggie Jackson. "Nothing bothers Claudell," remarked Jackson. "He won't be bothered by fame. He won't be screwed up by Charlie (Finley). He's in control of himself."[35] Washington's calm exterior became even more impressive given his teenage status. "I've never

seen a young player to secure," added Jackson. "He knows he's not
articulate; he knows he's no financial genius or mathematical wizard;
but he knows he can play baseball."[36]

"He's the best player for his age I've ever seen or known,"[37] said
Jackson, upgrading his praise further. Although Washington had yet to
show Reggie-like power at the plate, his speed and left-handed stroke
reminded some in the organization of a young Jackson, circa 1967. "In
two years," Sal Bando said of Washington, "he'll be a better ballplayer
than Reggie."[38] Jackson himself held an equally high opinion of Washington, whom he compared to Minnesota Twins" star Tony Oliva. "He's
going to be a better player than I am," said Jackson. "He runs better
than I do, and he's a better hitter at his age than I ever hoped to be."[39]

Washington would never became the superstar that Bando and
Jackson had so confidently predicted. He would hit .300 or better only
one more season (1988), would fail to hit more than 17 home runs in a
single season and would never match his total of 40 stolen bases in
1975. Washington's struggles against left-handed pitching and his overly
aggressive approach at the plate hindered his ability to produce runs.
Yet, Washington enjoyed a solid 17-year career as a line drive hitter
with both power and speed, and became a good defensive center fielder
with the Yankees in the late 1980s.

On September 1, the A's expanded their roster by four players,
adding pitcher Bill Parsons and three infielders: Manny Trillo, Phil Garner and veteran John Donaldson. The lefty-hitting Donaldson, who had
spent time with Oakland during the early-season wave of injuries to
various second baseman, needed only 24 more days of service time to
qualify for his full, four-year pension. As long as Donaldson remained
on the roster for the balance of the regular season, he would reach the
needed service time. In promoting Donaldson from the minor leagues,
Charlie Finley had shown a considerate nature for a journeyman player
who would likely contribute little to the pennant drive.

The same could not be said of Finley the following day, when the
A's hosted the Angels at the Oakland Coliseum. The game was marked
by Dick Williams' return to the Coliseum for the first time since his
post-World Series resignation. Reggie Jackson and Joe Rudi spoiled
the return for Williams by homering in support of Glenn Abbott, who
earned the win with relief help from Rollie Fingers. When Fingers retired the last Angels' batter in the ninth inning, the scoreboard at the
Oakland Coliseum exhibited the following message, in large lettering:

GOODNIGHT, DICK

The scoreboard order had been placed by none other than Charlie
Finley, who took extra pleasure in defeating a man he had considered
disloyal to him. The scoreboard message, left up for several minutes,
infuriated most of the Oakland players, especially Reggie Jackson. "If
they ever do that again," Jackson said of the scoreboard message, "I'll

walk off the field and they can fine me anything they want."[40] Even current manager Alvin Dark bristled at the lack of class shown by his employer. A few minutes later, Dark and Reggie Jackson walked to the Angels' clubhouse to personally apologize for the embarrassing message displayed on the Coliseum scoreboard.

The A's had won all five meetings with California since Dick Williams had been hired as Angels' skipper. Instead of deriving simple satisfaction from the wins, Finley had felt motivated to rub a few salt pellets into the wounds of his former manager. The scoreboard directive was childish and mean-spirited, continuing the same kind of vindictive personality that Finley had exhibited since his heart attack in August of 1973. Somewhere, Mike Andrews must have felt a special degree of sympathy for Dick Williams.

Proponents of fair play had to be pleased when the Angels, after 10 straight losses to the A's, finally defeated the defending champions two days later, grabbing a 5-2 decision at the Coliseum. The A's somehow managed to score only a pair of runs despite being the recipients of 10 walks by Angels' left-hander Andy Hassler. Sal Bando committed two errors behind a mediocre performance by Vida Blue, whose record dropped to 14-14. With the win, Dick Williams notched his first victory against his former club after six consecutive defeats.

In early September, relief ace Rollie Fingers endured his worst game of the season, perhaps in part due to his off-the-field problems. Fingers had separated from his wife earlier in the season, enjoyed a temporary reconciliation, and then another break-up. Fingers indicated to the Oakland media that the latest break-up had probably signaled the end of his marriage. On September 6, Fingers allowed four runs and nine hits in a stint of three and two-thirds innings, taking the loss in a 5-4 defeat to the Rangers. In the top of the 11th, Fingers allowed a leadoff single to Dave Nelson, who moved to second on Cesar Tovar's sacrifice bunt. With first base open and MVP candidate Jeff Burroughs scheduled to bat, an intentional walk seemed like reasonable strategy. Dark could have instructed Fingers to pitch carefully to the hot-hitting Burroughs, who had already accumulated three hits on the night and take his chances with a less dangerous hitter like Mike Hargrove. Instead, Dark ordered Fingers to pitch to Burroughs, who lined a run-scoring single to give the Rangers the lead. Steve Foucault retired the A's in the bottom of the 11th to saddle the A's with one of their toughest losses of the summer. For the umpteenth time in 1974, Oakland players and media engaged in widespread first and second-guessing of Dark, perhaps the most embattled first-place manager in the history of the game.

The next day, Dark and Darold Knowles argued on the mound, as part of an ugly 8-2 loss to the Rangers. Dark had come to the mound to remove Knowles and replace him with right-hander Bill Parsons.

Knowles, who didn't want to leave the game, shouted at Dark. The argument represented the second public dispute between the manager and the 32-year-old reliever. After the game, Dark apologized to his left-handed reliever in front of the other Oakland players. As much as the A's questioned many of Dark's in-game strategies and decisions, they could not criticize their manager for a failure to own up to his mistakes, something he had done frequently throughout the season.

The Rangers won their third straight against the A's on Sunday, as former Chicago Cub standout Ferguson Jenkins recorded his 22nd win of the season. Jenkins struck out 10, did not allow a run until the ninth and scattered seven hits in a 5-1 victory. With three wins in the four-game weekend series, the Rangers had given themselves some life in the American League West race, as they had pared two games off the Oakland lead. Although less than a month of the regular season remained, the Rangers had moved to within five and a half games of the A's, who had completely lost their momentum. The two teams would meet again in another week.

The A's moved on to Kansas City, where they first feared that they might be without one of their relievers for the balance of the season. Darold Knowles, struggling with a staff-high 4.56 ERA, was diagnosed with a case of bursitis in his right hip and leg. The pain struck Knowles so severely and suddenly that he had to crawl from the floor of his hotel room to the door in order to let trainer Joe Romo into the room.

Doctors prescribed medication and rest as a way of treating his bursitis, but acknowledged the possibility that the condition might sideline Knowles for the remainder of the season and the playoffs. All of a sudden, Knowles realized he may have made his last pitch as a member of the A's staff. "If Alvin (Dark) is here next year," Knowles predicted, "I very definitely will be traded. If he isn't around, I might stay."[41]

Knowles' fears turned out to be premature. Doctors determined that Knowles had not been afflicted with bursitis, but rather a viral infection. As a result of the chance in diagnosis, Knowles would be able to return to game action within a few days.

The A's lost Knowles temporarily, but gained two important victories against the Royals. Vida Blue and Catfish Hunter pitched back-to-back shutouts in a doubleheader sweep, allowing a combined six hits in the two games. Gene Tenace, Joe Rudi and Sal Bando each homered and Campy Campaneris collected four hits to lead the A's to 3-0 and 7-0 wins over the fading Royals. In the meantime, the Rangers split a doubleheader with the Angels, falling to six games back in the West. The Rangers lost the first game to none other than Chuck Dobson, who allowed only one run in pitching a complete game and earning his first win for a team other than the Kansas City or Oakland A's.

Six games separated the Rangers from the A's, as the two teams prepared to play the beginning of a three game set on Friday the 13th.

The series represented the last head-to-head meeting between the two rivals, meaning the Rangers needed to win all three games in order to have a more realistic chance of catching Oakland in the season's final two weeks.

Alvin Dark and Rangers' manager Billy Martin could not have planned their rotation any better for the series. In the first game, 22-game winners Catfish Hunter and Ferguson Jenkins took the mound at Arlington Stadium. In the top of the third, the A's broke through on singles by Billy North and Campy Campaneris and a sac fly by Reggie Jackson. The Rangers came right back with two runs on Lenny Randle's triple. Jenkins shut down the Oakland attack the rest of the way, preserving an imperative 3-1 win for Texas.

On Saturday night, Alvin Dark turned to the inconsistent Vida Blue to face 11-game winner Jackie Brown. The A's scored three runs in the first four innings to take a 3-1 lead. In the bottom of the fourth, the Rangers bounced Blue with a five-run inning, capped off by Jim Sundberg's bases-loaded single. Dark understandably removed Blue and then watched his offense swing feebly against Brown, who held the A's scoreless over the last five innings. An 8-3 Texas win drew the Rangers to within only four games of the A's.

Dark had taken his two best shots at the Rangers by using his two premier starting pitchers. Both had failed. With Ken Holtzman unavailable after pitching a complete game on Thursday, Dark had no recourse but to give the ball to inconsistent rookie Glenn Abbott. The A's would have to cope with Texas right-hander Jim Bibby, who had given them so much trouble over the past two seasons.

The two losses left Charlie Finley in a borderline panic mode. The owner called Dark, ordering him to re-institute the rotating second base strategy that Finley had imposed on Dick Williams during the 1972 season. Finley told Dark to start Ted Kubiak at second base, pinch-hit for him, and replace him with another second baseman, either Dal Maxvill or Dick Green. Under the plan, Dark would continue to pinch-hit for his second baseman as long as the A's needed to score runs.

The Rangers struck early against Abbott. Cesar Tovar led off with a single, advanced to second on Lenny Randle's bunt and scored on Mike Hargrove's two-out single. As Dark pondered how long to stay with Abbott, the A's responded with the tying run in the second, thanks to Billy North's two-out RBI single. In the third inning, Bibby walked Reggie Jackson and coughed up a two-run home run to Sal Bando. The captain's blast gave the A's a 3-1 lead.

Bando's next at-bat produced a few bad feelings between the two teams, whose rivalry had grown since the Rangers had replaced the more even-tempered Whitey Herzog with the highly combustible Billy Martin. In the fifth inning, Bando hit an infield grounder against Steve Foucault and ran hard to first base. As he crossed the bag, Bando landed on the foot of first baseman Mike Hargrove. Having recorded the out, Hargrove began yelling at Bando for what he considered an intentional spiking. The two men exchanged shoves and both dugouts emptied. Fortunately, most of the players concentrated on breaking up the fight between Bando and Hargrove rather than initiating their own skirmishes. Players returned to their dugouts, but the on-field display proved to all that these two teams didn't like each other.

With a 3-1 lead and the game of critical importance, Dark pulled Abbott with one out in the fifth. Instead of calling on long relievers Bill Parsons or Paul Lindblad, Dark summoned Rollie Fingers. The troubled right-hander pitched four and two-thirds brilliant innings, held the Rangers scoreless and picked up his ninth win. A 4-1 Oakland victory gave the A's a comfortable five-game lead in the West, with only two weeks remaining. In much the same way that they had done against the second-place White Sox in 1972, the A's had pushed away the Rangers at the last possible moment.

Just as Finley had ordered, Dark had started Ted Kubiak at second base, only to replace him with pinch-hitter Jim Holt. Dal Maxvill then took a turn in the field before being lifted for Angel Mangual. Dick Green entered the game and remained at second for the rest of the game. With the A's leading 3-1, and then 4-1, Dark had decided to keep his most experienced defensive second baseman in the field instead of taking chances with a journeyman like John Donaldson or rookies like Phil Garner and Manny Trillo.

The A's players didn't like the reincarnation of the Ferris wheel at second base but they realized the importance of salvaging one game against the Rangers. Perhaps too relaxed after the win, the A's dropped three of their next four. Yet, the Rangers also lost three of four, failing to capitalize on Oakland's mediocre play.

On September 26, the A's edged the Twins, 2-1, while the Rangers conceded both ends of a doubleheader to the White Sox. The day's results clinched at least a tie in the American League West divisional race. Catfish Hunter didn't walk a batter and allowed a mere seven hits in notching his career-high 25th win of the season. Yet, Hunter's pregame gesture ranked as even more impressive than his latest clutch pitching performance.

When he arrived at the Oakland Coliseum, Hunter presented a greeting card to backup infielder John Donaldson, who would officially complete his fourth year of service time upon completion of the game that evening. The card, signed by the Hunter family, read as follows: "From the four of us for your fourth."[42] Donaldson, now eligible for a full baseball pension, thanked Hunter for the card. "That shows what kind of class Hunter has,"[43] Donaldson told reporters. The national media had so often concentrated their reportage on dissension and conflict in the Oakland clubhouse. The exchange between Donaldson and Hunter,

which exemplified some of the camaraderie felt between Oakland players, received very little attention outside of the Bay Area.

The next day, the A's lost to Chicago, but ended up clinching their
fourth consecutive division title when the Rangers fell to the Royals.
Judging by the tepid celebration in the Oakland clubhouse, an unin-
formed observer would have had a difficult time recognizing that the A's
had won the American League West. For the first time in four seasons,
the A's had lost their game on the day of the clinching. The team had
played listless baseball for most of September, winning one, losing one,
winning two, losing two. Players like Billy North criticized the A's for
their repeated failures at playing fundamental baseball. Opposing scouts
offered a similar critique of the defending world champions. Alvin Dark
insisted that Oakland's problems resided in the area of run production,
not any poor execution of fundamentals.

Although the A's would not play another important game until the
playoffs, they could not escape another bit of controversy in playing out
the string. Dark pulled 19-game winner Ken Holtzman from his final
start, preferring to rest him before the Championship Series. As a result, Dark denied Holtzman his last chance at winning 20 games. The
move did not sit well with Holtzman, who did his best to control his
anger. "I plan to retire, anyhow,"[44] Holtzman said with resignation. Fortunately for the A's, Holtzman did not mean it.

On September 30, two days before the end of the regular season,
Charlie Finley exacted revenge on a local media that he felt had been
unfairly critical of him and his team. The A's informed Bay Area beat
writers that they would not be allowed on the team's charter flights
during the post-season. Finley also announced that the A's would no
longer make flight or hotel reservations for the writers. Under baseball's
standard operating procedure, teams usually booked accommodations
for local newspapers, who would then be billed for airline and hotel
expenses. The A's, at the behest of Finley, had decided to abandon that
courtesy.

Chapter Twenty-five:
A Rematch With The Birds

On October 2, the A's played their final game of the regular season. Even though the outcome of the game meant nothing to the playoff-bound A's, Alvin Dark still had one decision to make with regard to his post-season lineup. Who would start at catcher against the Baltimore Orioles in the American League Championship Series: Ray Fosse, a .196 batter during an injury-interrupted season, or Gene Tenace, the lesser of the two defensively?

Fosse had not displayed his usual mobility since returning from an injured cervical disk. While the lineup in the regular season finale contained backups like Jesus Alou, Angel Mangual, Jim Holt and Dal Maxvill, Dark decided to start Fosse behind the plate. Although Fosse went 0-for-3, he looked fluid behind the plate and threw out two potential base stealers, Morris Nettles and Denny Doyle. Fosse's performance convinced Dark to name him as the starting catcher for the playoffs, and potentially, the World Series.

For the third time in four years, the A's prepared to meet the Orioles in the American League playoffs. In 1971, the Orioles had swept the A's in three games. In 1973, the A's had rallied from a one-game deficit to post a dramatic series victory, three games to two. On paper, the 1974 Orioles featured many of the same players that they had used the previous season. Yet, the O's had won only 91 games, six fewer than in 1973. Injuries limited staff ace Jim Palmer to 26 games and a 7-12 record. After hitting over .300 as rookies, speedsters Al Bumbry and Rich Coggins had suffered under the weight of the sophomore slump. Bumbry had fallen off to .233 and Coggins to .243. Veteran infield mainstays Boog Powell and Brooks Robinson had combined to drive in only 104 runs, hardly the kind of run production expected from a team's first and third baseman.

While those numbers looked unimpressive, the Orioles entered the second season riding the momentum of recent fine play. Baltimore had won 28 of its final 34 games, including nine straight to complete the regular season. The Orioles carried that caliber of play into the first game of the Championship Series at the Coliseum. The Birds pecked at 25-game winner Catfish Hunter, scoring single runs in the first and fourth innings, before exploding for four runs in the fifth. Home runs by Brooks Robinson and Bobby Grich knocked Hunter from the game. The Cy Young candidate, who had pitched so well in September, surrendered a total of three home runs and six runs, while ending up on the short end of a 6-3 loss. Twenty-two game winner Mike Cuellar pitched eight solid innings to give the Orioles yet another Game One victory.

Rather than rely on the maddeningly inconsistent Vida Blue in the second game, Alvin Dark decided to use Ken Holtzman as his starter against Dave McNally. The two left-handers matched scoreless innings through the first three frames before the A's capitalized on an error by the usually impeccable Oriole infield. Bobby Grich dropped a foul pop-up off the bat of Sal Bando, giving the A's third baseman another swing against McNally. Two pitches later, Bando deposited a McNally pitch into the left field bleachers, giving the A's a 1-0 lead.

The A's tacked on another run in the sixth, which gave an effective Holtzman a larger margin for error. In the eighth inning, light-hitting Ray Fosse, who had hit only four home runs during the season, smacked a three-run dinger against reliever Grant Jackson. With Holtzman in command, the A's finished off the Orioles, 5-0.

The series moved to Baltimore, where Vida Blue and Jim Palmer mirrored the brilliance of Holtzman in a classic third game pitching matchup. Both pitchers had underachieved during the regular season, while Blue had never won a game in the playoffs or World Series. In Game Three, Palmer and Blue offered vintage performances. Palmer allowed four hits and Blue permitted only a pair of safeties. The game produced only one extra-base hit, a fourth inning home run by Sal Bando. Sal's blast accounted for the only scoring of the game, a 1-0 Oakland victory. For the first time in his career, Vida Blue won a game during the post-season.

One of Blue's teammates called it his finest pitching performance, better even than any of his games in 1971. "Vida pitched the best game of his career because this was a pressure game," said captain Sal Bando, "the third game of the playoffs tied at 1-1."[1] The complete game left

Alvin Dark amazed at Blue's ability to sustain velocity from start to finish. "He threw as hard for nine innings as anyone can possibly throw."[2] Except for a half-dozen curve balls, Blue threw only fastballs at the Oriole hitters.

As Blue tried to downplay the significance of his first playoff triumph, Gene Tenace tried to contain himself from strangling Alvin Dark. In the seventh inning, Tenace had drawn a one-out walk, only to be lifted for pinch-runner Herb Washington. Tenace marched into the dugout and fired his helmet into the ground. The helmet bounced and rolled — next to Dark's feet. "I wasn't trying to hit him,"[3] Tenace said, defending his intent with the helmet. A disgusted Dark picked up the helmet and hurled it onto the dirt in front of the A's dugout.

"I don't think you take one of your best defensive players out,"[4] explained Tenace, referring to the A's one-run lead at the time of his removal. When a reporter asked him if he thought Dark had unilaterally made the decision to insert Washington as a pinch-runner, Tenace pointed the finger at the owner. "It's definitely coming from Charlie," said Tenace. "He's the one who introduced the designated runner."[5]

Thus far, the playoffs had matched the pattern of the 1973 series — a Baltimore win in the first game followed by consecutive victories for the A's. In 1973, the Orioles had come back to win Game Four, pounding Blue and Rollie Fingers in the late innings. Alvin Dark hoped for a different scenario this time around, especially with his best starting pitcher on the mound.

Catfish Hunter met Mike Cuellar for the second time in the series. Unlike the first game, Hunter proved effective in the early innings, as he kept the Orioles scoreless over the first five innings. "He's the kind of pitcher that hitters are anxious to hit off,"[6] Alvin Dark had said of Hunter, whom he likened to Hall of Famer Robin Roberts and two other pitchers from an earlier era. "Howie Pollet was like that, and Preacher Roe. You think about how easy they are to hit off, but you never hit them."[7] Unfortunately for Hunter, the A's batters couldn't hit Cuellar, who no-hit them over the first four and two-thirds innings. In the fifth inning, however, Cuellar mysteriously walked four consecutive batters, including the patient Gene Tenace, whose base on balls forced in the first run of the game. The quartet of walks gave Cuellar, usually a control specialist, a total of nine for the game. Earl Weaver yanked the man known as "Crazy Horse," despite the fact that he had not yet allowed the A's a base hit.

Left-hander Ross Grimsley retired Claudell Washington to end the threat, but the A's struck again in the seventh, when Sal Bando walked and Reggie Jackson plated him with a double. Incredibly, Jackson's blow represented Oakland's only hit of the afternoon. The A's, with a two-run lead, needed only nine more outs to return to a third World Series. Hunter pitched a scoreless seventh, but allowed the first batter in the eighth inning to reach safely. Alvin Dark, who had utilized the quick hook all season long, signaled to his bullpen, where Rollie Fingers had concluded his warm-ups. With a man on first and no one out, Fingers set the Orioles aside in the eighth inning.

The A's maintained their 2-0 advantage heading to the bottom of the ninth. When Fingers retired the leadoff man, right fielder Rich Coggins, the pennant seemed inevitable. Fingers then committed a cardinal baseball sin. With the middle of the order coming up — Bobby Grich, Tommy Davis, and Boog Powell — Fingers walked Paul Blair. Grich followed with a single, pushing Blair to second. Davis, the former Athletic and the American League's best designated hitter, hit a slow grounder which the Oakland infield turned into a force play at second. With Blair at third and pinch-runner Enos Cabell at first base, Fingers needed one more out to clinch the pennant. Powell, reduced to platoon status at the age of 33, stepped in against Fingers. The lefty-hitting slugger, 0-for-7 in the playoffs, rocked a two-out single, scoring Blair with the Orioles' first run.

With the tying run now at second in the form of pinch-runner Jim Palmer, Don Baylor strode to the plate. The young left fielder, 4-for-14 in the series, wiggled his bat as he awaited the first delivery from Fingers. Baylor, pulling a major surprise, dropped his bat into bunting position but couldn't reach a slider that broke low and away from the plate. Baylor fouled off three pitches, including a very hittable fastball, eventually working the count to 2-and-2. Fingers had mixed his fastball and slider, trying to keep both pitches away from Baylor. What would Fingers throw now? Baylor might have expected Fingers to throw his trademark slider, his most effective pitch against right-handed hitters, toward the outer half of the plate. Instead, Fingers released a fastball, a pitch that he had allowed to gravitate toward the middle of the plate. Baylor swung through the fastball. The A's had succeeded the Orioles of 1969-71 as the winners of three consecutive American League Pennants.

How did the A's win, considering the persistent struggles of their most important hitters? Gene Tenace went hitless in 11 at-bats, Billy North garnered only one hit in 16 at-bats, Joe Rudi went 2-for-13, Reggie Jackson collected two hits in 12 at-bats and Campy Campaneris managed only three hits in 17 tries. Once again, the A's had won their most important games of the season with their two constants — pitching and defense, defense and pitching, in whatever order you preferred. Aside from two harmless errors committed by Dick Green in the 1-0 win in Game Three, the A's had played flawlessly in the field. Oakland's front-line pitching had been equally responsible for the three playoff wins. Although only five different pitchers made appearances in the four games, three of them did not allow any runs — Vida Blue, Ken Holtzman and reliever Blue Moon Odom. The other two — Catfish Hunter and Rollie

Fingers — had teamed up to win the clincher.

Even Alvin Dark had contributed to the Oakland cause. He had allowed Holtzman and Blue to pitch complete games, and had wisely concentrated the bulk of Oakland's innings on to the shoulders of his best pitchers. Dark had also been sparing in his use of Herb Washington, employing the pinch-running specialist in only two of the games, both Oakland wins. For one of the few times all season, several A's publicly applauded the work done by Dark. "I just wanted to win for Alvin Dark," disclosed Hunter, the winner in the clinching Game Four. "Alvin has received a lot of bad publicity and he's done a hell of a job."[8] Earlier in the season, Catfish and many of his teammates had second-guessed Dark's managerial decisions — especially his quick hooks of starting pitchers — a practice that Hunter now regretted. "Sure I got on him," Hunter admitted. "Sal (Bando) got on him, and it's bad to get on the manager. Everyone was against him, myself included. But he proved himself by winning. Believe me, it's tough to take over a championship team and win again."[9]

In retrospect, Bando says Dark struggled in his handling of the club over the first 50 to 60 games of the season, primarily due to his unfamiliarity with his players. From mid-season on through the post-season, Dark's managing improved considerably. "Once a third of the season was over," Bando says, "Alvin had a firm handle of the club and what guys can do."

Chapter Twenty-six:
The Freeway Series

A second consecutive Championship Series defeat of the Orioles landed the A's in the World Series against the surprising Los Angeles Dodgers. In the National League playoffs, the Dodgers had handled the Pirates fairly easily, winning in four games. LA's pitching, led by starters Don Sutton and Andy Messersmith, had pinned down a Pirate offense that featured a succession of hard hitters — Manny Sanguillen, Willie Stargell, Richie Zisk, and Richie Hebner.

Given the ease with which the Dodgers' pitching had retired the best of the Pirate hitters, the matchup against a weak Oakland offense did not bode well for the A's. Alvin Dark could count on his corps of Catfish Hunter, Vida Blue, Ken Holtzman and Rollie Fingers pitching well, but the manager had to wonder whether the A's would be able to score any runs against Dodger Blue. The oddsmakers must have harbored similar concerns, making the Dodgers the favorites against the two-time defending champions. Oakland's 90-win regular season and four-game playoff win over the Orioles had left much of the betting public unimpressed.

The A's had other concerns, as well. Rumors sprang up that Charlie Finley planned to move the franchise to New Orleans after the World Series, win or lose. Robert Nahas, the president of the Oakland Alameda County Coliseum, Inc., told reporters that the rumors had no merit. Nahas pointed to a document that contained incontrovertible proof — the A's lease with the Coliseum extended for another 13 seasons, through the year 1987.

Aside from the unsubstantiated discussion of a franchise move, three very real controversies struck the A's before the World Series even begun. The most minor of the events involved former Oakland infielder Mike Andrews. Still stung by Charlie Finley's shabby treatment of him one year earlier, Andrews filed a $2.5 million libel lawsuit against the owner, claiming Finley had slandered him by trying to remove from the A's roster during the 1973 World Series. The suit contended Finley had caused the former major league second baseman "severe mental anguish and emotional distress."

After the A's worked out at Dodger Stadium prior to Game One, Blue Moon Odom approached Rollie Fingers in the clubhouse. Odom made mention of Fingers' recent marital problems. "Rollie has been having trouble with his wife and a lot of guys on the team have been ribbing him about it," an anonymous teammate explained. "Real personal stuff. I guess he got fed up. About three weeks ago, he made an announcement. He'd had it with the cracks. No more. Cut it out, or he'll whip some butts."[1] Fingers' teammates had abided by Fingers' decree, until Odom decided to test the waters. Fingers threw his right fist at Odom, sending the pitcher sprawling into a shopping cart that doubled as a bat rack. Odom retaliated by ramming his head into Fingers' chest, pushing him backward into a locker. Fingers banged the back of his head against a metal hook contained inside the locker and suffered a large cut to his scalp which required five stitches. Odom emerged from the scuffle a bit more damaged than Fingers. Odom twisted his ankle, jeopardizing his availability for the start of the Series.

Fingers and Odom, good friends before the exchange of fists, quickly shook hands in an effort to put the fight behind them. Both players tried to minimize the severity of the fight and the injuries. Odom called the fight a "little thing, nothing to get excited about it," while Fingers described the incident as a "friendly scuffle."[2] Billy North hurried over to Odom's locker and entertained the pitcher with a few seconds of shadow boxing.

Alvin Dark did not hold such a humorous opinion of the latest fight involving Oakland players. "These players have been together so long — many of them all the way through the minors — that they may know each other too well," explained Dark. "There is more needling among players on this team than on any I know of. Sometimes the needling can get too serious."[3]

The largest controversy, however, involved staff ace Catfish Hunter. On October 11, the day before the start of the World Series, the *Chicago Sun-Times* reported that Hunter and his lawyer, Jerry Kapstein, had charged Charlie Finley with a breach of contract. According to the report, Hunter's two-year contract, which he had signed prior to the 1974 season, stipulated that Finley pay a $50,000 installment to the Jefferson Standard Life Insurance Company of Greensboro, North Carolina. Hunter claimed that Finley had refused to make the deferred payment, which amounted to half of the pitcher's $100,000 salary. The *Sun-Times* reported that Hunter had threatened to declare himself a free agent after the Series if Finley did not make the payment immediately.

Finley telephoned the *Sun-Times'* chief rival, the *Chicago Tribune*, in an effort to refute the story. "It's not even worth commenting on," Finley told the Tribune. "But you can be assured that we do not owe any player any money."[4] Hunter, for his part, refused public comment on the story, saying that he didn't want to distract from the team's goal of trying to win the World Series.

On October 12, the Sun-Times followed up on its original story by conducting an exclusive interview with American League president Lee MacPhail. In the follow-up, MacPhail explained that Charlie Finley had tried to make the $50,000 payment to Hunter on October 4, the day before the start of the playoffs, only to have Catfish reject the offer. MacPhail believed that Finley's recent offer of restitution weakened Hunter's case for free agency. "The fact that Mr. Finley did offer Hunter a check for the disputed $50,000 puts an entirely different light on the situation. I seriously doubt that Hunter will win his free agency."[5]

Others disagreed with MacPhail's assessment. Dick Moss, a lawyer for the Players' Association, said that Finley's last-minute offer did not make up for his initial refusals to make payment. Moss told reporters that Hunter's lawyers, back in mid-September, had informed Finley in writing of defaulted payment. Moss then quoted from the standard player's contract. "The Player may terminate this contract upon written notice to the Club, if the Club shall default in the payments to the Player provided for...and if the Club shall fail to remedy such a default within 10 days after the receipt by the Club of written notice of such default." In other words, Finley had failed to pay the deferred money within 10 days of receiving the letter from Hunter's camp; therefore, Hunter could declare himself a free agent.

Marvin Miller, the head of the Players' Association, informed Hunter that he could file for free agency beginning on September 26, 10 days after Finley had received written notice. With the A's still trying to fend off the Rangers for the Western Division title, Hunter did not want to file for free agency — at least not immediately. That same day, Hunter won his 25th game of the season. On October 4, Dick Moss sent Finley a telegram, informing him that Hunter's contract would expire the day after the A's season came to an end, be it the playoffs or the World Series. Moss' telegram made it seem fairly certain that Hunter intended to become a free agent.

Most of Catfish's teammates, and ex-teammates for that matter, couldn't blame the pitcher for wanting to leave a team owned by Finley. In an interview with Bay Area columnist Wells Twombly, Vida Blue charged Finley with racism, a claim that he had previously made in 1972. "He

treats his black players like niggers,"[6] Blue said bluntly. Cleveland Indians' catcher Dave Duncan, a former Athletic who had often sparred with
Finley, tried to offer Blue some twisted consolation. "Don't feel bad," Duncan
advised Vida. "He treats his non-black players like niggers, too."[7] Racist
or not, Finley's reputation had reached rock-bottom in the baseball world.

The resolution of the Hunter affair would have to wait until after the
final games of the season had been played. In the meantime, one Oakland
player did his best to downplay the generally turbulent image of the A's.
"We're really one big, happy family," maintained Gene Tenace. "And we
have the average family's trouble and flare-ups."[8] Tenace said that fights
between players did not signify dislike for each other. "We may fuss and
fight but we don't wind up hating each other. No cliques, nothing like
that. Sal Bando is sort of the leader of the team... If somebody needs some
advice, they'll probably go to Sal."[9]

Another player discredited the severity of the fight between Fingers
and Odom. "The fight yesterday was very mild," claimed backup infielder
Dal Maxvill, who disputed the notion that the two pitchers had tried to
punch each other. "No punches thrown, just some shoving. Rollie fell over
a basket on the floor and cut his head against the front of a locker."[10] A
reporter asked Maxvill if any other fights had taken place during the early
hours of the morning. "There have been no fights yet," Maxvill replied
wryly as the clock read 11:00 AM. "But, of course, it's still early."[11] The
visiting clubhouse attendant at Dodger Stadium, a man named Jim Muhe,
approached a few of the A's near the batting cage. "You guys haven't been
here half an hour and I already believe everything I've heard about you.
I've been around this clubhouse for 15 years and thought I'd seen everything, but in 10 minutes you showed me I hadn't."[12] Welcome to the world
of Charlie Finley and the Swingin' A's.

The A's had more tangible concerns than that of their traveling soap
opera. Injuries topped the list of worries for Alvin Dark. The fight between
Fingers and Odom had left the latter on crutches as he entered the clubhouse prior to Game One. Dark announced that Odom would spend most
of Game One in the clubhouse icing the foot. "He'll be my last resort if I
need a right-handed pitcher,"[13] Dark explained.

The status of the A's most feared power hitter ranked as an even
greater concern. The A's listed Reggie Jackson, bothered by a pulled hamstring throughout the Championship Series, as questionable for the first
game of the World Series. Unlike the playoffs, when the A's used Jackson
as a DH, Reggie would have to be able to run well enough to play the
outfield. For the second straight fall, World Series rules prohibited the
use of a designated hitter. Although Jackson categorized himself as only
85 per cent healthy, he insisted he would play in Game One.

On the afternoon of October 12, the A's and Dodgers took to the field
at Chavez Ravine, site of Dodger Stadium. Ken Holtzman, who had not
allowed a run in his one playoff start, opposed the Dodgers' Andy

Messersmith. Alvin Dark's last-second lineup included the following: Campaneris, SS; North, CF; Bando, 3B; Jackson, RF. Reggie's hamstring felt well enough for him to take his accustomed place in the cleanup spot.

After Wayne Newton performed the National Anthem as a late replacement for the ailing Sammy Davis, Jr., the A's and Dodgers made history by commencing the first all-California World Series. The A's reached Messersmith in the second inning, when Jackson led off with an opposite-field home run. In the fifth, Holtzman started another rally with a one-out double, advanced to third on a wild pitch by Messersmith and scored on a daring play called by Alvin Dark. With two strikes on Campy Campaneris, Holtzman broke from third and Campy bunted the ball precisely toward the mound, scoring the slow-footed pitcher. If Campaneris had fouled the ball off, he would have been called out on strikes and Holtzman would have been forced back to third base. If Campy had missed the pitch entirely, the Dodgers likely would have tagged Holtzman out for an inning-ending double play.

Oakland's defense, nearly impenetrable in the playoffs, made two critical errors in the bottom of the fifth. Campaneris fumbled a one-out grounder by Davey Lopes. When Bill Buckner followed with a hit-and-run single to right field, Jackson dropped the ball, allowing Lopes to score all the way from first base. Holtzman then walked Jimmy Wynn, moving Buckner into scoring position. An impatient Alvin Dark called upon Rollie Fingers to face Steve Garvey and Joe Ferguson, the Dodgers' fourth and fifth-place hitters. Fingers struck out Garvey, hit Ferguson with a pitch, and escaped further trouble by retiring Ron Cey on a fly ball to Joe Rudi in left field.

In the eighth inning, Campaneris lined a leadoff single against a tiring Messersmith. After a sacrifice bunt by Billy North, Sal Bando bounded a chopper to the left side of the infield. Third baseman Ron Cey fielded the ball cleanly, hurried his throw and fired wildly past Steve Garvey. The error allowed Campy to score, while pushing Bando to third base. Reggie Jackson lofted a fly ball to medium right-center field. Jimmy Wynn, the Dodgers' center fielder, glided over to make the catch, only to be cut off suddenly by right fielder Joe Ferguson, who possessed a much stronger throwing arm than Wynn. Ferguson caught the ball on the run and fired to the plate, on the fly. The perfect throw struck down Bando to complete the double play. "That was the best throw I've ever seen,"[14] said Wynn, who was now glad that Ferguson had charged in front of him to make the catch.

The A's took their 3-1 lead to the bottom of the ninth. Fingers retired the first two batters, Davey Lopes and Billy Buckner, with ease. Jimmy Wynn, the Dodgers' leading long ball hitter with 32 during the regular season, kept the LA cause alive with a home run to left-center field, just beyond the extended reaches of Billy North and Joe Rudi. Fingers then surrendered a line single to Steve Garvey. Having pitched four and a third innings of pressurized relief, a tiring Fingers gave the ball to Alvin Dark. Who would the manager call upon to face Joe Ferguson, a dangerous right-handed power hitter? Glenn Abbott, an unproven young right-hander making his first trip to the World Series? Not a chance. Dark called upon the team's latest center of the storm, potential free agent Catfish Hunter, who had pitched only three days earlier in the clincher against Baltimore. "The Cat" promptly struck out Ferguson, preserving a dramatic Game One victory on the road. "It was the perfect time to bring the Catfish in," said Dark, patting himself on the back. "He isn't scheduled to pitch until Tuesday (Game Three)."[15]

The A's had become accustomed to watch Hunter pitch brilliantly in the playoffs — as a starter. Now Hunter had entered a game under completely difficult circumstances and pitched effectively as a stand-in for a fatigued Rollie Fingers. Hunter had also set aside any thoughts of his potential free agency. "When I put this uniform on," Hunter warned, "I'm 100 per cent. I don't go out to lose, I go out to win. I don't care if it's a cow pasture game."[16] Other A's pitchers attested to his high level of effort. "I've never seen a man pitch with more determination," said Darold Knowles, Hunter's teammate since mid-1971. "He's a deadly professional."[17]

With Hunter slated to start the third game, the A's chose Vida Blue to pitch Game Two against Don Sutton, the Dodgers' best starter over the second half of the season and the playoffs. The curveballing right-hander, overshadowed by Andy Messersmith for much of the season, hadn't lost a game in two months. Los Angeles quickly supported Sutton by scoring a run in the second on Steve Yeager's RBI single. In the sixth inning, Steve Garvey reached on an infield single and scored on Joe Ferguson's long home run to the center field bleachers.

Sutton continued to hold the three-run lead into the eighth, when the A's loaded the bases with one out. Billy North, the fastest man on the A's, figured to score at least one run by simply hitting the ball on the ground. After all, the chances of turning a double play against North ranked low on the list of probabilities. North hit a ball on the ground all right, but in the wrong place. Dodger shortstop Bill Russell fielded North's grounder up the middle, stepped on the second base bag for one out and then threw to first. Russell's throw sank too quickly, short-hopping Steve Garvey. With a sweeping scoop of his glove hand, Garvey fielded the hop cleanly, completing the double play. It was the "key play of the game," assessed Sal Bando. "If he doesn't catch that ball, we have two runs and a man on second."[18]

Sutton ran into another jam in the ninth when he struck Sal Bando with an errant pitch. Reggie Jackson followed with a check-swing grounder, good for a two-base hit, down the left field line. With the tying run coming to the plate, Dodgers' skipper Walter Alston called upon his best relief pitcher, Mike Marshall, to face Joe Rudi. The A's left fielder roped a single to center, scoring both Jackson and Bando.

Marshall recorded the inning's first out by striking out Gene Tenace. Rudi, still standing on first base, noticed the presence of Herb Washington on the diamond. Much like he had done on Opening Day, Alvin Dark had decided to use his designated pinch-runner for his starting left fielder. This time, the strategy made some sense. Down 3-2 with one out and a runner on first base, the speed of Washington gave the A's a better chance of putting the tying run in scoring position via the stolen base.

The presence of Marshall on the mound, Washington pinch-running at first base, and Steve Garvey holding him on provided an intriguing triumvirate of Michigan State alumni. Both Washington and Garvey had graduated from Michigan State, while Marshall had worked there as a professor. Thinking aggressively, Washington took a big lead off first base. Marshall, a well-conditioned athlete with a quick spin move to first base, stepped off the rubber repeatedly, and then threw to first base. Washington dove back ahead of Steve Garvey's tag — safely but barely so. Marshall then tried another pickoff, twirling his body around quickly and firing to Garvey. Washington hesitated for a moment, his legs frozen, before turning back to first base. Garvey slapped the tag on Washington, who futilely dove head-first into the bag. First base umpire Doug Harvey made a decisive call — OUT!

The pickoff of Washington eliminated the A's most realistic hopes of tying the game. When Marshall struck out pinch-hitter Angel Mangual, the national media began the inevitable process of placing goat horns squarely on the head of Herb Washington. "It was a perfect set up," said Steve Garvey, explaining the pickoff of Washington. "Marshall stepped off the rubber three times and we froze Herb. The throw was on the money."[19] During spring training, Charlie Finley had boasted that Washington would prove directly responsible for at least 10 victories. In this case, he had at least indirectly contributed to a World Series loss.

As the A's waited for their plane at the Los Angeles Airport, Reggie Jackson approached Washington. "You'll bounce back," the superstar told the pinch-runner. "You made a mistake. You'll have to learn from it."[20] Alvin Dark came by next, patted Washington on the shoulder and offered him similar words of encouragement.

With an off-day scheduled between the second and third games, the A's flew upstate for the continuation of the Series in Oakland. Oakland players originally thought they had the option of attending a Monday workout at the Oakland Coliseum, but during the flight, Charlie Finley unilaterally decided to make the practice mandatory. "What do we have to work out for?" asked an irked Sal Bando. "we've played 190 games already. The day off would do us more good than the workout."[21]

An optional workout might have saved a 52-year-old sportswriter named Murray Olderman from the wrath of Reggie Jackson. During the Monday afternoon session, Vida Blue informed Jackson of Olderman's arrival on the Coliseum premises. Jackson left the batting cage and unfurled a vicious verbal attack on Olderman, shouting at him for about 10 minutes while the writer's 16-year-old son watched on. "You better not get around me," Jackson said in a threatening tone. "I want to embarrass you. You made me look like a bleep."[22]

Reggie and Vida had been angered by Olderman's feature article about Jackson which appeared in the October edition of Sport Magazine. Blue accused Olderman of quoting him in the article without ever speaking to him. Olderman later admitted that he had used second-hand quotes from Blue that had been given to him by other writers.

The cover of Sport showed Reggie wearing a military helmet and holster under a headline that read "Reggie Jackson: Blood and Guts of the Fighting A"s." Jackson had consented to the unusual pose and had allowed Olderman into his home, but didn't agree with some of the San Francisco writer's conclusions about his personality and lifestyle. In the article, Olderman alternately praised and criticized Jackson, describing him as "utterly charming or maddeningly harsh." Olderman lauded Jackson for being "glib and charming and witty and spirited," but pointed out that "he can be sullen and evasive and quarrelsome."[23] Olderman also portrayed Jackson as hypocritical, given that both a Holy Bible and a gun lay atop the television set in the right fielder's home.

The commissioner's office soon learned of Jackson's angry public display toward Olderman. Moments before Game Three, Major League Baseball's director of public relations, Joe Reichler, approached Jackson as he threw warm-up tosses to Jesus Alou. The aide to the Commissioner questioned Jackson about his threat to keep Olderman out of the Oakland clubhouse. "The Commissioner doesn't want anything like this ever to happen again," Reichler warned Jackson. "If it does, there's going to be a serious problem, a very serious problem, and I think you know what I mean by that."[24] In other words, Commissioner Bowie Kuhn might fine or even suspend Jackson for a similar outburst. Jackson nodded at Reichler, promising that he would avoid such confrontations in the future.

While many reporters applauded the commissioner's office for adopting a get-tough stance on media relations, one of the nation's most influential sports writers expressed a contrasting opinion. After the Series, New York Times writer Red Smith chided baseball officials for their reprimands of Jackson and Dodger relief pitcher Mike Marshall, a man notorious for belligerent treatment of writers and broadcasters. "Murray Olderman is a nice guy," Smith wrote in the October 20th edition of the New York Times, "but if Jackson doesn't like what he writes, he's entitled to tell him so. And there is nothing in the rules of baseball or Mike Marshall's contract that forbids him to be as bumptious a boor as he likes."[25] Smith's rather unexpected support of Marshall and Jackson struck some as rather strange and twisted but really came as no surprise, considering the legendary writer's history of criticizing management and supporting players.

With Jackson still in the lineup, the A's and Dodgers had to wait an extra 15 minutes to start the game due to national television coverage of President Gerald Ford's address to the nation in Kansas City. Prior to Game Three, the unflappable Catfish Hunter discussed the issue of nervousness with several members of the media. "A lot of guys get nervous before big games," Hunter acknowledged. "I've never been that way. I'm pitching, I just concentrate on the batter. If he hits me, the world doesn't come to an end. If I get him out, I'm still not in the Hall of Fame."[26]

Dodger manager Walter Alston might have had reason for nervousness in making his pitching selection for Game Three. Alston matched Hunter with former A's left-hander Al Downing, the choice over Doug Rau, who had pitched poorly over the final weeks of the regular season. Downing himself had won only five games during the season.

Alston's decision to switch to Downing prompted Oakland reporters to question Alvin Dark about possible lineup changes. Since the A's had faced two right-handed starters in the first two games of the Series, would Dark use a more heavily right-handed lineup in Game Three? Dark acknowledged that he was considering several changes, such as flip-flopping Campy Campaneris, the leadoff batter, and Billy North, the second-place hitter. Another possibility involved dropping North or Campaneris to the No. 6 position while moving Joe Rudi to the second spot. "Will you check it with Finley?" one writer asked Dark about the new lineup combinations. "I talk over all possible changes with the general manager," Dark said diplomatically. "Every general manager is entitled to that respect."[27] Of course, any one remembering the Deron Johnson-Vic Davalillo switch during the first week of the season already knew the answer to the writer's question.

Downing struggled badly in the third and fourth innings. Billy North, batting out of the leadoff spot for the first time in the Series, singled and moved all the way to third on a hit-and-run groundout by Campy Campaneris. After a walk to Sal Bando, Reggie Jackson topped a high bouncer in front of the plate. Catcher Joe Ferguson, the right fielder in the first two games of the Series, bobbled the ball, allowing North to score and Jackson to reach first base safely. Joe Rudi drove in the A's second run with a ground single up the middle, past the dive of second baseman Davey Lopes. In the fourth inning, Downing walked the light-hitting Dick Green to start the inning. With Green at second and two outs, Campaneris supplied a clutch, two-out single to center field. The official scorer charged Ferguson with his second error of the game when Jimmy Wynn's throw from center field caromed past him, allowing Campy to move up to third base. "The ball never should have been thrown," Ferguson surmised. "We had no chance at home plate. If the pitcher feels there is a chance, he should be backing up the plate. He was standing on the mound."[28] Both Wynn and Downing had committed mental mistakes on the same play. Campy's hit gave the A's a 3-0 lead and knocked an ineffective Downing from the box.

Hunter pitched brilliantly until the eighth, when Davey Lopes drove a pitch to deep center field. For a moment, Lopes seemed destined for a double or triple, only to have Billy North make a terrific back-handed catch. Momentarily spared by his defense, Hunter surrendered a line-drive home run to Billy Buckner. "There were a couple of people up here from North Carolina (Hunter's home state) that wanted me to give up a home run," Hunter joked later. "They'd never seen one before."[29]

The fans also saw the last of Hunter, as Alvin Dark called upon Rollie Fingers. The A's relief ace allowed a single to his first batter, Jimmy Wynn. Fingers then faced Steve Garvey, who represented the tying run. Garvey ripped a Fingers pitch to the right side of the infield. For a moment, the Dodgers seemed destined to enjoy a first-and-third, one-out situation. Oakland second baseman Dick Green dove for the Garvey liner, made the grab, and fired to Gene Tenace at first base for an inning-ending double play.

In the ninth inning, Fingers allowed a leadoff home run to right fielder Willie Crawford. With the Oakland lead down to one run, Joe Ferguson hit a hard-hit grounder to the left side, which Campy Campaneris failed to handle. Fingers then toughened, striking out Ron Cey. Bill Russell grounded to the right side, where Dick Green scooped up the ball quickly, starting a 4-6-3 double play. Thanks in large part to the defensive play of Green, the A's had taken the lead in the Series, two games to one.

Green's game-ending double play represented the third of the night for Oakland. The deft fielding second baseman tied a World Series record through his involvement in all three twin killings. When asked about the double plays, Green expressed surprise at matching the record, then fired several shots at the condition of Oakland's home field. "When you take into account how bad the infield is in the Oakland Coliseum, making three double plays in any game, let alone a World Series, is something. We've complained about our infield for years and sometimes I wonder why we keep bothering. No one is going to do anything about it."[30] Other Oakland players agreed with Green's rating of the Coliseum playing field. Even Joe Rudi, perhaps the most reserved of the A's, had ripped the quality of the Oakland sod earlier in the season. "The field is just awful," said Rudi. "I think the Oakland Coliseum field is the worst in the American League."[31] Yet, it hadn't derailed the American League's best defensive second baseman.

Another clutch pitching exhibition by Catfish Hunter had lifted the A's to a one-game lead over the Dodgers. One reporter asked him if his contract dispute with Charlie Finley had served to distract him on the mound. "No," Hunter replied, "and I won't think about it until our season is over. Our team fights in hotels and fights in the clubhouse, we get that off our shoulders and go out and play baseball."[32]

The continuing malaise of the Oakland offense had not prevented the A's from assuming a two-games-to-one lead in the Series. "We're not getting runs the way we did the first three months of the season," moaned Alvin Dark. "This team's not been hitting since the middle of the summer."[33]

Several Dodger players had noticed the generally unimpressive way the A's had won Game Three, expressing disbelief that the A's had managed to take a lead in the Series. On two occasions, Dodger hitters had laced line drives, only to have them caught by Dick Green, who then doubled off LA's Jimmy Wynn each time. "The A's are getting away with murder," fumed Dodger catcher Joe Ferguson. "They haven't beaten us yet. We gave them the game and hit three or four line shots that they caught. They are definitely a team of opportunity."[34]

Billy Buckner, in revealing his frustration over the Series' turn of events, insulted the caliber of the A's. "We definitely have a better team," snorted Buckner. "The A's have only a couple of players who could play on our club,"[35] continued Buckner, who mentioned Reggie Jackson, Sal Bando, Joe Rudi and the pitching staff as the only ones worthy of consideration for the Dodger roster. "Other than that, I think if we played them 162 games, we'd beat them a hundred times."[36] The newspaper clipping containing Buckner's quotes soon reached the hands of Charlie Finley.

Prior to Game Four, Finley called a team meeting to inform the players of Buckner's disparaging statements. As he held up the clipping, Finley exhorted his players to prove Buckner wrong. Some of the A's did not appreciate Finley's attempt at false motivation. "I don't need no pre-game dump," said Reggie Jackson, "to rev me up."[37]

In Game Four, Alvin Dark made news by omitting Gene Tenace from his lineup. Tenace's name appeared in the original lineup, but after a meeting with Charlie Finley, Dark unveiled a revised batting order. Several reporters overheard Finley talking to his manager. "Last night you had your way," bellowed Finley, referring to the Game Three lineup changes that Dark had instituted. "Tonight I have mine."[38]

Dark didn't want to keep Tenace on the bench but still had to explain the decision to the media as if he agreed with it. Dark told reporters that he wanted to make room for another left-handed hitter, Claudell Washington, against the righty-throwing Andy Messersmith. Tenace, having just completed batting practice, received official word of the change from third base coach Bobby Winkles.

The last-minute alteration did not sit well with Tenace, the MVP of the 1972 World Series. "Finley is trying to bury me," Tenace complained. "He treats me as just another number. I want to be treated like a man." Other players sympathized with Tenace's plight. "Personally," said Sal Bando, "I think he should have been in there."[39] Tenace also criticized Alvin Dark for his failure to resist Finley's lineup changes. "I have no respect for Dark, for not backing me up," Tenace complained. "I don't see how a man can let himself be dominated that way." Tenace added his desire to play for another team in 1975. "I'd like to be traded. I could continue to play for the A's, but I don't want to."[40] Yet, Tenace didn't believe that Finley would accommodate him. "I think he would get a big kick out of seeing me rot on the bench," seethed Tenace. "He's that kind of a man."[41]

Ken Holtzman made up for the absence of Tenace's right-handed power, once again proving his surprising value at the plate when he pounded a home run to left field against Messersmith. Holtzman almost didn't complete his route around the basepaths. "I was light-headed going around," said Holtzman, unaccustomed to hitting home runs and running the bases. "I remember tripping going over first base. I forgot where it was."[42] The home run, Holtzman's second extra-base hit of the Series, gave the A's a 1-0 lead. The Dodgers vaulted right back in the top of the fourth, however, scoring a pair of runs on Bill Russell's two-out triple.

The Dodgers held their 2-1 lead until the bottom of the sixth. Billy North drew a leadoff walk and moved to second on an errant pickoff throw by Messersmith. Sal Bando blooped a single in front of right fielder Joe Ferguson, scoring North with the tying run. Walks to Reggie Jackson and Claudell Washington, sandwiched around a sacrifice bunt by Joe Rudi, loaded the bases.

The intentional walk to Washington made sense for the Dodgers, considering that the next scheduled batter, Ray Fosse, had one hit in 11 World Series at-bats. Alvin Dark decided to take a chance on his weak bench, sending the lefty-hitting Jim Holt to the place to face Messersmith. Holt, a .143 hitter for the A's after being acquired in a trade with the Twins, had failed to deliver a single hit in 24 pinch-hit at-bats.

Alston might have considered a move to the bullpen, but a switch to a left-handed pitcher would have allowed Alvin Dark to employ Jesus Alou, a much better hitter than Holt. Alston left Messersmith in and watched Holt line a single to right field. The unlikely pinch-hit scored Bando and Jackson, while advancing Claudell Washington to third. A Dick Green forceout pushed across the A's fourth run of the inning, cementing a 5-2 Oakland lead. In the ninth inning, with Ron Cey on first and one man out, Green made a diving stop of a Von Joshua ground ball near the second base bag. Green corralled the ball, tossing to Campy Campaneris to start another game-ending 4-6-3 double play. "The last play might have been the best one of the Series," claimed Dodger manager Walter Alston., who then took his praise a step further. "That double play was one of the best I've ever seen."[43] The A's were fortunate, however, considering Green's poor positioning on the play. "Our book on Joshua says he hits them up the middle," Green admitted after the game. "I was out of position when he hit it and had to hurry for it."[44] Rollie Fingers, who had noticed Green played too far toward first base, considered motioning him closer to second base. "I noticed that Dick was seven or eight steps out of position," said Fingers. "I almost motioned him to move over, but didn't."[45] In spite of the judgment errors by Green and Fingers, the A's had pulled off a highwire double play.

After the game, Charlie Finley took his turn in the game of verbal-thrashing enjoyed so much by the A's. Gene Tenace's complaints over his omission from the lineup and his insinuations about Dark and Finley did not sit well with the owner. "When I took this club," Finley calmly began in run-on sentence form, "I told my players they could grow their hair down to their belly-buttons if they wanted and wear whatever clothes they wanted, but that I am the owner of the ballclub, and Mr. Dark is the manager of the ballclub, and if they don't like the way we run it, they can pack their bags and get the hell out, right now!"[46] It was Finley at his diplomatic best.

In order to win the Series in a taut five games, the A's would have to beat Don Sutton, the Dodgers' best starting pitcher. Campy Campaneris led off the first with a single and Billy North followed with a forceout grounder. North promptly stole second, and when Steve Yeager's throw caromed into center field, the Oakland center fielder popped up from the bag and raced to third. Sal Bando plated North with a sacrifice fly to left field.

In the second inning, Ray Fosse, with only one hit in the Series, lined a Sutton fastball into the left field bleachers. With Vida Blue pitching well and shutting out the Dodgers over the first five innings, Game Five seemed well in hand.

In the sixth inning, Tom Paciorek pinch-hit for Sutton, who had settled down to shut down the A's over the last three innings. Paciorek lined a double into left-center field, splitting the placement of Claudell Washington and Billy North. Blue walked Davey Lopes, putting the tying runs on base with no one out. Rather than play for the big inning, Walter Alston instructed Billy Buckner to lay down a sacrifice bunt. With runners on second and third, Jimmy Wynn flied out to left field, scoring Paciorek. Steve Garvey followed with a two-out ground single between Sal Bando and Campy Campaneris to score Lopes with the tying run.

Mike Marshall relieved Sutton and pitched a scoreless sixth inning. After the Dodgers failed to score in the top of the seventh, several fans at the Oakland Coliseum tossed debris onto the field. With objects like Frisbees, apples, beer cans and whiskey bottles falling all around him, Dodger left fielder Billy Buckner complained to left field umpire Doug Harvey. The umpires decided to halt play until the fans had ceased the latest round of garbage-tossing, allowing the grounds crew to clear the outfield. The unruly behavior resulted in a delay of six minutes before the A's could come to bat.

Rather than use the unexpected down time to throw warm-up tosses, Mike Marshall elected to join the umpires and players in conversation. Marshall then threw his first pitch to Joe Rudi, the A's leadoff batter in the seventh. Normally a strong opposite-field hitter, Rudi turned on the pitch quickly, launching it into the left field stands. The first-pitch home run gave the A's a 3-2 lead. Having noticed the Dodgers' strategy of trying to jam him with fastballs throughout the Series, Rudi anticipated a similar pitch from Marshall. "I hit an inside fastball, belt-high," Rudi said later. "Believe it or not, I was looking for it."[47] "When they had the mess in the outfield and he didn't take any warm-ups, I thought he might try to sneak one by me."[48] Marshall's strategy backfired, leading several writers to question his decision to forego warm-up tosses during the unusually long delay. After the game, the media asked Marshall if he regretted his decision not to warm up. "I only answer questions I'm interested in," Marshall responded rudely. One interrogator followed up by asking Marshall what kind of pitch he threw to Rudi. "When I don't answer a question," Marshall said after pausing for a moment, "it means I don't hear it."[49]

Alvin Dark made several defensive changes as the A's took the field in the top of the eighth inning. Gene Tenace, who hadn't started the game, moved in to play first base, with Joe Rudi retreating to his more accustomed left field position. Rollie Fingers relieved Blue Moon Odom, the successor to Vida Blue, who was still hoping for his first win in World Series play.

Billy Buckner led off with a line single to right-center field, which Billy North misplayed badly. The ball rolled to the wall, allowing Buckner to run to second. As North and Reggie Jackson scurried to retrieve the ball near the wall, Buckner rounded the bag at second and continued running to third. Jackson, the owner of a much stronger throwing arm than North, picked up the ball and fired to Dick Green, who made an on-line relay throw to Sal Bando at third base. Bando, the recipient of the perfect relay throw, applied the tag to a sliding Buckner for the first out of the inning. Instead of having the tying run at second with no one out, Buckner's base-running gaffe had demoralized the Dodger offense. Fingers then retired Steve Garvey and Joe Ferguson on routine fly balls.

"I saw them still chasing the ball and figured I had a good chance of going to third," Buckner said, attempting to defend his overly aggressive baserunning. "It took two perfect throws to get me."[50] Perfect throws aside, Buckner had committed a costly fundamental error in allowing himself to be retired at third base as the inning's first out.

The mistake brought the A's within one inning of their third straight world championship. Ron Cey, Bill Russell and Steve Yeager, the sixth, seventh and eighth hitters, represented the last three scheduled Dodger threats against Fingers in the ninth. Cey launched a fly ball deep to right field, pushing Reggie Jackson to the warning track. The 1973 Most Valuable Player backtracked and reached up for the first out. Willie Crawford, batting for Bill Russell, lofted a high pop-up behind second base. Dick Green, the A's best defensive player throughout the five games of the Series, called off Campy Campaneris and made the catch. Two outs. Walter Alston called upon Von Joshua, 0-for-3 in the Series, to pinch-hit for Yeager. Joshua reached for the Fingers delivery, tapping it softly back to the mound. Fingers snared the one-bouncer, crow-hopped two steps toward first base and fired to Gene Tenace. With that out, the A's joined baseball's most famous franchise, the New York Yankees, as the only team to claim at least three consecutive world championships. The Yankees had first turned the trick by winning four in a row (1936 to 1939) and had then bettered the mark by winning five straight championships (1949 to 1953). Other storied teams like the St. Louis Cardinals, Brooklyn Dodgers, New York Giants and Oakland's predecessor, the Philadelphia Athletics, had all enjoyed success over a long stretch of years, but none had won back-to-back-to-back World Series titles.

Red and green fireworks, set off at the moment that Rollie Fingers recorded the final out, filled the sky above the Oakland Coliseum. Hundreds of fans, mostly younger ones in their teens and twenties, streamed onto the field in a search for souvenirs. Forced to dodge the oncoming admirers, Oakland players raced to the dugout, which provided access to the victorious clubhouse celebration.

Oakland players and staff engaged in a frenetic but brief post-game party that lasted fewer than 40 minutes. Reggie Jackson good-naturedly poured champagne on the head of Bowie Kuhn, the commissioner who had indirectly warned the A's right fielder about his behavior toward the media just a few days earlier. Jackson also sprayed a combination of champagne and shaving cream on broadcaster Joe Garagiola, who had hosted the World Series pre-game shows for NBC. "We wait for the door to open," explained Reggie, "and when it does, we go through."[51] Relief pitcher Darold Knowles, a forgotten man in the '74 World Series after appearing in every Series game the year before, climbed atop his locker and poured wine and champagne on any teammates within reach.

Questions remained. Who would *Sport* magazine choose as its World Series MVP? In 1973, the magazine had made the controversial selection of Reggie Jackson over Campy Campaneris, who many sports writers had favored. Some of the attending media promoted Dick Green as the 1974 choice, based on his spectacular fielding in each of the five Series games. Green's defensive work had highlighted Oakland's defensive superiority over the Dodgers. "Fielding was the main difference between the teams,"[52] acknowledged Dodger manager Walter Alston. Yet, sportswriters obsessed with offensive numbers could not help but notice Green's paltry hitting. Green had not managed a single hit during 13 World Series at-bats. No Series MVP, outside of pitchers, had ever gone hitless for an entire Fall Classic.

Not surprisingly, *Sport* settled on a more conventional MVP selection: relief pitcher Rollie Fingers. Fingers saved two games, won one and held Dodger hitters to only two runs over nine and a third innings. But Sport did give Green heavy consideration. The Oakland second baseman finished a close second in the voting. Furthermore, the New York Baseball Writers named Green the winner of their World Series MVP award — the Babe Ruth Award. The New York Writers had never before handed an

MVP to a player who had endured a hitless Series. Green's defensive play
had been that good.

Green's fielding had contributed directly to three of the four A's victories. He had taken part in six double plays, tying a record for the most
double plays in a five-game World Series. As a younger player, Green had
been influenced by another World Series hero, New York Yankee second
baseman Bobby Richardson. When Green first entered the American
League in 1963, he considered Richardson the American League's best
defensive second baseman. Green sought advice from Richardson and
patterned his style of play after the Yankee veteran.

Throughout much of his career, Green had played second base with
a workmanlike grit that left him overlooked among writers and fans. "Dick

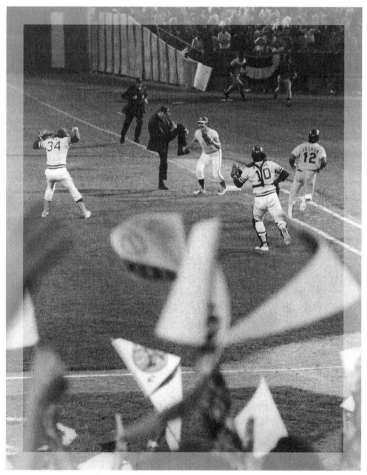

Dynasty complete. Rollie Fingers retires pinch-hitter Von
Joshua to end the 1974 World Series. As Ray Fosse looks on,
Gene Tenace registers the putout at first base.

Green was what we called a 'two outs in the ninth inning' player," says Jack Aker. "He was a guy that we wanted the ball hit to with two outs in the ninth inning when we were trying to hold the lead. He was not flashy, but any ball — routine balls that were hit to him — we always counted on being gobbled up." In the World Series, Green played the position with a more discernible flair that nearly matched his stylish clothing. "The best dresser on the team,"[53] Reggie Jackson once said. And perhaps the best defensive player on the team. Green's Richardson-like fielding in the World Series left such an impression that *Sport Magazine* writer Stanley Frank included him in an updated version of the famed baseball poem, Tinker to Evers to Chance.

> Enshrined in baseball's myth and romance
> Is Chicago's Tinker to
> Evers to Chance
> But that DP combo was never the menace
> Of the A's Campaneris to Green to Tenace[54]

While many of the A's happily shouted obscenities during the clubhouse celebration, manager Alvin Dark, not given to verbal profanity, provided a religious backdrop to the proceedings. "A lot of people won't understand this," Dark said in his first post-game interview, "but glory be to God."[55] One reporter followed up Dark's declaration with a more secular line of questioning. Would Alvin return to manage the A's in 1975? Dark replied by thanking Charlie Finley for allowing him to return to baseball and said that he would discuss his future with the owner at a later date.

Finley spent much of his time in the clubhouse directing players to a podium, where they would be interviewed by NBC on live television. A reporter asked Finley if he intended to bring Dark back for another season, given the friction between him, the owner and the players. "I will have to sit down and talk about next year with him," Finley answered in his usually cryptic, side-stepping way. "He did a real good job. He's a fine gentleman. We were very happy to have him."[56]

As the celebration continued, the media questioned the status of other Oakland personnel in the room. Several reporters surrounded Gene Tenace, who only four days earlier had asked to be traded. "There's no reason for me to leave this club," said Tenace, turning away his previous desire. Did Tenace expect to be traded? "No, I don't think they'll trade me. Claudell Washington is a hell of a ballplayer and he's got to play in the outfield, so Joe Rudi's got to play first base and you keep Fosse at catcher."[57] Under that scenario, Tenace would be left without a position, or at best, as a platoon player. "If that happens," Tenace continued, "they're going to platoon me. (Then) I've got to ask them to trade me."[58] The interview with Tenace left reporters thoroughly confused. In other words, Tenace wanted to stay and didn't think he would traded, but he felt the A's might platoon him, and if they did, then he preferred to be traded. Huh?

Few championship teams had so many lingering questions hanging over their immediate future. Would Tenace return? Would Alvin Dark resign, be fired, or brought back for another season of torture under Charlie Finley? Would Catfish Hunter, as had been reported prior to the Series, pursue free agency as a result of a contractual mistake by the owner?

Finley and Dark answered one of the questions quickly. One day after the World Series victory, Finley publicly announced his desire to have Dark return. Rather than accept the one-year deal immediately, Dark contemplated the offer for one night. Dark then agreed to return. The new contract contained an increase in pay, and offered Dark a bit more security than his 1974 deal. Under terms of the old contract, Finley could have fired Dark at any time and would not have been liable to pay his manager for the balance of the season.

The new contract still seemed like a small reward for leading a team to its third consecutive title. Although Dark had made many mistakes during the regular season, he had managed the playoffs and World Series with conviction, precision and the proper extent of aggressiveness. Dark had led the A's to the title with a weaker bench and a thinner bullpen than either of the championship teams managed by Dick Williams.

In rewarding Dark with a new contract, Finley couldn't resist taking another shot at Williams. The owner pointed out that the A's had beaten the Orioles in four games and the Dodgers in five, while Williams' teams had required the full five games to win the Championship Series and the full seven games to claim the World Series in each of the previous two seasons. Only Finley would nit-pick about the number of games it took his team to win the championship.

The status of Gene Tenace remained in doubt, especially after Finley continued his nearly annual off-season tradition of trading with the Cubs. On October 23, less than a week after winning the World Series, Finley sent three players — second baseman Manny Trillo and extraneous relievers Darold Knowles and Bob Locker — to Chicago for future Hall of Famer Billy Williams. "We feel he will be the finest designated hitter in the American League," boasted Finley. "He hits with authority and consistency."[59] While many Cub followers mourned the loss of one of their longtime stalwarts, Oakland fans — and players — reacted with favor to the trade. "This is not just some guy you pick up," said Reggie Jackson. "This is a Hall of Famer."[60]

As a ten-and-five player, Williams had the right to reject any trade attempt by the Cubs. Chicago management provided Williams with a list of six teams, five of which the lefty slugger rejected. Williams agreed to report to Oakland for two reasons: the A's gave him a stronger chance of playing in the post-season than the Cubs, and Charlie Finley agreed to give him a two-year contract worth $300,000. The rebuilding Cubs had indicated that they would only offer a one-year deal.

The A's had surrendered considerable talent to acquire Williams.

Although Locker had missed the entire season after elbow surgery and Knowles had pitched poorly for Alvin Dark, the willingness to include Trillo represented a greater risk. Trillo had struggled in brief trials as a major league hitter but his soft hands and limitless range made him the heir-apparent to Dick Green at second base. What would the A's do if Green went ahead with his latest retirement threat and left the game for good? The A's had already waived journeyman John Donaldson, now that he had reached his four-year pension, and would soon part ways with Dal Maxvill, whose large salary made him too expensive for Finley's shrinking budgetary tastes.

The addition of Williams filled a major need for the A's — a left-handed power hitter to protect Reggie Jackson in a batting order top-heavy with right-handed hitters. The 1972 National League batting champion possessed a lifetime batting average of .296. Although he had slumped in 1974, his .280 average and 16 home runs indicated he had ample productivity remaining in his slowing bat.

Aside from his sweet left-handed swing, Finley also liked Williams' reputation as an easygoing, likable person. "He's not a pop-off," Finley said proudly while using one of his pet phrases. "I've been watching him six and a half years and he's a team player."[61] Billy North had already attested to Williams' strong influence. As a young player with the Cubs, North had found Williams a willing helper. "Williams taught me how to play baseball," North said of his time in Chicago. "He's the best hitter there is. More important than that, he's a great human being. Pro isn't the word. He's a man — at his job and at living... Billy Williams is the man who's been more help to me than anybody."[62]

After praising Williams' quiet, professional nature, Charlie Finley delivered a not-so-subtle message to his outspoken players — principally Gene Tenace — who had complained about playing time in the past. "There seems to be players who think they can manage this club better than Alvin Dark," Finley exclaimed, perhaps forgetting that he himself felt he could manage better than Dark. "Those who think they're smart enough should come to me, put in an application and relate to me the reasons they should be managing."[63] Finley continued his diatribe against the team's most vocal complainers. "What this team needs is more talent and less pop-offs,"[64] sounded Finley, who promised to make more trades before the start of the 1975 season.

The trade for Williams also created a glut of first baseman, left fielders and designated hitters. With Williams penciled in as the DH, Alvin Dark would have to play Claudell Washington regularly in the field. Left field seemed like the obvious destination, with Joe Rudi moving to first base. Since the A's preferred the defensively superior Ray Fosse at catcher, the Williams deal left Tenace without a regular position, at least on the surface. The Oakland media circulated rumors that the A's would soon trade Tenace, perhaps in a deal for a second baseman.

The proposed shifting of Joe Rudi to first base made no sense. Rudi, who had just won his first Gold Glove award, ranked as the American League's best defensive left fielder. "It took me eight years to win a Gold Glove as an outfielder," Rudi said half-sarcastically, subtly expressing his displeasure with the possible position change. "Now they move me to a new position."[65]

Finley and Dark seemed too willing to tinker with Rudi, who had just completed his finest season. Rudi finished second to the Rangers' Jeff Burroughs in the American League's MVP vote, just ahead of more publicized teammates Sal Bando and Reggie Jackson, who placed third and fourth respectively. Rudi earned five and a half first place votes, while Burroughs picked up 10 first-place tallies. Several Oakland players wondered aloud how Burroughs, who had tailed off badly in September for the second-place Rangers, could win the award over a member of the first place A's. While Rudi conceded that Burroughs had enjoyed the better season, Bando suggested that the writers vote for two separate awards — the Most Valuable Player, and the Most Outstanding Player. Under such a system, the writers could have recognized Burroughs for compiling the best set of statistics while also rewarding a player like Rudi, Bando or Jackson for helping his team to the pennant.

In the meantime, Charlie Finley had promised to make more trades. On the same day that the A's added Billy Williams, Finley reacquired left-handed hitting first baseman Pat Bourque from the Twins. The interest in Bourque, a mediocre hitter and fielder, was mystifying enough. The talent that Finley sent to Minnesota to recover Bourque made the deal rather appalling from Oakland's perspective. Finley packaged two minor league prospects, outfielder Dan Ford and pitcher Dennis Myers, to the Twins for Bourque. Ford, perhaps the best outfield prospect in the Oakland system, would become a fine player for the Twins, Angels, and Orioles during an 11-year career. The dispatching of Ford would rank as one of Finley's worst trades.

Chapter Twenty-seven:
The Kingdom Begins To Crumble

Making trades made Finley happy; a decision by the Major League Baseball Players' Association had not. On October 17, only moments after the A's had defeated the Dodgers in the World Series, the Association had filed the first of two grievances on behalf of Catfish Hunter. The first grievance cited the American and National Leagues, and Commissioner Bowie Kuhn, for failing to recognize Hunter's free agency. The following day, the Association filed a grievance specifically against Finley, claiming the owner had violated Hunter's contract by not making the appropriate insurance payment of $50,000 during the 1974 season. Finley called his continuing disagreement with Hunter a mere technicality, but the pitcher and his agent suspected that they had caught the owner making a critical mistake.

On November 19, Finley and the Players' Association made their cases to arbitrator Peter Seitz. As the neutral member of the arbitration panel, Seitz would cast the decisive vote on Hunter's contract status in December after studying the contrasting arguments over the next few weeks. Hunter initially indicated that he wanted to return to Oakland under a long-term contract, even if Seitz awarded him free agency. Hunter said he preferred playing for a team in a city that he had become comfortable with. The pitcher later altered his stance. "If I become a free agent," Hunter said, sounding a warning to his owner, "I know I won't play for the A's. I don't think Finley appreciates what I've done for the A's."[1]

The two sides waited for Seitz's decision, which would be announced publicly on December 13. Seitz unveiled his bombshell ruling to Finley and Marvin Miller, the head of the Players' Association. Seitz instructed Finley to pay Hunter the $50,000 in question, at a rate of six per cent interest. In addition, Seitz announced that Hunter would become a free agent — immediately. For the first time in major league history, a player had become a full-fledged free agent without having been released by his previous team.

Seitz's decision shocked Finley, most of the other major league owners and American League president Lee MacPhail, while vindicat-

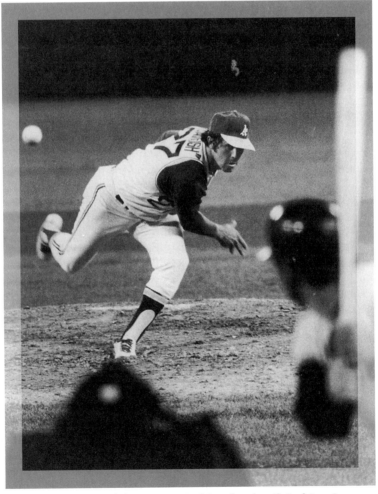

Hall of Famer Catfish Hunter pitching for the A's in his prime, well before a contractual violation called his Oakland career into question.

ing Hunter, his agent and the Players' Association. "I think it was fair and just, and I knew we told the truth," said a satisfied Hunter. "I had the feeling all the time it was going to come out way."[2] In theory, the ruling made him free to negotiate with any of the 24 major league teams, including the A's, with no compensation due Oakland should he sign with another club. Under the Seitz decision, Finley would not be allowed to match any offers made to Hunter. The independent arbitrator had done the unprecedented — making a player a free agent, with no strings attached. When a reporter asked him what he might not say to Finley, the pitcher responded with a smile, "I would say, 'Many thanks.'"[3]

Based upon Hunter's earlier remarks and the acrimonious negotiating style of Finley, Oakland players figured they had lost one of their most respected teammates, the team's best starting pitcher, and the 1974 American League Cy Young Award winner. Although Hunter refused to rule out the A's, his friends knew he had little interest in returning to Oakland, not with the opportunity to sign with large-market clubs in New York or Chicago, or free-spending teams in San Diego or Montreal, both of whom craved a marquee talent like Catfish.

The potential loss of Hunter did not please his former Oakland teammates, especially his catchers, who loved his easygoing nature and his willingness to defer to their knowledge in calling games. "When I went over to Oakland in '73," Ray Fosse revealed, "Catfish Hunter never shook me off. I asked him why and he told me, 'It's your job to know the hitters'"[4] Catchers like Fosse, Dave Duncan and Larry Haney appreciated the authority that a respected pitcher like Hunter bestowed on them.

Other Oakland players sounded off on the impending departure of their pitching leader. "With Catfish, we were world champions," declared Reggie Jackson. "Without him, we have to struggle to win the division."[5] Jackson had previously suggested that he himself might have to be traded to another team for a pitcher, someone comparable to Hunter. "If they traded Hank Aaron, Willie Mays and Babe Ruth, they can trade Reggie Jackson," the Oakland right fielder told the *San Jose Mercury News* only hours before Hunter's arbitration decision. "I expect to be traded in three weeks."[6]

Reporters quickly circulated a series of trade rumors. The A's asked the Phillies for half of their starting infield — Mike Schmidt and Dave Cash — in exchange for Jackson. The Phillies rejected the proposal. The Dodgers discussed the possibility of trading star first baseman Steve Garvey and utilityman Lee Lacy, or Don Sutton and Lacy. Another rumor indicated the Indians might offer starting pitcher Gaylord Perry and second baseman Jack Brohamer. The most frequently mentioned rumors involved the Orioles. Charlie Finley asked for Bobby Grich and one of two players, either outfielder Don Baylor or pitcher Ross Grimsley.

Yet, Finley was not ready to give up Jackson, or give up the notion of keeping Hunter. Nor was Bowie Kuhn. Finley announced that he would file a lawsuit against any team attempting to sign Hunter. Finley sought a temporary injunction to prevent Hunter from being courted by other teams but a Superior Court judge in Alameda County turned down his request. Finley then announced that he would appeal the arbitration panel's decision on the grounds that it had exceeded its authority in making Hunter a free agent. In the meantime, Kuhn advised the 23 other major league teams to refrain from negotiations with Hunter. The commissioner's directive angered Marvin Miller and Hunter's team of four country lawyers, headed up by 68-year-old J. Carlton Cherry.

A few days later, Kuhn reversed field and gave all teams permission to negotiate with Hunter. Within three hours of the commissioner's change of policy, 12 teams contacted Cherry's office in Ahoskie, North Carolina, in pursuit of Catfish Hunter, the game's first true free agent. As Christmas passed and New Year's neared, practically every major league team had called to make an opening offer. Both New York teams made it clear they wanted Catfish, while teams in smaller markets warned the small-town Hunter about the perils of playing in a large city. Several teams tried to use their own players and coaches — those who were friends of Catfish — to persuade Hunter to sign with them. The Brewers told Mike Hegan, a former Athletic, to meet with Hunter in an effort to lure him to the land of bratwurst. The Indians sent star pitcher Gaylord Perry, Hunter's frequent hunting companion during the offseason. The Padres dispatched a party of two — manager John McNamara and "executive" coach Bill Posedel, both former Oakland employees — to meet with their one-time pitching hand. In total, 48 baseball representatives descended on the small tobacco-farming burgh of Ahoskie, which had suddenly become the center of the baseball universe.

Hunter said he would consider proposals from any major league team. "I'll take the best offer,"[7] said Hunter. Catfish wanted the total package, taking into account such factors as salary, endorsement and investment possibilities, the stability of ownership, and the quality of the team. Hunter eventually narrowed his choices to eight teams, a group that surprisingly included the A's. Hunter's lawyers had heard that Charlie Finley might sell the team. In that case, Hunter might be interested in a return to Oakland.

Despite recent rumors of a sale of the A's to a group headed up by former Giants' manager Herman Franks, Finley was not about to sell the A's. Hunter thus eliminated the A's from all consideration and reduced his list of potential teams to five: the Braves, Indians, Padres, Royals and Yankees.

On New Year's Eve, the New York Yankees concluded the largest bidding war in baseball history. Needing a starter to replace the soon-to-be retired Mel Stottlemyre, the Yankees signed Hunter to an unprecedented five-year contract worth a record $3.75 million. The decision surprised some, given Hunter's previous comments about New York. In 1971, Hunter had expressed trepidation about leaving his hotel room during Oakland's stays in New York City. "New York still scares me to death,"[8] Catfish had told *Sport* magazine.

Three years later, a more mature Hunter had changed his mind. Even though teams like the Padres had made better financial offers, the endorsement opportunities of New York and his relationship with Yankee director of scouting Clyde Kluttz, the man who had originally signed him for the Kansas City A's in 1964, had swung him in the direction of New York. "He never lied to me," Hunter said of Kluttz. "He's my friend. That's why I signed with the A's, and that's why I signed with the Yankees."[9] Kluttz convinced him that New York was not only livable, but would provide him with the recognition that he could never receive in San Diego. Former teammates Curt Blefary and Mike Hegan suggested he could live in suburban areas around New York, such as northern New Jersey, which had no state income tax. The Yankees thus won out over 22 other major league teams, each of whom had placed bids on the 1974 Cy Young Award winner. Only the San Francisco Giants had refused to make Hunter an offer.

Although Hunter had developed close relationships with several of his A's teammates and had come to like the Oakland community, he expressed relief over his escape from Charlie Finley's clutches. Catfish had grown uncomfortable playing for a man who too often treated his players like possessions. In 1965, Finley had instructed Hunter to pose for an embarrassing publicity photo by sitting in the lap of venerable pitcher Satchel Paige, whom the A's had signed in an attention-getting stunt. Finley's subsequent badgering of Hunter to repay a $150,000 loan sooner than anticipated had also bothered him. "I'd felt like I just got out of prison," Hunter told *Sport* magazine of his feelings upon leaving the A's, "even if I did regret how the other players might feel about my leaving the club."[10]

The needless loss of Hunter resulted in the retirement of another player. Thirty-three-year-old Dick Green called it quits — again — saying that he did not want to return to a team that couldn't return to the World Series. "I'm just not coming back," Green declared. "Catfish is the best pitcher in baseball and we won't win without him."[11] Although Green had retired each of the past three off-seasons only to return in spring training, the veteran second baseman said he meant it this time.

The retirement of Green left the A's with only 31 players on their 40-man roster. Coupled with the recent trade of Manny Trillo to the Cubs and the release of Dal Maxvill, Green's departure also left the A's without a natural, everyday second baseman. Alvin Dark had only two options: utility infielder Ted Kubiak and converted third baseman Phil Garner, who had hit .330 as a minor league player in 1974. Kubiak had never hit well enough to merit regular playing time, while Garner lacked the range desired of a middle infielder. Garner had also been playing winter ball at third base, not at second base.

On January 18, more changes came to the A's. Finley announced the hiring of White Sox broadcaster Bob Waller, who had worked with Harry Caray over the past two seasons. Waller had angered White Sox manager Chuck Tanner with his frequent criticisms of the team's performance. Waller, the 15th announcer employed by Finley since 1961, would replace Jon Miller and team with Oakland fixture Monte Moore in the broadcast booth. The 23-year-old Miller had teamed well with Moore but was apparently not favored by KPIX-TV, the A's flagship station in San Francisco.

The configuration of the broadcast booth ranked far behind the largest concern facing the A's in 1975. How would the A's replace the annual 20-plus wins of the departed Catfish Hunter? "I've got to hit 10 more home runs this year," said Reggie Jackson, laying out the necessary formula of success, post-Catfish. "Sal Bando will have to drive in 25 more runs. Vida Blue will have to win six more games. Billy North will have to steal 25 more bases. The Catfish is gone, and everybody is going to have to do something to make up for those 25 games he won last year."[12] The A's also needed more production from veteran starter Blue Moon Odom, who had continued the inconsistent pattern of his career by winning only one game and posting an ERA of 3.83 in 1974.

Given the lack of proven commodities after Vida Blue and Ken Holtzman in their starting rotation, the A's extended spring training invitations to two aging starters. Charlie Finley telephoned former Athletic Lew Krausse, who had been released by the Braves over the winter. Finley also contacted a well-known Bay Area star, the former ace of the rival San Francisco Giants. Finley wanted to replace Catfish Hunter with another big name — that of future Hall of Famer Juan Marichal.

The 37-year-old Marichal had given up nearly five runs per nine innings for the Red Sox, but had won five of six decisions. As a one-time star in the Bay Area and a six-time 20-game winner, Finley believed that Marichal would serve as a drawing card for the A's. Furthermore, the signing of Marichal figured to deflect some of the criticism that Finley had been leveled with since his needless contract snafu with Hunter.

Finley felt so confident that he would be able to sign Marichal that he ordered his public relations staff to include the pitcher's biography in the team's organization book. Marichal's entry in the book became a curiosity when the Dominican right-hander rejected the overtures from Finley. The future Hall of Fame right-hander decided to sign with another California team — the Dodgers — the same team the A's had defeated in the 1974 World Series.

Chapter Twenty-eight:
The Perils of Arbitration

Perhaps Juan Marichal had decided to avoid Finley at all costs after watching the majority of Oakland's veteran players take their contracts to arbitration. Finley low-balled his top stars, Sal Bando, Joe Rudi, Reggie Jackson and Ken Holtzman, so severely that each player decided to take his chances in front of an arbitrator. The owner simply refused to budge from his initial offers, which in some cases, represented pay cuts for his best players.

Bando's arbitration case became especially nasty. Finley publicly demeaned his third baseman's abilities on every level, from his inability to hit for high average to his supposedly diminishing fielding skills. Bando tried to withdraw his case from the arbitrator in an effort to avoid a confrontation and try to reach a new contract through peaceful means. "Everything he does," Bando told Dick Young of the *New York Daily News*, "there must be a battle and I'm sick of it. I think most of our men are sick of it. You get to a point where hassling every day isn't amusing anymore. I want out."[1]

Yet, Finley would not allow Bando to withdraw his case from arbitration "unless I agree that he can. And the only way I will agree is if he signs the contract I have offered him."[2] Finley proceeded to call Bando ungrateful and unappreciative before launching a final insult. "If he wishes to become the village idiot," said Finley, "let him be my guest."[3]

In the past, Finley had reserved such vicious name-calling for only his worst enemies in baseball, namely Commissioner Bowie Kuhn. While some observers of the A's laughed off Finley's "village idiot" remark, Bando admits that it did sting him. "It hurts to a degree," admits Bando, "because no one wants to be talked about like that. But I also considered the source and the circumstances." Bando realized that Finley could become particularly nasty at negotiations time, sometimes saying things that he didn't necessarily believe in a desperate effort to save money. "Charlie was like that," says Sal. "He did not set a good example."

The arbitrator ruled in Finley's favor — a salary of $100,00 instead of the $125,000 that Bando sought. Finley gloated over his victory against his newfound enemy. "I'm extremely happy about it,"[4] exulted Finley, who had just saved himself $25,000.

Finley also defeated Holtzman in arbitration. Two weeks later, the veteran left-hander hinted that he might not pitch the entire 1975 season. "If a business opportunity I have works out right and everything is conducive to leaving at mid-season," Holtzman warned, "I'd quit then." Holtzman fired another shot in the direction of his owner. "I'd like to let him go out and find another 19-game winner."[5] Holtzman had been insulted by Finley's refusal to offer him a raise at the arbitration table.

Unlike Bando and Holtzman, Ted Kubiak came to understand Finley's way of doing business during negotiating sessions and arbitration hearings. "He was difficult, and I had my troubles with him in arbitration," admits Kubiak, who had lost his arbitration case with Finley in 1974. "He'd say I didn't belong in the big leagues and that he saved my career. You know, you want to choke the guy. And then it comes out after, and this is a true story. After the arbitration, he hands me a watch and he has a gift for my wife and he says, 'Don't worry about it. It's just business. Don't believe anything I said.' You learn what the guy's tactics were."

As the A's began spring training in Mesa, Alvin Dark examined his alleged 40-man roster. In reality, the list contained far fewer names. "We're supposed to have 40 men on our roster, right?" the disgruntled Sal Bando asked rhetorically. "We have 31 — and that includes Herb Washington, a pinch-runner who isn't worth a damn; Catfish Hunter, who is gone; and Dick Green, who is retiring. That gives us 28 men to start out with. So we ask ourselves, is our owner trying to win?"[6]

Dark made several adjustments to his lineup, in an effort to compensate for the dwindling number of players and improve the team's depreciating offense. Dark told Gene Tenace, his regular first baseman in 1974, to concentrate on catching. The move relegated Ray Fosse, a sub.200 hitter in 1974, to second-string status. Dark moved Joe Rudi to first base, clearing the way for Claudell Washington to play left field. Dark also delivered a surprising message to Reggie Jackson, telling his regular right fielder to work out at first base in spring training. Jackson had never before played the position — either in the majors or minors. Furthermore, Reggie's two greatest defensive attributes, his speed and throwing arm, would be wasted playing the infield corner.

Rudi, however, felt that switching Jackson to first base made more sense. "Why don't they move Reggie?" asked Rudi, emphasizing his displeasure with his own move to the infield. "He has bad legs. He gets hurt all the time. It would be much less demanding on him at first base."[7] Rudi then suggested an even more logical possibility. "Or they could move Claudell," Rudi said, hoping that Finley and Dark might pick up the hint. "Why can't they make him a first baseman?"[8]

"Rudi's a good left fielder," countered Finley, "but Washington's speed will enable him to reach balls that Rudi couldn't reach."[9] Perhaps Finley hadn't consulted with the voters of the Gold Glove Award. "I don't care how much Rudi pops off," Finley added venomously. "He can pop off every hour on the hour if that makes him happy."[10] Finley would soon realize the error of his changes. With Rudi at first and Washington in left field, the A's would prove to be a far inferior defensive team in 1975

Dark also decided to give Phil Garner plenty of work at second base. Having failed in their bid to convince Dick Green to return, the A's announced that they had given their 1974 World Series star his uncon-

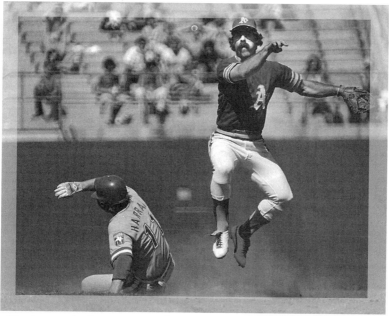

Having made the transition from third base to second, Phil Garner turns a double play against Toby Harrah and the Texas Rangers during a game in 1976.

ditional release. Charlie Finley also brought back Dal Maxvill — as a coach, not as a player — for the specific purpose of working with Garner on his transition from third to second. Garner had not played second base in five years, when he was still playing collegiately for the University of Tennessee.

The A's had hoped that Lew Krausse would provide a boost to the team's pitching depth but the one-time bonus baby pitched poorly in his early spring outings. In his first game, Krausse surrendered two home runs to a collegiate lineup, that of Arizona State, the alma mater of Reggie Jackson and Sal Bando. In his second appearance, Krausse allowed a three-run homer to Cubs' catcher George Mitterwald. Krausse's early struggles doomed him to a return to Triple-A.

The off-season loss of Catfish Hunter spurred on a desperate search for pitching, culminating in a flurry of trades and signings the final week of spring training. The A's latched onto veteran starter Roger Nelson, a one-time standout with the Royals who had been cut loose by the White Sox earlier in the spring. Finley also purchased two relievers, Horacio Piña from the Angels and Skip Lockwood from the Yankees. Both had previously spent time in the A's organization, Piña in 1973 and Lockwood when the franchise was still playing in Kansas City. Charlie Finley earmarked both hurlers for Triple-A Tucson, with the idea that they would be able to help the A's later in the season. As vested veterans, Lockwood and Piña had the option of rejecting minor league assignments, which they both did. As a result, both pitchers became free agents, with Piña opting to return to the Mexican League. Finley also tried to add veteran left-hander Claude Osteen, who had been cast off the Cardinals. One day after Alvin Dark remarked that the A's "were almost sure" of signing Osteen, the former Dodger ace signed a contract with the White Sox.

The final week of bargain basement hunting continued when the A's signed veteran infielder Billy Grabarkewitz, another former Cub. Grabarkewitz, a classic one-year wonder, had hit .289 with 17 home runs and 84 RBI's for the Dodgers in 1970. Since then Grabarkewitz hadn't batted above .226 for a full season in stints with the Dodgers, Angels, Phillies and Cubs. No longer an everyday player, the A's hoped that Grabarkewitz could fill in at third base and shortstop while providing Phil Garner with an experienced fallback at second base.

On March 28, the A's continued to make obscure pickups when they announced the acquisition of minor league outfielder Don Hopkins from the Montreal Expos. Hopkins, who had never played higher than Class-A ball, had batted .301 with 49 stolen bases for Kinston of the Carolina League in 1974. Listed as a non-prospect by most scouts, Hopkins had never hit a home run in five seasons of minor league ball. Did anyone say Allan Lewis?

Unbelievably, the A's announced that they would use Hopkins as a pinch-runner, much like their pre-existing pinch-runner, Herb Washington. Not satisfied with one pinch-running specialist, Charlie Finley felt he needed to have two-of-a-kind. "You're kidding," reacted a disbelieving Sal Bando. "Two pinch-runners? My only question is who are we going to hit when we pinch-run for the other guys."[11]

Jesus Alou was no longer available to pinch-hit. Finley decided to release Alou to make room for Hopkins, even though Jesus was in the midst of a terrific spring. In 1974, Alou had batted a respectable .268 in 220 at-bats and had led all Oakland reserves with seven pinch-hits. Alou could ask Tommy Davis how it felt to be released while enjoying one of his best springs at the plate.

The A's also released another bench player, first baseman Pat Bourque, after he refused to accept a demotion to the minor league camp. Charlie Finley now had nothing to show for the senseless off-season deal in which he had given up heralded prospect Dan Ford.

On the final day of spring training, the A's acquired relief pitcher Jim Todd, whom the Cubs had deemed expendable, in exchange for a player to be named later, which would turn out to be minor league outfielder John "Champ" Summers. At first, the A's told Todd that he would start the season on the major league roster, only to have Charlie Finley change his mind and send him to Tucson. When Alvin Dark scheduled him to pitch in an intra-squad game, Todd initially refused. Pitching coach Wes Stock advised Todd to pitch in the game, warning him that Finley might not take too kindly to such a refusal. "Finley is the kind of guy you can get off on the wrong side of,"[12] Todd said, already aware of his new owner's penchant for vindictiveness. Todd made the wise decision to pitch, giving up only one hit in an eye-opening three-inning relief stint.

The payment for Todd — Champ Summers — figured to spend another season at Triple-A before he was sent to the Cubs. The minor league veteran, who had come to bat only 24 times for the A's in 1974, appeared trapped in a logjam behind Claudell Washington, Billy North, Reggie Jackson and Joe Rudi. The trade to Chicago liberated him from his dead-end status in Oakland, giving him a chance to play a more prominent role with the Cubs. Shortly after his arrival in the Windy City, Summers took aim on what he described as a harmful atmosphere in the Oakland dugout and clubhouse. "The last time I struck out for Oakland," Summers said, "I felt like my world had dropped from under me. I came back to the bench and maybe somebody said something, but most of them looked away."[13] Summers said that his new Cubs teammates offered more support and camaraderie to struggling players, creating a more savory atmosphere for all players.

Finley's new-look A's finished the spring with a record of 7-11, despite a tidy .294 team batting average. The Oakland lineup had shown the ability to produce runs, but the departures of Catfish Hunter and

Dick Green had weakened both the pitching and defense. Angels' manager Dick Williams offered a surprising evaluation of the potential impact of the two key player losses. "I don't think losing Hunter is fatal," predicted Williams, who was expressing a minority opinion. "I think Green being gone will hurt you more than the loss of Hunter in the long run...I think he (Green) should have been the Most Valuable Player of the World Series, even though he didn't get a hit."[14]

What did the national media think of the A's chances in the post-Catfish era? A pre-season survey of baseball writers indicated that Oakland would win its fifth consecutive Western Division title but would lose in the playoffs. Who would the A's fall victim to? The New York Yankees, of course, who had added both Hunter and Bobby Bonds to their roster during the winter. Rangers' manager Billy Martin, a man once recruited by Charlie Finley to be Oakland's manager, thought even less of the A's chances than the national writers. "I thought we should be the team to beat even before Oakland lost Catfish," Martin said, boasting about a Rangers team that had surprised many by finishing second in the AL West in 1974. "Now I definitely think we should be favored."[15]

"We have a funny type of ballclub," Alvin Dark said, assessing the qualities of his A's. "We really only played for three and a half months last year. When we got ahead by nine games, we played about .500 ball in August and September. This year it will take a little more a little longer."[16]

Chapter Twenty-nine:
Still Good, But Not Great

As the season began, Charlie Finley tried to create extra incentive for his charges to win a fifth consecutive division title, a fourth straight pennant and their fourth consecutive world title. Finley offered to give all of his players diamond rings in the shape of four-leaf clovers — provided they were the only ones left standing come the final game of the World Series.

On April 8, the A's opened up the regular season at home against the White Sox. Three players not on the Opening Day roster the previous season started for the A's: Billy Williams at DH, Claudell Washington in left field and Phil Garner at second base. Vida Blue, who had not started on Opening Day since 1971, took the ball in place of the departed Hunter. The list of reserves and relief pitchers included five players — Billy Grabarkewitz, Jim Holt, Don Hopkins and Mike Norris — not with the team at the beginning of the 1974 season.

The new blood played a large role in defeating the White Sox. In the second inning, Williams doubled in his first-ever American League at-bat. Garner followed with a two-run single, giving Oakland the early jump against knuckleballer Wilbur Wood. Blue, whom Alvin Dark predicted would win 25 games during the season, pitched seven strong innings, followed by Rollie Fingers, who saved the 3-2 victory.

Gene Tenace hit a grand slam in the next game, but the A's lost when the bullpen combination of Blue Moon Odom, Paul Lindblad and

Rollie Fingers allowed four runs in the eighth and ninth inning. The following day, Mike Norris made his major league debut and stifled the White Sox with a three-hit shutout. Norris, a third-year pro who had never pitched above the Double-A level, displayed good control and a live, darting fastball. Reggie Jackson connected on a three-run homer, his first hit of the new season, helping Norris and the A's to a comfortable 9-0 win.

Alvin Dark, quoting the bible, compared Norris to the biblical figure Jeremiah. "Call unto me and I will answer thee, and show thee great and mighty things, which thee knowest not," Dark said, referring to Jeremiah 33:3. "Norris just might be the prophet sent down to save us,"[1] added Dark.

The A's compiled a pair of four-game winning streaks, helping them to a record of 12-8 in April. The record looked even more impressive considering an injury suffered by Campy Campaneris, who had strained his back on Opening Day, and the team's newfound defensive problems. The muscle strain sidelined Campy for seven of the A's early-season games.

With Campy out, the A's utilized Ted Kubiak at shortstop. Although sure-handed, Kubiak lacked the range and quickness of Campaneris in the field. In left field, Claudell Washington appeared uncertain, often letting looping line drives and short fly balls fall in front of him. As one teammate described of Washington, he "treats fly balls as if they were bombs."[2] Behind the plate, Gene Tenace struggled to throw out opposing runners, gunning down only one of the first ten players to attempt stolen bases. At first base, Joe Rudi played adequately, but nowhere near the Gold Glove level he had achieved in the outfield.

The A's also lost their most impressive young pitcher during the first month. Mike Norris had pitched brilliantly in his first two starts, allowing no earned runs and only four hits in 16 innings. In his third start, Norris faced only one batter before asking to leave because of pain in his right elbow. Although initial X-rays showed no abnormalities, doctors eventually found calcium deposits on his elbow. "If he can't pitch in two weeks," said Alvin Dark, "God will provide."[3] God would have to provide another pitcher. On April 29, Norris underwent surgery, ending his rookie season.

The season-ending injury to Norris forced the A's to dip into their farm system for pitching help. Charlie Finley and Alvin Dark called upon reliever Jim Todd, a last-second pickup in spring training. The Cubs had given up on Todd because they felt he did not throw hard enough to succeed against major league hitters. Todd notched saves in his first two appearances for the A's, before igniting a bench-clearing rhubarb in a game against the Angels. Bruce Bochte, who had homered and doubled earlier in the game, came to the plate against Todd in the sixth inning. Todd sailed a fastball up and in against Bochte, nicking him in the side of the helmet. Angels' manager Dick Williams led a surge of Angels from the dugout onto the field. Oakland and California players exchanged punches in two groups along the first base line. In one pile, Williams found himself double-teamed by Todd and backup outfielder Angel Mangual, who had not enjoyed playing for Williams in Oakland. "Everybody who work me over," said Mangual, "I get 'em sooner or later."[4]

After the umpires broke up the array of fights, Williams stood at home plate and yelled at Todd, challenging him to continue the fight. When Todd refused to leave his station on the mound, Williams called him gutless. Alvin Dark stepped from the Oakland dugout, walked toward Williams and tried to calm his managing counterpart. After the game, Charlie Finley blasted Williams for putting on a "bush show."

One day after the brawl with the Angels, the A's continued to add to their collection of pinch-runners. Finley sent minor league pitcher Howell "Buddy" Copeland to the Cubs for switch-hitting infielder-outfielder Matt "The Scat" Alexander, considered a non-prospect by most scouts. Cut from the mold of Allan Lewis and Don Hopkins, the 28-year-old Alexander had shown little ability to hit or field well, but possessed an abundance of footspeed. In order to make room for Alexander, the A's demoted another former Cub, Billy Grabarkewitz, to the minor leagues. Grabarkewitz had batted only twice in six games. Thus, Grabarkewitz joined the likes of long-gone A's Orlando Cepeda and Art Shamsky in the "Zero Club" — veteran players who failed to register a single hit during their brief, obscure careers in Oakland.

The addition of Alexander to the roster gave the A's three players who specialized in pinch-running. "The Scat" joined Hopkins and Washington on the Oakland relay team. Oakland writers, and Washington himself, wondered how long the A's could continue to carry such a large contingent of runners. The overload left Alvin Dark short of capable pinch-hitters and defensive replacements.

The A's opened up May with a dramatic 4-3 win in 12 innings. Oakland's speed blitzed the White Sox' catchers and pitchers, stealing four bases over the final five innings. "We beat you with the long ball, on defense, with speed, every way,"[5] said Billy North, who ended the game with an RBI single in the 12th.

The A's had plenty of speed on their 25-man roster, perhaps too much. One of the specialty runners would have to go. Since Matt Alexander had just arrived on the scene, he seemed safe. That left Don Hopkins and Herb Washington vulnerable to either a minor league demotion or outright unemployment. On May 5, the A's requested waivers on Washington for the purpose of giving him his unconditional release. Charlie Finley's great experiment had come to an end, an indirect result of the offseason departure by Catfish Hunter. Without Hunter, the A's faced added pressure to score more runs to support a thinner pitching staff. With a need to score more often, Dark needed to use pinch-hitters more frequently, making a non-hitter like Washington an unaffordable luxury. Alexander and Hopkins could play a position in the field and swing a bat. Washington could do neither.

A few A's expressed sympathy for Washington, citing his amiable personality and high level of intelligence. Others took a less sensitive approach. "I'd feel sorry for him if he were a player," said Sal Bando. "He got a bonus and a salary and a full World Series share, didn't he?"[6] Washington fired back at his critics among the players and the media, especially those who had questioned his credentials to serve a major league team. "The toughest adjustment was putting up with egocentric players," Washington said without naming names, "and a ton of bullbleep from front-runners on the team, front-runners in the media and front-runners among the fans...Some of the players are nice guys. Some are jerks, too."[7]

At first, the A's contemplated replacing Washington on the roster with veteran pitcher Roger Nelson, whom they had signed off the waiver wire scrap heap during spring training. Finley changed his mind, however, instead promoting backup catcher Charlie Sands from Triple-A. Like many of the Oakland players, Sands owned a World Series ring, having contributed as the third-string catcher to the 1971 Pittsburgh Pirates world championship effort. Finley had grown dissatisfied with the hitting of backup first baseman-outfielder Jim Holt and hoped that Sands might provide a better left-handed threat off the bench. As soon as Sands arrived in Oakland, Holt proceeded to smack two consecutive, game-winning pinch-hits.

On May 10, the A's reunited with Catfish Hunter for the first time since their former ace had discarded Charlie Finley's prison stripes in favor of the pinstripes preferred by the Yankees. During the warm-ups at the Oakland Coliseum, one A's fan taunted and booed Hunter for his lack of loyalty in leaving the A's. Catfish responded calmly, instructing the fan to boo Finley instead.

Hunter showed little anxiety in pitching before his former home-town fans. With his typically precise pitch-making, Hunter mastered the Oakland lineup, winning 3-0. "It's just like a trade," Sal Bando observed wryly, in preparing to throw a dagger at Finley. "Except we didn't get anything in return."[8]

The loss of Hunter had not affected attendance at the Oakland Coliseum, where larger crowds had shown up to watch the A's than during the championship season of 1974. Yet, Charlie Finley remained unsatisfied. In an interview with the San Francisco Examiner, Finley predicted that the Bay Area could not support two major league franchises over the long haul. Finley's warning spurred on another set of rumors about the A's relocating to greener pastures in any one of three cities: New Orleans, Seattle and Toronto.

Oakland's poor economy and the location of the Coliseum both worked against the A's in their quest to maximize attendance. "We might be better off having the stadium in the suburbs," suggested Sal Bando. "Baseball makes its money from the average-income people. There aren't enough of those in Oakland."[9] Even Oakland players, many of whom ranked in the above-average income bracket, stayed away from the downtown area, preferring instead to live in the suburbs.

In mid-May, the A's assembled their first five-game winning streak of the season. Billy Williams, who had scuffled in his transition to the American League and to the unfamiliar role of designated hitter, hit three home runs during the stretch. Vida Blue improved to 8-1 by pitching back-to-back wins over the Yankees, one in New York and one in Oakland.

Although the state of the A's pitching had ranked as the biggest concern in spring training, the eight-man staff succeeded in catapulting to the team to the best record in the American League through games of May 15. In addition to Blue's work anchoring the rotation, Ken Holtzman pitched brilliantly over his first nine starts, while Dave Hamilton and Glenn Abbott added solid contributions. In the bullpen, Jim Todd pitched so effectively that he temporarily took over the closer's role that had belonged to Rollie Fingers exclusively since mid-1971. Although Todd didn't throw hard, his sinking fastball, dubbed the "super sinker" by Alvin Dark, featured plenty of movement. Several opponents claimed that the movement on Todd's pitches was not created by natural forces, but rather by illegal ones. "It's a known fact he throws a greaseball,"[10] charged Tiger manager Ralph Houk. Both Todd and Dark denied the charge.

Only one member of the pitching staff had struggled through the first month and a half of the season. Blue Moon Odom, making five appearances, had given up 16 hits and nine walks in only nine innings. Dark didn't want to pitch Odom at all, but had been forced by a higher authority — namely, Charles Oscar Finley. "There were times when he ordered Dark to pitch John Odom when Odom shouldn't have been pitching," captain Sal Bando said after the season. "Odom would lose and it hurt us."[11] Odom's ERA reached such a bloated stage — 11.00 — that the A's finally asked him to accept a demotion to Triple-A, but the veteran right-hander refused the assignment. Nonetheless, Odom's career in Oakland seemed to be coming to an end. The A's signed veteran reliever Orlando Pena, recently cut by the Angels, and assigned him to Tucson. Pena and Roger Nelson gave the A's two experienced options at Triple-A should they decide to trade or release Odom.

Although the A's had played well over the first six weeks, their small lead over division rivals Kansas City and Texas left Charlie Finley concerned. Oakland's pitching had overachieved in the absence of Catfish Hunter, but Finley wanted more. On May 16, as the A's prepared to start a series in New York, Finley sent popular utility infielder Ted Kubiak to the Padres in a straight-up swap for right-hander Sonny Siebert. The 38-year-old Siebert had won three of five decisions for San Diego, but had given up over four runs per nine innings. The A's then replaced Kubiak with middle infielder Teddy Martinez, acquired in a trade with the Cardinals for minor league pitchers Mike Barlow and Steve Staniland.

With much the same flourish that he had exhibited during the whirlwind 1972 season, Finley continued his flurry of trades two days later. On May 20, the A's finally parted ways with Blue Moon Odom, sending the injury-prone pitcher and $15,000 in cash to the Cleveland Indians for two veteran starters. The deal netted the A's Jim Perry, the brother of Gaylord Perry, and former Washington Senators' ace Dick Bosman, who had frequently enjoyed success pitching against the A's.

When Odom heard about the trade, he beamed about the prospects waiting for him in Cleveland. "I always wanted to pitch for a black manager,"[12] Odom said of playing for Frank Robinson. As soon as Odom arrived in Cleveland, he would alter his gleeful stance and made a strange request of Indians' management. Figuring that he would lose about $8,000 in potential playoff and World Series money, Blue Moon asked the Indians to raise his salary by that figure. Not surprisingly, the Indians refused to give the struggling Odom any more money. Odom pouted, infuriating Frank Robinson. Indians' general manager Phil Seghi soon sent Odom packing to the Atlanta Braves.

The trade of Odom to Cleveland ended a run of service for one of the most senior A's. In grade school, a friend and high school football teammate had dubbed Odom "Blue Moon," due to the roundness of his face and his frequently somber expression. Sadness would follow Odom in his post-playing days. Unlike most of his Oakland teammates, Odom would encounter a series of struggles after his retirement: financial debt, drug use, severe depression, psychiatric treatment, and a jail term for threatening to kill his wife with a gun. In 1985, Odom hit rock-bottom when police arrested him for selling a gram of cocaine to a fellow employee at the Xerox Corporation. Odom refuted the charge of dealing drugs, but did not deny using cocaine. A jury later convicted him on two counts of selling cocaine. No longer the colorfully brash pitcher known as "Blue Moon," John Odom spent 55 days in a county jail.

Of the three players in the deal, Jim Perry was the most well-known. After winning 17 games for Cleveland in 1974, the veteran right-hander had suddenly lost six of seven decisions to start the 1975 season and seen his ERA rise above 6.00. Perry had pitched the bulk of his career with the Minnesota Twins from 1963 to 1972, and had won 44 games during the team's division-winning seasons of 1969 and '70. "A great, great seven inning pitcher," says former Minnesota writer Bob Fowler. "You know, in that era we had a pretty good bullpen with Ron Perranoski and Stan Williams. But he was a battler; he was a tough,

tough guy. Boy, he took the ball against anybody, never flinched."

Fowler says the Twins tended not to score many runs for Perry. "It seemed to me Jim Perry was always in 2-1 games," Fowler recalls. "I mean, he and Bert Blyleven. It was unbelievable. Where someone else would go out and with (Harmon) Killebrew and (Tony) Oliva, we'd score 28 runs or something. But with Jim Perry, it was always 2-1. Just a tough competitor." Throughout much of his career, Jim Perry had been overshadowed by his younger brother, Gaylord, a member of the National Baseball Hall of Fame. "(He was) very much like his brother Gaylord," Fowler says. "They came from the same stock. But not as notorious as Gaylord." Unlike Gaylord, Jim did not throw a spitball or a greaseball. The older Perry relied on a more standard repertoire of pitches, along with his inherent toughness, in his efforts to retire opposing batters.

The series of deals cost the A's a couple of prospects and some cash but greatly changed the structure of the pitching staff for the better. In addition to workhorses Vida Blue and Ken Holtzman, the A's could call upon three accomplished veteran starters in Perry, Bosman and Siebert. The trades also balanced the rotation, giving Oakland three right-handers to go with the two incumbent left-handers. The arrivals also took pressure off youngsters Dave Hamilton and Glenn Abbott. The A's sent Abbott back to the minor leagues for more seasoning, while Dark dispatched Hamilton to the bullpen, giving Oakland another left-handed pitching option in the late innings.

In the meantime, the A's hobbled through their worst stretch of the season, as they lost four straight games, including a three-game series in Boston. The A's played miserably during the set at Fenway Park, losing the first game, 10-5, in Blue Moon Odom's final appearance in an Oakland uniform. The Red Sox rocked Blue and Holtzman in the next two games, winning 7-0 and 7-3. The Boston series also provided the setting for a nasty confrontation between Sal Bando and Reggie Jackson.

Earlier in the season, Jackson had made a major baserunning error, when he broke late from first on an apparent bloop single to the outfield by Joe Rudi. Jackson was forced out at second, negating what should have been a safety for Rudi. In continuing his season-long troubles on the basepaths, Jackson made another baserunning mistake against Boston. The latest error in judgment prompted a dugout lecture from Bando, never shy to castigate teammates for poor play. Jackson, offended that Bando had criticized him within earshot of other players, shouted back at the captain. Several A's interceded, separating the two stars.

Alvin Dark, who claimed he heard racial remarks during the latest incident, called a clubhouse meeting after the game. Dark urged his players to refrain from allowing any of their disagreements to escalate into racial catcalling. Dark's speech smacked with irony, considering the accusations of racism that Orlando Cepeda and other players had leveled at him during his days in San Francisco.

Following the three losses to Boston, the A's moved on to Cleveland for a four-game series. Sonny Siebert, a one-time member of the Cleveland organization, made his Oakland debut against the Indians. Siebert threw hard in shutting out the Indians on one hit over five innings, winning a 3-0 decision over Gaylord Perry. Two days later, Jim Perry lasted only two innings in losing to his former teammates, 6-0. In the second game of the doubleheader, Dick Bosman concluded the triumvirate of pitching debuts with six and 2/3 innings of three-run baseball. Bosman, with relief assistance from the surprising Jim Todd, helped the A's to a 6-3 win, their third in four games against the Indians.

Bosman's victory initiated a five-game winning streak, helping the A's finish with a 16-10 record during the month of May, while improving their overall record to 28-18. Bosman added another win during the streak, beating the Indians for the second time in a week. As the A's headed to June, they held a slim one-game lead over the Royals and a three-game edge over the rival Twins.

Of the new pitchers, only Jim Perry showed any signs of his pre-Oakland difficulties. Perry had lasted fewer than five innings in his first two starts against Cleveland and Milwaukee, leading to speculation that the A's might try to demote him to Tucson. The 39-year-old right-hander refused the assignment and took his turn against the light-hitting Orioles on June 10. Perry walked Al Bumbry to start the game before retiring the next 17 batters in succession. In the sixth inning, Bumbry became the first Oriole to pick up a hit, a harmless two-out single. Perry allowed no other hits and only one more walk to polish off a complete game shutout. Gene Tenace and Claudell Washington touched Ross Grimsley for home runs, supporting Perry's first win as a member of the A's.

Perry's one-hitter was the A's second during the month. Two days earlier, Ken Holtzman narrowly missed a no-hitter against the Tigers when Billy North misplayed a catchable fly ball. With two outs and two strikes on Tom Veryzer in the ninth inning, the Tiger shortstop lifted a high fly toward deep left-center field. North broke late for the ball, which the wind dropped onto the warning track untouched. Since North had failed to come close to putting his glove on the ball, the official scorer properly ruled Veryzer's drive a double. Holtzman followed up the unsuccessful bid at his third career no-hitter by striking out Ron LeFlore to end the game.

Although Holtzman refused to blame the center fielder directly for his failure to preserve the no-hitter, several Oakland players claimed that North had broken in at first before retreating toward left-center on Veryzer's drive. After North retrieved Veryzer's double and fired back to the infield, he threw his glove several feet into the air. "I wanted that no-hitter," said an angry North. "I blame myself."[13]

Standout pitching kept the A's atop the Western Division, compensating for a lineup that had not fulfilled expectations. Three of the most important hitters — Sal Bando, Reggie Jackson, and Billy Williams — found themselves hitting below .240. The nagging futility prompted Jackson to come up with an unflattering nickname, referring to himself, Bando and Williams as a "wealthy ghetto."[14]

On June 15, just before the annual trading deadline, Charlie Finley continued his recent trend of adding veteran, thirtysomething pitchers to his staff. Finley acquired right-hander Stan Bahnsen from the White Sox for the hefty price of left-hander Dave Hamilton and outfield prospect Chet Lemon. Unlike the deal that netted Oakland Dick Bosman and Jim Perry from Cleveland, the latest trade seemed heavily tilted against the A's. Bahnsen, with an ERA over 6.00, had fallen victim to Chuck Tanner's ill-advised three-man rotation, which had placed too much of a burden on his right arm. The White Sox liked Hamilton, who was three years younger than Bahnsen, and possessed the versatility to start or relieve. Furthermore, most scouts considered Lemon, a talented hitter with power and speed, the best prospect in the Oakland system. Finley himself would later regret the deal. In the spring of 1976, Finley repeatedly called White Sox general manager Roland Hemond, hoping to reacquire Lemon. The trade reminded some observers of another Finley transaction — the offseason deal that had sent prospect Danny Ford to the Twins for mediocre first baseman Pat Bourque.

A week later, two of the A's most prominent players became involved in a disturbing off-the-field incident — through no fault of their own. As the A's hosted the Royals in a four-game weekend series, Reggie Jackson and Vida Blue received threats on their lives in the form of a frightening letter. The author of the letter claimed he would kill Jackson and Blue sometime during the series with the Royals. Charlie Finley informed both players that they could sit out the series if they wished. Blue and Jackson decided to play. Blue pitched well over a stint of eight and 2/3 innings, earning a no-decision. Jackson performed even better, rapping out six hits in 18 at-bats, collecting a home run and four RBI's. For the second time in the last three years, Jackson had decided to play under the specter of a death threat. Jackson had not only played, he had played spectacularly.

Spearheaded by their in-season pitching additions, the A's enjoyed their most successful month of the season in June. The team compiled winning streaks of four games, five games and eight games on their way to claiming 20 of 29 contests during the month. Dick Bosman and Jim Todd each won three games, while Sonny Siebert and Jim Perry added a victory apiece. Five pitchers not on the staff at the beginning of the season had accounted for 40 per cent of Oakland's victories during the month.

The bullpen continued to buttress the starters, while the offense showed improvement, as well. Paul Lindblad extended his streak of scoreless pitching to 22 1/3 innings and stretched his perfect record to 6-0. In one three-game series against the Twins, Campy Campaneris scored eight runs, Claudell Washington swiped a half-dozen bases and Reggie Jackson smashed three home runs.

By the end of June, the A's record stood at 48-27, giving them a seven and a half game lead in the West. At the same juncture in 1974, the A's lead was only three and a half games. Somehow, without Catfish Hunter, with phenom Mike Norris sidelined for the season and with half the staff acquired since Opening Day, the A's had managed to improve their club from their 1974 standing. Alvin Dark deserved some of the credit. Dark had decided to use only Vida Blue and Ken Holtzman in a regular rotation on three to four days rest, in an effort to maximize the number of starts they could make. Depending on off days and rainouts, Dark would then turn to his second-line starters: Dick Bosman, Sonny Siebert and, if necessary, Jim Perry.

Superior relief pitching and increased run production had played major roles over the first three months of the season. The bullpen, bolstered by the threesome of Rollie Fingers, Jim Todd and Paul Lindblad, had earned saves or wins in 40 of the 48 victories. Lindblad had not lost a single game despite being used frequently. "As the only left-handed reliever we have," explained Todd, "Lindblad has a real burden. He always has to get a guy out."[15] Lindblad's ability to warm up and quickly and pitch in the cold, damp air of Oakland made him an especially tempting option for Alvin Dark. Todd's presence had relieved the workload of Fingers, who had pitched too many long relief stints in 1974. "Todd has been the key," said Rollie. "He's given Paul and me a big break."[16] Now used more selectively and for shorter outings, Fingers' fastball appeared quicker and his slider more explosive. "He's the best I've ever seen," Todd said, praising Fingers. "With men on base...I've never seen anybody get out of jams better than he does."[17]

The offense, helped by the acquisition of Billy Williams and the graduation of Claudell Washington and Phil Garner to regular duty, had produced the second-highest run total in the American League behind only the Red Sox, who played in a ballpark much more favorable for hitters. Through games of July 1, Washington led the A's in batting average (.306) and in stolen bases (31), while Williams and Garner had improved the offensive production at DH and second base, respectively. Garner had also supplied surprisingly solid defensive play, prompting Alvin Dark to remark, "He's as good at making the double play as anyone in the league."[18]

The play of Washington, however, had stood out above all others in the A's lineup. His speed and line-drive hitting justified Alvin Dark's decision to use him as the No. 3 hitter in the Oakland order and earned him selection to the American League All-Star team. Only his fielding remained a concern, although even that had improved since his early season follies in left field. Washington's season had played itself out in dream-like fashion until July 11.

As Washington woke up from his sleep in his apartment, he felt dizzy and decided to go back to bed. Washington awoke a second time and proceeded to black out. As he fell to his bed, he sustained a small cut on his head. When Washington regained consciousness, he decided to call a local hospital and have himself checked out. Although doctors could not pinpoint an exact reason for the fainting spells, a scan of his brain showed no significant abnormalities. "They don't know what caused them,"[19] said a mystified Washington, who had first experienced fainting spells at the age of 16. Doctors nonetheless cleared Washington to return to the lineup. "I guess I'm just going to pass out every now and then,"[20] Washington conceded.

After struggling to hit .250 earlier in the season, Reggie Jackson continued his midsummer assault on American League pitching. On July 25, Jackson beat the White Sox with a game-ending two-run homer in the bottom of the 13th inning. Earlier in the game, Jackson singled, doubled, stole a base and also threw out a runner. "I guess I did it all,"[21] Jackson bragged in complete honesty. Close observers of the A's noted that Jackson had played much of the season with more hustle, intensity and intelligence than at any point in his career, including his MVP year of 1973.

Jackson's power surge, teamed with the sustained hitting and speed of Washington, had made up for the season-long slump of Sal Bando. With his average hovering near the unaccustomed .200 mark, the captain resorted to superstitious remedies. Bando removed the mustache he had worn since 1972, when the A's had first become known as the "Mustache Gang." Now clean-shaven, Bando went 1-for-10 over his next three games. The mustache would return.

In early August, the A's discovered an outside source of motivation when they learned of the comments of Cincinnati Reds' star Johnny Bench. The All-Star catcher predicted that his team would win the National League pennant and would easily handle the three-time defending world champions in the World Series. Bench added that only two A's — Reggie Jackson and Joe Rudi — would be able to crack the roster of the "Big Red Machine."

"Is that so?" said Rollie Fingers, one of several A's to react angrily to Bench's statements. "Why, Johnny Bench couldn't carry the catching gear over here."[22] Fingers further demeaned Bench's ability to handle a pitching staff. "I'd hate to pitch to him," Rollie said to a reporter. "He can't think behind the plate. All he knows is he has five fingers on his hand, but he doesn't know which ones to put down."[23]

Other players responded with more diplomatic disbelief to Bench's vitriol. "Bench says the only A's who could make the Reds are Reggie and Joe?" third-string catcher Larry Haney asked rhetorically. "Our whole pitching staff could make that team."[24] One could also make a strong argument for Billy North and Claudell Washington beating out either Cesar Geronimo or Ken Griffey in the Reds' outfield. Players like Gene Tenace, Campy Campaneris and Sal Bando might not supplant Cincinnati regulars Tony Perez, Dave Concepcion and Pete Rose, but would certainly make the Reds' 25-man roster as reserve or part-time players.

On August 4, Charlie Finley's undermanned front office became even smaller when John Claiborne, the team's director of minor league operations, announced his resignation. Finley shed no tears over Claiborne's departure, saying the team didn't require a minor league director because of their recent decision to join the major league central scouting bureau. "We just didn't need him anymore," Finley said, sounding like Ebenezer Scrooge to Claiborne's Bob Cratchett. "I told him at the start of the season to go ahead and look for another job. He will not be replaced."[25] Finley would soon change his mind, replacing Claiborne with Syd Thrift, a well-respected executive formerly with the Pirates and Royals.

Developments over the past year had hastened the 36-year-old Claiborne's departure. Since Finley had eliminated all but two full-time scouts, Claiborne had asked for permission to travel more often in order to evaluate prospects firsthand. Finley, not wanting to spend money on travel expenses, told Claiborne to stay in his office. Claiborne had also become increasingly frustrated by Finley's refusal to consult him on trades involving minor league prospects. Finley had traded Dan Ford to the Twins for Pat Bourque without seeking the advice of Claiborne. Finley had also included Chet Lemon in the package for Stan Bahnsen, also against the wishes of Claiborne. "Prospects are a dime a dozen,"[26] scoffed Finley in defending his recent trades. As a result of Finley's unwillingness to listen to Claiborne, the Oakland farm system was almost devoid of legitimate prospects at the upper minor league levels.

In spite of the front office turmoil, Oakland continued to play well. The A's won 18 of 29 games in July, giving them four consecutive months of winning baseball. Ken Holtzman paced the pitching staff, winning five of six decisions during the month. Vida Blue added three victories, including two against the rival White Sox. The continuing excellence of the pitching staff helped the A's build up a season-high 11-game lead over the second place Royals.

After reaching peak efficiency in June and July, troubles arose in August. The A's started the month by playing their closest pursuers, the Royals, who took two of three from them. The A's lost three of five to the Rangers before splitting a four-game set with the Red Sox. The 11-game lead soon shrank to five and a half games. Royals' manager Whitey

Herzog hinted at the fallibility of the A's, while taking a subtle poke at Charlie Finley and Alvin Dark. "It's a great team," Herzog said, in prefacing his criticism. "But eight of their guys have played 105 games, and another has played 99. They've got to be tired...Charlie Finley keeps making out the lineups and Alvin Dark keeps playing them. Dark knows they need a rest, but what can he do? And when something does happen, they haven't got any bench."[27]

Something did happen. Joe Rudi tore ligaments in the base of his left thumb while trying to check his swing. The hand injury would sideline him for most of August and September. The pitching also received a blow when Jim Perry continued to pitch poorly, forcing the A's to give him his unconditional release on August 13. Aside from his one-hit and three-hit efforts against the Orioles, Perry had been hit hard almost every time he took to the mound. The release of Perry ended the right-hander's 17-year major league career. He retired from the game with impressive numbers: 215 wins, 174 losses and an earned run average of 3.45.

On the same day that the A's released Perry, they announced the purchase of former American League stolen base king Tommy Harper from the Angels. With Rudi facing extended time on the sidelines and with the farm system lacking in first base prospects, the A's hoped that the aging Harper would be able to play first base in the interim. Harper made his Oakland debut on August 13, in the second of a three-game home series against the Yankees. Harper, playing first base and batting eighth in the order, went 0-for-3 against Catfish Hunter, who defeated his former mates for the third consecutive time.

The loss of Rudi left the A's vulnerable to left-handed pitching, especially given the season-long struggles of Sal Bando. After a nasty arbitration hearing with Charlie Finley, Bando had reported to spring training at just over 200 pounds, significantly trimmer than at any point

---

Former All-Stars Acquired By Charlie Finley (1970-76)

Felipe Alou	Billy Grabarkewitz
Matty Alou	Mudcat Grant
Mike Andrews	Tommy Harper
Rico Carty	Mike Hegan
Orlando Cepeda	Darold Knowles
Nate Colbert	Willie McCovey
Vic Davalillo	Denny McLain
Tommy Davis	Don Mincher
Al Downing	Jim Perry
Ron Fairly	Sonny Siebert
Ray Fosse	Billy Williams

during his major league career. The lost weight had not counteracted the pressure Bando had felt after hearing Finley denigrate him during the arbitration proceeding. "Maybe I'm not hitting because I'm trying too hard to make Finley eat his words,"[28] Bando conceded. By August 17, Bando's season average had fallen to .199, the lowest it had ever been at such a late juncture in a season.

On August 18 and 19, the A's reached their low point when they dropped two straight to the Tigers, a rebuilding team that had compiled the worst record in the American League. Their lead over Kansas City dropped to five and a half games.

The A's bounced back the next day, as Sonny Siebert salvaged the last game of the Tiger series with a 2-1 victory. Even in victory, the A's found another reason to squabble. As Campy Campaneris led off third base, Reggie Jackson prepared to face a two-strike pitch. Campaneris danced off the bag, feigning a steal of home plate. Distracted by the fake, Jackson swung and missed at the next pitch, completing the strikeout. As Reggie walked back to the dugout, he mouthed a few angry words in the direction of Campaneris. "I don't know what he's talking about," said an incredulous Campaneris, who often tried to distract opposing pitchers by making quick dashes down the third base line. "I'm just doing my job."[29]

The lack of recent clutch hitting by Jackson underscored the A's recent offensive problems, especially the lack of production from the middle of the order. The injury to Rudi, the continuing slump of Bando and the difficult American League transition experienced by Billy Williams also contributed to the difficulties in scoring runs.

On August 30, 1975, the A's entered their game with the Red Sox having lost four of their last five games. The A's, who had scored only ten runs combined during the four losses, found themselves trailing in another game. Red Sox slugger Jim Rice, not blessed with great running speed, attempted to steal second base. The throw by Gene Tenace appeared to beat Rice to the bag, but second base umpire Rich Garcia ruled the Red Sox left fielder safe. Alvin Dark argued the call fiercely with Garcia, who ejected the Oakland manager. As he walked back to the dugout, Dark loosened the third base bag from its mooring, carried it over to the third base stands and heaved it into one of the box seats. A's players laughed at Dark's comic demonstration.

The A's ended up winning the game, 7-6, in the tenth inning on an RBI single by Sal Bando, who credited Dark for spurring on the comeback. "We came to life after he did that," Bando said of Dark's humorous tantrum. "It was like a pep talk at half-time."[30]

In spite of the win, Charlie Finley went to work, trying to acquire a veteran hitter for the stretch drive, as he had done in '72 with Matty Alou, and in '73 with Rico Carty, Jesus Alou and Vic Davalillo. Finley set his sights on three players of varying talents: the Rangers' Jim Fregosi, former Athletic Deron Johnson (now with the White Sox) and the Twins' Tony Oliva, but was unable to complete a deal for any of them.

As the A's wrapped up August with a record of 15-16, their first losing month of the season, Finley did manage to swing a deal for an established player — albeit one with less potential for impact than either Oliva or Deron Johnson. On August 31, just before the deadline for freezing post-season rosters, Finley acquired versatile infielder-outfielder Cesar Tovar from the Rangers for a player to be named later.

Tovar, a veteran of 11 seasons with the Twins, Phillies and Rangers, was best known for playing all nine positions in a major league game. Tovar ironically matched a record originally set by the A's Campy Campaneris on September 8, 1965. In his first minor league season, Campaneris had actually pitched ambidextrously in a late-season game for Daytona Beach of the Florida State League. He later played left field, center field and third base. Remembering his unusual pitching stint and his minor league versatility, Charlie Finley decided to use Campaneris in a promotional stunt. With the A's hopelessly out of contention and the season winding down, Finley announced the staging of "Campy Campaneris Night" as a way of drawing more fans to the ballpark. Campy would start the game against the Angels at his accustomed shortstop position, then rotate around the infield and outfield before winding up at pitcher and catcher.

Campaneris played the seven infield and outfield positions without incident. In the eighth inning, Campaneris took to the mound. Throwing right-handed, Campaneris faced Angels' outfielder Jose Cardenal, who ironically happened to be his second cousin. Campy retired Cardenal on a pop-up before allowing two walks, a base hit and a run in a one-inning stint. Then in the ninth, Campaneris experienced even more adventure when he went behind the plate. Ed Kirkpatrick singled to lead off the inning. A sluggish runner, Kirkpatrick promptly stole second base against the inexperienced catcher. Later in the inning, with runners on second and third, the Angels attempted a double steal. Campaneris fired to second baseman Dick Green, who immediately returned the throw to Campy.

The throw had Kirkpatrick, breaking from third base, beaten by several feet. Kirkpatrick rammed into Campaneris as he tried to apply the tag. The slightly built Campaneris fell to the ground, bounced up quickly and challenged Kirkpatrick to a fight. Jose Cardenal, the next scheduled batter, separated Kirkpatrick and his cousin, but the collision left Campy with a painful shoulder. As the trainer carted Campaneris off the field, Charlie Finley fretted that his grand promotion had blown up in his face. Fortunately for the A's, X-rays on the shoulder proved negative. Finley would not have to invoke the $1 million insurance policy that he had taken out on Campaneris.

The nine position stunt irritated most of the veteran A's. "It ended up costing us the ballgame," recalls Jack Aker. "It was a close ballgame. He pitched in the eighth inning, gave up a run. He played catcher in the ninth inning and dropped a sure out, the sure third out." The A's eventually lost the game in extra innings. "The players were pretty much upset," says Aker. "Even though it was a great feat for Campaneris, that's not what we were out there for; we were out there to try to win the ballgame. We felt like we more or less gave a game away so just Mr. Finley could have a stunt."

Three years after the Campaneris promotion — at the urging of Twins' owner Calvin Griffith — Cesar Tovar played an inning apiece at each position, including catcher and pitcher. "Griffith thought it was a good idea," says Bob Fowler, the Twins' beat writer at the time. "It was a late September game as I recall it. The first position — he pitched — he was the starting pitcher, and he got them out. And then the second inning, he caught. And it was absolutely hysterical, because he came out in the catcher's garb with his chest protector — the bottom of his chest protector almost dangled on the ground. He looked like a Little Leaguer. It was just an hysterical sight. The place was just howling with delight at the sight of Cesar coming out of the Twins' first base dugout in the catching garb — it was just hysterical."

While Campaneris played primarily as a shortstop during his major league career, Tovar was a more legitimately versatile player. Tovar played second base, third base and the outfield regularly throughout his career, and also saw significant time at shortstop. "He played all those positions during games that were significant games," Fowler points out. "I mean he was not a stiff that you just threw at third base because Harmon (Killebrew) was hurt or something. I mean, he could play all those positions."

Now 35 years of age, Tovar didn't figure to bring much of a hitting dimension to the A's. In 102 games with the Rangers, Tovar had batted a mediocre .258 while drawing only 27 walks. Yet, Tovar could still run, having stolen 16 bases, and still displayed versatility, having played the outfield and second base for the Rangers.

In order to make room for Tovar on the 25-man roster, the A's finally parted company with Angel Mangual, their once-promising center fielder of the future. After an impressive debut season in 1971, Mangual had regressed in almost every phase of the game. Somehow Mangual had lasted five seasons in Oakland despite a continuing stream of fielding errors and an inability to produce at the plate. Once dubbed a "miniature Roberto Clemente," Mangual had fallen into the baseball oblivion known as "irrevocable waivers." Yet, Mangual felt no antagonism toward Charlie Finley. "I never had any problems with Mr. Finley," Mangual revealed. "And I would like to play for him all my life."[31] Mangual's major league career, however, had come to an end.

Fortunately for the A's, the Royals had failed to take full advantage of Oakland's August swoon. The Royals won 16 of 28 games during the month, but a pair of three-game losing streaks late in August prevented Kansas City from denting Oakland's lead. As the two teams headed into September, the Royals found themselves seven and a half games back in the West.

The Royals needed to pile together a long winning streak to pose a threat to the A's. After losing to the White Sox in the first game of a doubleheader on September 1, the Royals did just that. Kansas City strung together eight straight victories, sweeping consecutive four-game sets against the White Sox and Angels. The Royals' streak lopped two and a half games off the standings, placing Kansas City within five lengths of first place. Playing their best baseball of the summer, the Royals prepared to travel to the Oakland Coliseum where they would meet the A's in a most pertinent three-game series.

The A's had won three straight games of their own, but would have to play the Royals without two injured regulars: first baseman Joe Rudi and shortstop Campy Campaneris, who had been out of action since pulling his groin while running out a bunt attempt on August 26. In facing Royals' 12-game winner Dennis Leonard, who had won seven straight decisions, Alvin Dark prepared a makeshift lineup that featured Tommy Harper at first base and Teddy Martinez at shortstop. Martinez had played well defensively in Campaneris' absence, making only one error in the field. But his sub-.200 average and lack of speed had done little to help a slumping offense.

Rookie third baseman George Brett clipped Ken Holtzman with a solo home run in the top of the first, but the A's took the lead in the bottom of the third on Sal Bando's two-run blow. In the sixth inning, the A's assembled a five-run rally, highlighted by Gene Tenace's two-run homer. Claudell Washington added a solo blast in the eighth, his first longball since June, to complete an easy 8-2 victory.

With the lead now up to six games, the A's started the inconsistent Glenn Abbott in the second game. Abbott and Royals' lefty Paul Splittorff pitched creditably, each allowing a solo home run before giving way to their respective bullpens. The game remained tied at 1-1 through the regulation nine innings, and continued to be deadlocked for four more innings. Rollie Fingers pitched exceptionally well in relief, throwing six innings of pressurized, shutout ball.

In the bottom of the 14th, Kansas City reliever Marty Pattin retired Tommy Harper and Gaylen Pitts for the first two outs. Campy Campaneris, who had entered the game as a defensive replacement in the ninth inning, grounded a ball to the left side of the infield. Freddie Patek, who had homered for the Royals' lone run earlier in the game, allowed the grounder to go under his glove and through his legs, enabling a limping Campaneris to reach first base. Still bothered by the groin pull, Alvin Dark ordered Campy not to steal second base. Campy, noticing that Pattin was paying little attention to him, decided to ignore the manager's directive and headed for second. Campy stole second easily and then scored on Billy North's dribbling single to the outfield. The A's most important victory of the season, a 2-1 decision in 14 innings, had improved their lead to seven games while crushing the collective morale of the young Royals.

Campaneris' daring steal of second base captured much of the post-game attention, overshadowing the brilliant relief work of Fingers. "He's been doing this for four years," observed Paul Lindblad, Fingers' bullpen mate since 1973. "He's the greatest. The scouts in the National League all say he's the best. He's better than Mike Marshall, he's better than Clay Carroll. He's better than all of them."[32]

The extra-inning win lessened the importance of the next game, but the A's held little back in pounding the Royals, 9-1. Phil Garner went 4-for-4, Billy North added three hits, Sal Bando clubbed a three-run homer and Gene Tenace knocked a two-run shot to support Vida Blue's 19th win. Blue pitched a complete game despite walking six Royals, effectively resting a bullpen that had pitched eight innings the night before.

The three-game sweep of the Royals ended the pennant race. The A's now led by eight games with only three weeks remaining. The schedule looked favorable, as well, with sub-.500 teams like the Twins, Rangers, White Sox and Angels representing their opponents in 15 of their final 18 games. The A's would play the Royals only once more — a three-game set in Kansas City on September 19, 20 and 21.

With the A's magic number for clinching a tie reduced to one, Steve Busby outpitched Glenn Abbott in the first game of the series, winning a 5-4 decision. The next day, the A's clinched at least a share of the Western division title by clubbing the Royals, 16-4. Billy Williams, whose power production had risen over the second half, hit his 23rd home run in support of Vida Blue's 20th win.

The Royals rallied to win the third game, but the victory mattered little in the standings. On September 24, after three consecutive losses, the A's played the White Sox. In spite of the losses, the A's held a five-game lead over the Royals while their magic number for clinching the division outright remained at one.

Vida Blue, with a record of 20-11, faced White Sox rookie Jesse Jefferson in an overwhelming mismatch. The A's torched Jefferson for eight runs over the first four innings, before scraping relievers Rich Hinton and Pete Vuckovich for five more runs. Reggie Jackson slammed two home runs, his 33rd and 34th of the season. Claudell Washington drove in four runs and Sal Bando added three hits and three RBI's. The A's won the game, 13-2, to clinch their fifth consecutive Western Division crown.

Unlike their tepid clubhouse celebrations of 1973 and '74, the A's rejoiced their latest divisional championship more enthusiastically. Some of the newer A's, who had never before played in the post-season, felt special satisfaction in the Oakland clubhouse. Billy Williams, a 16-year veteran of also-ran teams in Chicago, drank from one of the 48 bottles of champagne supplied by Charlie Finley. "Beautiful," Williams shouted. "Absolutely magnificent. Ain't no feeling like this. Never knew champagne tasted so good. Fifteen years to pour champagne."[33]

Another newcomer to the A's had almost played as long as Williams without reaching the playoffs. "Thirteen years," said Tommy Harper, who had played in Cincinnati, Cleveland, Seattle, Milwaukee, Boston and California before finding solace in the Bay Area. "I knew I'd get to the right place if I kept moving around."[34]

Harper had been more than a passive bystander during the A's stretch run. As part of the Oakland bench, Harper had quietly replaced the injured Joe Rudi at first base. In 34 games with the A's, Harper hit .319 and stole seven bases. During his most productive stretch, Harper had collected 14 hits in 34 at-bats. Another backup, shortstop Teddy Martinez, had made only two errors while filling in for Campy Campaneris. Martinez' deftness in turning the double play had also drawn approval from second base partner Phil Garner. In 20 starts at shortstop during Campaneris' absence, the A's had won 14 games.

The versatility of the A's bench moved Charlie Finley to call the 1975 A's "the best ballclub we've had in the 15 years I've owned it. We've got two players, Tommy Harper and Ted Martinez, who can play six positions; another player, Cesar Tovar, who can play five positions; some who can play four, and a number who can play three."[35] One could forgive Finley for his overly exuberant assessment of the '75 A's in the afterglow of the division clinching. He had obviously forgotten that the A's no longer had a pitcher named Catfish Hunter. No matter how well the A's had played during the regular season, the loss of a 25-game winner would have an impact — eventually.

Although the September 24th game against the White Sox represented the last meaningful contest with regard to the pennant race, the A's added an historical footnote four days later. In the season finale against the Angels, Alvin Dark planned to give Vida Blue a five-inning tune-up before using him in the second game of the playoffs. Blue pitched five innings — five no-hit innings. Dark stuck to his original plan and removed Blue after the fifth. Glenn Abbott worked a hitless inning, as did Paul Lindblad. Dark then called on Rollie Fingers, who pitched two more scoreless and hitless innings to complete a 5-0 victory. For the first time in baseball history, four pitchers had combined to throw a no-hitter in a regular season game lasting at least nine innings.

In the past, Finley had paid bonuses to any of his pitchers who had thrown no-hitters. In 1968, Finley had rewarded Catfish Hunter with a $5,000 bonus for pitching a perfect game against the Twins. The price of a mere no-hitter was a bit less — $1500. When a reporter asked Finley if he would still pay the $1500 bonus, even though it had taken four pitchers to complete the no-hitter, the owner cursed angrily and repeatedly. Rollie Fingers, the last of the four no-hit pitchers, offered a possible solution. "I think we all ought to share $1500," Fingers said. "Vida should get five-ninths, Abbott and Lindblad one-ninth each, and I should get two-ninths."[36]

Chapter Thirty:
A Flop At Fenway

As well as the A's had played during a surprising regular season, the post-season matchup did not bode well. The Boston Red Sox featured an intimidating lineup, one headlined by Rookie of the Year and MVP favorite Fred Lynn and fellow rookie slugger Jim Rice. Thanks to a powerful offense, the Red Sox had claimed the American League East with 95 wins. Although the A's had forged a slightly better record than the Red Sox, they would have to play the first two games of the series at Fenway Park, a difficult stadium for road teams — and for left-handed pitchers.

During the A's final regular season visit to Fenway in August, Alvin Dark had used three right-handed pitchers as his starters, Stan Bahnsen, Glenn Abbott and Sonny Siebert. None of the three had pitched particularly well, but the A's had still won two of the three games. Would Dark repeat the trend of using right-handers at Fenway in the playoffs? After all, he no longer had the luxury of calling upon Catfish Hunter, one of the top five right-handed pitchers in the league.

Some members of the media speculated that Dark might use one of his right-handed relievers, either Jim Todd or Rollie Fingers as a starter in Game Two. Such a strategy seemed dubious. Fingers hadn't started a game since 1973, when he had made two starts for Dick Williams, and hadn't been a full-time starter since early in 1971. Todd had started six games for the Cubs in 1974, but with little success.

Ignoring the argument of left-handers vs. right-handers, Dark decided to use his two best starters — Vida Blue and Ken Holtzman — in the first two games of the series. Both happened to be left-handers, but Dark felt they gave him stronger chances of winning than lesser right-handers like Dick Bosman and Stan Bahnsen or relievers like Todd and Fingers. Dark did surprise the media when he announced that Holtzman would pitch Game One, followed by Blue in the second game. Blue, a 22-game winner, had pitched appreciably better than Holtzman during the regular season. But Dark considered Blue's poor record in the post-season. In previous playoff and World Series appearances, Blue had won just once while losing five.

In spite of the problems created by dispatching left-handers upon Fenway Park, the oddsmakers still made the A's slight favorites, based on their status as defending world champions and their fine regular season showing. Their previous experience in the playoffs far outweighed that of the Red Sox, a relatively young team. Only a handful of Red Sox — Carl Yastrzemski, Rico Petrocelli, Bernie Carbo, Dick McAuliffe, and former Athletic Deron Johnson — had ever participated in the post-season.

"The balls aren't the same balls, the bats aren't the same length, it's further between the bases,"[1] said Reggie Jackson in describing playoff baseball. In other words, pitching in the playoffs was better, hitting was tougher, and every defensive play took on added importance. A greater sense of tension enveloped each player. Playoff baseball was just different.

The A's also received a pair of breaks with regard to injuries. Joe Rudi, who had missed six weeks in August and September with strained tendons in thumb, had re-injured his hand in the final regular season game. Rudi deemed the second injury as far less serious, making him available to take part in the playoffs. The A's also discovered that rookie outfielder Jim Rice would be unable to play for the Red Sox due to a broken arm. The young right-handed slugger had led the Red Sox in home runs during the regular season, while finishing second only to Fred Lynn in batting average and RBI's. In addition, the first-game pitching matchup favored the A's. Holtzman, 18-14 with a 3.15 ERA would face fellow 18-game winner Luis Tiant, whose ERA had topped off at a fairly high 4.02.

Holtzman retired Juan Beniquez and Denny Doyle to start the game before allowing a single to Carl Yastrzemski, one of the few players still left from the Red Sox' "Impossible Dream" season in 1967. Holtzman then induced a sharp grounder from cleanup man Carlton Fisk, who bounded the ball to the left side of the infield. Sal Bando backed up on the ball slightly, allowing it to take an extra hop and skip past him for an error. Yastrzemski rounded the bag hard at second and headed for third, waved on by third base coach Don Zimmer. Claudell

Washington retrieved the ball in left field and overthrew the cutoff man, the throw bounding off Bando's glove. Yastrzemski scored on the throwing error and Fisk moved up to second. Fred Lynn followed with a ground ball to second baseman Phil Garner, who misplayed the ball so badly that it reached the outfield. Fisk scored the inning's second run. Two plays, three errors, and two unearned runs.

The game remained 2-0 until the bottom of the seventh, when Billy North dropped an easy flyball for an error and Washington misplayed Fred Lynn's high drive to left field. Thinking that the ball would bounce high off the "Green Monster," Washington retreated several steps toward the infield in order to play the carom. The ball dropped near the base of the wall, indicating that Washington could have made the catch had he stayed back. The Red Sox ended up scoring five runs off the combination of Holtzman and relievers Jim Todd, Paul Lindblad, Glenn Abbott and Dick Bosman, cementing a 7-1 victory for Boston.

Dating back to their 1971 playoff appearance against the Orioles, the A's had never played so badly in a Championship Series or World Series game. In making four errors, the A's had set a new Championship Series record. They had failed to make up for their defensive escapades with nonexistent hitting and shaky relief pitching, all of which had badly stained the first game of the playoffs. "The second game is the key one," said a calm and philosophical Alvin Dark, who had seen his team lose the first game of the '74 playoffs before rebounding to win the series. "We just need a split here,"[2] Dark said of the two games in Boston. Although the A's had lost the first games of previous Championship Series — in 1971, '73 and '74 — they had never played as sloppily as they did in losing the first game to the Red Sox. Major improvement would be needed to garner a split at Fenway.

Faced with a sudden post-season crisis, Dark made lineup changes for Game Two. He removed Claudell Washington from left field and installed him as the DH, where he could do little damage with his glove. Joe Rudi, more experienced in playing the "Green Monster" at Fenway, replaced Washington in left. Dark inserted Ray Fosse as his catcher, moved Gene Tenace to first base and benched his regular DH, Billy Williams, who had gone hitless in the first game.

The A's responded well in the early stages of Game Two. Reggie Jackson reached Boston starter Reggie Cleveland for a two-run homer in the first inning. The A's added a single run in the fourth inning to make it a 3-0 game. Vida Blue, cruising with three scoreless innings, seemed primed to hold the advantage and give the A's the tying game in the series.

The blueprint fell apart. In the bottom of the fourth, Carl Yastrzemski drew the Red Sox close with a two-run homer. Carlton Fisk followed with a ringing double and moved to third on Fred Lynn's clean single. With the right-hand hitting Rico Petrocelli coming to the plate, Alvin Dark yanked Blue, replacing him with right-hander Jim Todd. The sinkerballer induced a double play grounder by Petrocelli, but Fisk scored the tying run on the play.

In the top of the sixth, the A's tried to retake the lead, only to be held back by Boston's outfield defense. Carl Yastrzemski, playing a masterful left field throughout the series as Jim Rice's replacement, played a Sal Bando drive off the "Green Monster" perfectly. Yastrzemski returned the ball to the infield quickly enough to hold Bando, an average runner, to a single. Later in the inning, Joe Rudi swatted a drive to right-center field that seemed capable of scoring a run from first. Fred Lynn raced to the gap, cutting off the drive on his backhand side. Rudi reached second with a double, but Lynn's quickness in retrieving the ball and pitching it back to the infield prevented Bando from scoring. With runners on second and third and two out, left-handed reliever Rogelio Moret retired Claudell Washington to end the threat.

In the meantime, Todd had pitched only one inning before Dark had made a desperation move, summoning Rollie Fingers in the fifth inning. Fingers pitched a scoreless inning before running into trouble in the bottom of the sixth. The Oakland closer gave up a double to Carl Yastrzemski, and a run-scoring single to Carlton Fisk. The Red Sox now led for the first time, 4-3. Rico Petrocelli homered off a Fenway Park light tower in the seventh, giving the Red Sox a two-run cushion. Fred Lynn completed the scoring with a bloop RBI single in the eighth. The A's offense failed to score over the final five innings, completely shut down by relievers Moret and Dick Drago. As the A's completed an embarrassing 6-3 loss, Red Sox fans taunted Charlie Finley by chanting "Good-bye Charlie, Good-bye Charlie, we hate to see you go."[3] Finley stood up from his seat near the third base dugout, raised his arms to the fans and smiled uncomfortably.

The Red Sox had suddenly moved within one game of their first trip to the World Series since 1967. As Reggie Jackson said of the Red Sox, "Now they know they can slay the giant."[4] The A's could not draw comfort from past Championship Series. In the brief history of the playoffs, no team had come back from a two games-to-none deficit to advance to the World Series.

On the brink of playoff embarrassment, Finley ordered Dark to make more changes for Game Three. Finley demanded that Campy Campaneris bat leadoff in favor of the hitless Billy North (no hits in seven at-bats), who would bat eighth. In context, this was a relatively small adjustment; Finley had even bigger changes in mind.

After a day off for travel, the A's returned to the West Coast. The worst-case scenario had fully developed. In games one and two, Alvin Dark had burned Blue and Holtzman, his best starters, and had still lost twice. That seemingly left Dark with his best right-handed starter, Dick Bosman, to start Game Three. Bosman had won 11 of 15 decisions since joining the A's in the mid-season trade with the Indians.

Charlie Finley, however, lacked the confidence to pitch Bosman in the third game. At the behest of Finley, Dark informed Ken Holtzman that he would start the game against Rick Wise on only two days rest. Holtzman, who had pitched over six innings in the first game, had not made a start during the regular season on anything less than a three-day interval.

Dark's, or Finley's, decision to use Holtzman left the manager and the owner vulnerable to an array of second-guessing. In the first place, why hadn't Dark started Bosman, his best right-handed starter, during one of the games at Fenway Park? Since Bosman had pitched only one-third of an inning in Boston, how could Finley resist using him in Oakland? Didn't a relatively relaxed Bosman stand a better chance of pitching well than Holtzman on only two days rest? Why wasn't Catfish Hunter here? The last second guess, no fault of Dark's, was reserved solely for Charlie Finley.

Holtzman pitched well over the first three innings, keeping the Red Sox off the board to maintain a scoreless tie. In the fourth inning, another costly fielding mistake by Claudell Washington led directly to an unearned Red Sox run when Rico Petrocelli followed with an RBI single. In the fifth, the Red Sox broke the game open when Rick Burleson started the inning with a double, and Denny Doyle, Carl Yastrzemski, and Carlton Fisk each lashed singles. The three-run rally pushed Holtzman from the game while giving the Red Sox a 4-0 lead.

In the sixth, the A's threatened to make a run at Red Sox starter Rick Wise. Oakland scored one run before watching the rally stall. With two runners on and two out, Wise faced Reggie Jackson, representing the potential tying run. Jackson struck out, ending Oakland's best chance at making the game a close one.

The A's tried to mount another comeback in the eighth inning. With run already in, runners on first and third and one out, Jackson stepped to the plate to face a tiring Wise. Jackson went with the outside pitch, lining it into the left-center field gap. Carl Yastrzemski, the defensive star of the series, gave chase. "All I thought of was to cut the ball off," Yaz explained. "I didn't think I had a chance, but I just dove as far as I could and all of a sudden, the ball was in the webbing of my glove."[5] Yastrzemski leapt to his feet and threw to second base, holding Jackson at first. Although Yaz had not caught the ball on the fly, he had managed to cut it off before it bounded to the outfield wall. If the ball had eluded Yaz, the A's would have scored two runs and Jackson might have ended up at third with a triple. Thanks to another miraculous play by an aging but still skilled outfielder, only one run had scored, the runner from first had stopped at third, and Jackson had settled for a long single.

The A's now trailed, 5-3. Red Sox manager Darrell Johnson called on his best reliever, Dick Drago, to replace Wise. Drago threw one pitch to Joe Rudi, who promptly bounced into an inning-ending double play. Although the A's still had one inning to bat, their season had effectively come to an end. Gene Tenace drew a one-out walk in the ninth before Drago retired Billy North and pinch-hitter Jim Holt to finish the game and the series. With a 5-3 win, the Red Sox had finally ended Oakland's dynastic string of post-season victories.

Often criticized for acting like spoiled children in victory — as evidenced by their many post-game fights and arguments — the A's showed a different side to their character in losing. Several A's — Reggie Jackson, Sal Bando, Joe Rudi and Rollie Fingers included — all walked over to the Boston clubhouse to offer their congratulations to the new American League champions. Oakland's stars spent several minutes in the Red Sox clubhouse, discussing the series and Boston's status as a World Series participant.

In the aftermath of their first postseason loss since 1971, many players and writers sounded off on a common refrain: it might have been different if Catfish Hunter were still around. The A's could have used Hunter to pitch Game One at Fenway Park, while reserving Vida Blue or Ken Holtzman to pitch Game Three on full rest, rather than the paltry two days that Charlie Finley's panic had created. Veteran sportswriter Steve Jacobson, working for *New York Newsday*, asked Sal Bando if the loss of Hunter was the biggest blunder by a franchise in baseball history. After a short pause interrupted by laughter, Bando responded. "If it wasn't the biggest," answered Bando, "I haven't heard of any bigger."[6]

Chapter Thirty-one:
The Last Hurrah

Criticism of Finley's bungling of the Hunter affair soon gave way to discussion of the A's future and the ways for the team to improve. Given the failures of the Oakland left-handers at Fenway Park, the A's desperately needed another right-handed pitcher. "We've got to get someone like Don Sutton who'll go out there and pitch," said Sal Bando. "You can't get a Catfish Hunter in a trade, but you can go out and get someone who can win you 15 games."[1] Sutton, a 16-game winner for the Dodgers in 1975, would nicely fill out a rotation that already contained left-handers Vida Blue and Ken Holtzman and veteran right-hander Dick Bosman.

While Bosman had pitched well for the A's, another mid-season pitching acquisition had not fared as well. Although Sonny Siebert hadn't pitched terribly in an Oakland uniform, he had shown little durability, averaging fewer than five innings per start. Siebert's availability had also been affected by a series of groin injuries and continuing problems with his sinuses. Siebert's fragility had convinced Charlie Finley to cut him loose.

The A's pitching problems figured to get worse if Holtzman followed through on his retirement hints. Unlike most of his teammates, Holtzman's boyhood had not included dreams of becoming a major league player. "I didn't want to be a professional athlete," Holtzman admitted. "I thought maybe I'd like to be a lawyer, or something like that."[2] The owner of a masters degree in business administration, Holtzman told reporters of his interest in entering private business in the metropolitan areas of either Chicago or St. Louis. Over the last two years, Holtzman had speculated that his playing career might not last much beyond the 1975 season.

Holtzman was beginning to tire of the constant travel, which kept him away from his family for long stretches during the baseball season. "I figure I'll pitch maybe two, three more years," Holtzman had said in a 1973 interview with *Sport* magazine. "I'll have my 10-year pension then. I've never thought I'd be the kind of guy who would pitch 17 years. When the thrill is gone, when it's a chore to suit up, that's when I'll quit."[3] Holtzman had indicated that winning a World Series was his chief goal; and since he had achieved that, he regarded all else as "anticlimactic." Without Holtzman, the A's would have little to chance to repeat as divisional champs, much less even think of making it back to the World Series.

Aside from pitching, Charlie Finley craved another big hitter for the middle of the Oakland order. An examination of the playoff statistics revealed a lineup filled with unproductive players. The group included Gene Tenace and Billy Williams, the two key components behind Reggie Jackson, who had combined to go hitless in the three games against Boston. Finley had tried, and failed, to acquire Tony Oliva in August; now he set his sights on Brewers' first baseman George Scott, who had led the American League in RBI's but had been accused of selfishness by his Brewer teammates. Who would the A's trade to Milwaukee for a star like Scott? The Brewers needed a center fielder, so perhaps a package headed up by Billy North would suffice. North, who had been hampered by calcium deposits and bone spurs in his foot during the season, figured to be 100 per cent by 1976. If the A's acquired Scott, they could play him at first base, return Joe Rudi to left field and slide Claudell Washington over to center.

Such scenarios represented uncertainty for the A's. Finley created more uncertainty on October 17 when he announced that Alvin Dark would not return to manage the team. Finley refused to call the move a "firing," but the short statement issued to the press made it clear that Dark's contract would not be renewed. The decision may have been spurred by an article in the October 2nd edition of the *Hayward* (California) *Daily Review*. A story in the Review appeared under the following headline:

Alvin Dark Says That Unless He Changes His Ways,
Finley's Going To Hell

Dark claimed that the reporter had taken his comments out of context. When asked about the article, Finley reacted nonchalantly, saying that Dark's words had not bothered him. Finley did not attribute the "firing" of Dark to the newspaper article, but rather to the manager's heavy involvement with the church. "I believe that Dark's outside activities interfered with managing the club,"[4] Finley said, making a statement that was sure to infuriate Christian leaders.

Once again, Finley had failed to consult his players, many of whom felt Dark had done a better job of managing in 1975 than he had during the world championship season. Even Sal Bando, at one time Dark's staunchest critic on the A's, had become a convert. "He should have been named Manager of the Year," Bando said, a year and a half after claiming that Dark couldn't handle a meat market. "Alvin made a few mistakes his first year and admitted them. This past season he had the smarts and got the most out of the team."[5] Dark had taken a team with only two above-average starting pitchers — Vida Blue and Ken Holtzman — to its fifth consecutive appearance in the post-season.

Rumors immediately centered on one man as the successor to Dark. The name of Gene Mauch, most recently the manager of the Montreal Expos and the man at the helm when the Philadelphia Phillies experienced their late season collapse in 1964, came up again and again. Finley found Mauch appealing for two reasons: he liked that Mauch was a big name among managers and preferred a disciplinarian who stressed fundamental play, one of the weaknesses during the Dark regime.

If Dark had remained as manager, he was prepared to make certain changes. Dark wanted to move Joe Rudi back to left field — against Finley's wishes — and preferred to trade Billy Williams, who had finished the season with a career-low .244 average. Dark also wished to keep Ray Fosse, who had been rumored as the player to be named later in the trade that had netted the A's Cesar Tovar from the Rangers.

With Dark out of the picture, Finley set his sights on making his own changes. He hoped the Rangers would take Fosse off his hands, rather than take the cash option needed to complete the deal. Texas settled for money, but Finley still managed to unload Fosse, selling him to the Indians, his original major league team. In the meantime, Finley sought several star players in potential trades. Gaylord Perry headed up Finley's list of pitching help. Now with Texas, Gaylord had run afoul of manager Frank Robinson in Cleveland. The Red Sox' Rick Wise loomed as another target of Finley. The owner also desired two high-impact offensive players: Milwaukee's George Scott and Jimmy Wynn of the Dodgers.

Finley offered the Brewers Reggie Jackson in a one-for-one deal that would bring Scott to the Bay Area. In exchange for Wynn, the A's talked about giving up a package that would include Billy North and Paul Lindblad, who was also rumored to be part of a package for Gaylord Perry. Finley suggested Sal Bando as possible compensation to the Red Sox for Rick Wise, the man who had beaten the A's in the final game of the Championship Series. Unfortunately, the A's no longer had any high-level minor league prospects that could be used to pad any block-buster trades. Perhaps they could put together a trade for one of the players in the Scott-Wynn-Perry category, but probably not two of them, and certainly not all three.

One of the potential trades quickly fell through. Wynn would end up being traded, but to Atlanta, not Oakland, in a blockbuster six-player deal. The Brewers considered offers for Scott, but decided to hold on to the burly first baseman. The Rangers adopted a similar stance with Perry. The best Charlie Finley could do was send career minor league outfielder Charlie Chant to the Cardinals for speedy infielder Larry Lintz, who became the A's latest pinch-runner extraordinaire. Finley also parted ways with four veterans by cutting infielders Tommy Harper, Dal Maxvill and Billy Grabarkewitz and pitcher Sonny Siebert. For some reason, Finley didn't announce the departures of Harper and Siebert until February, nearly three months after the fact. The releases of Siebert, Maxvill and Grabarkewitz came as no great shock, but the decision to waive Harper smacked of Finley's typical cheapness. The veteran first baseman-outfielder had hit well and run well during his 34-game stint in Oakland, but made too much money for Finley's lik-ing. The owner didn't like paying utility players, even productive ones, at premium rates.

While Finley failed to add any big-name players to his stable dur-ing the offseason, he did find a marquee manager. The attempt to se-cure Gene Mauch fell through, however. Mauch apparently wanted the job, but wanted to bring in his own pitching coach. Finley insisted that his new manager retain holdover pitching coach Wes Stock, Finley's favorite on the staff. After considering one of his coaches, Bobby Winkles, and former Royals' manager Jack McKeon, Finley settled on Chuck Tanner, who had been fired by the White Sox only one day earlier.

"He'll be the best manager I've ever had,"[6] Finley said in his typi-cally understated way. Tanner, perhaps the most optimistic and up-beat manager in either league, used a strange choice of words in describing his reaction to the Oakland appointment. "I'm feeling out-standingly exotic, or whatever the word is,"[7] Tanner said breathlessly, while wearing an absurd ten-gallon hat bearing the A's logo.

Tanner had forged a reputation as an enthusiastic player's man-ager, a man who publicly defended and stressed the strengths of his players, even in the face of extreme criticism. During his tenure in Chi-cago, Tanner had accomplished what other managers had failed to do repeatedly — finding a way to extract the most from the talented, but moody Dick Allen. In 1972, under the guidance of Tanner, Allen had reached the limits of his extraordinary skills by batting .308 with 37 homers and 113 RBI's and winning the American League MVP Award.

In contrast to his handling of Allen, Tanner's use of the White Sox' pitching staff had drawn criticism from the Chicago media. In 1972,

Tanner and his pitching coach Johnny Sain had made a controversial decision to use a three-man rotation, often pitching knuckleballing left-hander Wilbur Wood and right-handers Stan Bahnsen and Tom Bradley on only two days' rest. In the short term, the unusual rotation had paid dividends. Wood won 24 games, Bahnsen established a career-high 21, and Bradley tied his best with 15 victories. The heavy workload may have taken its toll, however, on both Bahnsen and Bradley. In 1972, Bahnsen made 41 starts while Bradley started 40 games. Within two years, both right-handers saw their ERA's rise above 4.00 and their won-loss records dip below the .500 level. Both careers were near the end.

In Chicago, Tanner had dealt with several controversies, including the day-to-day presence of Dick Allen and the interference of general manager Stu Holcomb. Such problems figured to look minuscule in comparison to the soap opera style of the A's, where players fought and argued with regularity and the owner did his best to make life unbearable for his manager of the day. Tanner anticipated little difficulty in managing a team filled with loud, volatile personalities. "There are a lot of good kids who go to bed at eight every night, are no trouble at all, are great to be around, and hit .180," Tanner explained to reporters. "Give me the outspoken good player."[8]

Now that his managerial choice had been finalized, Finley started to concern himself with rumors of an impending move of the franchise to Seattle. Finley denied the speculation, instead proposing a plan that would improve the condition of his financially-ailing club. At the owners meetings in January, Finley championed one of his favorite causes — interleague play. "Think of the rivalries," Finley exclaimed. "There would be the A's and the Giants, the Yanks and Mets, the White Sox and Cubs, the Dodgers and the Angels."[9] Finley believed that interleague play — specifically a number of regular season series against San Francisco — would increase attendance at the Oakland Coliseum while cutting down on travel costs.

As usual, the other major league owners initially resisted Finley's attempt at change. Bob Fowler says Finley's idea of interleague play might have gained more immediate acceptance if had tried a gentler, more logical approach. "I think if he had not been such a character, if he had not been such a square-peg, round-hole kind of guy, he could have certainly gotten the people to do it. If he could have presented his ideas with charts and graphs to show how they could have made even more money than they were making, all of those things would have been rubber-stamped." Twenty-one years after Finley's proposal, and just months after his death from heart disease, the major leagues instituted a plan of interleague play similar to the one he had suggested.

One week after discussing interleague play, Finley introduced Chuck Tanner to the Oakland media at a press conference, where the owner officially refuted all rumors of the A's being moved to Seattle, or any other North American location. A few days later, Finley quietly announced through a press release that the A's had raised ticket prices for their top two levels of seats by 50 cents apiece. By not mentioning the ticket increase at the press conference, Finley hoped to minimize the negative feedback leveled at him by the Oakland writers.

Finley faced bigger problems than mere criticism of his ticket price hike. Many of his best players, including seven represented by powerful agent Jerry Kapstein, remained unsigned as spring training neared. Two of Kapstein's clients, Campy Campaneris and Ken Holtzman, wanted multi-year contracts. Finley explained that, as a matter of policy, he had no intention of handing out contracts for more than one season. Finley failed to mention that he had previously signed Campaneris, Billy Williams and Catfish Hunter to two-year deals.

Finley did not have to worry about any of the players taking him to the arbitration table, since arbitration had been suspended while major league players and owners continued to negotiate a new collective bargaining agreement. Still, Finley ran the risk of losing the players outright after the season. A recent landmark decision by independent arbitrator Peter Seitz had made veteran pitchers Andy Messersmith and Dave McNally free agents. With the old collective bargaining agreement having expired, the possibility existed that a new agreement would result in all unsigned players becoming free agents at the end of the 1976 season. By refusing to sign players beyond the upcoming season, Finley seemed to be playing with contractual fire.

In a related development, the unsigned Reggie Jackson told Finley that he preferred to sign a multi-year contract and remain in Oakland. Rumors persisted that Finley might trade Jackson to the Orioles for right-handed pitcher Mike Torrez and an unnamed outfielder. Although the A's held 20-year-old right-hander Mike Norris in high regard, the youngster had missed most of the 1975 season after surgery to remove bone chips from his pitching elbow. No one knew for sure if Norris would be able to return, given his history of arm trouble. Without a healthy Norris, the A's needed a front-line starter who threw from the right side. In order to acquire such a player, the A's would have to at least consider the possibility of trading a player the caliber of Reggie Jackson.

Jackson remained unsigned, as did fellow outfielder Billy North, starting infielders Joe Rudi, Campy Campaneris and Sal Bando, first-string catcher Gene Tenace and Oakland's three best pitchers — Vida Blue, Ken Holtzman and Rollie Fingers. Since arbitration had been temporarily removed as an option, Finley mailed each of the players automatically renewed contracts at the maximum 20 per cent pay cut. The pay decreased angered most of the players, whom the media began referring to as the "Oakland Nine." The players did have one recourse. They could play out their options and declare themselves free agents after the 1976 season. In other words, Finley ran the risk of losing his nine best players without any compensation in return.

Finley's salary tactics, which featured demeaning insults, telephone hang-ups and un-returned calls, proved especially frustrating to Holtzman. "All he would have to do," stipulated Holtzman, "is negotiate with me in good faith, in a civil tone of voice and I probably would sign. I like the Oakland area. I like the guys on the ballclub. I don't want to leave."[10] Holtzman recalled how Finley had cut his salary by 10 per cent after acquiring him from the Cubs after the 1971 season. Holtzman also remembered an incident in 1972, right after the A's had won their first World Series. As a large gathering of fans welcomed the players back to Oakland, Finley had scolded Holtzman, embarrassing him in front of his father-in-law. "Charlie just doesn't know how to treat people,"[11] said Holtzman, expressing the sentiments of many of his teammates.

Holtzman's life had become more miserable after assuming the role of Oakland's player representative from a beleaguered Reggie Jackson. Over the past 10 years, player reps had been subjected to more abuse from Finley than any other players. "I honestly believe it cost me my job with the A's," says Jack Aker, who served as Oakland's player representative for two seasons before being left unprotected in the 1968 expansion draft. "I think it cost me what should have been better years in '67 and '68 because I had so many problems with Mr. Finley. It was almost constant. Almost every day there was a problem of some sort." Finley frowned upon the idea of a Players' Association and warned many of the A's not to attend union meetings. Given his resentment of the Association, Finley harassed Aker, often over petty and trivial matters. "The real problem that I had with Mr. Finley was the little things," recalls Aker. "Maybe a player or two on the club did not autograph all the balls in the clubhouse before the game. I would be called into his office immediately the next day as soon as I got to the ballpark. It was little things like this; it was a constant thing." Finley also kept count of the number of bats used by the players and charged them each time they tossed baseballs into the stands.

Player rep Ken Holtzman and the rest of the unsigned — and unhappy — players reported to spring training on time. The A's also invited a few new players to camp, including veteran third baseman Ken McMullen. The former Senator, Angel and Dodger infielder had been released by Los Angeles during the winter. The A's planned to look at McMullen as a pinch-hitter and utility infielder, and as possible insurance should they decide to trade Sal Bando for a pitcher.

On April 2, as spring training narrowed to its last few days, the A's announced that they had made a trade. The deal did not involve Sal Bando. No, this trade would be even bigger, much bigger. Oakland's most recognizable player, perhaps the man most synonymous with their successful seasons of 1971 through 1975, was now gone. Charlie Finley had traded the unsigned Reggie Jackson, unsigned pitcher Ken Holtzman and minor league hurler Bill Van Bommel to the Baltimore Orioles for right-hander Mike Torrez, outfielder Don Baylor and pitcher Paul Mitchell.

Although a trade involving Jackson and the Orioles had been rumored for months, the official announcement of the deal still shocked a group of disbelieving Oakland players and writers. Jackson, the A's best left-handed power hitter and most recognizable player, had been with the organization since 1967, when the team still played in Kansas City. Holtzman, their second-best starter after Vida Blue in 1975, had been critical to the success of the 1972, '73 and '74 championship teams. The comments of Joe Rudi epitomized the feelings of many of the A's. "I don't think the guys we got from Baltimore are as good as Kenny or Reggie," Rudi explained. "Torrez isn't as good a pitcher as Kenny. And Baylor is no Reggie Jackson."[12]

Charlie Finley disagreed with Rudi's assessment, calling the trade the best he'd ever made. Finley added that he would have made the trade even if both Jackson and Holtzman had already signed contracts. "This trade was made because I feel this deal will lead us to another world championship," said Finley, before making a bombshell proclamation. "I feel that Baylor is the equal of Reggie Jackson."[13] In 1975, Jackson had totaled 36 home runs, 104 RBI's, 17 stolen bases and a .253 average. Baylor had hit for a better average and stolen more bases, but his 25 home runs and 76 RBI's hadn't come close to matching Jackson's power numbers. In addition, Baylor couldn't throw, the result of a severe shoulder injury which meant that he could only play left field and first base. Yet, Finley liked the potential of Baylor, who at 26, was three years younger than Jackson. "I don't mean this out of respect to Jackson. I think Baylor is outstanding and will be even more outstanding in the next few years."[14] Baylor remained unsigned, however, raising the possibility that he could leave the A's after the season.

In surrendering three unsigned players, Finley had acquired two

---

Charlie Finley's Worst Trades:

• Reggie Jackson and Ken Holtzman to the Orioles for Don Baylor, Mike Torrez and Paul Mitchell

• Chet Lemon and Dave Hamilton to the White Sox for Stan Bahnsen

• Dan Ford to the Twins for Pat Bourque

• George Hendrick and Dave Duncan to the Indians for Ray Fosse and Jack Heidemann

• Manny Trillo, Bob Locker and Darold Knowles to the Cubs for Billy Williams

• Don Stanhouse and Jim Panther to the Rangers for Denny McLain players — Torrez and Mitchell — who had already signed contracts and could not become free agents after the season. Finley pointed to Torrez' 20-win season in 1975 and said the inclusion of Mitchell was the key to the deal. In 1975, Mitchell had won 10 of 11 decisions for Rochester, the Orioles' top minor league affiliate. Considered one of the best pitching prospects in the game, the A's planned to use both Mitchell and Torrez in their revamped starting rotation.

One week later, Finley changed his mind concerning the rationale behind the trade. In an interview with Roger Williams of the San Francisco Examiner, Finley admitted that Jackson's lofty contract demands had bothered him. Finley had asked Reggie's agent to lower his asking price. When Jackson refused, Finley felt he had no other choice but to trade his superstar. Otherwise, the A's might lose Jackson — and receive nothing in return — at season's end.

Aside from shaking the emotional structure of the team, the six-player trade resulted in several lineup changes. Chuck Tanner returned Joe Rudi to left field, moving Claudell Washington to right field, his natural position in the minor leagues. Baylor would become the regular first baseman and occasional DH, filling in for Billy Williams when Tanner saw fit. Tanner also announced that Torrez would become his Opening Day pitcher, fitting into the assignment that he had originally given to Holtzman. Vida Blue would pitch the second game, followed by Stan Bahnsen, one of Tanner's best pitchers during their days with the White Sox. The surprising decision to use Bahnsen as the third starter left Dick Bosman wondering about his role with the team in 1976.

Tanner prepared to reunite with another one of his former White Sox pitchers when the A's acquired right-hander Tom Bradley from the Giants in a trade. Although the A's ticketed Bradley to start the season at Triple-A Tucson, Tanner hoped to see Bradley in Oakland before too much of the regular season had elapsed.

Perhaps distracted by the monstrous trade, the A's struggled in spring training. Oakland won just four of 14 exhibition games, the team's worst showing ever in the Cactus League. The A's fared better once the regular season began, winning their first three games, before dropping three straight to the rival Rangers. The pattern of .500 baseball continued over the first month of the season. Oakland finished April with a record of nine wins and eight losses.

Attendance at the Oakland Coliseum, always a problem for the A's, only worsened in the absence of Reggie Jackson. No longer featuring one of the American League's marquee power hitters, Chuck Tanner resorted to a different brand of baseball. Tanner instructed his fastest baserunners, Billy North, Campy Campaneris, Claudell Washington and Don Baylor, to attempt stolen bases at every opportunity. The strategy generally paid off, helping the A's to steal nearly two bases for every one game. Yet, the aggressive style of offense also brought a downside. In one game, Gene

Tenace tried to steal second base with the A's trailing by three runs. Tenace strained ligaments in his left knee. an injury that would sidelined him until July.

Heralded pitcher Paul Mitchell, facing pressure to justify the controversial Reggie Jackson trade, did not pitch well in his Oakland debut. Opposing hitters banged Mitchell badly in his first two starts, resulting in his demotion to the minor leagues. Tanner replaced Mitchell with Mike Norris, who had pitched well in early-season relief stints.

April's mediocre level of play soon gave way to an atrocious month of May. The A's started the month by losing five of their first seven. On May 17, the A's began perhaps their worst stretch of play since becoming division winners in 1971. A 5-4 loss to the Twins signaled the beginning of an eight-game losing streak. Jim Todd lost two straight games in extra innings. Starting pitchers lost six consecutive decisions. Don Baylor, the new cleanup man in the aftermath of the Reggie Jackson trade, struggled to raise his batting average above .200. At least Baylor had an excuse, having suffered a slight fracture in his left wrist. The injury, coupled with the cool early-season weather in the Bay Area, robbed Baylor of his usual power stroke. The newfangled lineup also had to make do without Billy Williams, sidelined by back spasms. Even when healthy, Williams hadn't hit, either. Like Baylor, his batting average rested uncomfortably under .200. Several writers suggested that Williams would retire after the season.

With Gene Tenace injured and Sal Bando also wallowing under .200, the once-powerful A's lineup had taken on the look of an also-ran. Other than Vida Blue and Mike Torrez, the pitching had done little to compensate. Except for a ten-strikeout game against the Angels, Paul Mitchell continued to experience major league shellings. Mike Norris pitched inconsistently in his return from the bullpen. Rollie Fingers fared so poorly that Chuck Tanner relegated him to the inglorious role of long relief. The A's of the early seventies seemed light years away.

On June 15, just hours before the annual trading deadline, the A's took an even larger step away from their glory years. With the team getting set to host the Red Sox at the Coliseum, Charlie Finley announced the sales of Joe Rudi and Rollie Fingers to Boston, one of the contending teams in the American League East. In exchange, the A's received a record $1 million apiece for their starting left fielder and best relief pitcher. Fingers and Rudi switched dugouts before the game and put on their new Red Sox uniforms, but did not play that night. After announcing the blockbuster sales, Finley told reporters, "the night's not over."[15] It certainly wasn't. Finley followed up the sales of Rudi and Fingers moments later when he sent Vida Blue to the Yankees for $1.5 million.

In one fell swoop, the A's had stripped themselves of three of their most important players. Why did Finley dispatch his best starter, his top reliever and his best defensive outfielder? Given that Blue, Fingers and

Rudi represented less than half of Oakland's impending free agent class, Finley considered the threesome unsignable beyond 1976. Finley also had to negotiate with Sal Bando, Campy Campaneris, Gene Tenace and Don Baylor, four other players also eligible for post-season free agency. Realizing that he had little chance (or perhaps desire) to sign Blue, Fingers and Rudi to long-term contracts, Finley decided to acquire something in return. Otherwise, the players would be able to leave as free agents without compensation, a la Catfish Hunter.

"It was a difficult decision," Finley admitted, "but I made every effort to sign them. I'm sorry to see Rollie and Joe go. They are two fine athletes and two fine gentleman. I'm very disappointed over having to do what I did."[16] Earlier in the day, Finley had actually signed Blue to a new four-year contract, before surprising the left-hander with the news that he had been sold to New York. Finley had signed Blue to the contract only as a pre-condition to his sale to the Yankees.

Finley's actions quickly caught the attention of Commissioner Bowie Kuhn. Disturbed and angered by Finley's firesales, Kuhn came down with a shockingly unprecedented ruling. On June 18, three days after Finley had made his transactions with the Red Sox and Yankees, Kuhn announced that all three sales were null and void. Kuhn ordered Blue, Fingers and Rudi, who had yet to debut with their new teams, to return to the A's. The commissioner condemned the transactions, in which the A's had received only cash, and no players in return. "Shorn of much of its finest talent in exchange for cash," Kuhn proclaimed, "the Oakland Club, which has been a divisional champion for the last five years, has little chance to compete effectively in its division. I would be remiss... if I did not act now... to prevent a development so harmful to baseball as this."[17] Kuhn, citing one of his powers as commissioner under Article One, Section Four of the major league agreement, declared that the player sales would not be allowed because they violated "the best interests of baseball." Those words would become Kuhn's common refrain until the end of his reign as commissioner in 1984.

Prior to selling the players, Finley had tried to make a trade with the Red Sox. He had discussed the possibility of swapping for players like Fred Lynn, Rick Burleson, Rick Wise and Cecil Cooper, but had been unable to come to an agreement. Finley had also approached the Brewers about a trade of Rudi for left-handed hitting catcher Darrell Porter. When Finley refused to allow the Brewers to negotiate a long-term contract with Rudi, Milwaukee turned down the deal. As a result, Finley settled for record cash compensation in return for Rudi and Fingers.

Finley responded to Kuhn's surprising decision by filing a $10 million lawsuit against the commissioner, claiming restraint of trade. Finley ordered Chuck Tanner not to use any of the three players in a game until the issue was settled in court. So, for the time being, Tanner was forced to make do with a 22-man roster, instead of the usual 25 players. Finley's attorney, Neil Papiano, explained the rationale behind the owner's decision. "If Charlie uses any of the players," claimed Papiano, "Then, in essence, he is ratifying the commissioner's position."[18] Papiano added that the three players shouldn't even be allowed into the Oakland clubhouse. Why? "The A's have been known to hurt themselves in the lockerroom,"[19] said a half-joking Papiano, referring to the fights that had taken place before and after games during the 1970s.

American League President Lee MacPhail questioned the wisdom of Finley's refusal to use the three players. "What bothers me is that they are not being played," MacPhail said. We can't let it go beyond another day or two. It is not fair to the players. They cannot be allowed to remain in limbo too long."[20] The absence of Rudi, Fingers and Blue was not only hurting the A's as a team, but was harming the bargaining power of each player. Each day missed translated into fewer chances for Rudi, Blue and Fingers to add to their usually impressive statistical totals.

Finley found allies in other camps. Yankee manager Billy Martin, angered by the ruling that had denied him the services of Blue, sarcastically compared Kuhn to the game's first commissioner. "What he's trying to be is another Judge (Kenesaw Mountain) Landis."[21] Marvin Miller, the head of the Players' Association, also criticized Kuhn, saying he had "singlehandedly plunged baseball into the biggest mess it has ever seen...It's raised the potential for litigation which would last for years. He is asserting a right to end all club owners' rights with respects to all transactions. Whenever there's a trade made, he can decide that one team did not get enough value and can veto the deal."[22]

Fingers, Blue and Rudi remained in limbo, unable to suit up for the A's because of Finley's edict, and prevented from joining their new teams in Boston and New York. Fingers remembers his disappointment over Kuhn's decision to negate his sale to the Red Sox. "At the time," Fingers recalls, "Charlie Finley knew that all three of us were playing out our options. We were gonna go to another ballclub. And all he was trying to do was to try to get some cash for us. I was happy to be going to Boston. I was going to a contending ballclub. They had some great players there, a good pitching staff. I loved pitching in Fenway Park. I was looking forward to going to Boston."

The forced inactivity frustrated all three players. "We were getting pretty disgusted with the whole thing," Fingers says. Finally, on June 24, nine days after the transactions had first been announced, Kuhn ordered Finley to "remove any restraints" against using the three players. Kuhn told Finley to allow Tanner to play Fingers, Rudi and Blue. Once again, the stubborn Finley refused to allow the players to suit up.

On June 27, the A's players decided to take the matter into their own hands. "It got to the point where we had a team meeting in the clubhouse (that day)," Fingers says, "and we told Chuck Tanner that guys weren't gonna play. Minnesota had come to town, and we were not gonna play the ballgame; we were gonna forfeit the ballgame to Minnesota if we were not activated."

Captain Sal Bando took a poll of Oakland players, who voted 21-0 in favor of striking, with two abstentions. Fingers vividly recalls the scene in the A's clubhouse just minutes before the scheduled first pitch against the Twins. "Everybody was in the clubhouse in their regular clothes, about 15 minutes before the game. Chuck Tanner called up Charlie Finely and said, 'The boys aren't gonna play unless you do something about it.' Chuck Tanner came out of his office and started reading the lineup." Tanner announced the following names: North, Campaneris, Baylor, Bando, Tenace, Rudi... "As soon as he said Rudi's name, the boys put their uniforms on," Fingers says. "We went out and beat Minnesota that day." Finley had finally given in, allowing Rudi to return to the starting lineup and Blue and Fingers to resume their roles on the pitching staff. The A's, perhaps motivated by the return of their three teammates, defeated the Twins, 5-3.

Although the players were relieved that they had been reinstated, the resolution to the scenario proved less than ideal. "I still had to play out the year in Oakland," Fingers points out. "The hardest part was sitting around for almost two weeks and not playing. I didn't pitch for two weeks because Charlie Finley felt as though he were right, and Joe Rudi didn't hit for two weeks, and Vida Blue missed about five starts in two weeks. We lost to Kansas City that year by one game." (actually two and a half). "I think if we'd been playing, and had the opportunity those two weeks, we may have won the pennant that year. That's probably the saddest part of that whole situation." The facts bear our Fingers' assessment. The A's went just 6-5 during the absence of the three players. The inactivity also had a prolonged effect on two of the players. Rudi struggled to regain his batting stroke. Blue did not win his next game until July 6, more than three weeks after Finley had initially tried to sell off his three players.

Finley's $10 million suit against the commissioner's office proved futile. In 1977, U.S. District Judge Frank McGarr came down with a ruling in favor of Bowie Kuhn. McGarr cited a pre-existing agreement between the major league owners and the commissioner. Under that agreement, owners had promised never to challenge a commissioner's decision in the courts. In 1978, Finley would file for an appeal. The Supreme Court refused to even hear the case, quietly bringing to an end a two-year saga that had begun so loudly with three blockbuster sales — sales that would never come to be.

Bolstered by the returns of three important players, the A's played their best ball of the season in July, winning 17 of 28 games. Sal Bando, who had hit two home runs on the day that Rudi, Fingers and Blue enjoyed their reinstatement, banged seven home runs during a seven-game stretch. On July 15, Gene Tenace returned to catching for the first time since straining his knee. With Tenace unavailable to play behind the plate, the A's had struggled to find adequate catching. On two occasions, the A's had botched rundown plays when their catchers had failed to cover home plate. The mental errors had contributed directly to two losses.

The A's bridged July and August by losing six straight games, including five to the Twins. "When you're a fan, you can laugh at this, but when you're an owner, all you can do is cry," Charlie Finley said, reacting to the sudden reversal of fortune. "The way they played against Minnesota, losing all five games, was a disgrace. I can't believe it happened."[23] Yet, Finley still believed the A's would catch the first-place Royals. "Kansas City is looking over their shoulders," claimed Finley. "In my opinion, they're going to choke."[24]

In the meantime, Chuck Tanner tried to fight off controversy in the clubhouse. Utilityman Cesar Tovar, on the disabled list since May 31, complained to Marvin Miller of the Players' Association that the A's had refused to activate him, even though he was now healthy. Tovar claimed that his broken right wrist had healed sufficiently. Throughout his career, Tovar took pride in playing hurt and returning quickly from injuries.

Knowing that he was no longer hurt, Tovar bristled at the A's decision to keep him disabled. After speaking to Miller, the A's finally relented and activated the veteran utilityman. In order to make room for Tovar on the 25-man roster, Tanner decided to option pinch-runner Larry Lintz to Tucson. Lintz did not take the news well, engaging Tanner in a shouting match over the demotion.

Another unhappy player, relief pitcher Jim Todd, did not pitch once during a 24-game stretch. Todd suggested that his status as Oakland's player representative had prompted Charlie Finley to mandate he not be used in any games. Todd asked Tanner for a meeting, but the manager insisted that Finley had played no part in his recent absence from games.

Shortly after Finley's diatribe, the A's assembled a season-high nine-game winning streak to move within seven games of the Royals. The win streak prolonged Sal Bando's career in Oakland. Finley had agreed to sell Bando to the Yankees, who were seeking a right-handed hitting DH to balance their lineup. When the A's pulled back into the pennant race, Finley canceled the sale of Bando to the Bronx.

The A's stayed within striking distance throughout August. On the next to last day of the month, Finley imported a veteran bat capable of designated hitting and providing some power off the bench. Finley purchased future Hall of Famer Willie McCovey from the Padres. "The reason for getting McCovey was for getting us to the playoffs,"[25] Finley explained.

Given McCovey's experience and the A's need for a left-handed bat, the deal made sense. Two days later, Finley tried to make another transaction, one that made no sense. With the A's only seven games back and Sal Bando sharing the league lead in home runs, Finley attempted to sell his captain to the Rangers. Finley actually completed a trade with Texas,

> **Hall of Famers Employed By Charlie Finley**
> Luke Appling — Manager
> Joe DiMaggio — Coach and Executive VP
> Gabby Hartnett — Coach and Scout
> Billy Herman — Scout
> Catfish Hunter — Player
> Reggie Jackson — Player
> Rollie Fingers — Player
> Billy Williams — Player
> Willie McCovey — Player

contingent on the Rangers' ability to sign Bando to a long-term contract. Bando asked for four years and $600,000. The Rangers said no, killing the deal. The same day Finley's attorney, Neil Papiano, told reporters that Finley planned to file an injunction in an effort to have Rollie Fingers and Joe Rudi sent to the Red Sox and Vida Blue dispatched to the Yankees. After previously indicating that he felt his team could still make the playoffs, Finley was now acting as if the post-season meant nothing to him.

Although McCovey had batted only .203 for the Padres, Chuck Tanner inserted him into the designated hitter role, replacing another slumping veteran, Billy Williams, who hinted that he would retire after the season. Williams remained on Oakland's 25-man roster for the moment, but the versatile Cesar Tovar did not. The A's released Tovar to make room for McCovey. Finley likely hadn't forgotten that Tovar had complained to the Players' Association about the A's refusal to reinstate him from the disabled list.

With 24 games remaining, the A's moved within five games of the first-place Royals. Six head-to-head matchups with Kansas City gave the A's hope that they could catch the Royals before the end of the regular season. On September 14, Finley once again reverted to his playoff-hopeful mode, acquiring first baseman-outfielder Ron Fairly from the Cardinals. Chuck Tanner planned to use "The Mule" as a left-handed pinch-hitter in the late innings, but would soon expand the role of the veteran National Leaguer.

On September 20, the eve of a showdown series between the two leaders in the AL West, the A's trailed the Royals by six games. With the A's no longer having a Catfish Hunter or Ken Holtzman to use in the biggest game of the season, Chuck Tanner fell back on eight-game winner Stan Bahnsen. Needing to win all three games to have a chance of coming back, the A's dropped the first game, 3-1. Doug Bird outpitched Bahnsen with six innings of one-run baseball and won for the first time since August 22.

The A's rallied to win the next two games, but remained five games out in the West. After splitting a two-game series with the White Sox and creeping within four and a half games, the A's hosted the Royals in a last-gasp series at the Oakland Coliseum. In the first game, Ron Fairly homered for the third time in two weeks and Sal Bando added his 26th HR to give the A's an 8-3 win. After Bando homered to lead off the sixth, Dennis Leonard hit Don Baylor with a pitch, precipitating a dugout-clearing brawl and Baylor's ejection. During the melee, Claudell Washington flattened Leonard with a punch to the head.

The A's drew within two and a half games when Mike Torrez outdueled Marty Pattin, 1-0. Torrez allowed only two hits and retired the final 14 batters he faced. The victory left the A's confident that they could sweep the series, since the Royals would pitch left-hander Larry Gura, one of the least used hurlers on the Kansas City staff.

Oakland starter Paul Mitchell lasted only two innings, having surrendered three runs and six hits. In the meantime, the soft-tossing Gura mastered the A's hitters, keeping them off balance with his mix of curve balls and change ups. Gura shut down the middle of the Oakland order — Joe Rudi, Gene Tenace, Sal Bando and Don Baylor — pitched a four-hitter and won a 4-0 decision.

The loss virtually eliminated the A's from playoff contention. The Royals needed just one more victory or Oakland loss to clinch the division

The A's aren't toasting another title here. Rollie Fingers, Joe Rudi, Don Baylor, Gene Tenace and Sal Bando celebrate their upcoming free agency — and impending departure from Charlie Finley.

title. Two nights later, the Royals lost to the Twins, 4-3, then waited out the results of the game later that evening in Oakland. Thanks to the pitching of Vida Blue and Frank Tanana, the A's and Angels played scoreless baseball over the first 11 innings. In the top of the 12th inning, Angels' center fielder Rusty Torres, batting .206, cracked a solo home run against Blue. Two singles sandwiched around an error by Billy North gave the Angels a 2-0 lead. Angels' reliever Dick Drago, the same man who had been on the mound for the Red Sox when Boston defeated Oakland in the '75 playoffs, came on to retire the A's in the bottom of the inning. For the first time since 1970, the A's had failed to make the playoffs.

After playing out the final two games of the season, the A's held a small champagne party in the Coliseum clubhouse. Even though the A's had no pennant to celebrate, they had found another occasion to commemorate. The A's seven impending free agents purchased 36 bottles of champagne for the players, coaches and manager Chuck Tanner. "This is to celebrate the liberation of the Oakland Seven,"[26] said Billy North, one of the A's players actually under contract for the coming season. "I feel sorry for anyone who has to play for this club next year,"[27] said Rollie Fingers, who had already announced that he would not return to Oakland. In addition to Fingers, players like Gene Tenace, Campy Campaneris, Sal Bando, Joe Rudi and Don Baylor couldn't wait to escape from Charlie Finley's prison. Even a relative newcomer like Willie McCovey seemed anxious to play elsewhere. The future Hall of Famer refused to start the final game in protest of his lack of playing time down the stretch. Like the others, "Stretch" would soon be saying goodbye to the Bay Area and to Mr. Finley.

Chapter Thirty-two:
Baseball's Last Dynasty

$\mathbf{E}$xcept for center fielder Billy North, whom he had re-signed to a two-year contract, Charlie Finley allowed almost everyone of his stars to leave while still in the prime of their playing careers. "No telling how many championships we could have won," Sal Bando said several years later. "We had everything on the field — speed, pitching, defense and power. But no management. Some of the things Charlie did were good. But he did more destroying. He destroyed the A's."[1]

Bando signed a contract with the Milwaukee Brewers. Rollie Fingers and Gene Tenace moved down to the coast to the San Diego Padres. Don Baylor and Joe Rudi also moved south to the California Angels. "Charlie Finley is going to wind up with nothing," Rudi said in 1977, his first year with California. "It's like the good man says, 'You reap what you sow.' And Charlie has sowed only garbage for a lot of years."[2]

Finley's inability and unwillingness to sign any of his free agents sowed a lineup filled with over-the-hill stars and mediocre prospects. Finley traded manager Chuck Tanner to the Pittsburgh Pirates for 32-year-old catcher Manny Sanguillen, who would succeed the tandem of Gene Tenace and Larry Haney. At first base, 35-year-old Dick Allen replaced the combination of Tenace and Don Baylor for 50 games before retiring. After designated hitter Billy Williams had decided to retire following the 1976 season, the A's signed veteran slugger Earl Williams, at one time a budding star with the Atlanta Braves. With Rollie Fingers gone, Finley traded for 37-year-old reliever Dave Giusti, the relief ace of the Pirates' 1971 championship team. The A's tried to fill other gaps with untested minor leaguers like Rob Picciolo, Jim Tyrone, Mitchell Page and Rick Langford.

The new mix proved disastrous. The 1977 A's finished last in the American League West, 38 and a half games back of the first place Kansas City Royals. To make matters worse, the A's finished one-half game off the pace of the Seattle Mariners, one of baseball's two new expansion teams. The dynasty, which had reached its peak only three seasons earlier, had given way to a full-fledged on-field embarrassment.

As much as the A's accomplished from 1971 to 1975, Sal Bando felt the team could have performed even better had Charlie Finley treated them differently. "I've seen how people respond to fair treatment," Bando said in 1985. "I know I would have been a better player treated fairly. Reggie (Jackson) was a very good player, but he would have been better. Campy (Campaneris) was such a sensitive person. As good as he was, he could have been better."[3]

Although Campaneris, Bando, Rudi, Jackson, Gene Tenace, Catfish Hunter, Ken Holtzman and Rollie Fingers had all turned 30 or older by 1977, the A's likely would have contended for the American League West title for at least two more seasons had they retained all of them. The Kansas City Royals, a good young team, would have posed a challenge, but the A's would have remained the favorites. The New York Yankees would not have had the services of Jackson, Hunter and Holtzman, and likely would not have won the American League pennant in 1977 and '78. The National League champions, the Los Angeles Dodgers, possessed a similar make-up to the 1974 pennant winners, which had lost to the A's in the World Series. This is all supposition, of course, but it is not unreasonable to say that without the effects of free agency the A's would have won two more world championships in 1977 and '78. If they had retained Hunter all along, they might have accomplished more in 1975 and '76, as well.

By 1979, age had caught up with several of Oakland's former stars. Catfish Hunter struggled to a 2-9 mark with the Yankees and retired after the season. Ken Holtzman pitched poorly in 23 games with the Cubs and also called it quits. Sal Bando slumped to a nine-home run, 43-RBI season in Milwaukee. Joe Rudi batted only .242 with 61 RBI's for the Angels. Rollie Fingers fell off to 13 saves and a 4.50 ERA in San Diego. Bert Campaneris split the season between Texas and California, batting .230 with a paltry 13 stolen bases. Only Gene Tenace and Reggie Jackson enjoyed productive seasons in 1979.

Of the slumping players, only Fingers would bounce back in 1980. Jackson remained a legitimate star, batting a career-high .300 while leading the American League with 41 home runs. The other Oakland ex-patriots, however, ceased being regular players or left the game entirely. For those speculating about continuing Oakland supremacy, the argument had become irrelevant.

Yet, the A's accomplished more during the 1970s than any other major league team at that time, or since. As owner and general manager in the sixties, Charlie Finley realized that he was a relative novice at baseball. He listened intently to his scouts — people like Joe Bowman, Dan Carnevale, Tom Giordano, Clyde Kluttz, Art Lilly, Don Pries, Jack Sanford and others — who told him which amateur players to pursue as free agents and which ones to draft. As a result, the A's developed future stars like Catfish Hunter, Vida Blue, Blue Moon Odom, Rollie Fingers, Campy Campaneris, Sal Bando and Reggie Jackson. In later years, a more confident and penurious Finley pushed out many of his veteran scouts and tended to ignore the advice of those he still employed. Yet, he still managed to exhibit a deft hand in making trades and signing bargain basement role players. "I have to give the guy a lot of credit," says Ted Kubiak. "I mean, he put some teams together. For someone who came into baseball that didn't know anything, he really developed and did a lot of talking, did a lot of phone calling."

In 1971, Finley made perhaps his best trade, sending an underachieving Rick Monday to the Cubs for the enigmatic Ken Holtzman, who would win 77 games over four seasons in Oakland. In 1972, Finley acquired Billy North for an aging Bob Locker. In his first four years with the A's, North would play a solid center field, steal 212 bases and become both a capable leadoff man and No. 2 hitter. Finley also engineered a five-player deal that brought a young left-handed power hitter (Mike Epstein) and an important left-handed reliever (Darold Knowles) to the Bay Area. Without Epstein, the A's might not have won in 1972. In 1973, the same could be said of Knowles, who pitched in all seven games of the World Series against the Mets. Finley also swung unheralded deals for key role players like Matty Alou, Deron Johnson and Horacio Piña, who would fill important holes in the outfield, at designated hitter and in middle relief during the 1972 and '73 seasons.

The A's of 1972, '73 and '74 tend to be grouped into one single unit. The core of the team — Gene Tenace, Campy Campaneris, Sal Bando, Joe Rudi, Reggie Jackson, Catfish Hunter, Vida Blue, Ken Holtzman and Rollie Fingers — played on all three championship teams. Yet, the secondary players on each of those teams were different, and each team faced unique obstacles in winning the World Series. Which one of the three was the best?

"I might have to say the first year," Kubiak says of the 1972 team, "only because we were not picked to win (the Series). We were facing the 'Big Red Machine' there that time, the beginnings of it anyway. We were the long-haired kids coming in there being the underdogs. It was a very tough Series." The 1972 A's also overcame serious obstacles in defeating the heavily-favored Reds. Oakland played all seven games of the World Series without its marquee position player, Reggie Jackson, and without its best left-handed reliever, Darold Knowles. "I personally thought that the Mets and the Dodgers were not that good a club that we played," Kubiak continues, "and I think everybody might say that...I don't know. We came back home from New York down three games to two, knowing that we had to win. It was up in the air, but I just really had the feeling we were gonna come back and win. And the Dodgers didn't show us anything; I don't think they showed us much at all. We didn't think they were that good defensively."

Sal Bando casts his vote for the team that defeated the New York Mets in the middle of the championship run. "We became more of a stable club in '73, an experienced club in '73," claims Bando, who says the '72 team suffered from so many player transactions and personnel changes. "I thought the '73 team, when healthy, was the best, simply because I thought we had more depth in the bullpen in '73. I thought we were a complete team; there wasn't anything we did not have. We had speed; we had power; we had defense; we had pitching. We had great depth in the bullpen; we had (Darold) Knowles and (Paul) Lindblad as left-handers, we had (Rollie) Fingers and (Horacio) Piña. I thought Horacio was kind of the difference." In 1973, the side-arming Piña pitched 88 innings as the primary right-handed long man in relief. Piña's 2.76 ERA ranked second among all A's relievers, and his effectiveness allowed Dick Williams to cut down Fingers' heavy workload during the season.

Were the A's the last true dynasty in major league baseball? First, we need to attach a definition to the word dynasty. According to the *American Heritage College Dictionary*, a dynasty is a "succession of rulers from the same family or line," or a "family or group that maintains power for several generations." Obviously, neither definition applies specifically to a baseball dynasty, a subjective term that has been created by sports writers and broadcasters in an attempt to describe teams that have won a number of championships and place those teams in proper historical context. Yet, if we apply the first definition from *American Heritage* and substitute the word champions for rulers, and replace the word family with organization, we may have come close to establishing an appropriate baseball definition of a dynasty: "a succession of champions from the same organization."

If we use this newly created definition, the key word becomes succession. A succession implies a sequence that is continuous and uninterrupted. Therefore, in order to achieve a dynasty, a team must reign supreme over several consecutive seasons, without interruption. Since the A's of 1971-75, only five teams have won as many as three consecutive divisional crowns — the New York Yankees, Kansas City Royals, the A's, Toronto Blue Jays and Atlanta Braves. No club has won more than two straight world championships, with the Cincinnati Reds, Yankees and Blue Jays each defending their titles before succumbing in the third season.

Since the mid-seventies, several teams have been categorized as "dynasties." In the 1990s, a few broadcasters and writers have argued that the Atlanta Braves deserve the dynasty distinction. From 1991 to 1997, the Braves won six out of a possible seven divisional titles, four National League pennants and one World Series. Yet, the Braves won no more than three divisions in a row, having finished second in the National League East during the strike-shortened season of 1994. The runner-up finish broke up a potentially dynastic string of consecutive division titles.

The Braves captured National League flags in 1991 and '92, but lost to an inferior Philadelphia Phillies' team in 1993 before recovering to win two more league titles. Most importantly, the Braves won only one World Series during the six-year span (not including the strike year), a "winning" percentage of only .166. Given any definition, one world championship in six years hardly qualifies a team for dynasty status.

The Toronto Blue Jays won three straight American League East crowns, two pennants and two World Series during their three-year reign from 1991 to 1993. A third-place, sub-.500 finish in the strike year of 1994 signaled the end of the Jays' success. The New York Yankees experienced a strikingly similar run in the late 1970s. After winning the American League pennant in 1976, the Yankees lost to the Cincinnati Reds in an embarrassing and one-sided four-game sweep. Bolstered by the addition of free agent right fielder Reggie Jackson, the Yankees won two more pennants in '77 and '78 and elevated themselves to the level of world champions. In 1979, the Yankees fell well short of the post-season, finishing in fourth place, 13 and a half games out in the American League East.

From 1976 to '78, the trophy count for the "Bronx Zoo" Yankees reads like this: three divisional titles, two American League pennants and two World series crowns. The numbers are impressive enough to put the Yankees — and the Blue Jays of '91 to '93 — close to dynasty contention. Close, but just a bit short. We might be tempted to classify the Yankees as a dynasty if they had put on a better show in the 1976 World Series or won another division in 1979. Two World Series titles, bookended by four division titles, would likely have been enough to place the Yankees or the Blue Jays at the dynasty level. Without a fourth division win or a third World Series championship, the Yankees and Jays fall just short.

Some baseball historians have classified the Cincinnati Reds of 1970, '72, '75 and '76 as a dynasty. Yet, the Reds lost the World Series in 1972 (to the A's, no less), and did not even qualify for the playoffs in 1971, or '74. How then, can the Reds of the 1970s be described as a true dynasty, when they did not continuously win world championships, much less division titles or pennants?

The Reds of 1975 and '76 represent two of the most dominant teams in major league history. The "Big Red Machine" featured one of the most fearsome offensive lineups ever, comparable to the 1927 and '61 Yankees and the 1930 Philadelphia A's. Yet, two straight world championships, with no surrounding divisional titles or pennants, hardly constitutes a succession. A succession can also be thought of as a sequence. One of the definitions of the word sequence involves the playing of card games, where a sequence occurs with at least "three or more playing cards in consecutive order." Therefore, if we continue to enforce this definition and line of reasoning, winning back-to-back World Series by itself does not qualify one as a dynasty. Especially when one considers that the Reds' teams of the preceding and succeeding seasons did not even make the playoffs. The Reds of 1974 finished four games back of the Los Angeles Dodgers in the National League West. In 1977, the Reds once again finished second to the Dodgers, a full 10 games back.

In contrast to the Reds of '76 and '77, the A's won three straight World Series and American League pennants, piggybacked by five consecutive divisional crowns. This succession of winning, much longer than that of the Reds, Yankees, Blue Jays, or Braves, smacks of a true dynasty. The A's won consistently over a period of five interrupted seasons, compared to two seasons for the Reds and three apiece for the Blue Jays, Yankees and Braves.

Yet, when historians refer to dynasties in recent baseball history, they inevitably mention the Cincinnati Reds first, followed by only a fleeting mention of the A's. Why? The answer can be found in the way the Reds won in 1975 and '76. The Reds won 108 games in 1975, a full 20 games over the second place Dodgers, before outlasting the Boston Red Sox in arguably the most compelling World Series ever. The following summer, the Reds won 102 games, 10 lengths in front of Los Angeles. The "Machine" then annihilated the Yankees in the Fall Classic.

In contrast, the A's of 1972-74 never won more than 94 games in the regular season and never staked claim to a divisional title by more than six games. In the World Series, the A's failed to sweep a National League opponent, twice winning in seven games and once in five games. Yet, the A's won when they had to. For example, Oakland snared two deciding fifth games in the American League Championship Series and two seventh games in the World Series. In fact, the A's never lost a decisive fifth game of a playoff series, or a Game Seven in the World Series during the 1970s.

A few years ago, Rollie Fingers provided an explanation for the A's ability to win such "elimination" games. "At the end of the season, we'd be really hungry for World Series checks because Charlie Finley didn't pay us much," Fingers said. "A lot of us there got a taste of it early in our careers, so we wanted to get there again and again and again."

Even if supporters of Cincinnati were to concede that the Reds were not a true dynasty, they might argue that the "Big Red Machine" teams of 1975 and '76 were better and more dominating teams than the A's. The two teams did not meet head-to-head — well, not exactly. In 1972, the A's, playing without the injured Reggie Jackson and Darold Knowles, defeated a Reds' team that was fairly similar to the clubs of '75 and '76. Of the eight regulars on the '72 Reds, six played for the championship teams of 1975-76 — Tony Perez, Joe Morgan, Dave Concepcion, Pete Rose, Cesar Geronimo and Johnny Bench. Ken Griffey, Sr. succeeded Bobby Tolan in the outfield, and George Foster essentially replaced third baseman Denis Menke, with Rose moving from left field to third base to accommodate Foster. On the pitching staff, the top three starters — Gary Nolan, Don Gullett and Jack Billingham — remained the same, as did two of the key relievers — Pedro Borbon and Clay Carroll. Therefore, the A's of 1972, playing without two of their most instrumental players, defeated a team that we might regard as the direct predecessor to the Reds of 1975 and '76.

Yet, the Reds of the mid-seventies were clearly better than the '72 team, thanks to the addition of George Foster's right-handed bat and a deeper bullpen that added Rawly Eastwick and Will McEnaney. Therefore, let's assemble composite lineups of the A's of 1972-74 and the Reds of 1975-76.

Position:	A's player	Reds' Player
Catcher:	Gene Tenace	Johnny Bench
First Base:	Mike Epstein	Tony Perez
Second Base:	Dick Green	Joe Morgan
Shortstop:	Campy Campaneris	Dave Concepcion
Third Base:	Sal Bando	Pete Rose
Left Field:	Joe Rudi	George Foster
Center field:	Billy North	Cesar Geronimo
Right Field:	Reggie Jackson	Ken Griffey, Sr.

The head-to-head analysis of the lineups favors the Reds — heavily. Cincinnati rates advantages at catcher, first base, second base, shortstop, third base and left field. The A's come out ahead at only two positions, center field and right field. While such an analysis is fun to create and provides a conversation piece, it really does little to tell us which is the better team. Baseball is not a game where position players match up, like they would in basketball or football. First basemen do not lock heads, second baseman don't guard each other and outfielders don't set picks on one another.

Baseball's matchups involve pitchers vs. hitters, and vice-versa. It is here where the A's gain an advantage. Oakland's superior starting pitching poses a problem — even for Cincinnati's stacked Hall of Fame lineup. In short series, teams with strong pitching tend to handcuff teams filled with power hitters. While Gary Nolan, Don Gullett, Jack Billingham and Fred Norman all rank as competent starters for Cincinnati, they would be hard-pressed to crack the Oakland rotation of Catfish Hunter, Vida Blue and Ken Holtzman. In the bullpen, relievers like Pedro Borbon, Clay Carroll and Rawly Eastwick would probably rate no higher than second best among the Oakland relievers, behind Rollie Fingers.

An examination of the benches also tilts in the direction of Oakland. A reserve corps of Dave Duncan, Mike Hegan, Don Mincher, Ted Kubiak, Deron Johnson, Vic Davalillo and Matty and Jesus Alou gives the A's speed, excellent defensive backups at catcher, first base and the middle infield, five solid pinch-hitters and two power hitters. The Reds' bench, consisting of Bill Plummer, Dan Driessen, Bob Bailey, Darrell Chaney, Ed Armbrister, Terry Crowley and Merv Rettenmund, is good, but not nearly as powerful or as deep as the Oakland contingent.

So which teams were better, the A's of the early seventies or the Reds of the middle seventies? Since they never played each other in real games, no one will know for sure. More to the point, a tangible examination of each team's accomplishments proves that the A's did achieve more over a longer period of time. When you add it up, two divisional crowns, two league pennants and two world championships in two years is not as impressive as five divisional crowns, three league pennants and three World Series victories over five years. The bottom line is this: two seasons do not make a dynasty; five seasons do.

Rollie Fingers offered little hesitation when asked about the best ballclubs he played on during his Hall of Fame career. "Those years, we were the best team I've ever seen," Fingers says of the A's of 1972 to '74. "We had a solid bench, pitching, hitting, speed, everything."[4]

"I can't explain that club," says Ted Kubiak. "It was just a unique club, as far as what they could do. It was almost like Dick (Williams) would send them out there and that was it. I mean he used to sit in the dugout and watch them play. Jesus Christ, pitchers getting guys out easy; players were always in the right position defensively."

In spite of off-the-field disagreements and never-ending controversies, the A's played to maximum efficiency once the games began. "When you were on the field," says Kubiak, "I mean, it was like one big gigantic unit. And the thing that amazed me was how well they played the game. You talk all the time about not making mistakes and hitting cut-off men and being able to pitch guys in a certain way. I mean, that club was just unbelievable."

Was the Oakland dynasty the last one in major league history, never to be duplicated again? "I would have to say so," says Rollie Fingers. "We won five straight division titles, three straight World Series championships. I don't think you're going to see that happen nowadays, simply because with free agency, ballplayers are jumping around all over the place. That's why I don't think you're gonna see teams repeating, repeating, repeating in championships. That's the main reason why."

The Oakland A's of 1971 to 1975. We may never see the likes of them again.

Footnotes

Chapter One
1. Ron Bergman, *The Sporting News* (October 17, 1970): p. 25
2. Ibid.
3. Associated Press (October 3, 1970)
4. Ron Bergman, *The Sporting News* (October 17, 1970): p. 25
5. Ron Bergman, *The Sporting News* (November 28, 1970): p. 25
6. National Baseball Hall of Fame Library File (1971).
7. Al Hirshberg, Sport (October 1973): p. 102
8. Ron Bergman, *The Sporting News* (December 12, 1970): p. 56
9. Ron Bergman, *The Sporting News* (February 13, 1971): p. 31
10. Ibid.
11. Ibid.
12. Ron Bergman, *The Sporting News* (April 17, 1971): p. 3
13. Ron Bergman, *The Sporting News* (February 13, 1971): p. 31
14. Glenn Dickey, *Sport* (July 1973): p. 54
15. Ed Rumill, *Christian Science Monitor* (March 18, 1968)
16. Ron Bergman, *The Sporting News* (December 9, 1970) p. 39
17. Ibid.
18. Ibid.
19. Ron Bergman, *The Sporting News* (February 26, 1971): p. 43
20. George Vass, *Baseball Digest* (January 1971): p. 37

Chapter Two
1. Ron Bergman, *The Sporting News* (March 6, 1971): p. 38
2. Ibid.
3. Ed Rumill, *Christian Science Monitor* (September 25, 1971)
4. Ron Bergman, *The Sporting News* (March 6, 1971): p. 38
5. Ron Bergman, *The Sporting News* (March 13, 1971): p. 47
6. Ibid.
7. Bill Jauss, *Baseball Digest* (April 1971): p. 42
8. Ron Bergman, *The Sporting News* (March 20, 1971): p. 40
9. Ron Bergman, *The Sporting News* (March 27, 1971): p. 40
10. Michael Haggerty, Oakland A's press release (undated)
11. Ibid.
12. Bill Libby, *Sports Today* (June 1971) 13 Ibid.
14. Arthur Daley, *New York Times* (July 23, 1969)
15. Ron Bergman, *The Sporting News* (April 19, 1969): p. 25

Chapter Three
1. Ron Bergman, *The Sporting News* (April 10, 1971): p. 34
2. Jerry Izenberg, *Sport* (October 1971): pp. 70-71
3. Dick Young, *New York Daily News* (October 2, 1971)
4. Ron Bergman, *The Sporting News* (April 24, 1971): p. 12
5. Ron Bergman, *The Sporting News* (November 14, 1970): p. 56
6. Ron Bergman, *The Sporting News* (April 24, 1971): p. 12
7. Murray Chass, *New York Times* (April 15, 1971)
8. Phil Pepe, *New York Daily News* (June 7, 1976)

Chapter Four
1. Larry Claflin, Boston Record American (April 24, 1971)
2. Ibid.
3. Ibid.
4. Marty Ralbovsky, *New York Times* (April 15, 1971)
5. Ron Bergman, *The Sporting News* (May 8, 1971): p. 6
6. Ron Bergman, *The Sporting News* (May 15, 1971): p. 6
7. William Leggett, *Sports Illustrated* (May 3, 1971): p. 20
8. Sandy Treadwell, *Sports Illustrated* (May 31, 1971): p. 73
9. Ron Bergman, *The Sporting News* (May 22, 1971): p. 12
10. Arnold Hano, *Sport* (November 1972): p. 87
11. Ibid.
12. Ron Bergman, *The Sporting News* (May 22, 1971): p. 12
13. Ron Bergman, *The Sporting News* (May 29, 1971): p. 7

Chapter Five
1. Roy Blount, Jr., *Sports Illustrated* (May 17, 1971): p. 66
2. Arthur Daley, *New York Times* (June 1, 1971)
3. Ibid.
4. Wells Twombly, *New York Times Magazine* (July 25, 1971)
5. Arthur Daley, *New York Times* (June 1, 1971)
6. New York Times, (June 1, 1971)
7. Super Sports, (October 1971)
8. Joseph Durso, *New York Times* (July 13, 1971)
9. Ron Bergman, *The Sporting News* (June 5, 1971): p. 3
10. Robert Vare, *Sport* (August 1971): p. 26
11. Ron Bergman, *The Sporting News* (June 5, 1971): p. 3
12. Robert Vare, *Sport* (August 1971): p. 28
13. Ron Bergman, *The Sporting News* (March 20, 1971): p. 40
14. Ron Bergman, *The Sporting News* (June 5, 1971): p. 3
15. Pat Jordan, *Sport* (November 1971): p. 76
16. Russell Schneider, *The Sporting News* (August 23, 1969): p. 21
17. Ibid.
18. Associated Press (May 18, 1971)
19. Ron Bergman, *The Sporting News* (August 19, 1972): p. 21
20. Phil Collier, *The Sporting News* (May 10, 1980): p. 10
21. Joe Donnelly, *New York Newsday* (May 26, 1971)
22. Ron Bergman, *The Sporting News* (June 19, 1971): p. 8
23. Ron Bergman, *The Sporting News* (June 26, 1971): p. 11
24. Ibid.
25. *New York Times*, (June 1, 1971)
26. Wells Twombly, *New York Times Magazine* (July 25, 1971)
27. Milton Gross, *Sport Scene* (November 1971)
28. *Newark Star Ledger* (July 6, 1971)
29. Dick Edwards, *Black Sports* (January 1974)
30. Ibid.
31. *New York Times*, (June 13, 1971)
32. Robert Vare, *Sport* (August 1971): p. 28
33. *New York Times*, (June 13, 1971)
34. Wells Twombly, *New York Times Magazine* (July 25, 1971)
35. Bill Ballew, *Sports Collectors Digest* (April 26, 1996)
36. Samuel J. Skinner, *Black Sports* (September 1971)
37. Len Koppett, *New York Times* (June 4, 1971)
38. Wells Twombly, *New York Times Magazine* (July 25, 1971)
39. Ibid.

40. Ibid.
41. Samuel J. Skinner, *Black Sports* (July-August 1972)
42. Ibid.
43. Ron Bergman, *The Sporting News* (August 19, 1972): p. 21
44. Ron Bergman, *The Sporting News* (March 3, 1973): p. 3
45. National Baseball Hall of Fame Library File (1972)
46. Ron Bergman, *The Sporting News* (July 24, 1971): p. 10
47. Ron Bergman, *The Sporting News* (July 17, 1971): p. 26

Chapter Six
1. *The Sporting News* (July 31, 1971): p. 8
2. Dick Young, *New York Daily News* (July 15, 1971)
3. Ibid.
4. Dick Young, *Cincinnati Enquirer* (July 15, 1971)
5. Ibid.
6. Ron Bergman, *The Sporting News* (August 14, 1971): p. 8
7. Ibid.
8. Ron Bergman, *The Sporting News* (June 21, 1969)
9. Ibid.
10. Marty Bell, *Sport* (July 1974): p. 68
11. Ibid.
12. Ron Bergman, *The Sporting News* (August 21, 1971): p. 6
13. Ibid.
14. Associated Press, (August 16, 1971)
15. Robert Vare, *Sport* (August 1971): p. 28
16. Larry Eldridge, *Christian Science Monitor* (August 21, 1973)
17. Ron Bergman, *The Sporting News* (August 28, 1971): p. 13
18. *Baseball Magazine*, (April 1980)
19. Ibid.
20. Ron Bergman, *The Sporting News* (September 11, 1971): p. 10
21. Ibid.
22. Ibid.
23. Joseph Durso, *New York Times* (August 16, 1971)
24. Associated Press, (August 18, 1971)
25. Ibid.
26. Ibid.
27. Ron Bergman, *The Sporting News* (September 18, 1971): p. 7
28. Ibid.
29. Ibid.
30. Ron Bergman, *The Sporting News* (October 2, 1971): p. 8
31. Bucky Walter, *San Francisco Examiner* (May 8, 1968)
32. Pat Jordan, *Sport* (November 1971): p. 92
33. Paul Hemphill, *Sport* (April 1975): p. 67
34. Ibid.
35. Pat Jordan, *Sport* (November 1971): p. 76
36. Ron Fimrite, *Sports Illustrated* (June 7, 1971): p. 75

Chapter Seven
1. Arnold Hano, *Sport* (November 1972): p. 66
2. Ron Bergman, *The Sporting News* (October 9, 1971)
3. Arnold Hano, *Sport* (November 1972): p. 68
4. Ron Fimrite, *Sports Illustrated* (September 27, 1971): p. 25
5. Murray Chass, *New York Times* (October 2, 1971)
6. Dick Young, *New York Daily News* (October 2, 1971)
7. Ron Bergman, *The Sporting News* (October 16, 1971): p. 17

8. Ibid.
9. Associated Press, (October 3, 1971)
10. Murray Chass, *New York Times* (October 2, 1971)
11. United Press International, (October 2, 1971)
12. Ibid.
13. Ibid.
14. Murray Chass, *New York Times* (October 3, 1971)
15. Ibid.
16. Ibid.
17. Associated Press, (October 5, 1971)
18. Ibid.
19. Joseph Durso, *New York Times* (October 7, 1971)
20. Phil Jackman, *The Sporting News* (October 23, 1971): p. 12
21. Joseph Durso, *New York Times* (October 7, 1971)
22. Ed Rumill, *Christian Science Monitor* (September 25, 1971)
23. Melvin Durslag, *Los Angeles Herald* (September 7, 1971)

Chapter Eight
1. *The Sporting News*, (January 1, 1972): p. 37
2. Glenn Dickey, *Sport* (October 1973): p. 58
3. Ibid.
4. Ibid.
5. Ron Bergman, *The Sporting News* (January 1, 1972): p. 37
6. Joe Gergen, *Baseball Writer's Assn. of America Scorebook* (1975)
7. Ron Bergman, *The Sporting News* (December 11, 1971): p. 47
8. Arnold Hano, *Sport* (November 1972): p. 66
9.Associated Press, (January 7, 1972)
10. Ibid.
11. Samuel J. Skinner, *Black Sports* (July-August 1972)

Chapter Nine
1. Dick Young, *New York Daily News* (March 24, 1972)
2. Red Smith, *New York Times* (February 18, 1972)
3. Eric Prewitt, Associated Press (February 25, 1972)
4. Ibid.
5. Associated Press, (February 27, 1972)
6. Ibid.
7. Dick Miller, *The Sporting News* (March 11, 1972): p. 34
8. Ibid.
9. Ron Bergman, *The Sporting News* (March 18, 1972): p. 32
10. Ibid.
11. Red Smith, *New York Times* (March 6, 1972)
12. Bill Verigan, *New York Daily News* (March 9, 1972)
13. Associated Press, (March 12, 1972)
14. Ibid.
15. Ibid.
16. Associated Press, (March 17, 1972)
17. Ibid.
18. William Leggett, *Sports Illustrated* (April 10, 1972): p. 70
19. Ron Bergman, *The Sporting News* (February 5, 1972): p. 44
20. Ibid.
21. Phil Pepe, *New York Daily News* (April 22, 1974)
22. Murray Chass, *New York Times* (March 26, 1972)
23. Ibid.
24. Bob Cottrol, *Black Sports* (August 1974)
25. Ibid.

26. Ibid.
27. John Eisenberg, *Baltimore Sun* (July 20, 1986)
28. *New York Times* (April 27, 1972)
29. United Press International, (April 30, 1972)
30. United Press International, (May 3, 1972)
31. Associated Press, (April 30, 1972)
32. Ron Bergman, *The Sporting News* (May 13, 1972): p. 8
33. Associated Press, (May 5, 1972)
34. Bill Ballew, *Sports Collectors Digest* (April 26, 1996)
35. Ibid.
36. Associated Press, (April 26, 1972)
37. Ibid.
38. Ron Bergman, *The Sporting News* (May 27, 1972): p. 19
39. Edgar Munzel, *The Sporting News* (March 20, 1965): p. 26
40. Don Delliquanti, *Sports Illustrated* (May 22, 1972): p. 55
41. Associated Press, (May 17, 1972)
42. *The Sporting News*, (June 3, 1972): p. 17
43. Arthur Daley, *New York Times* (May 18, 1972)
44. Associated Press, (May 17, 1972)
45. *New York Daily News*, (May 15, 1972)

Chapter Ten
1. Paul Brodie, *Palm Beach Times* (March 15, 1972)
2. Harold Peterson, *Sports Illustrated* (May 29, 1972): p. 74
3. Lawrence Linderman, *Sport* (October 1972): p. 73
4. Ron Bergman, *The Sporting News* (July 22, 1972): p. 3
5. Lawrence Linderman, *Sport* (October 1972): p. 73
6. Ron Fimrite, *Sports Illustrated* (June 19, 1972): p. 59
7. Ron Bergman, *The Sporting News* (July 22, 1972): p. 3
8. Ibid.
9. Phil Pepe, *New York Daily News* (March 25, 1986)
10. Oakland A's press release, (March 2, 1973)
11. *Chicago Sun-Times* (1984)
12. Associated Press (June 13, 1972)
13. Ibid.
14. Ron Fimrite, *Sports Illustrated* (June 19, 1972): p. 59
15. Ibid.
16. Dave Hirshey, *New York Daily News* (June 24, 1972)
17. Ibid.
18. *New York Newsday* (June 30, 1972)
19. Arthur Daley, *New York Times* (July 4, 1972)
20. Associated Press, (June 30, 1972)
21. Associated Press, (July 14, 1972)
22. Ibid.
23. Ron Bergman, *The Sporting News* (July 22, 1972): p. 4
24. Ron Fimrite, *Sports Illustrated* (July 31, 1972): p. 16
25. Bill Ballew, *Sports Collectors Digest* (April 26, 1996)
26. Ron Bergman, *The Sporting News* (July 15, 1972): p. 24
27. Thomas Rogers, *New York Times* (September 8, 1972)
28. Ron Bergman, *The Sporting News* (July 15, 1972): p. 3
29. Ibid.
30. Glenn Dickey, *Sport* (October 1973): p. 58
31. Ron Bergman, *The Sporting News* (August 5, 1972): p. 7
32. Ron Fimrite, *Sports Illustrated* (July 31, 1972): p. 16
33. Ron Bergman, *The Sporting News* (July 22, 1972): p. 3
34. Joseph Durso, *New York Times* (July 6, 1972)

35. Gerald Eskenazi, *New York Times* (July 4, 1972)
36. *The Sporting News*, (August 5, 1972): p. 21
37. Arnold Hano, *Sport* (November 1972): p. 88
38. Ron Fimrite, *Sports Illustrated* (July 31, 1972): p. 17
39. Ron Bergman, *The Sporting News* (August 5, 1972): p. 7
40. Ibid.
41. Bruno Sniders, *Rochester Times* (May 16, 1973)
42. Ron Bergman, *The Sporting News* (september 2, 1972): p. 9
43. Ibid.
44. Al Hirshberg, *Sport* (October 1973): p. 100
45. Ron Bergman, *The Sporting News* (September 2, 1972): p. 9
46. Ron Bergman, *The Sporting News* (September 23, 1972): p. 7
47. Ibid.
48. Ron Bergman, *The Sporting News* (September 30, 1972): p. 19
49. Ibid.
50. Charley Feeney, *The Sporting News* (Date unknown)
51. Pat Jordan, *Sport* (November 1971): p. 94
52. *New York Daily News* (October 16, 1972)

Chapter Eleven
1. Dave Nightingale, *Chicago Daily News* (undated)
2. Bill Hart, *Binghamton Press* (November 12, 1972)
3. United Press International, (October 9, 1972)
4. Bob Hertzel, *Cincinnati Enquirer* (October 14, 1972)
5. Joe Trimble, *New York Daily News* (October 10, 1972)
6. Dave Nightingale, *Chicago Daily News* (undated)
7. Associated Press, (October 12, 1972)
8. Ibid.
9. Ibid.
10. Ibid.
11. Phil Pepe, *New York Daily News* (October 13, 1972)
12. United Press International, (October 13, 1972)
13. Ibid.
14. Dwight Chapin, *San Francisco Examiner* (undated)
15. Dick Young, *New York Daily News* (October 15, 1972)
16. Al Hirshberg, *Sport* (October 1973): p. 102
17. Phil Pepe, *New York Daily News* (October 13, 1972)

Chapter Twelve
1. Joseph Durso, *New York Times* (October 18, 1972)
2. Ibid.
3. Ibid.
4. Reggie Jackson and George Vass, *Baseball Digest* (January 1974): p. 66
5. Dwight Chapin, *San Francisco Examiner* (undated)
6. Frank Dolson, *Baseball Digest* (January 1974) p. 24
7. Ron Bergman, *The Sporting News* (July 22, 1972): p. 3
8. Dwight Chapin, *San Francisco Examiner* (undated)
9. Peter Coutros, *New York Post* (October 17, 1990)
10. Joseph Durso, *New York Times* (October 15, 1972)
11. Ibid.
12. Ibid.
13. Ibid.
14. Bob Hertzel, *Cincinnati Enquirer* (October 15, 1972)
15. Peter Coutros, *New York Post* (October 17, 1990)
16. Phil Pepe, *New York Daily News* (October 15, 1972)
17. Bob Stevens, *San Francisco Chronicle* (October 16, 1972)

18. *San Francisco Chronicle*, (October 16, 1972)
19. Associated Press, (October 16, 1972)
20. *San Francisco Chronicle*, (October 16, 1972)
21. *Chicago Daily News*, (October 16, 1972)
22. Ibid.
23. Bob Stevens, *San Francisco Chronicle* (October 16, 1972)
24. Ibid.
25. Ibid.
26. Ibid.
27. Phil Pepe, *New York Daily News* (October 15, 1972)
28. *Chicago Daily News*, (October 16, 1972)
29. Red Smith, *New York Times* (October 16, 1972)
30. Dick Young, *New York Daily News* (October 19, 1972)
31. Al Hirshberg, *Sport* (October 1973): p. 104
32. Dwight Chapin, *San Francisco Examiner* (undated)
33. Arnold Hano, *Sport* (November 1972): p. 68
34. Red Smith, *New York Times* (October 19, 1972)
35. Sal Bando and Al Hirshberg, *Sport* (April 1973): p. 67
36. Ray W. Kelly, Gannett News Service (October 19, 1972)
37. Ibid.
38. Associated Press, (October 19, 1972)
39. Al Hirshberg, *Sport* (October 1973): p. 108
40. Joe Trimble, *New York Daily News* (October 20, 1972)
41. *San Francisco Chronicle*, (October 20, 1972)
42. Ibid.
43. Dave Nightingale, *Chicago Daily News* (October 20, 1972)
44. Larry Claflin, *Boston Herald* (October 21, 1972)
45. Bill Plaschke, *Los Angeles Times* (October 20, 1972)
46. Al Hirshberg, *Sport* (October 1973): p. 108
47. Earl Lawson, *Cincinnati Post* (October 21, 1972)
48. United Press International, (October 21, 1972)
49. Associated Press, (October 21, 1972)
50. Joseph Durso, *New York Times* (October 21, 1972)
51. Ibid.
52. Dick Friendlich, *San Francisco Chronicle* (October 20, 1972)
53. Murray Chass, *New York Times* (October 21, 1972)
54. Ibid.
55. Associated Press, (October 22, 1972)
56. Ibid.
57. Ibid.
57. Ibid.
58. Ibid.
59. Ibid.
60. Ibid.
61. Bill Plaschke, *Los Angeles Times* (October 20, 1972)

Chapter Thirteen
1. *New York Times* (October 22, 1972)
2. Murray Chass, *New York Times* (October 22, 1972)
3. Dick Young, *New York Daily News* (October 24, 1972)
4. Phil Elderkin, *Christian Science Monitor* (January 29, 1973)
5. *New York Post*, (October 17, 1972)
6. Associated Press, (July 22, 1973)
7. Dick Young, *New York Daily News* (October 24, 1972)
8. Ron Bergman, *The Sporting News* (November 4, 1972): p. 25
9. Lowell Reidenbaugh, *The Sporting News* (November 4, 1973): p. 3

10. Ibid.
11. *New York Times* (October 3, 1973)
12. Lowell Reidenbaugh, *The Sporting News* (November 4, 1973): p. 3
13. Ibid.
14. Ron Bergman, *The Sporting News* (November 11, 1972): p. 40
15. Joe Trimble, *New York Daily News* (undated)
16. Pete Swanson, National Baseball Hall of Fame Library File (November 4, 1972)
17. Joseph Durso, *New York Times* (October 24, 1972)
18. *New York Times*, (October 27, 1972)
19. Associated Press, (October 27, 1972)

Chapter Fourteen
1. *Cleveland Plain Dealer*, (July 21, 1974)
2. Murray Chass, *New York Times* (January 26, 1973)
3. Ron Bergman, *The Sporting News* (January 6, 1973): p. 3
4. Ibid.
5. Ron Bergman, *The Sporting News* (December 23, 1972): p. 37
6. Ibid.
7. Phil Elderkin, *Christian Science Monitor* (October 18, 1973)
8. Lenny Megliola, *Black Sports* (August 1973)
9. Ron Bergman, *The Sporting News* (June 23, 1973): p. 11
10. Ibid.
11. *The Sporting News Baseball Guide* (1974)
12. Ron Bergman, *The Sporting News* (February 10, 1973): p. 37
13. Ibid.
14. Ron Bergman, *The Sporting News* (February 17, 1973): p. 41
15. Arthur Daley, *New York Times* (June 3, 1973)
16. Arthur Daley, *New York Times* (June 6, 1973)
17. Arthur Daley, *New York Times* (June 3, 1973)
18. Ron Fimrite, *Sports Illustrated* (April 2, 1973): p. 71
19. Dick Young, *New York Daily News* (July 12, 1973)
20. Ron Fimrite, *Sports Illustrated* (April 2, 1973): pp. 71-76
21. Ron Bergman, *The Sporting News* (April 21, 1973): p. 4
22. Glenn Dickey, *Sport* (July 1973): p. 56
23. Ibid.
24. United Press International, (March 15, 1973)
25. Ibid.
26. Ron Fimrite, *Sports Illustrated* (April 2, 1973): p. 76
27. Ron Bergman, *The Sporting News* (April 7, 1973): p. 34
28. *New York Times* (April 15, 1973)
29. Ibid.
30. Phil Pepe, *New York Daily News* (October 15, 1972)
31. Ron Bergman, *The Sporting News* (April 14, 1973): p. 16
32. Associated Press, (March 18, 1973)
33. Ibid.
34. Ibid.
35. Associated Press, (March 28, 1973)

Chapter Fifteen
1. David Condon, *Baseball Digest* (January 1974): p. 23
2. Joe McGuff, *The Sporting News* (July 31, 1965)
3. Jim Kaplan, *Sports Illustrated* (April 23, 1973): p. 62
4. Associated Press, (June 8, 1973)
5. Ibid.
6. Ron Bergman, *The Sporting News* (May 19, 1973): p. 13

7. Ron Bergman, *The Sporting News* (May 26, 1973): p. 4

8. Ron Bergman, *The Sporting News* (May 26, 1973): p. 3

9. Ron Bergman, *The Sporting News* (June 2, 1973): p. 8

10. Ibid.

11. Ron Bergman, *The Sporting News* (June 9, 1973): p. 17

12. Ron Bergman, *The Sporting News* (July 7, 1973): p. 10

13. Phil Eldridge, *Christian Science Monitor* (August 21, 1973)

14. Ron Bergman, *The Sporting News* (June 16, 1973): p. 9

15. Ron Bergman, *The Sporting News* (June 23, 1973): p. 11

16. Ibid.

17. Will Grimsley, Associated Press (October 17, 1974)

18. *New York Times*, (May 31, 1973)

19. Ron Bergman, *The Sporting News* (June 23, 1973): p. 11

20. Associated Press, (June 2, 1973)

21. Ibid.

22. Ron Fimrite, *Sports Illustrated* (June 18, 1973): p. 21

23. *The Sporting News*, (June 30, 1973): p. 21

24. Ibid.

25. Glenn Dickey, *Sport* (July 1973): p. 53

26. Ibid. p. 54

27. Ibid. p. 56

28. Ibid. p. 56

29. Ron Fimrite, *Sports Illustrated* (June 18, 1973): p. 20

30. Ibid. p. 21

31. *The Sporting News*, (June 30, 1973): p. 21

32. Phil Pepe, *New York Daily News* (October 15, 1972)

33. Ibid.

34. Ron Bergman, *The Sporting News* (July 14, 1973): p. 7

35. Ibid.

36. *The Sporting News*, (July 21, 1973): p. 42

37. *New York Times*, (July 6, 1973)

38. Murray Olderman, *Sport* (October 1974): p. 50

39. Ron Bergman, *The Sporting News* (July 28, 1973): p. 27

40. *New York Times*, (July 6, 1973)

41. Ron Bergman, *The Sporting News* (January 12, 1974): p. 29

42. Ibid.

43. Jim Kaplan, *Sports Illustrated* (April 30, 1973): p. 62

44. Ron Bergman, *The Sporting News* (August 4, 1973): p. 12

45. Ron Bergman, *The Sporting News* (August 18, 1973): p. 8

46. Ibid.

47. Ron Bergman, *The Sporting News* (August 25, 1973): p. 8

48. *The Sporting News*, (November 22, 1975): p.55

49. Ron Bergman, *The Sporting News* (August 25, 1973): p. 8

Chapter Sixteen

1. Joseph Durso, *New York Times* (August 13, 1973)

2. Pat Jordan, *Sport* (November 1971): p. 92

3. Ron Bergman, *The Sporting News* (September 15, 1973): p. 3

4. Ibid.

5. Ron Fimrite, *Sports Illustrated* (September 3, 1973): p. 48

6. Morton Sharnik, *Sports Illustrated* (September 17, 1973): p. 101

7. David Condon, *Baseball Digest* (January 1974): p. 23

8. Ron Bergman, *The Sporting News* (September 22, 1973): p. 8

9. Ibid.

10. Glenn Dickey, *Sport* (October 1973): p. 59

11. Ibid.

12. Ibid., p. 60
13. Ron Bergman, *The Sporting News* (September 29, 1973): p. 4
14. Ibid.
15. Morton Sharnik, *Sports Illustrated* (September 17, 1973): p. 101
16. Dick Young, *New York Daily News* (November 11, 1973)
17. Ibid.
18. Associated Press
19. Ron Bergman, *The Sporting News* (October 6, 1973): p. 7
20. Ibid.
21. Ron Fimrite, *Sports Illustrated* (September 10, 1973): p. 93
22. Ibid.
23. Ibid.
24. Don Kowet, *Sport* (January 1974): p. 77
25. Phil Elderkin, *Christian Science Monitor* (1973)
26. Phil Elderkin, *Christian Science Monitor* (October 16, 1974)
27. Associated Press, (December 31, 1974)
28. Associated Press, (October 20, 1973)
29. Ibid.
30. Ibid.
31. Ron Fimrite, *Sports Illustrated* (October 22, 1973): p. 24
32. Parton Keese, *New York Times* (October 6, 1973)
33. Ibid.
34. Gannett News Service, (October 5, 1973)
35. Parton Keese, *New York Times* (October 6, 1973)
36. William Leggett, *Sports Illustrated* (October 8, 1973): p. 34
37. Don Kowet, *Sport* (January 1974): p. 75
38. Steve Cady, *New York Times* (October 7, 1973)
39. Ibid.
40. United Press International, (October 8, 1973)
41. Steve Cady, *New York Times* (October 7, 1973)
42. William Leggett, *Sports Illustrated* (October 8, 1973): p. 35
43. Ron Bergman, *The Sporting News* (October 27, 1973): p. 4
44. *New York Times*, (October 10, 1973)
45. Ibid.
46. Ron Bergman, *The Sporting News* (October 27, 1973): p. 4
47. Ibid.
48. Ibid.
49. Len Koppett, *New York Times* (October 9, 1973)
50. National Baseball Hall of Fame Library, (1973)
51. Phil Elderkin, *Christian Science Monitor* (1973)
52. Len Koppett, *New York Times* (October 12, 1973)
53. Ibid.

Chapter Seventeen
1. Wells Twombly, *San Francisco Examiner and Chronicle* (October 14, 1973)
2. Ibid.
3. *San Francisco Examiner and Chronicle*, (October 14, 1973)
4. Associated Press, (October 14, 1973)
5. Phil Pepe, *New York Daily News* (October 14, 1973)
6. Red Smith, *New York Times* (October 14, 1973)
7. Wells Twombly, *San Francisco Examiner and Chronicle* (October 14, 1973)
8. Red Smith, *New York Times* (October 14, 1973)
9. Ibid.
10. Joseph Durso, *New York Times* (October 14, 1973)
11. Len Koppett, *New York Times* (October 14, 1973)
12. Len Koppett, *New York Times* (October 15, 1973)

13. Ibid.
14. Tim Gartner, *San Francisco Chronicle* (undated)
15. Ibid.
16. Len Koppett, *New York Times* (October 15, 1973)
17. Ibid.
18. Ibid.

Chapter Eighteen
1. Ron Bergman, *The Sporting News* (November 3, 1973): p. 5
2. Red Foley, *New York Daily News* (October 16, 1973)
3. Red Smith, *New York Times* (October 17, 1973)
4. Red Foley, *New York Daily News* (October 18, 1973)
5. United Press International, (October 17, 1973)
6. Associated Press, (October 20, 1973)
7. Ibid.
8. *New York Times*, (October 17, 1973)
9. Ibid.
10. Associated Press, (October 20, 1973)
11. *New York Times*, (October 18, 1973)
12. Ibid.
13. Ibid.
14. Ron Bergman, *The Sporting News* (November 3, 1973): p. 5
15. Will Grimsley, Associated Press (October 1973)
16. Ibid.
17. Ibid.
18. *New York Post*, (October 17, 1973)
19. John Kuenster, *Baseball Digest* (January 1974): p. 5
20. Red Foley, *New York Daily News* (October 18, 1973)
21. Phil Pepe, *New York Daily News* (October 18, 1973)
22. Ibid.
23. Joseph Valerio, *New York Daily News* (October 18, 1973)
24. Murray Chass, *New York Times* (October 18, 1973)
25. Marty Bell, *Sport* (July 1974): p. 68
26. Furman Bisher, *The Sporting News* (November 10, 1973): p. 27
27. Reggie Jackson, *Guideposts* (October 1975)
28. Red Smith, *New York Times* (October 18, 1973)

Chapter Nineteen
1. George Ross, *Oakland Tribune* (October 20, 1973)
2. Phil Pepe, *New York Daily News* (undated)
3. Dave Anderson, *New York Times* (October 19, 1973)
4. Ron Bergman, *Oakland Tribune* (October 20, 1973)
5. Ibid.
6. Phil Pepe, *New York Daily News* (October 20, 1973)
7. Red Foley, *New York Daily News* (October 20, 1973)
8. Arthur Daley, *New York Times* (October 20, 1973)
9. Red Foley, *New York Daily News* (October 21, 1973)
10. Frank Dolson, *Baseball Digest* (January 1974): p. 26
11. Red Foley, *New York Daily News* (October 21, 1973)
12. George Vass, *Baseball Digest* (May 1974): p. 25
13. Neal Russo, *St. Louis Press-Dispatch* (October 22, 1973)
14. Dick Young, *New York Daily News* (undated)
15. Ibid.
16. Arthur Daley, *New York Times* (undated)
17. David Condon, *Baseball Digest* (January 1974): p. 22
18. *New York Daily News*, (October 21, 1973)

19. Dave Anderson, *New York Times* (February 28, 1974)
20. Associated Press, (October 21, 1973)
21. Larry Claflin, *Boston Herald* (October 23, 1973)
22. Maury Allen, *New York Post*, (October 18, 1973)
23. Ibid.
24. Ibid.
25. National Baseball Hall of Fame Library (1973)
26. Phil Pepe, *New York Daily News* (October 23, 1973)
27. Dave Hirshey, *New York Daily News* (October 23, 1973)

Chapter Twenty
1. Red Foley, *New York Daily News* (October 21, 1973)
2. Associated Press, (October 25, 1973)
3. Ibid.
4. Ron Bergman, *The Sporting News* (November 10, 1973): p. 27
5. Ron Bergman, *The Sporting News* (December 22, 1973): p. 38
6. Dick Young, *New York Daily News* (December 21, 1973)
7. Ron Bergman, *The Sporting News* (December 22, 1973): p. 38
8. Marty Bell, *Sport* (July 1974): p. 65
9. Dick Young, *New York Daily News* (December 21, 1973)
10. National Baseball Hall of Fame Library (1973)
11. Red Foley, *New York Daily News* (December 22, 1973)

Chapter Twenty-one
1. Ron Bergman, *The Sporting News* (November 24, 1973): P. 33
2. Russell Schneider, *The Sporting News* (September 14, 1974): p.16
3. Pete Swanson, National Baseball Hall of Fame Library File (November 4, 1973)
4. Ibid.
5. Ron Bergman, *The Sporting News* (December 29, 1973): p. 29
6. Ibid.
7. Neal Russo, *St. Louis Post-Dispatch* (October 22, 1973)
8. Red Foley, *New York Daily News* (October 26, 1973)
9. Dick Edwards, *Black Sports* (January 1974)
10. *The Sporting News* (January 5, 1974): p. 27
11. Ibid.
12. Deane McGowan, *New York Times* (January 30, 1974)
13. Milt Richman, United Press International (February 4, 1974)
14. Ron Bergman, *The Sporting News* (June 14, 1969)
15. Ron Bergman, *The Sporting News* (February 9, 1974): p. 74
16. Ibid.
17. Ibid.
18. Ron Bergman, *The Sporting News* (February 2, 1974): p. 29
19. Ron Bergman, *The Sporting News* (February 16, 1974): p. 33
20. Ibid.

Chapter Twenty-two
1. John Underwood, *Sports Illusrtated* (March 4, 1974): p. 22
2. Ibid.
3. Ibid.
4. Ibid.
5. Ron Bergman, *The Sporting News* (March 9, 1974): p. 29
6. Ron Bergman, *The Sporting News* (March 16, 1974): p. 42
7. Alvin Dark and John Underwood, *Sports Illustrated* (May 3, 1974)
8. Ibid.
9. Murray Olderman, *Sport* (October 1974): p. 54
10. Time, (June 3, 1974)

11. John Underwood, *Sports Illustrated* (March 4, 1974): p. 24
12. Ron Bergman, *The Sporting News* (April 13, 1974): p. 3
13. Ibid. p. 3-4
14. Wells Twombly, *New York Times Magazine* (July 25, 1971)
15. Ron Bergman, *The Sporting News* (March 23, 1974): p. 33
16. Ibid.
17. Dick Young, *New York Daily News* (March 6, 1974)
18. Ron Bergman, *The Sporting News* (April 6, 1974): p. 18
19. Bill Libby, *A Season without A Superstar*
20. Kenny Moore, *Sports Illustrated* (June 10, 1974): p. 69-72
21. Ron Bergman, *The Sporting News* (April 13, 1974): p. 3
22. William Leggett, *Sports Illustrated* (April 8, 1974): p. 55
23. Ron Bergman, *The Sporting News* (April 20, 1974): p. 5
24. Ibid.
25. Ibid.
26. Ibid.

Chapter Twenty-three
1. Ron Bergman, *The Sporting News* (April 27, 1974): p. 5
2. Ibid.
3. Ibid.
4. Associated Press (April 9, 1974)
5. Ron Bergman, *The Sporting News* (May 4, 1974): p. 5
6. Joe Jares, *Sports Illustrated* (April 22, 1974): p. 70
7. Art Spander, *The Sporting News* (May 4, 1974): p. 29
8. Ron Bergman, *The Sporting News* (May 11, 1974): p. 11
9. Ibid.
10. Ron Bergman, *The Sporting News* (May 25, 1974): p. 19
11. Pat Jordan, *Sports Illustrated* (May 20, 1974): p. 67
12. Ron Bergman, *The Sporting News* (May 25, 1974): p. 19
13. Ibid.
14. Ron Bergman, *The Sporting News* (June 1, 1974): p. 15
15. Time, (June 3, 1974)
16. Herman Weiskopf, *Sports Illustrated* (June 3, 1974): p. 50
17. Ibid.
18. Phil Elderkin, *Christian Science Monitor* (September 18, 1974)
19. Herman Weiskopf, *Sports Illustrated* (June 3, 1974): p. 48

Chapter Twenty-four
1. Dick Young, *New York Daily News* (June 8, 1974)
2. Murray Olderman, *Sport* (October 1974): p. 50
3. Dick Young, *New York Daily News* (June 6, 1974)
4. *New York Daily News*, (June 8, 1974)
5. *Time*, (June 3, 1974)
6. Phil Pepe, *New York Daily News* (June 9, 1974)
7. Dick Young, *New York Daily News* (June 6, 1974)
8. Phil Pepe, *New York Daily News* (June 9, 1974)
9. Clint Rosewell, *New York Daily News* (June 8, 1974)
10. John Kuenster, *Baseball Digest* (November 1974): p. 8
11. Ron Bergman, *The Sporting News* (July 6, 1974): p. 5
12. Murray Olderman, *Sport* (October 1974): p. 50
13. Ron Bergman, *The Sporting News* (July 13, 1974): p. 7
14. Don Kowet, *Sport* (February 1974): p. 95
15. Melvin Durslag, *Boston Herald* (June 20, 1974)
16. Dick Young, *New York Daily News* (June 6, 1973)
17. Ibid.

18. Ibid.
19. Ron Bergman, *The Sporting News* (July 27, 1974): p. 27
20. Ron Bergman, *The Sporting News* (August 3, 1974): p. 28
21. Ron Bergman, *The Sporting News* (July 27, 1974): p. 27
22. Ibid.
23. Ibid.
24. Ron Bergman, *The Sporting News* (August 3, 1974): p. 28
25. Ibid.
26. Ibid.
27. Glenn Dickey, *Sport* (March 1976): pp. 68-72
28. Ron Bergman, *The Sporting News* (August 24, 1974): p. 22
29. Ibid.
30. Ron Bergman, *The Sporting News* (August 31, 1974): p. 5
31. Ibid.
32. Ibid.
33. Ron Bergman, *The Sporting News* (September 7, 1974): p. 15
34. Ron Bergman, *The Sporting News* (September 21, 1974): p. 5
35. Glenn Dickey, *Sport* (March 1976): p 68-72
36. Ibid.
37. Ron Bergman, *The Sporting News* (September 28, 1974)
38. Dick Young, *New York Daily News* (October 18, 1974)
39. Glenn Dickey, *Sport* (March 1976): pp. 68-72
40. *The Sporting News*, (September 21, 1974): p. 22
41. Ron Bergman, *The Sporting News* (October 5, 1974): p. 13
42. Ron Bergman, *The Sporting News* (October 19, 1974): p. 31
43. Ibid.
44. Herman Weiskopf, *Sports Illustrated* (October 7, 1974): p. 118

Chapter Twenty-five
1. Augie Borgi, *New York Daily News* (October 9, 1974)
2. Ibid.
3. Associated Press, (October 9, 1974)
4. United Press International, (October 9, 1974)
5. Ibid.
6. Phil Pepe, *New York Daily News* (October 5, 1974)
7. Ibid
8. Associated Press, (October 10, 1974)
9. Ibid.

Chapter Twenty-six
1. Phil Pepe, *New York Daily News* (October 12, 1974)
2. Ibid.
3. Ron Fimrite, *Sports Illustrated* (October 21, 1974): p. 23
4. *Chicago Tribune*, (October 12, 1974)
5. *Chicago Sun-Times* (October 12, 1974)
6. Wells Twombly, *The Sporting News* (1974)
7. Ibid.
8. *New York Times*, (October 12, 1974)
9. Ibid.
10. Ibid.
11. *New York Daily News*, (October 13, 1974)
12. *New York Times*, (October 12, 1974)
13. *New York Daily News*, (October 13, 1974)
14. Ron Fimrite, *Sports Illustrated* (October 21, 1974): p. 23
15. Ibid.
16. Phil Pepe, *New York Daily News* (October 15, 1974)

17. Dave Anderson, *New York Times* (October 16, 1974)
18. Ron Fimrite, *Sports Illustrated* (October 21, 1974): p. 24
19. Ibid.
20. Phil Pepe, *New York Daily News* (October 15, 1974)
21. Ibid.
22. Art Spander, *San Francisco Chronicle* (October 15, 1974)
23. Murray Olderman, *Sport* (October 1974): p. 54
24. Milt Richman, United Press International (October 16, 1974)
25. Red Smith, *New York Times* (October 20, 1974)
26. National Baseball Hall of Fame Library File , (October 16, 1974)
27. *New York Times*, (October 15, 1974)
28. *New York Times*, (October 17, 1974)
29. *San Francisco Chronicle*, (October 16, 1974)
30. Ibid.
31. *The Sporting News*, (May 19, 1973): p. 28
32. *San Francisco Chronicle*, (October 16, 1974)
33. *New York Times* (October 17, 1974)
34. Ibid.
35. *New York Daily News*, (October 18, 1974)
36. *San Francisco Chronicle* (October 16, 1974)
37. Ron Fimrite, *Sports Illustrated* (October 28, 1974): p. 27
38. Lowell Reidenbaugh, *The Sporting News* (November 2, 1974): p. 7
39. Ibid.
40. *San Francisco Chronicle*, (October 17, 1974)
41. United Press International, (October 18, 1974)
42. *New York Times*, (October 20, 1974)
43. *New York Times*, (October 18, 1974)
44. Ibid.
45. Ibid.
46. Dick Young, *New York Daily News* (October 18, 1974)
47. Associated Press, (October 18, 1974)
48. *San Francisco Chronicle*, (October 18, 1974)
49. Ibid.
50. Ibid.
51. Ron Fimrite, *Sports Illustrated* (October 28, 1974): p. 27
52. Stanley Frank, *Sport* (April 1975): p. 72
53. Joe Gergen, Baseball Writer's Association of America Scorebook (1975)
54. Stanley Frank, *Sport* (April 1975): p. 72
55. *San Francisco Chronicle*, (October 18, 1974)
56. Ibid.
57. Ibid.
58. Ibid.
59. Ron Bergman, *The Sporting News* (November 9, 1974): p. 56
60. Ron Fimrite, *Sports Illustrated* (April 7, 1975)
61. Ron Bergman, *The Sporting News* (November 16, 1974): p. 41
62. Bob Logan, *Chicago Tribune* (June 24, 1973)
63. Ron Bergman, *The Sporting News* (November 16, 1974): p. 41
64. Ibid.
65. Ron Fimrite, *Sports Illustrated* (April 7, 1975)

Chapter Twenty-seven
1. Ron Bergman, *The Sporting News* (December 28, 1974): p. 39
2. Associated Press, (December 17, 1974)
3. Ibid.
4. Sid Bordman, *Kansas City Star* (July 13, 1986)
5. Paul Hemphill, *Sport* (April 1975): p. 69

6. *San Jose Mercury News*, (November 26, 1974)
7. Gerald Eskenazi, *New York Times* (December 19, 1974)
8. Pat Jordan, *Sport* (November 1971): p. 94
9. Paul Hemphill, *Sport* (April 1975): p. 63
10. Ibid. p. 69
11. Glenn Dickey, *Allegheny Airlines Flightline* (April 1975)
12. Associated Press

Chapter Twenty-eight
1. Dick Young, *New York Daily News* (January 31, 1975)
2. Associated Press, (February 16, 1975)
3. Ibid.
4. Associated Press, (March 5, 1975)
5. Ibid.
6. Dick Young, *New York Daily News* (Juanuary 31, 1975)
7. United Press International, (March 20, 1975)
8. Ibid.
9. Ron Bergman, *The Sporting News* (April 12, 1975): p. 12
10. Ibid.
11. Ron Bergman, *The Sporting News* (April 19, 1975): p. 5
12. Ron Fimrite, *Sports Illustrated* (September 8, 1975): p. 15
13. Roy Blount, Jr., *Sports Illustrated* (May 26, 1975): p. 30
14. Ron Bergman, *The Sporting News* (April 19, 1975): p. 5
15. Ron Fimrite, *Sports Illustated* (April 7, 1975): p. 44
16. Ibid.

Chapter Twenty-nine
1. Herman Weiskopf, *Sports Illustrated* (April 21, 1975): p. 72
2. Ron Bergman, *The Sporting News* (May 10, 1975): p. 7
3. Jim Kaplan, *Sports Illustrated* (May 5, 1975): p. 76
4. Ron Bergman, *The Sporting News* (May 17, 1975): p. 18
5. Jim Kaplan, *Sports Illustrated* (May 12, 1975): p. 58
6. Ron Bergman, *The Sporting News* (May 24, 1975): p. 13
7. Ibid.
8. Ron Fimrite, *Sports Illustrated* (May 19, 1975): p. 29
9. Ibid.
10. *The Sporting News*, (September 13, 1975): p. 9
11. Joe Giuliotti, *Boston Herald* (October 7, 1975)
12. Frank Robinson, *Sport* (May 1976): p. 64
13. Associated Press, (June 9, 1975)
14. Herman Weiskopf, *Sports Illustrated* (June 23, 1975): p. 52
15. Ron Bergman, *The Sporting News* (October 4, 1975): p. 3
16. Ron Fimrite, *Sports Illustrated* (Septmber 8, 1975): pp. 12-15
17. Ron Bergman, *The Sporting News* (October 4, 1975): p. 3
18. Ron Bergman, *The Sporting News* (July 26, 1975): p. 9
19. Ron Fimrite, *Sports Illustrated* (September 8, 1975): pp. 12-15
20. Glenn Dickey, *Sport* (March 1976): p. 70
21. Herman Weiskopf, *Sports Illustrated* (August 4, 1975): p. 40
22. *The Sporting News*, (August 16, 1975): p. 24
23. Herman Weiskopf, *The Sporting News* (August 4, 1975): p. 40
24. Ron Bergman, *The Sporting News* (August 16, 1975): p. 15
25. Ron Bergman, *The Sporting News* (August 23, 1975): p. 10
26. Ron Fimrite, *Sports Illustrated* (September 8, 1975): p. 12
27. Pat Putnam, *Sports Illustrated* (August 25, 1975): pp. 36-37
28. Ron Fimrite, *Sports Illustrtated* (September 8, 1975): p. 12
29. Ron Bergman, *The Sporting News* (September 13, 1975): p. 9

30. Ron Fimrite, *Sports Illustrated* (September 8, 1975): p. 15
31. *The Sporting News*, (May 14, 1977)
32. *The Sporting News*, (October 4, 1975): p. 3
33. Ron Bergman, *The Sporting News* (October 11, 1975): p. 17
34. Ibid.
35. *The Sporting News*, (October 11, 1975): p. 27
36. Ron Bergman, *The Sporting News* (October 11, 1975): p. 34

Chapter Thirty
1. Ron Fimrite, *Sports Illustrated* (October 6, 1975): p. 25
2. Peter Gammons, *The Sporting News* (October 18, 1975): p. 6
3. Ibid.
4. Ron Fimrite, *Sports Illustrated* (October 13, 1975): p. 38
5. Peter Gammons, *The Sporting News* (October 25, 1975): p/ 11
6. Steve Jacobson, *New York Newsday* (undated)

Chapter Thirty-one
1. Ron Bergman, *The Sporting News* (October 25, 1975): p. 5
2. Larry Elderkin, *Christian Science Monitor* (June 12, 1973)
3. Glenn Dickey, *Sport* (October 1973): p. 60
4. Ron Bergman, *The Sporting News* (November 1, 1975): p. 21
5. Associated Press, (October 31, 1975)
6. Ron Bergman, *The Sporting News* (January 3, 1976): p. 38
7. Ibid.
8. Ron Bergman, *The Sporting News* (February 14, 1976): p. 34
9. Ron Bergman, *The Sporting News* (February 7, 1976): p. 47
10. *New York Times*, (March 20, 1976)
11. Ibid.
12. Ron Bergman, *The Sporting News* (April 17, 1976): p. 16
13. Associated Press, (April 3, 1976)
14. Ibid.
15. Associated Press, (June 16,1976)
16. Ibid.
17. Associated Press, (June 19, 1976)
18. Ibid.
19. Ibid.
20. Associated Press, (June 23, 1976)
21. Norm Miller and Larry Fox, *New York Daily News* (June 19, 1976)
22. Ibid.
23. Ron Bergman, *The Sporting News* (August 28, 1976): p. 16, 30
24. Ibid.
25. Ron Bergman, *The Sporting News* (September 18, 1976): p. 8
26. Ron Bergman, *The Sporting News* (October 23, 1976): p. 22
27. Ibid.

Index